MW00987352

SUPERMOB

SUPERMOB

How Sidney Korshak and His
Criminal Associates Became
America's Hidden Power Brokers

GUS RUSSO

BLOOMSBURY

Published by Bloomsbury USA, New York
Distributed to the trade by Holtzbrinck Publishers

All papers used by Bloomsbury USA are natural, recyclable products made from
wood grown in well-managed forests. The manufacturing processes conform
to the environmental regulations of the country of origin.

Library of Congress Cataloging-in-Publication Data

Russo, Gus.
    Supermob : how Sidney Korshak and his criminal associates became America's
hidden power brokers / Gus Russo.—1st U.S. ed.
        p. cm.
    Includes bibliographical references and index.
    ISBN-13: 978-1-58234-389-1
    ISBN-10: 1-58234-389-6
    1. Korshak, Sidney Roy, 1907–1996. 2. Lawyers—Illinois—Chicago—
Biography. 3. Lawyers—California—Biography. 4. Organized crime—United
States. I. Title.

KF373.K67R87 2006
364.1092—dc22
[B]
                            2006015747

First U.S. Edition 2006

10 9 8 7 6 5 4 3

Typeset by Westchester Book Group
Printed in the United States of America by Quebecor World Fairfield

Contents

Cast of Characters

Antonino Leonardo Accardo (1906–1992)—aka "Tony," "Joe Batters," and "The Big Tuna." Served as boss of Chicago's Outfit, the most powerful underworld cartel in U.S. history, for over six decades in the twentieth century. A major force in national bookmaking, labor racketeering, the Teamsters Pension Fund, and Las Vegas casino gambling, Accardo treated Sid Korshak like a son.

Jacob "Jake" (or "Jack") Arvey (1895–1977)—Chicago-born attorney/political kingmaker who built one of the most powerful patronage "machines" in America. He served as a mentor to many of Chicago's most "well-connected" Jewish attorneys, and as a crucial vote deliverer for Democratic presidents such as FDR, Truman, and JFK. Key early supporter of the state of Israel.

David Lionel Bazelon (1909–1993)—Chicago tax attorney, originally in law firm with college buddy Paul Ziffren, but left private practice to become Truman's assistant attorney general in charge of the lands division, a position that he used to his advantage in his own real estate investments. He quickly advanced to become director of the Office of Alien Property, where he oversaw the disbursement of land (often to his Chicago pals) seized from the Japanese Americans sent to internment camps during World War II. Eventually became a chief judge in D.C.'s Court of Appeals.

Charles Bluhdorn (1926–1983)—aka "The Mad Austrian." Austrian immigrant who parlayed a successful auto parts distributorship into a conglomerate comprising over a hundred firms, all consolidated in 1958 when he formed Gulf & Western Inc. In 1966, Bluhdorn purchased struggling Paramount Pictures, named Sid Korshak's sycophant Bob Evans as production chief, then brought in the Mafia's Vatican money launderer Michele Sindona as a major "silent" investor in the movie studio. Bluhdorn utilized Sid Korshak's talents to oversee his Chicago racetracks' labor issues; invested in Korshak's mob retreat, The Acapulco Towers.

Albert Romolo Broccoli (1909–1996)—aka "Cubby." One of Sidney Korshak's closest Beverly Hills friends, and producer/owner of the James Bond movie franchise. When Broccoli produced *Diamonds Are Forever* in Las Vegas, Korshak was the "uncredited legal advisor," donating both his Riviera Hotel and his girlfriend Jill St. John to the production.

Edmund G. "Pat" Brown (1905–1996)—San Francisco–born attorney and respected governor of California (1959–67). Father of California governor Jerry Brown. Received important political and financial support early and often from Sid Korshak and friends. On board of directors of Bernie Cornfeld's Investors Overseas Services (IOS), which bilked investors out of hundreds of millions, before imploding after allegations of being a fraudulent pyramid scheme and money launderer for the mob. (Founder Cornfeld served eleven months in a Geneva jail, before charges were dropped, allowing him to move to Beverly Hills and date Heidi Fleiss.)

Jerry Brown (Edmund G. Brown Jr.) (1938–)—aka "Governor Moonbeam." Governor of California (1974–83) who received controversial labor support from Sid Korshak, allegedly in return for Brown's favored treatment of Korshak's California racetrack-owner clients. Later, a presidential candidate (1992) and mayor of Oakland, California. Dated Linda Ronstadt.

Delbert W. "Del" Coleman (1926–)—After selling his interest in Seeburg, Inc. (a jukebox manufacturer linked to the Outfit by the Chicago Crime Commission), the Chicago entrepreneur, an investor in Sid Korshak's Acapulco Towers, connived with Korshak to take over the Parvin-Dohrmann company as part of a master plan to buy the Stardust and other Vegas casinos. The affair ended with Coleman, Korshak, and others being rebuked by the Securities and Exchange Commission for stock manipulation. The experience also led to a permanent falling-out between Korshak and Coleman.

Morris Barney "Moe" Dalitz (né Dolitz) (1899–1989)—aka "Moe Davis" and "The Godfather of Las Vegas." The leader of Cleveland's Mayfield Road Gang, where he specialized in bootlegging and gambling. Moved to Las Vegas, where he owned mob-skimmed Desert Inn, before expanding into numerous other Vegas properties, and the formerly mob-friendly La Costa Resort in Southern California. Considered Sid Korshak his legal adviser.

Allen M. Dorfman (1924–1983)—For many years, did the Outfit's (and Sid Korshak's) bidding as manager of the Teamsters Pension Fund, disbursing over $500 million in low-interest loans, especially to Chicago hoods in Las Vegas. In return, he received kickbacks on the loans, and his insurance company was named carrier of the lucrative Teamsters' Health Care Fund. Soon after his convictions on the kickbacks and the bribery of Nevada senator Howard Cannon, he was murdered in the Chicago suburbs, amid contentions that he had been "flipped" by the feds.

Bob Evans (né Robert J. Shapera) (1930–)—Manhattan-born clothing salesman for his brother Charles's Evan-Picone clothing line. After a brief flirtation with acting, named by Gulf & Western chief Charles Bluhdorn as production head at Paramount Studios, which he gave a new life after producing hits such as *The Godfather* and *Love Story*. Well-known abuser of narcotics, Evans fell out with his longtime "consigliere," Sid Korshak, after being busted in 1980 for cocaine possession, narrowly escaping a trafficking charge. It was reported that he later came under suspicion when Roy Radin, an investor in Evans's *Cotton Club* movie, was murdered in 1983, amid a haze of massive cocaine purchases and thefts. When the case came to trial in 1989, Evans, under the guidance of his attorney, Korshak friend Robert Shapiro, took the Fifth Amendment and refused to testify. Evans was a close friend and promoter of child rapist and director Roman Polanski. Dated _____ *(fill in the blank with starlet names)*. Serial husband.

John Jacob Factor (1889–1984)—aka "Jake the Barber." British stock swindler, brother of Hollywood cosmetics baron Max Factor. After hiding out in Chicago, Factor faked his own kidnapping (with the Outfit's help) to avoid extradition to the UK (sending an innocent "kidnapper" to jail for life). Later, Factor fronted for the Outfit at their Stardust Hotel in Las Vegas. In Sin City, Jake took orders from Sid Korshak, while in Los Angeles, brother Max Factor employed Korshak to keep labor in line. Noted philanthropist.

Charlie Gioe (né Joye) (1904–1954)—aka "Cherry Nose." Bookie in the Capone Syndicate, co-owner of Chicago's Seneca Hotel (a key Supermob crossroads) with Alex Greenberg; convicted in the 1943 Hollywood extortion scandal, after which Sid Korshak, who had visited Gioe in prison twenty-two times, arranged for his parole supervision.

Alex Louis Greenberg (1891–1955)—aka "The Comptometer." Chicago bootlegger and real estate investor for the Capone mob and the Outfit, loan shark, and part owner of the Seneca Hotel. Partnered with Paul Ziffren and others in California land investments.

Al Hart (1904–1979)—Bootlegger in the Capone mob, distillery owner, backer of Bugsy Siegel in Las Vegas. After move to California, he owned the mob-friendly Del Mar Race Track and founded the mob-friendly City National Bank of Beverly Hills, later the largest independent bank in California. With Sid Korshak, an original investor in both the Bistro restaurant and Korshak's gangster getaway, The Acapulco Towers.

Conrad Hilton (1887–1979)—New Mexico–born patriarch of the Hilton Hotel dynasty, partnered with mob-front Arnold Kirkeby to expand his empire, which utilized Sid Korshak as labor consultant. Paid for his long association with Korshak when his bid to obtain a New Jersey casino license was rejected in 1985, largely due to Korshak's mob ties.

James Riddle "Jimmy" Hoffa (1913–1975?)—Rugged son of an Indiana coal miner who seemed predestined to head a violence-prone organization like the Teamsters, which he did from 1957 until his imprisonment for jury tampering in 1967. Hoffa was only able to attain his post thanks to the key backing of Outfit bosses such as Curly Humphreys, who had their sights fixed on the heavily endowed Pension Fund. When Hoffa allowed them Las Vegas loans, he had to answer to Sidney Korshak. Hoffa disappeared in 1975 after he announced he wanted to take back the Teamster presidency from a cabal that made Hoffa's relationship with racketeers seem benign by comparison.

Howard Robard Hughes (1905–1976)—Texas-born aviation-industry pioneer, film producer, Las Vegas–hotel magnate, recluse, and best-known sufferer of obsessive-compulsive disorder. Hughes tangled (successfully) with Sid Korshak over ownership of RKO studios in the fifties and unsuccessfully with Korshak's Outfit pals in Las Vegas in the seventies.

"Murray" Llewelyn Morris Humphreys (1899–1965)—aka "Curly," "The Hump," "The Camel," "John Brunswick," "G. Logan," "Mr. Lincoln," "Dave Ostrand," "Cy Pope," "Einstein," "Mr. Moneybags." Labor-racketeering, corruption, and bribery genius of the Chicago Outfit. Sidney Korshak's

direct superior and liaison to "the Chicago boys" after Korshak was sent West.

Burton W. Kanter (1930–2001)—Abe Pritzker's Chicago tax attorney, and a founder of the Castle Bank in the Bahamas, where the Pritzkers and other clients were able to dodge millions in taxes in the 1970s. Kanter, himself a multimillionaire, openly admitted to not paying taxes for decades. With the Pritzker dynasty, devised a kickback scheme involving Prudential Insurance and creative forms of offshore film financing used to bankroll some of Hollywood's biggest hits. At the time of his death, after a complicated ten-year IRS investigation, he was awaiting sentencing for massive tax evasion. Noted philanthropist.

Kerkor "Kirk" Kerkorian (1917–)—California-born, hugely successful dealmaker and conglomerate builder. After an early profitable airline venture, he purchased MGM and numerous Las Vegas hotels, including the Hilton International, MGM Grand, The Mirage, and Mandalay Bay. In his early career, he was linked by telephone wiretaps to Genovese crime-family enforcer Charlie "the Blade" Tourine.

Arnold S. Kirkeby (1900–1962)—Chicago real estate speculator who partnered with Conrad Hilton (openly) in numerous hotels and restaurants, and with hoods such as Meyer Lansky and Longy Zwillman (covertly).

Morris Jerome "Marshall" Korshak (1910–1996)—Sidney's kid brother and another Chicago-born attorney, one of the most successful elected politicians (liberal Democrat) in twentieth-century Chicago, and a lifelong supporter of the state of Israel.

Sidney Roy Korshak (1907–1996)—aka "The Fixer," "The Myth," "Mr. Silk Stockings," and "The Duke." Chicago-born attorney who was the point man in the Chicago Outfit's power plays in Hollywood and Las Vegas, often conducting business from his table at the Bistro restaurant in Beverly Hills, where he had relocated in the fifties. Middleman between the mob-controlled Teamsters and legit corporations who curried its favor for labor peace. In Vegas, he was in charge of a number of hotel-casinos, most notably The Riviera. Frequent escort of actresses Jill St. John (Oppenheim) and Stella Stevens (Estelle Eggleston), among others.

Irv Kupcinet (1912–2003)—aka "Kup." Iconic *Chicago Sun-Times* gossip columnist and Emmy Award–winning television host, Kup was a longtime friend of Sid Korshak's, with whom he shared Table One in the Ambassador East's Pump Room. Korshak came to Kup's aid when Kup's daughter was murdered in Hollywood in 1963.

Paul Dominque Laxalt (1922–)—Nevada-born U.S. senator (1974–87) and governor of Nevada (1967–71). Ronald Reagan's closest pal, and his presidential campaign chairman, he was also close to his own chief fund-raiser, Ruby Kolod of Cleveland's Mayfield Road Gang, and Chicago's Sid Korshak. When Laxalt needed a loan to build his Ormsby House Casino in Carson City (soon to be skimmed by the Chicago Outfit), Korshak allegedly had him write a character reference letter on behalf of imprisoned Jimmy Hoffa to President Nixon; Korshak then set him up with a loan from a friendly Chicago banker. When these associations and allegations were reported in the *Sacramento Bee*, Laxalt's long-planned presidential bid was torpedoed.

James Caesar Petrillo (1892–1984)—aka "Little Caesar" and "The Mussolini of Music." Longtime Chicago president of the powerful American Federation of Musicians (AFM). Often linked to the Chicago Outfit, Petrillo gave favored-fee status to Stein's fledgling MCA, enabling it to bury the competition. Target of three congressional investigations and two federal prosecutions for union corruption.

Abe Pritzker (1896–1986)—Chicago attorney (Pritzker, Pritzker and Clinton) and corporate mogul (Hyatt Hotel chain, the massive Marmon Group conglomerate). His firm's Stanford Clinton was a trustee of the mob's bank, aka the Teamsters Pension Fund, from which Hyatt made low-interest loans. Often linked to Chicago's Outfit, and L.A.'s "Capone," Jack Dragna, Pritzker employed lifelong friend Sid Korshak to keep labor unions in line. His company paid penalties of $460 million for a fraudulent bank failure and millions more to the IRS for tax evasion; the Pritzker empire was the largest depositor in the offshore Bahamian Castle Bank, which was developed by Pritzker's tax attorney Burton Kanter as a vehicle for tax dodging. Noted philanthropist.

Ronald Wilson Reagan (1911–2004)—aka "Dutch," "The Gipper," and "The Great Communicator." Sub-B actor from Iowa, who started out in

Outfit-controlled joints before being promoted by his agents, MCA's Stein and Wasserman, into the Screen Actors Guild presidency, the California governorship, and eventually the U.S. presidency. Lifelong hunter of commies, both real and imagined, and an informant on fellow actors for the FBI's J. Edgar Hoover. Told the Soviets, "Tear down this wall."

Harvey Silbert (1912–2002)—Chicago-born attorney; moved to L.A., where he was a partner in the powerful law firm Wyman, Bautzer, Rothman, Kuchel, Christianson, and Silbert, which represented many A-list celebrities; personal attorney for Frank Sinatra. Silbert was a stockholder in Korshak's heavily skimmed Riviera, which he managed for a time. (FBI sources alleged that Riviera skim was laundered through Silbert's law firm.) Silbert was also a director of the beleaguered Parvin-Dohrmann Corporation. Prolific philanthropist, especially to Jewish causes.

Michele Eugenio Sindona (1920–1986)—aka "The Shark" and "St. Peter's Banker." Charlie Bluhdorn's Sicilian alter ego, successful industrialist, banker, conglomerate builder; also a reputed made mafioso who laundered Gambino-family heroin profits through the Vatican Bank (one of his clients), and a member of the secret Italian Masonic Lodge, known as P-2. After investing heavily in Bluhdorn's Paramount Pictures, he was convicted of bank fraud in 1980 (sentenced to twenty-five years), then extradited to Italy, where he was convicted in 1986 of ordering the murder of an Italian prosecutor who was investigating Sindona's vast Mafia entanglements. Two days after his murder conviction, Sindona died in an Italian prison, poisoned under mysterious circumstances.

Dr. Julius Caesar "Jules" Stein (1896–1981)—Chicago ophthalmologist and founder of Music Corporation of America (MCA) and Universal Pictures, arguably the most powerful entertainment conglomerate in American history. Early friend of Al Capone, who helped Stein muscle his way into the business by smoke-bombing competitors. His MCA was continually investigated by the feds for six decades, with minimal repercussions. Noted philanthropist.

Lester Velie (1908–2003)—Classmate of Sid Korshak's at the University of Wisconsin, preeminent award-winning investigative journalist for *Collier's* and *Reader's Digest*; a lifelong organized-crime gadfly and the first to crusade against Korshak, Ziffren, and the Supermob.

Louis "Lew" Wasserman (né Weiserman) (1913–2002)—MCA president who, with Jules Stein, became one of the most powerful entertainment moguls in America. Tried hard to stay out of the public eye and was known as a brilliant visionary, tough businessman, and master of corporate tax avoidance through the use of the Dutch Sandwich scheme. Heavily reliant on Sid Korshak's sway over Hollywood unions and guilds. Together with Ziffren and Korshak, known as the Three Redwoods. Wasserman was an important West Coast supporter of many Democratic presidents.

Paul Ziffren (1913–1991)—Chicago attorney (and possibly the illegitimate son of Jake Arvey), specializing in tax law. Frequent real estate speculator, especially in postwar California, with the likes of Alex Greenberg, David Bazelon, Fred Evans, and Sam Genis. In his twenty-year run as California's Democratic national committeeman, Ziffren became, like his mentor Arvey in Illinois, a kingmaker for the Democratic Party in California in the mid-twentieth century. Brought both the 1960 Democratic convention (which nominated JFK) and the 1984 Olympics to L.A. His prestigious L.A. law firm, Gibson, Dunn and Crutcher, which specialized in tax matters, had a large celebrity clientele.

Abner Zwillman (1904–1959)—aka "Longy." New Jersey's most notorious gangster, founder of Murder Inc. Among his enterprises were gambling, prostitution running, and control of labor unions. Zwillman was possibly the first big gangster to "wash" his money in so-called legit businesses such as Kirkeby's Hilton Hotels, casinos from Havana to Las Vegas, and in Hollywood movie studios, where his interests (and girlfriends such as actress Jean Harlow) were often watched over by Sid Korshak.

Preface

Su-per-mob (soo-per-mahb) *n.* a group of men from the Midwest, often of Russian Jewish heritage, who made fortunes in the 20th century American West in collusion with notorious members of organized crime.

Two TYPES OF POWER dominated the twentieth century: the visible, embodied in politicians, corporate moguls, crime bosses, and law enforcement; and the invisible, concentrated in the hands of a few power brokers generally of Eastern European and Jewish immigrant heritage. Operating safely in the shadows, these men often pulled the strings of the visible power brokers. Although they remained nameless to the public, they were notorious among a smattering of enterprising investigators who, over decades, followed their brilliant, amoral, and frequently criminal careers. The late Senate investigator and author Walter Sheridan dubbed them the Supermob.

For all their power, this covert cadre of men had a surprisingly monolithic pedigree. They shared an ancestral lineage traceable from the former Russian-mandated Jewish ghetto known as the Pale of Settlement, emigrating first to the Maxwell Street–Lawndale sections of Chicago, and ultimately to what could be termed the Third Settlement, Beverly Hills, California. While they were nomadic to the degree that they followed the money, from Lake Shore Drive to the Vegas Strip to Beverly Hills, the Supermob largely succeeded in creating better, and more legitimate, lives for their offspring. In the process, they became quintessential capitalists, exerting such far-flung influence that the repercussions were felt by practically every American of their era, with an economic impact that could only be measured in the trillions of dollars. Through deniable, often arm's-length associations with the roughneck Italian and Irish mobsters imprinted in the

popular imagination, the Supermob and the hoods shared a sense of entitle-
ment regarding tax-free income. This "Kosher Nostra" stressed brains over
brawn and evolved into a real estate powerhouse, an organized-labor autoc-
racy, and a media empire. If power does, indeed, corrupt, then the Supermob corrupted absolutely. Through methodically nurtured political ties, the
Supermob effectively insulated itself from prosecution. They were above the
law.

They had names like Korshak, Arvey, Greenberg, Pritzker, and Ziffren.
Within this Supermob, Jake Arvey was the visionary kingmaker, the patriarchal Chicago ward boss who inspired his own young wards—prodigies like
Sid Korshak, the sphinxlike operator who quietly kept the wheels of the enterprise greased, or Alex Louis Greenberg, Paul Ziffren, and the others who
plunged into stealthy entrepreneurships that made up the engine of this hidden economy. Although they propelled the making of the movies we
watched, the music we listened to, the politicians we voted for, and the hotels and resorts we frequented, it is a testament to their genius that most
Americans never heard of any of them.

CHAPTER 1

The Lawyer from Lawndale

FADE IN
Beverly Hills. Present day.
INT STARBUCKS on BEVERLY DRIVE
At separate tables, a gaggle of aspiring screenwriters sip on their Frappuccinos as they ponder the next line to tap into their Mac iBooks. They all have a friend who has a friend whose sister works at Universal, or DreamWorks. They've all heard who is looking for new product and they aim to deliver. So here they sit, day after day, until they type the words FADE OUT on page 120 of the third draft of the mother of all screenplays. With any luck, they might soon actually *live* in Beverly Hills.

OVER THE LAST DECADE, a supposedly new type of office has emerged, wherein young entrepreneurs park themselves in a public coffee shop or restaurant for the better part of the day, as they work their cell phones and iBooks. With their Wi-Fi Internet connections, these "Laptopias" offer up-and-comers, whom the *Baltimore Sun* recently labeled the New Professionals, a more pleasant, and relatively low-cost, headquarters from which to launch their careers.[1] Little do they realize, the restaurant/office is nothing new—it was perfected, if not invented, by a shadowy man who plied his trade just two blocks from the Beverly Hills Starbucks, in The Bistro on Canon Drive. But this trailblazer never wrote a movie, and he never had to worry about someone's sister who used to work for a studio. He was on a first-name basis with the moguls themselves and could start up or kill movie productions with a quick call from one of two phones installed at his personal table at the restaurant.

In Hollywood, he was known as The Myth; his birth name was Sidney Roy Korshak, and his incredible reach said as much about his heritage as it did about the man, for Sid Korshak merely had to call one of a dozen men with whom he'd grown up on Chicago's West Side (and whose parents all hailed from a small parcel in the Russian West). In their lives, they accomplished the impossible, overcoming fierce anti-Semitism, making complex alliances with notorious underworld bosses, and emerging victorious, reinvented, and relatively unscathed in America's Garden of Eden, Beverly Hills, California.

Their common story began in Russia.

In 1791, Russian empress Catherine the Great established the Pale of Settlement. Meant as a territory for Russian Jews to live in impoverished sequestration from the rest of their countrymen, the encampment comprised the territories of present-day Latvia, Lithuania, Ukraine, Belarus, and parts of Poland. Jews living in the villages, or shtetls, of the Pale paid double taxes and were forbidden to lease land or receive higher education. After a brief period of liberalization in the 1860s, the restrictions were revisited with an even more vulgar ferocity, introducing a vile new word into the lexicon: *pogrom.*

The 1881 assassination of Czar Alexander II by radicals gave the Russian government, and the anti-Semitic factions within it, the excuse to crack down. *The Encyclopaedia Judaica* defines *pogrom* thus: "A Russian word designating an attack, accompanied by destruction, the looting of property, murder, and rape." After the assassination, and instigated by the government's resultant "May Laws," the Russian military carried out a wave of such pogroms, spreading throughout the southwestern regions. Two hundred state-sanctioned terror attacks took place in 1881 alone. In Kiev, home of the Korshak family, dozens of Jewish men were murdered, their houses looted, daughters raped, and almost a thousand families ruined financially. It is not surprising that such villainy left a powerful imprint in the collective memory of all who survived it. It would manifest itself in the West as a hunger for real estate, financial success, and higher education. The emphasis was on mind over muscle. Indeed, no other people valued education more than the Russian Ashkenazic Jews. To learn was a religious duty, and nothing was lower than ignorance, a belief that inspired a popular ghetto slogan: "Better injustice than folly." As Rabbi Edgar F. Magnin, founder of L.A.'s predominantly Jewish Hillcrest Country Club, was quoted: "We are Jews. We are a minority and a lot of people don't like us. We don't have to kowtow to anybody. We don't have to be weak . . . but we must use our heads. We are a very, very tiny minority in a tremendous majority."[2]

* * *

In the years 1882–93, Tevye and Bella Korshak, whose surname meant "kite," began sending their six sons to the western land of opportunity known as the United States, where they joined the wave of immigrants that hit American shores within months of the pogroms. After the requisite first landing at Ellis Island in New York, many proceeded farther westward, establishing their second settlement in America's Second City, Chicago. These arrivals were overwhelmingly young, but included a larger percentage of family groups, urban dwellers, people of skills and education, and permanent settlers than any other European group.

The first Jew, of the German sect, had actually arrived in Chicago five decades earlier. In 1838, a merchant named J. Gottlieb settled there briefly, then prophetically moved on to California in search of gold, unwittingly initiating a paradigm for Korshak and company. Before the immigration surge of the 1880s, the total Jewish population in Chicago was 10,000 out of 500,000. By 1920 that number had swelled to over 225,000, and by 1950 Chicago would have the second-largest Jewish count in America, numbering some 350,000.

The newest Americans quickly learned that German Jews like J. Gottlieb had arrived in Chicago at a more opportune time. On first arrival, the Russian Jews were met with a prejudice emanating, surprisingly, from their own religious kin, the origins of which were in internecine rivalries between Eastern and Western European Jews, and exacerbated by competition between new arrivals and settled, assimilated German Jews. These competing cliques even had their own discrete cemeteries. Perhaps worst of all, the Russian Jews were perceived as being unrelated to the original twelve tribes of the Torah.

The attitude of both the German Jews and the Spanish (Sephardic) Jews toward the Russian and Polish Jews was one of superiority and pity. German Jews thought themselves more intellectual and aristocratic. Many were professional businessmen, while the more orthodox, Yiddish-speaking, nomadic Russians were seen as only good enough to employ in the Germans' sweatshops. German Jews, hinting at their own Jewish self-hatred, regarded the Russians as inferior and illiterate, referring to them as schnorrers (beggars, or bums).

A manuscript entitled *Autobiography of an Immigrant*, written by an anonymous Ashkenazi, paints a dour picture: "When I first put my feet on the soil of Chicago, I was so disgusted that I wished I had stayed at home in Russia. I left the Old Country because you couldn't be a Jew over there and still live, but I would rather be dead than be the kind of German Jew that brings the Jewish name into disgrace by being a goy. That's what hurts: They parade around as Jews, and deep down in their hearts they are worse than goyim."[3]

The Germans' upper hand was temporary as they became outnumbered, within a brief but tumultuous ten years, by the Eastern European Jews (fifty thousand to twenty thousand), a change that forever altered the character of the Chicago Jewish community. On a macro level, Chicago's population grew from four thousand in 1840 to 1.7 million in 1900.

Invariably, the wanderers found Maxwell Street on the west side of the city.

Maxwell Street

Bereft of education, money, and property, these Russian Ashkenazic Jews packed into the poorest parts of Chicago to the west of the Chicago River—symbolic of the rift between themselves and the East Side–dwelling German Jews. In short time, they coalesced in an area that stretched from south of Taylor Street to the railroad tracks at about Sixteenth Street, and from Canal Street westward to Damen Avenue. This community, only minimally refurbished after the great Chicago fire of 1871, was centered around the intersection of Halsted and Maxwell streets, where the population was 90 percent Jewish. Over the next twenty years, an estimated fifty-five thousand Eastern European Jewish immigrants crowded into this tiny locus. So dense had this *ghetto* become that one social scientist determined that if the rest of the city were similarly clotted, Chicago would boast, instead of two million residents, over thirty-two million people, half the population of the entire country.[4]

Here, Yiddish was the language of the streets and homes, used for shopping, labor anthems, lullabies, and political debates. Although Maxwell Street included all the trappings of a shtetl—the open market bazaar being most popular—it was not yet a complete escape from the violence of the homeland. Maxwell Street was in fact known as Bloody Maxwell. In 1906, the *Chicago Tribune* published a description of the street:

> Murderers, robbers and thieves of the worst kind are here born, reared and grow to maturity in numbers that far exceed the record of any similar district anywhere on the face of the globe. Reveling in the freedom which comes from inadequate police control, inspired by the traditions of the criminals that have gone before in the district, living in many instances more like beasts than any human beings, hundreds and thousands of boys and men follow day after day year after year in the bloody ways of crime . . . From Maxwell come some of the worst murderers, if not actually the worst, that Chicago has ever seen. From Maxwell come the smoothest of robbers, burglars, and thieves of all kinds, from Maxwell come the worst

"tough-gangs." In general, it may be safely said that no police district in the world turns out such skilled and successful criminals.[5]

The atmosphere began to improve somewhat in 1899, after a Jewish peddler was killed, precipitating a protest meeting at Porges Hall at Jefferson and Maxwell streets. Attended by nearly five hundred, this mobilization led to the formation of the Hebrew-American Protective Association of Chicago. Subsequently, life within Maxwell Street was safer and familiar.

Lawndale

Turn-of-the-century immigrants to Chicago found a town that was a model of civic corruption. The city was divided into political wards, and power flowed up from the saloon-owning ward bosses directly to City Hall in an overt scheme involving payoffs and job patronage. Bosses like Michael "Hinky Dink" Kenna and John "Bathhouse" Coughlin were given exclusive rights to hire thousands of city workers, who, out of self-preservation, voted Kenna-Coughlin and their anointed mayors into office ad infinitum. It was a brilliant self-perpetuating corruption machine that had yet to assimilate the Jewish wave.

As Chicago's Russian Jews started to prosper at the turn of the century, they began moving out of the run-down Maxwell Street area, following Roosevelt Road west toward Ashland Street, then leapfrogging over the Damen Avenue rail yards, finally ending up four miles from the Lake Michigan shoreline in a community called Lawndale. They were barely two miles removed from the dregs of Bloody Maxwell Street, but their new home of Lawndale nonetheless seemed an eternity away. Now, instead of the crowded firetrap homes around Maxwell Street, the quiet streets of Lawndale featured brick homes with porches and backyards. So attractive was the locale to the Russian immigrants that by 1930 Russian Jews comprised 45 percent of Lawndale's population.

Called a "monument" to Jews who had successfully fled Maxwell Street, Lawndale was organized in 1857 and annexed to Chicago in 1869. The Chicago fire of 1871 sent the first wave of city Jews to Lawndale, followed by the Polish and Irish. When the Sears, Roebuck world headquarters, employing ten thousand workers, and the McCormick Reaper Company (International Harvester) were constructed in South Lawndale, many new inhabitants, especially the Russian Jews of Maxwell Street, took jobs there and found housing in eastern North Lawndale. Like Maxwell Street before it, Lawndale swelled from a population of 46,000 in 1910 to 93,750 in 1920, and 112,000 by 1930—50 percent of whom were Russian Jews. By the early forties, as the Jewish population of Chicago was approaching about 9 percent, about 110,000 of the 300,000 city Jews were living in the greater Lawndale area, the largest and most developed Jewish community that ever existed in Chicago.[6]

In truth, the name Lawndale was a misnomer—the apartment buildings and duplex homes were so tightly aligned that little room was left for lawns. (At its peak, Lawndale held the dubious distinction of having the highest population density in Chicago, earning it the moniker the Kosher Calcutta. By 1930, Lawndale's population density reached unprecedented totals at fifty-one thousand people per square mile.) Nonetheless, the locale was alive with outdoor activity, and the physical surroundings were a pleasant change from the chaos of Maxwell Street. What greenery existed was largely relegated to the large median on Douglas Boulevard and the bucolic expanses of Douglas Park. The boulevard was Lawndale's main thoroughfare, and the Jewish cultural center of the settlement, measuring 250 feet wide with a seventeen-foot-wide grass median. In a relative eye blink, some seventy synagogues and countless Jewish educational, medical, and convalescent facilities sprang up in this confined area, many of these facilities clustered around Douglas Boulevard.

Beneath the orthodox surface, subtle changes were mutating the culture of the Ashkenazim: They adopted an uncommon (for Jews) desire to assimilate, perhaps because they came to the collective conclusion that it was the only way to prosper in America. They started to affect German ways (so much so that this area of second settlement was often referred to as Deutschland), becoming increasingly less orthodox, or kosher. Lawndale Jews, as they were called, became lax about synagogue and began to frequent the Near North and the Loop for entertainment. The rabbi had been the most important person in their lives in the Pale and on Maxwell Street, but now, increasingly, the most important person was the precinct captain, who lorded over the vital patronage job allocations. The Jews even started producing athletes—Sidney Korshak was a school basketball and boxing star. But above all, they worked and studied tirelessly in an effort to ascend the social and economic ladder. In the words of Pulitzer Prize–winning journalist Wendell Rawls, "The Jews were called names, but they were smarter than the others. They knew math and percentages. They were the Asians of their day."[7]

Since Jews were not allowed to rent, they bought Lawndale—block by block—and they were thrilled to be able, for the first time, to do so. Their focus on acquiring real estate bordered on the obsessive and would play a major role in the success of the Supermob. The intense drive for improvement created a potent primordial soup that saw an extraordinary number of Maxwell Saint/Lawndale youths achieve greatness: there were entertainers such as Benny Goodman, whose father had taken him to the free band concerts in Douglas Park on Sunday afternoons; actors Wallace Beery, Tom Mix, Gloria Swanson, and Paul Muni; President Kennedy's secretary of labor, Arthur Goldberg; World War II military hero Admiral Hyman George Rickover; champion lightweight boxer Barney Ross; corporate moguls William S. Paley (founder of CBS) and Barney Balaban (founder of Paramount Pictures); Harry Hart, of Hart, Schaffner & Marx men's clothing; Julius Rosenwald, founder of Sears, Roebuck; Charles Lubin, of the Kitchens of Sara Lee; the Goldblatt brothers, founders of the fifty-store chain of Goldblatt's Department Stores; the Bensinger family of Brunswick Bowling; Abe Pritzker, founder of Hyatt Hotels and the massive conglomerate the Marmon Group; Henry Crown of General Dynamics and an owner of the Empire State Building; writer L. Frank Baum (*The Wizard of Oz*); and even the occasional infamous ne'er-do-well like Lee Harvey Oswald's killer, Jack Ruby, and a key member of Al Capone's brain trust, Jake Guzik.[8] Then there were the not-so-famous successes . . .

One year after the 1881 pogroms in Kiev, brothers Mendel and David Korshak, then young adults, set sail from Hamburg, Germany, on the SS *Suevia* and arrived in New York in 1882. They proceeded on to Chicago, followed over by Max, Abraham, Reuben, and, finally in February 1889, thirteen-year-old Harry, the youngest by almost a generation. It is believed that all the Korshaks in America today descended from these siblings. David Korshak, a saloonkeeper and a real estate investor, achieved ignominy when he became part of an arson-for-hire ring, and the first Korshak to be exposed in the *New York Times* (July 13, 1913). One of David's partners was an insurance adjuster named Joseph Fish, whose wife was heiress to the Brunswick bowling ball and billiards empire. That an old-line German Jew would have engaged in an arson conspiracy with an immigrant Russian Askenazi contradicted the conventional wisdom, but for a time, the partnership flourished. David, who was dubbed King of the Firebugs by the *Chicago Daily Journal*, even hooked up with an Italian for the schemes. With Fish's insurance ken and Korshak's talent with kerosene, the arson trust set up operations in Chicago, New York, and other large cities, defrauding numerous insurance companies out of tens of thousands of dollars. As friends and a

David Korshak, arsonist (Rich Samuels)

family photo album attest, David Korshak appeared to have a special closeness with Harry's middle child, Sidney.[9]

Also of interest was brother Max, the first of many Korshak lawyers. According to Korshak family historian Rich Samuels (husband of Judy Korshak), Max became one of the two protégés of Judge Harry Fisher. The other was a fellow young Ashkenazi named Jacob Arvey, about whom much more will be seen. According to Samuels, Max wanted to become the ward boss and kingmaker that Arvey eventually became, but only reached as high as the master of chancery in circuit court.*

Brother Abraham was found guilty, along with his son Jimmy, of beating a woman named Sophie White into unconsciousness on June 10, 1933, and a federal grand jury had earlier indicted Jimmy and a brother for violation of the Volstead Act (the federal law that outlawed the sale of alcohol from 1920 to 1933). Jimmy was not convicted, but his brother was.[10] Alluding to the less savory aspects of the family's history many years later, Harry's son Morris (later "Marshall") told the attendees at the second family reunion, "You know, in the old country we were horse thieves. In this country we became car thieves." When he noticed a journalist in the crowd, he suddenly changed the topic. Descendant Judy Korshak's husband, Rich Samuels, said, "I sometimes think my wife thinks she's still in the marketplace in Kiev. There's a certain toughness there. My wife says, 'Don't ever fuck with a Korshak.'"[11]

Harry's Atlantic crossing was followed in 1890 by that of his future wife, then seven-year-old Rebecca Beatrice Lashkovitz from Odessa. Young Rebecca barely survived a pogrom; her parents' landlord was a kindly gentile

---

*Charlie Korshak was another family lawyer, but his career was a bust. In his first case, the murder defendant he represented confessed on the stand. It was the first and last case he tried.

David with nephew Sidney at a 1927 Korshak family picnic (Rich Samuels)

who allowed her family to hide in his barn when the Cossacks searched the house. Harry and Rebecca married in Chicago in 1902, and Harry took work as a two-dollar-per-week laborer, before hiring on as a carpenter contractor, then starting his own company. When Harry's small construction enterprise began to flourish, the family, which quickly came to include five children, joined the Maxwell Street exodus to Lawndale, where Harry presided over a kosher home—son Marshall would continue the tradition, never having bacon or ham in his own home. Harry now operated his business out of his family's new Douglas Boulevard home (which he built), just down the street from Douglas Park, where Jake Arvey, too short to play basketball with the towering Korshaks, played tennis.[12] Named after Senator Stephen A. Douglas, Douglas Park was a large and beautiful landscaped refuge that saw the occasional nighttime turf war between Polish gangs and the new Lawndale Jews.

On June 6, 1907, Rebecca gave birth to Sidney Roy Korshak, the middle child among five: Theodore (1903), Minnie (1905), Sidney Roy (1907), Morris Jerome (1910), and Bernard (1913).[13] Morris, who went by the name Marshall, described his six-foot-two-inch father as a "cream puff," whereas his mother was "the strong one, an introvert like Sidney." Sidney may have been an introvert, but by all accounts he was a tough one. One schoolmate told the *New York Times* in 1976, "He was handsome and had a lot of ego and a lot of guts. He didn't let anybody push him around. Sid was a tough guy."[14] The famously outgoing Marshall noted, "Sidney and I are completely different."

Sidney's elder siblings were family tragedies. Theodore, known as Ted, fell into the throes of drug addiction and, using numerous aliases, amassed quite a rap sheet with the local police, often charged with narcotics violations and confidence schemes. For a time he ran a bookie joint at 217 North Clark Street for Tony "Joe Batters" Accardo, boss of the Chicago Outfit,

Tony "Joe Batters"
Accardo mug shot
(Chuck Schauer)

and his underboss, Charles "Cherry Nose" Gioe. (Sidney's cousin Pete Posner handled bookmaking for the Outfit in the Hyde Park section for Curly Humphreys's underlings Ralph Pierce and Hy Godfrey.)[15]

Minnie Korshak's tragedy was of a different kind. Shortly after her marriage to Harry Wexler, she died of an unknown cause on January 12, 1928, at just twenty-two years of age. Exactly one year later, the Korshaks paid tribute to her, placing a short poem in the *Chicago Tribune*'s death notices:

> *Thoughts return to days long past,*
> *Time rolls on, memory lasts.*
> *Your life is a beautiful memory.*
> *Your absence a great, great sorrow to us.*

—LOVING PARENTS AND BROTHERS[16]

Like many of the Lawndale Jewish youth, Sidney attended Herzl Grammar School, then Marshall High School, where he was an A student and a standout basketball player, his skills no doubt honed in Douglas Park, little more than a long jump-shot from his front yard. His academic success mirrored the business fortunes of his father, Harry, who was on his way to becoming one of the most successful contractors in Lawndale. "My father was a Jewish millionaire," recalled Marshall. "He was worth about two hundred thousand dollars, a fortune in the twenties."[17] From 1925 to 1927, Sidney went to the University of Wisconsin, enrolled in the College of Letters and Sciences. At UW, the Phi Sigma Delta pledge held an 82 average, but with a 98 in Phys Ed, not surprising given that he won the 158-pound title in the 1927 All University Boxing Championships. The school paper reported on the curious nature of Sidney's pugilistic success: "Korshak was awarded a verdict over Schuck at 158 pounds in an overtime period. Korshak, tall and with a long reach, was unable to withstand the heavy punching of Schuck, who hit him at a rate of six blows to one. However, an overtime period was required, and again Schuck sent Korshak reeling with a flock of stomach blows and kidney punches. Consequently when the judges awarded the fight to Korshak, there was a great deal of surprise in the crowd."

Korshak left UW for DePaul University, where he graduated in June 1930 with a law degree.[18] His grades had slipped to a C+ average, and, curiously, the only A's he received in two years were in Partnership, Trust, and Property Law—subjects well suited to his future successes. After Sidney's death many

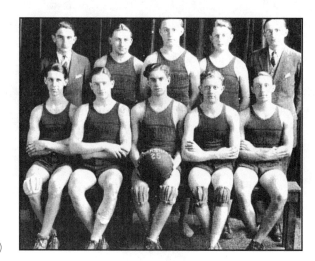

Sidney Korshak (front row, far left), the Marshall High School basketball team's star center (Francelia Herron)

Sidney Korshak's 1925 Marshall High School portrait (Francelia Herron)

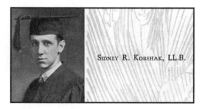

Sidney R. Korshak, LL.B.

Sidney Korshak's law school graduation photo (DePaul University Alumni Relations)

Frat boy Sidney Roy Korshak (top row, fourth from left), 1928 (David Null, University of Wisconsin Alumni Association)

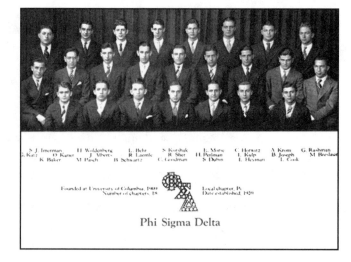

Phi Sigma Delta

years later, a collegetown scribe wrote ominously, "He left DePaul for the shadows, where he spent the next sixty years."[19]

Sidney Korshak was licensed to practice law on October 16, 1930,* and his younger brother Marshall followed Sidney to Herzl, Marshall High, Wisconsin, and DePaul. "I aped Sidney," Marshall remembered. At Wisconsin, Marshall was a privileged student, receiving $125 a week from his father. However, when Harry was hard hit by the Depression, Marshall's University of Wisconsin days were over. "My brother Sidney called and said, 'You'd better come home and tell Dad you don't want to stay,'" Marshall recalled years later. "He was telling me the old man was broke."[20] Marshall came home and sold programs at Soldier Field, putting himself though night school at the Kent School of Law ($175 per semester), where he earned his law degree. Their father, Harry, would die soon thereafter, on January 29, 1931, at age fifty-five, likely due to the combined effects of the Great Depression and his young daughter's death. Marshall would go on to build one of the greatest political careers in Chicago history, all the while keeping his thriving law practice going.†

Whereas Marshall's career remained squeaky-clean, Sidney would prove to have few qualms about subscribing to the maxim "The ends justify the means." Tom Zander (pseudonym), a former organized crime investigator with the Chicago office of the U.S. Department of Labor, said of the brothers' formative years, "I saw Sidney when he was moving up the ladder. I knew his brother Marshall very well. He was a great fifth Ward committeeman. I think Marshall was against the mob, but was very careful never to say it. In Chicago it wasn't uncommon for one brother to go straight while the other went with the boys."[21]

These two most enterprising of Harry's sons, Sidney and Marshall, were astute enough to deduce that the shortest road out of Deutschland was to ally with Uncle Max's fellow protégé of Judge Fisher's, and their neighbor of some six blocks away, the rising Twenty-fourth Ward star Jake Arvey. The Korshaks had been friends with the Arveys for as long as anyone could remember, and that kinship would come to benefit not only Sidney and

---

*In his application for membership in the Chicago Bar Association, Korshak listed the following references: David Silberg (111 W. Washington St.), Solomon P. Roderick (139 N. LaSalle St.), Philip R. Davis (188 W. Randolph St.), and his uncle Max Korshak (11 S. LaSalle St.).

†In his five-plus decades in the political arena, Marshall Korshak held down a staggering number of elected and appointed posts, such as Fifth Ward committeeman, state senator, Sanitary District trustee, state revenue collector, Cook County treasurer, Chicago city treasurer, city collector, and Police Board member.

Marshall, but also the majority of America's future Supermob. For in Lawndale's solar system, there was but one star for the up-and-comers to orbit, Jake Arvey.

The Patriarch

A man ain't going nowhere without he has his Chinaman.
—CHICAGO PROVERB

Jacob Meyer Arvey was born in Chicago in 1895, the son of Russian immigrants Israel and Bertha Arvey. Like so many other Russian Ashkenazim, Israel worked in the Maxwell Street marketplace. A hardworking street peddler and milkman, Israel inculcated his son with the need for self-improvement. Arvey described the times: "Where [my parents] came from in Russia, they were poor not only in money but poor in liberty and opportunity . . . They could not participate in who would govern them. And they were always in fear of the raids and assaults of hooligans and Cossacks . . . They were denied things. They had to grease the palms of authorities. Pay tribute in the *shtetls*. And the story of Maxwell Street is like the story of the Jews all over the world for centuries. They are raised amid violence, muscle, corruption, [and] distortion . . . Well, I was understanding that things could be better for the Jew. The opportunity was there. We needed the power."[22]

After his father's death when Jacob was just thirteen, Arvey located the power quickly: it was concentrated at the Roosevelt Road headquarters of the corrupt Twenty-fourth Ward Democratic organization, a model of miscreant efficiency, with sixty Jewish neighborhood precinct captains each responsible for a small section of the ward, where they knew everyone and almost everything. They befriended the voters, often bringing food, clothing, and coal to the needy, helped immigrants secure citizenship papers, and assisted people who had run afoul of the law or merely needed traffic tickets fixed.

This hands-on, in-person style of ward politics had been the brainchild of brothers Michael and Moe Rosenberg. The Rosenbergs, also sons of Russian immigrants, started out as junk dealers, but after forming an alliance with the notorious utilities baron Samuel "the Emperor" Insull, they prospered, becoming among the first Maxwell Street habitués to make the exodus to Lawndale.[23] Insull, a former private secretary to inventor Thomas Edison, and himself a genius in business, inherited Edison's General Electric power company and, thanks to massive political corruption, built it and his other holdings into a $2 billion empire. The Rosenbergs, in exchange for uncontested junk-hauling contracts from Insull, corrupted countless pols who happily allowed Insull to use monopolistic and predatory practices in exchange for "investment opportunities" in the power company—in other words, insider stock priced far below the market quotes. Ovid Demaris, the seminal historian of Chicago crime, described the unsavory climate thus: "[Insull] built his paper colossus on the hot coals of corruption. Corrupt politicians and predatory law firms kept it precariously fireproof for forty years in a continuing conspiracy that provided low taxes, and favorable legislation, plus safe judges, reasonable mayors, pliable aldermen, patronage officeholders, and anybody else who could serve Insull's undivided interest."[24]

Everyone got rich together, and when the stock market crashed in 1929, Insull merely sold overvalued stock to the public, costing investors over $2 billion in losses. So hated did Insull become that he hired Capone's musclemen to protect him from his countless enemies. Eventually, Insull's paper profits evaporated and he was charged with stock fraud and, separately, with embezzlement—he escaped conviction in both.[*,25] Years later Moe Rosenberg would serve a prison term for receiving stolen goods and was also indicted for tax evasion. In an effort to lessen his sentence, Rosenberg gave a full confession in 1933 regarding the massive political-corruption schemes he had entered into with Insull. However, Rosenberg died before the trial started, and a year later his sealed confession was made public.[26]

Although his father's death forced Arvey to work evenings after high school, and days while at night school at John Marshall Law School, he made time to grease the Rosenberg corruption machine. The Rosenbergs became Jake's "Chinamen," or sponsors. Arvey's was a year-round job, but he was especially visible among his neighbors before each election, when every home was visited more than once to convince and plead with voters to vote for the endorsed candidates. It wasn't uncommon to see Arvey escort semiliterate Jewish immigrants, ignorant of the complexities of white-collar gangsterism, into the voting booth, instructing them, "Vote this way." One of Arvey's successful protégés, Judge Abraham Marovitz, recalled in 1997, "They would give them matzos at Passover, and feed and clothe them, and, come election time, Arvey said, 'You vote for so-and-so,' and, 'You vote for so-and-so.'"[27]

The often-beholden voters turned out landslide majorities for the party machine, which sometimes garnered as much as 97 percent of the vote. Most Chicago Jews had voted Republican until the late 1920s, when they

---

*Sadly, the jury appeared glazed over by the staggeringly complex financial testimony and was, instead, moved by the simple rags-to-riches story of Insull.

started voting Democratic.[28] Jake Arvey once said of the Twenty-fourth Ward, "The only ones who voted Republican were the Republican precinct captains, election judges, and their families." Arvey's political prowess would soon garner him a national reputation. "In the election of 1936," Arvey later wrote, "President Roosevelt called our ward the best Democratic ward in the country."[29]

While too young to vote, a teenaged Jake Arvey nonetheless became a precinct captain for the Rosenbergs. The lifelong Democrat rang doorbells, developed personal relationships with voters, and learned about patronage, Ashkenazic style. Implicit in everything Arvey accomplished in his career was the attendant loyalty to all Jewish causes—a trait he would inculcate in his own protégés. He also insisted that his workers balance their lives with regular giving to the less fortunate. "I'm an intense Jew," Arvey later wrote. "I demanded that any man who was a precinct captain of mine had to belong to a church—Catholic, Protestant, or Jewish . . . I made them charity-minded, civic-minded, culture-minded, and sensitive to the needs of other people."[30] This charitable sensibility—*tzedaka* is the Hebrew word for giving back to the community—would become a paradoxical leitmotif in the coming decades for even Arvey's most corrupt students.

Arvey was admitted to the bar in 1916, at just twenty-one years of age, and then became the personal attorney for the Rosenbergs' junk business and Moe's Cook County Trust Company. Here, Arvey learned the beauty of the "receivership" game, the obtaining of foreclosed properties at fire-sale prices. Again, Demaris: "The fantastic earnings of receivers in six years in Chicago totally eclipsed the illicit profits of gangsters. One Congressional Committee investigating real estate foreclosures for a six-year period reported in 1936 that 'there appears in the State courts serving Chicago and its adjacent territory approximately 100,000 foreclosure cases filed since January 1930, representing approximately $2,000,000,000 in face value.' "[31]

Demaris concluded that local attorneys had accrued some $100 million in fees during the period. While working at the Trust Company, Arvey utilized the Rosenberg-controlled judges to obtain 272 receiverships. He and his emissaries, known as Arvey's Army, would revisit this scheme with a vengeance when Japanese Americans saw their California land confiscated during World War II.

When Mike Rosenberg died in 1928, Arvey was chosen to fill his spot as Ward committeeman. As such, Arvey ushered in a new era in Chicago politics, that of the politician/lawyer. It was now his turn to be the Chinaman. Previously, political power rested in the hands of saloonkeepers and bookies. Lawyering formed the bedrock of this new political sophistication, and

Korshak pals Jake Arvey (right) and
Arthur Elrod (center) with unidentified
associate (Chicago Historical Society)

years later Arvey would mentor and advise a young Richard Daley as to the
wisdom of earning a law degree. Daley had admired Arvey, who guaranteed
him great success in politics if he passed the bar. Daley followed Arvey's
advice and attained staggering power both in Illinois and the nation. His
biographers dubbed Daley the American Pharaoh.

With the help of Syndicate legend Al Capone, Arvey and Moe Rosenberg
elected Anton "Ten Percent" Cermak mayor of Chicago in 1931. In his quest
to "beat the Irish," Cermak focused on gaining the approval of the working
classes, and using Rosenberg's and Arvey's army of precinct captains, he un-
abashedly used patronage to gain the mayor's office. With Capone thugs
providing security, Arvey's Army stood in the polling places and reminded
the families of what they did for them, often accompanying the voter right
into the polling booth. "Let me put it to you in a crude way," Arvey advised
his young charges. "Put people under obligation to you."[32] By putting people
under obligation, especially those prone to legendary *ashmah*, or "Jewish
guilt," a self-perpetuating political machine was born. Patronage was king,
and Arvey's Army elevated the practice into an art form.

When Cermak was assassinated in 1933 in Florida by a lone shooter (who
some believe was actually aiming at the nearby President Roosevelt), Arvey
set about building his own legacy, solidifying his anointing as "The Kingmaker." With some seventy-five Arvey's Army precinct captains at his
command—many of whom went on to local and national success—Arvey
relished behind-the-scenes power. One of his precinct captains, Marshall
Korshak, remembered putting Arvey's style to work. "When I was a precinct
captain, I knew every one of the voters by their first name," Korshak said.
"I knew their wives. I knew their children. I knew their family."[33] When
Marshall set his sights on the Fifth Ward committeeman post years later,
his brother Sidney spoke to Arvey about it. Arvey appointed Marshall
committeeman, even though Arvey had to ask his own law partner, Barnet

Hodes, to vacate the position for Marshall. Putting Arvey's patronage rule foremost, Committeeman Marshall Korshak obtained jobs for over five thousand constituents in one ten-year period, according to one estimate.[34]

Arvey would spend twenty-eight years as ruler of the Twenty-fourth Ward before becoming Cook County Democratic chairman. His ward organization created absurd Democratic pluralities for Franklin Roosevelt—such as 29,000–700 (1936) and 29,533–2,204 (1944)—and his successor, Harry Truman. However, rumors of impropriety were never far beneath the surface. According to his obit, "Arvey's organization was at the top of the list in vote fraud charges, including ballot box stuffing, illegal voting and polling place violations."[35] By his own admission, Arvey took thousands of parking tickets to the mayor's office for scuttling.[36] He also freely admitted the election frauds perpetrated by his precinct captains. "Some of them went to illegal means to do it," he wrote. "I know it. I regret it very much, but they were inconsequential in relation to the ultimate result."[37]

With his expanding powers, Arvey extended the patronage system. It wasn't just the thousands of civil jobs that came under Arvey's thumb; applicants wishing to work at Lawndale's Sears, Roebuck headquarters knew better than to show up without a letter from Jake Arvey.[38] Other jobs were secured through Arvey's cousin George Eisenberg, a Maxwell Street Russian immigrant who made millions with his Northwest Side company, American Decal and Manufacturing.*

Not all of Arvey's triumphs were in the public arena, however. Congressional investigators learned that his law firm commanded a $24,000-per-year retainer from the infamous illegal national bookie service known as Continental Press,[39] itself the brainchild of fellow Russian Jewish émigré Moe Annenberg. Born in Prussia in 1878, Annenberg came to Chicago in 1885 and made his mark in the newspaper circulation wars of the 1920s that pitted William Randolph Hearst against Colonel Robert McCormick, not to mention the six other competing daily rags. Moe and his brother Max utilized the talents not only of well-connected Capone sluggers to gain the upper hand, but North Siders like Dion O'Banion. When Moe founded Continental, he again employed Capone's muscle to snuff out the competition. After Capone was sent to prison, Annenberg's alliance with the new Outfit was strengthened. In return, the Capone gang's bookies received the wire service free of charge. After his indictment for tax evasion on August 11, 1939, Moe Annenberg walked away from the wire business and the Capones took over. After the

*Like Arvey, Eisenberg espoused charity and donated many millions to over thirty-five institutions, including the Mayo Clinic, which received a $50 million bequest.

Capone takeover, Arvey began working for Continental.* After an in-depth investigation, the 1951 Kefauver Committee concluded, "The Continental Press national horsetrack service is controlled by the Capone mob in Chicago."

But there was an even more furtive association than that with the wire mogul. Early on, Arvey made a fortuitous alliance with a future powerful industrialist who would play a role in not only Arvey's financial success, but that of protégés such as the Korshaks. He was born Henry Krinsky, but was raised as Henry Crown.

Henry Crown, who spoke at a 1964 testimonial honoring Marshall Korshak,[40] had a long history with Jake Arvey. Henry was the third of seven children of Arie Crown (formerly Krinsky) and Ida Gordon. Crown's father, another Russian Jewish immigrant from the Pale, worked in the Maxwell Street market as a suspender maker, a foreman in a sweatshop, and a pushcart peddler. Like so many others, young Henry attended night school, where he took classes in bookkeeping. After persuading Chicago banks to extend him credit, he and his brother Sol formed the Material Service Corporation (MSC), a sand-and-gravel building-supply company—one of many conglomerates that would hire Sidney Korshak as its labor lawyer. Years later, Korshak told New Jersey gaming officials that, among his other successes, he'd intervened when Teamsters would not allow Crown's nonunion trucks to have access to his gravel pits in Indiana.[41]

As MSC prospered, Crown diversified into numerous raw-product and manufacturing entities, and real estate investing, which included the purchase of the Empire State Building in the 1950s.† With the political influence of his pal Arvey, Crown obtained lucrative city contracts in Chicago such as the award to furnish all the pencils and paper for the city's school system. He also supplied the coal for over four hundred schools, earning an additional $1 million per year.

---

*Moe Annenberg's son Walter, a partner in the race wire, joined the Chicago exodus to California and went on to great success, founding such publications as *TV Guide* and *Seventeen*. In 1969, Richard Nixon appointed Walter U.S. ambassador to Great Britain. Walter devoted the second half of his life to philanthropy, establishing a foundation valued at over $3 billion. In 1991 alone, he gave away $1 billion; likewise in 1993. In his father's honor, Walter endowed the prestigious M. L. Annenberg School of Communication at the University of Pennsylvania and at the University of Southern California.

†In 1952, with an investment of $3 million, Crown joined a partnership to buy the Empire State Building. He used his earnings to buy out other shareholders, reduce the mortgage, and improve the property to draw new office tenants to the landmark skyscraper at Fifth Avenue and Thirty-fourth Street. When he sold the building in 1961 for $65 million, his profit amounted to nearly $50 million.

The Two Colonels

After Japan attacked Pearl Harbor, Jake and Henry enlisted in the U.S. army. Arvey, aged forty-six, served four years as a judge advocate, including two years in the South Pacific, and when he came home in late 1945, he carried the rank of lieutenant colonel. However, during his military hitch, Arvey managed to become, with no small thanks to friends in the Roosevelt administration, the overseer of the countless international post exchange (PX) facilities on military bases. Soon, the military was supplying these PXes with commercial goods purchased from buddy Col. Crown's Material Service Corporation.

As for Crown, he was assigned to duty as a procurement officer for the Western Division, Corps of Engineers. Crown's service took him first to Los Angeles, where he directed the purchasing of military supplies. Eventually reassigned to the Great Lakes Division as chief of procurement, he was stationed near Chicago and promoted to full colonel. In that position, he supervised over $1 billion in military purchases. One month before his 1945 discharge, MSC was sued for more than $1 million by the Office of Price Administration for price-gouging a number of Chicago City and State of Illinois agencies.[42] Four years later, a Mrs. Dora Griever Stern began a fourteen-year legal struggle to obtain her share of MSC. Incorporation papers filed in 1919 proved that she had invested her life savings ($4,250) for 170 shares (of 800) of the fledgling company. Her investment should have earned back approximately $100 million. She had received nothing. Ultimately the courts decided that she had waited too long to file.

MSC would go on to become one of the largest government contractors in history. By any measure, it was the forerunner of the present-day Hal-

Captain Jake Arvey (Chicago Historical Society)

liburton and Bechtel conglomerates. In 1962, three years after Crown negotiated the merger of Material Service Corporation as an autonomous division with General Dynamics Corporation, it was awarded the largest
governmental contract ($6.5 billion) in world history—that for the TFX
fighter plane development. General Dynamics had been everyone's second
choice (after Boeing) for the contract, and a four-month Senate investigation
obtained testimony that political payoffs were made to ensure Crown's successful bid. This scandal-ridden project ended with the plane being one of
the great design failures in history.

In 1949, Arvey used insider information about soon-to-be-condemned
property to purchase land that the city would soon need to build the Congress Street thoroughfare. With a $1 million gift from Crown (a "loan" that
was never repaid), Arvey purchased a square block of property including
twenty-seven buildings for $900,000. A small portion of this property was
sold back to the city in 1949 for $1,206,452.62 for the highway construction.
Arvey's syndicate kept the remaining office buildings.[43]

Propinquity

"Within the Jewish West Side political community, everybody knew everybody else," said Korshak family historian Rich Samuels.[44] Without doubt,
two of the closest Lawndale families were the Korshaks and the Arveys. It
was Marshall Korshak whom the *Chicago Sun-Times* referred to as "the
worthy successor to Jack Arvey."[45] Marshall later said about Jake/Jack
Arvey, "He was the guy that impressed me the most. I learned from him. He
understood the problems of our people."[46] When Arvey was honored by
the Israel Bond Organization years later, Marshall served as chairman of the
event. Arvey was especially fond of Sidney. According to a retired Chicago
attorney who was close to the Korshak brothers, "Jake just loved hanging
with Sidney."[47]

Both Korshak brothers freely admitted their closeness with Arvey, Sidney to the FBI,[48] and Marshall to the local newsmen. And Jake Arvey returned the compliment, telling journalist Lester Velie in 1950, "Sidney
Korshak is one of my best friends in the world." The ward boss proceeded
to prove that to Velie. When Velie interviewed Arvey, the writer tipped him
that he had just left Korshak's law office, where he had noted the names of
many of his "clients" who had phoned the barrister's switchboard. Returning to Korshak's the next day, Velie found that all the callers were now
mysteriously using code names such as Mr. Black or Mr. White or Mr.
Green.[49]

The past is never dead. It's not even past.[50]

—WILLIAM FAULKNER

Like every other college grad set loose in the world, twenty-four-year-old Sid Korshak had life choices to make. He had lived through family tragedies and was just one generation removed from officially sanctioned Russian violence perpetrated against his family and everyone they knew back in the Pale. It is safe to assume that Sid and his brother Marshall were determined that such privations would never visit them or their offspring again. They opted for the kind of power that would grant just such assurances, and if that choice meant walking an ethical or legal tightrope, so be it. As Jake Arvey put it, "You have to be unmindful of everything except the ultimate goal. This is what we must attain. If anybody stands in the way, out with them! . . . It's a rough, tough game."[51]

In the post-Capone Chicago of the 1930s, the underworld heirs to Capone known as the Outfit, labor unions, and politicians were the ones with power, but they blurred together in murky alliances so as to increase their prosperity. All was for sale in Chicago as long as you had the muscle, brains, education, and economic and/or political power to take it. The Jews and the Italians who ran the Outfit were connected not only by their thirst for power, but by the value they placed in family. The only question was, how could the Outfit's power paradigm be altered to include these new Jewish up-and-comers? The answer was simple and elegant: the Jews would stay in the background. Throughout history, the Jews were never the public leaders; they were always the kingmakers and the power brokers. They knew from experience that a Jew would not get a top spot, however low the level, because of the existing anti-Semitism, even in America. They were always aware that their wealth and position in society could be noticed and another pogrom would ensue. Thus they worked surreptitiously, choosing to focus on the substrata of a business or event.

The Russians were fully confident that they possessed the drive and resilience to succeed in the shadows. They had only to look at recent history in Chicago for proof: German Jews hadn't allowed their Russian counterparts into The Standard Club, so the Russians had formed The Covenant Club; the Russians couldn't get on the board at Michael Reese Hospital, so they built Mount Sinai; unable to join the Illinois bar, they formed the Decalogue Society in 1935, the oldest and largest Jewish legal fraternity in America, today consisting of sixteen hundred Jewish lawyers.*[52]

---

*H. Burton Schatz, one of the society's founders, cited racial slurs in court, discrimination in hiring, and newspaper ads excluding Jews from applying for jobs as reasons for creating

The fields they chose to conquer were, in hindsight, predictable. Historically excluded from many professions such as politics and civic functions, Jews naturally gravitated to becoming bankers and merchants—they were not prohibited by religion from dealing in money. And trade was an abstraction that didn't require social assimilation—enemies often trade. Also, due to their historical wanderings, the Jews were worldlier than their adversaries, and far less provincial. Their wide-ranging travels brought the additional benefit of language skills, which engendered international connections. The Jews' historical Diaspora (dispersion) and relative lack of national roots helped them to identify and exploit more quickly the most lucrative emerging markets. Jewish merchants had operated in Venice, destined to become the first great epicenter of Europe's economic revival, long before it emerged into prominence in the thirteenth century.

Lastly, Jews were forced to toil in WASP sweatshops, ironically becoming the leaders of the labor union movement, the ascendancy of which brought about a tail-wagging-the-dog economy. It was a successful garment workers' strike by Chicago's Russian Jews in 1910 that established collective bargaining in the clothing industry. Among the most notable accomplishment was the founding of the Federation of Jewish Trade Unions in 1930.

Unable to compete in the higher circles of industrial capitalism, the Jews fixed their attention on many of the emerging niches of the developing world economy, for which participation they are now best known, such as diamonds, communications, fashion, retailing, entertainment, and the medical-legal professions. But those who came to comprise the Supermob steered toward law, real estate, finance, and partnerships with the gangsters of lore.

Footnote cont'd
the society. It was formed so "the judges, newspapers, businesses, and the public would get to know that Jewish lawyers are just as decent, just as effective as other lawyers are."

CHAPTER 2

From Lawndale to the Seneca . . . to the Underworld

> *You want diplomatic? . . . Greatest diplomats the world ever saw
> were the German Jews. Where did diplomacy get them? A ticket to
> Auschwitz.*
>
> —RABBI SCHLOMO CUNIN, CHABA HOUSE, LOS ANGELES[1]

WITH THEIR LAW DEGREES and chutzpah, Korshak, Arvey, Crown, and the others began to envision a world beyond Lawndale, itself a community that was always intended as a temporary way station on the road to bigger things. The young Turks of Lawndale, imbued with the "moving spirit," were keenly aware of socioeconomic heights to be scaled. Thus, these entrepreneurs and dreamers alike left their childhood homes, as transitional neighborhoods changed complexion almost overnight. Irving Cutler wrote, "This acculturation happened among some of the more radical, irreligious immigrant Jews as well as many younger Jews, usually American-born . . . But the Jews left the area because . . . they were interested in areas with better amenities, schools, higher status, more space and single family homes . . . The exodus was facilitated by the automobile and the government loans that were readily available, especially to veterans . . . [Some went] to Albany Park and Rogers Park, but more to West Rogers Park (West Ridge)."*,[2]

---

*The population of Lawndale dropped from 112,000 to approximately 100,000 between 1930 and 1950. This was due to the Jewish migration northward to communities like Albany Park and Rogers Park. During the decade that followed, European whites fled Lawndale in droves, many succumbing to racial fears, which were easily manipulated by unscrupulous Realtors. In 1960, 91 percent of the population was black. The newest residents of Lawndale encountered a series of community catastrophes after 1960, which resulted in a stagnated economy and a deteriorating social fabric. The riots after the King assassination in 1968 destroyed many parts of the Roosevelt Road shopping center,

Although many of the Jewish institutions of greater Lawndale were reestablished on the North Side, they would never approach the previous scale. By 1950, Lawndale's population had declined significantly, as the young left in pursuit of their dreams—first stop, downtown Chicago. Rabbi Saul Silber intoned, "Our children are running away from us because we have nothing to hold them with, to make them worthy of their Jewish heritage."[3] In truth, the dispersing young Lawndale Jews did not entirely cast off their heritage. Imbued with centuries of tradition, they held on to beliefs such as those crystallized in the paintings of Russian artist Marc Chagall, whose depiction of the fiddler on the roof shows an oval-shaped violinist floating in space over the roof of a peasant village, playing traditional songs. "The Jews sit precariously as the fiddler on the roof" goes the expression, and that notion bound the Lawndale Jews to their traditions until their own passing. For the rest of their lives, the Supermob associates played major roles in Jewish causes of all manners. Interestingly, as a retiring adult in Beverly Hills decades later, Sid Korshak collected Chagall originals.

As seen, many Lawndale evacuees achieved successful (and legitimate) careers in a variety of fields. But, invariably, some coveted a quicker—and guaranteed—path to success. These members of the future Supermob concluded that there was no future without some accommodation and/or alliance with the post-Capone Outfit, which seemed to hold a vise grip over Chicago and a powerful influence in many cities to the west, all the way to Los Angeles. Soon, associations would also be forged with East Coast boss Lucky Luciano and his "shadow Jew," Meyer Lansky. Noted New York Police organized crime expert Ralph Salerno wrote, "There is a happy

---

Footnote cont'd
making store owners relocate. The closing in 1969 of the International Harvester Company's tractor works led to an estimated loss of thirty-four hundred jobs. The riots and the racial turnover resulted in a loss of 75 percent of business establishments and 25 percent of the jobs in Lawndale. During the 1970s, 80 percent of the area's manufacturing disappeared, as Zenith and Sunbeam electronics factories closed. The deteriorated conditions are the legacy of structural aging, real estate speculation during the years of racial transition, inadequate building inspection, lax enforcement of building codes, and the disregard of property by the tenants. In 1990, 55 percent of all housing units were located in structures more than fifty years old. In 1987, the Chicago Economic Development Corporation's efforts to build a small-business "incubator" building collapsed, amid charges of mismanagement, misappropriation of $1.7 million in grants and loans, and fraudulent collusion between a local construction company and the area alderman. Health care is still provided by Mount Sinai Hospital, which has modernized and expanded Saint Anthony's on Nineteenth Street.

marriage of convenience between Jewish and Italian gangsters. It represents the three M's: Money, Moxie, and Muscle. The Jews supply the moxie. The Italians take care of the muscle. And they split the money between them."[4] According to Ira Silverman, NBC's longtime producer and organized crime specialist, "The Jewish lawyers were like 'house counsel' to the mob before the term was invented. They were on lifetime retainer."[5]

Jewish lawyers of the period made no apologies for their cozy relationships with the hoods. Typical of their philosophy is the statement of one retired Chicago Jewish attorney who was close to both Korshak and the crime bosses. "In those days it was so much different than today," said the attorney, who asked for anonymity. "In the early thirties, a Jewish kid right out of law school didn't have a lot of opportunities. All he could do was get into some kind of 'collection' practice, like a collection agency. Where else do you go? So he gets this opportunity to make the kind of money the WASP lawyers were pulling in and he took it. We all took it if it was offered to us. Sidney was just the best of the bunch."[6]

Former Chicago FBI agents Fran Marracco and Pete Wacks experienced the mob-Supermob alliance firsthand. According to Marracco, "The Italians knew that if you wanted something done, you didn't get an Italian accountant or lawyer. You got Jews. On the wiretaps we'd hear the Italians and how they stereotypically described the Jews' abilities with money. They respected their work ethic. They knew that the Jews came from this bad situation in Europe and they were hungry for success. They didn't want to be without. We used to call it the Kosher Nostra, the Jewish Mafia."[7] Wacks heard one hood remark, "If we didn't have the Jews, we'd still be hiding money under the mattress."[8]

Lawndale's Supermob evacuees were likely cognizant of Jewish proverbs such as "God help a man against gentile hands and Jewish heads" and "Heaven protect us against Jewish *moach* [brains] and gentile *koach* [physical force]." The successful use of *sechel* (smarts) rather than mere brute force was the only option. More important, for the Supermob, organized crime—or an association with it—was not a moral choice, but a political and economic reality, which translated into power and a "seat at the table." It was also pure Arvey, who later wrote, "I knew some men who were bookies in the old days who were well-respected—real estate operators, capitalists, and very acceptable in high society . . . They weren't degraded at all. They weren't demeaned by the fact that they were doing an illegal act . . . This was a different sense of morality."[9] In their Faustian bargain, the Supermob founders were making money and security for the family the fastest way they knew how, a rationale fueled by the insecurity of their position in America (or any other country throughout history).

Later in life, Sid Korshak bragged to friends about how, while still studying law at DePaul, he made his liaison with the Outfit by advising Al Capone. Bob Evans, a Korshak pal, protégé, and later production chief at Paramount, called Korshak Capone's consiglieri.[10] Movie executive Berle Adams recently recalled, "I heard that Sidney was Capone's chauffeur. Everybody heard it."[11] One of Korshak's closest friends in the Hollywood legal whirl, Greg Bautzer, informed editor Tom Pryor of *Daily Variety* that Sid told him he drove for Capone. Few in Chicago accept that proposition, given that a don's driver doubles as a bodyguard, the most trusted position in the crew, and is always an Italian. Often, the driver inherits the role of boss, as was the case with both Joe Batters Accardo and Sam Giancana. But there was, in fact, a Capone connection to Korshak's early work for the Outfit.

According to a retired Chicago attorney who was close to Korshak, the original link surfaced many years later, when the attorney (who asked not to be identified) had a chance encounter with a retired Abe Teitelbaum, formerly Al Capone's personal lawyer. (Teitelbaum had often stated, "Alphonse Capone was one of the most honorable men I ever met."[12]) When the source mentioned his friendship with Sid Korshak, Teitelbaum smiled and said, "I gave Sidney his first business clients. I was returning the favor because his uncle Max had started me in the law business." It is not a stretch to assume that many of those clients were from Capone's Syndicate, later called the Outfit.

With his chosen clientele now arranged, Korshak formed an early partnership with a fellow DePaul alumnus, attorney Edward King, lawyer for Capone's heir Frank Nitti. However, King, who was also cocounsel with Marshall Korshak at Windy City Liquors, soon found greener pastures in New York, working for Mob Commission boss Meyer Lansky and his adviser Moses Polakoff. From that point, according to others like former Chicago reporter James Bacon and Chicago FBI man Bill Roemer, Jake Guzik became Sid's chief liaison to "the boys." Guzik was born in Russia in 1887, making him an elder in the Capone organization. He had the dubious distinction of being part of a family that was entirely devoted to white slavery—his parents were imprisoned on that charge, and all six of their children were pimps. Breaking out of the world of whoring, Guzik was likely the first Ashkenazi to find his way into Capone's inner sanctum, becoming both his bookkeeper and political-payoff wizard. Guzik was imprisoned for tax evasion in 1931, the same year the IRS nailed Capone.

Abe Teitelbaum escorting Al Capone from court (Library of Congress)

Korshak's recruitment origins aside, there was no argument about whom Sid Korshak ultimately served. Judge Abraham Lincoln Marovitz, another Arvey protégé, recalled just before his death in 2001, "Sidney and I were rivals in the thirties. He had silent partners in his law firm—he was with the hoodlums. He almost never took a case to trial—he was always making

Jake Guzik, undated mug shot (Chicago Crime Commission)

deals."*,[13] Marovitz remarked that Arvey had played a role in getting him the seat on the federal bench years earlier.[14] "Jake Arvey picked me up when I was nineteen and helped me every step of the way," Marovitz would say at Arvey's funeral. "I owe him a lot."[15]

Not quite a year after his graduation, Sidney Korshak made his first known appearance in a court of law—but not to use his law degree in defense of a client. In May of 1931, Sidney, apparently influenced by his older brother, Ted, was arrested with his senior sibling after an early-morning brawl at a Loop club called The Showboat. The arrest came about when Sidney tried to stop the arrest of Ted. "You can't arrest him, he's my brother," warned Korshak. "Don't you know who I am?" The unimpressed cops promptly added Sidney to their paddy wagon. Although Sidney was held on $2,400 bail when he was discovered packing a pistol, the charges were eventually dropped.[16]

In October of 1931, Sidney finally appeared in court to exercise his legal muscle. It was an unimpressive debut. Hired to defend young toughs Joe Carbona (twenty-two) and Louis Cadulo (twenty-four) for grand theft auto, Korshak quickly lost the case and the two were sentenced to six months in the House of Corrections.

Korshak's next known appearance before the bench was no improvement. On May 2, 1933, Korshak was secured to defend one Jack Niedle for assault with a deadly weapon. Niedle was found guilty, sentenced to a year in jail, and hit with a $500 fine.[17] In September, Korshak appeared with his associate Ed King in defense of Sam Battaglia, a notorious Capone racketeer. At the time, the chief of detectives was cracking down on known mobsters, often citing them with nuisance vagrancy citations. Korshak and King had failed to deliver their client for an earlier appearance, and on September 5, Judge Thomas A. Green lit into them. "You attorneys are in contempt of the court," Judge Green bellowed. "The bailiffs will take you into custody." One lawyer was held in an anteroom and the other in the jury box. Green then turned to the court reporter and dictated to her for the record: "Policemen, lawyers, and some judges seemed to be under gangster influences." He ordered the $10,000 bond of Battaglia forfeited and set new bonds at $30,000. He then instructed the police chief that if other judges ever reduced bail, he should make a list of such judges and publish it. Then he directed the bailiffs to free attorneys King and Korshak.[18]

---

*Arvey promoted Marovitz to ward supervisor, then state senator, superior court judge, and federal district-court judge, appointed by JFK. "I think that was largely due to my friend Jack Arvey," Marovitz said in 1997. (Transcript of interview by ABC News for 1997's program "Dangerous World: The Kennedy Years")

James Bacon, renowned Associated Press reporter in Chicago at the time (later in Hollywood), recently recalled the gangster-crackdown period. "That's when I first became aware of Korshak," Bacon said. "They would arrest these guys for vagrancy. They might have twenty grand on them, but they were arrested for vagrancy. Sidney was always the lawyer down there defending them."[19] In Korshak's FBI file, the Bureau noted Korshak's "close contact with police officials and judges in the Police Courts in Chicago." Simultaneously, the Bureau noted, "Sidney Korshak was one of the Chicago attorneys used most frequently by the Syndicate."

Despite his courtroom failings, or perhaps because of them, Korshak's underworld bosses stuck with him. But it was apparent to all that his particular skills were of better use outside the bright lights of the city's courtrooms. The adjectives most often used to describe the young barrister—*suave, slim, tall,* and *imperious*—were the same attributes that made him the perfect corporate liaison for the most powerful underworld organization in the history of the nation. "Korshak was considered to be a fair-haired boy in the organization with the blessings of [Outfit boss] Tony Accardo," said veteran Chicago columnist (and Korshak friend) Irv Kupcinet. The gang had just emerged from the financial high of the bootlegging era, anxious to exploit new treasures such as labor, casino gambling, and entertainment. Aware that it would take someone with much more refinement than that of its typical crew member to mix with legitimate society, the bosses began headhunting for the right man with a law degree to smooth the transition into the next evolution of their enterprise, and the short list of candidates was topped by Sidney Korshak.

These were the years when Chicago's Outfit, under the direction of its "Einstein," Murray "Curly" Humphreys, was perfecting the science of labor racketeering—the takeover of unions so as to cut sweetheart deals with industry. Among others, Humphreys worked closely with Korshak mentor Abe Teitelbaum, Jake Guzik, and Al Capone in the takeovers of Chicago's dry-cleaning establishments.[20] Teitelbaum, who first met Capone due to the friendship of his and Capone's mothers, was a labor-relations attorney, hired by the Chicago Bar and Restaurant Association in 1932. His labor counsel was therefore invaluable to the Capones. Years later, a congressional investigation concluded that the Chicago Restaurant Association engaged in "terrorism" and functioned "principally to defeat and destroy legitimate unionization and has callously and calculatedly used men with underworld connections to make collusive arrangements with dishonest union officials. There is additional undisputed testimony that gangsters and hoodlums were employed to handle the association's labor relations." It added that

Teitelbaum was nothing more than a mob front, funneling corporate money to the Outfit in exchange for labor peace and protection from arson.[21]

In the case of unions not directly under the mob's control, it was often just a simple matter of paying off the union bosses to persuade them to accept a substandard deal, a modus operandi adopted by Sid Korshak. "He made cash payoffs to business agents—five thousand dollars here, three thousand dollars there," said Leo Geffner, a Los Angeles attorney who negotiated with Korshak years later. "I *know* that. That's the way it was—to keep labor peace, you'd find a corrupt business agent and pay him off."[22] Of course, in doing so, the racketeer stabbed both the workers and their employers in the back. Ironically, this was the very abuse suffered by Korshak's grandparents in Kiev. The ever-vigilant Korshak gadfly, journalist Lester Velie, succinctly described how the treachery worked: "The deal may be to bring a 'friendly' union in, or to keep a union out, or to accept substandard wages . . . In the deals that the go-between arranges, the union's function is perverted. Instead of serving as an instrument to win better wages and working conditions, it becomes a tool for keeping the worker in line. Thus, it performs the same function as the unions do in Communist Russia."[23]

Thus, by the early 1930s, it was decided that Korshak would be groomed to oversee labor matters when the Outfit expanded outside Humphreys's Chicago home base. Korshak later admitted to the FBI that he met Humphreys in 1929. As overheard by FBI "bugs" planted years later, it was Curly Humphreys who indeed approved Korshak's recruitment.

A retired detective from Chicago's Police Intelligence Division, who wished to remain anonymous, witnessed something of the Korshak-Humphreys

Curly Humphreys (Don Llewellyn)

relationship: "There used to be this joint on Rush Street many decades ago. It was a lavish seminightclub. A guy I knew was sitting at the bar with Sidney. I don't think Sidney drank, but he was sitting at the bar. Out of the back room of this joint came a man shouting all sorts of four-letter words at Sidney, demanding that Sidney come into his office in the back. And Sidney got up and went back. The significance of the story is that the man sitting at the bar said that the man doing the yelling and demanding was Murray 'the Camel' Humphreys."[24]

Humphreys scholar Royston Webb concluded, "Obviously Humphreys considered Korshak several rungs below, and I think he used Gus Alex as an intermediary for a while. He'd bloody well tell Korshak to remember on which side his bread was buttered or words to that effect."[25]

His niche now established, Korshak occasionally turned back to his original benefactor, Abe Teitelbaum, whenever a labor problem proved especially vexing. "Whenever the going got tough, Sidney called Abe in," said a close family friend of the Teitelbaums.[26] (This counsel would continue for decades.) Soon, Korshak and King were working out of the office of attorney Philip R. Davis at 188 W. Randolph Street, a notorious point of convergence for Syndicate members, their lawyers, and paid-for officials. The building had an interior connection to the equally notorious Bismarck Hotel, where mob boss Frank Nitti and his next-in-command, Paul "the Waiter" Ricca, maintained their headquarters. Thirty years later, 188 W. Randolph was still an unmolested underworld crossroads. Jim Agnew, an elevator operator in the building in the 1960s, saw teamster head Jimmy Hoffa, Outfit boss Tony Accardo, and underbosses Gussie Alex, Eddie Vogel, Phil Alderisio, and Marshall Caifano, all making the trek up to the mobsters' top-floor dominion. Mob-friendly judge, and Arvey protégé, Abe Marovitz also attended powwows on the upper floors. "They used the back

Gus "Slim" Alex, Korshak's pal and Outfit liaison (Kefauver Committee Evidence File, Library of Congress Legislative Archives)

Jake Arvey with Judge Abraham
Lincoln Marovitz (Chicago Jewish
Archives, Spertus Institute)

entrance and took the freight elevator up to Postl's Health Club on the
twenty-seventh floor," Agnew recently recalled. "They had meetings in the
steam room, which they didn't know was bugged illegally by FBI."[27]

The Chicago Crime Commission's legendary director, Virgil Peterson,
wrote:

> Korshak's connections were known ever since he could run from the bar-
> bershop two doors west of Henrici's where Fischetti and Gioe were kept
> waiting while Sid would hold a conference with "Tubbo" Gilbert [of the
> State's Attorney's Office]. This brazen messenger would commute from
> the barbershop to Gilbert's Sherman Hotel room four or five times a
> week. This was twelve years ago [1938]. But what about the supposed
> owner of St. Hubert's Grill on Federal Street? Where almost every goon of
> consequence would meet every Thursday evening, where, during the lunch
> hour, a number of federal judges including Igee would relax, not with the
> real owner, Jake Guzik, but with the "front" who has a "place," Tommy
> Kelly . . . Fischetti and wives would meet Campagna's wife and Gioe's
> wife, who were escorted by Sid Korshak.[28]

Peterson was referring to the investigator from the State's Attorney's Office's police labor detail, Dan "Tubbo" Gilbert, directed by the corrupt head of
the office, Tom Courtney. Gilbert had amassed an astounding $300,000 nest
egg, much of it by betting with Outfit-controlled bookies, and running his
own handbook on the side. In later years, when his congressional executive-
session testimony was leaked to the press, the local papers dubbed Gilbert "the
world's richest cop." Under intense questioning before a congressional tribu-
nal, Gilbert admitted that he had in fact earned big winnings by gambling on
baseball, football, prizefights, and even elections. He also conceded that he
placed his bets with the Outfit-connected bookie John McDonald.

During the Courtney-Gilbert reign, thousands of felony charges lodged against Outfit bosses and crew members were reduced to misdemeanors. But more importantly, Gilbert was in charge of the police labor detail, a position of critical importance to the efficient running of the city. The bottom line was that the city's business community depended on Courtney and Gilbert working closely with the Outfit as Murray "Curly" Humphreys took over one union after another. Frank Loesch, then president of the Chicago Crime Commission, said, "Few labor crimes have been solved in Chicago because of the close association between labor gangsters and law enforcing agencies." Many years later, mob-fighting federal judge John P. Barnes described the arrangement between the Outfit and a compliant State's Attorney's Office: "The [Capone] Syndicate could not operate without the approval of the [State's Attorney's] office . . . The relationship between the State's Attorney's Office, under [Tom] Courtney and [Dan] Gilbert, and the Capone Syndicate, was such that during the entire period that Courtney was in office [1932–44], no Syndicate man was ever convicted of a major crime in Cook County."

The entire scheme was facilitated by Courtney-Gilbert's alliance with none other than the gang's young labor lawyer, Sidney Korshak. An associate of Gilbert's recently said, "Gilbert worked both sides—labor and business—and he took to Sidney. Sidney learned at his knee." With Korshak representing the Humphreys-controlled unions, Gilbert became a powerful voice in Chicago's power structure. The troika represented a sort of parallel-universe version of City Hall. One Gilbert acquaintance recently recalled, "Dan Gilbert was the only guy in town who could stop a strike with a phone call." A call to Sidney Korshak, to be exact.

With such important consorts, Korshak not only controlled the city's Outfit-unionized workforce, but also was able to negotiate practically all gang criminal citations down to misdemeanors. Before long, Korshak had no need of the courts at all, since his clients had their cases resolved with a phone call. The all-solving telephone would become a leitmotif of Korshak's "practice." As one of his fellow lawyers said, "Sid Korshak is a lawyer who tries few cases—but he has one of the most important law practices in town."

The "Kosher Nostra" Finds a Home

Now suitably connected, the dashing Korshak joined the Lawndale exodus and made the move to the big city. Still in his midtwenties, Korshak was nonetheless wise to the power of networking. He therefore chose as his first out-of-the-nest home the most highly charged, vibrant abode in Chicago's upscale Near North district, the Seneca Hotel, a sixteen-story, four-hundred-room edifice on 200 E. Chestnut Saint, just two blocks from Michigan Avenue to the west and one bock from Lake Michigan to the east.

At the time, Jews leaving Lawndale preferred to live in residential hotels, with the North Shore becoming known as Jewish Hotel Row. Author Louis Wirth wrote, "The middle-class businessmen among the Jews moved into these hotels originally, not merely because their wives wanted to be free of household duties, nor merely because they had reached a station in life where they could afford the luxuries of hotel life, but rather because they wished to be taken for successful businessmen or professional men—not merely successful Jews. The hotels offered anonymity."[29]

When one hotel manager was found to have joined the Ku Klux Klan, the Jews banded together, bought the hotel, and hired a new manager. They continued to buy hotels, one being the Seneca, new home to Sidney Korshak, and arguably the nation's most dynamic underworld networking site.

To tourists, the Seneca was known for its amenities and legendary marathon poker games played by the city's upper class. But to knowledgeable Chicagoans, the hotel represented a critical intersection for Syndicate members anxious to invest the mob's lucre in legitimate or semilegitimate operations. And it wasn't just the tenants who raised local eyebrows; the very ownership represented a who's who of the local underworld. In hindsight, the financial cross-pollination that occurred at the hotel resulted in a cascade of immense business transactions that spawned numerous Fortune 500 companies, many of which were tainted by mob money, and not coincidentally represented by former criminal lawyer, now "labor consultant," Sid Korshak.

As one might expect, Jake Arvey's presence was felt at the Seneca: his son Buddy kept his ex-wife and son there, as well as his current flame, actress Lila Leeds. The hotel was also known to be home to a dozen racketeers and hit men, including Hymie "Loud Mouth" Levin.[30] And although it was rumored that Korshak was seduced into the mob's circle with stock in the Seneca, this was never followed up or proven.[31] But the partners of record were interesting enough to local law enforcement officials. One co-owner and tenant of the Seneca was Charlie "Cherry Nose" Gioe (also spelled Joye), a Capone underboss and client of Korshak's. Gioe admitted under oath that he owned $12,000 of stock in the Seneca, which, in a pattern that would prove typical for underworld investments, was placed in his wife's name.[32]

The Seneca
(author photo)

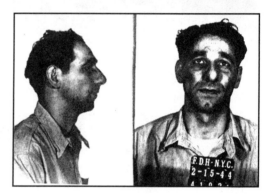

Charlie Gioe after his 1944 arrest
in the Hollywood Extortion
Case (author collection)

Gioe testified that he had grown up and gone to school with top Chicago mob boss Tony Accardo. In that same testimony he added that he met Korshak soon after he came out of law school, "through some fellows on the West Side when he just opened his office." Gioe further testified that he had frequent meetings with Korshak at the Seneca, as well as with bookie Hymie Levin, who lived across the street. According to a source of the Chicago Crime Commission's, Gioe enlisted Korshak's advice when immigrant Outfit boss Paul Ricca applied for (and received) his naturalization using a false identity.[33] Korshak later told the FBI that he was the attorney for Gioe's Don the Beachcomber restaurant in 1939 and represented him in his divorce from his first wife.[34] Simultaneously, one of Gioe's bookie joints, at 217 North Clark, was run by Korshak's brother Bernie for Gioe and "Joe Batters" Accardo, boss of the Chicago Outfit.

Like so many others involved with the Seneca, Gioe's tentacles reached far and wide. With the Calimia brothers, notorious hoodlums from Nebraska, Gioe was heavily invested in the Reddi-Whip Corp., based in Los Angeles—the Calimias became president and VP of the company. The company was the parent of over ten subsidiaries that within a decade counted over $1.5 million in assets.*

Gioe also partnered with Supermob member Alfred S. Hart, a Hungarian Jewish immigrant (born Alfred Harskovitz in 1904) who started out as a beer runner for Capone, then managed Gold Seal Liquors for Gioe and his partner Joe Fusco. Hart was among the earliest of the group to make the move to California, where in the 1920s he prospered by first forming Glencoe Distilleries and the Pacific Brewing Company. He was arrested two times in 1928, four times in 1929, and twice in 1931, all in connection with his running of an illegal punchboard operation out of an L.A. cigar store.† In the thirties, Hart owned Central Liquor Distributors, the San Angelo Wine and Spirit Corporation, and the Alfred Hart Distilleries, using their profits to purchase the Del Mar Race Track, where he struck up a lifelong friendship with racing fan—and FBI director—J. Edgar Hoover, this despite the fact that Hart's FBI file notes, "Hart has a reputation of associating with known hoodlums."

In 1949, a San Bernardino grand jury was convened to investigate two of Hart's partners in Alfred Hart Distilleries, Edward Seeman, the slot-machine king of San Bernardino, and State Senator Ralph E. Swing, for soliciting a bribe from a citizen who wanted to obtain an auto racing concession.[35] However, the grand jury returned no indictment.

There was more. According to the LAPD, Hart became first an investor, then a majority owner, in the Maier Brewing Company. In that endeavor, he partnered with one Paul Kalmanovitz, who was in turn part of mobster Mickey Cohen's local syndicate. Kalmanovitz operated bars, such as Keith's Café in downtown L.A., that were key meeting places for the Cohen organization. In 1945, Hart sold Maier to his old Capone partner Joe Fusco.[36]

In 1948, Hart invested $75,000 in the infamous Flamingo Hotel in Las Vegas, run by legendary hoodlum Benjamin "Bugsy" Siegel for a consortium of Chicago and New York gangsters. At the time of the partnership with Hart, Siegel maintained a booth at Hart's Del Mar Turf Club, which he shared

---

*Reddi-Whip, the first aerosol food product in the United States, was owned by Capone associate Marcus Lipsky, who was, in turn, fronting for Capone boss Ross Prio. In the 1930s, they formed L&P Milk Co. (Lipsky and Prio). According to federal and Texas authorities, Lipsky masterminded the Chicago Outfit's takeover of the Dallas rackets, after planning the murders of four established top Dallas gamblers as a Machiavellian show of strength. Like so many others, Lipsky ended up in Beverly Hills after selling Reddi-Whip to Hunt & Wesson for $6 million in 1970. He died in 1980.
†See second footnote on p. 128 for details of the operation.

Del Mar president (and former Capone bootlegger) Al
Hart presenting jockey Willie Shoemaker with a trophy
for his 300th win, September 1, 1953 (Corbis/Bettmann)

with Virginia Hill. Hart was also known to have loaned money—$7,000 on
one occasion—to L.A. mob kingpin Meyer "Mickey" Cohen. Hart would
go on to dabble in real estate speculation in San Bernardino (which landed
him in stir for fraud), become a director at Columbia Pictures, and finally
create the City National Bank of Beverly Hills, currently the largest independent bank in Los Angeles and the bank of choice for movie moguls,
celebrities, and the Supermob (pals like Sid Korshak were among the original
stockholders).[37]

Another co-owner (25 percent) of the Seneca was Jake Arvey's brother-in-
law, Benjamin Cohen, who also owned the DuSable Hotel, which featured a
grill that was called "a common whorehouse" by the Chicago PD. He also
owned ten buildings, including the Pershing Hotel, in the heart of Chicago's
"Bronze Belt," a province handed down by Al Capone to the "white syndicate" for the express purpose of preying on the city's black population. According to an FBI source, Cohen, who died in Los Angeles in 1943, "had
been an integral part of the Capone investment machinery."[38]

But the importance of Gioe's and Cohen's Seneca ownership pales in
comparison to that of the majority owner, and one of the most important
architects of the Supermob, Alex Louis Greenberg. It was Greenberg's financial partnerships that would taint the reputations of numerous political,
corporate, and judicial icons, not only in Chicago, but also in Chicago's
soon-to-be outpost, Southern California.

The Comptometer

Chicago gossip writer, and Korshak pal, Irv Kupcinet called him The Comptometer, and "one of the most interesting characters I ever met."[39] According

to "Kup," for Alex Louis Greenberg, "like almost everyone who became rich through racketeering, respectability was what he sought most."[40] His son-in-law, a scientist named Nathan Sugarman, was accustomed to seeing Greenberg studying books in Sugarman's vast library. "Imagine knowing all them words!" he once told a friend. In his quest for success, Greenberg would become key to the Supermob's massive, hidden investments in, and control over, the Golden State.

Born in Russia on December 10, 1891, Greenberg was an émigré from the 1905 pogroms, journeying first to New York, then to Chicago in 1908. Greenberg liked to boast of how he journeyed from Russia alone at age fourteen with just "sixteen cents in my pocket."[41] Sensitive about his lack of formal education, Greenberg was driven to succeed, and in wide-open Chicago he worked his way up from a mugger of drunks to expert jewelry thief, with Big Al Capone's right hand, Frank Nitti, acting as his fence. He admitted under oath to being friends with Capone since about 1920. "He used to be my barber," Greenberg sarcastically testified. He said he had met Nitti the same way. "We all get acquainted with good barbers," Greenberg told the Kefauver Committee in 1951.[42] At only twenty years old, he opened his first saloon, which provided him with a steady stream of suitable drunks/victims. Greenberg relocated to Lawndale (4013 W. Roosevelt, at Pulaski) within walking distance of pals Jake Arvey, Moe Rosenberg (2051 S. Hoyne), and the Korshaks.

Greenberg was first arrested in May 1910 for theft of barrels of whiskey; he was one of ten defendants indicted by a grand jury for larceny and receipt of stolen goods. During Prohibition he operated a speakeasy at Lawndale and sixteenth and was arrested in a raid there in 1921, caught with forged whiskey permits.[43] In 1925, he was charged in what the IRS described as "the biggest booze plot since the advent of Prohibition." The scam, which

Alex Louis Greenberg testifying before the Kefauver Committee, January 19, 1951 (Corbis/Bettmann)

included a police captain, three bankers, and Prohibition personnel, involved hijackings, counterfeit medicinal-alcohol certificates, spurious Prohibition Department stationery, and phony withdrawal permits. The partners had grossed millions in the enterprise.[44]

Greenberg's career really began to accelerate when he decided to enter the world of finance. Starting off small, he first loan-sharked his own mugging victims at 20 percent vig* per week. Those who were tardy in their payments were seen frequenting emergency rooms complaining of broken arms. Greenberg may have learned the ropes from his brother-in-law, Izzy Zevlin, another financial wiz, responsible for hiding millions of embezzled entertainment union funds. As personal secretary to George Browne, the president of the International Alliance of Theatrical and Stage Employees (IATSE), Zevlin would soon figure in a massive extortion of Hollywood studios.

By this point, Greenberg had mastered the political payoff, greasing the palms of the notoriously corrupt Kenna-Coughlin regime in order to quash the few indictments that he received. He later testified that he made a point of bribing both Democrats and Republicans. "They both want money," he said. "You pay them for what you want. Then you get it."[45] His money-lending scheme thrived and gave rise to Roosevelt Finance, which became, according to Greenberg's testimony, the third-largest company in Chicago.[46] The company obtained start-up funds (used to finance mortgages) by borrowing as much as $50,000 at a time from notorious bootlegger Dion O'Banion, the Arvey-Annenberg ally in the circulation and wire wars.[47] Greenberg had previously loaned O'Banion and Hymie Weiss money to start their bootlegging Manhattan Brewery (later Canadian Ace Brewery), where one of O'Banion's partners was Joe Adonis, underboss for New York Mafia chief Frank Costello.[48] For his distribution needs in the West, Greenberg was represented by mafioso Tony Gizzo in Kansas City, and Luigi Fratto in Des Moines.[49]

After the Capone Gang killed O'Banion and Weiss, Greenberg took over the brewery with Nitti, helping Canadian Ace become the most popular beer in Chicago, grossing over $10 million a year by 1950. That success was not based merely on the brew's sudsy appeal. When the Outfit started to muscle in on the Bartenders Union, union official George McLane said that he was ordered by Nitti and Greenberg to have his men push sales of Manhattan/Canadian beer.[50] Such an order was not to be taken lightly, since

---

*Vig, or *vigorish*, is street slang for the compound interest that accrues to a gambling debt or loan—a principle later adopted by credit card companies.

Greenberg's Chicago distributor was Ralph Buglio, the gunman for Capone's patriarch, Johnny Torrio.

Greenberg diversified again when he opened Realty Management, which managed, among other properties, Capone's Cicero headquarters, The Towne Hotel. With Capone's backing, Greenberg opened a cigar store in the lobby of another Capone installation, the Lexington. The store was merely a front for an off-track betting parlor, started with $110,000 fronted by Nitti. Under the Realty banner, Greenberg bought stock in the Seneca, the shares actually purchased from the wife of Charlie Gioe. At the time of his death decades later, Greenberg owned, by his own testimony, $579,632 of stock in the Seneca, for which he also served as president.[51]

Another of Greenberg's significant real estate partners was Fred Evans, regarded by the Chicago Crime Commission as "the financial brains of the Capone gang." Evans worked closely with Frank Nitti, Paul Ricca, and Louis Campagna, but his staunchest Capone partner was the legendary Murray Humphreys, the labor and legal strategist for the Capone Syndicate, and occasional Public Enemy Number One. The two were so close that Evans named his only son, Robert Murray Evans, in tribute to Humphreys. Evans and Greenberg were coinvestors in a number of commercial properties, such as buildings at 5100 Cornell Saint, the Monterey Hotel, and Ruby Cleaners.[52] These investments were but a warm-up to the massive land grabs that Greenberg, Evans, and the rest of the Supermob would institute in California and elsewhere. (For a biography of Evans, see chapter 4.)

Still another diversification was the founding of Lawndale Enterprises, which saw Greenberg fronting for Nitti in a partnership with Jake Arvey and Moe Rosenberg.[53] Another partner in the business, which operated theaters and exhibitions, was Joseph G. Engert, a co-owner with future Outfit boss Joey "Doves" Aiuppa, owner of Capone's Towne Hotel.[54] Not surprisingly, Lawndale Enterprises had its downtown Chicago office at 188 W. Randolph.[55]

As though he needed any more underworld connections, the driven Greenberg helped finance the San Carlo Italian Village at the 1933 World's Fair, held on Chicago's lakefront. The village was run entirely by members of the Chicago Outfit, including Fred Evans, Paul Ricca, Joe Fusco, Ralph Capone, Murray Humphreys, James Mondi, and Charlie Fischetti.[56]

When interviewed by congressional staffers, Greenberg admitted that he and Nitti had loaned each other tens of thousands of dollars over the years.[57] On the occasion of Nitti's suicide on March 19, 1943, Greenberg had to pay back the money to Nitti's estate. During the probate hearings after Greenberg's subsequent death, it was disclosed that *Nitti had loaned*

Greenberg over $2 million in mob money for investment purposes. Nitti's widow, Annette, told the court that Greenberg had been investing Nitti's money for over twenty-five years. Some of the stocks purchased included American Air Lines, the *Chicago Daily News*, Marshall Field & Co., United Air Lines, Standard Oil, and US Steel.[58] Greenberg appeared to share the investment-adviser role with Sid Korshak. As the FBI later noted, "Korshak advised top racketeers in Chicago concerning their investments in legitimate enterprises and was in close contact with [Murray] Humphreys and handled many matters for Humphreys and his Chicago hoodlum associates."[59] According to James Ragen, president of the Continental Wire Service prior to the Outfit's takeover, Greenberg also peddled Continental's "blue sheet" racing form. Ragen added, "Louis [Greenberg] is Capone to some extent. He is probably Capone to a larger extent than he wants to be. He would like to break away and he is having a hell of a time doing it."[60] (Six weeks after making these and other disclosures to the U.S. attorney in Chicago, Ragen was shot to death in his car on June 24, 1946.)

As a final side endeavor, Greenberg managed many of the Capone-run unions. One such guild, the waiters' union, had Greenberg reach accommodation with the owner of the Folies-Bergère, a topless dance revue that was the hit of the 1933 World's Fair. That proprietor, Jules Stein, like so many other Greenberg contacts, would play a large role in the future success of Sid Korshak and the Supermob. Through his founding of the entertainment power agency Music Corporation of America (MCA) on May 24, 1924, Stein would give his Chicago brethren entrée—once they moved to the next settlement in Los Angeles—into the highest echelons of twentieth-century entertainment. With his enabling pal, James Petrillo, supplying the talent, Stein turned MCA into the most powerful entertainment conglomerate in American history.

The Czars of Music

Julius Caesar Stein was born in 1896, another son of Jewish immigrants from the Pale (Lithuania). Growing up in Indiana, he studied violin for a time, but soon gravitated to saxophone. In 1913, at age seventeen, Stein moved to Chicago, where he played in, and organized, dance bands to pay for his schooling. Stein's diminutive, 140-pound frame was no barrier to attracting the ladies—his wit more than made up the difference. He entered Chicago's Rush Medical School on a scholarship, but when Prohibition became law in 1920, Stein was seduced by the money that flowed not only to the speakeasies, but also to the bands that were enlisted therein. Like Arvey, Greenberg, Korshak, and so many of his friends, Stein soon struck up a

Jules Stein (Marc Wanamaker/Bison Archives)

friendship with Big Al Capone, with whom he was also a bit player as an illegal-whiskey supplier.

"Mr. Stein was friends with Al Capone," recalled Charles Harris, Stein's butler and confidant for over four decades.[61] Actor Robert Mitchum said, "Everyone knew that Stein worked for Al Capone in Chicago. That's how MCA got into the band business."[62]

In return for the supply of whiskey, Stein obtained Capone's muscle to force holdout clubs to book his bands. It is also known to insiders, such as columnist Irv Kupcinet, that Stein gave Capone a piece of MCA, which regularly took as much as 50 percent of the client's earnings.[63] Stein fine-tuned Capone's bookkeeping model, maintaining murky ledgers in order to render accurate royalty statements impossible. MCA entertainers such as Bing Crosby, needing relief from freelance Black Hand extortionists, turned to Stein, who would use his connection with Capone to call off the dogs.* When the Outfit started placing its newly invented coin-operated jukeboxes in clubs, Stein came up with the top-forty list of most-often-played songs. Of course, the accounting was far from accurate and jukes were rigged, so soon entertainers became beholden to the Outfit and Stein's MCA for the career push afforded by the machines.[†,64]

---

*According to Ruth Jones (pseudonym), "Machine Gun" Jack McGurn's golfing partner, McGurn told her how Crosby asked Stein to help with two particularly worrisome Black Handers. Stein enlisted the Outfit's McGurn, who beat the two to within an inch of their lives.

†It was Stein who encouraged fellow Lawndale entrepreneur William Paley to boost his new network, the Columbia Broadcasting System (CBS), by putting Stein's music acts on the air live, turning the rigged *Top Forty* into a national phenomenon. The success of CBS would lead Stein to open an MCA office in New York.

Stein's hardball modus operandi included the use of an Indiana labor union racketeer named Fred "Bugs" Blacker to "take care of " nightclubs that refused to hire MCA bands. Under Stein's orders, Blacker hurled stink bombs into the holdout clubs, along with his trademark bag of roaches— hence the nickname Bugs. Stein's dirty tricks came to an abrupt end on November 26, 1937, when Blacker and his wife stepped out of Chicago's Argo Theater and were killed by three masked gunmen.[65] MCA had grown so notorious that a series of federal investigations into MCA (over a dozen) were begun in 1938 and would continue periodically for the next five decades, albeit with minimal success. Stein was also close to entertainment union honchos Willie Bioff and George Browne, who would soon figure in a headline-grabbing extortion of Hollywood studios.

Stein was also known to be an owner of the 650-seat mob hangout the Chez Paree Club, which opened in 1932. "I know Jules had an interest [in Chez Paree] because I represented [co-owner] Mike Fritzel," said Chicago's legendary Judge Abe Marovitz. "Jules made deals with Fritzel and [Joey] Jacobson to provide the entertainment, and then he demanded a piece. Jules was very powerful."[66] However, it was common knowledge that the Chicago Outfit was the silent partner behind not only Stein, but also the owners of record, Fritzel and Jacobson. It was also understood that the Outfit handed the club over to the Fischetti brothers to run it.

The new club instantly became a "meeting place for the Outfit," according to columnist Irv Kupcinet. It was at the Chez that Arvey protégé and Harry Truman pal Arthur X. Elrod apparently sanctioned a murder. Elrod, who overlooked the gang's bookie operations in exchange for a $700-per-month payoff from boss Louis "Little New York" Campagna, was witnessed meeting with Outfit members who were at war with a bookie competitor named Willie Tarsch. At the sit-down, Elrod told the boys to "take care of it your own way." A few days later Tarsch's bullet-ridden corpse was found on W. Roosevelt Road.[67]

Of course, up-and-comers like Sid Korshak were regulars at Outfit-frequented clubs like Stein's Chez Paree. "Korshak and Stein met each other in the band-booking business," a former FBI agent remembered. "They were introduced by Joe Glaser, a mutual friend who ran his own talent agency [Associated Booking]. Stein knew that Korshak was connected [to the Outfit], and he went to him when he wanted to get a message to someone or wanted something done."[68] Club singer Tony Martin began his career at the Chez, where he met his lifelong friend Sid in the midthirties.[69]

The cross-pollination that occurred at connected clubs like the Chez was well-known, and much of it would figure in the Supermob's future hold over

Southern California real estate, politics, and the entertainment industry that made its home there. Illinois-born actor and future California governor and U.S. president Ronald Reagan was one of Stein's early and lifelong MCA clients, booked into the Outfit-controlled Club Belvedere in Iowa. Joe Glaser got his start managing Capone's interests in the Sunset Café and a small prostitution ring, before obtaining a $100,000 loan from Stein to create Associated Booking, which specialized in black musicians like Louis Armstrong and Duke Ellington, both Capone favorites. Jazz authority Burton Peretti points out that unscrupulous club owners maximized their profit by muscling their names as coauthors onto Ellington compositions, and patenting a trumpet mute that was actually created by their black acts. When Associated moved to L.A., it developed a strong roster of both white and black talent, funneling many to Las Vegas showrooms. Of course, by that time, Sid Korshak had taken over the company.[70]

The through-line of the Supermob continued from Jules Caesar Stein and his Chez Paree to the man who contracted the local musicians that played there. While Stein concentrated on band bookings, his childhood pal James Caesar Petrillo, who was also a friend of Sid Korshak's, lorded over Chicago's individual musicians. His rise to the top was littered with stories of clubs that were firebombed and stink-bombed for using musicians not represented by Petrillo. Born in Chicago's Little Italy section in 1892, Petrillo's first job was that of union muscleman. An amateur musician, Petrillo soon gravitated to the musicians' union, where he found a career. With the mob's backing, the man who was known as Little Caesar and the Mussolini of Music became and remained president of the Chicago Federation of Musicians for over forty years, and the president of the American Federation of Musicians (AFM), with its 250,000 members, for another eighteen. Petrillo regularly gave Stein exclusive sweetheart deals, including waivers that allowed MCA alone to book its acts on radio shows it produced. These favors, in contravention of AFM bylaws, were a boon when MCA ran into problems with Petrillo's union rule forbidding out-of-town bands from performing for money on local radio stations. This unique treatment given to MCA by the AFM greatly accelerated MCA's rise to predominance.

"Both Stein and Petrillo made their deals with the major mob guys in this town," a veteran Chicago investigator advised.[71] Not only was it impossible to run a business without some mob accommodations, such alliances tended to minimize the ongoing kidnapping epidemic. At the time, local bootlegging powers supplemented their income with the occasional grabbing of a thriving businessman. There were also fake kidnappings. Petrillo was said to have been kidnapped in 1933, although some musicians believed it a con devised in order to allow Petrillo to keep the $100,000 ransom paid by his union. Stein also received threats, but both he and Petrillo always pointed the finger at Capone's North Side rival, Roger Touhy.

But the truth may have been even more convoluted: not only were there fake kidnappings, but also false accusations—railroading someone for a kidnapping that never occurred was a convenient method for having a rival put away. "I was pretty sure the Touhy gang was behind it," Stein had said of one threat against him.[72] But informed Chicagoans were, like Petrillo's union rank and file, skeptical. "Touhy was nothing next to Capone and his boys, and that's where Stein and Petrillo's connections were," the Chicago investigator adds. "All the rest of that stuff about kidnappings was nothing more than high drama, well contrived and acted out." Touhy was soon to learn the worst consequence of a false kidnap accusation.

Sid Korshak's friendship with Petrillo came to a crashing halt in 1933, when Petrillo, for reasons unknown, made a weak attempt to distance himself from the Outfit. In December 1933, Korshak represented two union musicians in a suit against Petrillo, alleging that he stole the ransom money from his "kidnapping" earlier that year.

Petrillo's AFM weathered three congressional investigations and two federal prosecutions, both of which came up empty. Petrillo died in Chicago in 1984, at age ninety-two.[73]

Like the rest, Stein would move his operation to California, but not before he brought a worthy heir into the MCA fold. On December 16, 1936, Stein hired the publicist for Cleveland's Mayfair Theatre and Casino, Lew Wasserman. Louis, as he was originally named, was the son of Isaac and Minnie Weiserman, Yiddish-speaking Ashkenazim who had arrived in Cleveland from Russia in 1907.[74] His family name changed to Wasserman, young Lew, as he was now called, entered the workforce as a theater usher, eventually rising to the level of publicist for Cleveland's Mayfair Casino. The Mayfair was nominally run by Lew's mentor, Harry Propper, but the man who sold it to him in 1933, Herman Pirchner, knew the truth. "He was the front man," Pirchner admitted. "The casino was owned by the Syndicate—four Jewish gentlemen." Those men were Moe Dalitz, Lou Rothkopf, Morris Kleinman, and Sam Tucker, all members of Cleveland's notorious Mayfield Road Gang, which had the local monopoly on vice, gambling, and bootlegging. These men would all work in league with Korshak in the coming years in Las Vegas. According to a congressional committee, the Mayfair had still more silent partners, including the city's Mafia representatives, the Polizzi brothers.[75]

When the Mayfair went bankrupt in 1936, Wasserman moved to Chicago to work for Jules Stein's MCA. The move to Chicago would prove momentous, given that Wasserman began to socialize with Stein's friends, such as Sid Korshak and Ronald Reagan, the two men most key to his future success. The disparity in income between a green Wasserman and the flush Korshak didn't prevent them from becoming soul mates. "It didn't matter that Reagan was making two hundred dollars a week, and I was making three hundred dollars, and Sidney much more," Wasserman recalled. "We didn't know just what Sidney was making, or what he was doing. He was a good lawyer, very accepted in the community. And he was a good friend of mine for fifty years."[76]

Los Angeles attorney Leo Geffner recalled that Sidney commented years later about Reagan, "Ronnie says he's so pure. He's really phony with this big

Lew Wasserman (Cleveland Public Library)

Early Ronald Reagan headshot (Irv Letofsky)

moralistic platform—he and I used to be with hookers in the same bedroom!" Korshak told Geffner that they had maintained a strong friendship for many years, often mentioning recent phone chats with the future president.[77]

Wasserman, who has been likened to a rarely smiling funeral director, would come to rule over the Hollywood production machine, all the while in daily contact with his close friend and adviser Sid Korshak; other chums, such as Ronald Reagan, were lodged in political positions high enough to ensure that the Supermob was untouchable. Henry Denker, who worked closely with Stein, Wasserman, and MCA producing television programs for CBS in the earliest days, recently recalled, "Wasserman was a guy in a gentleman's suit with a mob mentality. He was the shrewdest guy in all of show business. He used that shrewdness in many, many ways." Denker added that Mrs. Doris Stein had her own calculating style: "All the antique furniture in Stein's offices was bought by Mrs. Stein in Europe and rented to MCA. She was getting a terrific paycheck every week. They didn't miss a trick."[78]

While Stein, Greenberg, Arvey, and Korshak for the most part kept their questionable associations in the background, one Supermob associate was so reckless that he barely made the coming gang exodus to California. John Jacob Factor was born Iakow Factrowitz in the Polish sector of the Russian Pale in 1889, the tenth child of a Polish rabbi. In 1905, the family relocated to Chicago's Maxwell Street, where Factor's father joined many other breadwinners as a street peddler.

After a teenage job as a barber, his nickname was secure; Iakow Factrowitz had become Jake "the Barber" Factor. Not one to resist the allure of the quick buck, the Barber left a trail of lawlessness that even Capone could envy. Among his indictments: in 1919 for stock fraud in Illinois; in Florida twice for land fraud (one elderly Florida woman was relieved of her life savings of $280,000); twice for mail fraud; and for stock swindles in Canada and Rhodesia. Factor returned to Chicago and in 1923 convinced New York's most brilliant criminal mind, Arnold Rothstein, to front $50,000 toward what would be the largest stock swindle in European history. They started off small, selling worthless penny stocks, in London, then graduating up to bilking British investors out of $1.5 million.

Yet even these were mere preludes to the main event, in which Factor and Rothstein sold worthless African land, which they claimed was home to Vulcan Diamond Mines, to tens of thousands of investors, many of them elderly. The pair made off with $8 million, a staggering amount in 1930. The U.S. Justice Department called Factor "absolutely ruthless." Tried in absentia in

Jake Factor after his alleged 1933 kidnapping
(Library of Congress)

England, Factor was sentenced to eight years at hard labor. But he had made his way to Chicago, where it is believed he cut Murray Humphreys in on the booty for the protection of the Capones. Factor managed to delay the extradition hearing for three years and, thanks to his deep pockets, had his high-powered legal team appeal the case up to the Supreme Court.

In 1933, cracks began to appear in the wall of protection built by the Outfit for Factor. That spring, federal authorities made it clear that Factor would have to appear in court in preparation for extradition to England. Since the lawyers had exhausted their legal bag of tricks, it was up to the hoods to show how to delay a court appearance, permanently. According to a source close to both Tom Courtney and Tubbo Gilbert, fair-haired boy Sid Korshak, with Curly Humphreys's approval, was instrumental in devising a strategy to keep Factor out of prison. Consequently, the first show-up was scuttled when Factor's son Jerome was "kidnapped," only to be found healthy eight days later, with no "kidnappers" ever charged. When the feds reset the date to late June, Jake Factor himself disappeared after leaving an Outfit-controlled saloon in the northwest suburbs.

Jake Arvey, a close friend of both Korshak's and Factor's, was seen running in and out of Factor's elegant fortieth-floor suite at the Morrison Hotel, trying to arrange his ransom.[79] However, after twelve days, Factor surfaced, like his son, in excellent health. But this time, a kidnapper was named. In rapid succession, Tom Courtney's goons arrested the enemy of Stein, Petrillo, and Capone: Roger Touhy.* Courtney persuaded the Washington authorities to cancel Factor's extradition proceedings now that he was a material witness in a capital case. Touhy was tried twice in the

---

*Touhy had further alienated the Capones by protecting union leaders threatened when the Capones muscled in on the Building Services Employees Union (see next chapter).

Factor case, the first jury being unable to reach a decision. Although Factor identified Touhy, his admission was suspect given that he had earlier testified that he had been blindfolded the entire time. Two weeks later, the second trial produced a surprise witness, Isaac Costner, or Tennessee Ike, a man who when asked under oath to state his occupation replied, "Thief." Ike stated that he was with Touhy during the kidnapping, but he was against the idea. Factor chimed in that he remembered Ike as the "good man" among the kidnappers. Touhy was found guilty this time around and sentenced to ninety-nine years in prison. Meanwhile, Jake the Barber was allowed to stay in the country as "a friend of the court." (Twenty years later, Ike filed a deposition in which he admitted that he was put up to the false testimony by U.S. assistant attorney general Joseph B. Keenan, who promised to cut Ike a break on a thirty-year sentence for mail robbery if he agreed to testify against Touhy. When Keenan reneged, Ike filed the damning deposition.)

Now free to resume his larceny, Jake the Barber continued scamming until his luck ran out in 1942, when he was found guilty of swindling three hundred individuals in Iowa out of almost $500,000. The scheme, which involved the sales of fraudulent whiskey receipts, finally sent Factor to prison for six years. After his release, he would first relocate to Vegas, where he managed, under Korshak's and Humphreys's close supervision, the Outfit's Stardust Hotel, then go on to self-reinvention in Los Angeles, joining the rest of the Supermob.

Meanwhile, Jake's brother, Max, single-handedly reinvented the look of Hollywood movies with his development of Pan-Cake makeup (*pan* because of its small, flat, panlike container, and *cake* because of the form in which it was made). Prior to this, stars were painted with vaudeville-style grease-paint, which tended to crack. Max Factor was also the originator of the pouty-lip look and is widely considered the father of the cosmetics industry. When his cake makeup was mass-produced, Factor revolutionized the way everyday women presented themselves (prior to this invention, women rarely used makeup). Max Factor, who was immortalized in the Johnny Mercer song "Hooray for Hollywood," died in 1938.[80] His company is now owned by Procter and Gamble and continues to be one of the worldwide leaders in cosmetics.

As the Supermob continued to coalesce, the unanswerable question was which, if any, of its constituents viewed their association with the underworld as merely a means to an end, and which ones embraced the criminal life without reservation? Much as James Ragen had hinted that Greenberg was trapped by his alliance with the Outfit, there were those who would echo a similar sentiment about Korshak. Among the first to notice some misgivings (if only slight) on Korshak's part was Harry Busch, a fellow attorney who also worked out of 188 W. Randolph. Looking back, Busch commented recently, "However Sidney got his start, I think it was inadvertent. Something that was just too tempting, and then he couldn't get out." It was a theory expounded by any number of Korshak's friends, of which there were many, over the years. But Busch actually heard Korshak voice it.

One day, Busch encountered Korshak at the Randolph entrance. They exchanged pleasantries, and Busch informed Korshak that, with court in recess, he was on his way to pick up his car.

"How I envy you," Korshak said to his friend.

"Why? I know you're making far, far more money than I," replied Busch, to which Korshak said, "I'd rather be making less money and be out of this."

Busch didn't ask what "this" was because he knew. "The thing was," Busch concluded, "by then, he couldn't get out."[81]

It was a refrain Korshak would repeat thirty years later.

Hollywood Escapades

While Korshak was busy in Chicago learning the ropes as liaison between Courtney's office and the Outfit, events were unfolding in Hollywood that would test his abilities in the art of damage control. The gang Korshak so often represented was about to become embroiled in one of its few missteps, and a potentially fatal one at that.

In the early thirties, the Outfit began making inroads into the exploding movie business. It first became interested in the local variation, specifically in the thriving company founded by Barney Balaban. The oldest of seven sons of Maxwell Street Russian immigrants Goldie Manderbursky and Israel Balaban, Barney had partnered with his brother-in-law, Stan Katz, in 1917 when they opened the Central Park Theatre, Chicago's first picture palace. The pair revolutionized the film exhibition business by indulging in lavish buildings, combined with reasonable ticket prices, which made the movie experience accessible to middle-class filmgoers. In addition, they personally oversaw the design of massive air-conditioning systems that allowed theaters to stay open, for the first time, throughout the hot Midwest summers.

Soon the B&K theater chain was prospering. That's when the Chicago Outfit enlisted the business manager of the stagehands union, George E. Browne, and a Russian-born pimp named Willie Bioff, to extort B&K out of $20,000 or else have stink bombs tossed into their theaters. Pressure was also applied to John Smith, president of Local 110, the Motion Picture Operators Union. Smith later testified that Korshak showed up, for no fee, and asked if his union wanted protection. "I said no," Smith said. "He thought I was going to hire him as an attorney, and since there is trouble here, I don't want no part of Korshak."[82]

Of course, Smith was unable to forestall the gang's momentum, and before long everybody was paying the boys for protection. When the local putsch proved successful, the mob began coveting the movie business itself, then the fourth-largest industry in America. Later testimony revealed that the plot was devised at a series of meetings at the mob's Colony Club. "I think we can expect a permanent yield of a million dollars a year," Capone's heir Frank Nitti, who had to authorize the proposal, was heard to say. According to an unnamed source of the Chicago Crime Commission, Sidney Korshak was present at the Colony meetings every night.[83] In later testimony, George Browne confirmed Korshak's attendance.[84]

The Outfit was hopeful of success in large part because it already had a good man in place: Johnny "the Hollywood Kid" Rosselli had been dispatched from Chicago by Capone's Syndicate in the twenties to oversee the Outfit's race wire, which, thanks to the massive gambling habits of the movie crowd and corrupted L.A. mayor Frank Shaw, was turning a big profit. Rosselli simultaneously become the personal bookie for studio honchos like Joe Schenck (United Artists), Harry Cohn (Columbia), and Joseph Kennedy (RKO and Film Booking Office).

Rosselli and friends were also engaged to break a few legs when the industry's labor unions made demands. Columbia's Harry Cohn became one of Rosselli's best employers and friends. In return, the Chicago gang was allowed to begin their infiltration of the business—first through silent partnerships in actors' careers, and later in the various craft unions.*

The Hollywood Kid flew back to Chicago and explained how the studio bosses had him emasculate the leading trade union, the already corrupt International Alliance of Theatrical and Stage Employees (IATSE), making it ripe for a takeover by the mob. It shouldn't have surprised anyone. As director Orson Welles put it, "A group of industrialists finance a group of mobsters to break trade unionism, to check the threat of Socialism, the menace of Communism, or the possibility of democracy . . . When the gangsters succeed at what they were paid to do, they turn on the men who

---

*Actors such as George Raft, Chico Marx, Jimmy Durante, Jean Harlow, Cary Grant, Clark Gable, and Marilyn Monroe were among the most often rumored to have benefited from hoodlum associations.

paid them . . . [The] puppet masters find their creatures taking on a terrible life of their own."[85]

Rosselli's wish and Welles's analysis came to fruition on June 24, 1934, at IATSE's annual convention in Louisville, Kentucky. With the mob's gunmen ringing the perimeter of the convention hall, George Browne ran for the IATSE presidency unopposed. Once Browne was installed, Alex Greenberg assigned his factotum Frank Korte to be vice president, and his brother-in-law, Izzy Zevlin, to manage the crooked books.[86] Then it was Bioff's turn. The convicted panderer and whore-beater went door-to-door in Hollywood, letting the studio heads know that unless they ponied up large quantities of untraceable cash, IATSE would shut down production. The moguls had no choice, and the "majors" (Fox, MGM, Warner, and Paramount) as well as the "minors" (RKO and Columbia) each began paying $50,000 a year to Bioff and the mob-run IATSE to keep the cameras rolling. Only Rosselli's pal Harry Cohn at Columbia was spared.

Of course, the studio heads were far from lily-white victims: they watched their profits soar when IATSE's mob bosses slashed worker salaries by up to 40 percent; the Schenck brothers utilized their new underworld partners to divert theater profits away from their stockholders; Fox had Bioff make insane union demands of rival independent theater owners to drive them out of business. Harry Warner admitted under oath that "it was just good business" to have a relationship with Bioff. Writer Stephen Fox concluded, "Bioff did not have to 'corrupt' Hollywood any more than he needed to corrupt the stagehands union. In both instances he merely folded smoothly into the environment."[87]

When Bioff made an attempt to go independent and seize the actors' union for himself, he was promptly summoned back to Nitti's Bismarck Hotel headquarters, where he was informed that Charlie Gioe, Sid Korshak's pal from the Seneca, was now in charge of that union.*

In 1936, at the suggestion of adviser Joseph Kennedy, the presidency of Paramount (the Balaban & Katz parent company) was offered to Barney Balaban. He moved to New York City to take over the corporation and remained there for thirty years, while his brother John Balaban ran the studio in Hollywood and Stan Katz became a VP at MGM. In 1958, Balaban raised additional capital by selling the company's backlog of pre-1948 films to Jules Stein's Music Corporation of America for $50 million.[88] In 1966, Balaban was eased out as Paramount came under control of Gulf & Western.

---

*For a detailed description of the Outfit's takeover of IATSE, see my earlier book *The Outfit*, pp. 121–55.

Meanwhile, Sidney Korshak was engaged in his own private showbiz enchantments. In the midthirties, Korshak balanced his intense "mob lawyer" duties with the occasional representation of a helpless young babe, such as twenty-one-year-old model Dorothy Zink, who was immersed in a property dispute with her estranged husband.[89] This is one of the earliest examples of Korshak's mixing of business and pleasure—the young barrister was seen squiring Zink around the Windy City. A more lasting enchantment began when, during his association with attorney Phil Davis, Korshak was brought in to handle the nuisance lawsuit of Hollywood starlet Dorothy Appleby. A native of Portland, Maine, Appleby was a beauty queen (not to mention a drama queen), crowned Miss Maine in 1923 by matinee idol Rudolph Valentino. The brush with Hollywood royalty inspired Appleby to become an actress, so she packed her bags and hit the road as a greasepaint gypsy, appearing in stage plays around the country before landing work in Tinseltown. In a fit of retribution against a former lover, she hastily married a fellow actor in 1931, then one week later attempted suicide in New York's Central Park Lake. "He called me a lousy actress in front of my friends," a distraught Appleby said of her husband to the divorce court not long after.

The brunette heartbreaker next fixed her sights on Chicago furniture-empire scion Sidney M. Spiegel Jr., formerly married to Fay Lamphier, Miss America 1925. When he broke off his 1935 engagement to Appleby at the last minute, she sued under a soon-to-expire "breach of promise" statute, and Korshak was hired to represent her in the specious $250,000 claim, unaware that he would soon join the long list of men to succumb to Appleby's charms. The suit was settled out of court (for $1,000 in expenses, according to Spiegel's attorney; $5,000, according to Korshak). One week later it was announced that twenty-eight-year-old Korshak and twenty-nine-year-old Appleby were engaged.

Dorothy Appleby circa 1929 (Corbis/Bettmann)

CHICAGO LAWYER TO WED ACTRESS DOROTHY APPLEBY ran the September 22, 1935, *Chicago Tribune* headline. The article noted that Sid had just taken the train back to Chicago from L.A., where he had spent two weeks. According to Korshak, the romance developed during this, his first visit to California. Plans were announced for a December wedding in Harrison, New York, but for reasons unknown the marriage was postponed and, after three more years of dating, canceled outright. "Something about Hollywood makes love fade away," Appleby had once said.*,[90]

But the relationship gave Korshak the opportunity to experience his future West Coast home, and also likely to get to know one of Appleby's costars in *Riffraff*, white-hot actress Jean Harlow, the stepdaughter of Chicago mobster Marino Bello, and lover of New Jersey gangster Abner "Longy" Zwillman. Two decades later, Korshak would provide counsel to Mrs. Zwillman after Longy's passing. Pulitzer Prize–winning journalist Wendell Rawls, who researched Jules Stein for years, recently opined, "Korshak was like Zwillman. The entertainment world is very appealing to guys who grew up poor. There was great access to women."[91]

In 1938, Korshak's partner Ed King moved to New York, but before doing so transferred one hundred shares in the Industrial Trading Corporation to Korshak's Chicago bank account.[92] In New York, King worked with fellow attorney Moses Polakoff for Meyer Lansky and was said to have tried to convince Korshak to move to New York and join Team Lansky, but Sidney was already smitten with California girls.

Before making the move West, Korshak partnered with a number of local attorneys, including Jack Oppenheim, who later became a partner in Arvey's firm. Their offices were at 100 N. LaSalle, another favorite spot of the Outfit's political connection guys such as Guzik, Humphreys, and Gussie Alex.[93] In December of 1939, Korshak became partners with Harry A. Ash, a former Cook County inheritance-tax attorney general of Illinois. That same year, Korshak briefly flirted with political office, running, with Tom Courtney as his endorser, unsuccessfully against Robert C. Quirk for the nomination of alderman on the Democratic ticket for the Forty-eighth Ward. Interestingly, Korshak admitted to the FBI that Charlie Gioe, Outfit bookie and co-owner of the Seneca, donated $100 to the cause.[94]

---

*Appleby went on to appear in over fifty-six B movies and seven Three Stooges shorts, and had a bit part in one class movie, 1939's *Stagecoach*. She eventually married big-band leader Paul Drake in 1944—they divorced in 1980. She died on Long Island, New York, in 1990.

CHAPTER 3

Birds of a Feather

A prudent ruler can not and should not observe faith when such observance is to his disadvantage.

—MACHIAVELLI

THE YEAR 1940 GOT off to a bad start and only seemed to get worse, as Sidney Korshak became embroiled in two major scandals involving his Outfit-controlled union clients. Thanks to the efforts of crusading 132-paper syndicated columnist (and future Pulitzer Prize winner) Westbrook Pegler, the true agendas of Willie Bioff and George Scalise, president of the seventy-thousand-member Building Services Employees Union, would be revealed.

By sheer coincidence, Pegler, who had once worked the crime beat in Chicago, attended a 1939 party in Los Angeles where he was introduced to "Willie Bioff of IATSE." But Pegler knew better—he remembered Bioff as the whore-beater of Maxwell Street, on the lam for an outstanding pandering indictment. In November 1939, Pegler outed Bioff, and in early 1940, Pegler gave his information to the Screen Actors Guild, which had an open investigation of Bioff and IATSE, the result of Bioff's terrorizing of guild members with tire slashings—he also sought to control their union. SAG notified Chicago authorities, and Bioff was remanded to Chicago in April 1940 to answer the pandering charge. In the current vernacular, Bioff had been "Peglerized."

It came out in later testimony that while Bioff was in Chicago waiting to be jailed for the pandering charge, he attended a series of conferences with Nitti, Ricca, Korshak, and Alex Greenberg, held at their various homes and at the Bismarck and Seneca hotels. At a Bismarck Hotel meet, Bioff was first introduced (or so he testified) to the Supermob's Sid Korshak. Prosecutors doubted this was the first time the two had met, since Bioff admitted under oath that he was involved in the Scalise affair, which also involved Korshak. In any event, at the Bismarck powwow, Charles "Cherry Nose" Gioe introduced his Seneca Hotel–mate Korshak to Willie Bioff.

"Willie, meet Sidney Korshak. He is our man," Gioe declared. "I want you to do what he tells you. He is not just another lawyer. He knows our gang and figures our best interest. Pay attention to him, and remember, any message you get from him is a message from us."

Over the next few weeks, Bioff said, he met with Korshak about a dozen times at cafés and hotels. Years later, when a California friend asked if he had defended Bioff in court, Korshak exploded, "Are you nuts? Of course not! I only counseled the bastard!"[1] In early April, Bioff began serving out his five months in Bridewell Prison, after which he returned to L.A. to continue IATSE thuggery.

But Westbrook Pegler had not yet finished his haunting of the Outfit and Sid Korshak. In his January 19, 1940, column, Pegler exposed George Scalise as another ex-convict and panderer. Pegler's article revealed that Scalise was a convicted white slaver who had served four and a half years in prison on that charge and had long been associated with gangsters such as Lepke Buchalter and Jacob Shapiro of New York's Murder, Inc.*

One week after Bioff's imprisonment, George Scalise was arrested in New York and indicted on fifty-two counts of embezzlement. The new Scalise charges were based on the discovery of phony accounts set up to siphon union money to Scalise, and by implication, to the New York mob and its partner in the scheme, the Chicago Outfit (the union was headquartered in Chicago and taking orders from Murray Humphreys). Another part of the scheme involved the establishment of new bylaws that permitted Scalise to gerrymander the union locals in ways that would consolidate his power. It was learned that in the previous three years, over $1.5 million had found its way from the union treasury into Scalise's private account. Not only was Sidney Korshak the union's counsel, but, what was more telling, authorities found evidence that he had helped set up the phony accounts.

Grand juries were convened in both New York and Chicago on the Scalise matter, and in Chicago, Sidney Korshak caught a break, simultaneously experiencing firsthand the importance of political connections. Korshak must have had to stifle a grin as he took the witness stand before the Chicago grand

---

*Other associates were Peter Rienzi, Frankie Yale (Uale), Anthony Carfano, Joey Amberg, and James Plumieri. He had worked for both the Lucchese and Genovese crime families of New York.

jury, waiting to be grilled by none other than his great friend, and the man who had just sponsored him for alderman, State's Attorney Tom Courtney.

Under less-than-hostile questioning, Sidney explained that the fees he had received—$5,000 as retainer and $3,750 for drawing up the bylaws that established the phony accounts—were not, to his knowledge, for the furtherance of Scalise's scheme. Thanks to Courtney's "grilling," Korshak emerged from the incident unscathed, whereas Scalise was ousted from the union, convicted on five counts, and sentenced to ten to twenty years in the federal penitentiary.[2]

But Korshak's problems had just begun. In the fall of that year, one Louise Morris, a tenant of the Seneca, informed Chicago police captain John Howe that a group of men had been seducing underage girls in one of the building's apartments, coercing them into "immoral and perverse sexual acts." Upon further investigation, Howe learned that five men in the building had previously been arrested for sex offenses against two underage girls. The men were Lou Pelton, a Capone associate connected with the Bartenders Union, a restaurateur named Gibby Kaplan, Joel Goldblatt, owner of the sixteen-location Goldblatt Brothers Department Store chain, and lastly, law partners Harry Ash and Sidney Korshak.

The Domestic Relations and Delinquency Court scheduled the case to be heard before Judge Victor A. Kula on December 16, 1940. However, when the Chicago Crime Commission checked the court records over the next few weeks, the case had simply disappeared. Although the names of the alleged female victims were located, the five men's names had vanished along with any record of how the case was resolved. It seemed apparent that, in this so-called most corrupt city in the world, money had changed hands in an amount that satisfied all concerned.[3] (Ironically, Sidney's brother Marshall would become chairman of the Illinois Sex Offenders Commission, which sought to determine—with input from consultant Dr. Alfred Kinsey—the best treatment for sex offenders and the prevention of sex crimes.)

No sooner had the vice charges been dealt with than it was back to the Bioff business, which was about to explode again, forcing Korshak to deliver another "message from us" to Willie Bioff. In 1940, as the result of an ongoing IRS probe, MGM's Joe Schenck was indicted for tax evasion to the tune of $400,000. Facing 167 aggregate years for conspiracy and tax fraud, the movie honcho cut a deal and informed the authorities of the payoffs to Bioff and Browne.[4] Schenck's disclosures led to the May 23, 1941, indictments of Bioff, Browne, and Nick Circella, at whose Colony Club the plot was hatched; Circella also functioned as the Outfit's watchdog over Bioff. While Bioff and Browne utilized legal stalling maneuvers, Circella went on the lam, only to be caught six months later hiding out with his girlfriend and Colony hostess, Estelle Carey. In late May, Sid Korshak, who was in Los Angeles pursuing his latest flame, a beautiful twenty-two-year-old Ice Capades skater named Bernice "Bee" Stewart, met with Bioff at the Ambassador Hotel to make certain he didn't "give up" his Chicago bosses.

At the meeting, Korshak was accompanied by two young women, one of whom was believed to have been Bee Stewart. Excusing themselves, the men spoke in private. "You will admit to being Schenck's bagman and do your time like a man," Korshak explained to Bioff—there would be no mention of Nitti or the others. "He advised me to lie," Bioff later testified.

Bioff knew that defying Korshak meant defying the Outfit. He accepted his fate and prepared for the trip back to New York to plead guilty. Korshak obtained $15,000 from Gioe, which he delivered to Bioff to defray his attorney fees.

Bioff did exactly as Korshak had advised him when the trial convened later that year: yes, he took some money, but it wasn't extortion, and it went no further than himself. Browne and Bioff were both found guilty of all charges and sentenced to ten years in federal prison, while Circella received eight. Prosecutors, however, knew the culpability went far beyond Bioff and Browne, since during the trial, studio head Harry Warner blurted out that Bioff had told him the money was "for the boys back in Chicago." However, without a cooperating witness, prosecutors were unable to vet the lead.

On December 7, 1941, two months after the trial, the Japanese attacked Pearl Harbor, forcing the United States into World War II. Although it couldn't be known at the time, the effect of the conflict on Japanese Americans would prove fortuitous for the Supermob. In the meantime, prosecutors in New York spent all of 1942 prodding at Bioff, Browne, and Circella to try to learn more about "the boys in Chicago." If their intuitions were correct, the truth about "the boys" could be a career-maker for all the young feds. After months of fruitless questioning, their luck changed, albeit in a most tragic way.

At 3:09 in the afternoon on February 2, 1943, Chicago firemen were called to an apartment at 512 Addison Street on the North Side near Lake Michigan, where neighbors had smelled smoke. Racing up the stairs to the third-floor apartment, they found on the dining room floor the still-smoldering corpse of a redheaded young woman. Her remains were in a horrid state: she had been stabbed with an ice pick, beaten, and set afire after being doused with a flammable liquid. The "flash fire" had burned the flesh off her legs up to her knees. The apartment's condition bespoke a fierce struggle. The woman's blood and hair covered the walls and floors in the kitchen and dining room. In the kitchen, investigators found the bloody objects used to assault the woman before she was set ablaze: a blackjack, ice pick, knife, electric iron, and broken whiskey bottle.

The police concluded that the crime had occurred just hours before their arrival. The victim, it was later learned, was known to have been alive just two hours earlier, as she had been on the phone with her cousin when she had to answer the door. "I'm expecting someone" were her last words as she hung up. Although two fur coats were missing, the victim's much more valuable jewelry was untouched. Police wondered if the coats were taken to give the appearance of a robbery. Also, it was determined that the bottle of flammable liquid found in the ashes did not belong to the deceased or her roommate, and burglars are not typically known to carry combustibles with them to a heist.[5] The last thing learned was the victim's identity—Estelle Carey, Circella's girlfriend.

Although it was far from certain that Carey's murder had anything to do with Circella's involvement with the extortion scheme—she maintained a slew of dangerous liaisons with jealous lovers—the three men held in stir were convinced of the connection.

"As soon as [Carey] was killed, that was the end of it," prosecutor Boris Kostelanetz recalled. "[Circella] turned off, boom, just like an electric light."[6] When Murray Humphreys's aide Ralph Pierce was questioned in connection with the Carey murder, Sid Korshak represented him.[7] Unlike Circella, Willie Bioff, fearing for his beloved wife, Laurie, and their children, reacted with rage, saying, "While we do time for them, they are murdering our families." Bioff proceeded directly to the prosecutor's office, asking, "What do you want to know?" For his part, George Browne took the middle ground, cooperating only minimally with the investigators.

Within days, on March 18, 1943, conspiracy and extortion indictments were returned against Johnny Rosselli, Frank Nitti, Louis Campagna, Paul Ricca (De Lucia), and Charlie Gioe, as well as Phil D'Andrea, Frankie Diamond (Maritote), and a New Jersey union boss named Louis Kaufman, who'd helped engineer Browne's takeover of the Kentucky IATSE convention.

Six hours after the indictments were delivered, Frank Nitti, who was ultimately responsible for the scheme, put a gun to his head rather than face prison time or the wrath of Outfit bosses Tony Accardo and Murray Humphreys. At the time of Nitti's death, Alex Greenberg was in possession of $100,000 of Nitti's money, which he eventually returned to Nitti's estate.

* * *

Indictments, brutal murders, sex scandals, suicides—Sid Korshak probably thought it was a good time to "get outta Dodge." On April 4, luck appeared in the unlikely form of a draft notice. Five days later, Korshak showed up at seven thirty A.M. and took his physical for induction into the U.S. army, in advance of being stationed at Camp Lee, Virginia, where he served throughout the war as a military instructor and a "paper-pushing" desk sergeant. One of his duties included vetting prospective candidates for officer candidate school (OCS), where he promoted one recruit by the name of Morris Dalitz, who would play a large role in the future success of Korshak.

Corporal Korshak took a leave on August 17, 1943, to marry Bee Stewart at the Ambassador Hotel in New York City, before returning to active duty.

While Sidney was off learning how to break down an M1 rifle (and likely shopping in Arvey's PXes), the trial of the original "Chicago Seven" commenced on October 5, 1943. During the New York trial Bioff told the court that Sid Korshak was "our man in Hollywood." In Chicago, the headlines hit: CHICAGO LAWYER "OUR MAN" SAYS BIOFF AT MOVIE TRIAL, declared the *Sun.* BIOFF NAMES SID KORSHAK AS MOB AIDE, echoed the *Herald-American.* The reportage would nag at Korshak for the rest of his life.

Eventually, Ricca, Campagna, Rosselli, D'Andrea, Maritote, and Gioe were sentenced to ten years in prison plus $10,000 fines. Louis Kaufman, the New Jersey union strong-arm, was given seven years.

After Korshak was discharged as a corporal in 1945, he and Bee set up their first home at the Seneca, and together they threw the best parties in pre–Hugh Hefner Chicago, where their female party guests presaged a Playboy Club–like atmosphere. As a former judge told the *New York Times*, "Sidney always had contact with high-class girls. Not your $50 girl, but girls costing $250 or more." Rumors of Sidney's associations with "working girls" would follow him for decades.

The marriage put nary a dent in Korshak's prewar bachelor lifestyle, as he became a regular at the coveted Table One in the Ambassador East Hotel's Pump Room, and Outfit-attended boîtes like the Chez Paree and Eli's Restaurant. He struck up a lifelong friendship with *Chicago Sun-Times* entertainment/gossip columnist Irv Kupcinet, with whom he often shared Table One. The relationship between the two former Lawndale Russian Ashkenazim was symbiotic: Kup made certain Sidney and the rest of the Korshaks were portrayed in a good light in his daily "Kup's Column," while Sidney, after his eventual move to Beverly Hills, helped Kup gain access to Hollywood celebrities and gossip. "Irv Kupcinet was always kissing Sidney's ass," said former Chicago FBI

Irv Kupcinet holds down the fort at the Pump Room's Table One (Library of Congress, *Look* Magazine Collection)

Table One at the Pump Room today (author photo)

man Fran Marracco. "Irv got his free meal. I'd bet a pension check that Sidney probably helped get Irv's son Jerry started as a director out in Hollywood."*,[8]

"When Sidney sat at Table One in the Pump Room, you'd see him with city politicians," recalled Labor Department Chicago investigator Tom Zander.[9] "At the Ambassador East, they treated Sid like he owned the place," echoes Joel Goldblatt's widow, MJ.[10] And while Sid schmoozed, his wife, Bee, was teaming up with Gussie Alex's gorgeous professional-model wife, the former Marianne Ryan, to produce fashion shows in the Chicago area.

134 North LaSalle

I really have no power. All I have is friends.

—PAUL ZIFFREN[11]

In hindsight, it now appears that Korshak was being groomed—the mob had decided to use the Supermob to help them go legit. What Willie Bioff

---

*Jerry Kupcinet directs the television series *Judge Judy* and *Judge Joe Brown*.

had told the court about the Outfit's recruitment of George Browne could just as easily have applied to Sidney Korshak: "They said they could use a man like him. He has a nice clean background, and they need a front man like him—it is very important to them."[12] Conversely, and perhaps more importantly, the Supermob was using the mob to further *its* own agenda. The symbiosis, or mutual parasitism, had its roots across the street from City Hall, where a number of Supermob associates, including Sidney Korshak, had recently moved their offices.

Upon his return to Chicago, Sidney Korshak took up with his brother Marshall in Suite 400 at 134 North LaSalle Street (aka the Metropolitan Building), a twenty-two-story office building directly across from City Hall, and just around the block from his former office at 188 W. Randolph. It seemed that the mob had its locus on Randolph, while the Supermob was a block away at LaSalle, which fittingly was the street on which Jake Arvey was born in 1895.[13] "There were three offices in Suite 400, Marshall's, Sid's, and an associate," recalled Chicago FBI agent Pete Wacks. "Interestingly, their suite was the only one with a back-door emergency exit."[14]

Number 134 was known to be the place where the secret deals were cut with the pols like Tom Courtney working across the street; it was the *other* City Hall. As such, the building was under the routine scrutiny of well-meaning but impotent law enforcement officials. Among the numerous brokers networking in the halls of 134 was a close friend of both Korshaks' who had also opened an office there in 1945, as well as one in Los Angeles, a man whom "Colonel Jack Arvey," as he now preferred to be addressed, treated like a son. His name was Paul Ziffren, and he would become a key architect in the Supermob's successful infiltration of Southern California.

Six years younger than his friend Sid Korshak, Paul Ziffren always claimed he was born in Davenport, Iowa, on July 18, 1913, to Jacob Ziffren

134 North La Salle Street (Karen Laurencell)

of Russia and Bella Minnie Rothenberg of Lithuania. Like Korshak, Ziffren had four siblings, brothers Lester and Lee, and sisters Betsy and Annette. Despite claiming this lineage, Ziffren (or anyone else, for that matter) could never produce his birth certificate from Davenport (Scott County), although a delayed birth certificate was filed in *Des Moines* in 1940. This was curious for at least two reasons: all the other Ziffren siblings had their birth certificates filed in a timely manner, and Iowa law permits a delayed birth certificate only for *adopted children*, and adoption court records are sealed.

A former Chicago political operative for Richard Daley has related a remarkable story that he said explains the curiosities. "In the early fifties I was working for the Daley camp at a time when Arvey had refused to endorse Daley for president of the Cook County Board," the operative recently recalled. "I took it upon myself to tap Arvey's phones to see if he was on the take." The tap relayed one conversation in which a local precinct captain was asking Arvey to have Ziffren, by then a force in California, intercede for a friend in hot water in Los Angeles. Referring to Ziffren, the caller then said, "C'mon, Jack. Look, we know Paul's your kid. You can talk him into it." To which Arvey responded, "Don't bring that up. It's old history."[15]

Interestingly, the possibility of Paul Ziffren being Arvey's illegitimate son has been bandied about for years by old Chicago pols that traveled in Arvey's sphere.[16] Ziffren's FBI file notes informants who point out that Paul doesn't resemble his siblings, who were, unlike Paul, all delivered by the same physician. Conversely, when photo comparisons are made, Ziffren, although much taller than Arvey, bore an uncanny facial resemblance to the ward boss. Also, there is no record of the attending physician at Paul's birth. Shockingly, both Ziffren's grade school and high school records appear to have been written in one hand, and in one sitting, although they were for a number of different schools. Ziffren's FBI file concluded, "The natural parentage of Paul Ziffren, if ever learned, could explain his exceptional and early acceptance in Chicago political and organized criminal circles—upon which associations, coupled with his acknowledged intelligence, are based his phenomenal economic and political career."[17] (As a curious footnote to the adoption allegation, in 1937 law school student Ziffren spoke at the Chicago Philanthropic Club's "Orphans' Outing" at the Congress Hotel.)[18]

A brilliant student, Ziffren attended Northwestern University Law School and financed his grad schooling thanks to a Pritzker Foundation scholarship (much more to be seen about the Pritzkers). In 1938, Ziffren passed the bar and immediately began working for the U.S. Attorney's Office for Northern Illinois, where he was the tax law specialist, handling over 130 civil tax cases and several major criminal prosecutions. Ziffren spent a brief period on the staff of the chief counsel of the IRS just before going into private practice in 1941. One of his cases was the government's ongoing effort to obtain $350,000 in back taxes from Al Capone.[19] In 1941, Ziffren joined Gottlieb and Schwartz, where he was a tax case specialist at a time when crime syndicates were employing lawyers, accountants, and former IRS employees to oversee their investments. At this firm of thirty-two lawyers, Ziffren shared a suite with occasional Sid Korshak law associate Jack Oppenheim. When the FBI checked into Ziffren's background, a "number of persons" informed the investigators that "Ziffren was a shrewd, promoter-type attorney [who] placed his personal interests above those of the law firms with which he had been associated."[20]

Alex Greenberg's tax records disclose that Paul Ziffren handled Greenberg's taxes at Gottlieb and Schwartz, and that in 1943 Greenberg made an inappropriate deduction of some $27,265 paid to Ziffren.[21] Those same records indicate that in 1946 Greenberg wrote checks to Ziffren totaling $25,000, Fred Evans ($20), and gave contributions to others in Arvey's Army, such as Arthur Elrod ($2,041) and Judge Abe Marovitz ($500).

Ziffren next became a full partner in his mentor's firm, Arvey & Mantyband, and was said to have been engaged to Jake Arvey's daughter. The engagement was broken off, but Jake Arvey stayed close, considering Ziffren to be, according to associates, like a son. After marrying the former Dorothy Kolinsky in 1937, Ziffren began traveling constantly, often to SoCal. The FBI had also learned that Ziffren was the tax specialist for American Distillers, which also retained lawyers Edward King, Sid Korshak, and his brother Marshall.

Sid Korshak and Paul Ziffren were friends to the end. Writer and former studio executive Dominick Dunne recalled meeting Korshak at Ziffren's home a few years after his own 1957 move to California at a party given for the writer Romain Gary and his wife, actress Jean Seberg. "Sidney was there, and I remember Natalie Wood was there," remembered Dunne. "I mean, it was a jazzy Sunday-night group." (Dunne was known to bring his camera to these parties. Unaware that he was not permitted to photograph Korshak, he casually took a picture from across the room. "I could hear this collective gasp. I didn't know what I had done, and then someone said, 'Don't take a picture of Sidney!' He was the presence in a room. There's always that wonderful feeling of knowing someone in the underworld.")[22]

Regarding Sidney Korshak, Ziffren said, "My relationship with Sid is essentially a social relationship. I consider him a friend of mine, but he never discusses business with me, nor do I with him"[23] Ziffren's friendship with Korshak would reach the height of its symbiosis decades later, when both

David Bazelon, attorney (private collection)

were engaged in political kingmaking in Los Angeles. Before that, there was another friend of Ziffren's—perhaps his closest friend in life—who would be instrumental in facilitating the expansion of the Supermob. His name was David Bazelon.

"My Best Friend in the World"

The youngest of nine children, David Lionel Bazelon was born on September 3, 1909, in Wisconsin. His father died destitute when David was two, precipitating the family's move to the North Side of Chicago. Although his schooling was punctuated by periods of being forced to work—as a movie usher and store clerk—young Bazelon was considered an academic wunderkind, and, like Ziffren, some called him a genius. Bazelon attended DePaul and Northwestern undergraduate schools in 1926–27, then Harvard Law for one week, having to return home to care for his sick mother. In 1931, he transferred to Northwestern Law School, where he became undergrad Paul Ziffren's schoolmate and lifelong best friend, as Bazelon freely told the FBI.[24] In 1935, Bazelon married the former Miriam Kellner, who, according to congressional informants, was related to Jake Arvey.[25] On the same day in 1938, the two best friends were hired by the U.S. attorney's office, then, in 1941, they were hired together by the firm of Gottlieb and Schwartz, where they were both tax law specialists. Both Bazelon and Ziffren quickly became senior partners at Gottlieb, where Bazelon was said to be the attorney for Alex Greenberg's Canadian Ace Brewing Company.[26]

The Pritzkers

Also commanding a suite at 134 was another firm critical to the expansion of the Supermob, not to mention the legitimizing of massive amounts of

Outfit lucre. The amazingly long reach and ambition of Pritzker, Pritzker and Clinton would dwarf its role as a law firm and fold neatly into the world of the Supermob.

Nicholas Pritzker, another 1880s Jewish immigrant from Kiev, was so poor that he was taken in by Michael Reese Hospital the day it opened, treated for a cold, and given a $9 overcoat by the hospital. "Best investment they ever made," said his son Abe. "I paid them back for that coat—about a million times."[27]

In 1902, Nicholas founded the Pritzker & Pritzker law firm, which later added Stanford Clinton to the partnership. Clinton later became the general counsel to the mob-controlled Teamsters Pension Fund and also represented Capone gang members like Al Hart's partner, Joe Fusco. Years later, when Fusco moved to Palm Springs, he was seen hosting the likes of son Abe Pritzker, as well as mob bosses Tony Accardo, Frank Costello, Rocco Fischetti, Jake Guzik, and Phil Kastel (Kastel had fronted for Frank Costello in introducing slots and big-time gambling in New Orleans during the Huey Long era). The Pritzkers' firm also represented Jake Guzik, and the family were friends with the Korshak clan.[28] The FBI made note of the friendship of Korshak and Pritzker.[29]

Patriarch Nicholas Pritzker was on the board of the department store chain owned by the Goldblatt brothers, also good friends and clients of Korshak's.[30] "I met Korshak when he was attorney for Goldblatts' department store," Abe recalled. "You know something? I like him."[31] Then, contradictorily: "He's done favors, but I've never used him because I'm afraid of his reputation."[32] Most insiders are convinced that Pritzker's statement is disingenuous at best, and one longtime attorney friend of Korshak's and Pritzker's knew it for a fact. Not long after his own passing of the bar, one young Chicago lawyer who stayed a lifelong friend of both men went to Abe Pritzker to try to secure his business for his fledgling practice. The attorney, who wished to remain anonymous, has a vivid memory of the encounter: "When I went to Abe Pritzker to try to get his account for my new law practice, he said he didn't need me. 'We hire the best attorney in America,' he said. 'Sidney Korshak.' "[33]

As will be seen, Korshak himself later told the Securities and Exchange Commission of his work for the Pritzkers, and Melville Marx also told the SEC that he believed Korshak was the Pritzkers' labor lawyer in Chicago.[34] Marx's statement begs the question: Why would a law firm require a labor lawyer? The answer is that the successful legal practice was but the tip of the iceberg of a vast Pritzker commercial and real estate empire that would come to be worth billions, much of which would be hidden in

Abe Pritzker (Chicago Jewish Archives, Spertus Institute)

offshore bank accounts to avoid paying taxes. Their varied interests included the Marmon Group, which oversaw dozens of corporations with diversified holdings in basic industries, natural resources, and real estate. The Pritzkers also came to own the Hyatt Hotel chain, with its hundred-plus international hotels. The *New York Times* noted, "Pritzker holdings are too numerous for any one member of the family to recall at any given moment."[35] (For a more thorough accounting of the Pritzker holdings, see appendix B.)

> *Behind every great fortune there is a crime.*
> —HONORÉ DE BALZAC, FRENCH REALIST NOVELIST (1799–1850)

What is most relevant to the Pritzker role in the Supermob is the large number of Pritzker transactions that involved known crime figures, Supermob partners such as fellow 134 tenants Paul Ziffren and Sidney Korshak, as well as other notables including David Bazelon, Alex Greenberg, Murray Humphreys, and Teamster boss Jimmy Hoffa.

Allegations of Pritzker-mob links have dogged the family from the earliest times. Jack Clarke, a renowned Chicago private investigator, recently recalled what he heard on the streets: "Frontier Finance was used and owned by the Pritzkers as a holding company and is believed to be the secret to the origins of the family's involvement with criminals. Pritzker lent to immigrants 'five for seven,' or five dollars lent against seven dollars repayment with interest. It was started on the West Side and the Pritzkers let the mob run it for them. This company office was where the mob held their meetings."[36] Frontier Finance was a state-licensed loan company, with a number of legit investors, such as the postmaster of Chicago, a former chairman of the Cook County Republican Party, and a retired Chicago police captain.

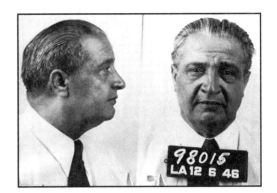

Jack Dragna in a 1946 LAPD
mug shot (author collection)

But curiously, the president of the firm was Frank Buccieri, brother of the
notorious Fiore "Fifi" Buccieri, one of the Outfit's top gambling bosses and
a dreaded "juice" collector.[37]

Stronger evidence was surfacing on the West Coast, where the LAPD
observed Abe Pritzker meeting with Louis Dragna, brother of "L.A.'s
Capone," Jack Dragna, in the Los Angeles office of attorney Louis Hiller, a
Korshak associate. Louis Dragna was a made mafioso, who later ran the
L.A. family with Jimmy "the Weasel" Fratianno."* The LAPD developed information that Pritzker and Hiller were fronting for "gangland money." The
supposed purpose of the meeting was to bring the Dragnas, who had a million dollars to invest, together with the Pritzkers.[38]

In the late forties, the Pritzkers, like most other savvy Chicago hoteliers,
joined the new Chicago Hotel Association, a powerful group of approximately thirty owners that was somehow immune to strikes by the equally
powerful Hotel and Restaurant Employees Union (HRE), a guild whose
leaders were handpicked by the Chicago Outfit, and whose reach would
soon extend to the West Coast. Not surprisingly, the labor negotiator for the
HRE was Sidney Korshak, who told investigators that he was recommended
for the job by Henry Crown's vice president, Patrick Hoy.[39] (Future players in
the gambling mecca of Las Vegas occupied the 134 suite immediately adjacent
to the Pritzker firm. Thanks to loans from the Outfit-Korshak–controlled
Teamsters Pension Fund, Bernard Nemerov and Sam Tucker would become part owners of the Riviera and the Desert Inn, respectively—
although many reported that Korshak was a silent partner in both. Lastly,
Benjamin Cohen of Cohen, Berke and Goldberg maintained a suite at 134.

---

*After being named in a federal extortion case in 1981, Louis Dragna flipped and became
a government witness.

Cohen, as well as eight other 134 tenants, would join Paul Ziffren in future hotel investments.)

> *If you want to get something fixed in Chicago, the person to see is Korshak, and it doesn't matter where he is at the time—all a person has to do is mention Korshak's name.*
>
> —FBI INFORMANT[40]

Sidney Korshak was, meanwhile, gaining experience in the labor-counseling game—Chicago style—while helping a man who would become one of his alleged Seneca "sex party" pals, department store owner Joel Goldblatt. Over the years, the friendship deepened, with the Korshaks and Goldblatts traveling to Europe together several times. Joel's widow, MJ Goldblatt, recently recalled, "Anti-Semitism was a motivating factor in the drive of both Joel and Sidney. Joel treated Sidney like a god. When Sidney came into the office, you'd think the pope was coming. Joel would disconnect the phones, close the doors, and order kosher hot dogs or corned beef."

In 1946, Goldblatt engaged Sidney after labor organizers threatened him with strikes and extortion. It appears that the Outfit had two prongs of attack with regard to business targets: either force one of their unions on the business, or allow the owners to pay a fee to keep the unions out. Korshak was given the role of collector. Investigative reporter Sy Hersh, who would later interview Goldblatt and write the seminal exposé of Korshak for the *New York Times*, recently said, "After World War Two, [Korshak's] new, classier thing was to fix unions. He would get unions to strike, and then he would go to the people, say, 'I can take care of it,' and he would get a lot of money."[41] Mrs. Goldblatt remembered, "Goldblatts' had union problems with delivery trucks. Sid had the know-how and the contacts to end any labor problems at the store."[42] The FBI looked into Korshak's alleged role with

Two on the town: Mrs. Sidney Korshak (l.) and Mrs. Joel Goldblatt, 1955 (*Chicago Tribune*)

Murray Humphreys in the Goldblatt-union affair, but unable to find records of payoffs or testimony from witnesses, the Bureau declined prosecution.[43]

Korshak resolved Goldblatts' labor difficulties so smoothly that his name quickly circulated among other entrepreneurs hoping to fend off the unions. These clients were trying to avoid aggressive attempts by honest labor unions to organize their employees. They also wanted to avoid doing business with the mob-dominated unions that would keep wages low but demand heavy extortion payments. Korshak's growing reputation led to a relationship with an established banker, Walter M. Heymann, then a vice president of the First National Bank of Chicago and Joel Goldblatt's personal banker. Initially critical of Goldblatt's association with Korshak, within a year Heymann was recommending his most important clients to do business with Korshak; he continued in this for the next twenty years. One businessman described Sidney as "a consolidation of the payoffs." Within a year Korshak had secured a number of furniture and manufacturing companies as clients.

Brian Ross, the iconic TV network investigative reporter—and to this day the only member of his profession to produce a televised exposé of Korshak (1978)—recently summed up Korshak's delicate position: "A guy like Korshak is essential for that bridge between polite society and criminal society. He's the one who can bridge that, one way or the other. Neither side quite knows what he's doing. It's a dangerous game for him, but that's where his place was."[44]

In 2003, Sandy Smith, the longtime dean of Chicago crime reporters, spoke at length about Korshak's place in the mob-Supermob hierarchy:

Actually, Sidney functioned as a gangster. He was their straight man. He would go to the corporations and those places that the gangsters couldn't get into, simply because they were such slobs. For instance, Giancana could not go in on his own. Nobody would want to get anywhere near him. Actually at the time, there were thirty-nine or forty police districts in Chicago—the mob operated in maybe half of them. The mayors knew exactly what was going on because on the street the collections from the mob were made each month. In other words the mob had to pay off people each month. There was a political payoff and a police payoff, separate ones. That's how the system worked. A lot of reporters knew exactly what was going on. In most of those thirty-nine districts I could've identified the cop who was collecting money for the captain from the mob joints and also who was collecting the political payoffs. Sometimes one collector handled both payoffs, but more often than not, given that Chicago was a place where nobody trusted anybody, there were separate collectors. That system existed for an awful long time in every police district in Chicago. The mob was into almost anything that was making money in any of those districts. There were payoffs for that. And every now and then, some cop who was handling the payoffs would disappear, go to Mexico and live there for the rest of his life. But this went on in every district in the city. But that's what made the Korshaks so strong. They played right into that. I'm not sure that there was anything in any other big city that was as tight as the relationships between the Korshaks and the mob and all that in Chicago. They were a force to be reckoned with.[45]

Marshall Takes Chicago

While Sidney grew accustomed to his middleman role, his brother Marshall Korshak was well on his way to becoming Chicago's city treasurer, the second most powerful Democratic Party official in Chicago. The FBI noted, "His control of top city patronage jobs was regarded as absolute." Attorney Timothy Applegate, who was the liaison between Hilton Hotels and its labor consultant Sidney Korshak, recently remembered Marshall's growing hold on the city's finances: "Marshall used to represent Hilton on property tax matters, and he received fifteen percent of whatever he saved us when our taxes were reviewed every four years. I became suspicious when the assessor started reviewing us every year for no reason—and of course Marshall then got his cut four times as often. So I went to see him in Chicago, where he and Sidney shared a big, palatial office. A few minutes later Marshall walked in the front door with his arm around the Cook County tax assessor, and Marshall said to me, 'Tim, I want you to meet my best friend.' It was an education as to how things worked in Chicago."[46]

Jack Walsh, the former Chicago-based IRS organized crime investigator who oversaw the 1980s prosecution of corrupt Chicago judges (Operation Greylord), knew the setup well. "Whoever holds the money strings in Chicago is the most important person in the city, other than Daley," Walsh has said. "We found people in the treasurer's office connected to the hoods. Marshall had his own connections with organized crime."[47] Chicago FBI agent Pete Wacks heard stories that Marshall was even run in on the occasion when suburban gambling spots were rousted. "There were hidden poker games, very typical," said Wacks. "Certain people would be taken aside so their names wouldn't surface."[48]

"Marshall always had a police driver with a city car," remembered former Chicago FBI agent Fran Marracco. "He had a lot of control in the Chicago police commission—who was hired, who was fired, promoted. He was very tight with old man [Mayor Richard] Daley. There was no way to delineate between the Korshak brothers—they were *both* tight with the Outfit. But that is Chicago."[49] Lastly, another former Chicago FBI man, the late Bill Roemer, seemed to agree with Marracco when he told *Vanity Fair* magazine in 1997, "Marshall was an important legislator and politician, and of course we always felt that he was put in there because he was the younger brother of Sidney."[50]

In the ensuing years, Marshall Korshak would come to define the classic and articulate liberal politician, as he championed increases in workmen's compensation, increased benefits, aid to dependent children, and training facilities for the mentally handicapped. His popularity saw him voted one of the four best state senators by the Independent Voters of Illinois.

Although brother Sidney was prospering in his own way, his growing Chicago client base didn't prevent him from continuing his love affair with California. He was now spending so much time on the West Coast that he rented a house in the Coldwater Canyon area just north of the city; he would soon buy property at 17031 Magnolia, in Encino.[51] At the same time, thanks to the increased scrutiny brought on by the Hollywood extortion scandal, plans were being made to invest some of the hoods' profits in SoCal real estate, while simultaneously infiltrating both the political and corporate substructure of the state—this time without the burden of a Willie Bioff. This time they'd get it right: they'd use the Supermob.

In postwar Los Angeles, Korshak was received with open and familiar arms: Al Hart, Jake Factor, Lew Wasserman, Jules Stein, Ronald Reagan, and Walter Annenberg (Moe's son) had all relocated there; Abe Pritzker, Fred Evans, and Paul Ziffren were keeping a presence in Los Angeles, with Ziffren opening a satellite office on Spring Street downtown and renting a house in Coldwater Canyon near Korshak. Everything was in place for a massive reallocation of funds from Chicago to California, and with it, a near-total usurping of the state's political and economic system.

All of these Chicago émigrés were bent on proving F. Scott Fitzgerald wrong when he said, "There are no second acts in American lives." Indeed, California seemed to mandate that its citizens re-create themselves. Not only would they adopt new identities, but they would do it in a state that virtually invited the Chicagoans to hijack it. The Supermob had done its homework; there was not a chance of finding a better locale in which to build "Chicago West."

CHAPTER 4

Kaddish for California

Watch that fucking Bonanno . . . he wants what's ours—what's always been ours, California. He can't have Arizona, and he sure as hell can't have California!

—CHICAGO OUTFIT BOSS TONY ACCARDO SPEAKING TO HIS ENFORCER
TONY SPILOTRO ABOUT THE ENCROACHMENT OF NEW YORK MAFIA
CAPO JOE BONANNO, IN 1978[1]

THE MOVIE EXTORTION CASE left the Chicago underworld shaken and more resolute than ever to transfer its cash westward, into real estate and other legitimate business. California, with its lax law enforcement and legal double standard for the wealthy, was the most heavily invaded. It had the perfect climate, literally and figuratively, to expand their enterprise. All that the hoods needed was a front. Enter the Supermob, a cabal that had its own sights fixed on the Golden State.

For numerous reasons, Southern California was the ideal place for transplantation of the mob-Supermob alliance. Los Angeles, in particular, was known as a city receptive to both hoodlums and Jews. And, like Chicago, Los Angeles seemed to encourage corruption on a massive scale.

Founded in 1781, Los Angeles was incorporated as an American city on April 4, 1850. A census taken that year showed a population of 8,624, among them only eight Jews. However, one of those eight, M. L. Goodman, was elected to L.A.'s very first city council in 1850, and another, Arnold Jacobi, was elected in 1853—only eight Jews, yet two served on the city council. Isaias Hellman, who had arrived in 1859, went from a poor immigrant to clothing store owner to banker. In 1871, he partnered with former governor John Downey to found the Farmers and Merchants Bank, Los Angeles' first bank. In 1890, Hellman left Los Angeles to become the president of Wells

Fargo in San Francisco.[2] So influential was this small minority of Jewish businessmen that fully 40 percent of the housing constructed in Los Angeles since the end of World War II was financed and built by Jewish developers and bankers.

By 1908, some seven thousand Jews lived in Los Angeles, a city that mirrored Chicago in every way sociologically, while in no way climatically; it was like Chicago for people who preferred short sleeves to winter parkas. Like Chicago, Los Angeles' power elite was historically anti-Semitic, with Jews similarly excluded from private clubs, law firms, and boards of institutions. This discrimination remained in place far longer than in most American cities, typified by the policies of the Jonathan and California clubs, which didn't admit their first Jewish members until the 1980s. Early-arriving Jews bent on assimilating lived and worked in downtown L.A., like the German Jews in Chicago living east of the Chicago River. As had happened in Lawndale, L.A.'s Jews became less and less kosher, with only one in five attending synagogue.

In the early twentieth century, when the Russian Ashkenazic wave hit the West Coast, it merely ignored the downtown status quo and developed its own shtetl ten miles to the west, a sort of West Coast Lawndale. The area was comprised of towns named Hollywood, Santa Monica, Brentwood, Malibu, and Beverly Hills, with countless Jewish-owned law firms and accountant offices springing up on Wilshire Boulevard and its environs. Historian Kevin Starr has written of the assimilated "Mid-Wilshire Judaism" that oversaw the building of the stunning Wilshire B'nai B'rith Temple at Wilshire and Hobart. "Wilshire Boulevard anchored the emergent Jewish Los Angeles," Starr wrote.[3] Among the Supermob associates who would also gravitate to Wilshire were Korshak, Hart, Ziffren, and Glaser. From then on, these two L.A.'s—downtown and Westside—would have almost nothing to do with each other.

Adding to the allure of the Westside for new Jews was the fantastic success of a new industry created by the first Jews to arrive there. With a determination rarely seen in an oppressed class, the Jews had always created their own economy. In Chicago, they had established their own banks, schools, hospitals, country clubs, legal societies, and indeed their own sophisticated version of organized crime. In Los Angeles, they did much the same, with one profound addition: they seized an unwanted commodity originally called flickers; we now call them motion pictures. The only major studio not founded by Jews was RKO, which was primarily a British venture.

Like Chicago's Supermob, practically all of L.A.'s motion picture sachems had their roots within a hundred-square-mile area in Russia's Pale of Settlement. Their families had all emigrated to the United States within ten years of one another, failed at a first career, then found the flickers, at the time considered an unseemly business by the WASP upper class. Among the titans of the new business were:

• **Louis B. Mayer**—He said that he'd forgotten exactly where and when he'd been born in Russia, but arbitrarily made the Fourth of July his birthday. With Samuel Goldwyn, he later headed Metro-Goldwyn-Mayer.

• **Joe and Nick Schenck**—The brothers were born in Rybinsk, Russia (Joe in 1878, and Nick in 1881), and emigrated to the United States in 1893. Joe founded United Artists (with Mary Pickford, Charles Chaplin, Douglas Fairbanks, and D. W. Griffith) and was CEO of Twentieth Century-Fox, while Nick lorded over Loew's Theaters and MGM. Joe sponsored the creation of Todd-AO recording and Cinemascope.

• **Jack and Harry Cohn**—Sons of Joseph Cohen, a German Jew who ran a tailor's shop in New York's Upper East Side, and Bella Joseph Cohn, a Russian Jewess from the Pale of Settlement on the Polish border. Harry became president of Columbia Pictures.

• **David O. Selznick**—The son of Lewis J. Selznick, a Ukrainian Jew who'd immigrated to Pittsburgh and entered the jewelry business, a partner in the founding of Universal Pictures.

• **Harry, Sam, Albert, and Jack Warner**—Decided to buy a movie projector together and eventually started Warner Brothers. Their father, Benjamin Warner, had left his wife and daughter in Poland and gone to Baltimore as a cobbler until he settled in Youngstown, Ohio, and brought his family over.

Among the motion picture elite, expatriate Chicago Ashkenazim were everywhere:

• **Barney and A. J. Balaban**—The sons of a Russian immigrant grocer, they owned a string of large movie palaces before Barney became the chairman of Paramount Pictures.

• **Adolph Zukor**—Born in a small Hungarian village in the Tokay grape district. Orphaned early in life, he left for America and later founded Paramount Pictures. Zukor remained in Chicago and impressed another fur trader, Morris Kohn, and they became partners, and Zukor married Kohn's niece, Lottie Kaufman. By 1899 they moved the company to New York.

• **Carl Laemmle**—Born in 1867 in Laupheim in southwest Germany, he founded Universal Pictures with Selznick. Laemmle came to America in 1883 after his mother's death and ended up off and on throughout the beginning of his career in Chicago, where he owned the White Front Theater (1906) on Milwaukee Avenue.

• **Irving Thalberg**—Born in a middle-class section of Brooklyn in 1899. His father was a lace importer who had emigrated from a small town near Coblenz, Germany. Laemmle was impressed by Thalberg and offered him a job at Universal, where he quickly rose to the top of the studio's writer pool.

And there were more Chicagoans, such as Leo Spitz (RKO) and Sam Katz (VP of MGM). Chicago-born (or -bred) actors included Wallace Beery, Tom Mix, Gloria Swanson, Jean Harlow, and Paul Muni, many of whom started out at Chicago's Essanay Studios.

Screenwriter Michael Blankfort, who worked for many of the Jewish movie moguls, described their demeanor: "They were accidental Jews who rejected their immigrant background to become super-Americans. They were interested in power and profit. They would hardly ever touch a story with a Jewish character, and if they did, they cast a gentile for the part." Harry Cohn added, "Around this studio, the only Jews we put into pictures play Indians."[4]

The Land of Milk and Honey—and Sun

California was virtually exploding, its population growing from 1.48 million in 1900 to 3.4 million by 1920, and 2 million more by 1930. But no city epitomized the spurt more than Los Angeles. Between 1920 and 1940, L.A. grew from 577,000 citizens to over 1.5 million. In just one four-year period in the 1920s, the self-proclaimed City of Destiny saw real estate transfers that amounted to $2.7 billion; building permits totaled an astounding $500 million between 1923 and 1927.[5]

Within this maelstrom, the Jewish film moguls sought to carve out their own territories. All that the thriving film sachems needed was a paradise in which to live unfettered and raise their children. Many of the most successful chose the Westside tract known as Beverly Hills. Originally the abode of the peaceful Gabrielino tribe, the region's native population was decimated in 1844 when European invaders introduced them to smallpox, wiping out two thirds of the Gabrielinos. Those who survived the epidemic soon succumbed to mistreatment by the European settlers.

The 5.69-square-mile subdivision was opened in January 1907, whereupon Wilbur D. Cook, influenced by landscape designer Frederick Law Olmsted, created a garden city, with wide, curving streets leading to narrow switchbacks that hugged the hills just above. The city's first streets (Rodeo, Canon, Crescent, Carmelita, Elevado, and Lomitas) were constructed, and these winding roads were lined with palm, acacia, eucalyptus, jacaranda, and pepper trees. Developer Burton Green named the new city Beverly Hills on a whim, after noticing a news story on President Taft's recent vacation in Beverly Farms, Massachusetts. Sales of lots were languid until Green built a world-class resort hotel, The Beverly Hills Hotel, in 1912.

Douglas Fairbanks and Mary Pickford led the wave of movie stars to Beverly Hills when they built their mansion, Pickfair (1143 Summit Drive), in 1919. Stylish mansions began to spring up overnight, built by a torrent of new celebrity homeowners, among them Gloria Swanson, Will Rogers (the city's honorary mayor), Charlie Chaplin, Tom Mix, Carl Laemmle, Ronald Colman, King Vidor, John Barrymore, Buster Keaton, Harold Lloyd, Jack Warner, Clara Bow, Marion Davies, Harry Cohn, and Rudolph Valentino. By century's end, there would be 8,269 mostly well-to-do families residing within the city limits, among them Chicago's transplanted Supermob.

The Club

All that was missing was a place for the Jewish elite to schmooze. As in Chicago and elsewhere, the Jews were confronted with the entrenched WASP clubbism, prohibiting them from joining the established local watering holes/golf courses. The ongoing joke was that Groucho Marx was once invited to visit the "restricted" Los Angeles Country Club, and while his children were splashing in the pool, the president of the club quietly informed him that the club was restricted and his young ones would have to leave the pool.

"They're only half-Jewish," Groucho replied. "Let them go in up to their waist."

The club problem was rectified in June of 1920, when "Rabbi to the Stars" Edgar Magnin and a group of German Jews formed the Hillcrest Country Club on a 142-acre plot out in western Los Angeles just south of Beverly Hills on Pico Boulevard. Today the club boasts over six hundred members, who each pay a $40,000 annual membership fee. In addition to the fees and requisite sponsors, new members are said to have to document at least $50,000 given by them to charitable causes. On the occasion of an important new cause being defined, meetings of the membership were held wherein they had to stand up individually and tell the amount of their pledge. Such was the case when they raised $34 million to build Cedars-Sinai Hospital (where a wing is now named after Jake Factor's brother, Max). Regarding Hillcrest's strictures, Groucho remarked, "I wouldn't want to join a club that would have a person like me for a member." That was only for laughs—Groucho became one of the club's stalwarts.

The new Ashkenazic Jews were first admitted when the 1929 Depression decimated the membership, making Hillcrest not merely a club for the assimilated downtown Jews, but a place where all Jews, and even a smattering of non-Jews, could congregate. Hollywood chronicler Neal Gabler noted the importance of this distinction: "Hillcrest forged an alliance between these groups that would strengthen the entire Jewish community, especially when it was confronted by the virulent anti-Semitism of the thirties or when it was needed to raise funds for Jewish causes." The new openness paved the way for light moments (such as Harpo Marx playing a round of golf in a gorilla suit) and serious power brokering. Countless movie deals and business transactions were hatched in the club's dining room or on its putting greens. Gabler called it "the klavern from which all power emanated."[6]

In addition to the moguls and movie stars like the Marx Brothers, Milton Berle, Jack Benny, Danny Kaye, and George Burns, after their arrival in the forties, virtually the entire Supermob were spending their leisure time at Hillcrest.[7] And although Sidney Korshak was seen there, he was less than enthusiastic about its true raison d'être. When Beverly Hills restaurateur Kurt Niklas offended Hillcrest president Arthur Sinton by asking him not to bring his pipe into his eatery, Sinton responded by calling Niklas a Nazi and orchestrated a Hillcrest boycott of his establishment. Niklas's pal Sid Korshak gave his apt assessment of the clubbers: "Fuck 'em! . . . Listen, the guys that started that place, George Jessel and L. B. Mayer and Harry Cohn and the Warner brothers, guys like that—they wanted to be plain old rich Americans. They thought a country club would help them assimilate, be like everybody else. But now we've got a second generation that's spoiled to the core and thinks being a Jew is something special. I say, fuck 'em! You don't need Hillcrest!"[8]

An offshoot of Hillcrest was soon constructed to quench the one major vice that prevailed among the Jews. Although there was the occasional womanizing and even less alcoholism, the real Jewish weakness was gambling. Not allowed in Santa Anita Race Track, they built Hollywood Park in Inglewood. This "Hillcrest with furlong markers," as it was called, was founded in 1938 by Jack Warner and six hundred shareholders that included Sam Goldwyn, Darryl Zanuck, Walt Disney, and stars such as Al Jolson, Bing Crosby, George Jessel, and Wallace Beery. For forty years, the director of the park was Mervyn LeRoy. Here again, the Supermob, especially Sid Korshak, would come to wield power conferred on him by the alliance with the underworld-controlled unions.

Neal Gabler aptly summed up the Jewish milieu in Los Angeles when he wrote, "Their own lives became a kind of art. They lived in large, palatial homes, became members of the country club Hillcrest, subscribed to a cultural life, centered around the Hollywood Bowl, that simulated the cultural life of eastern aristocracy. They organized a system of estates, a rigid hierarchy."[9]

Not only had Southern California proven hospitable to Jews, but it was also no less amenable to gangsters, who seemed virtually exempt from prosecution, just as in Chicago. In Los Angeles, Ben Siegel's successor as the mob's local wire-service boss, Mickey Cohen, was close friends with municipal officers at all levels. Artie Samish, a Cohen childhood friend and California lobbyist, who was called more powerful than the governor by Governor Earl Warren,[10] remained a powerful ally of Cohen's. As Cohen explained in his autobiography, "See, if I had any problems with legislators in Sacramento on things like slot machines on premises, he nipped it in the bud. I was his right hand, and he was my godfather, my senior statesman."[11] Cohen's friendly influence did not stop at the state capital—it extended into every important agency, including the police force and the mayor's office. "At one point in the 1940s and 1950s, I had the police commission in Los Angles going for me," Cohen recalled. "A lot of the commissioners didn't have any choice. Either they would go along with the program, or they would be pushed out of sight . . . It was all the way up to the box at certain police stations . . . When I was in the mayor's corner, see, a certain amount was put into his campaign each time through my lawyers, Sam Rummel and Vernon Ferguson." Cohen had the private numbers of the mayor's home and office to boot.[12] He also knew Richard Nixon, who, before running for Congress, demanded that Cohen come up with a $75,000 "contribution" to assure Nixon's leniency toward the local bookies. Cohen held a dinner with all the local hoods and came up with the money.[13]

Mickey Cohen (r.) with his enforcer, Johnny Stompanato
(author collection)

The mobsters bonded not only with the local pols, but also with the moguls and their stars. It was yet another symbiotic relationship: the mob wanted the executives' money and broads, and the Hollywood elite wanted the swagger they thought would rub off by association with hoods, in addition to the muscle they could bring to bear on the nascent labor movement. Much has been written about Frank Sinatra and Sam Giancana, George Raft and Bugsy Siegel (and later Sid Korshak), and Johnny Rosselli and moguls like Harry Cohn, who proudly wore the ruby pinkie ring given him by Rosselli, and proudly kept a framed picture of his idol, Benito Mussolini, on his desk. But there was more: Joe Schenk's earliest investors included New York underworld genius Arnold Rothstein; Longy Zwillman provided Harry Cohn with start-up money to take over Columbia; and Louie Mayer's "closest friend" was said to be hood Frank Orsatti.

One employed the other, and in return mobsters were favorably portrayed on-screen. The gangster fraternization went beyond the moguls to the actors themselves. Sam and Chuck Giancana alleged that the mob sponsored numerous stars, including the Marx Brothers, George Raft, Marilyn Monroe, Jimmy Durante, Marie McDonald, Clark Gable, Gary Cooper, Jean Harlow, Cary Grant, and Wendy Barrie. Jimmy Fratianno and Mickey Cohen both claimed that they knew half the movie people on a first-name basis. Robert Mitchum and Sammy Davis Jr. acted as character witnesses for Cohen during his numerous trials. The hoods bedded an endless parade of young actresses, such as Jean Harlow, who enjoyed the affections of Longy Zwillman, and Lana Turner, who lived with Cohen's boy Johnny Stompanato.

The camaraderie between the moguls and the hoods caught the eye of noir writer Raymond Chandler, who, after seeing a herd of moguls returning from lunch, wrote, "They looked so exactly like a bunch of topflight Chicago gangsters moving in to read the death sentence on the beaten competitor. It brought home to me in a flash the strange psychological and spiritual kinship between the operations of big money business and the rackets. Same faces, same expressions, same manners. Same way of dressing and same exaggerated leisure of movement."[14]

When hedonistic studio chiefs or their stars risked potential vice or gambling scandals, they were happy to call on their new pals like Rosselli to make the problems go away. As Rosselli's biographers observed, "The sudden and enormous success of movies spawned an orgy of vice that threatened to shatter the industry. Drug use was widespread, including cocaine, heroin and illegal alcohol. Sexual favors were demanded by casting directors and became a sort of alternative currency."[15] When actresses such as Joan Crawford were blackmailed with porno reels shot in their youth, Rosselli and friends put the hammer to the extortionists. When the celebs or their employers got juiced up at Santa Anita or at Jack Dragna's offshore gambling ship *The Rex*, the hoods often took care of their markers.

At least that was on the surface. Behind the scenes, a subtler, criminal incursion was beginning, when into this dynamic mix of prospering Jews and mobster chic was added the post–World War II Supermob arrivals. Indeed, the Jewish population of Los Angeles exploded following the war, doubling by 1948, and doubling again by 1960. Jewish newcomers were so predominant that by 1950 only 8 percent of adult Jews in L.A. had been born here. But without doubt, the most important of the new arrivals hailed from Chicago, and they had names like Korshak, Ziffren, Hart, Factor, Stein, Wasserman, Evans, Pritzker, Annenberg . . . and a non-Jew named Reagan. These men represented a new kind of L.A. mogul, one that had ready access to the clout and lucre of the Chicago underworld. In no time, the new arrivals seized not only the entertainment juggernaut, but also the political clout that accompanied real estate investment on a massive scale.

The Taking of California, 1-2-3

> *The Chicago group took over. We used to sit around and wonder how they all got here.*
> —CONNIE CARLSON, ORGANIZED CRIME INVESTIGATOR IN THE
> CALIFORNIA ATTORNEY GENERAL'S OFFICE IN THE FIFTIES AND
> SIXTIES[16]

While the land grab in the Western world is as old as Columbus, its place in California history provides a study of its sophisticated evolution. After the destruction of the native population, questionable legal precedents separating the Mexican population from their property established a sympathetic relationship early on between the territorial courts and the newly arrived white immigrants. Later, rampant land-title abuses, fraudulent mining claims, and water-rights disputes schooled an investing elite whose financial interests would parade under the guise of public welfare concerns aided and abetted by a compliant court system. The history of California is inseparable from its land or what lay beneath.

In the twentieth century, California land grabs were exemplified by the actions of the privately owned Los Angeles Water Company. Under the leadership of William Mulholland and former L.A. mayor Fred Eaton, the company bought large tracts of land from farmers in Owens Valley, 230 miles north of Los Angeles.* The sellers had been told that the purchases were needed to advance a study on the best ways to irrigate the valley, when the truth was just the opposite: the actual intent of the land grab was to build an aqueduct with which to drain the local Owens River down to the exploding L.A. metropolis. When the spigots were opened in 1913, the Owens Valley farmland quickly turned into a dust bowl, as the water supply evaporated. In addition to the human toll, native wildlife and vegetation were devastated. But the water supply allowed L.A. to modernize, and the San Fernando Valley to exist at all.

"The Rape of Owens Valley," which inspired the fictionalized 1974 film *Chinatown*, was yet to experience its most tragic consequence. On March 28, 1928, one of the many dams linked to the aqueduct, the St. Francis, collapsed, sending a forty-foot wall of water into the Santa Clara Valley, claiming over four hundred lives. The subsequent investigation determined that an engineering flaw and "an error in regard to fundamental policy related to public safety" was the cause of the dam's failure. Mulholland was so distraught that he took a pair of pliers and pulled out all his teeth, then withdrew from the public until his death in 1935.[17]

Three decades after Owens Valley was denuded, it became the Supermob's turn to relieve unknowing Californians of their land. The decade from 1943 to 1953 was known as the Suede Shoe era, a time when FHA home-improvement-loan scandals swept the country, and returning GIs, anxious to purchase or improve their homes, were victimized by con artists who funneled mob money into collateral loans with the FHA. The mob too was investing much money in commercial real estate, especially hotels. With seemingly respectable attorneys and accountants as fronts, they channeled monies gained from gambling, vice, narcotics, extortion, etc., into legit properties that earned legit profit. The returning "clean" profits inspired the term *comeback money*. The gang that set the standard for this money laundering hailed from Chicago, and although much has been written about their self-admitted conquest, Las Vegas, few seem to want to discuss their first major target: the sunny expanses of Southern California.

What made California such an easy target for the mob-Supermob alliance was a classic example of good intentions gone awry. Lester Velie, one of the

---

*The valley was named after Richard Owens, a member of a U.S. platoon that wiped out the local native population.

great investigative reporters of the century, wrote, "The late Senator Hiram Johnson, seeking to bar political bosses and machines forever, had designed California's open primary. Aspirants could run in Democratic or Republican primaries—or both—without party labels. Boss control of primaries withered, and then died altogether as reform laws barred parties from endorsing primary candidates. But something that Reformer Johnson didn't bargain for took the boss's place: money power."[18] Art White, a tireless political reporter with the *Los Angeles Mirror*, wrote about how this arrangement played into the hands of outside corrupters in the post–World War II period in California:

> California was to become a state full of strangers, political waifs and mavericks who registered in their party of preference only to find that they had come to a place where political ideology was of no importance. Republicans ran as Democrats and Democrats ran as Republicans. With disconcerting regularity, Republicans, having won both party nominations, were elected in the primaries.
>
> Since party designations had no meaning to the electorate, elections were won by the candidate with the most money, the greatest number of billboards, direct mail pieces, and the most radio time.
>
> Any individual who could devise a system to furnish these campaign necessities on a sustained basis was on his way to becoming a political boss, California style. The boss . . . could have a say, perhaps the final word, in the appointment of judges from the municipal courts to the state supreme court. Other appointive jobs included inheritance tax appraisers, deputy attorneys general, state department heads and commissioners of departments. With a handful of such appointments in his pocket, the boss could protect his economic interests.[19]

In short, California was, by design, the perfect place to export Chicago-style patronage and political corruption. Fletcher Bowron, L.A.'s mayor throughout the war years, was a Republican reform politician often at odds with diehard business coalitions and organized crime cartels. Among his other powerhouse enemies, Bowron was at war with *Los Angeles Times* publisher Norman Chandler, who controlled the do-nothing police commission. For a time, Bowron and Chandler held an uneasy truce—Bowron promising not to reveal what his intel unit learned of Chandler's marital infidelities, and Chandler agreeing not to publish stories of police transgressions. But the truce broke when Chandler, at odds with Bowron's desire to obtain federally funded housing projects, began financing opposing candidates.[20]

Mayor Bowron described the sociopolitical climate in 1940s California thus: "Los Angeles potentially is the most lush field for the activities of those connected with organized crime; with particular reference to commercialized gambling and vice, it is probably more true than for any city in America. We have considerable wealth here. We have a large population. We have free spenders here. We have people that like that sort of thing. It means constant and eternal vigilance to keep the city clean. We can't keep it entirely clean."[21]

Adding to the city's woes was an understaffed police department that, according to the Association of National Chiefs of Police, was two thousand police short of the six thousand it needed to monitor the 453-square-mile sprawl.[22] Incorporated towns, like Beverly Hills, thus sprung up with their own police departments that redefined the term *lax*.

When Bowron's political enemies attempted a recall in 1948, there were rumors of outside instigation. Bowron later testified, "Many of those behind [organized crime] were connected directly or indirectly with the recall movement. I don't merely mean that they had to eliminate me, but they have to eliminate those people that I try to represent, those who want laws enforced and want to see a clean city."[23] Soon, rumors were flying that a mysterious group of non-Californians called The Big Five, hoping to open up the state to underworld control, were financing the recall. One associate of that group, a bookie and co-owner of the offshore gambling ship *The Rex*, James Utley, sent a courier named Polly Gould to Bowron in an effort to cut a deal: Utley said he couldn't pull out of the recall because the other participants were "bigger shots" than he, but he would quietly work for Bowron at the same time in exchange for a promise from Bowron not to raid his nightclub, The Tropics. Bowron replied, "I don't make any deals."[24]

Soon thereafter, based on a tip, the Los Angeles Police Department (LAPD) began looking into the people behind the Hayward Hotel at 20 E. Sixth Street, the headquarters of the anti-Bowron movement. At the time, LAPD chief William H. Parker ran the most sophisticated police intelligence division in the country. Writer Frank Donner rightfully called him "probably the most respected public figure in Southern California and, next to J. Edgar Hoover, the most celebrated law-enforcement official in the country."[25] Parker's investigation opened a Pandora's box of immense proportions, but one that to this day has been little known outside SoCal environs. And even there, the facts are so obfuscated that only the most determined investigators have grasped the full implications.

Chief Parker first entrusted LAPD Intelligence commander James Hamilton, and his chief investigator, Walter J. Devereux, with the Hayward Hotel inquiry. Hamilton worked closely with FBI agent, and later investigator for the DA's office, Julian Blodgett. When the evidence trail showed its labyrinthine complexity, involving countless shell and holding companies (all recorded in the L.A. county clerk's records warehouse), Hamilton shared the immense workload with top-notch *Pacific News* reporter and CBS News producer Robert Goe, who amassed hundreds of hours trolling through real estate and corporate filings, both in L.A. and Chicago. "Robert was a workaholic and was meticulous," his widow, Wanda, recently recalled. "Whatever he did at any time would consume him. He was obsessed with the mayor's office. It kept him looking over his shoulder until the day he died—he was very aware of the truth of California politics."[26]

Goe in turn passed his findings over to *Mirror* and *Times* reporters Art White and Jack Tobin. Ridgeley Cummings also conducted corroborative research in the journal the *Government Employee.*[27]

According to the FBI, the Goe-White research was funded "by certain well-to-do Democrats who became concerned over the emergence in California of forces within the Party who were foreign to the California political scene and were suspected of injecting machine politics of such a nature as to pose a threat to the nominal Party hierarchy here." Both the FBI and the U.S. Congress investigated some aspects of this takeover,[28] but the investigations were allowed to whither when neither the White House nor the attorney general showed any interest in pursuing the story.

The daunting private investigation in California would take even more years than the team was able to devote to it—it might never be fully explicated—but their findings painted a clear and consistent picture of a territory engulfed by Chicago money, much of it tainted. What was most disturbing was the degree to which high public officials, some of whom later became icons, appeared to facilitate, and profit from, these investments. Not surprisingly, the key players' trails all seemed to lead back to the Seneca and Sidney Korshak.

Author and former investigative reporter for the *Los Angeles Times* William Knoedelseder summarized the style of California crime that never seemed to make the newspapers: "In Los Angeles, organized crime has always operated as a more subtle, almost invisible force, employing more lawyers, bankers, and investment brokers than leg breakers and button men." This climate bears much resemblance to corrupt Chicago, so much so, Knoedelseder writes, that "organized crime is often indistinguishable from legitimate business in Los Angeles."[29]

The Hayward Hotel Nexus

The first clue as to the scope and tainted pedigree of the massive Chicago investments in SoCal was the name listed as a co-owner of the Hayward, none other than Chicago Jake Arvey's boy Paul Ziffren. By this time, Ziffren was spending most of his year in California, soon to be a full-time resident. At the same time, Paul's younger brother Lester attended school at UCLA, where he romanced Jake Arvey's daughter, Helen Sue, also a student there.[30] The two were later married, and Lester established his own legal reputation in L.A., albeit much less controversial than Paul's.

A congressional informant noted that Paul Ziffren even added Arvey's name to his West Coast shingle. However, "Arvey made a special trip to Los Angeles 'to have his name taken off,' he having heard how 'hot' Ziffren was at the time."[31] Many astute Californians saw Ziffren as an emissary of Arvey's, dispatched westward to organize the California Democratic Party along Illinois "machine politics" principles. However, even these observers failed to grasp the full scope of Ziffren's business in their state.

"Ziffren made a big thing of his connection with Arvey when he first came out here," said an old-time California pol. "He just mushroomed."[32] Attorney David Leanse, who worked with both Korshak and Ziffren after their moves to the West Coast, said, "Arvey's protégé in Chicago was Paul Ziffren. He didn't have the contacts with labor that Korshak had, but Ziffren represented savings and loans and lenders, and that put him in touch with the entertainment business a lot."[33] But even that description misses perhaps the most important aspect of Ziffren's impact: his partnership in the reallocation of tainted Chicago money in his new home state. What Leanse and the others failed to see was, however, seen by those investigating the Hayward Hotel.

Connie Carlson, the retired organized crime specialist for the California attorney general's office, closely monitored the world of Ziffren and his

The Hayward Hotel today
(author photo)

other Chicago transplant pals. She recently spoke of Ziffren's appearance on the California scene: "When I first heard about him, it was negatively. When Ziffren came here in the forties, it was like he was dropped out of the sky, and he became one of the top Democratic advisers to the Truman administration. Ziffren usurped all of the top Democrats overnight, and somebody in the White House went along with it. First Chicago exported the mob here, then the machine. The takeover was so quiet that no one ever knew it happened. Paul Ziffren became a social leader, sharing the Chandlers' [owners of the *Los Angeles Times*] box at the Hollywood Bowl. He put every bit of his past behind him, whatever it was, good or bad."[34]

Elevating the Hayward-Ziffren link beyond the mere suspicious were the unassuming names listed with Ziffren's among the shareholders of the hotel: Mathilda B. Evans and Esther Greenberg. In short order it was determined that Mathilda was merely lending her name in the place of her notorious husband, a genuine Capone Syndicate heavyweight and partner with Murray Humphreys, Fred Evans.[35] Fred had learned that the hotel's liquor-license application would require his fingerprints, a vetting he tried to avoid.

Evans, another Jewish brainiac, moved to Chicago as a child from St. Louis, turning into a financial hood with an impressive variety of income sources. He graduated from the University of Chicago as an accounting major and also studied architecture and engineering. He would soon earn the distinction of being Chicago's only college-educated Syndicate functionary. After the Depression, the distinguished-looking Evans sold jewelry, loan-sharked—loaning money to Syndicate bosses, such as Louis Campagna ($20,000), when they ran into tax difficulties—became a Loop banker, and bought and sold distressed merchandise, which he fenced with Capone Syndicate wunderkind (and an early Public Enemy Number One) Murray Humphreys. Their operation was housed in a Twenty-fourth Ward garage at Halsted and Van Buren streets, a few blocks north of the Maxwell Street Market. After his first wife, Donna Levinson, divorced him in 1924 on cruelty charges, he hooked up with Mathilda.

Evans was convicted of a crime only once—storing illegal alcohol—and was known to favor the criminal use of the trained mind over the trained trigger finger. With Humphreys, Evans took over the mob-controlled laundry rackets, cornering the market on sheets and towels dispensed in Chicago's countless hotels and brothels. In November 1940, he was indicted with Humphreys for embezzling the Bartenders Union out of $350,000 (he skated when Humphreys fixed the jury). In 1959, he was implicated in the 1953 kidnapping-murder of six-year-old Bobby Greenlease—Evans was caught purchasing a money order (paid to the Outfit's Lenny Patrick) with marked bills that had been paid out in the botched Greenlease ransom.[36]

Like Mathilda Evans, Esther Greenberg was performing the same signatory function for her spouse, the notorious Alex Greenberg.[37] When he testified under immunity in Chicago, Greenberg related how he had become enticed into the world of real estate by Manhattan Brewing's former president Arthur C. Lueder, also a former postmaster for the city of Chicago. "Leuder would appraise real estate in bankruptcy proceedings at a low figure," he told a federal grand jury on February 29, 1944. "Several of us would form a pool to buy up these properties, then we took care of him with a share. That was good for one hundred thousand a year for each of us."[38]

Bit players in the Hayward included Joseph Best, also on the Seneca board with Greenberg, and the president of Hayward Hotel; and Sam Levin, believed by Chicago authorities to have purchased seventy-five jukeboxes from Capone hood Joe Peskin, also known as Sugar Joe Peskin.[39] In addition to the Hayward connection, Ziffren and Evans were linked when police found that they were coholders of a liquor license for another hotel owned by the consortium.[40]

Chicago Crime Commission director Virgil Peterson informed both the Kefauver Committee and the LAPD of the implications: "It is quite likely that the Hotel Hayward may be a mob-owned hotel. In any event, it would appear likely that the stock allegedly held by the wife of Fred Evans is probably actually held by Evans himself."[41] In fact, Evans admitted to Congress that he owned 14 percent of the Hayward, brought into the investment by Paul Ziffren's brother-in-law, and Hilton Hotel executive, Joseph Drown. He further testified that he put a 10 percent interest of another hotel, the San Padre in Bakersfield, California, in his children's names. Evans explained that he first met Alex Greenberg during the 1933 Chicago World's Fair, when Greenberg asked him to place Manhattan Brewery ads on popcorn boxes sold at Evans's concession (run with Murray Humphreys). He also informed Congress of three other Chicago properties he co-owned with Greenberg.[42]

The same year as the Hayward purchase, Ziffren divorced his wife, Phyllis, despite, according to the LAPD, Alex Greenberg's intervention to try to save the marriage. Ziffren continued to invest that year, when he became trustee and executor for lawyer (and Greenberg's Seneca partner) Benjamin Cohen. Together, Ziffren and Cohen held stock in the San Diego Hotel and the Morris Hotel in Los Angeles. But the realization of the notorious Evans's partnership with the notorious Greenberg and the supposedly clean Paul Ziffren inspired an investigation of California real estate transactions that would be passed down to two generations of public and private investigators for the next two and a half decades. It turned out that the Hayward investment was just the beginning of a frenzy of tainted California hotel and real estate purchases. What most disturbed investigators was the appearance of assistance coming from Ziffren's closest friend, David Bazelon, by then a high-ranking member of the Truman administration—who just happened to control millions of dollars' worth of recently seized real estate that was in need of new owners.

CHAPTER 5

The Future Is in Real Estate

What we call real estate—the solid ground to build a house on—is the broad foundation on which nearly all of the guilt of the world rests.
—NATHANIEL HAWTHORNE (1804–1864)

BY THE MIDFORTIES, Paul Ziffren was already a California resident, although for the next six years he remained listed in Chicago as working out of Arvey's office at One North LaSalle, and he still had a listing at 134 N. LaSalle. In Los Angeles, Ziffren represented celebrities with tax problems, such as actor Errol Flynn, who the IRS declared owed $333,000 in back taxes and penalties.[1]

Picking up on Ziffren's drive and intellect, a West Coast friend asked him, "Why don't you go into politics?" To which Ziffren responded, "I want to make money first."[2] And Paul Ziffren knew just how he was going to do it: by joining up with his Supermob pals in a glut of property investments with some of Chicago's most notorious Syndicate financiers.

Not long after his friend Paul Ziffren left the Gottlieb firm for California, David Bazelon followed suit, leaving the practice in 1946 for a position as Attorney General Tom Clark's assistant attorney general, promoted a year later to being in charge of the lands division, giving up a $50,000-a-year private practice for the $10,000-a-year post.[3] According to a later congressional probe of Bazelon, the word in Chicago was that the firm was happy to see Bazelon depart "because of their fear that Bazelon's client, [Capone's financial whiz] Arthur Green [*sic*], might get them into serious trouble."[4] At the time of the job change, Bazelon supposedly told one intimate that he was worried about the IRS looking into his work for Alex Greenberg's Canadian Ace Brewing Company, and that he "needed a federal judgeship to get himself cleaned up."[5]

From his lands division vantage point, Bazelon was well aware of recently seized properties, and real estate that was in tax arrears. Perhaps not coincidentally, pals Bazelon and Ziffren went on a property buying-and-selling spree that appeared to be blessed with the Midas touch. But close scrutiny of these investments gives a telling clue as to how the American underworld discreetly, and successfully, laundered its money in the twentieth century, the massive financial shift occurring soon after World War II.

In 1947, Abe Pritzker and Paul Ziffren (whose college tuition was financed by the Pritzker Foundation) partnered with Assistant Attorney General Bazelon to form the Franklin Investment Company in Ohio. With Ziffren as VP of Franklin Investment, the intent was to invest in debt-ridden hotel properties such as the 650-room Neil House and the 1,000-room Deshler-Wallach Hotel in Columbus. During this period, Franklin controlled virtually all of the first-class hotel rooms in Columbus. One participant in the Franklin deal told the Bureau that Pritzker was a silent partner, through Ziffren, and that "his participation came as a surprise to the other parties in interest."[6]

David Bazelon owned 25 percent of Franklin, which Abe Pritzker apparently gave him. At a meeting six years later, Pritzker claimed he gave Bazelon the stock because he "was just feeling good and generous and was grateful to Bazelon for things he had done for his son, Jay Pritzker."[7] The favors also likely included the original tip that the Deshler and Neil hotels were in deep tax troubles with the federal government, information to which both Bazelon and Ziffren would have been privy. Conflicting records had shown that Bazelon paid $6,200 for the stock, but Pritzker denied this. "Bazelon hadn't paid a penny for his stock in the Franklin Hotel Company," Pritzker insisted. "That stock was given to him."[8]

The Deshler-Wallach Hotel (from a postcard)

Franklin's taint went beyond the previously noted Pritzker connections; it more importantly swirled around the fourth partner in the enterprise, a close friend of Pritzker's named Arthur Greene, the man who lent Ziffren $11,500 to purchase his shares of Franklin and caused so much concern about Bazelon at Gottlieb and Schwartz.

Investigative author Ovid Demaris referred to "Abe & Art" as "the most mysterious financiers in Chicago."[9] Another Jewish émigré like his pal Abe Pritzker, Arthur Greene was described by the Chicago Crime Commission as "the financier for Jake Guzik of the Capone organization." The CCC went so far as to refer to Greene as "the brains of all the Chicago rackets." Greene headed up a dozen companies, most notably the Domestic Finance Corporation, a small loan corporation. Well-placed informants told the CCC that Greene's Domestic was instrumental in setting up Charlie Gioe's Reddi-Whip underworld partnerships. Greene was also the investment agent for Charles and Rocco Fischetti, and East Coast bosses Meyer Lansky and Abner "Longy" Zwillman. Interestingly, Greene was close to the Roosevelt White House, via FDR's businessman son James Roosevelt.

According to LAPD information, Greene somehow figured in the California expansion of Jules Stein's MCA, through a relative named Edwin Greene, who was an MCA VP. "Abe and Art" were also on the deed of trust of the Ronan Investment Company property at 5050 Pacific Boulevard in Vernon, California, having loaned hundreds of thousands of dollars to the purchase of Ronan, which had at least seven subsidiaries. Ronan had been formed by William Ronan of Chicago, who had been fired from the Civil Service Commission (a post he attained through the offices of Arvey) in 1942 when it was found that he had whitewashed the investigation of four police captains accused of being on the dole of the Syndicate's gambling bosses.[10] On July 15, 1957, Greene supplied $173,000 to his Ronan Investment Company to purchase the Davis Warehouse, a property that the county tax assessor's records show to have had an actual value of $2 million.

Greene's stock in Franklin was, per underworld custom, placed in his wife Shirley's name, although the Ohio secretary of state's records show Arthur Greene as secretary of the company. Simultaneously, Pritzker, Ziffren, and Greene formed Lakeshore Management Company, one of whose officers named M. Woolen also held stock in the Seneca Hotel with Alex Louis Greenberg.

The Franklin investing group named Julius Epstein as president of Deshler Hotel. Epstein also co-owned the Hollenden Hotel with slot king Nathan Weisenberg in Cleveland; the hotel was the headquarters for the Mayfield Road Gang (one member of the gang was Thomas McGinty, who operated Meyer Lansky's Nacional Casino in Havana). Epstein was also one of Greene's principal real estate agents in Chicago, and by the midfifties, Epstein and Greene controlled $85 million worth of property in Chicago, New York, and California, including dozens of Midwest shopping centers (American Shopping Centers Inc.) valued at over $65 million, and over eight thousand hotel rooms. Pritzker's law partner Stanford Clinton was listed as secretary of Deshler.

When the Franklin Corporation was dissolved on October 25, 1949, then federal judge Bazelon sold his Franklin/Deshler stock back to the tax-exempt Pritzker Foundation for $190,000. An insider to the deal told the FBI that Pritzker remarked, "You know, it's always the way when you give somebody something and when you want it back, they want a big price for it."[11] The FBI concluded that any violations of the law that may have occurred involving the sale back to Pritzker were not within the jurisdiction of the Bureau but, nonetheless, deemed the buyback "suspicious."[12] Ziffren sold his shares simultaneously for a tidy $25,000 profit.

But there was even more to the Deshler setup than the questionable partnership members and the $190,000 stock gift from Pritzker to Assistant Attorney General David Bazelon. Corporate records in Ohio show that the new Deshler Corporation sublet the premises of the hotel to the Hilton Hotel Corporation, of which Paul Ziffren's thirty-nine-year-old brother-in-law, Joseph Drown, was a vice president, it becoming the Deshler-Hilton—and Hilton opened up its own can of underworld worms.

The Supermob's rush to buy hotels as investment properties was officially on.

The Hilton Nexus

To understand why a Ziffren/Bazelon relationship with Hilton Hotels should have raised eyebrows, it is necessary to trace the origins of the Hilton empire. Hilton Hotels Inc. was created in 1946 when Paris Hilton's great-grandfather Conrad Hilton merged with Arnold Kirkeby to form the new venture. At that time, fifty-nine-year-old New Mexico native Conrad Hilton had already established a chain of ten hotels, predominantly located in the Southwest.[13] Hilton was anxious to expand eastward and internationally and thus agreed to a merger with another hotel scion, Arnold Kirkeby.

Arnold S. Kirkeby was born in Chicago in 1900. In 1928, he married Carlotta Maria Cuesta, the daughter of a wealthy Tampa, Florida, cigar maker. In Florida, he dabbled in real estate under the banner of the Chicago-Florida Realty Company, and his career in hostelry began with the formation of the National Cuba Hotel Corporation Inc. in the 1920s, incorporated in Delaware as the National Hotel of Cuba Corporation. In the mid-1930s, National Hotel of Cuba merged with Eastern mob boss and Cuban casino owner Meyer Lansky and opened an office on Flagler Street in Miami—Lansky later admitted his participation with Cuba National in his testimony before the 1951 Kefauver Committee investigating organized crime. Under the Kirkeby umbrella, Lansky, Frank Costello, and New Jersey boss Abner "Longy" Zwillman operated the Nacional, then the largest gambling casino in the world, in Havana. Meyer's brother Jake was the Nacional's floor manager.[14]

When he appeared before the Kefauver Committee in 1951, Jules Endler, a bar owner in Newark, New Jersey, admitted that he acted as a go-between in securing Longy Zwillman's interest in Kirkeby and the Nacional. As he told committee counsel Richard G. Moser, "Kirkeby called me and told me how many bonds I could have . . . and he gave Zwillman half of what I got . . . I invested ninety-two thousand dollars." (Endler also noted other partnerships he had entered into with Zwillman, such as a real estate venture—a former U.S. post office building worth $1.4 million—in Louisville, Kentucky; and Hollywood production deals with luminary partners such as Harry Cohn at Columbia, Fred Allen, Morrie Ryskind, Jack Benny, Sam Wood, Claudette Colbert, and Don Ameche, in which Zwillman held an 8 percent investment stake; and $41,000 invested in New York's Sherry Netherland Hotel, owned by Kirkeby.)[15]

Among the Chicago shareholders in Kirkeby was one Jules Stein, MCA founder.[16] Other Hilton partners of record from Chicago were Blanche Greene and Shirley Greene, Arthur's wife and daughter, respectively. Of course, they were fronting for Arthur, much as Alex Greenberg's wife had fronted for him in the Hayward Hotel deal.[17] Under this thin guise, Greene and Hilton acquired the Sir Francis Drake Hotel in San Francisco in 1944 and the Plaza Hotel on Vine Saint in Hollywood. Jake Arvey's pal Colonel Henry Crown put up $3 million for Hilton to buy New York's Waldorf-Astoria.[18] Crown ultimately owned 150,000 shares, or 8.7 percent of Hilton's stock. The FBI received information that Chicago Outfit boss Tony Accardo and underbosses Gus Alex and "Strongy" Ferarro had obtained large blocks of the Hilton chain. According to an FBI report, "These individuals had apparently penetrated into the Hilton chain through Jake Arvey, Sidney Korshak and Henry Crown in the days when Hilton was starting to acquire numerous hotels."[19]

LAPD Intelligence files revealed that on April 16, 1940, Arnold S. Kirkeby became president of Cuba National, and Ernest Ponterelli of the Capone Syndicate became VP (his brother Michael was said to be a high-ranking member of the Mafia's ruling clique, The Unione Siciliana).

A S S I G N M E N T

WHEREAS, the undersigned, JULES ENDLER, has succeeded to an undivided 8% interest in and to certain assets of GREENTREE PRODUCTIONS, INC., a dissolved California corporation, and by reason thereof is the owner, as trustee, of an undivided interest in and to the motion picture photoplay entitled "GUEST WIFE", and the producer's net proceeds to be derived therefrom, all as more specifically set forth in that certain disbursing agency agreement dated on or about January 2, 1946 executed by and between the Bank of America National Trust & Savings Association in its trust capacity, hereinafter referred to as "Agent", and the former stockholders of Greentree Productions, Inc., a dissolved California corporation; and

WHEREAS, said interest held by JULES ENDLER as trustee (which interest will hereinafter be referred to as the "trust interest") is in addition to an interest held by JULES ENDLER in his individual capacity and not as trustee (which interest will hereinafter be referred to as the "Endler individual interest"); and

WHEREAS, JULES ENDLER holds the trust interest as trustee for ABNER ZWILLMAN;

WHEREAS, said JULES ENDLER is desirous of transferring his trust interest, but not the Endler individual interest, to ABNER ZWILLMAN; and

WHEREAS, ABNER ZWILLMAN is willing to accept and consents to the assignment of the trust interest as aforesaid,

NOW, THEREFORE, the undersigned, JULES ENDLER, does hereby transfer, set over and assign the trust interest hereinabove described to ABNER ZWILLMAN, and does hereby direct that any and all payments which would hereafter be made but for this assignment by any person, firm or corporation whatsoever to JULES ENDLER for and on account of the trust interest, shall be made from and after this date to ABNER ZWILLMAN.

Dated:

June 13th 1950   _Jules Endler_
Jules Endler

Abner Zwillman
Abner Zwillman

RECEIVED the original of this Assignment June 20, 1950.

BANK OF AMERICA NATIONAL TRUST & SAVINGS
ASSOCIATION,

By:

With this 1950 document, Longy Zwillman became one of first hoods to secretly invest in Hollywood (Kefauver Committee investigative files, Library of Congress)

Predictably, Paul Ziffren became the attorney representing Hilton in L.A. and within three years handled approximately $1 million in transactions for the expanding corporation. Joseph Drown, another Chicago native, came to California in 1939 and acquired controlling interest in twenty-nine hundred acres above Sunset Boulevard, then called the Botanical Garden. It would later become known as Bel-Air and the Brentwood Estates. In 1944, the day his daughter was born, Drown partnered with his brother-in-law Ziffren and Conrad Hilton in acquiring the U.S. Grant Hotel in San Francisco, as well as The San Diego Hotel, in partnership with no fewer than eight tenants of 134 N. LaSalle,* including future Supreme Court justice Arthur J. Goldberg and Seneca co-owner Benjamin Cohen. Sid Korshak's L.A. attorney pal Greg Bautzer was also involved. Drown went on to develop vast acreage in the Santa Monica Mountains and was also an owner of El Rancho Casino in Vegas with G. Sanford Adler, a known associate of mob boss Joseph "Doc" Stacher. With Johnny Rosselli, Drown also founded in 1947 the short-lived Beverly Club, a dining room and bar (with secret gambling in the back).

Eventually, Kirkeby Inc. obtained some of the crown jewels of hostelry: The Kenilworth, and Belle Aire, in Miami; Chicago's Drake, Stevens, and Palmer House hotels, and The Blackstone Restaurant; the Warwick, Gotham, Waldorf-Astoria, Roosevelt, Plaza, Astor, Hampshire House, and Sherry Netherland hotels in New York; the Nacional, which was openly run by Lansky in Cuba; in Los Angeles, The Sunset Towers, Beverly Wilshire, Hilton, and Town House on Wilshire Boulevard; and in the nation's capital, The Willard, Mayflower, and D.C. Hilton hotels.[20] Not surprisingly, Hilton was, according to the Korshak brothers, the largest client (by room count) of their Chicago Hotel Association, a membership that rendered them virtually immune from union strikes.[21]

Police files in L.A. and Chicago point to many of the Kirkeby holdings in those cities as meeting spots for the underworld elite: Frank Costello maintained a suite on the thirty-seventh floor of the Waldorf in New York (where he was often seen with Joseph Kennedy); the Blackstone and Drake in Chicago were overrun with Outfit members; and Bugsy Siegel had an apartment in the Sunset Towers, where he was once busted for bookmaking. Don Wolfe, an author who grew up among the Beverly Hills elite, has vivid memories of Arnold Kirkeby's world. "My brother was a close friend of Buzz Kirkeby, Arnold's son," Wolfe recalled in 2005. "I used to go up to the

*The others were Max Krauss, Minnie Krauss, Janet Krauss, Marion Krauss, Harry Fertig, and Samuel Berke.

mansion to swim in their tropical pool, which had a waterfall. Several times I'd see Bugsy and Virginia Hill there with Arnold. I later found out that Kirkeby used a lot of Syndicate money. Within a certain crowd in Beverly Hills it was common knowledge that the Kirkebys were swimming in mob money."[22]

Indeed, that crowd included the FBI, which noted in its Bugsy Siegel file, "The Mafia operates through its New York headquarters, where Frank Costello and Joe Adonis, using Siegel as a front, have put themselves in the hotel business though Siegel and under the trade name of the Kirkeby Hotels."[23]

As an aside, the Kirkeby properties served as convenient places for assignations coordinated by others in the Supermob. LAPD intel files refer to Paul Ziffren delivering call girls to Tahoe gambler Mandel Agron at Kirkeby's Beverly Wilshire; Ziffren's name appeared in the "trick books" of a number of L.A. call girls (Carol Brandi, Paula McNeil, and Marilyn Anderson), according to LAPD files. Under Ziffren's phone number was printed the word "French."[24] Various sources described Ziffren as a womanizer, one saying, "Paul had a lot of girlfriends around town who might sing for you." Another said that he "knew from Bonanno's mistress, a former prostitute who serviced Ziffren often, that the great Democrat led a secret life of diapered sexual infantilism."[25]

There were numerous Kirkeby subsidiaries as well, among them:

• Kirkeby Realty and Grant Realty, both of which employed Paul Ziffren's secretary Edith Cutrow as executive secretary, and which held over $4 million in assets.
• Kirkeby Ranch Corp. This time, Paul Ziffren's brother Leo's secretary, Jean Staley, was on board.
• The CVC Company, which, with a loan from Kirkeby, financed development of three hundred lots in Beverly Hills. Leo Ziffren handled the loan, which was negotiated by City National Bank of Beverly Hills, of which Arnold Kirkeby was a director, Sid Korshak a shareholder. City National's founder was none other than Chicago's Al Hart, who had parlayed his distillery profits into his new banking endeavor.

In July 1953, Kirkeby-National changed its name to Beverly Wilshire Hotel Corp., and by 1954 Kirkeby's Hilton Inc. would comprise twenty-eight hotels when it merged with Statler Hotels on October 1 of that year. By 1979 that number would explode to 185 domestic and 75 international facilities, and at century's end Hilton had a value of $6.2 billion. Arnold Kirkeby died on March 1, 1962, when the American Airlines flight he was on crashed into

Jamaica Bay, New York.* His body was never recovered, and all ninety-five passengers perished, making the crash the greatest civilian U.S. air tragedy to that point.[†,26]

Conrad Hilton died of pneumonia in 1979 at age ninety-one.

Ziffren's investments in the Hayward, Deshler, Kirkeby-Hilton, and Franklin were just the beginning. A year before the attack on Pearl Harbor, a new corporation had appeared on the Los Angeles scene, a real estate holding company called Store Properties Inc., headquartered at 714 S. Hill Street in Los Angeles. Store's owner of record was one Sam Genis, a known associate of mob bosses Longy Zwillman, Doc Stacher, Frank Costello, Joey Adonis, and Meyer Lansky. Genis's criminal record showed that he had been arrested for bad checks in Florida, embezzlement in New York, and mail fraud and securities law violations in Georgia. When he died in a 1958 auto accident in L.A., his probate (which was handled by Paul Ziffren and Al Hart) revealed that he had started Store with a $93,000 loan from none other than Paul Ziffren. In 1947, Genis transferred half the stock in Store, worth $720,000, to Ziffren.

By 1957, Store Properties had bought thousands of acres of land in over three hundred transactions worth $20 million in Los Angeles alone. When Store's other California purchases are factored in (in San Bernardino, Fresno, Oakland, and San Francisco), the estimate approaches $100 million. Then there were the additional investments in such states as Arizona, Utah, Colorado, Oklahoma, Florida, Illinois, and New York. One of the properties in the Store umbrella, a plush motel in Phoenix, Arizona, was co-owned by Jake Arvey's chief Chicago protégé, Arthur X. Elrod.[27]

But just as in the Hayward and Deshler deals, Ziffren's Store Properties venture was tied to the notorious Alex Greenberg, who, in so many words, informed the Kefauver Committee in 1951 that he was a "silent owner" of Store Properties. This was backed up by Kefauver Exhibit #70, which included Greenberg's tax returns and detailed his income from Store Properties. Those same records list among his income for 1947 $4,338.34 from his

---

*Kirkeby had been living in Bel-Air, California, in an estate built in 1938 and valued at $27 million, the most valuable single-family home in the world. It featured a silver vault, two 250-foot tunnels leading to the gardens, a 150-foot waterfall, gold-plated doorknobs, and a library with hidden bookshelves. From 1962 to 1971, the Kirkeby Estate on Bel-Air Road was the setting for the *Beverly Hillbillies* TV show. (*Los Angeles Times*, 2-9-86)
†Also perishing was Linda McCartney's mother, Mrs. Lee Eastman.

"Partnership with Paul Ziffren."[28] Greenberg admitted that he was the actual owner of a square-block building at 333 E Street in San Bernardino, valued at $900,000. The trouble was, Greenberg's name appeared nowhere on the deed of trust involved. The "official" owner was Genis's and Ziffren's Store Properties. (See appendix C.)

Store also partnered with FDR's son James Roosevelt and San Francisco real estate mogul James Swig, who later became Pat Brown's statewide finance chairman in his successful California gubernatorial campaign.[29]

By 1948, Ziffren had placed his Store stock in his new wife Muriel's name (he had been introduced to her by Bazelon);[30] likewise, Genis transferred his shares to his wife, Sayde.

Central to the Ziffren issue are the legal ramifications of forming a business with the full knowledge that one's partner's contribution was obtained through criminal activities or was being used to launder the lucre of organized crime. Andrew Furfaro, the former organized crime and corporate-corruption chief for the Western Division of the IRS, has no doubt about the culpability of such a "clean" entrepreneur. "If you have knowledge that the money was stolen or contraband, you're still liable," Furfaro said emphatically in 2004. "It's called aiding and abetting."[31]

It is impossible to know whether any or all of the above investments were the result of insider information from Bazelon's land office about the fiscal or proprietary health of the properties involved. But there is little doubt that the investments that followed bore the taint not only of underworld partnerships, but also of inside information that allowed the purchasers to profit off the misery of 120,000 innocents.

The December 7, 1941, attack on Pearl Harbor by the Japanese provided an inadvertent boost for the fortunes of the Supermob. The payoff was not immediate, taking three and a half years to transpire, but it was profound—a direct result of profiteering from the misery of thousands of wrongfully detained Americans.

The Rape of the Nisei

Imagine the tragic effect had the United States confined every American-born and foreign-born Muslim to a three-and-a-half-year imprisonment after the September 11, 2001, terrorist attacks on the country. Add to that horror the impact on these innocents had all their property, which had been earned over two generations, been seized and auctioned off for pennies on the dollar, much of it going to buyers with inside information about the choicest parcels. In 1942, this is exactly what happened to the nisei, or Japanese Americans, and the Supermob was the insider. Ironically, the process by which this largely Jewish cadre acquired Japanese property bore a resemblance to the Aryanization of Jewish property in Nazi Germany.

The first Japanese arrived in the United States in 1869, establishing the Wakamatsu Colony in Gold Hills, California. Although initially welcomed as a form of cheaper labor than even the irascible Chinese, they soon became pariahs when, through backbreaking hard work, they saved enough to purchase land, mostly in the form of farms, small hotels, and other commercial real estate; and what they couldn't buy, they leased for farming. Soon, the Japanese became a major economic force in the state: in 1940, the 535,000 acres of nisei farms, situated on the state's most fertile property, were worth $72 million plus $6 million in equipment; California's ninety-four thousand Japanese raised 41 percent of the state's staple "truck" crops, such as celery, carrots, onions, lettuce, and tomatoes.[32] Other commercial real estate in downtown areas was valued in the millions, but would be worth much more in the near future as the city populations were unknowingly on the verge of a postwar explosion. The success of the Japanese in California brought out so much latent racism and xenophobia among the whites that in 1913 California passed the Alien Land Law, which prevented noncitizens from buying any more land.

The impressive ascendancy of the nisei came to a screeching halt almost immediately after the Pearl Harbor attack; within two hours, police were arresting everyone who looked Japanese in the L.A. district known as Little Tokyo.[33] The next day, the U.S. Treasury froze Japanese bank accounts and seized all Japanese-owned banks and businesses; two days after the attack, Japanese-language schools were closed. But the U.S. citizenry called for much more. Fueled by reports of "magic cables," intercepts of communications among Japanese diplomats that allegedly discussed the recruitment of nisei spies, the American paranoia, especially in California, reached a fever pitch.

Columnist Westbrook Pegler led the outcry in the national press, writing, "The Japanese in California should be under armed guard to the last man and woman right now—and to hell with habeas corpus."[34] Syndicated Hearst sportswriter Henry McLemore wrote of the Japanese Americans, "Herd 'em up, pack 'em off and give them the inside room in the badlands. Let 'em be pinched, hurt, hungry and dead up against it . . . Personally, I hate the Japanese. And that goes for all of them."[35]

California's attorney general (and future governor and Supreme Court chief justice), Earl Warren, voiced the hysteria for Californian politicians in congressional testimony:

There is more potential danger among the group of Japanese who are born in this country than from the alien Japanese who were born in Japan. We believe that when we are dealing with the Caucasian race, we have methods that will test the loyalty of them, and we believe that we can, in dealing with the Germans and the Italians, arrive at some fairly sound conclusions because of our knowledge of the way they live in the community and have lived for many years. But when we deal with the Japanese, we are in an entirely different field and we cannot form any opinion that we believe to be sound . . . I believe, sir, that in time of war every citizen must give up some of his normal rights.[36]

Thus, ten weeks after the outbreak of war, on February 19, 1942, President Roosevelt signed Executive Order 9066, which gave to the secretary of war the power to exclude any persons from designated areas in order to secure national defense objectives against sabotage and espionage. More specifically, the order mandated the detaining of all persons believed to be a possible danger, especially the West Coast nisei. Over the objections of FBI director J. Edgar Hoover, whose Bureau was tasked with arresting religious and community leaders, all 120,000 West Coast Japanese were placed in temporary facilities and given less than two weeks to make arrangements for the sale of their property before being transported to concentration camps in the desert Southwest, where they would spend the next three and a half years. The incarcerations initiated a lifelong, and historically significant, behind-the-scenes feud between Hoover and Warren.* Interestingly, during his tenure as chief justice of the Supreme

---

*Hoover launched the first salvo in 1952. Presidential candidate Dwight Eisenhower had made a deal with then governor Warren that if California's "favorite son" presidential candidate delivered the California delegation to Eisenhower at the Republican convention, *President* Eisenhower would nominate Warren to the Supreme Court at the next vacancy. Warren did as asked, and when Eisenhower nominated him in late 1953, Hoover gave a scathing background report to the Senate Judiciary Committee, which had to approve the nomination (the report dealt with a Warren love affair with a staffer). Committee chairman William Langer (R-North Dakota) was already bent on holding up the nomination as political blackmail against Eisenhower. (Langer wanted more say in Dakota patronage appointments. Langer had also received citizen complaints, one charging that Warren had permitted "organized crime to establish itself in California.") After three months of stalling by Langer, Warren was confirmed as chief justice on March 1, 1954. Nine years later, when Warren chaired the investigation into JFK's 1963 assassination, Hoover again had to vet the commissioners. He found what he felt were questionable right-wing associations of three of the Warren Commission staff nominees, but

Court (1953–69), one of Warren's favored law clerks was Ken Ziffren, son of Paul.[37]

> *Like a man without a nation*
> *In a camp of concentration*
> *With a stamp of degradation and shame*
> *To a place they call it Manzanar by name*
> —VAN DYKE PARKS, "MANZANAR"[38]

Initially, the Japanese were given a mere forty-eight hours to leave their homes for transport to temporary holding stations. Said one victim, "The evacuation was unquestionably harsh and pitifully unjust. To command bewildered women with children suffering in mental agonies through internment of their husbands by the FBI to pack and evacuate in forty-eight hours was inhumanly harsh and unjust . . . Children were crying, boys and girls dashing in and out to help their mothers on whose shoulders the world came crashing."[39] (The roundup was so thorough that for the next four years the movie moguls had to settle for Caucasian actors made up to look oriental for the spate of war movies that followed. Peter Lorre's portrayal of "Mr. Moto" and Paul Muni as an Asian peasant were most memorable.)

After a few days of that humiliation, the "detainees" were ordered onto transport buses with no room for their few salvaged belongings. One federal official reported on what was left behind at the Japanese community on Terminal Island in Los Angeles harbor: "One of our workers who was on the island the day after the evacuation said that fishing nets, fishing trucks, rubber boots, household goods, and all kinds of equipment, enough to fill at least eight trucks, had been abandoned."[40]

The government then delivered the nisei to "relocation centers" in desolate interior regions of the West where they were housed in hastily built, barbed-wire-ringed desert barracks, the largest in California (Tule Lake,

---

Footnote cont'd

Warren had already announced their appointment publicly—too late for Hoover to have them pulled. Warren fired the last barb when he rejected the staff report on the FBI's performance and had one of the staff that Hoover had wished to reject (Norman Redlich) write a second version. Based on a 4–3 vote, this scathing report was incorporated into the *Warren Report* and noted that, had the Bureau been "an alert agency," Lee Harvey Oswald would have been put on a list of potential threats to the president. (Int. of FBI agent Jim Hosty, 7-22-03, who was given the details by Hoover; Hosty's book, *Assignment Oswald*, 136–38; *Warren Report*, U.S. Government Printing Office version, 443; Cray, *Chief Justice; Time* and *Newsweek*, 3-1-54)

19,000) and Arizona (Poston, 17,814). Ironically, some of the Japanese were housed in the same Owens Valley (the Manzanar Camp) that had had its water stolen four decades earlier by Mulholland et al.—forcing the military to find ways to bring water back to the valley to sustain the prisoners.*

Surrounded by armed guards in barracks that measured 20 by 120 feet, the internees were divided into four or six rooms, each from 20 by 16 to 20 by 25 feet, with two families of six each often sharing but one room. A visiting reporter from the *San Francisco Chronicle* described the quarters at Tule Lake: "Room size—about 15 by 25 . . . Condition—dirty." The rooms had no running water, and some center's evacuees lived without electric light, adequate toilets, or laundry facilities. Mess halls planned for about three hundred people had to handle six hundred or nine hundred for short periods.

And then there was the weather.

The detainees endured temperatures as low as 35 degrees below zero in winter and 115 above in summer. In July, evacuees doused their cots with cool water in an effort make sleep possible. In the Arizona camps, dust storms regularly sent torrents of sand through wide cracks in the poorly constructed barracks. Nisei Monica Sone described a dust storm on her first day at Minidoka Camp: "We felt as if we were standing in a gigantic sand-mixing machine as the sixty-mile gale lifted the loose earth up into the sky, obliterating everything. Sand filled our mouths and nostrils and stung our faces and hands like a thousand darting needles. [Inside] the dust poured through the cracks like smoke." One visiting journalist to the Manzanar barracks wrote that "on dusty days, one might just as well be outside as inside." Of course, the outside held the additional thrill of rattlesnakes and other poisonous desert wildlife.[41]

As if the nisei collective memory needed more trauma, there was one last insult to weather: when they emerged from their concentration camps over forty months later, all their possessions were gone.

The Sell-Offs

The issue of the nisei's abandoned property was dealt with in the same harsh manner as the prisoners themselves. Suddenly without employment, they could not afford mortgage payments or indefinite storage for their possessions. Given mere days to sell their homes, businesses, and all the belong-

---

*The ten "relocation centers" were built by the future king of the Las Vegas hotel builders, Del Webb.

ings they could not carry, their plight defined a "buyer's market." Victims told Congress's Tolan Committee of their losses:

- The $125 sale of a new pickup truck with $125 worth of new tires alone.[42]
- A federal official collected solid stories of victims "selling three- and four-hundred-dollar pianos for five and ten dollars, of selling new refrigerators and new stoves for small amounts."[43]
- One Japanese American sold his strawberry-farming operation for $2,000; the purchaser resold it for more than $10,000.[44]
- Nisei owners of an ice cream parlor had a $10,000 inventory plus $8,000 in equipment, but sold it all for $1,000.[45]

One victim lamented, "It is difficult to describe the feeling of despair and humiliation experienced by all of us as we watched the Caucasians coming to look over our possessions and offering such nominal amounts knowing we had no recourse but to accept whatever they were offering."[46] And not all property losses were monetary. The army forced victims to sell, give away, or euthanize family pets.[47]

But for speculators with deep pockets, the real bargains were in houses, undeveloped nisei land, and commercial property such as stores, warehouses, and hotels. In February 1942, one American official directing internments noted that victims could "either turn over their business to their creditors at great loss or abandon it entirely." This official referred to "commercial buzzards" who took "great advantage of this hardship, making offers way below even inventory cost, and very much below real value."[48] Initially, the Federal Reserve Bank had authority to act as a go-between, matching prospective buyers with Japanese American sellers. If sellers wished, the Federal Reserve Bank would act as their agent and liquidate property on their behalf. In the rush to make a sale, property was unloaded for a fraction of its value.

Los Angeles mayor Fletcher Bowron assured a U.S. congressman, "Property within this city formerly occupied or used by the Japanese will not remain idle or fall into a state of disrepair."[49] And a May 1942 congressional report noted, "Liquidation of real and personal property held by evacuees is proceeding at a rapid pace." Nisei who owned property that could remotely be viewed as in a strategic location, such as near a port or a military base, were in an even worse position. Once Executive Order 9066 was in effect, and the military had designated the land that the Japanese held to be strategically vital, all Japanese property claims to the land were null and void; in many cases, the military either kept the land for its own use or sold it to presumably loyal white farmers. A representative of a grower association in

Salinas said, "We're charged with wanting to get rid of the Japs for selfish reasons. We might as well be honest. We do. It's a question of whether the white man lives on the Pacific Coast or the brown man."[50] What gives credence to the allegation of a hidden Anglo agenda to take over the Japanese land is the obvious and damning fact that the United States did not inter Germans and Italians, with whose homelands we were also at war.

When the Japanese were released from the camps in 1945, they were not quickly reimbursed for their property losses, and when they were finally "compensated," the dollar figure was puny. The Federal Reserve estimated that the direct property seizures from the nisei were worth $400 million (in 1942 dollars), approximately $2.7 billion today, and the Commission on Wartime Relocation and Internment of Civilians estimated the total income and property losses at between $810 million and $2 billion (inflation-adjusted). Insultingly, in 1948 Congress passed the Evacuation Claims Act, which gave the detainees seventeen months to make a claim from a paltry $31 million fund. Kotkin and Grabowicz wrote, "For the most part, the war all but wiped out Japanese-owned business in California, long the goal of many Anglos."[51]

Enter the Supermob

Despite their best efforts, the Japanese could only sell a fraction of their holdings in the brief time allotted. Thus, on March 11, 1942, FDR signed Executive Order 9095, establishing the Office of Alien Property. This new office, under the umbrella of the Department of Justice, spent the next few years seizing, inventorying, and finding buyers for millions of dollars' worth of property taken not only from the Japanese but also from German nationals. Even more disturbing, many of the seized properties were sold via no-contest sealed bids, overseen by a key appointee of President Harry Truman. When Truman became president after FDR's death just weeks after his 1945 inauguration, he undertook the cronyism typical of a new leader, making payback appointments favored by key power brokers and supporters. Predictably, he made a number of appointments at the suggestion of one of the most powerful pols in America, Colonel Jack (Jake) Arvey, and one of those appointments would have a profound impact on the success of the Supermob's Western investments, and the tragic plight of the nisei.

Truman and Arvey

"The most human president, for whom I have affection like that for my father, is Harry Truman," Jake Arvey once said. "I am prouder of his friendship for me than I am of any political associations I have."[52] Arvey's tribute was not an understatement, for the ward powerhouse believed Truman saved his life during World War II. "I was a member of the 33rd Division which was supposed to make the invasion of Japan," Arvey wrote. "We might have been annihilated—[Truman's] dropping of the bomb averted that."[53] Less than a year before, Arvey and his "Bloody 24th Ward" minions had used Outfit muscle to turn out the widest margin of victory of any ward in the entire country for the 1944 Roosevelt-Truman ticket: 29,533 for FDR to 2,204 for Dewey. In that effort Arvey assigned two of his ward's most notorious committeemen, Peter Fosco, and Arthur X. Elrod, who had gained notoriety for, among other things, turning out absurd Democratic electoral pluralities in the precinct where he was captain, to seal the deal. Fosco was an admitted close friend of Outfit boss Paul Ricca and a dominant figure in the Building Laborers' Union, where he manipulated the city's labor force with the likes of Curly Humphreys and Sid Korshak. Elrod had come up in the 1920s as a business front and bail bondsman for the North Side Moran gang. He later worked as a private secretary for North Side gunman and vice king Jack Zuta, who became the most notorious brothel owner in Chicago.*

The Truman-Arvey relationship grew stronger due to their beliefs concerning the Jewish homeland. Arvey had been passionate about a pending UN resolution on the founding of the state of Israel and had worked tirelessly in the Israel bonds movement.[54] Cook County state's attorney Ralph Berkowitz recalled, "Jack Arvey told Truman that if he does not recognize the state of Israel, then he couldn't guarantee that he could carry the Twenty-fourth Ward [in the 1948 presidential election]. Let alone the county and the state. When Truman came around and endorsed the resolution on March 16, 1947, Arvey delivered. "I worked harder for him in '48 than I have ever worked for a candidate in my life," Arvey recalled.[55]

In 1948, Arvey's push was considered critical to Truman's eventual victory, with Truman's campaign chairman saying that they would only declare victory when they won Illinois. Truman carried the state of Illinois by 33,612 votes (.9 percent). However, his margin of victory in Cook County, where Elrod's precinct gave Truman a 300-to-1 victory, was 200,836 votes (9 percent). When the final count was tallied, Truman received 303 electoral votes, with 266 needed to win. Illinois had 28 votes. Irv Kupcinet, not only

* Elrod eventually bought his own ballroom, the Club Dorel (an anagram of his last name), which contained a fake wall that concealed a hidden room used as a casino and bookie parlor. When New York Commission partner Frank Costello's phone records for 1945 were obtained by authorities, they noted numerous calls to Elrod.

(Left to right) Jake Arvey, Averell Harriman, Estes Kefauver, Harry Truman, Richard Daley (Corbis/Bettmann)

Korshak's dining pal, but also a close friend of both Truman's and Arvey's, wrote, "Arvey's work . . . laid the groundwork for the surprising victory of Harry Truman in 1948 . . . [Arvey] worked night and day for Truman's nomination at the 1948 convention."[56]

When Truman appeared at a party in Chicago after the election, Elrod presented him with the precinct tally sheet displaying the ludicrous totals. Truman jokingly asked Elrod, "Who was the one?" To which Elrod replied, "I don't know, I'm still looking for him."

Two years later, Elrod and Fosco organized a torchlight parade for Truman, with Elrod acting as chauffeur for Sid Korshak's friend Vice President Barkley in the motorcade.* In 1952, the IRS investigated Arvey for possibly having been given tax concessions because he was so close to Truman.[57]

---

*Korshak often bragged about his friendship with Kentuckian Barkley, and the FBI noted that when the VP visited Chicago, he and Korshak were often seen at the Outfit-infested Chez Paree nightclub, where Barkley nonetheless refused to be photographed with Korshak. (FBI memo from DELETED to SAC, Chicago, 6-15-59, Korshak file)

Part and parcel of the Arvey-Truman symbiosis was Truman's obliging of Arvey's wishes when it came to federal appointments. At Arvey's urging, Truman appointed Arvey protégé Michael Howlett, then the Illinois secretary of state, to be the regional director of the Federal Office of Price Stabilization. Another Truman-Arvey appointment was that of Chicago attorney Daniel F. Cleary to the chairmanship of the War Crimes Commission.

But by far the most controversial Truman-Arvey appointment now appears to have been a major boost for the investment wishes of the old Capone mob and their allies in the Supermob, giving them their turn at the California land grab.

"Ex-Chicagoan in Control of Enemy Assets"
—*CHICAGO TRIBUNE* HEADLINE, JUNE 1, 1947

On June 1, 1947, Assistant Attorney General David Bazelon, who had been a top Democratic Party fund-raiser in the 1944 elections, was promoted to custodian of Alien property, prompting him to declare, "I am probably in a sense one of the largest businessmen in the country. On top of that I'm my own lawyer."[58] Once installed, Bazelon hired Pritzker's son, Jay A. Pritzker, who became the special assistant to the director in the Alien Property office.[59] Jay was, like Paul Ziffren, a former classmate of Bazelon's at Northwestern. It was now clear why Abe Pritzker had been "grateful" to Bazelon and therefore gave him his Franklin stock. Jay's acceptance of the new post raised eyebrows, since the wealthy Pritzker heir was lowly paid and resided in the pricey Willard Hotel for the duration of his one-year employment. Speculation arose that since Jay's bill at the Willard dwarfed his meager paycheck, there must have been some other purpose for his taking the position. That contention was buttressed when, according to congressional investigators, Jay utilized his new insider information to purchase stock in a knitting-machine

David Bazelon, director of the Office of Alien Property (Corbis/Bettmann)

manufacturing company that had been vested (seized) by the Alien office. His $73,000 investment was said to be worth $1 million.[60]

Bazelon's assessment of his new clout was not an understatement. The Office of Alien Property (OAP) confiscated 415 businesses with a total valuation of $290 million in tangible assets alone, and over six thousand German patents (worth exponentially more than the businesses) that would be given to U.S. businesses. One congressman spoke of the businesses and capital under the control of the OAP, saying, "They are the biggest plums in the entire Truman administration."[61] Journalist Robert Goe wrote, "The Alien Custodian could use his discretion as to whether properties were put out for sealed bid, or negotiated . . . it is clear that there is much room for preferential treatment by the Custodian."

Preferential treatment is exactly what happened, and, not surprisingly, among the earliest recipients were Paul Ziffren and other "connected" Chicagoans. When the FBI searched the Alien Property Custodian Office files five years later, it found letters showing that Ziffren and Bazelon had been interested in obtaining four commercial buildings in L.A. from the OAP at least as early as August 23, 1946. Even prior to that, in April 1941, when Ziffren and Bazelon were at the Gottlieb firm, Ziffren had inquired of the Treasury Department about the regulations concerning "freezing the funds of certain foreign countries."[62] This was a full two months *before* the United States actually froze the funds of the enemy Axis powers, in solidarity with those already at war with Germany, leading to speculation that Ziffren had insider information of what was about to occur. The FBI further learned that "Bazelon and Ziffren had been involved in numerous transactions over a period of years and frequently had made each other partners in such transactions."[63]

According to a U.S. Department of Interior report of 1944, 216 hotels in California were seized from the nisei by the government. By war's end, that number had risen to 1,265. It was the responsibility of David Bazelon to find buyers for these properties, the most highly valuable being in California, which was in the midst of a postwar boom. A number of the choicest parcels went to Bazelon's best friend, Paul Ziffren, in partnership with his regular unsavory clique.

Almost immediately after Bazelon assumed his new post, Jake Arvey's great friend Colonel Henry Crown purchased a twenty-six-thousand-acre abandoned coal mine in Farmersville, California, from the OAP for $150,000.[64] The coal alone on the property was valued in the tens of millions.

Another purchase from the OAP seizures was the Los Angeles Warehouse Properties Co. on 326 N. San Pedro Street. This was a massive building and

Ben Weingart, 1950 (photographer unknown)

lot, previously owned by a Japanese national, purchased in January 1948 by Bazelon's best friend, Paul Ziffren, and seven partners. One of the senior partners, Ben Weingart, was a major purchaser of alien land, including dozens of parcels and hotels in the Wolfskill tract, the skid row area of L.A. Weingart also acquired Japanese properties in Whittier, Santa Ana, Pasadena, Southgate, Bakersfield, Fresno, and Stockton.[65] In the late 1940s, Weingart bought thirty-five hundred acres of land north of Long Beach and oversaw the building of seventeen thousand homes on the site, thus giving birth to the city of Lakewood. Weingart also built the Lakewood Shopping Center, the first large-scale shopping center in the country.*

Almost immediately, the OAP came under suspicion of being an insider gravy train, prompting a Senate investigation of its methods. On March 7, 1948, the *Chicago Tribune* summarized the allegations Congress hoped to investigate:

> At least a score of former New Dealers, close friends of the administration and former federal employees, have been put on the payrolls of the firms the United States operates or placed in strategic positions as directors. Some of them draw as much as $50 thousand a year. In half a dozen multimillion dollar corporations, former government workers and their political pals are in on the ground floor in anticipation of the time these firms are sold to private management . . . Some concerns, such as the $80

---

*In the 1950s, Weingart founded the Weingart Foundation, which today has total assets of $490,350,000. The primary recipients of grants were to be the down-and-out people of skid row, where Weingart had made his fortune in alien real estate. The foundation helps underprivileged groups with education, youth programs, health and medicine, crisis intervention, disaster relief, and community programs. Weingart died in 1980.

million General Aniline Film Corporation, are suffering from undercover jockeying of powerful political and financial groups which hope to get these lush properties when Uncle Sam puts them on the auction block . . . The alien property investigation will inquire into reports that law firms and lawyers with right connections have found a "paradise" in rich fees and costly litigation involving seized properties.[66]

As damning as these allegations were, they were far from representative of the worst secrets hidden behind the doors of the OAP.

> *Several of us would form a pool to buy up these properties, then we took care of him* with a share.*
> —ALEX LOUIS GREENBERG, DESCRIBING HIS REAL ESTATE MO[67]

The most troublesome aspect of the Warehouse deal was that seven years later, on March 14, 1955, Ziffren's name on the deed was replaced with that of David Bazelon, who now held 9.2 percent of the multimillion-dollar real estate holding company—with no record of any cash outlay.[68] Interestingly, Bazelon's name was deleted from a number of official records, although it appears in some as early as 1948. Journalist and investigator Robert Goe wrote, "Title Insurance Trust officials have stated for the record that they knew of the Bazelon roles in the Warehouse Properties deal. Since their information is not reflected in their own reports to the City of Los Angeles, it may be that someone high in the Trust office has caused this knowledge to be removed from the files."[69] Goe called it "a deliberate attempt to cover up the ownership of the property."

In August of 1959, the City of Los Angeles, reportedly due to the influence of Paul Ziffren, purchased the massive Warehouse Properties parcel for $1.1 million in furtherance of its Civic Center Master Plan. The Warehouse lot was situated in the center of a location earmarked for purchase by the federal government for the new $30 million Customs Building. Brother Leo Ziffren had also been seen massaging the deal in the office of the city's chief of the Bureau of Right of Way and Land.[70] David Bazelon's cut was over $100,000.[71]

It wasn't just Japanese property that was seized by the OAP then directed to the Supermob. Friends of Bazelon's profited off German seizures as well. In

---

*Him referred to Illinois state auditor Arthur Lueder, who, like Bazelon, gave Greenberg advance tips on real estate he had underappraised.

a purchase that was not divulged for other bidders, the Ziffren group relieved the Office of Alien Property of the Luxembourg-based Rohm Haas Chemical Corporation in Philadelphia for $40 a share, when it was worth $125. Their $1 million investment in 1948 was worth $40 million by 1954.

Since the purchase was not divulged to others, only the custodian, David Bazelon, would have known of it.[72] Interestingly, one of Bazelon's and Ziffren's associates at Gottlieb, William J. Friedman, became the director of Rohm Haas after the purchase. The FBI in Los Angeles was informed years later that Jake Arvey and Sidney Korshak divided about $12 million worth of the Haas stock.[73] When Custodian Bazelon appointed a friend's law firm to handle the legal aspects of one German seizure, Truman's Attorney General James Howard McGrath refused to pay their exorbitant bill, reportedly saying he "dare not approve the fee because the situation is so ticklish in the Department of Justice right now that he doesn't know what furor it might cause."[74]

On May 16, 1957, Attorney General Herbert Brownell wrote Hoover asking him to investigate the Rohm Haas acquisition by a "Chicago group" and the possibility that Bazelon was paid off with the Warehouse Properties stock gift. "The Chicago group included Ziffren, Sidney Korshak . . . and Jacob Arvey, the well-known Chicago politician with whom Ziffren formerly shared a law office." After only two weeks, the FBI delivered its conclusion: Bazelon's OAP indeed controlled 70 percent of Rohm, while the group headed by his best friend, Paul Ziffren, held the remaining 30 percent. The Bureau, incredibly, was not asked to see if Ziffren's $40-per-share price was (as it appeared) well below the true value.

The FBI's conclusion to its inquiry was a tribute to bureaucratic buck-passing: "If by some arrangement or 'deal' this purchase was actually done, it would appear to have been a private transaction and does not fall within the scope of this inquiry."[75] A top Wall Street stock analyst recently reviewed the FBI's file and translated the obtuse stockbroker jargon: "There is clearly the possibility of impropriety. Bazelon was in a position to know the true worth of the [Rohm] company and to influence whom they sold it to. The only way to know is if Bazelon did something to help Ziffren buy it for cheap—like telling the original owners, 'I'm going to fuck you if you don't sell to my friend for such and such a price.' . . . The FBI is saying, 'We had a very limited investigation.' Nobody asked them to go further. It was totally not a complete investigation. There were enough ways for them to get to the bottom of it, but they weren't asked to."[76]

On October 21, 1949, David Bazelon became, at age forty, the youngest federal judge in history, appointed by President Truman to the most important circuit court in the United States, the Washington D.C. Court of Appeals.[77] Bazelon's new posting was made as a "recess appointment," a presidential ploy often used to secure a controversial enlistment while potentially disapproving congressmen are on break.* It was believed by some that Arvey arranged the appointment as payback for his support of Truman in the 1948 election.[78] Former secretary of the interior Harold L. Ickes, writing in the *New Republic,* called the appointment "deplorable" and showed great prescience when he advised, "Certainly the Senate would do well to investigate closely Bazelon's conduct of the Office of Alien Property." He added that he'd assumed that the Truman administration's appointment of Tom Clark to the Supreme Court was as bad as it would get, but he added regretfully that Bazelon's naming was an "all-time low." Ickes next wrote Truman in a last-ditch effort to sink the nomination, arguing, "I happen to know a good deal about Bazelon and I consider him to be thoroughly unfit for the job that he holds, to say nothing of a United States judgeship, either on the Court of Appeals or on the District Court."[79] (Ickes was also a former Chicago newsman and outspoken opponent of political corruption and collusion with the Capone Syndicate.)

Los Angeles Mirror journalist and tireless researcher into the L.A. real estate purchases Art White summarized the importance of the expansionist decade:

> During these years some hundreds of associates of Greenberg, Evans, and others of the Capone crime syndicate, and of Arvey and Ziffren, poured hundreds of millions of dollars into California. They bought real estate, including hotel chains through apparently unrelated corporations from San Diego to Sacramento. They invested in vast tracts of land, built or bought motels, giant office buildings, and other commercial properties. More importantly, they invaded the loan field, establishing banks and home loan institutions. By 1953, Ziffren and his associates had gained control of an enormous block of California's economy. They could finance political campaigns with the best of the native barons.[80]

When the FBI reviewed White's research into the extent of the relationship between the Capones and Ziffren, it concluded with a rare declaration vindicating White's conclusions: "The extraordinary success of this adventurer [Ziffren]—and by the same token his backers, who can be traced right

---

*The recess appointment was most recently utilized in 2005 by George W. Bush in his naming of firebrand John Bolton as U.S. representative to the United Nations.

into the Midwest and East Coast hoodlum world—*has been proven and documented.*"[81] (Author's italics.)

For a more detailed, but still partial, list of the properties acquired by the combine of Chicago's Supermob associates, see appendix A.

Along with Chicago's tainted money and mob-controlled unions now flooding the West came a need to manage the requisite labor and political issues that accompanied them. Who better for the role of underworld liaison to the upperworld than the suave Chicago attorney already comfortable with the Capones, and already schooled in the intricacies of labor "negotiating"? Who better than Sidney Roy Korshak?

CHAPTER 6

"Hell, That's What You Had to Do in Those Days to Get By"

The future always looks good in the golden land, because no one re-
members the past.

—JOAN DIDION[1]

B Y THE LATE FORTIES, the Supermob's takeover of the Golden State was
well under way: Paul Ziffren had relocated his law practice from 134 N.
LaSalle Street in Chicago to 9363 Wilshire Boulevard in Beverly Hills and,
through pal David Bazelon, had helped his Chicago friends invest their profits in numerous tracts of West Coast land; Al Hart was a thriving California
distiller, racetrack owner, and soon-to-be bank owner; Joe Glaser had
moved his Associated Booking to L.A., and likewise, Jules Stein and Lew
Wasserman (who had been elevated by Stein to MCA president in December
1946) opened their MCA headquarters there and absorbed the 250-client
talent pool of the Zeppo Marx Agency when they purchased that Hollywood powerhouse; MCA client Ronald Reagan was now in Hollywood, a
bad actor, but a better politician who was about to become president of the
Screen Actors Guild (1947–52, 1959), where he would protect MCA's interests; Jake Factor was finally in prison, but would soon land in Las Vegas before settling in L.A., with his brother Max, as a prominent real estate
investor and philanthropist; Philadelphian Walter Annenberg expanded his
publishing empire and built his palatial 392-acre estate, Sunnylands, in Rancho Mirage, California, going on to become a key supporter of both Ronald
Reagan's and Richard Nixon's political careers; and Hilton scion Arnold
Kirkeby had landed in the tony Bel-Air enclave, where he built the most expensive private home in America.

Remaining behind in Chicago—although financially connected to
California—were Jake Arvey, the Pritzkers, Henry Crown, Alex Greenberg,

and Arthur Greene. Sidney Korshak was still dividing his time between the two outposts, due in large part to his advisory role with the Outfit, which was now trying to secure an unthinkable early release for its brethren incarcerated in the Hollywood extortion case.

By the late forties, Bioff, Browne, and Schenck had already been released from prison, but the rest were still cooling their heels in stir, while their confreres on the outside lobbied the Truman administration for an early release. According to Bureau of Prison records housed at the National Archives, Sidney Korshak visited Charlie Gioe in Leavenworth twenty-two times. Korshak was not Gioe's attorney of record, and it is widely assumed that he acted as an information conduit, updating Gioe on the negotiations with Truman's parole board. Korshak told the FBI that the visits were merely to update Gioe on the status of an Antioch, Illinois, real estate sale by Gioe's wife, whom Korshak was helping.

Among other services rendered, Korshak admitted that he solicited letters of character reference for Gioe and enlisted one of his law associates, Harry Ash, to agree to act as Gioe's parole supervisor. Since Ash was also Chicago's superintendent of crime prevention, he was considered by Korshak to be above reproach.[2]

After intense pressure applied to politically vulnerable President Truman and his parole board, the convicted Outfit felons were indeed released early (over the objections of prosecutors and prison wardens) on August 18, 1947, their terms cut by a third. The subsequent uproar led to a major congressional investigation and forced Harry Ash to resign his Chicago civic post.* Although the Hollywood extortion convictions gave the outward appearance of rescuing the movie business from the underworld, it actually distracted the public from a handoff to the more sophisticated Supermob, which would control huge segments of the business with remnants of the underworld. The new partnership was, like the Bioff gambit, mutually beneficial, especially when entertainers found themselves in the mob's crosshairs. Such was the case in November of 1947, when the nascent comedy team of Dean Martin and Jerry Lewis were appearing in Chicago at the Chez Paree. When on the road, the duo famously partook in the female temptations that presented themselves; however, when Martin and Lewis sought to make whoopee with two lovelies that were already spoken for—by Joe Accardo's boys—they took their very lives in their hands.

---

*For a complete discussion of the Outfit's links to Truman and his parole board, see my previous book, *The Outfit*, chapters 10 and 11.

"I got them out of Chicago about two steps ahead of Dean getting killed," recalled their agent, Abbey Greshler. "I did it with the help of Sidney Korshak. He's a very dear man, but some people say he's the mob's attorney. I never asked him that. You learn not to ask." It was to be one of countless rescues Korshak would perform over the years for celebrities who thought they could play ball with the boys in the big league.

It wasn't as if Martin and Lewis were naïve as to whom they were entertaining. Lewis had first run afoul of a loudmouthed front-table thug when Lewis grabbed his shoulder and said, "Hey, pal, the show is up here!" The "pal," who turned out to be Outfit enforcer Charlie Fischetti, shot back "the look" and warned, "If you don't move away right now, I'll blow your fuckin' head off." When Lewis realized whom he had crossed, he apologized profusely. (For decades thereafter, the Fischetti family sent substantial checks each year to Lewis's muscular dystrophy telethon.)[3]

One year later, Lew Wasserman decided he wanted Martin and Lewis in the MCA stable. The MCA boss ordered two men to break into Greshler's office to steal their contract, whereupon MCA made them a better offer. Although the duo ended up at MCA, Greshler obtained a huge legal settlement in the subsequent lawsuit filed against MCA. Of course, no one was about to charge Wasserman or Stein criminally, which should have occurred.[4]

As the second half of the century began, trouble for both the underworld and the Supermob loomed in the persons of journalist Lester Velie and ambitious politician Estes Kefauver, a freshman U.S. senator from Tennessee.

Forty-two-year-old Velie, an award-winning New York–based crime reporter, was an unlikely foe for the forty-one-year-old Korshak, given that he also hailed from Kiev and the University of Wisconsin, where he and Korshak were 1926–27 classmates. By 1950, Velie was writing crime exposés for *Collier's* magazine, where he was an associate editor. His most recent investigation, aided by Chicago Crime Commission director Virgil Peterson, was an in-depth profile of the Capone heirs' political connections. The seven-page article appeared in the September 30, 1950, *Collier's* issue and devoted the first-ever investigative ink to Sidney Korshak. The article noted Korshak's association with Jake Arvey, Alex Greenberg's Seneca, Charlie Fischetti, and others. During his research, Velie visited Korshak's LaSalle Street office, where he eavesdropped on visits and phone calls from Arvey, Arthur Elrod, George Scalise, Dan Gilbert, and "layoff" bookie Joe Grabiner.

The Velie investigation intrigued Kefauver, who was about to embark on a mammoth congressional probe of organized crime, with the subject of Sid

Dalitz testifying before the Kefauver Committee in Los Angeles, February 28, 1951 (Cleveland State University, Special Collections)

Korshak. A legislator with presidential aspirations, Kefauver had persuaded Congress to have him oversee an ambitious, and first-ever, probe into the murky underworld. The senator and his investigators announced that they would crisscross the country in their efforts to clarify the state of American lawlessness.

Before Kefauver visited Chicago in October of 1950, he made it known that one of his prime targets would be one of Lester Velie's prey, the Supermob's Sidney Korshak. In July, shortly after receiving Velie's draft, Kefauver announced his committee staff 's September trip to the Second City and obtained Korshak's tax records for 1947–49 from Secretary of the Treasury John Snyder.[5] Those records showed that Korshak was declaring an average yearly income of approximately $94,000 ($1.4 million converted to 2004 dollars).[6] His brother Marshall reported a $46,000 average for the same period. Committee investigators in Chicago also subpoenaed Korshak's financial records from 1945 to 1948, and Korshak promptly complied with the request. The full-court press continued as former Chicago detective William Drury was enlisted by a Miami newsman to monitor Korshak's movements, the reports of which were shared with Kefauver's investigators. The Drury surveillance operation ended abruptly on September 25, 1950, when Drury was shot to death in his garage. Thus, when the committee touched down in Chicago, the prospects for a Korshak inquisition were expected to intensify.[7]

Another potential pitfall for Korshak was the committee's interest in Dan Gilbert, Korshak's key connection in the Chicago State's Attorney's Office. Under oath, Gilbert admitted his gambling links with the Chicago Outfit, a disclosure that had to heighten the investigators' interest in his associates such as Korshak. But by the time the Kefauver Committee arrived in Chicago to conduct formal hearings, Korshak and the Outfit had devised a scheme to ward off the committee's namesake. Just like other Washington insiders, the Supermob was aware of Estes Kefauver's vulnerabilities.

Prior to his marriage to the former Nancy Pigott in 1935, Estes Kefauver had a reputation as a stereotypical Southern ladies' man, a landed-gentry Lochinvar. After his marriage, Kefauver cleaned up his act—at least in Tennessee. Charles Fontenay, who covered Kefauver for the *Nashville Tennessean*, wrote, "A lot of people knew of his propensity for women, but he was clean as a whistle in Tennessee."[8] However, in Washington, and wherever else his travels took him, Kefauver was known as a legendary drinker and womanizer. William "Fishbait" Miller, the longtime House "doorkeeper," who supervised some 357 House employees, called him the "worst womanizer in the Senate." On Kefauver's premature death of a heart attack, Miller wrote, "He must have worn himself out chasing pretty legs."[9] The senator himself provided the fuel for the talk. When on tour in Europe, Kefauver caused a scandal after escorting a famous call girl to a society ball. On another occasion, he trysted with a woman in Paris who was not told of his wife in Tennessee. Afterward, Kefauver recommended his courtesan to a friend who was about to tour France.[10]

On future campaign junkets, Kefauver became infamous for dispatching his aides to procure women. *New York Times* columnist Russell Baker recalled one night with the candidate on the tour bus when Kefauver was feeling particularly randy. On arrival in a small town "in the middle of the night," Baker overheard Kefauver telling one of his minions, "I gotta fuck!"[11] Irv Kupcinet called Keef "the worst womanizer I've ever known. Whenever he came to town . . . he let the word out: 'Get me a woman!' He would have put Gary Hart to shame."[12] Capitol Hill lobbyist Bobby Baker, who would become the first American to have a scandal named after him, wrote that Kefauver regularly put himself "up for sale." According to Baker, "[Kefauver] didn't particularly care whether he was paid in coin or in women."[13]

On October 4, 1950, Kefauver and his senior staff descended on Chicago, where Kefauver took a room in the Kirkeby-owned Palmer House, while the rest of the staff and investigators stayed at the hotel that was also home to Outfit mastermind Curly Humphreys (as well as being the Outfit's former meeting place), the Morrison. Perhaps not coincidentally, Chief Counsel Rudolph Halley complained that the staff's phones were tapped. However, he never learned of the Outfit's planned setup of the committee's chairman. In June 1976, reporters Seymour Hersh and Jeff Gerth began to unravel the inside story of Kefauver and Korshak in a four-part profile of the well-connected Supermob lawyer in the *New York Times*. A close friend and business associate of Korshak's told the writers how Korshak and the Outfit blackmailed the ever-randy Kefauver. The informant, unnamed in the article, related that he had seen compromising photos of the senator taken in a suite at the luxurious Drake Hotel, which was of course owned by the Kirkeby–Cuba National–Lansky consortium. Recent interviews have shed more light on the incident.

The source who was shown the photos turned out to be none other than Joel Goldblatt, who, by the time he was approached by Hersh, had had a falling-out with his pal Sidney over Sidney's standing up for Joel's ex, Lynne Walker Goldblatt, in their divorce proceedings.[14] Goldblatt was notoriously jealous, and Korshak's friendship with Lynne put him over the edge. "Sidney double-crossed him," remembered Goldblatt's then secretary and future wife, MJ Goldblatt. "He came into the courtroom and kissed Joel's ex on the cheek."[15] It is now understood that Kefauver was enticed to the Drake, where two young women from the Outfit's Chez Paree nightclub entertained him. "The Outfit had a guy at the Drake, a vice cop who moonlighted as the hotel's head of security," a friend of the Korshak family recently divulged. "Korshak got the girls; the security guard set up an infrared camera and delivered the prints to Korshak." Sandy Smith, the veteran Chicago crime reporter, recently said, "I knew that district and its cops and the other people who were involved in that kind of thing."[16]

The confidential source added that a private meeting was arranged between Kefauver and Korshak. In the brief encounter, Korshak flung the incriminating photos on Kefauver's desk. "Now, how far do you want to go with this?" Korshak asked. Kefauver never called Korshak to testify before the committee, despite his being the first of eight hundred witnesses subpoenaed. A committee internal memo noted that they had hoped to interview Korshak, "but were forced to forgo that pleasure because of the chairman's recall to Washington."[17]

Finally, in October 1950, committee investigator George Robinson, who had merely intended to return Korshak's subpoenaed files, interviewed Korshak. Korshak told Robinson, and reporters afterward, that the committee's interest in him was generated by Lester Velie's article in *Collier's*. Korshak informed Robinson that Velie not only exaggerated the facts, but often invented them. According to Sidney, Velie had a hidden motive for his broadside: he'd held a twenty-four-year grudge against Korshak since their college days at Wisconsin, where boxing champion Korshak punched Velie—then Levy—in the nose. Incredibly, Korshak told the press that he never met Scalise (whom Velie saw with him in Korshak's office) and never represented Charlie Gioe (Korshak had handled his Hollywood extortion difficulties). In a brilliant choice of words, Korshak declared, "My records will show that I never represented any hoodlums." Of course, Korshak was famous for his lack of record keeping. He called Velie's piece "a series of diabolical lies," and Velie "a journalistic faker and an unmitigated liar." Korshak's words to the press would be his last. If he had been discreet before, from now on he would be near invisible, his name all but vanishing from the public consciousness.[18]

Kefauver's kid-glove approach to Korshak was trumped by his virtual incompetence in dealing with another key Supermob member, Alex Louis Greenberg. On January 19, 1951, Greenberg testified before Kefauver and admitted to his co-ownership of both the Seneca and California's Store Properties with Paul Ziffren, Sam Genis, James Roosevelt, et al. His IRS statements in the committee's possession corroborated the partnerships. To what should have been an eye-opening revelation, Kefauver merely remarked, "I just marvel that you can have so many businesses." Greenberg replied, "Thank you."

Greenberg ended his testimony by offering the committee an invitation: "The next time the committee comes to Chicago, I would like to have the committee stop in the Seneca Hotel . . . We operate a very nice hotel . . . [we have] very liberal rates. We got good food over there. Might as well give the Seneca a boost."[19] There was no follow-up questioning about Greenberg's investment role for Nitti, Capone, and the rest; no interest in the partnership with the notoriously connected Sam Genis or the myriad of properties obtained from Ziffren's close friend who headed the Office of Alien Property, Judge David Bazelon.*[20]

Move to the West Coast

With Velie and Kefauver summarily dismissed, Sidney Korshak set about joining his compadres in California, albeit now with greater respect from the Chicago hoods.

"Sidney became a legend after the Kefauver incident," remembered a top Chicago PD detective. "It was the key thing that impressed [boss Tony] Accardo and the others."[21]

Korshak's gossip-writing pal Irv Kupcinet recently said about his high-flying friend, "He knew and had the backing of Tony Accardo. Tony Accardo

---

*Interestingly, many of the Kefauver Committee's files, including some of the most sensitive, were looted before being transferred to the Library of Congress (*Washington Daily News*, 3-17-55). When the holdings were opened for the first time for this writer, much of the Korshak and Greenberg files were gone, as were the photos the committee had obtained of Frank Sinatra in Cuba at a Mafia convention with Luciano, Lansky, et al.

Tony "Joe Batters" Accardo (author collection)

loved him; he depended on him. [He] was considered to be the fair-haired boy in the organization with the blessings of Tony Accardo."[22]

Korshak's future success would require a delicate balancing act consisting of serving his Outfit patrons in Chicago, who felt they'd "made" him, and promoting the interests of himself and the rest of the Supermob, now becoming entrenched in California business and politics. It is one of the many great "unknowables" in Korshak's life: how much of his West Coast relocation was based on his own desires and how much came from an Outfit dictum. "Turned" mobster Joe Hauser voiced his opinion to a House subcommittee in 1983, saying, "Organized crime leader Tony Accardo, who I have known for many years as Joe Batters, told me on several occasions that he had sent Korshak to Los Angeles to represent the mob there." Frank Buccieri, brother of infamous Outfit juice collector Fifi Buccieri, recently said, "Sidney paid homage to Accardo. Accardo was telling him what to do. When Sidney was in California, he was still taking orders from Accardo. Absolutely."[23]

Leaving his sponsors behind, Korshak said good-bye not only to bitter Illinois winters, but also to the normal workplace. As the new fixer for both the Outfit and the Commission, Korshak only required a telephone, which he wielded like a scepter in the coming years, playing the highly compensated middleman between corporate supplicants and the hidden Eastern powers in Chicago's Outfit and New York's Commission.

By this time the Korshak family had expanded to include not only Sidney and Bee, but also their two young sons, Harry (b. 1945) and Stuart (b. 1947), on whom Sidney doted. For relaxation Hollywood-style, the Korshaks often joined the Ziffrens and pals at the hottest Hollywood nightspot, the Mocambo, located at 8588 Sunset Boulevard, and later immortalized in James

Ellroy's *L.A. Confidential*. A sort of West Coast Chez Paree, the Mocambo, which opened in 1941, was described as "a cross between a somewhat decadent Imperial Rome, Salvador Dalí, and a birdcage." The latter reference was to the club's aviary, which housed macaws and cockatoos. In addition to virtually every notable Hollywood actor,* mobsters such as Mickey Cohen, Ben Siegel, Johnny Stompanato, and Johnny Rosselli frequented the club and were in fact rumored to have a stake in it. Author and Beverly Hills native Don Wolfe said that, among the "in crowd," the Mocambo's true ownership was well-known. "Charlie Morrison had Bugsy as a silent partner," said Wolfe. "That's why it was one of the hoods' favorite hangouts."[24] In 1943, Frank Sinatra made his L.A. singing debut at the Mocambo.

In August 1952, Korshak pal Harry Karl threw a bash at the club in honor of Sidney Korshak and Jake Arvey, who flew out West for the event. The *Chicago Tribune* covered the Korshak-Arvey lovefest at the club and reported, "The guests numbered some 300 from the Hollywood blue book, or telephone book, and some politicians."[25] Karl, the adopted son of Russian immigrants Pincus and Rose Karl, had inherited his father's $7 million estate (and shoe factories and three hundred retail outlets) and moved from New York to Beverly Hills.[†,26] According to a Karl family member, Korshak and Karl were "as close as brothers" since the 1930s, when both were chasing starlets in Hollywood. According to the LAPD, there were hidden dimensions to the Karl-Korshak friendship. An informant told officials (just before he was blown up) that "Karl's Shoe Store was a front for the Chicago mob and that Korshak was the contact man."[27]

Professionally, Korshak continued to network with the best of them, not skipping a beat when it came to courting important L.A. lawyers, judges, police officials, and corporate moguls. During these years, Korshak was also often seen at Hillcrest, working the power-wielding clique, as opposed to the celebrities who drew the attention of most.** While the showbiz types

---

*Celebrity regulars included Errol Flynn, Marilyn Monroe, Henry Fonda, Jimmy Stewart, Burgess Meredith, Clark Gable, Carole Lombard, Lucille Ball and Desi Arnaz, Louis B. Mayer, Humphrey Bogart and Lauren Bacall, and Lana Turner.

†IRS investigator Andy Furfaro watched Karl's career closely and recently opined, "Harry Karl didn't exist. It was what they called the orphan train. A lot of these guys like Ziffren and Karl had no parents; suddenly they're adopted by these high muckety-mucks. A big shoe man from New England adopts Harry Karl."

**One FBI memo called Korshak "a director of the Hillcrest Country Club." (Memo from DELETED to SAC L.A., 12-8-75)

frequenting the "men's only" dining room were entranced by iconic regulars such as Groucho or Milton Berle or George Burns, Korshak was buying lunch for brokers he might need at some future time. Fellow L.A. attorney and Korshak friend Leo Geffner recalled meeting him for lunch one day: "This guy sits down with us—I didn't catch his name. He was very friendly with Sid. After he left, I asked who he was. The Beverly Hills chief of police!"[28]

Among Korshak's earliest dining partners was San Francisco district attorney and future governor of California Edmund "Pat" Brown, whom he met in the midforties. The commonalities of Korshak and Brown included their lenient views toward the underworld. Korshak's ethics were well-known nationally, and Brown's were certainly familiar to San Franciscans. Among his other curious actions, in 1947 Brown asked that murder indictments be dropped against three Colombo crime-family members, after a jury was already thirty hours into deliberations. He then promised the prosecutors that he would resubmit the case—he never did.[29] Brown, the son of a San Francisco gambler, would display this curious attitude as a private citizen in 1977, when he wrote a character reference letter for New Mexico organized crime boss John Alessio when Alessio applied for a racetrack license.[30]

By 1947, a new lunch partner, attorney and future L.A. Superior Court judge Laurence "Larry" Rittenband, had joined Korshak's entourage. After Korshak introduced Brown to Rittenband that year, the two formed one of L.A.'s most powerful law firms. Rittenband went on to become the most senior judge in Santa Monica. According to former *Sacramento Bee* reporter Richard Brenneman, who interviewed Rittenband extensively in 1976, "Rittenband topped the Santa Monica courthouse seniority list, where he handled his pick of the criminal cases—he loved mysteries—and presided over the courthouse's weekly Friday-morning law and motion calendar, ruling on all pretrial motions and arguments for all the Superior Court civil departments in the building."[31] Two decades later he would officiate at the marriage of Sidney's son Stuart. Pat Brown became California attorney general in 1951, and then governor of the state in 1959. Sid Korshak was a key supporter of both Pat's and his son Jerry's future political careers.

When Brenneman asked Rittenband how he justified his association with Korshak, given his ties to the Chicago underworld, the judge seethed. As Brenneman later noted, "His face burning, he made a dismissive wave of the hand and muttered, 'Hell, that's what you had to do in those days to get by.'"

Another new and important Korshak L.A. friend was the prominent Hollywood divorce lawyer Gregson "Greg" Bautzer. A Los Angeles native and son of a Yugoslavian fisherman, Bautzer began his legal career in the thirties, calling studio mogul Joe Schenck "my mentor." A partner in the Beverly Hills law firm of Bautzer, Grant, and Silbert, he was the prototypical Hollywood ladies' man: a handsome, impeccably dressed defender of maligned actresses caught up in nasty divorce squabbles. Among his clients were Lana Turner, Joan Crawford, Marion Davies, Ginger Rogers, and Jane Wyman (Reagan's ex). He never tired of telling his tale of deflowering Lana Turner ("I didn't enjoy it at all" was Turner's less-told side of the story). Male clients included George Raft, Clark Gable, Rock Hudson, and Arvey partner Henry Crown. Bautzer was also a volatile drunk, kicked out of places like the Beverly Hills Hotel dozens of times for besotted behavior. His name appeared regularly in the local rags, which reported on his babe of the month, usually a beautiful young starlet, or his long-running relationships with A-listers such as Turner and Crawford. (The term *A-list* was coined by gossip columnist Joyce Haber in reference to revelers on Sidney Korshak's invitation list to his sumptuous holiday parties.)

As in any good networking friendship, the benefits were mutual. When Bautzer client Susan Hayward was scheduled to be the focus of a 1955 *Confidential* magazine exposé, Korshak had it spiked. (Hayward tried to kill herself that year during a bitter child-custody battle, and public screaming matches with her ex were grist for the local media.)[32] On November 29 of that year, *Confidential* publisher Bob Harrison, a Korshak pal, wrote Korshak at his 134 N. LaSalle office, "Dear Sidney, In accordance with your request, we are dropping the Susan Hayward story from the upcoming issue of *Confidential*. Love and Kisses, Bob." For his part, Bautzer introduced Sidney to up-and-coming film producer Albert "Cubby" Broccoli and his cousin Pat DeCicco, a hard-partying Hollywood agent, and an alleged Hollywood front for New York's Lucky Luciano.[33] Broccoli went on to produce the lucrative James Bond film franchise, occasionally with the labor-consultation expertise of Sid Korshak.

Eventually, Bautzer graduated from the divorce courts to the world of corporate law, which opened up vast new possibilities for himself and his friends such as Korshak. Later, he formed the L.A. powerhouse law firm Wyman, Bautzer, Christianson, and Kuchel.[34] Thomas Kuchel, a protégé of Earl Warren's, would become a U.S. senator from California, a position from which he introduced tax legislation at the urgings of Lew Wasserman that allowed huge tax write-offs for the movie industry. Bautzer helped Bugsy Siegel and Meyer Lansky set up the corporation from which the Flamingo Hotel-Casino was born. Bautzer had actually been deeded the land by Moe Sedway and then transferred it to Siegel. At the Flamingo,

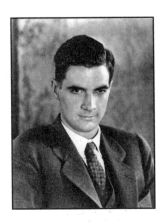

Howard Robard Hughes (Library of Congress)

Bautzer associated with another investor, Al Hart. The two had known each other since at least 1937: it was Bautzer who originally owned Maier Brewing and sold it to Hart that year.[35]

By far the most brilliant, powerful, and eccentric person that Bautzer brought to Korshak was a Susan Hayward boyfriend and Bautzer client soon to be dubbed "the billionaire kook," Howard Robard Hughes. The Texas-born Hughes had taken a sizable inheritance from his father, the founder of Hughes Tool Company, and parlayed it into numerous profitable endeavors when he started Hughes Aircraft, a major World War II contractor, and Trans World Airlines (TWA). In the early 1920s, Hughes entered the world of motion pictures through his uncle, Rupert Hughes, a famous author and movie producer. Howard produced twenty-six films, each of poor to average quality. However, he excelled in the role of producer-cum-babe-magnet, dating an enviable roster of the most desired women in Hollywood.*

Greg Bautzer met Hughes in 1947, when the competing cocksman made a pass at Bautzer's latest flame, Lana Turner. Hughes not only landed Turner, but also engaged Bautzer as his Hollywood attorney. Within a year, Hughes had achieved the producer's dream, acquiring his own studio, the Joseph Kennedy–created RKO, for $8.8 million. The purchase was a steal, as RKO was one of the most powerful studios of its time. But Hughes's Midas touch deserted him as a studio honcho, leading to massive financial losses and employee layoffs. Part of the reason for the decline was that Hughes's interest in the studio was, like that of many moguls before and after him, motivated

---

*Peter Brown's book *The Untold Story of Howard Hughes* contains an appendix (p. 394) that lists forty-four of the most well-known Hughes lovers, among them Jean Harlow, Jane Russell, Ava Gardner, Ginger Rogers, Bette Davis, Lana Turner, Yvonne DeCarlo, Gloria Vanderbilt, Rita Hayworth, Jean Peters, Terry Moore, and Kate Hepburn.

by factors other than the bottom line. Noah Dietrich, Hughes's right hand, and director of Hughes Tool Company, described his boss's connection to RKO: "Howard's involvement with RKO had other motivations than the pursuit of profits and furtherance of the art of the cinema. It also aided the exercise of his libido. I was never certain throughout Howard's long association with the motion picture industry whether his amours were an offshoot of that activity or film production was a screen for his romantic adventures."[36]

By 1952, Hughes, who was enduring endless complaints from the company's stockholders, was ready to sell RKO. Hollywood had "grown too complicated," he said. Bautzer's firm was to handle the details of the sale.[37] When Bautzer passed Hughes's dictum on to Sid Korshak, the former Chicagoan seized the opportunity to solidify his entrenchment in the movie business. While not yet possessed with pockets deep enough to contribute to the $1.25 million down payment,* Korshak was happy to be the behind-the-scenes facilitator, putting together a purchasing syndicate, with the understanding that he would become the new owners' "labor consultant" at a rate of $15,000 per year. He proceeded to convince Bautzer's law partner Arnold Grant to become chairman of RKO (for $2,000 per week), if Korshak could assemble a group of investors. When Grant (who was already the president of Al Hart's Del Mar Turf Club) agreed, Korshak set about synthesizing a motley group of investors hailing from his corrupt Midwest stomping grounds.

First there was Ray Ryan of Evansville, Indiana. Ryan was a gambler and a partner in a Texas oil venture with New York mafioso Frank Costello, his lieutenant Frank Erickson, and George Uffner, an ex-con and underworld leader.[38] Other Korshak recruits were the regionally notorious Ralph Stolkin and his father-in-law, Abe Koolish. Chicagoan Stolkin had amassed a fortune by selling a sort of take-home lottery contraption known as the punchboard, which had been invented in 1905 in Chicago.† This easily rigged contraption, although legal, paid off so rarely that complaint letters about Stolkin filled boxes in Better Business Bureau offices nationwide. The

---

*Hughes was so anxious to unload the albatross that he let it be known that he would hold the mortgage on the remainder of the $7 million price tag, in addition to loaning the new buyer(s) $8 million in transition capital.
†The punchboard consisted of an eight-inch-square, half-inch-thick piece of cardboard with hundreds of holes drilled into it, some of them supposedly containing a prize slip. The holes were covered with a sheet of paper, and the purchaser would punch out a hole with a nail in search of a prize—usually a cheap wristwatch, a pair of sunglasses, a pocketknife, or—rarely—cash.

device, like the modern lottery, preyed on the poorest people and predictably drew its share of mob and small-time con-man purveyors. For a time, the hapless Chicagoan Jack Ruby ran a punchboard con before moving to Dallas, where he would take out JFK's assassin Lee Harvey Oswald in 1963. But Stolkin turned the scheme into an art, earning over $4 million as the "Punchboard King of America" in the 1930s to 1950s.

The third partner, Stolkin's father-in-law, Abe Koolish, was no shrinking violet himself, having been indicted in 1948 after years of warnings by the Federal Trade Commission in a mail-order insurance fraud scheme. The charge was dropped only because the indictment was "faultily drawn."* With Stolkin, Koolish also plied the old con of running "charity drives" that were actually profit-making machines wherein the managers siphoned off most of the donations for "expenses." It is a classic con that is still ongoing. Rounding out the quintet of investors were a Ryan partner, Edward "Buzz" Burke, and Sherrill Corwin, a Los Angeles–based director of the Theater Owners of America.

After negotiations, the RKO sales agreement was signed in Hughes's Beverly Hills Hotel bungalow on September 23, 1952, and within three weeks it started to fall apart. On October 16, the *Wall Street Journal* began a series of exposés regarding the new owners. RKO'S NEW OWNERS: BACKGROUND ON GROUP WHICH NOW CONTROLS BIG MOVIE MAKER: A PUNCHBOARD KING, A MAIL ORDER CHARITY MOGUL, AND A GAMBLING OILMAN blared the first headline. Describing Sid Korshak as the "catalytic agent" in the sale, the story recounted all the aforementioned details about the new owners' true professions. Over the next few days, the *Journal* and *Time* magazine continued to pound away at the new owners, citing, among other evidence, Frank Costello's recent Kefauver testimony wherein he disclosed his partnership with Ryan.

Six days after the first *Journal* piece, the new owners began resigning from the RKO board; none of them could easily afford the glare of increased public (or official) scrutiny. Sid Korshak and Arnold Grant were the last to go, on November 13. For the next few weeks, RKO was in disarray, as the syndicate defaulted on their next installment. However, by February 1953, Hughes had named a new board and taken control of the stock. In what the *Journal* called "the financial feat of the year," Hughes also kept the $1.25 million down payment proffered by the Korshak syndicate, moved to

---

*A typical Koolish scam involved advertising, in bold letters, **$25 A WEEK DISABILITY BENEFITS**. But buried in the fine print were the terms: "For eight weeks after the seventh day of confinement in your home if you are over 60 and under 80, for chicken pox, mumps, diphtheria, measles, typhoid, yellow fever and undulant fever."

Las Vegas, and continued to search for new buyers. But he had ignited a lifelong feud with Sid Korshak that would play out over the next two decades in the Las Vegas gambling mecca.[39]

Years later, Korshak disclosed the reason for the depth of the vitriol to a business partner. "Korshak told me that Hughes himself had leaked the [Stolkin] story," the associate wrote, "knowing it would kill the deal and make him over $1 million richer, the down payment that Hughes never returned to the potential buyers. Hughes had bested Korshak, a fact that the latter neither forgot nor forgave."[*,40] A former Hughes employee seemed to corroborate Korshak's intuition, saying, "Howard Hughes knew the kind of people he was dealing with; he knew their backgrounds, and he knew their associations. That was the way he operated. In the case of the Stolkin group, he took their down payment and then waited. At the right time, he leaked the story to the press."[41] Former L.A. private detective Ed Becker agrees, saying, "Howard Hughes and his entourage had about ten trained security people, and they of course would have checked out Korshak immediately because Hughes obviously killed the RKO deal."

Another possible reason for Hughes's alleged leak was that in January 1953, Sidney Korshak filed a divorce suit on behalf of Chicagoan Theodore Briskin against his wife, twenty-one-year-old starlet Joan Dixon, an actress under contract to Hughes.[42] (Typically, Korshak would get the last word when he brokered the sale of five of the Outfit's hottest Vegas hotel-casinos to Hughes on April Fools' Day, 1967. The underworld, however, kept its boys in the pits and count rooms and, over the next three years of Hughes's custodianship, relieved the recluse of over $50 million of his profits.)

RKO continued its free fall, as stockholder lawsuits began piling up. The troubled studio's featured player Dick Powell chided, "RKO's contract list is now down to three actors and one hundred and twenty-seven lawyers." Hughes finally sold RKO in 1955, netting himself a $6 million profit.

Stolkin bounced back quickly, but temporarily, hawking a thirty-two-hundred-acre Florida pastureland he dubbed Coral City.[†,43] Abe Koolish and his son had a more ignominious future, continuing their bilking of unsuspecting charities. From 1952 to 1959, the Koolishes siphoned an astounding

---

*Korshak may also have had ill feelings for Hughes because of Hughes's 1932 movie production *Scarface: The Shame of the Nation*, which portrayed Korshak's friend Al Capone as a one-dimensional beast. He and his associates come off like ignorant, remorseless, and childish criminals.
†Now known as Carol City (changed when Stolkin was threatened with a suit by the city of Cape Coral), the development today boasts a population of fifty-nine thousand.

$11 million from the Sister Elizabeth Kenny Foundation of Minneapolis, their fee for soliciting $19 million in contributions to the fund for polio-afflicted children. The Koolishes' plundering of Sister Kenny prompted a state prosecutor to later say, "The Kenny Foundation was like a subsidiary of Koolish." The scam was finally broken in 1960 by thirty-two-year-old Minnesota attorney general Walter Mondale, making headlines for a year, and catapulting Mondale into prominence. "I went into office in May unknown, untested and very young and inexperienced," Mondale later said, "and within a month I was a very well-known state figure . . . It was a major source of strength to me." Mondale went on to become a leading Democratic senator (1965–76), vice president of the United States (1977–81), and a Democratic presidential nominee (1984). The Koolishes spent seventeen months in the federal penitentiary in Terre Haute and repaid a mere $1 million to the Sister Kenny Foundation.[44]

Of course, much more would be heard from Howard Hughes as well. In the aftermath of the RKO sale, Hughes personally authorized a $205,000 loan to Vice President Richard Nixon's brother, Donald, allegedly to boost the sagging finances of Donald's restaurant (which featured the appetizing-sounding "Nixonburger") in Whittier, California. However, just days after the December 1956 "loan," Hughes's TWA airlines was granted a lucrative route to Manila, then a route to Frankfurt, and a fare increase. Within a few months more, according to the director of the Hughes Tool Company, Noah Dietrich, the IRS granted Hughes tax-exempt status for his Hughes Medical Institute, a shell organization created to foster the illusion that Hughes Aircraft was controlled by a public trust. On the first day alone that the exemption took effect, Hughes saved $1 million. Two decades later, the loan would play a huge role in the careers of both Richard Nixon and David Bazelon.[45]

With the advent of the Velie and Kefauver investigations, the Supermob was beginning to lose its cloak of invisibility, if only to a few far removed from the nation at large. The most public difficulties centered on a Supermob partner in the Ohio Franklin Investment deal. In 1952, Art Greene was found guilty of stock fraud by the Securities and Exchange Commission and sentenced to two years in prison. Considering his affiliations with notorieties such as Gioe, Zwillman, and Lansky, Art Greene, the Franklin partner of Pritzker, Bazelon, and Ziffren, got off easy.

Most of the attention to the Supermob was occurring well behind the scenes, especially in Washington, where both Congress and the FBI were receiving disturbing reports about the workings of David Bazelon's Office of Alien Property. Among the protestations arriving on Capitol Hill was one from a confidential informant who advised, "Bazelon, while with the Office of Alien Property, saw to it that concerns in which he had an interest received preferential treatment in obtaining material from sources under the control of the Office of Alien Property."[46] The first reports found their way to the House Judiciary Committee, which oversaw the OAP.

At the time, popular forty-six-year-old Kentucky Democrat Frank Chelf, who went on to serve ten successive terms, chaired the committee. Chelf initially assigned a subcommittee to look into the possibility that OAP had favored certain companies in making allotments of materials recovered from seized enemy properties. The congressional investigators chose to begin by focusing on two specific allegations: (1) whether Bazelon had obtained lucrative stocks in German banks seized by the Custodian Office, and (2) if it was a mere coincidence that as custodian he appointed a Chicago friend to appraise a seized German coal mine and that when the mine was auctioned, it was purchased by another friend of Bazelon's.

However, during the committee's investigation, highly placed confidential sources attested to a litany of disparaging allegations about the OAP custodian, including:

• Bazelon saw to it that concerns in which he had an interest received preferential treatment in obtaining property and goods under the control of the Office of Alien Property.[47]

• Bazelon was given his judgeship thanks to an inner circle of the Democratic Central Committee, which regularly met with Bazelon in "an unidentified room in the Mayflower Hotel."

• Bazelon appointed attorney friends such as Democratic Party honcho William Boyle, Harold Horowitz, and Arnold Shaw (Shapiro) to be the legal representatives of vested companies, which resulted in their obtaining lucrative fees.[48] According to the president of the Norfolk and Southern Railway, Joseph Kingsley, Boyle had paid large sums of money to Bazelon, who, to conceal it, used the name Weld in his dealings with Boyle. Kingsley added that Bazelon was "scared to death" that this information would be disclosed.[49] Shaw was a former assistant to Bazelon and was "said to have done the 'dirty work' for Bazelon."[50]

• Bazelon, according to "reliable information," had "obtained control of certain hotel interests on the West Coast, formerly in the hands of [Office of] Alien Property," and "Ziffren and Bazelon formed a partnership for the purpose of administering warehouse properties which were under the control of Alien Property."[51]

• Bazelon "shows up in San Francisco in a shady manner as aligned with a Los Angeles lawyer [Ziffren] in owning or being equal counsel for hotels in Stockton, Modesto, San Francisco, Fresno, Bakersfield, etc., *which were formerly handled by OAP after being taken over from Japanese and others.*"[52] (Author's italics.) (Note: Bazelon's benefactor Abe Pritzker was also heavily invested in San Francisco. According to a former Department of Justice Strike Force officer, Pritzker worked in partnership there with hotel and real estate tycoon Donald Werby, who the source believed was dispatched westward from Chicago by none other than Al Capone.)*

• David Bazelon's brother Gordon, also an attorney, appeared to be the recipient of special treatment when he was indicted by the IRS for income tax evasion. The committee noted that "the case was extremely good from a prosecutorial viewpoint." However, when the case was forwarded to the Department of Justice, where brother David was assistant attorney general, it simply vanished. Recall that David had previously been assistant U.S. attorney in Chicago in charge of federal tax matters. (There were also uninvestigated reports that David Bazelon's father-in-law, corporate executive M. J. Kellner, relied on David when he got into tax trouble.)[53]

The "Chelf Committee" declined to publish a report of its findings, opting instead to forward the material directly to the Justice Department for further disposition. In those days is was not uncommon for a committee to avoid writing a report on a politically sensitive investigation. Pulitzer Prize–winning journalist and racketeer specialist Clark Mollenhoff wrote of how Congress demurred when investigating labor corruption: "It is often forgotten that pitfalls were there for committee members or staff investigators who tackled the job . . . Where investigations could not be stopped, union influence was used to cripple the investigators by sharply limiting their funds or curtailing their jurisdiction . . . One of the finest investigators to tackle the union racket was out of a job for six months because he was blackballed

---

*In 1990, Werby avoided child rape charges in their entirety by pleading guilty to two misdemeanor charges of contributing to the delinquency of a minor. Werby agreed to pay a $300,000 fine and was sentenced to three years' probation. Originally, a grand jury had indicted Werby on twenty-two felony sex and drug charges stemming from his hiring of underage prostitutes and furnishing them with crack cocaine for sex. All the felony sex charges, with their potential for prison time, sex offender registration, civil commitment, etc., were quietly dropped.

by union-influenced Congressmen . . . The heroes of the 1953 to 1957 period were Republicans and Democrats, liberals and conservatives. Some had their investigations ended by political pressure; some gave up in frustration."[54]

With the buck thus passed, the responsibility to act shifted to the Department of Justice. After receiving the Chelf data, Attorney General James McGranery on August 8, 1952, instructed J. Edgar Hoover to look into the Bazelon affair, but drastically limited its scope to just the Franklin Hotel allegations—understandable since McGranery was Bazelon's boss and friend at the department.[55] The FBI thus opened a new subject header: "Judge David L. Bazelon; Misconduct in Office." Their investigation proceeded quietly for the next five years and, as noted in the previous chapter, corroborated the accuracy of the Goe/White research, labeling the Bazelon-Ziffren dealings in Rohm Haas and other OAP transactions "suspicious." But since their initial charge was to conduct a narrow investigation of just the Franklin deal in Ohio, they conservatively refused to expand the probe. The FBI's liaison to the Department of Justice, Courtney Evans, wrote, "We will take no action in this matter in the absence of a request from the Attorney General [Herbert Brownell]."[56] Brownell and his Justice Department, however, declined to pursue the evidence against a sitting federal judge (Bazelon) and the man who had, by the report's closing, become the Democratic National Committee chairman from California (Ziffren). Interestingly, after an exhaustive search by National Archives staff, all Justice Department records on the Bazelon investigation have turned up missing.[57]

David Bazelon successfully weathered the 1952 House Judiciary probe, the protracted five-year investigations by the FBI (which yielded a 561-page report), the LAPD investigations, and a two-decade, if below-the-radar, investigation by reporters Robert Goe and Art White. Bazelon's future accomplishments as a jurist were groundbreaking, transforming the U.S. Court of Appeals (where he mentored clerks such as Alan Dershowitz) into the second most powerful judicial jurisdiction after the Supreme Court. Among his many praised opinions: he extended the rights of the accused and the breadth of the insanity defense to include those with inborn mental defects; in 1973, as head of the nine-judge appellate panel ruling in the Watergate case, he ruled that President Nixon had to hand over the infamous White House tapes; and he ruled that patients confined to public mental institutions were entitled to treatment, as opposed to being merely warehoused.

In 1962, Bazelon would briefly be considered for a Supreme Court post by the Kennedy administration, which was considering candidates to replace the retiring Judge Felix Frankfurter.[58] However, for reasons unknown, the

Judge Bazelon (far right) and fellow members of Big Brothers of America meet
President Kennedy, April 4, 1961 (Corbis/Bettmann)

Bazelon nomination was never proffered,* and another Chicagoan, Arthur
J. Goldberg, got the nod. Goldberg was not just another friend of Abe
Pritzker's, having been a partner in his law firm, but more interestingly, an
investor with Paul Ziffren and Benjamin Cohen in the San Diego Hotel.

In February 1970, according to the FBI, Bazelon stayed at the mob-
frequented La Costa Resort, his bill comped by the hotel. David Bazelon
passed away in February 1993, whereupon the D.C.-based Mental Health
Law Project changed its name to The Bazelon Center for Mental Health.[59]

Meanwhile, undeterred journalists Lester Velie, Robert Goe, and Art White
continued the thankless job of poring over real estate records and business filings, stored in clerks' offices and corporate records warehouses around the
country. They were energized by the realization that Paul Ziffren was becoming

---

*According to the JFK Library, it would be likely that Robert Kennedy had some input
into the decision not to proceed with the Bazelon appointment. Regretfully, the Kennedy
family continues to withhold forty boxes of RFK's files, including voluminous "name
files" that might provide the answer.

a major political force in California and in the nation. In truth, his ascension was nothing short of meteoric.

Ziffren's early strength came from his ability to raise money for Democratic candidates. When he solicited funds for Helen Gahagan Douglas in her senatorial campaign against Richard Nixon, Ziffren's methods were mysterious, but few Democrats cared. When a naïve young Colorado businessman was recruited by Ziffren to be Douglas's campaign finance chairman, the Coloradan knew something was wrong. "Paul was really the finance chairman," the businessman candidly admitted to Lester Velie. "I was the front. When I tried to determine the sources Paul was tapping, I got nowhere. He wasn't going to let me know the sources." The young man recalled how he could hardly pry Ziffren away from his long-distance phone calls to Chicago. He never learned who was on the other end.[60]

In 1953, Ziffren had been elected the Democratic national committeeman for California, a position that saw him hailed for "reinventing" the California Democratic Party, which captured both houses of the state government for the first time in seventy-five years. National Democratic Chairman Paul Butler said, "Paul Ziffren has been the greatest single force and most important individual Democrat in the resurgence of the Democratic Party in California."[61] That same year, Bautzer-Korshak pal Pat Brown became attorney general of California, and Lester Ziffren, Paul's brother, became Brown's assistant attorney general for the Southern California Region, where he would serve for seven years.

If anyone doubted that the Supermob was now untouchable, these developments should have proved dispositive. In fact, the goings-on were still far from public scrutiny. However, the trio of investigators remained undaunted and labored to stop what they perceived as a legitimizing of shady operators and mob-tainted money in California. Often their discoveries were forwarded to the FBI and absorbed into its investigation of the Supermob. The problem for the tireless reporters was getting their work into print. A veteran Chicago newsman who followed Korshak's career recently recalled two instances when he was ordered by a senior editor to remove Korshak's name from unfavorable articles. And articles about Korshak specifically were never even green-lighted. "You couldn't get a story about him in the paper," the *Chicago Tribune* scribe said. "How many battles do you have to lose before you get the message? There was something special about Korshak."

With these investigations ongoing, sources kept a steady stream of Korshak intelligence flowing into various agencies:

• In July 1951, an informant reported that Korshak was making an effort to fix the case of an arsonist.

• Virgil Peterson of the Chicago Crime Commission noted that just after Christmas, 1954, Jake Arvey flew to New Orleans to meet Frank Costello's slot machine and jukebox partner, "Dandy" Phil Kastel, at Kastel's palatial Louisiana estate. In noting "unimpeachable sources," Peterson reported that Arvey's travel arrangements were made by Korshak, who drove Costello to the house.[62]

• LAPD intel sources in 1954 reported that, even on the West Coast, Korshak was "currently in touch with Capone Syndicate members."

• Other sources reported that Korshak was "sponsoring" First Ward alderman John D'Arco's Anco Insurance Company, a partnership of D'Arco and Buddy Jacobson (an aide to Korshak mentor Jake Guzik). Anco had been set up as a means for funneling graft money to First Ward secretary Pat Marcy, and from there to the Outfit.*

By 1954, the yeomanlike work of Goe, White, and Velie was gaining more adherents. In addition to the Judiciary Committee's and FBI's plumbing of the Bazelon allegations, the LAPD opened its investigation of the Hayward Hotel.[63] The directors of the LAPD intel division also began corresponding with the Chicago Crime Commission regarding the Hotel Hayward ownership.[64] LAPD intel chief James Hamilton also sought Peterson's advice regarding Bazelon, Ziffren, and Warehouse Properties.[65] Suddenly, Los Angeles authorities were interested in all things Chicago. LAPD intel chief Hamilton wrote Peterson with a query about Abe Pritzker after he was prompted by an intel division report that noted suspicious movements by Pritzker in Los Angeles:

Abe Pritzker, a Chicago attorney with offices at 134 N. La Salle Street, which is the same address as that of Sidney Korshak's office, has been closely connected with members of the Capone syndicate, Tony Accardo, and other underworld characters. It is believed by the undersigned that Pritzker may be active locally, as a front for eastern hoodlum money to be invested in the Los Angeles area. Pritzker was at the office of attorney

*Typically, if a Chicago businessman wanted patronage contracts or help with striking unions, he was advised to buy insurance policies from Anco, and—presto!—their problems would go away.

Once the FBI had installed bugs in the First Ward offices, they listened as Marcy and D'Arco received their marching orders from the Outfit bosses, especially Humphreys and Sam Giancana, who often strategized over which judges and police officials were corruptible. The Bureau also noted D'Arco meeting with the hoods at Postl's Health Club at 188 W. Randolph. (See especially Roemer, *Man Against the Mob*, chs. 13, 22.)

Louis Hiller, 6399 Wilshire Blvd., LA; was there discussing the investment money without the definite plan being indicated. Those present at the meeting included Hiller, Pritzker, and Louis Tom Dragna [L.A. Mafia underboss, brother of "the Al Capone of Los Angeles," Jack Dragna]. Hiller indicated that he had a million dollars available for investments.[66]

Meanwhile, the business aspirations of the Pritzker legal clan began to explode. In 1957, they created the Hyatt chain of hotels when Jay Pritzker bought a small motel near the Los Angeles airport from Hyatt von Dehn, a real estate developer. Pritzker's intuition was that business executives craved luxury hotels near major airports—and time would prove him correct. The seminal purchase was initiated in a coffee shop named Fat Eddie's outside LAX, where Jay scribbled down his $2.2 million purchase price on a napkin.

The Pritzkers soon developed a reputation for their canny business modus operandi, being fast to move into a deal and quick to get out if they had to minimize a loss. They also became the avatars of a business technique called asset management, wherein the backer does not directly manage the property and the managers do not directly fund the projects. Since it is so expensive to build hotels and takes three to five years to see profits, the Pritzker family and the management teams of the Hyatt hotels only invest $400,000 to $800,000 per hotel and then get a backer like Prudential Insurance or the Ford Motor Company, companies with "staying power" to foot the several-million-dollar bill to actually build the hotel. Five decades later, the Hyatt chain (with over seventy-four hotels in twenty-seven countries), and other Pritzker holding companies, are worth anywhere between $5 billion and $7 billion, with annual revenues of $1.3 billion. The Pritzkers also became one of the country's largest hospital operators, acquiring six of their own and operating fifteen more under lease and contract management.[67] (See appendix B for more examples of Pritzker business interests.)

Profits, however, were not the only constants in the Pritzker saga. Rumors flew that, as with their questionable real estate partnerships in the forties, the Pritzkers' new Hyatt endeavor was similarly tainted. One IRS informant who was quoted as saying that "the Pritzker family of Chicago through their Hyatt Corp. initially received their backing from organized crime" was later identified as F. Eugene Poe, the late president of a bank in Perrine, Florida, and vice president of the offshore tax haven where the Pritzkers hid their wealth known as Castle Bank, about which more will be seen.

Michael Corbitt, who was recruited as a teenager into the operation of Outfit slot boss Pete Altieri, got a glimpse of what lay beyond the Hyatt façade. After he was promoted into the world of mysterious Chicago slot king Hy Larner, who trafficked in drugs, guns, and gambling machines in far-flung locales such as Spain, Japan, Iran, and throughout Central America, Corbitt kept running into the name Hyatt. As he later wrote in his book, *Double Deal*, "Whenever possible, Hy wanted us to put his guests up at a Hyatt . . . It was common knowledge that most of the Pritzkers' financial backing at that time came from the Teamsters, meaning pension fund manager Allen Dorfman."[68] Corbitt, who ran a Chicago security company as his "day job," elaborated about the Hyatt connection shortly before his death in 2004:

"My first job was the construction of the Hyatt at 151 East Wacker. After the Hyatt was built, I became the security director for the Hyatt chain in Chicago. They were a big Chicago chain—they weren't around the world like the way they are now. I had very close ties to the Pritzker family only through my Outfit connections. Our connections to the Hyatts all over the country were solid. At the time, we were dealing directly with Abe Pritzker. We could get in places that were sold-out; even if they were sold-out, we'd get the presidential suite. I know for a fact that we never got a bill. There is no way Larner wasn't with the Pritzker family."[69]

Like James Hamilton, Los Angeles district attorney Thomas C. Lynch wrote to the CCC's Virgil Peterson for information on Paul Ziffren and Jake Arvey.[70] That same year, it had been disclosed that Ziffren was the subject of a federal probe into the activities of Enterprise Construction and its subsidiary, United Credit Corp., of which Ziffren was VP and tax attorney. A high government source reported that Enterprise, which had made over $10 million in loans to home buyers, would be charged with misuse of FHA mortgage funds, including kickbacks from loan proceeds, failure to require down payments, exorbitant prices, etc. The source noted that the statute of limitations might inhibit prosecutions for crimes that may have been perpetrated in the late 1940s. Ziffren was reported to have financed United Credit with a fund set up for his wife, Muriel.[71] One U.S. senator referred to Enterprise/United as "the top racketeering outfit in the fleecing of home owners in the Los Angeles area."[72]

When an FHA officer investigating so-called suede-shoe artists visited Enterprise and attempted to warn them that they were on the verge of getting into a legal quagmire, he was quickly advised as to exactly who was calling the shots.

"I went to United Credit to induce them to be more careful in choosing their contractors," said FHA officer William Murray Jr. "Morrie Siegel, a vice president of Enterprise, tried to impress me by mentioning names of influential people he knew. He intimated he could make things uncomfortable for me. There was a signed picture of President Truman on the wall. I couldn't see to whom it was autographed, but Siegel and the others of the company there kept looking at it, as if to leave me draw the conclusion how important they were."

If the show-and-tell failed to impress, what happened next certainly did, when Murray was reassigned and demoted. "Later I heard that United Credit was responsible for my being banished to the salt mines of Long Beach [California] because I had gotten in the company's hair," he told a Senate committee investigating FHA fraud.[73] Eventually, Enterprise saw its California contracting license revoked and was forced out of business.

Investigators' interest in Ziffren heightened when they noticed the removal of Ziffren's name from the Warehouse Properties partnership papers in exchange for that of his best friend, David Bazelon, the man who was in charge of selling it for the government eight years earlier (see chapter 5). There is no public record that Ziffren received even one penny for his interest. The new partnership papers state candidly that the purpose of the partnership is "for convenience, in connection with the contemplated sale to the City of Los Angeles."[74] The notary on the papers of incorporation was Leo Ziffren, Paul's brother. As previously noted, the Warehouse property sale to the city eventually netted Bazelon a $100,000 windfall.

As the Supermob prospered, investigators noticed another curious trend under way in 1954: Sidney Korshak and Frank Sinatra, who were by now good friends, began directing their pals to a recently opened bank, guaranteed to be friendly to the Supermob. In no time, studio moguls and A-list celebrities closed accounts in their former institutions and opened them with the City National Bank of Beverly Hills, founded on January 1, 1954, by none other than Al Hart with the intent of servicing the real estate and entertainment industries.[75] Initial capitalization for the bank was provided, according to Dunn & Bradstreet, by Chicago's American National Bank, the same institution that provided additional financing for the likes of Arthur Greene and the Hilton chain. According to the IRS, Sidney Korshak held stock in American National, and, completing the circle of insiders, the American National officer who facilitated the capitalization was William J. Friedman, the same man who was Ziffren's partner at Gottlieb, and who became the director of the Rohm Haas enterprise that was seized by David Bazelon's OAP.

One of Hart's partners in the new venture was Samuel W. Banowit, who was in turn partners with both Alex Greenberg in the Spring-Arcade Building,

A young Francis Albert Sinatra (Library of Congress)

and with David Bright, associate of Gerry Restituto, the Mafia boss of San Joaquin Valley, with whom he invested in the three-hundred-thousand-acre Bright-Holland Ranch in Lassen County, California.

Hilton's Arnold Kirkeby was also a director of the bank, and Sidney Korshak a major stockholder.[76] Paul Ziffren's son Ken, himself a future L.A. power attorney, would eventually join the bank's board of directors as well.

An LAPD memo of August 3, 1958, lists City National Bank among a dozen businesses believed to be fronting for and/or doing business with the mob. Robert Goe's sources stated that the bank had "a number of directors who appear to be nominees or 'front men' for such individuals as Joseph Fusco."[77] However, given the extreme laxity of law enforcement in L.A., not to mention Hart's great friends in the attorney general's office, the bank was never adequately investigated, and it would become the largest independent bank in Los Angeles, with $3 billion in capitalization and a total of fifty-four offices throughout California.[78]

Like so many other mysterious Chicagoans now doing business in L.A., Al Hart was a mystery to some in law enforcement, but not all. David Nissen, former chief of the L.A. division of the U.S. attorney's office, recently said, "Al Hart was a big Democratic fund-raiser. I always thought he was with the mob people, but I never had any actual basis for that."[79] Nissen was likely unaware of the FBI's file on Hart, which noted his partnership with Bugsy Siegel, and numerous convictions with the Chicago mob. But others had no doubt about Hart's leanings. "Hart was Korshak's banker and he was the banker for the Democratic Party in California and later the Republican Party—whichever side they decided to support," said veteran Chicago private investigator Jack Clarke recently. "Hart was the major banker and a major player in politics, and he was well-known among the organized crime guys because when they were investigated, they would put money in his bank. They knew he wouldn't allow the IRS inside the front door of the bank, and he wouldn't turn over his records. Hart and Korshak were really tight. All the friends of Korshak who wanted to protect their money but to still have it close at hand put all their money there."[80]

Pulitzer Prize–winning journalist Wendell Rawls, who spent years investigating corruption in the Southern California entertainment community, heard the same thing. "You could deposit any amount in Hart's bank without letting the IRS know," said Rawls. Hart's unusual business practices were well-known in the state attorney general's office in Sacramento. "We had a joke that City National Bank was the closest thing to a Swiss bank in the United States," said the AG's investigator Connie Carlson. "Al would handle any transaction that you needed handled discreetly."[81] A 1970 FBI memo summarized, "Cleaning up [mob] money by a bank is an old trick, but an effective one and the City National Bank is as uncooperative [with IRS] as the bank of Las Vegas and a known front for the mob in Los Angeles."[82]

When he was tipped to Hart's possible connection to Meyer Lansky, L.A. district attorney crime investigator James Grodin did a background check and learned a fraction of the true story. "I went to the DA's office and ran a criminal history on Hart," Grodin remembered. "I learned that he went to prison in the thirties for some kind of land fraud in San Bernardino." Further proof of Hart's dubious associations comes from former L.A. private detective Ed Becker. When he needed a $10,000 loan, Becker was advised by Chicago's Johnny Rosselli to "go see Al." Becker said that Hart came through, despite being unable to read the business proposal. "He was illiterate," said Becker.[83]

With his client-friendly banking practices, Hart became the banker to the stars, often seen socializing with them. "Al Hart was a great friend of everybody," said acclaimed television comedy producer George Schlatter recently. "I managed Ciro's, and when we were running short, Al Hart would delay payment of the bill for liquor—which was not totally legal, but very friendly."[84] Helping his friends with investments was just part of what made Hart a good friend. He was said to have had a $250,000 investment in the Broadway musical *My Fair Lady*, among others, and that he often tipped his friends and bank clients to similar opportunities. Hart's celebrity clients were, and are, countless, from Frank Sinatra on down. Sinatra's (and later JFK's) girlfriend Judy Campbell recalled a 1959 Hawaiian vacation with Frank, Peter and Pat Kennedy Lawford, and Al Hart, whom she described as a "koala bear," with his "paunch and saddlebags" protruding from an unfashionable pair of swim trunks.[85] Jim Grodin remembered seeing Hart around town and had a vivid recollection of his persona: "Hart was a member at Hillcrest, but he was a real 'dee's, dem's, and doe's' guy—a gangster type, so he didn't fit in. He was always using foul language, even in front of women. But the members tolerated him because he gave them no-interest loans from his bank."

Despite the lack of deference to the distaff side, Hart had a reputation as a player. "Al Hart had many mistresses," said Peter Lawford's longtime manager Milt Ebbins. "And he made them a lot of money in investments."[86] Sid Korshak's daughter-in-law Virginia Korshak is more blunt, saying that Hart was a serial womanizer: "Al Hart was a little dog. He was a little weasel."[87] MCA starlet Selene Walters, whose great looks made her one of Hollywood's most in-demand dates, knew Hart and went on one date with him.* "Hart took out very young starlets while he was married," said Walters. "I didn't like him—he was crude and sinister. I was wary and afraid of him. His bank was the only one that terminated my account because he said it wasn't large enough. That hurt me very much because I had gone out with him."[88]

Among those most frequently linked to Hart were actresses Martha Hyer and Pier Angeli. According to Hart's FBI file, one of his women reported that her home had been burglarized of $79,000 in furs, jewelry, and paintings on the evening of October 31, 1959. It was being widely reported that Hart, who admitted to the LAPD that he had a key to the house, had engineered the break-in after the affair fizzled. He allegedly told one friend, "[Name deleted] was no damn good, and if he [Hart] went to her house and took his things back, it would not be burglary since, after all, he had given them to her in the first place."[89] The FBI was not allowed to pursue the case because there was no evidence of an interstate crime, and the Beverly Hills police typically treated Hart with the same preferential treatment afforded celebrities.

With the exception of Charlie Gioe, who was gunned down on a Chicago street in August, 1954 was notable for Supermob close escapes. The next year was not so fortuitous. Among those whose luck ran out in 1955 was Willie Bioff, who had assumed a false identity after his Hollywood-extortion prison term and lived for a decade in Phoenix, where he befriended and advised Senator Barry Goldwater, who only knew him as William Nelson. In 1955, Bioff had the temerity (or lunacy) to take a job under the name of Nelson as an entertainment consultant for Las Vegas' new

---

*Among Walters's many suitors were George Raft, Howard Hughes, Frank Sinatra, Gary Cooper, and Greg Bautzer.

Riviera Hotel and Casino, built with $10 million in Outfit money, behind a front group of Miami investors. Interestingly, the Riviera land was leased from an L.A. consortium that included Greg Bautzer's law partner Harvey Silbert, who was also Frank Sinatra's personal attorney, and a close Korshak friend. When the Chicago Outfit ID'd Bioff, his days were numbered. On November 4, 1955, as Bioff left his Phoenix home's front door and entered his pickup truck parked in the driveway, he had no idea that the Chicagoans were onto the man who'd testified against them. If he had had that knowledge, he would never have cranked the ignition that blew him into a hundred pieces.

A month later, on December 8, 1955, sixty-five-year-old Alex Louis Greenberg, the man who could link so many California up-and-comers to questionable Chicago investment money, was killed gangland-style as he and his wife, Pearl, were leaving Chicago's Glass Dome Hickory Pit Restaurant on the South Side's Union Avenue. As the couple walked to their parked car, two gunmen emerged from the shadows and dropped Greenberg with four .38-caliber bullets before calmly walking away; Paul Zifrren's real estate partner had been hit in the forehead, chest, left arm, and groin. Just months earlier, Greenberg had orchestrated the merger of Wisconsin's Fox Head Brewing Company, which was heavily invested in by Murray Humphreys and Joe Batters Accardo, and Fox Deluxe Beer Sales of Chicago. The new company served as a legit front and money-laundering sieve for the Chicago Outfit.[90] At Greenberg's funeral, one of Frank Nitti's cousins stayed on to make sure the body was properly disposed of. He reported back to his family, "Now he's the richest son of a bitch in hell."[91] In the coming weeks, police rousted over seventy-one hoods in their attempt to break the case. They never did.

The *Chicago Tribune*'s obituary concisely described Greenberg's legacy, although it has long since been forgotten: "Under his guidance, it is understood, the mob moved into ownerships of hotels, restaurants, laundries, cleaning establishments, and bought stock in banks, major industries, and entertainment enterprises."[92]

> *Alex Louis Greenberg handled all investments and financial matters of every type for and on behalf of Frank Nitti.*
> —NITTI'S WIDOW, ANNETTE, IN HER PROBATE LAWSUIT AGAINST THE
> GREENBERG ESTATE (1957)

With so many diverse holdings, Greenberg's probate took over five years to sort out. However, as expected, the final accounting stated that the estate included $964,252 in stock in the Seneca, over $1 million in liquid assets, dozens of real estate parcels, and thousands of shares in a variety of blue-chip stocks. It came as no surprise to those familiar with the financial connection between the mob and the Supermob that the family of Frank Nitti, Al Capone's successor, made claims against the estate. The *Chicago Daily News* wrote, "The widow of Frank 'the Enforcer' Nitti charged that Greenberg failed to repay more than $2 million entrusted to him by Nitti *for investments*." (Author's italics.) The probate also noted that Paul Ziffren owed Greenberg's estate $19,939.50.[93] Annette Nitti finally agreed to a $35,000 settlement in 1960.

While Greenberg's murder hogged the Chicago headlines, Sidney Korshak continued to fight his battles in private. In 1955, he narrowly escaped prosecution for possible violation of the Labor Management Relations Act of 1947. He and Murray Humphreys had been implicated in their dealings with Goldblatt Brothers, accused of using strong-arm tactics to prevent Goldblatt employees from unionizing.[94] The Bureau learned that Pritzker was Goldblatt's attorney of record, but Pritzker would defer to Humphreys and Korshak whenever a stalemate occurred.[95] Federal agents also noted that one union organizer at Goldblatt's had been murdered in 1933.

Korshak was first put on Goldblatt's retainer in 1950 for $6,000 a year, increased to $10,000 by 1954. According to the FBI, the IRS had carefully been watching Korshak's finances for at least four years, but found nothing out of order. When interviewed by Bureau agents, Korshak admitted that he had known Humphreys since about 1929.[96] Indeed, Korshak had been seen for years meeting with Humphreys at Fritzel's Restaurant. Prosecution of Korshak was ultimately (and typically) declined by the Department of Justice.

Like the reporters whose editors blanched at the prospect of a Supermob exposé, FBI agents knew all along that their superiors did not share their interest in men like Korshak. One memo generated by the L.A. Field Office stated the obvious: "Due to his position as a prominent attorney, and because of the Bureau's previous instructions that any Korshak investigation be handled in a circumspect manner, [the L.A. office] does not desire to write a report or make Korshak the subject of an active investigation under the Criminal Intelligence Program."[97]

Sidney Korshak was not alone in his feeling of legal invulnerability. The same FBI kid-glove approach applied to Ziffren, despite what the LAPD was telling them. "He is considered by officials in the Los Angeles Police Department as a vociferous enemy of law enforcement," an FBI memo noted, "and has been described by LA Chief of Police William H. Parker as a 'force of evil.' "[98] But Paul Ziffren had little to fear from the FBI, Chief Parker, Hamilton, or the rest—he simply informed his brother, the assistant attorney general, and his pal the attorney general, that he was upset. On May 22, 1956, Ziffren wrote a letter to his brother's boss, Attorney General Pat Brown, saying, "I want to congratulate you upon your decision to investigate law enforcement in Los Angeles . . . I have been increasingly alarmed by the activities of the Chief of Police of the city of Los Angeles, with particular reference to the mysterious and highly secret intelligence division operated under his direction."[99] However, on this occasion, Ziffren's impressive connections failed him. Brown, who now seemed to want to distance himself from the Ziffren taint, responded vehemently, calling his blast "unfortunate . . . unjudicious . . . and unwelcome." It was to be merely the first salvo in Brown's attempt to discard any negative baggage that might forestall his quest for higher office.

The national political stage was no less bothersome for Ziffren as Estes Kefauver, who was attempting to parlay his crime-probe celebrity into a presidential candidacy, began blasting Ziffren from the stump—something he had avoided in his vaunted investigation. In a speech given in San Diego on May 30, 1956, Kefauver singled out Ziffren in a stinging condemnation of "bossism" in California. Noting Ziffren's backing of his Democratic opponent, Adlai Stevenson, Kefauver declared that if Stevenson won, Ziffren and his associates would become "the czars of California democracy." Kefauver referred to Ziffren as "Arvey's protégé here."[100] A *Chicago Tribune* columnist wondered, "How much of a piece of Stevenson does [Arvey] own, and, by extension, how much of a piece of the candidate does Korshak own? And, if they have a piece, how much of that piece can the mob call theirs?"[101]

CHAPTER 7

Scenes from Hollywood, Part One

SID KORSHAK'S LIFE IN Beverly Hills was developing into a contradictory combination of sphinxlike mysteriousness and high-profile socializing with the world's most famous celebrities.

As Sid's gatekeeper to the underworld, Chicago's Curly Humphreys decreed that no one besides himself be allowed to communicate directly with the gang's golden boy. Korshak was so valuable that he had to stay insulated from gangsters. Soon, the Chicago FBI would succeed in wiretapping the Outfit's meeting places and discover that when Korshak communicated with Humphreys by phone, the two spoke in code, Korshak referring to his superior as "Mr. Lincoln."

One of Korshak's closest Hollywood pals described how Korshak's wife, Bernice, obtained a glimpse of Sidney's furtiveness early on. After returning from the honeymoon, Mrs. Korshak read from a list of coded messages that awaited her new husband.

"George Washington called, everything is status quo. Thomas Jefferson called, urgent, please call ASAP. Abraham Lincoln must speak with you, important. Theodore Roosevelt called three times, must connect with you before Monday."

"Your friends sure have a strange sense of humor," said Bernice. "Who are they?"

"Exactly who they said they were" was Sidney's terse response. "Any other questions?"

According to producer Bob Evans, who was told the anecdote by Bernice, "Fifty years later, Bernice has never asked another question."[1]

For his part, Korshak remained as low-key, blended-with-the-woodwork as possible. Among those few who traveled with him, Korshak's avoidance of cameras was notorious, as Dominic Dunne had discovered.

Given that Los Angeles was, and is, an "industry town" with the Supermob pulling many of its strings via MCA, Al Hart's bank, and the cadre's links to so many swank hotels and properties, Sidney Korshak and associates now counted the country's top celebrities among their closest friends, among them Cyd Charisse and Tony Martin, the Kirk Douglases, Dinah Shore, David Janssen (Sidney was the best man at Janssen's 1975 marriage to Dani Greco, who called Korshak Janssen's "surrogate father"), Jack Benny, John Gavin, Vincente Minnelli, Dean Martin, John Ireland, Donna Reed (and husband Tony Owen), George Montgomery, Warren Beatty, Korshak mistresses Rhonda Fleming, Stella Stevens, and Jill St. John, and James Bond producer Albert "Cubby" Broccoli. Hollywood gossip columnist Joyce Haber wrote, "Sidney Korshak is probably the most important man socially out here."

Near the top of Sidney Korshak's list of chums was the skinny Italian crooner from Hoboken, New Jersey, Frank Sinatra. By the 1950s, Frank and Sid were already fast friends. Although the details of their initial meeting are unknown, they shared so many friends and commonalities—Giancana, Accardo, Humphreys, Wasserman (Frank's agent), the Chez Paree, and Las Vegas—that the two likely knew each other since the earliest times. Interestingly, although Sinatra projected the tough-guy "Chairman of the Board" persona, by all appearances one of the few men he deferred to was Sid Korshak. "Frank was definitely subservient to Sid," said one friend of both who asked not to be named. "They would say Sid was the only one even Frank Sinatra knew not to fool with," recalled screenwriter Tom Mankiewicz.[2] George Jacobs, Sinatra's valet from 1953 to 1968, saw an almost brotherly bond between the two. "Sidney and Frank were good friends," Jacobs said recently. "They were very dear friends. They used to hang out at La Costa [Country Club] because there was a lot of money from 'the boys' there."[3] Early Korshak law partner Edward King told an acquaintance that he knew for a fact that Korshak interceded directly with Harry Cohn to land Sinatra the role that saved his career, some say his life, in 1953's *From Here to Eternity*.[4]

Legendary television comedy producer George Schlatter remembered the informality of the relationship. "Frank used to call Bee [Korshak], Dinah [Shore], and his wife 'lady broads,'" said Schlatter, "which was the best of all worlds. You can't say that today."[5] One friend of both men, who asked for anonymity, spoke at length about the relationship:

Sidney would talk about how Frank and his father's friends from the firehouse in Hoboken would sit around in the living room, tossing firecrackers at one another and roaring with laughter. Sidney also talked about Frank's mother, Dolly, and how she dominated the world's greatest lover's life. And the only peace the great man would ever have was during that time of the year when she'd go to her cottage at [Al Hart's] Del Mar. Sid used to say that when Dolly died in 1977, Frank was finally on his own.

When Sidney and Bee visited Frank and Barbara [Marx Sinatra] for the evening, Sidney would insist on going upstairs and watching his favorite TV program, which was *Kojak*. Sidney would go to watch *Kojak* while Frank was making spaghetti. I guess he was rather annoyed and offended that Sidney had left the table.[6]

Of course, the parties at Sinatra's were not immune from Korshak's demand for privacy. One exceptional faux pas was committed when the press was given a list of guests at a Sinatra birthday bash, a release that inadvertently included Korshak's name, which was supposed to have been redacted; according to one reveler, Korshak made his irritation known to Frank.

It was inevitable that a volatile performer like Sinatra would occasionally seek out Korshak's professional expertise, and his periodic wise counsel only strengthened their bond. Irv Kupcinet, who named Sinatra as one of Korshak's closest friends besides Wasserman and Ziffren, saw evidence of the tutelage. "I know Frank leaned on him a lot for political and legal advice," Kup said in 1997.[7]

One of the earliest known examples of this occurred when Sinatra was compelled to testify before a grand jury in 1955. It seemed that on November 4, 1954, Sinatra had driven a blind-with-jealousy Joe DiMaggio to Marilyn Monroe's place, where the ex–Yankee slugger had hoped to affect their pending divorce by catching Monroe in a sapphic assignation. When the duo and their two detectives forced their way into a neighbor's apartment by mistake, the incident became known as the Wrong Door Raid. Before long, Sinatra's personal thugs had beaten one of the detectives for leaking the story to the press. And Florence Kotz, the unaware neighbor, wanted her shattered door replaced.

The day after Sinatra was subpoenaed to testify before a March 1955 grand jury looking into the affair, the singer abandoned his legal team of record and called the Fixer, Sidney Korshak, who coached him for the appearance. Sinatra escaped indictment and started dating Monroe himself. He settled with Florence Kotz out of court.[8]

Korshak's rescue of Sinatra was just one of countless such interventions for which Korshak would become famous among the "in crowd." It seems that his snatching of Martin and Lewis from the mob's clutches in the forties was just the beginning of his Tinseltown altruism. Anecdotes abound describing Korshak's quick fixing of a problem for a celebrity or his or her child, especially when one of them fell behind with their bookie debts or crossed the legal line with powers that be. In 1958, when Kupcinet got pinched in L.A. for drunk driving, Korshak came to his rescue, referring him to his nephew, attorney Maynard Davis, who represented Kup in court as Uncle Sidney sat through the entire trial as a spectator—one of the few times he actually appeared in a courtroom. Although the judge intoned, "There's been an attempt to fix this case . . . cases cannot be fixed in L.A. Being from Chicago, the defendant may not be aware of this. But this is not Chicago!" Kup was acquitted.[9]

One of the most often cited celebs for whom Korshak played protector was a tough-guy actor from New York's Hell's Kitchen, George Raft (born Rollo). After a stint as a driver for bootlegging kingpin Owney Madden, Raft came to Hollywood, where gangster chic held sway, and quickly found film work portraying the stereotypical hood. His depictions were nothing if not authentic, benefiting from his friendship with the likes of Bugsy Siegel, who lived with Raft when Siegel first came out West to run the Chicago Outfit's race wire. By the 1950s, Raft was fronting a Cuban casino, the New Capri, for Meyer Lansky and New York mafioso Charlie "the Blade" Tourine. In 1965, Raft was convicted of tax evasion, but a benevolent judge fined him $2,500 instead of ordering a prison term.[10] According to crime expert Hank Messick, "Raft became involved in some complicated crime deals that ultimately led to the murder of syndicate accountant Benjamin Berkowitz."[11] (In 1967, Raft was barred from England as an undesirable after fronting for a large casino in London.)[12]

Although he occasionally acted in bona fide hits like *Scarface*, *Ocean's Eleven*, and *Some Like It Hot*, Raft was notorious for making horrendous career choices, among them turning down lead roles in such "bad scripts" as *High Sierra* (1941), *The Maltese Falcon* (1941), *Casablanca* (1942), and *Double Indemnity* (1944). No doubt due to his friendship with occasional Korshak client Bugsy Siegel, Raft became friends with Korshak and thereafter fell under Korshak's protective umbrella.

"George spent many Sundays at Korshak's, and Sidney often helped him out financially," said Raft biographer Dr. Lewis Yablonsky.[13] Attorney friend Leo Geffner recalled a later period when Raft seemed to live at the Korshaks' home. "George had no money so he became Sidney's gofer," said Geffner. "He would answer the phone or just sit around like one of the family."[14] Fellow Korshak pal Kirk Douglas recalled one such Sunday at Chez Korshak. "After a barbecue at Sidney Korshak's house one day, I walked into

Korshak pals Bugsy
Siegel and George
Raft (Library of
Congress)

Irv Kupcinet interviews George Raft (Library of
Congress, *Look* Magazine Collection)

the kitchen and was astonished to find George Raft doing the dishes," Douglas wrote in his autobiography. "I backed out and mentioned this to Sidney. He said, 'Oh, George likes to do that.'"[15] When Yablonsky's authorized biography of Raft was published in 1974, Korshak was among only two people cited for special thanks by Raft. Calling him a "special friend," Yablonsky wrote, "Sidney Korshak has generously helped George through many difficult periods in recent years; without his compassionate support and wise counsel this book might never have been completed."[16]

Movie producer Fred Sidewater also took note of Korshak's charity toward Raft. "Sidney actually gave George a job as a messenger because his career was gone," Sidewater remembered in 2003.[17] When there was talk of a potential Raft biopic, auditioning actors, such as Bob Evans, were submitted to Korshak for his approval.[18] On the occasion of Raft's death in 1980, Korshak delivered the eulogy, saying, "He came from poor beginnings, but he never turned his back on anyone." Graciously calling Raft an "industry giant," Korshak added that Raft was actually a modest man who considered himself "such a lousy actor he never saw any of his pictures."[19]

Among other examples of "Sidney to the rescue":

• Lounge singer and girlfriend of Johnny Rosselli, Betsy Duncan Hammes, recently recalled Korshak's help for an ill-planned singing engagement: "I'd never been to Hawaii, so I took this awful job there, but I had to book my own room. When I got there, every place was sold out, so I was stranded. I called Sid at the Polo Lounge and he called over and got me a room at the Surfrider, one of the best places in Honolulu at the time. Then my friend Rita May, of the May Co., who came with me, was unable to cash her checks there until Sid made another call and set them straight. Sid helped out friends of friends too. I know this guy in Chicago who got caught writing bad checks. He was part of the Rosenwald family [Sears Roebuck Inc.]. I called Sid, who knew the family well, and he made a call and took care of it."[20]

• Jan Amory, former wife of Korshak client/partner Del Coleman (Seeburg Inc.), recalled a weekend she spent with a movie producer who began acting "weird" and started to frighten her. Amory called Korshak at one in the morning. "I'll be right over," Korshak said. As she waited by the open door for Korshak, the producer tried to pull her back inside. Amory then told him that someone was coming to pick her up. "Who is it?" he demanded. Suddenly Korshak appeared and said, "It's me, and move away from her. I'm taking her back with Bee and myself now." The producer immediately cowered and said, "I'm so sorry, Sidney." According to Amory, "All of the sudden, it was like the Red Sea parted."[21]

• Amory also recalled that when she and husband Freddie Cushing, a banker with Lehman Brothers, were living in Paris, Freddie lost his driver's license after a speeding conviction. Amory called Korshak in L.A., and he asked for the name of the French prosecutor. "And all of the sudden, a week later Freddie's license was returned," Amory said with astonishment.

• One Korshak friend, who wished anonymity, joined the chorus with his story: "Once, when I took a photo to the best framer in L.A., somehow in conversation it came up that I was close to Sidney. The framer told me, 'I'd be dead if it wasn't for Sidney. The French Mafia had put a contract out on me, and a friend of mine got in touch with Sidney, who got his Italian friends to get it called off.' He absolutely refused to accept payment from me."[22]

• Recently deceased world-famous comic Alan King recalled being turned away from a posh European hotel that claimed it had no vacancies.

King calmly walked to a lobby phone to call his Vegas pal Sid Korshak in Los Angeles. According to King, before he hung up the phone, the hotel desk clerk was knocking on the phone booth door—as if by magic, a luxury suite had become available.[23]

There was, according to some, one glaring exception to Korshak's Hollywood altruism, and surprisingly, it involved one of Sinatra's best friends, Sammy Davis Jr. By 1956, the African-American Davis was a bona fide song-and-dance star, with hit albums, a sellout live act in Vegas and elsewhere, and a legion of A-list friends. Even a 1954 auto accident that cost him his left eye failed to derail his skyrocketing career. But Davis was also on good terms with the hoods who had a lock on the country's nightclub business; he was known to be especially well connected in Chicago, where, in leaner years, he had often borrowed money from Sam Giancana. It was believed by many that the mob had their hooks so far into Davis that they practically owned him. George Weiss, the composer of Davis's breakout 1956 Broadway musical *Mr. Wonderful*, spoke of witnessing how Davis had to obtain the mob's permission to appear in the show.[24]

Sammy Davis was able to balance his mob flirtations, but not those with Caucasian blond women, for whom he had powerful attraction. Of course, midcentury America was the last place a black man wanted to be caught in an assignation with a white woman, but Davis forged ahead as though he were living in a more tolerant European capital. When his affections were aimed at the hottest ingénue in the Columbia stable of hotheaded Harry "White Fang" Cohn, it was quickly made clear that he had crossed the racial Rubicon.

Having just come off film triumphs *Picnic* and *The Man with the Golden Arm* (opposite Frank Sinatra), the Chicago-born Marilyn Pauline Novak, aka Kim Novak, was being groomed to be a huge earner for the mob-connected Cohn. But soon after a brief first meeting in Chicago at the Chez Paree, then a date at the home of Korshak's friends Tony Curtis and wife Janet Leigh, the twenty-three-year-old blond "sex symbol" Novak and the thirty-one-year-old black entertainer Davis had (according to Davis) fallen in love. The affair was fueled by the excitement of having to arrange furtive meetings wherever possible. But despite their best efforts, the word got out, and it got out first to Harry Cohn, who, rightly convinced that the affair would destroy Novak's career, immediately hired detectives to follow the lovers. The racial flames were fueled when Irv Kupcinet wrote in his January 1, 1958, column in the *Chicago Sun-Times* that the two were engaged, and that Kup had a copy of the marriage license to prove it (he never produced it).[25]

Cindy Bitterman, a close friend of Davis's, who was employed in Columbia's publicity department, recently recalled a dinner party she attended at the time with Cohn and other Columbia honchos. "At dinner, the names of Kim and Sammy came up," Bitterman told Davis biographer Wil Haygood. "Cohn had no idea of my relationship with Sammy. He asked somebody at the table, 'What's with this nigger?' My stomach started cramping. 'If he doesn't straighten up,' he starts saying about Sammy, 'he'll be minus another eye.' I went to the bathroom and threw up. I threw up out of fear and greed and Hollywood moneymaking."[26]

"Harry Cohn wanted him dead," said comic Jack Carter, Sammy's Broadway costar in *Mr. Wonderful*. "What he was cocking around with was the mob," said Jerry Lewis. "They had a lot of money in Columbia—namely Harry Cohn—and I knew it."

Among the first warnings came from Steve Blauner, an agent with General Artists Corporation, who railed at a nonplussed Davis, "You stupid son of a bitch! How long you think it'll be a secret? They'll kill you!" Soon, Harry Cohn summoned Davis's adviser Jess Rand to his office. "I know the right people," Cohn bellowed. "I'll see that he never works in a nightclub again." Back in Chicago, where Davis was doing a gig at the Chez Paree, a mysterious stranger paid a visit to Davis in his hotel room and warned the singer that his remaining eye was on the line because of the affair.

"If you fuck with my right eye," Sammy shot back with uncharacteristic bravado, "I'll kill you." Before leaving, the man made certain Davis saw his gun, saying, "Don't ever say that, kid, unless you mean it."[27]

Cohn, who apparently was not about to wait for Davis to fall in line, decided to confront Novak. In an interview thirty years later, Al Melnick, Novak's first agent, said, "There's no doubt about it. Harry called a very highly placed attorney, a man in with the mob, and he arranged a serious action against Sammy."[28] For most knowledgeable insiders, that could only mean one man: Sid Korshak. According to actress Dana Wynter, the ex-wife of Korshak's close friend Greg Bautzer, the fixing talents of Korshak were indeed brought into play. In a recent interview, Wynter recalled a confrontation that bore the earmarks of an earlier power play with Estes Kefauver:

Harry Cohn called her in and said, "Look, knock it off." Apparently Kim didn't feel like obeying orders and it came down to calling her in again, this time with Sidney sitting behind the desk with Harry Cohn and saying to her, "Look, you absolutely got to stop this." And she said, "Why should I? It's my private life." At which point Sidney asked her to look at some pictures. Apparently Sammy Davis had cameras set up in the bedroom and had a whole file of these things, with various prominent white actresses, and this was his thing, and she looked at them and then started to tear them up, and then Sidney said to her, "Don't bother to tear them up, because we have the negatives." Then he said, "We're telling you, if he doesn't stop it, he'll lose his other eye."[29]

After the meeting, Korshak met with Greg Bautzer and laughed about the incident. "I heard Sidney say it, and to Greg and to me," said Wynter. "He had just come from Columbia and was crowing about it."

Screenwriter Tom Mankiewicz, who came to work alongside Korshak years later, heard another version of the story from Korshak. "We were sitting up late at night at the Riv in Vegas," remembered Mankiewicz, "and someone mentioned Sammy Davis, which I said may not be the best place to talk about it 'cause Sidney was sitting right there. So Sidney said, 'What, the I'll-put-your-other-eye-out story?' I turned red as a Coke machine. He said, 'I never said that. I threatened Sammy with something much worse. I told him if he ever saw Kim Novak again, he'd never work in another nightclub for the rest of his life. For a compulsive performer like Sammy, that's way worse than death.' "

This version is supported by Bob Thomas, Cohn's biographer, who said, "Sammy was presented with simple alternatives: end this romance or find himself denied employment by any major nightclub in America."[30] And Sid Korshak was the attorney most connected to the lucrative venues of Las Vegas, Chicago, and elsewhere.

Whatever the details of Korshak's threats, the fact was that they were beginning to take effect. "What is it they want me to do?" Davis asked his longtime agent, Arthur Silber Jr. "Are they telling me that I'm not good enough to be seen with a white woman? Do they want me to get my skin bleached white? What is it? I'm a human being. Why can't I be with the woman I love?"[31]

Sinatra's valet, George Jacobs, an African-American, remembered when Sinatra heard about the Cohn threats. "When Sinatra got wind of it, it brought up a lot of bullshit," Jacobs said. "Frank came to his defense when that happened. He didn't call them, but he wouldn't hang out with the guys from Columbia anymore. He never invited them to anything he had going on. Frank would see them at parties at Romanoff's and he'd walk right by them like they weren't there. He didn't like them at all. Sammy was like a little brother to him, and he took very good care of him. The only time I saw Frank angry with Sammy was when Sammy was smoking weed. Sinatra was against narcotics."[32]

The word was now out that Davis not only had to break off with Novak, but also had to marry a black woman to end the threats once and for all. "The gossip," remembered Annie Stevens (the wife of Sammy's conductor Morty), "was already backstage: Sammy has to get married—or he'll be killed." According to Arthur Silber Jr., Davis's father was warned by L.A. mobster Mickey Cohen that Harry Cohn had put out a mob contract hit on his son. "He said Harry Cohn is going to send some guys to break both my knees," said a hysterical Sammy Davis, "and put out my other eye if I don't find a black girl to marry within forty-eight hours!" With that, Davis quickly offered $10,000 to a black Las Vegas singer he barely knew if she would agree to marry him for one year only—and just for appearances. The girl, ironically named Loray White, had a crush on Davis and quickly agreed, thinking (wrongly) that the bond might last.[33] Davis's mother, Elvera, later said, "He married her because, if he had not, they would have broken his legs." According to Davis's autobiography, *Yes I Can*, just before the wedding, Davis received a call from his friend Sam Giancana, who told him, "You can relax, kid. The pressure's off." However, on their wedding night, Davis got blind drunk and tried to strangle his new bride.

On February 27, 1958, six weeks after the Davis-White vows, Harry Cohn died of a heart attack. When over a thousand showed for the intimidating mogul's funeral on the Columbia lot, comedian Red Skelton quipped, "Well, it only proves what they always say—give the public something they want to see and they'll come out for it."[34] Sammy and Kim continued to sneak around for a few months, but the situation proved untenable and the affair ended. "I don't think Sammy ever took anything harder in his life than the breakup with Kim Novak," wrote Arthur Silber. And one year after it began, the marriage to Loray White was over.

Movie Business

Just as he had with the stars, Korshak solidified his relationships with the movie moguls. With the studios at the mercy of the mob-controlled craft unions and talent agencies, dealing with Korshak became the first order of business for any studio that wished to stay solvent. Korshak's indispensable mediating skills set a trend in Hollywood that exists to this day. As many a producer can attest, in modern Hollywood, the entertainment business is now virtually run by attorneys. And the Teamsters are still ubiquitous on movie sets. One Hollywood insider recently joked, "In Hollywood, they cast a lawyer like they cast an actor. And they probably cast the lawyer first."

Typical of Korshak's clout was his effort on behalf of an anonymous Hollywood agent who recalled being threatened by mob muscle over an entertainment deal that had fallen through: "I went to Sidney and explained the situation, told him I was concerned, and he made a phone call, I never heard from them again."[35]

Former Los Angeles FBI agent A. O. Richards recently recalled what he was told by informants regarding Korshak's utility in Hollywood: "We knew he was strong and he had a lot of power and was a big man and all of that, but he kept a fairly low profile out here. The two big areas that Korshak was close to, that we could determine, were the unions and the movie industry. That was his forte. It was one of those things we knew, that he was practically behind everything that happened and knew about everything that happened. He could control them so that there wouldn't be a strike. That was his style—behind the scenes."[36]

Fellow L.A. FBI man Mike Wacks exhibited some frustration when he remembered the industry collusion with the Fixer. "It was well-known in the industry that if you were going to make a movie, the talk around town was that you'd have to use the Teamsters," Wacks said. "Of course, you better get it straightened out with Sidney before you get those Teamsters over there, or you could have problems. He'd get a consulting fee from both ends—the producers as well as the Teamsters. I wish we could have proved that, but that was what the talk around town was, that he got paid off by both sides."[37]

Certainly Korshak's strongest and most potent mogul friendships were those with Jules Stein and Lew Wasserman. According to Roy Brewer, the IATSE representative in L.A. in the fifties, Korshak helped MCA obtain Teamsters Pension Fund loans when it ramped up its production wing after Reagan and SAG granted the all-important waiver.[38] A measure of how much Korshak was revered by Stein was reported by L.A. County district attorney investigator Frank Hronek, a story confirmed by veteran *Los Angeles Times* reporter Jack Tobin and others. "Frank Hronek was our 'overcover' Hollywood guy in the DA's office," recalled former DA John Van DeKamp. "He and his colleague would go from bar to bar and pick up all the gossip."[39] Hronek, a former Czechoslovakian freedom fighter in World War II, had befriended Stein's Czech secretary, who became the first to tell him of a revealing incident in Stein's MCA suite. According to the secretary, when Korshak entered the office, Stein stood up from behind his desk and walked around to Sidney, saying, "Sidney, you sit there. That's your chair, not mine. You sit there. That is your chair behind the desk." Korshak, without hesitation, made himself comfortable in the chairman's seat.

"The woman was flabbergasted!" Hronek later recalled. "Here's the man who created MCA and he is saying to Sidney, 'That's your chair!' And of course Sidney didn't say, 'Oh, no.' He went over and sat down." According to the secretary, a short time after Korshak made himself comfortable, another visitor entered the room, a man of diminutive stature. After serving coffee and liqueurs, the secretary left the room with Stein. Now, Korshak and "the little man" were alone together behind closed doors for about twenty minutes, after which the man left, met downstairs by a waiting limo, and Korshak summoned Stein back into his own office.

Alone with the secretary later, Hronek showed her some photos, hoping she might be able to identify "the little man." One police mug shot caused the secretary to nod her head vigorously; she was certain that this one man, whoever he was, was the man alone with Korshak in Stein's office. The man in the photo was Meyer Lansky.[40]

Interestingly, it is believed by some that Stein drew the line at being seen publicly with the lawyer so obviously in league with the Chicago Outfit. The late Chicago judge Abe Marovitz, himself no stranger to "the boys," said just before his passing, "Jules had to do certain things to not be harmed, to be able to do business . . . Jules wouldn't want someone like Korshak bragging that Jules is his friend."[41]

Stein's MCA heir Lew Wasserman was, if anything, closer to Korshak than to Stein himself. Several people who knew both men asserted that Korshak was Wasserman's closest friend, period. Former senior MCA executive Berle Adams said that the tall trio of Wasserman, Korshak, and Paul Ziffren were together so often that they were nicknamed the Three Redwoods.[42] When NBC News obtained Wasserman's MCA phone logs years later, they revealed that Wasserman spoke with Korshak religiously at the beginning and the end of each business day. "Lew and Sidney were joined at the hip in the fifties," former MCA agent Harris Katleman told Wasserman biographer Connie Bruck. "Sidney did whatever Lew needed."[43]

Former Los Angeles DA John Van DeKamp was well aware of the Korshak-Wasserman relationship. "Wasserman used to go to Korshak quietly when

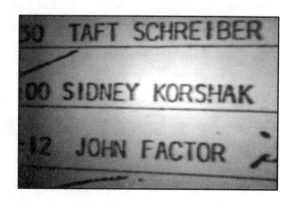

Typical entry from Lew Wasserman's daily MCA phone logs (confidential source)

there were labor problems in the industry," Van DeKamp explained recently. "And for some reason he was regarded as the person who could fix these things, and how he'd fix them you never knew. Of course, you can be a mediator without being a criminal fixer. On the other hand, the suspicion always was that some money must have changed hands. But you could never prove it."[44]

Occasionally, Korshak's favors for Wasserman were only partially related to business. "Sid did something really interesting for Lew Wasserman once," remembered Jan Amory, "when Lew and Edie wanted to go to the Hôtel du Cap in Antibes [French Riviera], which Sidney also loved, at a time when the unions were threatening a strike. Lew said to Sidney, 'I don't know what to do. Edie is dying to go to the Hôtel du Cap.' And Sidney said, 'When do you want them to strike?' Lew said, 'Well, we'll be back September second.' Then Sidney said, 'Okay, they'll be striking on September third.' And that was it."

If Korshak and Wasserman were somewhat considered equals, another Korshak relationship is usually described in clear paternal terms. His camaraderie with then actor (and co-owner with his brother Charles and tailor Joe Picone of women's pants manufacturer Evan-Picone) Bob Evans would grow stronger from their first meeting in the fifties until their estrangement four decades later, during which time Evans rose to the top of Hollywood moguldom, only to crash and burn in the hedonistic excesses of the 1980s. According to Evans, during the intervening years, Korshak was, in Mafia patois, "my consiglieri." Evans adds, "He said he was my godfather too."[45] He maintains that, for the next thirty-plus years, the two met every day for an hour when they were in town, or, if one was not in L.A., they spoke by phone daily. Journalist, and later Paramount executive, Peter Bart explained Evans's attraction this way: "Evans idolized gangsters, but he was fascinated with Jewish gangsters—Bugsy Siegel—not Italian ones."*[46]

Bob Evans (born Robert J. Shapera), the son of a successful Harlem dentist, has described a vivid memory of his first glimpse of the man he reverently calls The Myth one blistering-hot Palm Springs afternoon in the early fifties. The occasion was a mixed-doubles tennis match at the Palm Springs

---

*Evans likely had a familiarity with the hoodlum element from his experience in the New York clothing business, where his company was somehow allowed to flourish with nonunion workers in a town where that industry was totally controlled by gangster-dominated unions.

Racquet Club, where Evans observed the four players finish their match and walk over to an elegant man "as if they were looking for approval." In his autobiography, Evans described the barely smiling sphinx as a "ruggedly handsome man, at least six foot three," wearing a black silk suit, with a starched white shirt and tie. "He wasn't even perspiring," wrote the infatuated Evans. "In all the years I'd gone to Palm Springs, never had I ever seen anybody dressed this way." When the quintet headed into the clubhouse, Evans inquired of him at the reception desk.

The desk clerk was barely able to utter the name. "S-S-S-S . . . Sidney K-K-K-K . . . Korshak," he stuttered.

"Who is he? What does he do?" asked Evans. But the clerk rushed off without answering, thinking the better of it. Nonetheless, the two soon met and initiated a long friendship.[47]

A few years later, Korshak assumed his "protector" role for Evans when Sid and Bee dined with Evans at Le Pavilion in New York, which at the time was the finest and most elite French restaurant in the city. Another couple, unknown to Evans, were also in the party, the male half of which "made John Gotti look like a fruit." Evans, nothing if not narcissistic, began flirting with the man's beautiful date, much to Korshak's consternation. The next thing he knew, Evans was being kicked hard in the shins by the Fixer, who then played out a scene with the randy young actor.

"Bobby, you're late," Korshak said, looking at his watch. "The script— you were supposed to pick it up twenty minutes ago."

"What script?" asked an obtuse Evans, who was soon blasted with an even more painful kick under the table. "Then I got the look, the Korshak look," Evans later wrote. "Houdini couldn't have disappeared quicker."

The following morning, Korshak called Evans and let him know how close he had come.

Robert Evans, actor, 1958 (Photofest)

"Schmuck, if you'd stayed one more minute, you'd have gotten it to the stomach," Korshak informed him. "Not a punch—lead!"

"Who's the guy?" asked Evans.

"It's none of your fuckin' business," Korshak answered. "His broad's got one tough road ahead. Been married a week and the doorman won't even say hello to her—that's how tough the guy is. And you, schmuck, you're coming on to her. Tony was gettin' hot—I could see it. You're lucky your eyes are open." (The epilogue was that after the woman and her tough husband divorced a few years later, no matter where the divorcée relocated—Chicago, Los Angeles, Hawaii—no one had the guts to date her, despite that she was drop-dead gorgeous.)[48]

This incident was to be the first of many of Korshak's rescues of the reckless Evans over the next thirty-plus years. When Evans's brief acting star began to fade in the late fifties, Korshak tried to resuscitate it by interceding with Columbia chief Harry Cohn to hire Evans. "Are you kidding?" Cohn supposedly said. "The kid's a bum. He never even called me back when he was big."[49]

"Sidney was like a godfather to him," suggests Jan Amory. "I think he was trying to set him on the straight path. I just don't know, but I think Sidney liked the glamour and the girls at Bobby's, but Sidney was not into any of the drugs or any of that stuff. He would have two whiskeys and that would be it."

Evans relished the vicarious thrill of being in the company of a force such as Korshak. "We were at '21' one night," Evans recounted. "Sidney used to stay at the Carlyle, and he said, 'Let's walk.' He had two hundred thousand-dollar bills in his pocket. I said, "Are you *crazy*? How can you walk with all that money?" And he said, "Who's gonna take it?"

CHAPTER 8

Jimmy, Bobby, and Sidney

WHILE ZIFFREN, GREENBERG, and the rest continued their assault on Western real estate, Sidney Korshak was practically living out of airports and hotels as he expanded the Supermob's inroads into American labor. With the Chicago underworld fast establishing outposts on the West Coast, the gang increasingly relied on Korshak to represent its unions in L.A. one day, and in Chicago the next.

In the early fifties, the Supermob's "labor consultant" racket was largely confined to Chicago and Hollywood, where the remnants of the Bioff-Browne takeover still held sway over many craft unions. In fact, the Bioff-Browne template was what likely inspired the Supermob's move to expand its labor power nationally, giving Korshak his Platinum Club frequent-flier status. The Hollywood takeover strategy came so close to succeeding—brought down largely by the inclusion of Willie Bioff—that the Chicago Outfit and the Supermob thought it was worth another try. This time the target would not be just Hollywood, but every city dependent on keeping peace with organized labor. Instead of IATSE, the target would be the International Brotherhood of Teamsters (IBT); and in place of Willie Bioff and George Browne, the new facilitators would be a Detroit Teamster leader named James Riddle Hoffa and a Chicago insurance salesman named Paul "Red" Dorfman.

In operation since 1903, the International Brotherhood of Teamsters, Chauffeurs, Warehousemen and Helpers of America, commonly known as the International Brotherhood of Teamsters, or simply the Teamsters (named after the wagon drivers who commanded a "team" of horses), was involved in numerous violent strikes during a period when employer abuse of workers enjoyed a free rein. In one 1905 example, a tragic hundred-day strike against the Chicago-based Montgomery Ward Company left twenty-one dead and cost about $1 million ($20 million in 2006 dollars). After establishing strongholds in Detroit and Chicago, the Teamsters set about forcing independent unions to capitulate and antiunion companies to reconsider. Often these "negotiations" utilized violence as a tactic of first choice. Teamster rank-and-file passions were fueled by the success of their union in creating better working conditions, including standardized contracts, shorter workweeks, and the right to overtime pay. When the automobile came into widespread use in the twenties, the IBT expanded to include truck drivers, and its membership skyrocketed to over 1 million by the time Sidney Korshak became involved in the early fifties.

The Supermob infiltration strategy consisted of providing underworld support for amenable Teamster leaders in exchange for a deal wherein Korshak would become the union's key "labor negotiator" (of course, Korshak would secretly cut sweetheart deals with employers). The Teamsters would set up a fund from which the mob and Supermob could make massive low-interest commercial loans. In return, the fund accrued the interest on the loans, and the chosen Teamster leaders would receive not only financial kickbacks, but also mob muscle with which to guarantee their leadership positions. Few underworld eyebrows were raised when the chosen instruments turned out to be Red Dorfman and Jimmy Hoffa.

Red Dorfman's willingness to partner with the underworld was a given. As titular head of a number of labor unions including the Waste Handlers Union (controlled by Sid Korshak's immediate superior, Murray Humphreys), Dorfman was, according to the FBI, one of the five or six closest men to boss Joe Accardo. A Chicago Teamster described him as "a hood's hood," while another Teamster said, "He was a small, thin, red-haired guy who'd walk in and throw two bullets on a guy's desk and tell him, 'The next one goes in your fuckin' head.'" He had been indicted in 1928 for election fraud and in 1942 for a brass-knuckle assault on a fellow union boss.* Dorfman's purchase with the mob made him a perfect match for Teamster up-and-comer Jimmy Hoffa when the two met in 1949.

James Riddle "Jimmy" Hoffa was born on February 14, 1913, in Brazil, Indiana, the son of a coal driller who died of an occupational respiratory

---

*For a couple of months in the late 1930s, Dorfman's scrap-iron union had one temperamental slugger who would go on to infamy after he moved to Dallas in 1947. Known in Chicago as an emotional powder keg, Jacob Rubenstein, aka Jack Ruby, would avenge President Kennedy's November 22, 1963, assassination by whacking his killer, Lee Harvey Oswald, two days later.

disease when Hoffa was only seven. Quitting school after the ninth grade in order to help support his family, Hoffa went to work in a grocery warehouse, where he first became involved in the labor movement at age seventeen when he organized a strike. This was during the era when company goons, labor goons, and police goons were constant physical threats. "When you went out on strike in those days, you got your head broken," Hoffa remembered to the *Detroit News*. "The cops would beat your brains out if you even got caught talking about unions." In these formative years, Hoffa's car was bombed, his office smashed, and he was once arrested eighteen times in a single day.

But Hoffa was a tough fireplug of a man, seemingly born to lead the fledgling labor movement. Rising quickly up the ranks, Hoffa was appointed by Teamsters president Dan Tobin as a trustee in charge of examining the union's financial books in 1943, an appointment that would be key to his appeal to the Supermob. In 1946, Hoffa became president of a Teamsters local in Detroit, working under the corrupt union president Dave Beck. In this position, Hoffa was involved in a second critical Teamster evolution when he helped restructure the previously autonomous locals to consolidate power within the central organization. By 1952, Hoffa had won election as international vice president of the Teamsters under Beck, who was already under investigation by federal agencies.

Hoffa formed his first known coalition with organized crime when he requested help from some of Detroit's east-side gangsters to roust an opposition union, the Congress of Industrial Organizations (CIO). By the late forties, with his ambition to ascend the Teamster national power structure in overdrive, Hoffa knew that to achieve his goals he would require the allegiance of the all-powerful Chicago Outfit, which by now had a vise grip not only on Chicago's influential local Teamsters, but on the locals of numerous cities west of Chicago.[1]

Tom Zander (pseudonym), a retired organized crime investigator for the Chicago office of the U.S. Department of Labor, remembered well the takeover days. "The Chicago Teamsters were very corrupt, except for one or two locals," Zander recently said. "The mob took the Teamsters over in small ways: first they'd pinpoint certain locals and go after the treasurers and members of the joint council. They did it principally by payoffs or threats. Once they got one or two key guys, they were in. They got to the pension fund real quick. It was their bank. They used the money to build Las Vegas, and Sidney was in it very deep."[2]

An FBI intelligence report noted, "The labor racket's web had at its center Sidney Korshak, and around him were Murray Humphreys, Gus Alex, Joey Glimco, and Jake Arvey."[3]

Joey Glimco, 1959 (Chicago
Crime Commission)

In 1949, through a union-busting Michigan steel hauler named Santo
Perrone, Hoffa met Dorfman, who then introduced Hoffa to boss Accardo,
Humphreys, Ricca, and the rest. Hoffa also became close friends with
Korshak underling Joseph Glimco (né Guiseppe Glielmi), appointed by
Humphreys in 1944 to run the fifteen powerful Teamster taxicab locals of
Chicago. Predictably, Hoffa and Korshak developed a powerful association.
"Sid was the closest person to Hoffa," recalled Leo Geffner, an L.A. attor-
ney who associated with Korshak.[4] Andy Anderson, who became the head
of the Western Conference of Teamsters, remembered Korshak in constant
contact with Hoffa until Hoffa's imprisonment in 1967: "[Hoffa] checked
with Sidney on everything he did, and he still got in trouble."[5] In an interview in 2003, Anderson hinted at the kind of power Korshak held over
Hoffa: "He knew Hoffa well. In fact, he used to say to me, 'Do you want a
job with Hoffa? I'll get you promoted and you can get a job with Hoffa.'
And I'd say, 'No, I don't like him.' He said, 'Okay, thanks for telling me.' "[6]
MCA agent Harris Katleman went so far as to say, "Sidney Korshak controlled the Teamsters."[7]

According to the FBI, Red Dorfman suggested to Humphreys that if the
Outfit's Teamster locals, which Humphreys controlled, would back Hoffa's
advancement, Hoffa would return the favor by making Sid Korshak the
Teamsters' national labor negotiator. Simultaneously, all businesses dealing
with Korshak would be required to take out insurance with Dorfman's
agency, the newly constituted Chicago branch of the Union Casualty insurance company, run by Red's son, Allen. During the ensuing years, father and
son Dorfman were estimated to have received over $3 million in annual com-
missions, $5 million by 1963. A government asset manager, brought in to
clean up the operation in the 1970s, reflected, "It looks like it was an un-
written rule that when you got a loan from the fund you bought insurance
for your property from Allen Dorfman."

After the 1952 Teamster convention, where Hoffa was seen schmoozing Glimco and other hoods, it was understood that Hoffa would be the real power behind the "front" president, Dave Beck. According to Johnny Rosselli's friend L.A. mobster Jimmy Fratianno, Beck agreed to retire after one five-year term, while Hoffa worked behind the scenes to broaden his own power base, simultaneously proving to his underworld sponsors that he was capable of ruling. Among his first decrees was the anointing of Dorfman's insurance agency as the carrier for the Teamsters' Central States Health and Welfare Fund.

In 1954, aware of the windfall about to descend on Dorfman's insurance company, Sidney Korshak purchased $25,000 worth of stock in the agency. The stock soared one year later when, in March 1955, Hoffa created the Central States Pension Fund. Employers paid $2 per employee per week into the new fund (or $800,000 per month), which accrued to $10 million the first year; by the early sixties it held $400 million in its coffers, eventually topping off at $10 billion. In creating the fund, Hoffa also fought for more union leaders on the Teamsters' board of directors, and the fine points of the deal dictated that Hoffa would appoint Red's son, Allen, a college phys ed teacher, to administer the pension fund loans. Technically, a Teamster fund board of trustees, with Allen as a "consultant," had to authorize the loans, but in actual practice, Allen with his intimidating underworld sponsors called the shots on loan approvals. Of course, applicants were "strongly urged" to buy business insurance from the Dorfmans.

Under the new protocols, the hard-earned dues of truckers, warehousemen, and taxi drivers from the twenty-two states comprised by the Central Fund would subsidize business ventures of questionable pedigree in Nevada, California, and elsewhere. And for the next twenty-five years, Allen Dorfman disbursed the assets of a fund that by 1961 had lent over $91 million in low-interest (6 percent) loans. In all, some 63 percent of the fund's holdings were made available to borrowers.

Two retired trustees of the pension fund stated that Korshak was in the critical position of anointing prospective trustees, and James C. Downs attested that Korshak got him an appointment with Hoffa to apply as a loan analyst for the fund, a position he later resigned. "I don't know if I could have seen Hoffa if it wasn't for Sid," Downs said. One Teamster associate recalled that Korshak was responsible for appointing Abe Pritzker's law partner Stanford Clinton as the general counsel for the Fund.[8] Clinton, who represented Outfit boss Joe Batters Accardo, introduced Pritzker to Jimmy Hoffa and Dorfman and received a piece of Pritzker's Burlingame (California) Hyatt Hotel for his efforts.[9] Journalist Knut Royce located two letters from Abe Pritzker to Red Dorfman's son, Allen, asking for help in obtaining Teamster loans.[10] Consequently, between 1959 and 1975, the Pritzkers would obtain $54.4 million in Teamster loans, some for use in Las Vegas casino construction. A circumspect Sid Korshak told the SEC in 1970, "It is possible that Hyatt Hotels talked to me about the possibility of making an acquisition in Nevada."

Federal documents obtained by Sy Hersh in 1976 showed that Korshak played a huge role in arranging many of the fund's other loans. Reportedly, Korshak used Donald Peters, head of Chicago Teamster Local 743, as a key liaison to the Teamster board. Korshak and Peters, according to one source, had been close since the 1940s, and Peters had, like Korshak, been one of the early investors in Red Dorfman's insurance agency. "He was always Sidney's boy," said one prominent Chicago businessman. "Sid dealt with nobody as much as Don Peters."

Actor-singer Gianni Russo (no relation to the author), who came up in the world as a courier for New York mob boss Frank Costello, remembered Korshak's power when he shared Table One with him at the Pump Room. "He'd negotiate all the deals with the pension fund money," said Russo. "Whatever it was, whoever it was for, Sidney would be the guy who'd come and polish it up."[11]

The timing for Korshak's putsch with the pension fund couldn't have been better, since his sweetheart deal-making was soon to be diminished by the 1959 passage of the Landrum-Griffin Act. This legislation gave union members more power and compelled unions to file hundreds of written reports about all aspects of their activities with the Department of Labor, making sweetheart contracts negotiated quickly by the likes of Korshak impossible. Korshak's success now depended more on his ability to ensure freedom from strikes than his furtive negotiations of low-wage settlements.

Due to the Teamster connection, Sidney Korshak's workload grew exponentially. He was now in a position to broker countless Teamster loans, control strikes, and begin the creation of his own mythic legacy, of which by all accounts he was quite proud. With the Chicago mob's labor genius "Curly" Humphreys slowing down as he approached age sixty, Korshak likely assumed the time was right to stretch his wings and emerge from Humphreys's long shadow—or so he hoped.

The entire Humphreys-Korshak labor scheme had recently been facilitated by the passage of the Taft-Hartley Labor Act of 1947, which prevented employers from cutting deals with union leaders. This dictum, however, left the playing field open to the middleman, who was happy to take the bribes himself after seizing control of a particular union.

By now, all who sought to make good with the Teamster juggernaut courted Korshak. In 1955, Anthony Inciso, a Capone- and Accardo-affiliated racketeer and United Auto Workers union boss, gave pricey gifts (including $1,000 diamond rings) to five Teamster officials, and a symbolic $360 money clip to Sidney Korshak. Inciso admitted to a Senate Labor Committee that he gave the gifts to "anyone that had done us a favor. It wouldn't be honest to bring them money, so we bring them a token of appreciation." Inciso's honesty notwithstanding, he was convicted on twenty-two counts of a federal indictment charging him with violation of the Taft-Hartley Act. On June 23, 1960, he was sentenced to ten years and fined $22,000. He began serving his sentence on December 4, 1961. Senator Paul Douglas, Democrat of Illinois, had allegedly told Inciso that he had disgraced the labor movement.[12]

Korshak's Teamster dealings were next in the public spotlight in 1956, when he was listed on both the Sponsors' Committee and the Entertainment Committee for an April 20 testimonial dinner held to honor Jimmy Hoffa in Detroit.[13] Sidney's party pal Joel Goldblatt headed the sponsoring committee for the $100-a-plate dinner, with the $250,000 take used to build a children's home in Israel.[14]

Back in California that same year, Jake "the Barber" Factor's brother, Max, who was trying to weather a move to unionize his cosmetics company, engaged Korshak. Royston Webb, the company's British attorney, remembered Korshak at the firm:

I was the general counsel for Max Factor in the UK and also the director of personnel. I remember going across to the old Max Factor headquarters, which was on Hollywood Boulevard, opposite the Chinese Theater, to see my counterparts in Los Angeles—a chap named John McKenna. We were just talking of general personnel and union issues, which I handled in the UK, and I said to John, "Well, who deals with them over here, John?" He said, "Sidney Korshak." I think they were paying him about fifty thousand dollars a year. I said, "Is he coming in today?" I was told, "Oh, no. He doesn't come in. He's not coming in today."

"Well, when will he come in?"

"He doesn't come to the office at all," McKenna said.

So I said, "How does he deal with any union problems you have?"

He said, "You don't understand. Sidney is connected."

I just thought, "This is not how we would do business in England, but then, this isn't England."[15]

As his workload became burdensome, Korshak created a new paradigm for himself, wherein he would act as a referral service, shuffling the hard work off to a chosen colleague and keeping a healthy share of the fee just for making the call. Such was the case when he engaged Nathan Shefferman's Industrial Relations Associates of Chicago to handle the labor troubles of the Indiana plant of the Brooklyn-based Englander Mattress Company, which had Korshak on retainer. When the workers wanted to form a Teamster local, in the face of a company that was strongly antiunion, they turned to Shefferman, whose close friend Korshak was consulted only to put the fine points on the contract. After it met with Korshak's approval, it was sent up to Hoffa for his imprimatur.

Suddenly, Englander seemed eager to recognize the new Teamster local, and few who were privy to the deal questioned why. It seemed that Korshak had arranged for the workers to receive $37 take-home pay weekly, far below the national average of $53 for factory workers. Englander was now more than happy to allow workers at its Alabama, Illinois, New York, Washington, and Texas plants to become Teamsters.[16] For his role in backstabbing the workers, Shefferman was paid $76,000. (When Korshak, who claimed to have received only a $2,000 fee, was informed of this by Bobby Kennedy during later congressional testimony, Korshak feigned poverty, saying that, by comparison, "I am being grossly underpaid." Few would agree.)

But the truth was more complex. From the perspective of most Teamsters, their lot was far better than at any other time in history. Although some workers were receiving less pay, many others experienced just the opposite, with safer working conditions, guaranteed overtime pay, health benefits, etc. Also, from this point on, many Teamsters were paid handsomely to featherbed, wherein the union dictated that more workers were hired than were actually needed for a job. Some investigators, such as Pulitzer Prize–winning journalist Wendell Rawls, asserted that middlemen such as Sid Korshak had little difficulty in rationalizing their actions. "Korshak didn't think he was stealing from workers because he believed he was getting more money for the Teamsters than they ever dreamed they'd get," Rawls recently said. "And he deserved his commission. These negotiators got more sit-around Teamsters hired. If one worker complained about that, another would hit him with a crowbar."[17]

Occasionally, Korshak's double-dealing went sour and led to frayed relationships, such as with Charles W. Lubin, the innovator who conceived of freezing baked goods for later sale in supermarkets. Lubin's brainstorm led to the founding of his now famous Kitchens of Sara Lee brand, and predictably, the improvement sent jitters throughout bakers' unions, who feared their orders would decline. Lubin enlisted Korshak to work out the difficulties, and he did so with his trademark one or two phone calls. However, one year later, after Lubin learned that Korshak was playing both sides, he fired him. According to a Korshak associate, Korshak was furious. "He called Charlie [Lubin] up and threatened him by saying that he'd better not 'walk alone at night.'" The source added that Lubin was badly shaken by the warning.[18]

Bobby Kennedy's Version of Kefauver

A great deal of my business is transacted on the telephone
—SIDNEY KORSHAK TO ROBERT KENNEDY

By the end of 1956, the nation's lawmakers were swamped with reports that Teamster officials were looting the members' pension fund and forging alliances with the underworld. In December, the Senate Select Committee on Improper Activities in the Labor or Management Field was established to investigate the contentions, holding its first hearings on January 30, 1957. Chaired by a devout Baptist Democrat from Arkansas, Senator John J. McClellan, the "rackets" investigation would eclipse even the Kefauver probe in its scope, lasting over two and a half years and hearing fifteen hundred witnesses whose recollections (or lack thereof) were laid out over twenty thousand pages of testimony.

Chairman McClellan made it clear early on that his investigation would be a continuation of the xenophobic battles of the pre-Prohibition era, with Italian and Irish hoods cast as the country's chief law enforcement adversaries. He viewed the prospect of twentieth-century immigrant witnesses in self-righteous disgust, saying, "We should rid the country of characters who come here from other lands and take advantage of the great freedom and opportunity our country affords, who come here to exploit these advantages with criminal activities. They do not belong in our land, and they ought to be sent somewhere else. In my book, they are human parasites on society, and they violate every law of decency and humanity." In fact, most were charged with transgressions that paled in comparison to those being committed right under his nose by his party's national committeeman Paul Ziffren.

In his Supermob advisory role, Sidney Korshak called and met with his cronies and, by their own admission, ordered them to stonewall Kennedy, which they did. "I called Sid," one such associate told Sy Hersh in 1976, "and said, 'Robert Kennedy is asking to see me.' He said, 'Don't say anything, and call me when he leaves.'" The witness said he was "tough and uncooperative"

JIMMY, BOBBY, AND SIDNEY 171

with Kennedy and, as was demanded of him, called Sidney with the news. According to the unnamed witness, Korshak was "overjoyed."[19]

The many inherent ironies of McClellan's probe surfaced almost immediately, when the "McClellan Committee" chose as its chief counsel Robert F. Kennedy, the seventh child of Boston millionaire and former Roosevelt administration diplomat Joseph P. Kennedy. Over the years, countless firsthand witnesses have attested to Joseph Kennedy's pattern of working in consort with the underworld to establish his fortune. Bobby Kennedy, who had cajoled McClellan into forming the panel, quickly commandeered the probe, on which his brother Jack served as a Senate member, with a style alternately described as either forceful or bellicose. When the thirty-one-year-old Kennedy traveled back to Massachusetts for Christmas in 1956, he excitedly announced the full-blown inquiry to his father. Papa Joe, fully cognizant of the extent of the upperworld-underworld alliance that had helped build his dynasty, was not impressed.

According to Bobby's sister Jean Kennedy Smith, the argument that ensued at Hyannis Port that Christmas was bitter, "the worst one we ever witnessed."[20] Kennedy adviser Arthur Schlesinger Jr. described the row as "unprecedentally furious."[21] The politically savvy father warned that such an upheaval would turn labor, especially Hoffa's powerful Teamsters, against Jack in his presidential quest. Longtime Kennedy confidant Lem Billings recalled, "The old man saw this as dangerous . . . He thought Bobby was naïve."[22] Bobby, however, saw things differently, believing such a crusade would actually enhance the family's image.

One of Kennedy's key targets, Teamsters VP Jimmy Hoffa, said years later, "You take any industry and look at the problems they ran into while they were building it up—how they did it, who they associated with, how they cut corners. The best example is Kennedy's old man . . . To hear Kennedy when he was grandstanding in front of the McClellan Committee, you might have thought I was making as much out of the pension fund as the Kennedys made out of selling whiskey."

Despite the committee's concentration on Hoffa and typical low-life mob thugs, Bobby Kennedy felt compelled to make a cursory show of interest in the Supermob types. "Bobby was always interested in Korshak," said Tom Zander, a Labor Department investigator who funneled evidence to Kennedy during the hearings. "When he was on McClellan, he asked me about Korshak."[23] Consequently, committee investigator James J. P. McShane obtained files on Marshall Korshak and Gus Alex, and, according to a Chicago Crime

Commission (CCC) memo, "Bobby Kennedy was fully briefed on the contents." Brother Sidney was next. On March 28, 1957, Kennedy investigators Walter Sheridan and Pierre Salinger met with Sid Korshak in his 134 N. LaSalle office for a preinterview, in anticipation of Korshak's eventual testimony in Washington.* Regarding the Shefferman-Englander dealings, Korshak explained that he had received a paltry $2,000 for mediating a dispute between the Coca-Cola Company and Englander's unions. In Salinger's background report to Kennedy, he described Korshak as being "extremely close to the old Capone mob."[24]

After his polite chat with the investigators, Korshak returned to business as usual. His reverie was only briefly disturbed by another blast from his college rival, Lester Velie. In the July 1957 issue of *Reader's Digest*, Velie, who was likely leaked material by either Sheridan or Virgil Peterson of the Chicago Crime Commission, wrote an article entitled HOW INFLUENCE-PEDDLERS SHORTCHANGE THE UNION WAGE EARNER. In the piece, Velie recounted Korshak's friendships with Charlie Gioe, Nathan Shefferman, and his role in arranging sweetheart contracts for employers such as Englander.

Meanwhile, the Teamsters were preparing to name a new international president to replace Dave Beck, who stepped down in May after receiving federal tax and larceny charges, the result of McClellan Committee revelations. Throughout the summer, Korshak's underworld associates set about assuring that their man Hoffa was guaranteed the open position. When the word came down to Dorfman, he instructed his close friend Johnny Dio (Dioguardi) of New York to organize Teamster "paper locals," which had the sole purpose of ensuring Hoffa's control of the New York Joint Council of the Teamsters.

Any doubts that Hoffa would be a determined leader were dispelled on August 22, 1957, when he did verbal battle with firebrand Bobby Kennedy. In what was a classic example of the immovable object meeting the irresistible force, Hoffa, who viewed Bobby as a spoiled rich kid, sparred for two days with Kennedy, who in turn believed Hoffa to be evil personified. "We were like flint and steel," Hoffa wrote in his autobiography. "Every time we came to grips the sparks flew."[25] The great theater that was expected by millions of television viewers was delivered in spades, with name-calling and high sarcasm in great abundance.

"It was just a match of two absolutes," commented historian Ronald Steel. "Bobby Kennedy saw Hoffa as absolute evil. And so he could elevate

---

*Korshak later said that Robert Kennedy also paid him a visit at his N. LaSalle office. (IRS report of Furfaro int. of Korshak, 10-23-63)

this struggle against Hoffa into some kind of titanic moral issue, which is why he became so dedicated to it."

Hoffa's nonstop evasion was met with Kennedy's mocking, superior attitude. When the two brawlers needed a breather, there was no bell to save them, so they just stared at each other for minutes at a time, ending only when Hoffa winked. "I used to love to bug the little bastard," Hoffa recalled.

Even during lunch breaks, Hoffa made certain Kennedy knew he meant business as the jousting spilled out into the Senate office building hallways and nearby restaurants, at one point escalating from the verbal to the physical. According to Hoffa, he was walking to a table at a nearby restaurant when he heard someone yell, "Hey, you!" Before he could respond, a hand grabbed him and spun him around. It was Bobby Kennedy. Hoffa's tough union pedigree made him act instinctively.

"My hand shot out and grabbed him by the front of his jacket and bounced him up against the wall—hard," Hoffa wrote. " 'I'm only gonna tell you this one time. If you ever put your mitts on me again I'm gonna break you in half.' "[26]

When Hoffa's testimony resumed that afternoon, the altercation led to the following Q&A:

Kennedy: Did you say, "That SOB, I'll break his back"?
Hoffa: Who?
Kennedy: You.
Hoffa: Say it to who?
Kennedy: To anyone?
Hoffa: Figure of speech . . . I don't even know what I was talking about and I don't know what you're talking about.
Kennedy: Uh . . . Mr. Hoffa, all I'm trying to find out, I'll tell you what I'm talking about. I'm trying to find out whose back you were going to break.
Hoffa: Figure of speech . . . figure of speech.

For all intents and purposes, the interrogation duel ended as a draw.

On August 28, 1957, one month before the Teamster convention, the OCID (Organized Crime Intelligence Division) unit of the Los Angeles Police Department (LAPD) watched surreptitiously as the Teamsters' executive board met with Jimmy Hoffa and three powerful residents of the Windy City at L.A.'s Townhouse Hilton Hotel. An LAPD memo in the files of the Chicago Crime Commission gives further details of what the OCID witnessed: "According to information given to the LAPD, three men are with Hoffa for the purpose of aiding his cause in becoming President of the Teamsters Union.

It is claimed that the men in question are: Murray Humphreys, Marshall Caifano, and [Humphreys aide] Ralph Pierce—all of whom are well-known Chicago hoodlums. It is stated that a member of the Executive Board is being taken before these men singly, and they are advising members of the Executive Board in no uncertain terms that Hoffa is to be the next President of the Teamsters Union."

To no one's surprise, Hoffa became president at the October 4, 1957, Miami IBT convention. Allen Friedman, a muscleman for the Cleveland Teamsters local, described a coronation that mimicked the 1934 IATSE convention that anointed George Browne. "The delegates who elected Hoffa, usually the business agents, trustees, secretary-treasurer, and presidents of the various Teamster locals, had been carefully rigged," Friedman wrote. "Hoffa's men had meant to cover their tracks. They had stolen ballots that went against them and rigged both the seating and voting so inappropriate voting took place. Then they tossed the documents into the incinerator, blaming the maid for the action."[27] According to one report, Curly Humphreys, who was known to frequent the Sea Isle Hotel in Florida, was on hand one month later at Miami Beach's luxurious Eden Roc Hotel to watch from the shadows as Hoffa accepted the Teamster presidency before seventeen hundred roaring delegates.

In the aftermath of Hoffa's election, the Chicago underworld's personal friendships with Teamster officials only grew stronger. The wife of Korshak's controller, Curly Humphreys, witnessed the goings-on. Jeanne Stacy Humphreys remembered that Curly became close to John T. "Sandy" O'Brien, the international vice president of the Teamsters, whose wife, Marge, just happened to be the secretary of the Teamsters Pension Fund. Humphreys also maintained a close personal relationship with Hoffa, who often vacationed at Humphreys's Key Biscayne home. FBI bugs heard Curly tell Joey Glimco, "Hoffa was the best man I ever knew." According to Humphreys, whenever the Outfit told Hoffa to do something, "He just goes boom, boom, boom, he gets it done." Humphreys added, "One thing I always admired about the guy, they tried to fuck him, but he never took a bad attitude about it." On occasion, Humphreys even lent his legal expertise to Hoffa. "I worked on this case for him," Humphreys said, "and paid out a lot of money for him and never got it back." Despite the warming relationship with the new Teamster boss, both the hoods and the Supermob would wait a suitable amount of time before making withdrawals from their new bank. But once they commenced, they would be ravenous.

*   *   *

On October 30, 1957, barely four weeks after Hoffa assumed the Teamster presidency, Korshak appeared before Bobby Kennedy and the full committee. With Kennedy conducting all the questioning, Korshak deftly explained his dealings with Shefferman and Englander by pointing out that the lower wages were complicated by the variant costs of doing business in different areas of the country. Surprisingly, Kennedy seemed satisfied with Korshak's answers.

The only other major point of interest was Korshak's labor assistance given to Jake the Barber's brother, Max Factor, in Los Angeles. The union organizer at Max Factor Cosmetics, Michael Katz, knew enough to find Korshak at the Beverly Hills Friars Club, where he was lunching with Jake the Barber.

"I believe I was in the Friars Club in California," Korshak explained. "I received a telephone call from Mr. Katz. He met me in front of the place. He told me that he was organizing the company, and that he was having difficulty getting together with management. He understood that one of the Factors was from Chicago. He asked if I would arrange a meeting with management."

Korshak giving testimony before the McClellan Committee, October 30, 1957 (Corbis/Bettmann)

"Which Factor was that?" Kennedy asked.

"This was a Mr. John Factor [Jake the Barber]. Mr. John Factor was in the club at this particular time. I asked Mr. Katz to wait. I walked in and told Mr. Factor what I had just learned from Mr. Katz. Mr. Factor said the only one that he knew at the plant was his half brother, and that he was in Europe at the time, so he couldn't or wouldn't talk to anyone else. I went out and communicated that to Mr. Katz."

Korshak explained that his contact with Katz was accidental and should not be taken to mean he was in the employ of Max or Jake Factor, Royston Webb's observations notwithstanding. Korshak said that he probably told Katz as much. "I would have told him I have no interest whatsoever in the Max Factor Company, and that John Factor wasn't interested in the Max Factor Company," Korshak told Kennedy.[28]

For reasons unknown at the time, Kennedy's "interrogation" of Korshak came off as a lovefest in comparison to his treatment of Hoffa. At the close of questioning, Kennedy went so far as to compliment Korshak, calling him "very cooperative." And when Kennedy wrote his memoirs of the probe, *The Enemy Within*, he failed to mention Korshak's name at all—this despite the fact that both the FBI and Kefauver had made Korshak one of their chief labor-corruption targets.

With Bobby Kennedy's crusade behind him, Sid Korshak returned to business as usual. In January 1958, Korshak, Joe Accardo, Curly Humphreys, Sam "Mooney" Giancana, and Jackie "the Lackey" Cerone met at Giancana's Armory Lounge in Chicago's Forest Park suburb to work out Accardo's looming problems with the IRS. It seemed that the most powerful underworld boss in America was having difficulty explaining his vast income—he needed a legit job quick. Also in attendance were representatives from the Fox Head Brewing Company, which was heavily invested in by Humphreys. The FBI's informants revealed that Korshak drew up a bogus contract for Accardo, saying that he was a "salesman" for Premium Beer Sales Inc. For his services, Korshak received a $500 fee, but later told the FBI that he only reviewed the contract.[29] Interestingly, Accardo's daughter Marie Judith Accardo would soon be seen working as a secretary in Korshak's Chicago office.

"Sidney and Accardo were extraordinarily close," said a longtime Chicago attorney friend of Sidney's. "When Marie was growing up, Accardo wanted her protected when she went into the workforce, so he sent her to work for Sidney and Marshall. The point is that Sidney was so close that Accardo trusted his daughter with him. And Sidney was not a guy to trust around women."[30]

While in Chicago, Korshak attended to his legit clients as well. When the *Chicago Sun-Times* newspaper moved its headquarters in 1958, circulation director Louis Spear called Korshak to halt a strike by paper haulers who refused to unload papers that were now shipped by river to the new shorefront location. As Spear recalled in 2004, Korshak placed one call, and the strikers returned to work.[31] In New York that year, Korshak helped restaurateur Toots Shor resolve problems with his workers' union.[32]

Gus Hops on the Bus

Although Bobby Kennedy seemed quite satisfied with Sidney Korshak's testimony, he was nonetheless spoiling for a fight with one of Sidney's early sponsors, Gussie "Slim" Alex, ostensibly a "salesman" for the mob-owned Atlas Brewing Company. He later claimed to work for Blatz Brewing of Milwaukee, owned by Schenley Industries, a Sid Korshak client. A Greek hood who ran vice rackets in Chicago's Loop district, Gussie was, like Korshak, a direct subordinate of the gang's labor and political Einstein, Curly Humphreys, and was soon to become the Chicago Outfit's master courier, supervising the transportation of the Las Vegas casino skim to Swiss banks. The committee drew up a subpoena for the vaunted hood, but the trouble was, the committee staff couldn't find him to serve it. Alex and his wife, the former Marianne Ryan, had disappeared from their beautiful riverfront 4300 North Marine Drive apartment in late October. Just as the hoods had gone into hiding during the Kefauver probe—tabbed Kefauveritis—they did much the same when Bobby called, and one of those suffering from "Kennedyitis" was Gussie Alex.

Committee investigators in Chicago were told that the best way to find Alex was to talk to Sid Korshak, who was known to all to be tight with Gussie. In Chicago, local investigators referred to Korshak as "Gussie's man."[33] It was quickly determined that Alex's sister was married to Korshak Teamster associate Joey Glimco, and that Alex had taken over numerous Outfit financial machinations from Jake Guzik, for whom he used to bodyguard, when Guzik died in 1956. A confidential 1958 FBI report stated, "Gus Alex had moved up to an important position in the crime syndicate of Chicago . . . Sidney Korshak, well-known Chicago attorney, was the person who advised top racketeers in Chicago insofar as their legitimate enterprises were concerned . . . Gus Alex was the hoodlum closest to Korshak and . . . this was the basis for the belief that Alex had moved into a high echelon of the syndicate."

Once when Gussie applied for an apartment in an exclusive Lake Shore Drive complex, attorney Korshak wrote a letter of recommendation, saying about the infamous gangster, "He is a man of excellent financial responsibilities who will be an excellent tenant."[34] On another occasion, Alex used Sidney's brother Marshall's name when applying for memberships in Chicago's exclusive Standard Club and Whitehall Club. According to the FBI, Alex had claimed employment with Marshall as a front "for the last five years."

In fact, the relationship had only strengthened over the years, thanks in part to the friendship of their spouses. Alex and Ryan had met in the late forties, when Alex happened into the College Inn, where Ryan was moonlighting from her contract modeling gig at Marshall Field's Department Store. By all accounts, there was an instant attraction between the handsome, debonair hood and the copper-blond beauty, who was well aware of Alex's line of work. When word of their relationship got back to Marshall Field's, Ryan was fired. After Gussie Alex and Marianne Ryan were married in Santa Barbara, California, in 1950, Alex introduced his bride to Sidney, whose wife, Bee, was an established model. Over the next decade, Bee and Marianne produced numerous fashion shows in the Chicagoland environs.

The new Mrs. Alex was a perfect match for Korshak's wife, Bee. Not only were they married to "connected" Chicago men, but they were both drop-dead beautiful, young, blond models. Just as Gussie had used the Korshaks for references, his wife similarly used Bee Korshak's name when applying for modeling work. *Chicago Tribune* crime reporter Sandy Smith recalled that the paper ran a picture of Bee with Marianne when they attended a theater opening together. When Smith showed the picture to Sidney Korshak, he candidly admitted to Smith that he had known Gus Alex quite well for many years.[35] Throughout the fifties, the Alexes and the Korshaks became

Bee Korshak striking a pose, 1957 (*Chicago Tribune*)

Model behavior: Bee Korshak(r.) and Marianne
Ryan Alex attend a 1953 Chicago premiere (*Chicago
Tribune*)

best pals, often seen dining together at Table One of the Pump Room and
vacationing in Europe. The association held other benefits for Ryan, who,
after her eventual divorce from Alex, moved to California, where she became a wardrobe assistant for one of Bee Korshak's best friends, singer and
television star Dinah Shore.

When Korshak moved in on Las Vegas, he often booked Shore into prime
lounges via his ABC Booking Agency. In a 1963 FBI interview, Korshak told
the agents that he, his wife, and their two teenage sons "were taking off
with Dinah Shore, television entertainer, and her oldest child, for a two-
month tour of Europe." George Schlatter, the executive producer of Dinah's
hit TV series, recently described Dinah's friendship with the Korshaks. "Dinah was close to Sidney and Bee, who is a hell of a lady," recalled Schlatter.
"Very, very funny, gaudy—she and Dinah were like the Green Berets of fun.
When I became the producer of the *Dinah Shore Show*, we started using
couturier clothes, and Dinah and Bee would go to Europe and come back
with a boatload of clothes. They just had the best time ever."[36] When Shore
wrote her cookbook *Someone's in the Kitchen with Dinah* in 1971, she used
a number of Bee's recipes, calling her "indefatigable," and "a dear friend of
longstanding." Shore added, "Once we even traveled through Europe—not
by road map—but by the stomach, literally deciding where we wanted to go
and when, according to what restaurant we'd heard about."[37]

When Korshak hosted a fifty-first birthday party for Chicago Ford dealer
Charley Baron at Las Vegas' Tropicana Hotel, he enlisted Dinah to perform.[38] In 1962, when Dinah divorced George Montgomery, Bee was her
"corroborating witness," testifying that Montgomery was "remote and
withdrawn."[39] Dinah described her friend Sidney Korshak to the *Los Angeles Times* in 1969, calling him a "friendly man, sweet and sort of shy. He's
not the kind you'd catch doing the Watusi." Like Korshak's other friends,

Dinah Shore with Bee Korshak at Shore's divorce hearing
(photographer unknown)

Shore couldn't help but be aware of the furtive side of his life, saying that, at a party, Korshak would suddenly get an important phone call. "He disappears," Shore said. "He's gone for the evening."[40]

Pursued by both committee staff and FBI in 1958, Gussie Alex took off on an international tour that saw him elude his hunters for ten full months. Using his wife's maiden name, Gussie traveled under the name Michael Ryan and set a new standard for high living while on the lam. Always one step behind, the Bureau ascertained that the couple had frequented luxurious places the agents would likely never experience:

- Arnold Kirkeby's Beverly Hilton Hotel and his Continental Hilton in Mexico City.
- The mob-connected Flamingo, Sands, and Desert Inn hotels in Vegas.
- The high-end shops on Rodeo Drive, where owners said that he was a regular customer.
- The baths at Desert Hot Springs, California; also at Korshak's leased Villa #32 at Palm Springs' Ocotillo Lodge.
- The Palm Springs Racquet Club, where the Korshaks were members.
- He was seen driving both a Cadillac and a white Lincoln Continental Mark III convertible, the plates of which traced back to Sidney Korshak.

When Chicago FBI agents contacted Korshak on July 14, 1958, at his 134 N. LaSalle office, he initially claimed to have neither a social nor a business relationship with the known Outfit boss. However, when confronted with the license plate traces, the witnesses to Alex in Korshak's Palm Springs getaway, and Alex's alleged employment with Korshak's brother Marshall,

Korshak opened up and admitted that he knew Alex, but only because of his wife's friendship with Marianne Alex. Yes, he knew Alex was in California, where he had given Marianne free use of his luxury cars, but only because his wife's friend Marianne was visiting her mother in Montrose—not because Alex was avoiding the subpoena. When Chicago FBI man Bill Roemer then asked Korshak about the whereabouts of his wife, Bee, he pointedly replied, "I'll tell you where you can reach her. She's having dinner at the Mocambo [in Los Angeles] with Peter Lawford and his wife—you know, Bobby Kennedy's sister." When Roemer reported the intelligence to his superiors in Washington, he assumed that they would authorize a confrontation with Bee Korshak at the upscale eatery. Johnny Leggett, the THP (Top Hoodlum Program) coordinator at headquarters, responded, "Are you kidding, Roemer? They wouldn't touch that with a ten-foot pole."[41]

According to the FBI report of the interview, "Korshak indicated that he would attempt to get word to Alex that he should accept the subpoena." Just over one week later, Alex returned to Chicago, where on July 23 he was served with his subpoena in front of his apartment building. On July 31, at ten thirty A.M., Alex finally appeared before Bobby Kennedy in Washington. After almost a yearlong, expensive search for the elusive hood, Alex gave no more than his name and the following phrase (thirty-nine times): "Under the Fifth Amendment to the Constitution of the United States, I decline to answer on the ground that my answer may tend to incriminate me."[42] (Alex was next surveilled by the Bureau visiting Korshak's new Bel-Air manse. On September 9, 1959, Alex was grabbed by the LAPD and questioned about why he was in L.A. Alex was uncooperative, but made a point of saying he would call his lawyer, Leo Ziffren, Paul's brother. "That and ten cents will buy you a cup of coffee," responded one of the officers. Alex paid a $10 fine, was photographed and released.)

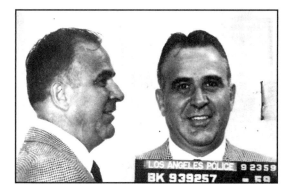

Gus Alex's, 1959 mug shot taken after being picked up on the lam in L.A. with Sid Korshak (Chicago Crime Commission)

Four months after Korshak's friend Gussie Alex came off the lam, Korshak dealt with a family tragedy when his troubled fifty-five-year-old brother, Ted, died on November 18, 1958.[43] According to the Chicago Crime Commission, Ted, who often used an alias, was a narcotics addict and somewhat of a con man. He had been arrested often over the years and had spent time in a narcotics hospital in Lexington, Kentucky.

The Aftermath

Although the McClellan hearings led to indictments against some ninety-six hoods, curiously absent was any criticism of their white-collar and Supermob partners. Opinions vary as to why men like Korshak again escaped unscathed. Tom Zander, Bobby Kennedy's Labor Department contact, recently defended Kennedy's performance. "We had to be very careful because the mob was wiretapping *us*," Zander said. "I had to get one phone, a direct line to Bobby, which was specially rigged to go directly to a central box. Bobby Kennedy was no-holds-barred. When he treated Korshak with kid gloves at the hearings, he must have had a reason for it. It was a feint. Bobby was very good at that."[44]

Attorney Adam Walinsky, Robert Kennedy's legislative aide and speechwriter during President Kennedy's administration, explains Kennedy's benign approach to Korshak as a function of the social learning curve. "The committee saw Dave Beck and he was clearly a crook," Walinsky said. "But the connections between the Teamsters and the pension fund and the families and all that, they don't get to understand that until much later. They're shoving a stick into an anvil. They have no idea what's going on there. During our Senate campaign in 1964, people on the inside were discovering for the first time that the building that was leased by Joint Council 16 of the Teamsters [the very one used by Dio to fix Hoffa's election] belonged to Joe Kennedy. People were first discovering who's connected to whom in that respect as late as 1964."[45]

But Jerry Gladden, both a former chief investigator for the CCC and a Chicago police intel officer, saw a different rationale for Kennedy's performance. "It had been Kennedy's policy throughout the hearings to shy away from matters concerning possible political corruption," Gladden explained in 1997. Gladden said it was the same policy that was employed in the Chicago PD. "We didn't look at any political guys if we wanted to stay in the unit."[46]

Others detected darker hidden political considerations in Kennedy's demonization of Hoffa and his seeming disregard of the Supermob. Chicago investigator Jack Clarke, who headed the investigative unit for Chicago's

Mayor Richard Daley, and occasionally counseled Bobby Kennedy, detected Bobby's personal agenda. "If Bobby really wanted to investigate organized crime, he never had to leave Boston," Clarke recently said. "The McClellan thing was a show. Bobby thought it was just good politics."[47] Clarke's view was supported by Bobby's friend, anticrime journalist Clark Mollenhoff, the Washington editor of the *Des Moines Register*. Mollenhoff, who had prodded Bobby Kennedy for months to spearhead such an investigation, met with little success until he called Bobby and introduced his brother Jack's presidential aspirations into the debate. "Kefauver did his investigations five years ago and it got him enough clout to beat your brother's butt [at the 1956 Democratic National Convention]," Mollenhoff wrote. Suddenly, Bobby's interest was piqued. "Well, why don't you come down and we'll talk about it."

Even more suspicious was the friendship of the Kennedy and Korshak families. The *Chicago Tribune* noted, "Among [Marshall Korshak's] friends over the years were members of the Kennedy family."[48] When Marshall was honored at the Palmer House as the 1967 Israel Bond Man of the Year, the keynote speaker was Bobby's sister Eunice Kennedy's husband, R. Sargent Shriver, who'd managed Papa Joe Kennedy's Chicago Merchandise Mart since 1945.*[,49] The Shrivers and the Sidney Korshaks were often seen together at theatrical openings at such venues as the Shubert Theater, and "Sarge" was a regular at the Pump Room—where Korshak held court at Table One—of the Ambassador East, where Joe Kennedy maintained an apartment. As seen, Sidney's wife Bee socialized in Los Angeles with Bobby's other sister Pat and her husband, Vegas Rat Packer Peter Lawford.

"It is true that the Korshaks were very close with the Kennedys," said one of Korshak's closest and oldest Chicago attorney friends. "When [JFK's brother-in-law] Sarge Shriver came to Chicago, Marshall took him under his wing and became his number one adviser in politics. Marshall got Shriver on the Board of Education, that's how it started. Later, Marshall ended up with Joe Kennedy's Merchandise Mart account for his firm. Sidney was also friends with them. Part of it has to do with Judy Campbell, but there's also a Marilyn Monroe consideration. I won't say any more about that."[50] There were many linkages between Sid Korshak and the Kennedy-Monroe affair, the most obvious being Korshak's friendship with Peter Lawford, JFK's brother-in-law and Monroe's closest confidant at the time of her August 1962 overdose.

---

*Marshall was also the recipient of B'nai B'rith's National Humanitarian Award on September 30, 1967. For the gala at the Palmer House, some 950 people paid $100 each to attend. Among the featured guests was Colonel Henry Crown.

Marshall Korshak escorts Bobby
Kennedy on the stump in Chicago
(Chicago Jewish Archives, Spertus
Institute)

Marshall was also close to intimate Kennedy family adviser Hy Raskin, an attorney for MCA who was soon to play a key role in maneuvering Bobby's brother Jack into the White House.[51] Chicago journalist Roy Harvey wrote in 1979, "In addition to bringing to the Police Board his many years of experience, Korshak is also hailed for his top-flight Zionist and Kennedy connections."[52] When he was campaigning in Chicago on October 17, 1962 (staying at Kirkeby's Blackstone Hotel), Bobby's brother Jack, by now president of the United States, was invited to attend a reception in Marshall's honor slated for Sunday the twenty-first.[53] Although Kennedy had planned to remain in Chicago through the weekend and would likely have accepted the offer, he was unable to attend because, unbeknownst to Marshall (and the rest of the country), Soviet medium-range ballistic missiles (MRBMs) had been discovered in Cuba on the fifteenth and Kennedy had to cut short his visit and return to the White House to manage the crisis. Kennedy announced the missiles to the world on Monday the twenty-second.[54]

Connie Carlson, former longtime crime investigator and Supermob watcher for the California Attorney General's Office, remembered well the Kennedy-Korshak axis. "Joe Kennedy was friends with Sid Korshak," said Carlson. "Before the Kennedy campaign of 1960 became really big, Joe had contact with Korshak, we had heard. There was a time when JFK came here for a fund-raiser, then went to Vegas with the Rat Pack. I think Korshak was involved in that."[55]

Veteran investigative reporter Wendell Rawls recently opined that, in Bobby's zeal to "get Hoffa," he all but ignored Hoffa's contributions to American labor. "Hoffa gave them respect, made them indispensable," Rawls argued. "Bobby Kennedy drove the Teamsters to Nixon [in 1960] by his treatment of Hoffa. RFK thought Hoffa was a thug, but they lost sight of where these guys were before Hoffa. But Bobby was always rich, so he didn't get that."[56]

The focus on Hoffa as the devil incarnate also distracted the committee from the shenanigans of the Supermob types. Philip Manuel, an investigator for the McClellan and other federal probes, recently spoke at length about the committee's work in that regard:

> That's really why I got the McClellan Committee into the hearings on stolen and counterfeit securities, because while the mob guys made the papers, it took the financial guys on the other end to really make it work. One of my pet peeves was that I thought the committee really had a golden opportunity to go after people such as the non-Italians. They really provided the cover and support and the chutzpah to make a lot of the mob activity a reality. I wanted to expose both ends of that. So I got into that and started proving my case before a lot of people knew what I was up to. I'm not talking exclusively about the Italians, because it's much more complex and interesting than just that.
>
> The first person that you have to point to, to make the case of simplification, is Bobby Kennedy. And while he was going after people that he wanted to go after, I think a lot of his father's friends got detected. That's been my thesis all along.[57]

Manuel would make the same case, again in vain, three decades later when he was an investigator for the President's Commission on Organized Crime.

If nothing else, the hearings positioned both Kennedy and Hoffa squarely in the national public consciousness. Kennedy's book on the hearings, *The Enemy Within*, became a brief best seller, with Joe Kennedy personally optioning the film rights to Twentieth Century-Fox for $50,000—the talk was that Paul Newman would play the role of RFK. Of course, given Hollywood's entrenchment with Sid Korshak and Hoffa's Teamsters, the idea that a film that portrayed Hoffa as the bad guy would actually be produced was little more than a fantasy. No sooner had the deal been reported than Fox producer Jerry Wald began receiving threatening phone calls and letters from Teamster leaders and rank-and-file members. One labor thug warned the studio that if the picture was made, Teamsters would refuse to deliver the print to theaters.[58]

Ralph Clare, the founding president (in 1930) of Studio Transportation Drivers Local 399 of the Teamsters, the oldest and most powerful Teamsters

Philip Manuel, commissioner, President's
Commission on Organized Crime, 1986 (National
Archives, commission files)

organization in Hollywood, went so far as to call the L.A. field office of the
FBI to complain. Clare, who lunched regularly with Sidney Korshak and
was in a position to shut down every studio in Hollywood, told the Bureau
"that a picture of this type would cause unfavorable reaction within many
of the labor organizations in Hollywood and that it would disparage labor
unions in general." Clare added that Barney Balaban at Paramount had
been offered the film, "but had rejected it because Paramount did not wish
to get into a controversial situation."[59]

For his part, Hoffa retained Korshak friend and Washington power
lawyer counterpart Edward Bennett Williams for the purpose of filing a
multimillion-dollar lawsuit, should the film actually get made. Predictably,
the film was scuttled, although a completed script was delivered in April
1962 by the Oscar-winning scripter of *On the Waterfront*, Budd Schulberg.*

Although Kennedy's McClellan investigator Pierre Salinger wrote a background report describing Korshak as being "extremely close to the old
Capone mob," he had no qualms about asking Korshak for a campaign contribution seven years later when Salinger ran unsuccessfully for the California State Senate (Korshak donated over $10,000). "The fact is that I needed
to raise $2 million," Salinger later said.[60]

There was one last curious cross-pollination. When he became attorney
general of the United States in 1961, Robert Kennedy hired Jules Stein's
thirty-year-old son-in-law, a bright New York lawyer named William J.
vanden Heuvel, as special counsel to the Justice Department. The hiring was
especially peculiar because the Justice Department was waging a massive
antitrust investigation of vanden Heuvel's father-in-law. (Jules had met

---

*Today, the script gathers dust in Box 98 at the University of Iowa Library's Twentieth
Century-Fox Script Collection.

vanden Heuvel in Bangkok in 1954 and years later introduced him to his daughter Jean, who was fresh from a four-year affair with writer and Nobel laureate William Faulkner.[61] The Stein–vanden Heuvel marriage produced two daughters, one of whom, Katrina vanden Heuvel, would inherit $8.5 million upon Jules's death in 1981[62] and go on to become editor and publisher of the *Nation* in 1995.)

The Bobby Kennedy nuisance had no effect on Korshak's skyrocketing career. According to the LAPD, Korshak wisely added to his investment portfolio during the period: "In 1959, Korshak had an interest in the American National Bank of Chicago. Held 1,500 shares in Merritt, Chapman & Scott Co. [a large building contractor]. Had shares in the [Al Hart's] City National Bank of Beverly Hills and had an oil partnership with Roy Huffington, Inc., 2119 Bank of the Southwest, Houston, Texas."[63] He now maintained swank residences in the Beverly Hills Hotel, New York's Carlyle Hotel, an undisclosed Paris location,* the Drake in Chicago, and a condo in Palm Springs' Ocotillo Lodge—these in addition to his primary Beverly Hills abode. In an FBI interview in June 1959, Korshak indicated "that he and his law partners maintain on a permanent basis Room 2001 in the Essex House in New York City."

As the decade waned, Korshak attended to still other obligations. Among the more bizarre favors Korshak performed in 1959 was the hosting of the marriage of Joan Cohn, widow of Columbia Pictures mogul Harry Cohn, to shoe-store magnate Harry Karl in his (Korshak's) Chicago apartment, with Korshak's friend Judge Joseph Drucker presiding.[64]

An FBI document reported, "After about three weeks, Joan Cohn Karl filed divorce proceedings against Harry Karl in Los Angeles Superior Court . . . The speculation was that Harry Cohn was fronting for Chicago investors in Columbia Pictures and when he died [in 1958] his $4 million estate went into probate and the marriage of Karl and Cohn was contrived as a method through which the real investors in Columbia Pictures could regain title to their property without disclosing themselves on public records." Essentially, the gambit, most assuredly concocted by Korshak, gave Joan time to shift Cohn's assets and not pay inheritance tax. The suspicion of an arranged marriage was fueled by the fact that just three days before the marriage to Cohn, Karl had proposed marriage to actress Debbie Reynolds, a friend of the Korshaks'.[65] (Only a year earlier, Karl, with the advice of Korshak, had divorced—for the third time—the fragile actress Marie McDonald. After the third divorce, McDonald, who was carrying on a long affair with

---

*The FBI noted a Korshak home "in the suburb of Paris." (Report 92-738-48, 2-26-62)

Bugsy Siegel, was supposedly kidnapped, and Korshak was photographed accompanying Karl to his ex's home.[66] She was soon returned safely, and no explanation was ever given for the abduction. Soon thereafter, the distraught actress began trying to kill herself, finally succeeding in 1965.)*

Harry Cohn, it will be recalled, received start-up money for his studio from New Jersey mobster Longy Zwillman, one of the East's most successful bootleggers, and a cofounder of Murder, Inc. Zwillman's lover, Jean Harlow, was the costar of the movie *Riffraff* with Korshak's former fiancée, Dorothy Appleby. Zwillman's links to Korshak also included his use of Arthur Greene (partner of Korshak's Chicago pals Ziffren, Pritzker, and Bazelon) as his investment adviser, leading Zwillman into dabbling in Hollywood productions, Vegas' Sands Hotel, and Kirkeby-Hilton stock purchases.

Korshak's connivance for Joan Cohn was not his only visit to widow's walk that year, and his next rescue was also connected to Zwillman. In April, Korshak came to the aid of Zwillman's widow, Mary. The fifty-five-year-old Longy had hung himself on February 26 in the basement of his Newark, New Jersey, mansion rather than face hard time for tax evasion.†
According to his FBI file, Sidney Korshak accompanied Mary Zwillman to Las Vegas, where he helped her dispose of Longy's interest in the Sands Hotel and Casino. Thanks to Sidney's intercession (for another hefty fee), Mary Zwillman paid minimal inheritance tax, and most of Zwillman's assets simply vanished.

Much as midcentury represented the high point of the mob's long run, so too it was for the Supermob, and Sid Korshak played it for all it was worth. He was now frequently seen at the exclusive Beverly Hills Friars Club on Santa Monica Boulevard, described by the FBI in 1960 thus: "The Friars Club continues to operate as a plush gambling joint and lists among its members such notorious characters as Johnny Rosselli, Jake Factor, [DELETED], and others. Also among the membership are numerous Las Vegas hotel owners and pointholders. There are also legitimate people in the entertainment and

---

*The Karl-McDonald relationship was the basis for the 1991 Neil Simon film *The Marrying Man*, starring married couple Alec Baldwin and Kim Basinger, who soon ended up in a nasty divorce à la Karl and McDonald, albeit with no kidnapping.
†Zwillman's funeral attracted 350 mourners, among them notables from the worlds of politics, business, entertainment, and the rackets, and 1,500 onlookers outside. Among the crowd of 1,500 on the street were Zwillman's boyhood pal the Hollywood producer Dore Schary, and Toots Shor, owner of the famed New York restaurant that bore his name.

business field who are members, but these people seldom appear at the club."[67]

By the late fifties, the Korshaks were also part-time residents of Palm Springs, where they had a condo, Villa 32, at the Ocotillo Lodge, built by the "Singing Cowboy" Gene Autry on 1111 E. Palms Canyon Drive. The lodge was known as a celebrity retreat; however, it was located in a town that was also fast becoming an underworld retreat, a place where the nation's hoodlum elite convened to plan their crime conspiracies. The Korshaks would eventually purchase a home there and become regulars at elite watering holes such as Charlie Farrell's Racquet Club on North Indian Canyon Drive.

In addition to the powerful Chicago Outfit boss (and close Korshak friend) Joe Batters Accardo and Al Hart's former partner Joe Fusco, over a hundred known gangsters boasted homes in the sun-drenched town located at the base of the San Jacinto Mountains. The town's local paper called Palm Springs "the second home" to top officials of the Hotel and Restaurant Employees Union, a client of Korshak's, and a body under constant scrutiny by the feds, who believed the low-paid union officials were bilking their union treasuries to purchase the pricey desert getaway abodes.[*,68] Former Riverside County sheriff Ben Clark opined, "Some big hoodlums may put their heads together in Coachella Valley and plan a crime, but the actual crime they're planning won't occur here; it may happen in Chicago, Detroit, Kansas City, New York, or New Jersey."[69]

In addition to the hoodlum element, already owning homes in Palm Springs were Korshak friends such as Harry Karl, Lew Wasserman, Greg Bautzer, Dinah Shore, Swifty Lazar, Max Factor, Kirk and Anne Douglas, Tony Curtis and Janet Leigh, Tony Martin and Cyd Charisse, Moe Annenberg's son Walter, and Frank Sinatra, who had homes there dating back to 1947, when he built a house on Alejo Road, and who, in the mid-fifties, lived on Wonder Palms Road, situated along the seventeenth fairway of the new Tamarisk Country Club, the main house later outfitted by Bee Korshak.[70]

Korshak's Ocotillo Lodge acquisition was but a prelude to the main event: in June of 1959, Korshak purchased a secluded mansion, built in

---

*Among those with Palm Springs addresses were John Lardino and Frank Calabrese, gunmen from the Chicago Outfit; Rene "the Painter" Piccarreto, a money launderer for the Rochester, New York, mob; and Vincent Dominic Caci of the Buffalo Mafia family. Labor bosses with shady connections also called Palm Springs their second home, among them Hotel and Restaurant Employees Union president Ed Hanley (Sid Korshak's connection to that union); its VP, Anthony Anselmo; Local 309 head Anthony Scimecana; and its business manager, Pat Battista.

1948, from Harry Karl for the astonishingly low price of $53,000.*,71 (On his 1961 application for homeowner's insurance, Korshak gave the assessed value of the home as $300,000. In 2004, the property was assessed at over $3 million.) The new Korshak home was located at 10624 Chalon Road, a switchback that boasted elite Hollywood homeowners such as Henry Fonda, John Gavin, Neil Simon, and Gene Wilder. Located in the upper reaches of exclusive Bel-Air, the semicircular, gated home, which borders the property of auto tycoon Lee Iacocca, was a tasteful blend of art deco and classical. The marble-floored manse is situated on a two-acre parcel, replete with gardens, guesthouses, and pool. The entrance, in the inner part of the semicircle, is windowless, contrasting with the outer rim and its floor-to-ceiling windows that overlook the gardens and flowing streams.

Completely hidden from the road by a gated, eight-foot wall, the site became legendary not just for the Korshaks' annual Christmas Eve dinner parties, but also for its extravagant amenities. Bee Korshak took great pride in her interior-decorating abilities, later outfitting the homes of a number of SoCal bourgeoisie, including the Palm Springs pad of her great friends Frank and Barbara Sinatra.[72]

Kurt Niklas, owner of the celeb haunt Bistro restaurant in Beverly Hills, attended many of the Korshak soirées and wrote of their extravagance in his memoir, *The Corner Table*: "Four hundred people minimum, maybe more; it was hard to estimate because it lasted all day and you could come and go at your leisure; you could stay five minutes or five hours, the Korshaks didn't care. Anyone who was anybody was invited, and a few people who preferred anonymity. There was always an orchestra, comprised of some of the finest musicians in Los Angeles, and the caviar and champagne was the best that money could buy . . . The Korshak mansion had a grand dining room with three tables that sat eight people each."[73]

Other Chez Korshak luxuries included one of the best wine cellars in Los Angeles, a walk-in vault,† chauffeurs' quarters, and a world-class art collection. Virginia Korshak, the ex-wife of Sidney's son Harry, recalled, "There were Rembrandt sculptures, original Picassos, Renoirs, and Chagalls. But it was all very tastefully done."[74] Ron Joy, an L.A. photographer who dated Frank Sinatra's daughter, Nancy, remembered his visits to the manse. "I attended a couple parties there with Nancy. The house contained a fabulous

---

*The grantor-grantee records of Los Angeles County show that the property was granted to Korshak by deed from Karl's Shoe Stores, Limited.
†Years later, when new owners drilled open the vault, they were shocked to find one empty gun holster and just one bullet.

10624 Chalon Road (various views, author photos)

art collection that had to be valued in the millions."[75] Fellow L.A. attorney and Korshak friend Leo Geffner recalled that not a room was left unadorned; no matter where one went in the Korshak home, one was reminded of the owner's success. "You'd go to the bathroom in his house, and you'd see a small Degas, a Cézanne, a Matisse!" said Geffner. "He didn't know anything about art. I think it was more, this is what you do when you're rich, you have art."[76] Geffner, clearly stunned by the collection, which included pre-Colombian art, recently added, "I can't exaggerate what that collection was like. Sidney had a New York curator on retainer whose job was to find art for the collection."[77]

Whether to protect the art or the family from enemies of Korshak's mob associates, one bizarre fixture at the house left guests a tad unnerved: armed guards. Hollywood producer of *The Godfather* Gray Frederickson, who co-produced the 1973 film *Hit!* with Korshak's son Harry, remembered his forays to Camp Korshak: "It was walled and gated, with armed guards on the grounds. Harry told me the guards were there to protect their art collection."[78] Former *Sacramento Bee* reporter Dick Brenneman, who followed Korshak's life closely, recalled, "I was told that the guards were former

Korshak party invitation and reminder (Dominick Dunne)

Israeli army members, brought in to 'to protect the Degas.' "[79] Former studio executive turned writer Dominick Dunne was invited to the Korshaks' annual holiday bash and came away shaken. "That was the first house I ever went to in my life where there was a guard with a gun at the door," Dunne said in 1997. "It gave me the creeps, if you want to know the truth . . . I went to visit Phyllis McGuire once in Las Vegas—incredible woman. A guy with a machine gun answered her door. But it was at Sidney's that I saw that first."[80] Friend Leo Geffner added that, in later years, one of the guards was often seen driving Sidney around Los Angeles. "He had a dual-capacity bodyguard/chauffeur who hung around the house," remembered Geffner.[81] More typically for this locale, the grounds boasted a sophisticated electronic security system as backup to the armed protectors.

The sale by Harry Karl would not go unappreciated by Korshak, who returned the favor when he discovered that Karl had a boyish crush on actress Debbie Reynolds, who just happened to be a friend of Sid and Bee's. Reynolds had met Karl when she'd raised funds for the Thalians, a group of actors who donated to various children's charities. Among the many donors were the Sid Korshaks and Al Harts. But the softest touch in town, according to Reynolds, was playboy heir Harry Karl. For months Karl had been sending flowers and begging Reynolds for a date, only to be rebuffed by the actress, who was just recuperating from her breakup with Eddie Fisher. Thus, in December 1959 Sidney played the yenta, calling Reynolds with a request.

"Won't you please accept a call from Harry, Debbie? It's eating him up inside. He just wants a chance to talk to you."

"No, Sidney," Reynolds replied. "I don't need this."

After another call from Sidney, Reynolds relented and went for a dinner date with Karl. Surprisingly, the duo clicked, and soon they rented a Malibu beach house together and married in 1960. When the couple attempted to buy the MGM backlot, their personal banker, Al Hart, raised $5 million for them, but the deal fell through nonetheless. Between introducing her to Karl and booking her regularly into his Riviera Hotel, where he reportedly negotiated a million-dollar deal for her debut, Korshak helped to make Debbie a wealthy woman. However, that wealth disappeared when the marriage fell apart fourteen years later.*

It was a time when all was splendid in the Korshak world: behind the gate, the tiled, circular Chalon driveway was jammed with the finest cars available—a personal obsession of Sidney's—that numbered at least six at

---

*Regrettably, Karl was an inveterate womanizer and gambler, losing hundreds of thousands in Vegas and at the Beverly Hills Friars Club.

one time: Rolls-Royces, Jaguars, Porsches, Bentleys, Cadillacs, and Bee's Karmann Ghia convertible; Bee became a club tennis player and world traveler; teenage sons Stuart and Harry were seen being chauffeured to Pasadena's Polytechnic School, where Stuart was student body president; Sidney even began collecting the requisite mistresses, the most obvious expression of male power and success, who were openly invited to the Korshak holiday parties. When Korshak applied for homeowner's insurance, he stated that his net worth was now $2 million, a gross understatement.[82]

Given the hedonistic trappings, one would think that the fiftyish Korshak might have turned into a Hefner-like hermit and enjoyed his Garden of Eden exclusively. But by all accounts, sybaritic Sidney was rarely there to enjoy the paradise he had crafted in the hills of Bel-Air. Not only was he keeping a hectic schedule with trips to Europe, New York, Chicago, and Palm Springs, he began wearing out a trail to a city that epitomized the most recent successful partnership of the underworld and the Supermob: Las Vegas.

CHAPTER 9

Forty Years in the Desert

If you worked in Vegas, you worked for the mob, because Vegas was all mob money. It was two different groups down there, from Chicago and New York, who invested money down there. Vegas was a piece of shit. A desert hole.

—GEORGE JACOBS, PERSONAL VALET FOR FRANK SINATRA[1]

THE COMMON MISPERCEPTION IS that the mob's association with Las Vegas began when New York boss Meyer Lansky's partner Ben "Don't Call Me Bugsy" Siegel built his Flamingo Hotel-Casino in 1946. But the town's history is more a product of the machinations of Chicago's crime syndicates and dates back more than a decade earlier than Bugsy's desert adventure.

The prehistory of the area began in the early nineteenth century, when Spanish explorers discovered an artesian spring in the southern part of the region. They christened the area Las Vegas, or the Meadows, and, after the conclusion of the Mexican-American War in 1848, ceded the territory to the new nation called the United States of America. There followed periods of domination by Mormon missionaries, and temporary gold and silver rushes. When the mineral deposits petered out, locals considered ways to rejuvenate the state's stalled economy. The state was given a second life thanks to two occurrences in the same year of 1931: the beginning of the construction of the Hoover Dam and the passage of the Wide Open Gambling Bill.

For over twelve years, federal officials had argued over what to do about the disastrous periodic flooding of the fourteen-hundred-mile Colorado River. Finally a bold plan was adopted that would, if successful, not only tame the Colorado, but provide water and hydroelectric power throughout the West: the government moved to construct the world's largest dam thirty miles to the southeast of Las Vegas. Since no city can grow without an adequate water supply, the construction of the massive Hoover Dam, which broke ground in 1931, went a long way toward making the idea of Las Vegas viable. With some five thousand dam workers looking for somewhere to squander their discretionary income, Nevadans started talking of legalizing gambling.

The Chicago–Las Vegas Connection

The modern notion of Las Vegas as the planetary mecca for casino gambling was conceived in large part by Sidney Korshak's closest Chicago cronies. The reasoning behind the hoods' interest in legalizing casino gambling was simple: not only would criminals now have a believable, and legit, explanation for their huge incomes, but they would attain a sublime and seemingly undetectable means to steal directly from the government: by skimming massive profits from the casinos' count rooms before the gross take was reported to the IRS. The only obstacle to this utopian scheme was the pesky fact that casino gambling was still illegal in the United States. But the mob had inside knowledge that one locale was primed for a reassessment of the gambling statutes—the same state that feared the loss of five thousand dam workers. Therefore, Curly Humphreys, the mob's Einstein and payoff master, was dispatched to the Nevada statehouse to make certain that it happened.

The FBI's massive file on Sid Korshak's underworld link Curly Humphreys (4,949 pages) notes Humphreys's constant interstate travel to grease the skids for the expanding Outfit enterprises. In one example, Humphreys traveled to New York State to bribe legislators to repeal the Sullivan Act, which forbade ex-cons from carrying a weapon.* Humphreys frequently journeyed westward, where he built a getaway home in Norman, Oklahoma, the hometown of his wife. Irv Owen, a Norman native and retired attorney who had known Humphreys's extended family and friends since 1937, recently stated emphatically that he knew how Nevada's Wide Open Gambling Bill came to be enacted: "In the 1930s, Humphreys and his protégé Johnny Rosselli [who worked closely with Korshak in Los Angeles] bribed the Nevada legislature into legalizing gambling. Las Vegas owes everything to Murray Humphreys."[2]

---

*Humphreys often visited St. Louis, Kansas City, Los Angeles, and Dallas, where he helped expand the gang's numbers racket; in Oklahoma, he was believed to have masterminded the flow of booze into that dry state; he made frequent trips to the nation's capital to visit with the "mob's congressman," Roland Libonati.

John Detra, the son of one of Las Vegas' earliest gambling-club owners, recently corroborated Owen, specifically insofar as Outfit money passing under the table at the Carson City statehouse. John Detra's father, Frank Detra, had moved from New York to Las Vegas in 1927. A year later, according to John, thirty-one-year-old Frank Detra and family began receiving visits from none other than Chicago's Al Capone, then twenty-eight. Although John had no knowledge of how the two met, it was clear to him that they were close friends. (It is possible that the friendship goes back to New York, since both men were there at the same time and were of a similar age.) The younger Detra still retains a gold pocket watch Capone gave his father, the back of which bears the inscription FRANCO AMICI ALPHONSE, which translates as "Frank and Alphonse are friends." Detra and Capone were obviously planning a business partnership, said John.

After a brief stint in Las Vegas as a dealer in downtown's Boulder Club, Detra was staked by a still-unidentified Eastern entity to build his own club five miles outside the city line, on a section of Highway 91 that would later be named The Strip. His club, The Pair-O-Dice, would make history as the Strip's first upscale carpet joint. In the vicinity at the time, there only existed The Red Rooster sawdust roadhouse. Although Detra's club was a speakeasy of sorts (a code word was needed to enter), it boasted all the refinements of Vegas lounges that would hold sway three decades later. Open only at night, the Pair-O-Dice featured delicious Italian cuisine, jazz and dance bands, fine wine, and of course, table games. To keep the operation afloat, the requisite bribes were in force. "The old man went to town every month with envelopes, several of them, and came back without the envelopes," John remembered.

When the 1930 debate over gambling legalization was joined, young John began accompanying his father as he made deliveries of cash-stuffed briefcases and envelopes to influential Nevadans across the state. Frank Detra admitted to his son that the money was being spent to ensure the passage of the Wide Open Gambling Bill. John believed the money had to have come from the Capone gang, since Capone was the only major player close to his father. John was aware that some monies were being paid to state legislators, but his father's role may have been even more critical to the pro-gambling strategy: Frank Detra's contacts superseded the local power brokers. "They were all federal people, top-drawer people who influenced the state people," John remembered. On one trip to Reno, John was asked to make the delivery himself. "Dad gave me a little briefcase and said, 'See that house over there? Go ring the bell.' I went over and rang the doorbell, and a man came to the door and said, 'Oh, thank you,' took the suitcase, and closed the door."[3]

After Nevada governor Fred Balzar signed the law legalizing gambling on March 19, 1931, Frank Detra openly operated the Pair-O-Dice until 1941, when he sold the business to Guy McAfee, who incorporated the club's structure into his Last Frontier Club. Detra, who died in 1984, went on to operate clubs in Reno and Ely.

In the early years, Las Vegas city commissioners issued only seven gambling licenses for downtown clubs, most of which had maintained illegal gambling operations for years. Among the licensed clubs was the Boulder Club, where Frank Detra had worked briefly as a dealer, and the Las Vegas Club.* Other club owners with Chicago affiliations were among the first to cash in on the Las Vegas gambling rush. On May 2, 1931, Johnny Rosselli's bootlegging partner from Los Angeles Tony "the Hat" Cornero opened Las Vegas' first legal hotel-casino, The Meadows, just east of the city. Unlike the small, sawdust-coated downtown casinos on Fremont Street, Cornero's place was a Lansky-like "carpet joint," but combined with well-appointed hotel accommodations. The May 3, 1931, *Las Vegas Age* newspaper described the Meadows: "Potent in its charm, mysterious in its fascination, the Meadows, America's most luxurious casino, will open its doors tonight and formally embark upon a career which all liberal-minded persons in the West will watch closely."

Although visionary, the Meadows was a huge gamble during the Depression. In southern Nevada especially, there were not yet enough well-to-do patrons to sustain the business. In just a couple years, the Meadows closed, only to reopen as a high-class bordello. Cornero would resurface in the 1950s to open another Vegas hotel-casino, the Stardust, which was quickly appropriated by the Outfit.

Cornero, Humphreys, Rosselli, and the rest were ultimately the victims of bad timing. The nation's depressed economy kept the number of available affluent high rollers to a minimum. The economic conditions around Las Vegas were even worse, since after the Hoover Dam was completed in 1935, the area saw the exodus of the five-thousand-man workforce and their families. The situation thus remained in stasis as Vegas once again became synonymous with low-rent dude ranches, cowboy casinos (with gamblers' horses harnessed out front), and sawdust-floored gambling roadhouses. Out-of-towners were dispossessed of a bit more cash by state legislators, who passed no-fault quickie divorce codes. But roadhouse gambling and quickie divorces were not panaceas for a flat state economy. However,

---

*The others were the Northern, the Rainbow, the Big Four, the Railroad Club, and the Exchange Club.

redemption would come soon after World War II in the form of an ambitious New York hoodlum who had been peddling the Outfit's Trans-America wire service to the downtown gambling joints. The movie-star-handsome thug came up with the best scam idea of his life: he decided that the time was right for Las Vegas (and the Chicago mob) to revisit the hotel-casino notion pioneered by Tony Cornero in 1931. With the Chicago–New York Commission's financial backing, Ben Siegel gave new life to Nevada while ironically sacrificing his own. In doing so, the fortunes of Nevada, and particularly Las Vegas, would improve forever.

Benjamin Siegel, Meyer Lansky's childhood pal and New York crime partner, had been exiled to the West Coast when his violent temper threatened to start a gang war. In Los Angeles, Siegel began fronting for the Chicago Outfit's Trans-America betting wire service, scattering agents throughout the Southwest. Siegel guaranteed his new empire's success by bribing countless state politicians and law enforcement officials, all the way up to the state Attorney General's Office. Among the men handling his legal affairs were Greg Bautzer and Sid Korshak.

Bugsy Siegel's selection as the Outfit's wire representative in the Southwest was understandable: he had known the gang's patriarch Big Al Capone since both their formative days in the Williamsburg section of Brooklyn, where they had worked in consort as strike-breaking thugs for garment-industry scions.

In 1941, just after the race wire was legalized in Nevada, Siegel sent his aide and lifelong Brooklyn friend Moey Sedway to Las Vegas with a charge to install the Outfit's Trans-America wire service in the downtown Vegas haunts of the serious gamblers—casinos such as the Golden Nugget, Horseshoe, Golden Gate, and Monte Carlo. The task was virtually effortless, since the "Glitter Gulch" casino owners saw bookie wagering as a draw and hoped that in between races the bettors would sample the other games of chance on-site.

The money was huge. In no time, Siegel was receiving a $25,000-per-month cut from the Las Vegas wire alone, which he called the Golden Nugget News Service. Sedway became a civic-minded philanthropist, who, for a time, considered running for public office—that is, until Bugsy set him straight. In a typical fit of rage, Siegel screamed at Moey, "We don't run for office. We own the politicians."

The second incarnation of Las Vegas casino gambling was about to occur. At the time, Willie Wilkerson, the publisher of the *Hollywood Reporter* and the owner of successful L.A. nightclubs on the Sunset Strip, hoped to create a new "strip" on the Las Vegas outskirts. Years later, the FBI would learn that there was also a hidden partner in the Flamingo project. As Chicago FBI agent Bill Roemer recounted, "We learned how Hump [Curly Humphreys] went there in 1946 to assist 'Bugsy' Siegel in establishing the first hotel-casino on what is now known as the Strip."[4]

By 1948, Virgil Peterson of the Chicago Crime Commission had determined the exact amount that Sid Korshak's Chicago bosses had invested in Siegel's operation. In a letter to the Nevada Gaming Commission, Peterson noted that, via the Fischetti brothers, Chicago had transmitted over $300,000 to Bugsy. If the figure is accurate, it would make the Chicago Outfit the most substantial shareholder in the Flamingo, since the largest investor of record (Siegel) had endowed only $195,000. As previously noted, Supermob associate and longtime Korshak friend Al Hart invested $75,000 in the Flamingo,[5] even more than Meyer Lansky, who chipped in an initial $25,000, adding $75,000 more later. Del Webb, the Phoenix-based builder who constructed many of the Japanese internment camps, was again enlisted to lend his talent in the furtherance of the Supermob's expansion.

Now, investors anxiously awaited the casino's grand opening, and when the big day arrived on December 26, 1946, everything seemed to conspire against Siegel, who at the time was involved in a tempestuous affair with a favorite Chicago moll and skim courier Virginia Hill. Bugsy had spared no expense for entertainers such as George Jessel, Rose Marie, George Raft, Jimmy Durante, and Xavier Cugat's Orchestra, but despite his best efforts, he was thwarted by Mother Nature and local politics, the combination of which guaranteed the Flamingo's opening would be a disaster. In Los Angeles, a winter storm grounded the two planes Siegel had chartered to ferry celebs to the gala; those who did arrive, such as Clark Gable, Lana Turner, and Joan Crawford, either drove the 350 miles from L.A. or took a train. While in Nevada, most local gamblers, accustomed to the sawdust joints, had no desire to don dinner jackets and buy overpriced drinks merely to play a round of blackjack.[6]

In the face of massive cost overruns, it came as little surprise that Siegel was the victim of a mob rubout on June 20, 1947, or, as Flamingo comic Alan King put it, "Bugsy took a cab." Twenty minutes after the shooting, before police even arrived, the Outfit's Phoenix bookie chief, Gus Greenbaum, along with Moey Sedway and Morris Rosen, walked into the casino at the Flamingo and announced that they had taken over. The next day, the Outfit's Joe Epstein arrived to do the books. Over the next year, Greenbaum used $1 million in borrowed Outfit money and Mormon bank loans to enlarge the hotel's capacity from ninety-seven to over two hundred rooms. It turned out to be a good investment, since in its first year the Flamingo showed a $4 million profit, skim not included. Although Greenbaum did a brilliant job as the Flamingo's manager, his own alcohol and gambling addictions would ultimately produce tragic results. In the meantime, Greenbaum was proclaimed the first mayor of Paradise Valley—or the Strip.

The widely held perception that Siegel was killed over finances was later dispelled by many, among them Sidney Korshak, who occasionally represented Siegel's legal affairs in Los Angeles. "Ben [Siegel] introduced me to Sidney Korshak, who said he was his consigliere," said screenwriter Edward Anhalt.[7] Anhalt (*The Pride and the Passion, Becket, Jeremiah Johnson, Not as a Stranger,* etc.) recently recalled a conversation with Korshak when Anhalt had sought out Korshak years later with the intent of getting background for a possible film on Siegel.

"You know all that bullshit about Ben being killed because he spent too much money?" Korshak asked. "Absolute fiction." The man who ordered the contract, according to Korshak, was Virginia Hill's first lover, "the guy from Detroit . . . the guy from the Purple Gang." The only man from the Purple Gang with the power to order such a hit was none other than future Las Vegas sachem Morris Barney "Moe" Dalitz.* "He was very offended by it [Siegel's battering of Hill]," said Korshak. "He warned Siegel," Korshak said, "and Siegel paid no attention to the warning, and they whacked him."[8]

Korshak's allegation of Siegel's abuse of Hill was corroborated by other hangers-on as well as by the FBI, which noted in their Siegel file, "Early in June, 1947, Siegel had a violent quarrel with Virginia Hill at which time he allegedly beat her so badly that she still had visible bruises several weeks later. Immediately after the beating she took an overdose of narcotics in a suicide threat and was taken unconscious to the hospital. Upon recovery she immediately arranged to leave for an extended trip to Europe."

After Bugsy's demise, the Flamingo began delivering big-time. In addition to the millions in legit profit, the partners were sharing a count-room skim estimated in the hundreds of thousands of dollars per month. With dollar signs now occupying their complete field of vision, the ravenous hoods

---

*Before forming his Mayfield Road Gang, Dalitz had been associated with Detroit's Purple Gang.

quickly looked for their next cash cow, but this time they would improve the scheme by choosing a better front man than Bugsy, and one with no criminal convictions to attract the government's radar. Thus when the New York and Chicago mobs made their post-Bugsy foray into the Nevada desert in 1949, they concocted a bold game plan: they would hide behind intentionally arcane casino investment partnerships so as to obfuscate the true nature of the endeavor. Casino owners of record rarely indicated the true powers behind the thrones.

"The owner names on file at the Nevada Gaming Commission in the early days were a joke, and everybody knew it," said one retired local attorney familiar with the lax licensing procedures. In one wiretapped conversation, East Coast mob investor Doc Stacher summed up the strategy nicely for the eavesdropping feds. "We worked out a deal that gave each group an interlocking interest in each other's hotels," Stacher explained, "and our lawyers set it up so that nobody could really tell who owned what out there."[9] Even Nevada's then governor, Grant Sawyer, was aware of the "hidden interests" and the casino theft that was transpiring right under his nose. Sawyer said that "there is probably considerable unaccounted-for vagrant cash going somewhere," and that both state and federal governments are "being deprived of unknown amounts of taxes."[10]

With Sid Korshak in place to broker these complex hidden casino ownerships and to mediate disputes among the partners, the hoods needed owners of record whose IRS statements reflected legitimate wealth. The obvious first choice for the ownership role was the non-Chicago Supermob associate Moe Dalitz, a lifelong friend of MCA heir Lew Wasserman's, Jimmy Hoffa's, and Meyer Lansky's. The addition of Dalitz to the fold would herald a three-decade Supermob affair with Sin City.

"A Man of Gargantuan Contrasts"[11]

Born on December 12, 1899, in Boston, the son of Russian immigrants Jacob and Anna Cohn Dolitz (later Dalitz), "Moe" Dalitz and family relocated to Michigan, where Moe's father opened a successful laundry business. Moe developed into a wiry young tough, with few scruples about with whom he associated in his quest to rise above his current situation. One associate of Dalitz's, a Midwestern attorney, recently described him: "Dalitz had gray eyes that never blinked. He walked like a cat—on the balls of his feet."[12]

When prohibition hit in 1919, laundry trucks became a useful commodity in the world of the bootleggers, and the enterprising Moe used his father's trucks to deliver the hooch. Relocating to Cleveland, Dalitz bought

Dalitz testifying before the Kefauver Committee in Los Angeles, February 28, 1951 (Cleveland State University, Special Collections)

the best barges money could buy, floated his trucks across Lake Erie to Canada on what he called his Little Jewish Navy, and brought them back loaded to the gills with prime Canadian liquor. Because his trucks disembarked at Cleveland's Mayfield Road dead end on the shores of Lake Erie, Dalitz's gang was christened the Mayfield Road Gang. The key members of Dalitz's gang included Morris Kleinman, Lou "Uncle Louie" Rothkopf (Rhody), Ruby Kolod, Sam "Sambo" Tucker, and Tom McGinty. When Senator Estes Kefauver's committee questioned his bootlegging, Dalitz said, "If you people wouldn't have drunk it, I wouldn't have bootlegged it."

Often working under the moniker Moe Davis, Dalitz and the gang branched out to run gambling "gyp joints" such as the Pettibone Club, the Thomas Club, and the Arrow Club. High-roller clients were chauffeured by drivers such as Jimmy "the Weasel" Fratianno, who would go on to become one of the biggest Mafia turncoats in history. As local illegal gambling czars (with racing books in Ohio, New York, and Florida) and former bootleggers, the gang worked closely with Detroit's Purple Gang bosses Al Polizzi and the Milano brothers, New York's Meyer Lansky, Bugsy Siegel, Lucky Luciano, and Lepke Buchalter of Murder, Inc., and New Jersey's Longy Zwillman. In addition, Dalitz and Kleinman leased L.A.'s Moulin Rouge Nightclub (6230 Sunset Boulevard) from Lansky's partner Joseph "Doc" Stacher.

When questioned by the FBI in 1960, Dalitz said he met most of these hoods when he was stationed at New York's Governors Island during World War II. No one actually believed that Dalitz's criminal associations were just a matter of casual happenstance, since it was said that anyone who questioned Dalitz's power "would have to deal with Lucky, Meyer and Bug."[13]

Not surprisingly, most of the Mayfield Road Gang had criminal convictions: Kleinman served three years at Lewisburg federal penitentiary for tax evasion; Lithuanian-born "Sambo" Tucker boasted a Kentucky gambling conviction; McGinty served eighteen months in the Atlanta federal penitentiary for violating the National Prohibition Act (NPA); Kolod served three years in New York for unlawful entry, after previous bootlegging and assault-and-battery arrests; and Rothkopf/"Rhody" was the prime suspect in the murder of Cleveland councilman William "Rarin' Bill" Potter.

Another Dalitz associate was Henry Beckerman, whose name appeared on the liquor license for the Mayfair Theater, which was run by the Mayfields, and which provided early work for MCA's Lew Wasserman. In 1936, Beckerman was charged as an arsonist, but the corrupted officials refused to extradite his fellow arsonists from out of state, allowing the charges to be dropped. One week after the dismissal, Beckerman's daughter Edie, who referred to Dalitz as "Uncle Moe," married Lew Wasserman.[14]

Thanks to corrupted officials, Dalitz managed to have all their "yellow sheet" police records destroyed,[15] and Dalitz himself seemed to be coated with prosecutorial Teflon. That, and the fact that he had local officials well compensated, gave him a clean record with no convictions. Nonetheless, Dalitz was the prime suspect in the shooting murder of bootlegging rival Morris Komisarow in May 1930. When Komisarow's bloated body surfaced on Lake Erie a month later, it was tied to an anchor that belonged to Dalitz's boat, *The Natchez*. The anchor was stamped NAVY, also hinting of Dalitz's Little Jewish Navy.[16]

Many years later, Dalitz had the audacity to threaten drunken heavyweight boxing champion Sonny Liston. After the two exchanged words in Hollywood's Beverly Rodeo Hotel in 1964, Liston made a fist and reared back, then a mild-voiced Dalitz cut him off, "If you hit me, nigger, you'd better kill me. Because if you don't, I'll make one telephone call and you'll be dead in twenty-four hours."[17]

The Mayfield Gang made its headquarters in Suite 281 in the Hollenden Hotel, whose owner, Julius Epstein, would become a partner with Ziffren, Pritzker, Bazelon, and Greene in Franklin Investment Company (see chapter 5). From that vantage point, the gang expanded its operation and interstate mob alliances. In 1929, when Chicago's Al Capone decreed that there should be an organized crime convention, Dalitz offered to host it in Cleveland, but was overruled. Dalitz and the Mayfields attended the convocation, which was ultimately held in Atlantic City and attended by over thirty underworld bosses.[18] During the 1932 Democratic National Convention in Chicago, Dalitz appeared in Lucky Luciano's suite in the Supermob-invested Drake Hotel, where the New York boss was lining up delegates for

FDR.[19] Fourteen years later, Dalitz attended the farewell bash for Luciano, who was being deported to Italy.[20]

As Dalitz's friendship with Lansky grew, the two entered into major investment partnerships, the most visible being the building of molasses-alcohol distilleries throughout the Northeast, a venture that began in 1933, immediately after Prohibition was repealed.[21] The move exemplified the Supermob credo that emphasized a major presence in the legit world. Dalitz converted his profits into lucrative legitimate businesses, including linen supply companies, steel companies, and even a railroad.* His Detroit investments inevitably brought him into contact with Teamsters leader Jimmy Hoffa, whom he met in the mid-1930s through Hoffa's mistress, Sylvia Pagano. In 1949, when the Teamsters threatened to strike the Detroit Dry Cleaners Association, another Dalitz dry-cleaning racket, Dalitz slipped Hoffa $17,500 to get the union off his back.

His legit businesses notwithstanding, Dalitz was never more than a wink and a nod away from his underworld roots, and when the call came to join the Supermob's first major flirtation with Las Vegas, Dalitz, who realized its vast potential, jumped at the chance. According to the late Chicago FBI agent Bill Roemer, after World War II, Lansky dispatched Dalitz to Las Vegas to check on Siegel. Bugsy's murder came soon after Moe made his report.[22] As Dalitz later said, "All in all, the opportunity in Las Vegas seemed too good for me and my associates to pass up. I was fifty years old then and I could breathe easier in this climate."[23]

With Dalitz's lungs thus relieved, the Supermob's thirty-year affair with Vegas had its first tryst in a getaway named the Desert Inn.

The "DI"

The Desert Inn was the dream child of Wilbur Clark, a gambler from San Diego, California, with the personality of a showman. When Clark came up $90,000 short for the initial construction in 1947, work was halted and the wooden structure sat unfinished on the future Strip for almost two years. In 1949, a partnership bailout offer miraculously arrived from an unlikely locale: Cleveland, Ohio—Dalitz's Mayfield Road Gang. The Little Jewish Navy offered to put up the outstanding $90,000 start-up, plus $3.4 million,

---

*Among Dalitz's many holdings: Michigan Industrial Laundry Co. in Detroit and the Pioneer Linen Supply Co. in Cleveland, Colonial Laundry, Union Enterprise, Buckeye Catering Co., and percentages in the Reliance Steel Co. and the Detroit Steel Co. And there was Milco Sales, Dalitz Realty, Michigan Modern Land Co., Berdene Realty and the Liberty Ice Cream Co., River Downs Race Track, and the Coney Island Dog Track. Dalitz even owned a piece of the Chicago & Rock Island Railroad.

in exchange for 74 percent ownership, and they would be more than happy to let Clark call it Wilbur Clark's Desert Inn—so much the better for the hidden owners.

Dalitz's proposal to Clark embodied the proverbial "offer he couldn't refuse." Two years later, the Kefauver Committee's Senator Charles Tobey asked Clark about the men who'd come to his "rescue."

"Before you got into bed with crooks to finish this proposition, didn't you look into these birds at all?" asked the senator.

"Not too much. No, sir," answered Clark.

"You have the most nebulous idea of your business I ever saw. You have a smile on your face but I don't know how the devil you do it."

"I have done it all my life," Clark replied.

Wilbur Clark thus became the first major front for the Vegas Supermob contingent. In short order he went from being the gregarious "Ambassador of Vegas" to a frightened shell of a man who provided cover for the man later called "the Godfather of Vegas," Moe Dalitz. When the Nevada Tax Commission hesitated to deliver the requisite license (thanks to a damning report on Dalitz submitted to the commission members by the Chicago Crime Commission's Virgil Peterson), "juice" was promptly supplied by Galveston mafioso (and DI investor) Sam Maceo to Senator Pat McCarran, and the precious document appeared as if by magic.[24] Dalitz became vice president of the resort, while Ruby Kolod assumed the coveted casino manager post. Interestingly, 13 percent shareholder Sam Tucker opened an office in Chicago at 134 N. LaSalle, home turf of the Korshaks, the Supermob, and the Teamsters Pension Fund. Real estate entrepreneur Allard Roen, the son of Cleveland gambler Frank Rosen, came aboard as manager; Roen would later plead guilty to a $5 million stock swindle.[25]

Finally, after an over-three-year gestation, the $6.5 million, three-hundred-room Desert Inn opened on April 24, 1950. Guests of the new resort were greeted by the DI's exterior trademark, a Painted Desert scene highlighted by a large Joshua-tree cactus. The hotel's rooms featured a modified Western décor, and the countless amenities included:

- Five hundred air-conditioned rooms and suites
- The luxurious 450-seat Painted Desert Room
- A twenty-four-hundred-square-foot casino, one of Nevada's largest
- A ladies' salon/health club
- The Strip's only eighteen-hole golf course, situated on its 272 acres of property
- The Sky Room Lounge

- For those with more bizarre tastes, the hotel offered choice viewing of A-bomb mushroom clouds when the nukes were tested a mere sixty-five miles away.

For the opening gala, Dalitz's pal Lew Wasserman sent MCA's Edgar Bergen, the Donn Arden Dancers, and the Ray Noble Orchestra. Van Heflin, Bud Abbott, and Lou Costello were among other MCA clients sent as audience shills.

"That's when all the gangsters started coming," said Barbara Greenspun, publisher of the *Las Vegas Sun*.[26] She was right: also in the crowd that night to protect the interests of hidden investors were mafiosi such as Black Bill Tocco, Joe Massei, Sam Maceo, Pete Licavoli, and Frank Milano.[27]

On the first Saturday after the opening, the Desert Inn casino lost $87,000 in one eight-hour shift, $36,000 to one lucky winner. But it was the best publicity any resort could ask for. People flocked to the resort, and by the following Friday, the casino had recouped its losses, with the first week's profits totaling $750,000.

In the coming years, the DI featured some of the most exciting acts in show business, among them one Frank Sinatra, who made his Las Vegas debut in the DI's Painted Desert Showroom on September 13, 1951. "Wilbur Clark gave me my first job in Las Vegas," the Voice recalled in 1992. "That was in 1951. For six bucks you got a filet mignon dinner and me."*

The Supermob's presence at the DI was not limited to Moe Dalitz. *The Godfather* movie producer Gray Frederickson said there was at least one more notable stockholder. "Sid Korshak owned a piece of the Desert Inn," Frederickson said recently. "We went to Vegas one time, and I remember that Johnny Rosselli was running the hotel the time Sid introduced us."[28]

"Korshak knew Rosselli very well," said former DI public relations man Ed Becker. "He was working with Korshak. They were part of the same crime family, with the tough guy. Rosselli told me this personally." Becker remembered that it was Rosselli who first introduced him to Korshak. "Rosselli said to me, 'Sid is the labor guy. I'm the guy who makes the decisions, and the labor problems are up to Korshak.' Of course, he took care of Korshak. Rosselli also said, 'I'm this representative of the motion picture industry. And Korshak is the labor organizer.'"[29]

---

*Other DI regulars over the years included Tex Beneke, Paula Kelly, Hal Dickinson and the Modernaires of Glenn Miller fame, Jimmy Durante, Sonny King, Danny Kaye, Peggy Lee, Tony Martin, The McGuire Sisters, Patti Page, Louis Prima & Keely Smith, Eddie Fisher, and *The Ed Sullivan Show*.

Luellen Smiley, the daughter of Bugsy Siegel's L.A. partner Allan Smiley, also remembered Korshak with Rosselli. "I met Sid at La Costa [Country Club in California] when we went down with Johnny Rosselli. Sid helped my father, who they tried to scapegoat after Ben was killed. They wanted to deport him. I also remember that Gus Alex was a good friend of both Dad's and Sid's."[30]

The FBI reported that when he was in Vegas in those early years, Korshak stayed either at the DI, or at Dalitz's home. When at the DI, both Korshak and his friends were comped.[31] Dalitz himself, in a moment of candor, admitted to the FBI that Korshak not only represented some of the "big name acts" that played the hotel, but he also "represents some of these Chicago hoodlums."[32]

MCA's Lew and Edie Wasserman were frequent guests at the Desert Inn, where, according to MCA executive Berle Adams, Lew was a big gambler. According to Wasserman's former son-in-law Jack Myers, Dalitz used to bounce Lew's daughter Lynne on his knee. "Lynne used to call him Uncle Moe," said Myers.[33]

The money came so easily now to Dalitz that he reached out to his old distillery partner for an offshore expansion of the business. In 1956, Meyer Lansky, who had been functioning as Cuba's gambling czar for its dictator, Fulgencio Batista, since the midthirties, gave Dalitz the stewardship of Havana's Nacional Hotel and Casino, a jewel of the Kirkeby-Hilton empire.[34] And like many other Supermob associates, Dalitz would be among the first to hide his vast casino skimming profits in an untouchable offshore Caribbean bank, the notorious Castle Bank in the Bahamas (account number 50436), also a favorite of Abe Pritzker and his partner Stanford Clinton—Pritzker's lawyer Burton Kanter had founded the tax-dodging institution (see chapter 19).[35]

After years of watching Dalitz, and compiling a 2,729-page file on him, the FBI described his Las Vegas career thus: "Dalitz has long been one of the top hoodlums directing Las Vegas operations and allegedly may be a front for various other top hoodlums throughout the United States and elsewhere . . . It is noted that he is allegedly in close contact with numerous national and international hoodlums such as Meyer Lansky, Doc Stacher, Sam Giancana and others."*,[36]

Soon, more gang-controlled facilities such as the Sands (owned by numerous New York Commission members, the Outfit, Frank Sinatra, and Korshak's mentor Abe Teitelbaum) and the Sahara (Al Winter of Portland) opened for

---

*When the California Crime Control Commission issued its report in 1978, it listed Dalitz, as well as Sid Korshak, as "one of the top organized crime figures in California."

business. In most cases, the hotels were owned, or fronted, by an upperworld consortium, while the hoods managed the all-important casinos. "The hotels and the lounges were just window dressing," said one Outfit member. "All that mattered were the casinos." The FBI was fully aware of the sham ownerships, describing the owners of record in one memo: "These men have been or are acting as fronts for certain unnamed and undisclosed owners in these hotels and casinos. The fact that these men can meet either at Palm Springs or in Beverly Hills in relative privacy gives them the opportunity to plan further moves, move funds, and work out financial and real estate plans with their attorneys."

During this period, Chicago's interests, as coordinated by Korshak mentor Curly Humphreys, were limited to minor investments in the casinos. In partnership with the New York Commission, the Chicagoans began investing in other Sin City casinos, such as the New Frontier (formerly the Last Frontier) and the Thunderbird. By 1952, with newly empowered local crime commissions placing gangsters in many major cities under the microscope, the hoodlum exodus to Nevada increased dramatically. The Kefauver probe only fueled the hoods' desire to go more legit, except now the Chicagoans coveted an increasingly bigger piece of the pie than they enjoyed at the DI. They got it when they built the Riviera Hotel in 1955, arguably the hotel where Sid Korshak's presence was most strongly felt.

"The Riv"

I have all the big bosses at my place.

—SIDNEY KORSHAK[37]

At the very time they were looking to expand, the shady Midwestern investors descending on Las Vegas were given an unlikely boost by the Nevada statehouse. In 1955, in an attempt to create a public relations blitz extolling the beauty of "gaming," the legislators passed a regulation that barred large publicly held corporations from owning stock in the casinos. Las Vegas historian Hal Rothman described the consequences, writing that "[the regulation] had a dramatic unintended consequence. Instead of freeing gaming from the influence of organized crime, the state inadvertently strengthened its power."[38]

The Chicago Outfit and the Supermob rushed through the opening created by their new best friends in Carson City. With a group of Miami investors such as Sam Cohen as fronts, the Chicagoans secretly financed the $10 million Riviera Hotel & Casino, which opened next to the Thunderbird on April 19, 1955. The Riviera's ostensible Miami backers formed the Riviera

Hotel Company, which in turn leased the land from the Gensbro Hotel Company, a corporation operated by the Gensburg brothers of Los Angeles and Greg Bautzer's law partner Harvey Silbert, also from Los Angeles. Lesser L.A. stockholders included Arthur "Harpo" Marx (5 percent), Milton "Gummo" Marx (3 percent), Julius "Groucho" Marx (percentage unknown), and former Chez Paree singer Tony Martin (2 percent). All were close friends of Sid Korshak's, and all believed him to be a senior partner, albeit one with no written record to prove it.

"The Riv" represented the Strip's first high-rise resort, its nine stories comprising the casino, shops, three hundred deluxe rooms, and a style that changed the desert skyline radically. An architectural departure for Las Vegas, the neomodern Riviera looked as if it belonged on Collins Avenue in the Miami Beach home of its "investors." Besides the requisite casino, the Riv showcased the Starlight Lounge, with a 150-foot, free-form stage bar, and a ceiling from which hung brass lighting fixtures in a starburst design set against a teal-blue sky canopy. With Sid Korshak's "intervention with the Chicago Family," singer Dean Martin would be given points in the Riv and his own lounge, Dino's Den, from where he would hold court in his inimitable style.[39] There was the ten-thousand-square-foot Clover Room—the largest Vegas showroom yet—with six separate elevations and a forty-by-eighty-foot stage, the first to use four large, revolving turntables. On opening night, the Clover Room, which sat five hundred for dinner and seven hundred for the late show, featured pianist Liberace, who was being paid a whopping $50,000 a week (an unheard-of sum at the time, considering homes could be bought for less than $10,000). Liberace's absurd paycheck established a precedent that would forever alter nightclub economics, setting a benchmark that world-famous haunts such as the Copacabana in New York, the Coconut Grove in Los Angeles, and even the Chez Paree in Chicago, without the gaming tables to underwrite the entertainment packages, couldn't approach.

For evening dining, the wormwood-paneled, Western-styled Hickory Room Restaurant offered an open hickory fire and a large rotisserie blazing in view of the diners. Less formal fare was afforded in the coffee shop, later called Café Noir.[40]

What all these rooms had in common was that Sid Korshak, when in town on one of his frequent trips from Beverly Hills, was a fixture in each. Hollywood screenwriter Tom Mankiewicz recently described Korshak's Vegas world. "Sidney would hold court in his booth in the Riviera coffee shop, a wonderful restaurant which served great Chinese food," said the successful movie scribe. "It was like a bad scene out of *The Godfather*; people

The Riviera (courtesy John Neeland, the Riviera Hotel)

Dean Martin (center) at a Riviera roast (John Neeland, the Riviera Hotel)

would stop by the booth to talk to him and move on. He did business from booth one in the Café Noir coffee shop. He'd sit down, and for an hour and a half people would come and pat him on the arm, or someone else would come sit down. He was quite genial."[41] Legendary Riviera lounge singer Sonny King, who worked the Starlight Lounge from the opening days, remembered Korshak calling the shots at the Riv. "Korshak was the 'head administrator' of the Riviera," King recalled in 2004. "He was too expensive a lawyer to pay him hourly. So he got this sort of VP job."[42]

Korshak soon began referring to the Riv as his "club," becoming, according to a government source, "boastful about his wealth and influence . . . stressing to his friends how he hires and fires most of the entertainers at the Riviera."[43] Korshak's clout at the Riv also served to demonstrate his increasing hold over the Teamsters and its new president, Jimmy Hoffa. In October 1961, when Korshak checked into the Riviera unexpectedly during the conference of the International Brotherhood of Teamsters, he was quickly given the presidential suite of the hotel, necessitating the unceremonious removal of Hoffa from said suite. An irate Hoffa was relocated into smaller quarters down the hall.[44] That same month, Korshak repaired Hoffa's bruised ego when he arranged for Hoffa's stay at the Beverly Hills Hotel.[45]

Korshak's string-pulling at the casino-resort was well-known to law enforcement personnel, although finding proof of the financial kickback was something else again. Dean Elson, the retired FBI special agent in charge (SAC) of the Bureau's Nevada outpost, remembered the cat-and-mouse game he played with Sidney. "I ran the Nevada office for eight years in the sixties, and we never got any directive from Chicago that we should surveil him," Elson said recently. "But my friends always informed me when he was coming and going. When a guy like Sid Korshak comes to the Riviera and they move Jimmy Hoffa out so that Korshak can have his suite, you realize his importance. I had friends who informed me when it happened. If I had to bet on it, I would say that Korshak was a silent partner in some casinos. But he was bright—I couldn't catch him."[46] Despite Washington's seeming lack of interest, Elson's field office generated a memo that stated, "The Las Vegas Office believes that Korshak is one of the keys to the Riviera Hotel and Casino operation . . . any investigation of Korshak should definitely be discreet and circumspect in every detail."[47]

Connie Carlson of the California Attorney General's Office had a source close to Riv investor Harvey Silbert, who told him, "A syndicate headed by Sidney Korshak leased the casino at the Riviera Hotel." Silbert added that since he was the attorney for the hotel ownership, "he was in a position to know."[48] Senate investigator Walter Sheridan heard the same thing from a

Vegas source who told him, "Sidney Korshak has become the front man for the Riviera Hotel in Las Vegas with the title of executive director or manager."[49] The FBI noted, "Telephone calls made in 1960 indicate the probability that the undisclosed owners in the Riviera were James Hoffa through Allen M. Dorfman and Paul Dorfman and Sidney Korshak."[50] Lastly, the Bureau had two other sources that named Korshak as one of "the behind-the-scenes operators of the Riviera."[51] These sources also witnessed Korshak attending Riviera board meetings.[52]

Often, Korshak's position at the Riv enabled him to bail out friends who were tanking at the tables. One such Hollywood pal, Paramount's production chief Bob Evans, recalled a night when he was down a bundle at the craps tables, when Sidney showed up and called the bloodletting to a halt. Evans wrote that Korshak, "the silent owner of the Riviera," first asked the croupier how much Evans had lost.

"Forty-three thousand, Mr. K.," came the answer. With that, Korshak lectured Evans about the stacked odds at the craps tables.

"I could take the markers and use them for toilet paper," Korshak said. "But you're payin' every fuckin' cent. Before you shaved, you shot crap better than you do today. No one stands at the table all night and ends up winning."

"Cut it out Sidney, will ya?" Evans pleaded.

"Listen, schmuck," Korshak continued to lecture, "if I didn't brass knuckle ya now, within a year you'd not only be out of a job, you'd be on the lam from the collectors. Flicks is a tougher gamble than craps. Instead of doing your homework, you're standin' here like a pigeon."[53]

Korshak's control of the Riv's credit lines was also observed by the FBI, which noted in his file that on November 13, 1962, Korshak berated Riviera croupier Dave Halper in front of the cashier's cage for approving credit to some unknown person. The FBI also observed that Korshak extended $350,000 in casino credit to Debbie Reynolds; the credit was held by Al Hart at his City National Bank of Beverly Hills.[54] For gamblers not in Korshak's favor, running up a casino debt was known to be a dangerous game. One FBI informant overheard Riviera executives discussing a bettor who owed the casino $205,000, prompting one to remark, "There is one guy who is not going to lose out on money owed by [DELETED], and that's Sidney Korshak. [DELETED] had better pay the club or he'll be swimming in Lake Mead."[55]

A Chicago-based police intelligence officer who watched Korshak for years remembered following him out to Vegas on occasion, where he learned that Korshak was comping old Chicago friends, such as former law partner

Ed King, at the Riv. "You could see him in the coffee shop of the Riviera," said the officer, who wished to remain anonymous. "Supplicants would line up waiting for Sidney to nod for them to step forward. Once I went to the Riviera when Barry Manilow was singing. This was about '77 or '78. I was in my own private business at that time, and I went to see who was ostensibly the PR man for the Riviera, Tony Zoppi. I went in, sat down, and we started to talk. I don't know how it came up, but I said something about Sidney. Suddenly he leapt up from his desk and ran over and drew the blinds and lowered the window and he said, 'Don't talk so loud.' God, I wouldn't have thought . . . I mean I was retired and I had no antagonisms toward Sidney, but just to mention his name . . ."[56]

The seemingly melodramatic sentiment is echoed by many, including Dean Shendal, a former debt collector for the casino owners. "When Korshak entered the room in Vegas, everything stopped," Shendal recently said. "You'd hear people saying, '*Korshak* is here!' "[57]

Private-investigator-turned-author Ed Becker, who, for a time, was the Riv's director of publicity, was still another professional crime watcher with vivid memories of Korshak's swagger. "I didn't really get to know about him until 1955," said Becker. "I was in Las Vegas at that time and I heard that he was the 'big guy'—that he was one of the powers behind the Riviera, behind everything. Anywhere the money went, he was a part of it, especially the Teamster money."[58] After Becker left the Riv, Korshak hired Richard Gully to replace him in the publicist post, as Gully has readily admitted.[59] Years later, Benny Binion, owner of "Glitter Gulch's" (downtown) Horseshoe Casino, told an FBI source that he was interested in buying Korshak's interest in the Riviera, while another source reported that Korshak fired Riviera president Ben Goffstein for "dishonesty and incompetence."[60]

In 1955, the FBI was informed that Korshak and Jake Guzik were silent partners in many other Vegas casinos, and it concluded that Korshak's role involved watching out for Guzik's and the Outfit's interests.[61] Korshak told the FBI of his friendship with Guzik and admitted that, as a favor to Guzik, he hired his son-in-law, Billy Garret, to work in a law firm with which Korshak had an affiliation.[62] A 1963 FBI summary of Justice Department records on Korshak stated that he "primarily represented a group in Las Vegas which might be loosely termed the 'Chicago Group,' who were in the opinion of this source the biggest single factor on the Las Vegas scene."

When the IRS commissioned a special study two decades later to determine the truth of the long-rumored "silent" owners of Vegas casinos, they made the same conclusion as the FBI and others. The IRS investigation, known as Strike Force 18, headed by Robert Campbell, concluded that

Korshak was one of three behind-the-scenes directors of organized crime's investments in Las Vegas.[63]

Of course, the primary purpose for the Riv, like the very reason for Vegas itself, was to skim the casino count room for the Chicago Outfit and its various partners. And this prime directive, according to the FBI, appeared to be one of the key responsibilities of Sid Korshak. One FBI memo that noted Korshak's "hidden ownership" of the Riv's casino also advised that a source within the Chicago organization informed, "Sidney Korshak maneuvers the skim money back to Gus Alex in Chicago, who in turn distributes [it] to other Chicago organized crime people, Joe Aiuppa and Tony Accardo among them."[64] Another Bureau document referred to Korshak as "a courier for the Chicago LCN [La Cosa Nostra] of Las Vegas skim monies. Korshak reportedly travels to Chicago once a month to deliver or make arrangements for delivery of Las Vegas casino proceeds."[65]

The Riv's Miami-oriented front operators were unaccustomed to gaming while being simultaneously skimmed and ran into trouble immediately, with the casino sustaining such large losses that the resort went bankrupt in July of 1955, just three months after it opened. As a result, Gensbro Hotel Co., the Riviera's landlord, assumed control and immediately began a search for new operators. The Chicago mob made the call and decided to turn to an old friend with a proven track record, Gus Greenbaum, the man who turned around the Flamingo after Bugsy's untimely demise. As Chicago boss "Joe Batters" Accardo had been advised, Greenbaum, in failing health, had recently stepped down from the ownership of the Flamingo, taking with him the casino's ledgers, which held the identities of the Flamingo's Gold Club high rollers. After burying the valuable dockets in the Nevada desert, Greenbaum retired to Phoenix, Arizona, where he struck up his friendship with Vegas swinger Senator Barry Goldwater.

Greenbaum had scant time to settle into his new life, since Accardo needed a good man at the helm of the Riviera. Accordingly, Accardo and Jake Guzik (mentor of Sid Korshak) visited Greenbaum in Phoenix and ordered him out of retirement. Greenbaum initially refused the edict, but events yet to occur would change his mind. A few nights after Accardo and Guzik took their leave, Greenbaum learned that his sister-in-law, Leone, had received a telephone threat. " 'They' were going to teach Gus a lesson," she told her husband. In a few days, Leone herself was found dead, apparently smothered in her bed. And Gus Greenbaum packed for Vegas to manage the Riviera.

Most likely ordered by Accardo, Greenbaum drove back out into the desert, where he dug up and dusted off the ledgers containing the priceless list of Flamingo Gold Club members, the screed he had buried just months earlier. With the Flamingo list as a foundation, Greenbaum's secretaries were soon busied with mailing out new memberships for the exclusive, well-comped high-rollers' club at the Riviera.

As previously noted, Greenbaum's fatal decision to hire his and Goldwater's Phoenix pal "Willie Nelson" Bioff as entertainment director was the beginning of his undoing.* Bioff's November 4, 1955, murder for testifying in the movie extortion case stunned Gus Greenbaum, whose personal demons now grew to include heroin addiction. Greenbaum's "horse" problem only exacerbated his health woes, poor gambling abilities, and his growing infatuation with prostitutes. When these distractions began to affect the Riv's profit margins, Greenbaum's days were numbered.

In the late morning of December 3, 1958, Gus Greenbaum's housekeeper happened upon a grisly scene in the Greenbaum bedroom. Still in silk pajamas, Gus Greenbaum's corpse lay across his bed, his head nearly severed by a vicious swipe from a butcher knife. On a sofa in the den fifty feet away was found the body of Gus's wife, Bess, also the victim of a slashed throat. Although no one was ever charged in the murders, it was widely believed that the killings represented a Bugsy redux, i.e., the fastest way to effect a managerial change in Sin City. Barry Goldwater and three hundred others attended the Greenbaums' funeral in Phoenix.

By 1959, the Riviera was sold to a group headed by Ed Levinson of the Fremont Hotel, and Carl Cohen and Jack Entratter of the Sands Hotel, although Korshak and the boys from Chicago were still understood to be in control. The Riviera was financially solvent from then on.

The Vegas expansion was now growing exponentially. The same year the Riv debuted, the Dalitz-fronted mob consortium moved in on another local operation. From the Chicago Outfit's perspective, the idea started out as another substandard partnership with Dalitz, but soon tilted in Chicago's favor with the introduction of a new co-owner who owed the Outfit a huge favor. His name was Jake "the Barber" Factor. As a way of paying back the Outfit for rescuing him from a certain life sentence in a British jail, Factor accepted his new job as front for the Stardust Hotel.

The Stardust

Three months after the first die was thrown in the Riv's casino, Tony Cornero made his second grab at Vegas' brass ring, with decidedly mixed results

---

*As one of Goldwater's first contributors when he ran for Congress (to the tune of $5,000), Nelson and his wife, Laurie, were among the senator's closest friends.

Jake Factor's Stardust today
(author photo)

for him personally. Taking his California gambling-ship fortune to Vegas, Cornero announced that he was finally going to build his dream hotel in the heart of the Strip. The result was the 1,032-room Stardust Hotel and Casino.

Cornero's concept for the Stardust once again displayed his visionary genius. He rightly concluded that elegant joints like Moe Dalitz's Desert Inn had a finite clientele, whereas a casino designed for the low-roller masses would attract gamblers by the busload. Although the hotel's frontage would boast the Strip's largest (216 feet long) and most garish lighted sign (7,100 feet of neon tubing and over 11,000 bulbs), the hotel itself would be little more than a warehouse, where guests could stay for a mere $5 per night. The Stardust's all-you-can-eat buffets and practically free lodging would become a Sin City staple.

A variety of factors caused Cornero's Stardust dream to go bust. Complicating the typical Las Vegas cost overruns was Cornero's own gambling addiction, which quickly depleted his bank account. Just weeks before the scheduled August 1955 opening of the hotel, Cornero learned he was out of money, unable to pay staff or purchase furnishings and gambling instruments. On July 31, Cornero paid a morning visit to Dalitz's Desert Inn, where it is believed Cornero hoped Dalitz would make him an emergency loan. According to one telling, Dalitz met with Cornero for several hours; however, Dalitz ultimately declined to get involved. On his way out of the Desert Inn, Cornero could not fight the temptation to hit the craps tables, where he went quickly into the hole for $10,000. When Dalitz's crew not only refused to extend his marker, but had the audacity to charge him for his drinks (a monumental affront in the pits), Cornero went ballistic. Within minutes, sixty-year-old Tony Cornero was clutching his chest with one hand even as he clutched the dice with the other. He was dead of a heart attack, with less than $800 to show for the estimated $25 million he had made in his lifetime.

The Outfit's traveling emissary, Johnny Rosselli, promptly reported the new vacancy back to his Chicago bosses. According to the files of the LAPD's intelligence unit, which had been tailing Rosselli for years, Rosselli had been making the trek to Sin City regularly, cutting deals, and brokering complex intergang partnerships. George Bland, a retired Las Vegas–based FBI man, disclosed that one of the Bureau's illegally placed bugs revealed that one major casino had the skim divided twelve different ways. One partner later called Johnny "the Henry Kissinger of the mob," and Rosselli's business card from the period said it all, and simply: "Johnny Rosselli, Strategist." Rosselli's biographers described his role in Las Vegas as "nebulous, but crucial . . . He maintained open channels to all the different out-of-town factions, as well as to the California-based operators downtown, and served as a conduit to political fixers like Bill Graham in Reno, and Artie Samish, known in California political circles as "the Governor of the Legislature."[66]

Rosselli was soon living full-time in Vegas, dividing his time between his suites at Dalitz's Desert Inn and the Outfit's Riviera. Armed with the news of Cornero's cardiac, Rosselli flew to Chicago, where he met with Accardo, Humphreys, and Guzik at Meo's Restaurant. It was decided that the gang would finish construction and assume the debt of the Stardust in a partnership with Moe Dalitz. However, this time the Outfit would run the operation, with the Supermob's Jake Factor at the helm. Five years later, Johnny Rosselli described the arrangement to longtime friend, and L.A. mafioso, Jimmy Fratianno. "Jake Factor, an old friend of Capone . . . shit, I used to see him when he came to the Lexington to see Al," Rosselli recalled. "So I went to Sam [Giancana] and told him we could move into this joint. Listen, Jake owed Chicago a big one. Moe Dalitz wanted in on it and so it's a fifty-fifty deal."[67]

Over the next two years, Factor and the Outfit poured money into the Stardust operation, while Jake continually lobbied the newly formed Gaming Control Board for a casino license, where he was consistently rebuffed. Consequently, Humphreys recruited an already licensed Outfit ally from Reno, Johnny Drew, to run the casino temporarily. Eventually, paperwork was filed that showed Factor leasing the Stardust casino to Dalitz's gang for $100,000 per month. When the Stardust finally opened for business on July 2, 1958, it proved well worth the effort. After the grand opening attended by guests of honor then-senator and future president Lyndon Baines Johnson and his trusty sidekick Bobby Baker, the money began arriving in Chicago almost faster than it could be counted.

"They're skimming the shit out of that joint," Rosselli later told Fratianno. "You have no idea how much cash goes through that counting room every day. You, your family, your uncles and cousins, all your relatives, could live the rest of their lives in luxury with just what they pull out of there in a month. Jimmy, I've never seen so much money."[68] Coming from a man who lived though the phenomenal profits of the bootlegging era, this speaks volumes about the lure of Las Vegas. Carl Thomas, an expert on the skim, estimated that the Stardust was contributing $400,000 per month to the Outfit's coffers. Rosselli would rightfully brag for years, "I got the Stardust for Chicago," and for his role in setting up this windfall for the Outfit, Johnny was also well compensated. "I'm pulling fifteen, twenty grand under the table every month," Rosselli said.

Whereas Korshak was allowed to own a piece of the Riv and Desert Inn with the Dalitz group, this was forbidden at the Stardust, as the Chicago gang tried to keep their connection to Korshak as secret as possible. An FBI informant reported that Curly Humphreys told him that because Humphreys had an interest in the hotel, "therefore, Korshak was not allowed to have any interest therein."[69]

Since their earliest association, the Outfit had strived to give Korshak, whom Irv Kupcinet called their "fair-haired boy," a layer of deniability. Years later, boss Joey "Doves" Aiuppa upbraided Jimmy Fratianno for making direct contact with Korshak.

"Look, Jimmy, do me a favor," Aiuppa instructed. "If you ever need anything from Sid, come to us. Let us do it. You know, the less you see of him the better. We don't want to put heat on the guy . . . Let me explain something, Jimmy. Sid's a traveling man. He's in everybody's country but he's our man, been our man his whole life. So, you know, it makes no difference where he hangs his hat. Get my meaning? . . . He's got a permit. We gave him one, understand? . . . Don't put any heat on Sid. We've spent a lot of time keeping this guy clean. He can't be seen in public with guys like us. We have our own ways of contacting him and it's worked pretty good for a long time."[70]

The success of the DI, Riv, and Stardust paved the way to still more acquisitions. In a feat of ambassadorial legerdemain that rivaled the latter-day shuttle-diplomacy efforts of President Jimmy Carter, Rosselli brokered a complex partnership in the $50 million Tropicana, designed to be the most luxurious facility on the Strip. And once again, the talents of Sidney Korshak appear to have been involved. The intricate ownership trust of the Tropicana, which opened for business on April 3, 1957, included the Chicago Outfit, Frank Costello of New York, Meyer Lansky of Miami, and Carlos Marcello and Frank Costello's slot machine and jukebox partner

"Dandy" Phil Kastel of New Orleans. Recall that just after Christmas, 1954, Jake Arvey flew to New Orleans to meet Kastel at Kastel's palatial Louisiana estate. In noting "unimpeachable sources," Virgil Peterson reported that Sid Korshak, who, according to the sources, drove Costello to the house, made Arvey's travel arrangements.[71] Peterson and others concluded that these were in fact the preliminary meetings that resulted in the "Trop" partnership.[72]

In 1958, the *Chicago Tribune* reported that Korshak hosted the fifty-first birthday bash for Chicago Ford dealer Charles "Babe" Baron at the Tropicana. Associated Booking, which Korshak co-owned with Joe Glaser, furnished entertainers such as Dinah Shore and Sammy Davis Jr.[73] What the *Trib* failed to mention was that Babe Baron, a Trop stockholder, had ties to the Capone gang and was included on an IRS list of forty-two powerful mobsters.[74] In his early Chicago days, Baron was not only a confidant of Jake Arvey's, but also a violent credit enforcer, and the primary suspect in two murders.[75] For a time, Baron managed Lansky's Riviera Hotel in Havana, and the FBI reported that he met regularly with Curly Humphreys and Sam "Mooney" Giancana. The Bureau's source added, "Giancana advised Baron that he was to consider himself as Giancana's representative in Las Vegas, Nevada . . . not only Giancana's representative, but Humphreys' representative as well and if any matters were to arise in that area which could not personally be handled by Baron, he was to immediately report to Humphreys and/or Giancana pertaining to the situation."[76] On one occasion when Johnny Rosselli was acting up, Baron informed him that he (Baron) "had an obligation to the Chicago people, and that he would discuss the incident with them. According to Baron, Rosselli turned white and attempted to smooth the situation over."[77]

Another curious partner in the Trop deal was Irish tenor Morton Downey, the best friend and business partner of Kennedy family patriarch Joseph P. Kennedy. In 1997, Morton Downey Jr. said that the Trop investment, as well as numerous others made by his father, was conceivably a hidden investment of Joe Kennedy's, with Downey acting as the front. "Joe was my dad's dearest friend," Downey Jr. said. "My father owned ten percent of the Tropicana. I wouldn't be at all surprised if he was fronting it for Joe. That's how they worked. My father often had someone 'beard' for him also. I remember when he would jump up screaming at the dinner table when his name surfaced in the newspaper regarding some deal or other. 'They weren't supposed to find out about that!' he'd yell."[78]

A Kennedy investment in the Tropicana would not be a unique casino interest for Joe Kennedy. Compelling evidence has surfaced in recent years that Kennedy, using a front, had also heavily invested in Lake Tahoe's

Cal-Neva Lodge, where his co-owner was Chicago mob boss Sam Giancana, who was similarly fronted in his ownership by Frank Sinatra.*,[79]

For appearances, the same man who fronted for the New York Commission's interest in Miami Beach's Fontainebleau Hotel, Ben Jaffe, also directed the Trop operation.

All these operations had one executive in common: Sid Korshak, who was placed in the critical position of handling labor relations between the unions and the Vegas hotel owners, arranging favorable contracts for any establishment owned by the Outfit or their New York Commission peers. Korshak, known in Vegas as "the Chicago Juice," handled labor affairs for the Sands, the Desert Inn, the Riviera, the Stardust, the Trop, and others. During the boom years, Korshak prevented strikes from all corners of Sin City's workforce, including waiters, taxi hacks, entertainers, and casino employees. And of course, part and parcel with these activities were the backstabbing sweetheart deals for which Korshak was notorious in the Midwest. "Sid, as a consultant to casino owners, went to owners of casinos and told them how to defeat the unions and form company house unions," remembered Joe Longmeyer, a veteran Chicago labor organizer who fought pitched battles to try to free the Teamsters from their takeover by the Supermob and the underworld.[80]

A top Hollywood agent recalled Sidney's tenure in Vegas, saying, "Whoever the front guys were, it was Sidney who ran Vegas. He kept it away from any significant labor disputes and he did the same thing for the motion picture industry. That was his great ability."[81]

Occasionally, a labor problem would perplex even Korshak, such as an ongoing four-year dispute between unions and the Las Vegas Ramada Inn. In such intractable cases, Korshak placed a call to Abe Teitelbaum, asking him to come to the rescue. (The Chicago-based owner of Ramada, Marion Isbell Sr., had a long relationship with Teitelbaum.) In the Ramada dispute, Teitelbaum settled it with two phone calls, an intervention for which Teitelbaum, at that point in need of cash to settle with the IRS, sent a bill for $50,000. According to a source close to Teitelbaum, the hefty fee elicited a

---

*Other evidence suggests that Kennedy also had some involvement in the Flamingo and Dalitz's Desert Inn, according to Desert Inn former employee Annie Patterson. In two letters to Moe Dalitz, Patterson informed him that Joe Kennedy had told her of his close friendship with Meyer Lansky and how Lansky informed Kennedy that "he was not receiving his full share of the take [skim]." According to Patterson, this was the original reason for the wiretapping of the Desert Inn under Bobby Kennedy. (Letters from Patterson to Dalitz, 9-5-66, and 9-9-66, in National Archives, JFK Collection, Rec. #180-10020-10133, airtel from SAC Las Vegas to director, 3-2-67, HSCA, FBI Investigative File, Box 21, Sec. 115)

call from Korshak, who told his early mentor, "Hey, Abe, fifty thousand dollars is a lot for thirty minutes. That's really steep." It was an ironic statement from a man infamous for outlandish fees for his minimal intervention. However, an unfazed Teitelbaum replied, "It's not the thirty minutes. It's the fact that it took me thirty years to learn how to do it."

Shecky Greene, the iconic Vegas comic credited with "saving the Riv,"* and who interestingly shared a common Lawndale origin with Korshak, remembered how Korshak carried power around his dominion. "He always walked like he had a broom up his ass," Greene recalled. "I had a cheap five-dollar watch around my neck one day, and Korshak, who usually fancied high-priced watches, said to me, 'I want that watch.' I gave it to him. Everything he saw he wanted. Another time, he said to me, 'You know why I don't care to see your show? It's because if I saw you in the old neighborhood, I'd beat the hell out of you.' "[82]

To the employees of these hotels like Greene, Korshak was Mr. Big, the man who gave orders, not took them. Although Korshak was happy to foster the illusion, he knew the truth was far different—he was still Curly's vassal. Years later, when the FBI had succeeded in placing surveillance bugs in the Chicago mob's headquarters, they overheard Curly Humphreys berating Korshak for not responding quickly enough to an Outfit Las Vegas directive. In 1962, Korshak booked one of his singers, Dinah Shore, into a Vegas hotel not controlled by the Outfit, a move for which he was dressed down over the phone by Humphreys, and overheard by the FBI. Since 1961, Korshak had been booking Shore into the Desert Inn, supposedly obtaining a $1 million Vegas contract for the Southern songstress.[83] After Curly complained to his Chicago peers that Korshak was "getting too big for his britches," he got Korshak on the line and let him have it.

"Anything you want to do for yourself, Sidney, is okay," Curly explained. "But we made you up and we want you to take care of us first . . . Now we built you up pretty good, and we stood by you, but anything outside of [your] law business is us, and I don't want to hear you in anything else. Anytime we yell, you come running."[84]

For the first three weeks, things proceeded swimmingly at the Trop. But on May 2, 1957, investor Frank Costello was caught holding a piece of paper

---

*The Riv's PR director Tony Zoppi credited the highly successful Starlight Lounge for supporting the resort, saying, "Shecky Greene was almost single-handedly responsible for keeping the hotel in business."

describing the skim payouts, prompting the local Mormon-controlled banks to begin denying loans to questionable entrepreneurs.[85] Likewise, the Mormon-controlled Gaming Control Board suddenly became even more stingy, and discriminatory, with its licensing approvals. Until this time, the gangster owners had financed much of their start-up costs with monies supplied by the Mormon-owned Bank of Las Vegas. Although they certainly had more than enough disposable income to afford the costs, the hoods' decision to go with a more traditional method served a more important function by not calling the attention of the IRS to their immense hidden nest egg. Luckily for the mob and Supermob, a new, well-endowed bank had just opened in Chicago, and it curiously seemed to prefer gangster clients.

When Jimmy Hoffa assumed the presidency of the Teamsters in 1957, the mob was finally able to avail itself of the billion-dollar Teamsters Pension Fund cash cow. With Supermob functionaries like Sid Korshak handling the details, the hoods raided the fund and embarked on a five-year Vegas casino-building spree. But first, an emergency Teamster loan of sorts was made in 1959, when the Teamsters "purchased" the Indiana farm owned by Chicago boss Paul Ricca—this despite labor union ownership of property being illegal in Indiana. Hoffa later said that the property was to be converted into a school for Teamster business agents. At the time, Ricca was facing an IRS deadline for payment of tax penalties, so the Teamsters paid Ricca $150,000 for the spread, which was valued at only $85,000. In addition, the Riccas were permitted to live in the house free of charge for over a year.

Not surprisingly, the first fund loan in Las Vegas went to Moe Dalitz, but what shocked observers was that the money was earmarked for construction of a hospital. On September 3, 1959, a new Las Vegas partnership recorded a deed of sale in Nevada's Clark County Courthouse for a desert tract consisting of hundreds of acres situated two miles southwest of the Strip. On the same day, papers were entered in Chicago to obtain a 6-percent-interest, $1 million loan from the pension fund, with Jimmy Hoffa and his fourteen trustees signing on as beneficiaries.

The resultant hundred-bed Sunrise Hospital, a for-profit undertaking with built-in guarantees for the investors, would be but a prelude to an even bigger Sin City investment. The partnership chose as the hospital's president Mervyn Adelson, the transplanted son of a Beverly Hills grocer, and currently the "clean" owner of the Strip's Colonial House club (known locally as a magnet for Sin City hookers). Adelson had teamed up with local Realtor Irwin Molasky to build the much needed hospital, but, not unlike Wilbur

Clark and Tony Cornero, the partnership came up short before they could realize their dream. Thus, like Clark, Cornero, and others, Adelson and Molasky turned to Moe Dalitz with his Chicago Teamster connections. "We ran out of money and had to take in some investors," Molasky explained to the *Las Vegas Review-Journal*.

The hospital's success was guaranteed when Jimmy Hoffa decreed that the Teamsters and Culinary Unions' medical fund would only pay for treatment if the rank and file were treated at Sunrise. Thus, the new hospital saw an influx of thousands of "captive" patients. Irwin Molasky called it "an early form of managed care."[86] The lucrative facility also boasted the Sunrise Hospital Pharmacy Inc., the Sunrise Hospital Clinical Laboratory, and the Sunrise Hospital X-ray Lab, the only one in the county. Adelson and Dalitz would later parlay their huge Sunrise profits, with the aid of thirty-one separate loans totaling $97 million from the Pension Fund, into the construction of the luxurious Rancho La Costa Resort in Carlsbad, California. Dalitz hired Wallace Groves, a Bahamas associate of Meyer Lansky's who had been convicted of mail fraud in 1941, to handle the resort's land sales.[*,87] The golf course and country club opened on July 1, 1965, with homes and condos welcoming new owners soon thereafter. The resort, which came to cost about $500 million, became a favorite vacation and meeting spot for Sid and Marshall Korshak, Dalitz, Hoffa, and hoods such as Chicago bosses Tony Accardo and Sam Giancana, Meyer Lansky, Joey "the Clown" Lombardo, and Tony and Salvatore Provenzano; Chicago's Johnny Rosselli and Allen Dorfman both lived at La Costa during its heyday.[88] The preponderance of evidence prompted federal officials to refer to La Costa as "a playground for the mob." One FBI report alleged that La Costa "is used as a clearinghouse for bookie operations. The phones are used to receive incoming lay-off bets." Interestingly, Judge David Bazelon and Jake Arvey were also comped guests at the resort, according to the FBI.

Adelson's share of the Las Vegas and La Costa profits were in turn utilized in 1966 to bankroll his Hollywood juggernaut, Lorimar Telepictures Productions, which produced television's *Dallas* and *The Waltons* series.[†]

---

*According to a February 3, 1967, investigation by *Life* magazine, Groves controlled gambling in Freeport, Bahamas, and fronted three casinos for Lansky.

†Other Lorimar credits include *Eight Is Enough, Knots Landing, Family Matters, I'll Fly Away, Falcon Crest, Sybil,* and *Alf*—all for television. On the big screen, Lorimar produced *Billy Budd, Being There,* and *An Officer and a Gentleman.* Merv Adelson, briefly married to TV journalist Barbara Walters, recently merged Lorimar into Time Warner and placed his money in East-West Capital Associates, which invests in digital motion picture infrastructure.

Adelson and Molasky would also make the original land bequest that endowed the University of Nevada at Las Vegas.

But there was one other service the hospital provided, and this one was to the underworld. Ed Becker, the former public relations man for the Riviera Hotel, recently disclosed one of the hospital's most appealing hidden advantages. According to Becker, Accardo and associates used the hospital to fill the void left when their skim courier Virginia Hill fled to Europe to escape the IRS. "They would send a man out and he would be met at [Las Vegas'] McCarran Airport," Becker recently recalled. "He was put in an ambulance, driven to Sunrise Hospital, spend a few days there; [then] back in the ambulance, back to the airport, then back to Chicago. That's where the skim was going."[89]

Sunrise Hospital remains a highly regarded Las Vegas moneymaker. The Sunrise Hospital Mediplex, one of the largest hospitals west of Chicago, with over three thousand beds and one thousand four hundred doctors on staff, was but a prelude to an even bigger moneymaker, the Paradise Development Company. Employing great foresight, the Sunrise partners began developing the adjacent land tract, with the kind assistance of $5 million in government-guaranteed Federal Housing Authority (FHA) loans. With names like Paradise Homes, Desert Palms, and Paradise Palms, the consortium's homes, in the $22,000–$42,000 range, sold by the hundreds. During one two-year stretch, the abodes were selling at a rate of one per day. Authors Roger Morris and Sally Denton wrote accurately, "The Paradise Development Company shaped the emerging commercial and residential map of the city."[90] The company's profits would be used in the future to underwrite even more massive withdrawals from the Teamsters Pension Fund, the result of which transformed Las Vegas from a gambler's getaway into a vibrant Western city.

By the time the Labor Department took over two decades later, the fund had loaned approximately $600 million to the mob nationwide, out of $1.2 billion in total loans made.[91] Of those monies, $91 million went to Las Vegas between 1959 and 1961, and $300 million by the late seventies—one sixth of the fund's total assets. The money went for construction and/or improvements for the Stardust, Fremont, Desert Inn, the Dunes, Landmark, Four Queens, Aladdin, and later Circus Circus and Caesars Palace.

But the obtuse, entangled documentation on the loans render a complete understanding impossible, and the loan ledgers were so poorly kept that the actuary brought in by the feds reported that making sense of them was "like starting from scratch to reconstruct a bank's books after there had been a fire." The Labor Department noted that the files on the nine hundred loans would stack up to over twenty-four stories high if piled atop one another. Interestingly, Teamsters expert Steven Brill noted, "Organized crime loans were not necessarily 'bad' loans."[92] The true downside for the Teamsters rank and file stemmed from the lower interest rates given to Korshak's friends, often half the prime rate, as opposed to a point or two above it. The Labor Department estimated that this discrepancy amounted to $100 million in lost profit for the Teamsters.

Since the underworld began to develop the town in the early fifties, the county's population has exploded from under fifty thousand to 1.5 million in 2005. Former Clark County sheriff Ralph Lamb succinctly summarized the importance of the underworld on the development of Las Vegas. "Don't forget this town owes something to these people," Lamb said. "Without them there wouldn't be a Las Vegas."

CHAPTER 10

The Kingmakers: Paul, Lew, and Ronnie in California

WITH KORSHAK, FACTOR, AND Dalitz shoring up the Supermob's interests in Las Vegas, Ziffren, Wasserman, and Reagan saw to it that California government would be well under control when the Vegas contingent eventually settled there. This meant attaining a vise grip over the state's political heart, and given the previously noted anarchy in California's party system, the takeover by the Chicago trust was accomplished practically overnight. All this would occur while Ziffren-Greenberg, Pritzker, Weingart, and Kirkeby-Hilton gobbled up hotels and commercial property, with Al Hart's City National Bank usually handling the monetary details.

Although ideology and money meant more than party alignment in California, Paul Ziffren was working to change that climate in favor of the Democrats. With the wealth and political connections that naturally accrued to major California real estate investors like Ziffren, he and his associates were able, ironically, to use the state's anemic party system to create strong parties—albeit with them in control. As the Supermob's hold on the state strengthened, it was not uncommon to find them in league with pols of both parties, many of whom would switch to the other party.

Like Ziffren, other transplanted Midwesterners were throwing their weight around in California's political inner sanctums. Among them were Jules Stein and Lew Wasserman, who had long since relocated their Chicago MCA headquarters to Los Angeles—Stein had planned the move for decades, having sent his trusted VP Bernard Taft Schreiber westward in the twenties to open the market. Much as Korshak and Ziffren had aligned with the career of Pat Brown, Stein and Wasserman were about to increase the Supermob's virtual invincibility with their nurturing of another California political wannabe, Ronald Wilson Reagan.

The Creation of Ronald Reagan

"Ronnie" Reagan, as he was then known, had moved to California in the late thirties, after a stint as a sportscaster for WOC Radio in Iowa, bent on transforming his career from radio announcer to movie star. After Reagan's marriage to actress Jane Wyman, Stein and Wasserman guided his career at Warner Bros., where he made a string of B pictures. With titles such as *Swing Your Lady, Cowboy from Brooklyn, Girls on Probation*, and *Brother Rat and a Baby*, Reagan, who was once credited as Elvis Reagan, rightfully attained the moniker The Errol Flynn of the B's. MCA was always more adept at deal-making and solidifying power than it was at creating great art.

When World War II broke out, Wasserman and Jack Warner persuaded the War Department to delay Reagan's draft induction in order to let him star in what would arguably be his best movie, *Kings Row*.[1] After the war, Lieutenant Reagan picked up where he'd left off in Hollywood, joined Hillcrest Country Club, divorced Jane Wyman, and was forced to reassess his acting vocation, which was descending faster than a two-thousand-pound bunker buster.

In October of 1946, Reagan visualized his next career move when he spoke in Chicago at an American Federation of Labor (AFL) convention. Rousing the union members with anticommunist bombast, Reagan would learn, like other would-be pols such as Richard Nixon, that he could use red-baiting to craft a career in politics. Robert K. Dornan, nephew of comedian Jack Haley, recalled seeing Reagan venting at "Colonel" Jack Warner's house. "Ronald Reagan would be in a room talking a lot, even at parties, about how to keep the Communists out of Hollywood."[2] His obsession with Communism led him to barnstorm in an effort to destroy the liberal Conference of Studio Unions (CSU), a federation of Hollywood craft unions; that quest sided him with the corrupt IATSE and MCA in order to combat fictitious "commies" in Hollywood. This clash in the labor-intensive movie industry is widely perceived as one of the pivotal labor struggles of the postwar era. Reagan's demonization of the CSU was not new; labeling the leftist unionizers "parlor pinks," George Browne had employed the tactic a decade earlier when he fronted for the Outfit's takeover of IATSE.[3] Of course, the lefties were not aligned against the United States, but were merely a reaction to World War II fascism, and Reagan and cohorts surely knew it. Nonetheless, once the opportunistic Reagan picked up the anticommunist theme, he never let it go—it would be his ticket to success.

Reagan's stance was not without its drawbacks, however, as verbal jousts often threatened to turn physical. One former CSU operative, George Kuvakis, remembered how Reagan "had a limousine pick him up at his house, take him to work, and they were all armed . . . and they brought him home at night undercover."[4]

But Reagan's jingoism was even more ugly than people knew: in an attempt to curry favor with the FBI, Reagan undertook an insidious and secret anticommunist mission. According to a massive FBI file released in 1998, Reagan began meeting with FBI agents at his home in 1946, whereupon he gave the Bureau the names of actors Howard da Silva (*The Lost Weekend*), Larry Parks (*The Jolson Story*), and Alexander Knox (*Wilson*) as supposed Communists. Those and other names (deleted from the FBI documents) given by Reagan to the Bureau were eventually blacklisted in Hollywood. For the icing on the cake, Reagan publicly claimed that Hollywood liberals caused his lackluster film career to stall out as punishment for his hysterical anticommunist crusade.[5]

Ironically, Reagan's hand-wringing may have been a classic example of the maxim "He doth protest too much." According to the recent file release, the Los Angeles FBI Field Office reported that Reagan may have had his own "commie" connections: in 1946, Reagan was a sponsor and director of the Committee for a Democratic Far East Policy, which had been designated as subversive by the attorney general; he was also a member of the American Veterans Committee, cited as "communist dominated." Those were just the sorts of associations Reagan reported to Hoover that resulted in ruined careers for his fellow actors. Fellow actor Karen Morley, who knew Reagan at the time, opined, "It isn't that he's a really bad guy. What's so terrible about Ronnie is his ambition to go where the power is. I don't think anything he does is original, he doesn't think it up. I never saw him have an idea in his life. I really don't think he realizes how dangerous the things he really does are."[6]

Reagan's drive to free the acting community from the clutches of the Red Menace (coupled with a nudge from Lew Wasserman) motivated him to run for the presidency of the Screen Actors Guild (SAG), where he could become the endangered actors' father-protector. Years later, he verified the rationale in his autobiography, writing, "More than anything else, it was the Communists' attempted takeover of Hollywood and its worldwide weekly audience of five hundred million people that led me to accept a nomination as president of the Screen Actors Guild (SAG)."[7]

Although Reagan attained the post, not all in the acting community were convinced by his zealous rhetoric. Actor Alexander Knox commented, "Reagan spoke very fast . . . so that he could talk out of both sides of his mouth at once."[8] Another SAG member said, "Reagan was a conservative, management-sweetheart union president and ran SAG like a country club instead of a militant labor union."[9] And in a style that would presage his presidency, Reagan often seemed confused when tough questions were posed. But he was actually dumb like a fox, for as Hollywood labor expert and Fulbright Scholar Gerald Horne wrote, "[He] almost seemed to use this confusion as a tactic: he had converted bafflement into an art form . . . he misstated dates and events at meetings. At one point he said jokingly, 'Pat [Somerset, another SAG official] says I am mixed up.' "[10] Reagan would use the "kindly idiot" strategy not only in the presidency, but in future federal testimony when he was repeatedly quizzed about his furtive dealings with Wasserman. (It would also come in handy during the arms-for-hostages and Iran-contra gun-smuggling scandals of the eighties.)

Ronald Reagan's career in politics might have ended before it began were celebrities not virtually immune from prosecution in their Hollywood sanctuary. In February 1952, the actor with whom Sid Korshak occasionally went on the prowl set his sights on MCA starlet and single mother Selene Walters. According to Walters, a twenty-one-year-old combination of Kim Novak and Carole Lombard, it all started when Reagan introduced himself to her in the wee hours at Slapsy Maxie's nightclub. Walters recently recalled:

> I was very impressed because he was such a big star. He asked for my address and phone number and I gave it to him. After my date took me home to my apartment, I got undressed, put on a housecoat. Then there was a bang on my door—it was about three A.M. I was afraid to open it at that hour.
>
> "Who is it?" I asked.
>
> "It's Ron—I just met you an hour ago. Let me in."
>
> So I let him in. "I want to talk about my career," I told him. But he didn't want to talk about my career at all. So there was a lot of shuffling around on the sofa. I was struggling and kept saying, "Stop!" but he wouldn't. He forced himself on me and did what he wanted to do—in like a half a second, staining my nice housecoat in the process.
>
> He said, "Listen, kid, I'll be in touch. We'll talk about your career later."
>
> He never called me because he married Nancy Davis two weeks later. I didn't want any scandal so I never reported it. Besides, you couldn't sue a big star in those days. You still can't.[11]

Indeed, on March 4, 1952, Reagan married divorcée and actress Nancy Luckett Davis, and although his career was in the dumps, he refused to allow his new bride to live in anything but grand style. Living well beyond his means, Reagan purchased not only a home in Pacific Palisades, but also a 290-acre Malibu parcel for the amazing price of $65,000. Reagan was now under great pressure to afford his lifestyle, as well as pay a large tax bill that accompanied the land purchases. That pressure was soon to be relieved in the aftermath of one of Hollywood's greatest controversies, an episode that smacked of a Wasserman-Reagan-Korshak power play.

At the time, MCA and all other talent agencies were forbidden by SAG from becoming producers, for obvious conflict-of-interest reasons—a talent agent is at natural odds with a producer over the fees obtained by the talent.* With the recent arrival of the medium of television, which was centered in New York, all Hollywood-based businesses, including MCA, were feeling the pinch. Stein, Wasserman, and MCA decided that they had to get into television production if MCA was to continue expanding, and to do that, the long-standing SAG rule had to go. Although MCA had been granted an occasional waiver from the rule, they now coveted a "blanket waiver" for *all* productions. They had the admittedly brilliant foresight that MCA could pioneer the filming of television programs that could be resold, as opposed to the live variety emanating from New York.

With Reagan's divorce lawyer Laurence Beilenson representing MCA, SAG began considering the unprecedented blanket waiver. MCA frightened the union's membership by warning that all TV production would stay in New York unless MCA was granted the exemption. Rumors were rife that Sid Korshak was also involved in the dealings on behalf of his friends Lew Wasserman and Reagan. Thus, in his fifth and lame-duck term as SAG president, Ronald Reagan, with his new wife, Nancy, on SAG's board, granted a blanket waiver to MCA on July 14, 1952, allowing Stein's exploding MCA juggernaut a unique immunity from the SAG rules.

Much as James Petrillo's Chicago music-union waivers for MCA had given Stein the advantage in that city, the latest favor gave MCA an insurmountable edge over competing agencies in Hollywood. In the aftermath, MCA, now the only entity capable of "packaging" the product from top to bottom, began to exponentially increase its hold over the entertainment industry. (The company's production income would skyrocket from $8.7 million in 1954 to

---

*In fact, MCA had been breaking the rule for at least two years, producing such television programs as *Your Hit Parade, Starring Boris Karloff, Stars over Hollywood*, and *The Adventures of Kit Carson*.

almost $50 million in 1957, some of which was used to purchase the 327-acre Universal Pictures backlot for $11 million in 1958.) MCA could now demand that outside producers package more MCA talent into a production or take none at all. According to a source for the Justice Department, which began still another investigation of MCA, the mega-agency "has a representative stationed at every studio" who tipped the agency for future negotiations. The result of the spycraft was that if a studio wanted any MCA client (writer, actor, director, singer, comic, etc.), it had to fill all the positions with MCA clients.[12] This dictum extended to nightclubs as well, and businessmen who refused to succumb to the strong-arm tactics were often forced to hire grade B talent. When the Department of Justice investigated MCA for antitrust violations in 1962, it concluded that the 1952 waiver became "the central fact of MCA's whole rise to power."[13]

Both Hollywood professionals and law enforcement officials were certain that the deal involved collusion between Reagan and MCA. Former MCA executive Berle Adams euphemistically noted, "Lew got close to Reagan on that SAG deal."[14] But law enforcement was somewhat less discreet. One Department of Justice source later remarked, "Ronald Reagan is a complete slave of MCA who would do their bidding on anything."[15] And although no one in government formally charged that Reagan and MCA had conspired beforehand, many observers assumed that it had happened, especially given what happened next.

The Payback

What added fuel to the Reagan-Wasserman charges was the sudden and dramatic upturn in Reagan's fortunes at MCA. On a small scale, the agency cut a deal for Reagan to work at the Outfit-owned Last Frontier Hotel in Las Vegas to cover, as Reagan himself admitted, his back tax debt. Of considerably more importance was MCA's transfiguring of the washed-up actor into

Reagan takes Vegas (Irv Letofsky)

a national television star, a nod that would make Reagan not only a million-aire, but give him an audience that would later be receptive to his increasingly right-wing political aspirations.

A firsthand witness to the accommodation was Henry Denker, a pioneering New York–based television producer for CBS who helmed the weekly dramatic anthology show *Medallion Theater*, which premiered in 1953. Denker recently spoke of how the shows were put together: "Our advertising agency, BBD&O, asked us to work closely with MCA, because they had the biggest reservoir of stars. 'Work with Taft [Schreiber] and Lew [Wasserman] and Freddie [Fields],' we were told." And MCA delivered, producing such stars as Charlton Heston, Henry Fonda, and Jack Lemmon for Denker.

Occasionally MCA came to Denker asking for a favor in return, usually in the form of adding a new talent they were representing to the cast of the show. Denker had no problem with the quid pro quo, but was quizzical when one MCA request seemed odd: "One day I got a call from Freddie Fields. 'We might get you Ronald Reagan,' he said. Well, I knew by that time Ronald Reagan was over the hill. It was no secret in show business. They said, 'Find something for Reagan to do.' So, I wanted something that was surefire that nobody's ever missed with. I found something that had been produced three or four times—never failed. It was called *Alias, Jimmy Valentine*, about a safecracker who gets out of jail and decides to go straight."*

Denker remembered Reagan arriving prepared in New York, adding, "You couldn't have met a nicer guy in your life." At the end of Reagan's yeomanlike performance, a series of events occurred that clarified Freddie Fields's pitch for Reagan. According to Denker, at the end of the live broadcast, the director didn't call for the hot lights to be turned off. Denker thought, "There's something very strange going on here." In a couple of minutes, the situation became odder still when the director had Reagan, who had changed into a suit, stand in front of a gray velour drape and perform the introduction to *Alias, Jimmy Valentine*—but by now the show was off the air.

"What this really was about came out after the show aired," said Denker, who realized that MCA was using his show and soundstage to film a pilot

---

*Denker described the surefire plot thus: "Valentine, the former safecracker, gets a job in a small town and everything is fine, and the banker's daughter falls in love with him. And everything is just going great until one day when the banker's young son got stuck in the timed walk-in vault. And the only person who can open that vault before the oxygen runs out is the ex-safecracker Jimmy Valentine. But he has to expose his past and lose the girl to save the kid. So he opens the safe—great finish."

for a new weekly series that they eventually sold to General Electric. That audition evolved into *General Electric Theater*, a weekly series for which MCA hired Ronald Reagan at $125,000 per year as host, program supervisor, occasional star, and producer of the show. *GE Theater* was a top hit, running for nine years.

"I thought about bringing a lawsuit," Denker said years later. "They stole the show. What was going on was they needed a spot for Reagan because it was a payoff for something. They owed him something. This was the payoff for the waiver that he gave to MCA—an incredible conflict of interest. Every favor MCA did, like getting Reagan the GE job, was in exchange for something they got in return. Take my word for it. I know those guys. They were the shrewdest bunch of guys that have ever been in show business, and Lew Wasserman was the top of them all."

Denker later spent a year in Hollywood working at MCA's Universal Pictures production wing, where he saw firsthand why SAG had outlawed the agent-producer role for so long, the rule that was overturned during Reagan's tenure at SAG. "I found out—and here is the real evil in this thing," Denker recalled, "that the Universal writers represented by MCA were being paid less than the writers who are represented by outside agents. They sold their writers down the river."[16]

In 1972, Denker published one of his thirty-four novels, *The Kingmaker*, a thinly veiled roman à clef about a superagency that maneuvered one of its actors into the California governor's mansion. In the book, Dr. Isadore Cohen of Chicago creates the Talent Corporation of America (TCA), relocates to Los Angeles, where he lunches at Hillcrest, and promotes a washed-up actor and SAG president, Jeff Jefferson. After passing a SAG waiver for TCA, Jefferson performs in *Alias, Jimmy Valentine*, and TCA rewards him with the job of hosting the TV show *CM Theater*. At the end of the book, when a television commentator mused that Jefferson could actually become president of the United States, Cohen recoiled in fear that he might have created a monster. In just eight years, Cohen's fictitious nightmare would become a reality.

"My book is the true story," Denker has said. "I lived through it." True or not, when a prominent Hollywood producer wanted to adapt the book to film, Wasserman put his foot down. "Lew told him, 'Absolutely not!'" remembered Denker.* It would not be the last time that a Supermob boss

---

*After moving back to New York, Denker produced six plays on Broadway, two for the Kennedy Center, and published thirty-four novels, with more titles chosen by Reader's Digest Book Club than by any other author.

would interfere with a writer that dared expose their story. MCA's control over so many A-list talents allowed the firm to play hardball over the years with clients whose politics ran counter to Wasserman's and Stein's. In 1954, when SAG again threatened to retract the waiver, Reagan and SAG negotiator John Dales went into closed session and extended MCA's waiver to 1960. "Ronnie Reagan had done Lew another good turn," said Denker.

With Reagan's career back on track, MCA spent the remainder of the fifties building an entertainment monolith. In 1958, the company bought television distribution rights to over 750 pre-1948 films from Paramount Pictures for $35 million. Now MCA could add "distributor" to its list of services. The company also entered into an exclusive relationship with underdog network NBC. Robert Kitner, NBC's vice president, devised the arrangement with his MCA counterpart, Sonny Werblin. "Sonny," Kitner told him, "look at the [NBC] schedule for next season; here are the empty spots, you fill them in."[17] By 1959, MCA was producing fourteen NBC shows, for a total of eight and a half hours in prime time.

A potential problem arose in 1959 when SAG's seventeen thousand members threatened their first strike in sixty years, over televised-movie residuals—$60 million of which had already gone to MCA as a result of the Paramount film acquisitions. With their contract with producers scheduled to expire on January 31, 1960, the beleaguered actors prevailed upon SAG board member Reagan to take the SAG presidency again in the mistaken hope that he would provide a strong voice for them in negotiations with MCA. "That's why Reagan was elected president of SAG again in 1959," said a SAG board member. "We knew how close he was to MCA and thought he could get us our best deal."[18] (Of particular note was that Reagan was on the board illegally, since he was also a producer of *GE Theater*. Three years later, Reagan lied to the 1962 grand jury when he said he had not been a producer. Not only have writers for the show recalled his producer role, but Reagan himself admitted it to the *Hollywood Reporter* for its November 14, 1955, issue.)

SAG rules notwithstanding, Reagan decided to retake the presidency, especially after his Svengali weighed in. "I called my agent, Lew Wasserman," Reagan said. "Lew said he thought I should take the job."[19] It is widely believed that Sidney Korshak entered the picture at this point, helping to steer MCA through the shoals of the potentially disastrous SAG negotiations. Then IATSE president Richard Walsh told author Dan Moldea, "Korshak's involved in that whole proposition you're talking about there, and it would tie back into Reagan . . . Reagan was a friend of, talked to, Sidney Korshak, and it would all tie back together . . . I know Sidney Korshak. I know where he comes from, what he is, and what he's done. He's a labor lawyer, as the term goes."[20]

With Korshak's counsel, Reagan recommended that SAG strike against the producers, but with a twist: MCA would be immune from the strike action. What happened was, Milt Rackmil, president of MCA's production arm, Universal, secretly met with Reagan and promised that MCA would endow $2.65 million toward an actors' pension fund in exchange for immunity from any work stoppage. Furthermore, in a sweetheart deal that bore all ten fingerprints of Sidney Korshak, SAG would agree to drop its demand for the pre-1960 residuals. After a perfunctory six-week strike, which started on March 7, 1960 (and exempted MCA), the SAG membership agreed to the terms proffered by Rackmil.

MCA's retaining of its huge movie catalog, eventually worth hundreds of millions, dwarfed the $2.65 million donated to the SAG fund. The settlement created a schism in SAG, as some of the membership were overjoyed by the prospect of a pension and welfare fund, while others, especially the older stars of the pre-1960 films, felt as though they had been sold out. "In no way did we win that strike—we lost it," said one member.

As first chronicled by authors and latter-day Supermob gadflies Dan Moldea and Dennis McDougal, a legion of actors went public with their feelings:

• Bob Hope, one of Reagan's closest friends, bitterly stated, "The pictures were sold down the river for a certain amount of money . . . and it was nothing . . . See, I made something like sixty pictures, and my pictures are running on TV all over the world. Who's getting the money for that? The studios. Why aren't we getting some money . . . ? We're talking about thousands and thousands of dollars, and Jules Stein walked in and paid fifty million dollars for Paramount's pre-1948 library of films and bought them for MCA . . . He got his money back in about two years, and now they own all those pictures."
• Gary Merrill: "Reagan sold us down the river."
• Gene Kelly: "Reagan didn't pump for residuals at all."
• June Lockhart: "Reagan and MCA sold us out."
• Mickey Rooney was among the most passionate when he said, "The crime of showing our pictures on TV without paying us residuals is perpetuated every day and every night and every minute throughout the United States and the world. The studios own your blood, your body, and can show your

pictures on the moon, and you've lost all your rights. They own you, and they own the photoplay. We're not human beings, we're just a piece of meat."[21]

Two months after "The Great Giveaway," and with SAG members calling for his resignation, Reagan suddenly remembered that he could not legally hold the SAG presidency since he was also a 25 percent owner and occasional producer of *General Electric Theater*. Reagan resigned his post on June 6 and quit the SAG board on July 11. At the time, Reagan said, "I know I came back for a purpose, and it's been accomplished."

Over the next few years, Ronald Reagan cashed in on his *GE Theater* while becoming more politically active and increasingly conservative. In 1960, Reagan supported Republican presidential candidate, and fellow red-baiter, Richard Nixon, warning that the Communist Party "has ordered once again the infiltration" of the movie industry. "They are crawling out from under the rocks," Reagan intoned.

While Wasserman and Stein nurtured the career of Ronald Reagan, fellow Supermob associate Paul Ziffren was seeing to it that the former Chicagoans were well entrenched with the state's Democratic up-and-comers. In 1958, Ziffren backed his brother's boss, and Korshak's friend, California attorney general Pat Brown, in his gubernatorial run against incumbent Republican senator William Knowland, scion of the Joseph Knowland *Oakland Tribune* empire. To this end, Ziffren formed the highly secretive Southern California Sponsoring Committee, unregistered with any state regulatory agency. Ziffren told one wealthy Democrat that the idea was to enlist one thousand of his friends to donate $1,000 each, and to function as an emergency fund for the Democratic Party. The group opened an account in Al Hart's City National Bank in Beverly Hills.

That year, Sid Korshak was observed in a meeting with Ziffren at the home of actress Rhonda Fleming, known to have been *very* close to Sidney. Also participating was Superior Court judge Stanley Mosk, a University of Chicago graduate.[22] The purpose of the meeting was unknown at the time, but would become obvious soon after the election.

Although Ziffren raised eyebrows with his secretive sponsoring committee, Brown's opponent, Knowland, sank even lower and attempted to tarnish Brown in a classic "guilt by association" charge—an association with Ziffren, to be exact. To understand how Knowland would be aware of Ziffren's associates, it is first necessary to scrutinize Knowland's. Knowland was a political bedfellow of Richard Nixon's, and the two shared the

Paul Ziffren (Library of Congress)

friendship of Beverly Hills attorney Murray Chotiner, who had, at age thirty-three, masterminded Earl Warren's campaign for the governorship and Nixon's 1950 congressional bid. In that contest, Nixon smeared opponent Helen Gahagan Douglas with red-baiting charges that often appeared in the form of flyers written by Chotiner. Knowland repeatedly sparred with Nixon over who was the most aggressive commie fighter.

By definition a member of America's Supermob, Chotiner specialized in representing underworld types, such as Pennsylvania Mafia boss Marco "the Little Guy" Reginelli, and Angelo "Gyp" DeCarlo, in their legal battles with the feds. As might be expected, the two Beverly Hills attorneys Korshak and Chotiner were close friends, with Marshall Korshak telling a friend, "Every client Chotiner had, he first checked out with Sidney."[23] Interestingly, Chotiner, the son of a Pittsburgh cigar maker, and Sid Korshak shared the friendship of New York lobbyist Nathan Voloshen, who in turn was close to future Speaker of the House John McCormack.[24] Through Korshak's New York associate George Scalise, Voloshen obtained underworld clients such as Salvatore Granello, Manuel Bello, and Anthony DeCarlo.[25]

As mentor to both Nixon and Knowland, Chotiner toured the country in 1955, giving secret lectures to GOP "political schools" at the request of the Republican National Committee. A copy of the Chotiner lecture was leaked to the Democrats, one of whom described the transcript as "probably one of the most cynical political documents published since Machiavelli's *The Prince* or Hitler's *Mein Kampf*, . . . a textbook on how to hook suckers."

Not long after Chotiner became Knowland's campaign manager, Knowland came into possession of real estate records linking Pat Brown's backer Paul Ziffren to Alex Greenberg, Sam Genis, and the rest of Chicago's underworld. With Chotiner's unsavory connections, it is likely that Knowland had inside information on the deals. It is also possible that the damning material came from journalist Robert Goe, who was eager to expose the Arvey-Ziffren infiltration of the state.

In the campaign, Knowland attacked Brown's keystone supporter Ziffren with the Capone-Greenberg, Hayward Hotel, and Seneca connections, etc. Although there was no evidence that Pat Brown had knowledge of or condoned Ziffren's business partnerships, Knowland tried to make the mud stick. In speeches widely covered by California newspapers, Knowland warned of "the existence in California of a shadowland powerful force infiltrating our political and economic life." He called it "an overworld." (Compounding the bad news that year for Ziffren was word from Chicago that in November 1958, after a two-and-a-half-year investigation, Ziffren's forty-one-year-old brother, Herman, was arrested in Illinois on three counts of violating the White Slavery Traffic Act. Specifically he was charged with transporting three women across state lines for immoral purposes. Fifteen months later he received a $4,000 fine.)[26]

Of course, Knowland was correct about what Ziffren was pulling off, even though Brown may not have realized it. Veteran *New York Times* L.A. Bureau chief and California political scholar Gladwin Hill pointed out, "Whatever his shortcomings, Knowland was given neither to falsehood nor to gratuitous aspersion."[27] For his part, Ziffren called the charges "scurrilous nonsense" and implied that Knowland was anti-Semitic.[28]

After the Knowland charges appeared in the press, the FBI's L.A. Field Office opened what would become a 386-page file on Paul Ziffren. The file, which remained open for five years, represented a compendium of allegations against Ziffren, with virtually no editorializing, and no conclusions made by Bureau headquarters. There was no indication that the material was forwarded to the Department of Justice for action.

Knowland's attack on Brown had little impact, but the senator's anti-union, pro open shop (right-to-work) platform infuriated organized labor. In addition, Knowland's wife (known as the Martha Mitchell of the sixties*) sent a caustic seven-page letter to two hundred Republican leaders throughout the state, calling organized labor "a socialist monster." Thus it was no surprise when Brown won the election by a huge 20 percent margin, with over five million votes cast. It was a momentous win for the revitalized Democratic Party, which captured not only the governorship for the first time in twenty years, but both houses of the legislature for the first time in seventy-five years. For Knowland, the defeat initiated a long downward

---

*Martha Mitchell, the wife of President Nixon's attorney general John Mitchell, became infamous for her unbridled media outbursts.

spiral, both professionally and personally. When Knowland's wife, Ann, initiated divorce proceedings in 1972, she threatened to hire Paul Ziffren as her representative. "He hates your guts," Ann told Knowland.[29] The 1958 defeat also gave Nixon sole claim to the state's red-baiting pedagogy, making him the official right-wing standard-bearer from California.*

Governor Brown quickly appointed Judge Mosk, the man who had recently huddled with Ziffren and Korshak, as attorney general. The *Los Angeles Mirror* editorialized that Mosk would never have become AG "were it not for the strength he gained from Paul Ziffren."[30] The FBI echoed the conclusion when it noted in Ziffren's file that "[Mosk] owed his job at least in part to the genius of Ziffren."

Despite his candidate's winning the governorship, Paul Ziffren was still dogged by Knowland's Supermob allegations. On April 20, 1959, when Ziffren, in his capacity as the California Democratic national committeeman, lobbied in Sacramento for bills that would place stricter regulations on police arrest procedures, he was questioned in the open legislature about his Capone affiliations. One senator intoned, "I don't intend to let the Capone mob tell us how to write a law of arrest. I think we're entitled to know where these bills came from and who's behind them." Ziffren's only reply was "My own background has nothing to do with the merit of these bills."[31]

To the press, Ziffren said it was "ghoulish" to bring up the names of his business partners. (Greenberg had already been gunned to death, and Evans was about to be. On August 22, 1959, Evans was shot to death in Chicago, and typically for that city, no one was ever charged. At his probate hearing, it was estimated that his nonliquid real estate holdings approached $11 million.)

"I don't believe in character assassination," Ziffren informed the media. "Greenberg was honorable in all the dealings I had with him."[32] Ziffren also pleaded ignorance of what Evans's and Greenberg's underworld connections might have been. This contention borders on the ludicrous for numerous reasons: Ziffren's mentor, Arvey, was Greenberg's longtime partner in Lawndale Enterprises; Ziffren's college classmate, best friend, investment partner, and law partner, David Bazelon, had helped in the tax case against Greenberg's investment client Frank Nitti and handled Greenberg's Canadian

---

*Knowland went back to Oakland, where he took over his father's *Oakland Tribune*, but quickly fell into debt and depression. Ironically, much of the debt was incurred in Las Vegas at the Supermob's Riviera, Tropicana, and Stardust casinos. On February 17, 1974, he committed suicide by means of a .32-caliber Colt automatic.

Ace Brewery legal affairs; the longtime cohort of Ziffren's partner Fred Evans, Murray Humphreys, was Public Enemy Number One in the 1930s, and their indictment for embezzling the Bartenders Union out of $350,000 was front-page news in Chicago just a few years before the Hayward purchase, while Ziffren and his firm were Greenberg's tax lawyers; Greenberg's mob ties were well-known to the U.S. Attorney's Office, where Ziffren previously worked; Ziffren's partner in Store Enterprises, Sam Genis, was a convicted check kiter and associate of Lansky, Zwillman, and Costello; at the Lansky infiltrated Kirkeby-Nacional organization, Paul and Leo Ziffren handled legal matters, while their executive secretaries sat on the board, and Paul's brother-in-law was the VP of the company; lastly, Ziffren was Greenberg's tax attorney at Gottlieb and Schwartz, filing returns that showed his payments to Evans—this was in 1943, when Greenberg paid Ziffren for help in dealing with Greenberg's being implicated in the massive front-page-news Hollywood extortion scheme by the Capone mob.

Considering that Ziffren was an unquestioned genius in both tax law and investing, it strains credulity that he was unaware of the connections of his numerous tainted partners.

Despite the allegations, Ziffren's power was at such a zenith that he was able to accomplish the unthinkable, convincing the Democratic National Committee to hold their 1960 presidential convention in Los Angeles, wresting it from the proponents of favored cities including Chicago, where Jake Arvey lobbied for the event. With this move, Ziffren was stepping out from Arvey's shadow once and for all, letting it be known that he was now an independent kingmaker.

In recognition of Ziffren's contributions to the party, the California Democratic Committee rewarded him with a fête in his honor at Arnold Kirkeby's Beverly Hilton Hotel on June 23, 1959. Among the two thousand in attendance were a sponsoring committee that included all the partners (except for Bazelon) in the L.A. Warehouse Company, Sidney Korshak, Eugene Wyman, and Jonie Tapps (a producer pal of Johnny Rosselli's). In the festivities, Ziffren was saluted by Stanley Mosk and regaled by a performance from Korshak's great friend Rhonda Fleming.

The glow would not last long. The gala at the Beverly Hilton masked a growing tension in the Brown-Ziffren camp. Ziffren was becoming a lightning rod for controversy, and while he had undeniably played a huge role in the Democratic Party's resurgence, not all party faithful sang his praises. "I dislike him with a passion," said one Democratic legislative leader.[33]

Not long after his election, Governor Brown started to distance himself from Ziffren, warning him to not take credit for the election. "I am the architect of my own campaign," Brown told local scribes. In part motivated by Brown's desire to avoid contamination with the Greenberg deals, the rift would last years and lead to Ziffren's retirement from the Democratic Committee's top post. Brown, however, felt no such need to part company with Sid Korshak, since the Fixer was virtually unknown to the public at large. Not only were they frequently seen dining together, but also, according to some, were making critical state government decisions. Dick Brenneman, who developed well-placed sources when he investigated Korshak for the *Sacramento Bee*, was informed by a judicial source that Brown had convened with Korshak since the early fifties at Harry Karl's mansion (which Korshak later purchased) on Chalon Road in Bel-Air. According to the source, one purpose of the meetings was for Brown to vet his judicial appointments with Korshak.[34] Brenneman was further told by LAPD lieutenant Marion Phillips, who often surveilled the Korshak crowd for LAPD intel chief Jim Hamilton, that there were also numerous such Brown-Korshak huddles at Chez Karl.

In January 1960, Attorney General Mosk announced his intent to go after white-collar crime, especially in real estate investment. The implications of such a probe were not lost on knowledgeable California journalists, who knew that such a crusade by Mosk would likely expose the Ziffren-Greenberg nexus. As the *Hollywood Citizen News* wrote, "If Attorney General Mosk isn't careful, he may find himself soon treading on the toes of his political mentor, California National Committeeman Paul Ziffren, whose phenomenal economic penetration of California and criminal affiliation is a matter of record."[35]

Circumstantial evidence suggests that Ziffren may later have acted to short-circuit Mosk's agenda in 1964, when Mosk was the presumed Democratic front-runner in the California senatorial race—and yet mysteriously dropped out of the contest that spring. Thirty years later, in a 1994 cover story in the *L.A. Weekly*, Charles Rappleye and David Robb reported that Mosk's sudden exit was the direct consequence of an extramarital affair he'd been having with a young woman deeply involved in the world of organized crime. Chief William Parker's LAPD had reportedly come into possession of compromising photos of Mosk and the young woman. Interestingly, the LAPD's files reference Ziffren's own dalliances with hookers. Connie Carlson, one of Mosk's most trusted investigators in the AG's office, recently said, "Mrs. Edna Mosk told me about how Ziffren tried to block Mosk's advancement."*,[36]

---

*In the 1964 senatorial race, two sources—one of them a prominent Democratic newspaper publisher—told the *Weekly* that Democratic state comptroller Alan Cranston had shown them those photos in the spring of 1964 in an effort to get Mosk to drop from the race. Cranston said their memory was playing tricks on them.

Edmund "Pat" Brown, Paul Ziffren, and John F. Kennedy during the 1960 presidential campaign (TimeLife)

Brown's people also accused Ziffren of having tried to persuade Massachusetts senator John F. Kennedy to run in the California primaries against "favorite son" Brown. (Kennedy, a well-known pal of the Vegas Supermob, told an adviser that support from Ziffren and his Democrats was critical to his presidential ambitions.)[37] Finally, on June 19, 1960, the party's delegates voted 115 to 3 to replace Ziffren as party chairman. Stanley Mosk was voted to replace him. It had been rumored that Brown promised Mosk the state's Supreme Court chief justice post if he would go up against Ziffren.* The press interpreted Ziffren's defeat as a big victory for the governor, "who had gone all out to oust the incumbent committeeman. It ended a bitter fight which has torn the Democratic ranks, particularly in Southern California."[38] Another paper ran an editorial stating, "Last Saturday the chickens came home to roost."[39]

When Mosk stepped down from his Democratic National Committee post in 1961, he was replaced by yet another Chicago-born attorney, Eugene

---

*In 1964, as predicted, Brown appointed Mosk chief justice of the California Supreme Court, where he would serve for a record thirty-seven years. Writing over fifteen hundred decisions, he was rightly called "one of the most influential figures in the history of California law."

Wyman, Greg Bautzer's law partner. As chairman, Wyman proceeded to entice contributions to the party from his closest well-heeled pals, chief among them Al Hart, Jake "the Barber" Factor, and Sid Korshak. All were said to be major contributors, although Korshak rarely gave in his own name. "He had to do something with all that cash!" remarked one friend.[40]

As if to rub salt in Ziffren's wounds, perennial Supermob gadfly Lester Velie weighed in once again. In the July 1960 issue of *Reader's Digest*, Velie launched a broadside at Ziffren entitled "Paul Ziffren: The Democrats' Man of Mystery." In the biting seven-page article, Velie not only surfaced Robert Goe's research about Ziffren's fronting for the Capones via Greenberg, but he worried how much influence the mob would have in the White House if a Democrat supported by Ziffren won in 1960. One did, and the mob was happy to help him get elected. After Kennedy's July 11, 1960, nomination in L.A., Ziffren's lawyer Isaac Pacht was alleged to be preparing a libel complaint against Velie.[41] Sid Korshak's advice was also sought out, and he was said to have remarked to a friend, "Paul is always getting himself into hot water and I have to pull him out."[42]

When the FBI learned that Velie was about to excoriate Ziffren, the SAC of the L.A. Field Office wrote Hoover, "The big question is will Velie's piece destroy Ziffren or will the public remain as apathetic as it did when gubernatorial candidate William Knowland attempted an exposé in November 1958?"[43] The SAC went even further when assessing the Democratic Party rift caused by the Ziffren revelations: "Ziffren, hoodlum-founded though he is, is probably the shrewdest, most cunning, far-sighted, behind-the-scenes political manipulator ever encountered in California—where kingmakers have historically ruled politicians."[44]

Meanwhile, in D.C., an unnamed political journalist informed an FBI pal that David Bazelon was being groomed to be nominated to replace Judge Felix Frankfurter on the U.S. Supreme Court.[45] That would turn out to be the case after the upcoming presidential election. At the same time, the City of Los Angeles was feathering Bazelon's financial nest: reportedly due to the influence of Paul Ziffren, the city purchased the massive Warehouse Properties parcel for $1.1 million in furtherance of its Civic Center Master Plan. The lot was situated in the center of a location earmarked for purchase by the federal government for the new $30 million Customs Building. Leo Ziffren had also been seen massaging the deal in the office of the city's chief of the Bureau of Right of Way and Land.[46] Bazelon's cut was over $100,000.[47]

Paul Ziffren began spending more time expanding his law practice, specializing in tax and divorce law and representing numerous Los Angeles celebrities and moguls. He was regularly seen driving around Beverly Hills in his silver Rolls-Royce, at a time when they weren't nearly as ubiquitous as they are now in the affluent city.

CHAPTER 11

The New Frontier

By 1960, Korshak's influence surged beneath the surface of Holly-wood like an underground river.

—DENNIS MCDOUGAL, AUTHOR AND EXPERT ON

HOLLYWOOD HISTORY[1]

WITH REAGAN, WASSERMAN, STEIN, Hart, and Ziffren moving fast to create a Supermob-friendly California, Sid Korshak, Moe Dalitz, and Jake Factor saw to it that Las Vegas similarly reflected the wishes of the cadre and its even less savory partners. The city in the desert was exploding, thanks to the massive cash infusion from the Teamsters Pension Fund, and the Eastern gangs that created it were realizing their dream of going legit (or semi-legit), with the contingent from Kiev handling the paperwork. Additionally, Kennedy family patriarch Joe Kennedy had numerous investments in the state, and his presidential candidate son Jack was considered an honorary member of Sinatra's Rat Pack, which was ensconced in Sinatra's Sands and Korshak's Riviera in January-February 1960 while filming *Ocean's Eleven*.*

***Ocean's Eleven*, in addition to boasting JFK's visits to the set, provided a sneak peak into the world of the Supermob—for those who knew what to look for. The casino portions of the film were shot largely in Korshak's Riviera, and Korshak saw to it that his great friend George Raft was given a role in the movie as a casino owner; the opening scenes took place in Drucker's, the Beverly Hills barbershop preferred by Korshak, Rosselli, Siegel, Raft, et al.; Frank Sinatra's character "Danny Ocean" was married to "Bee," played by Angie Dickinson; the five casinos robbed by Sinatra's gang were the five most closely rumored to have been run by "the boys"—the Flamingo, the Sands, the Desert Inn, the Riviera, and the Sahara. But, for the knowledgeable, the most memorable moment in the movie came when actor Akim Tamiroff, referring to the gang's enlistment of an ex-con in their scheme, uttered one of the most absurd examples of high sarcasm ever memorialized on celluloid: "A man with a record can't get near Las Vegas, much less the casinos."

Sinatra's official Riviera portrait (courtesy John
Neeland, the Riviera)

When the Pack sobered up in the Sands steam room after an all-nighter, Jack
Kennedy often joined them, wearing his bathrobe, a gift from Sinatra, em-
broidered with his Pack nickname, Chicky Baby.

"We practically considered Jack to be one of the boys," one erstwhile
Chicago Outfit associate recently said. For decades a handwritten note from
Jack hung in Sinatra's "Kennedy Room" in the Voice's Palm Springs home
(later redecorated by Bee Korshak), reflecting Kennedy's reliance on Sin City
in the upcoming contest. "Frank," the barely legible scrawl began, "How
much can we expect from the boys in Vegas? [signed] JFK."[2] He got plenty.
In addition to massive "anonymous" Vegas donations, Jacqueline Kennedy's
uncle, Norman Biltz, who built Kennedy's Cal-Neva Lodge in 1926, traipsed
up and down the Vegas Strip collecting some $15 million from "the boys"
for Jack's war chest.[3] The Stardust's Jake Factor contributed $22,000 to the
campaign, becoming JFK's single largest campaign contributor.[4]

The Supermob's Fear Factor

There was, however, one storm cloud looming that threatened to spoil the
elysian setup: Jake Factor's nemesis Roger Touhy had just been released (in
November 1959) from his wrongful twenty-seven-year incarceration for Factor's "kidnapping"—and he wanted payback.*

Touhy published his autobiography, *The Stolen Years* (written with veteran Chicago crime reporter Ray Brennan), simultaneous with his release
from prison, prompting Chicago boss Accardo to make certain that Teamster truckers refused to ship the book, and Chicago bookstores were frightened off from carrying the memoir. Undeterred, Touhy also announced that

---

*When Judge John Barnes finally reviewed the case, he concluded, "The kidnapping never
took place." The parole board agreed.

he intended to sue Factor, Sid Korshak's Chicago point man Tom Courtney, Korshak's mentor Curly Humphreys, and Accardo for $300 million for wrongful imprisonment.

The threat couldn't have come at a worse time. Stardust front Factor, the man most directly vulnerable to Touhy's offensive, was in the midst of a massive and determined reputation face-lift. Since the midfifties, Factor had been drawing on the great fortune he had amassed during his early British stock swindle to embark on a successful PR campaign aimed at creating the persona of Jake the Philanthropist. With the Stardust humming along, Factor dabbled in California real estate and life insurance, exponentially increasing his wealth. His frequent six-figure donations to various charities earned him numerous humanitarian awards. The Barber/Philanthropist was simultaneously engaged in a seven-year battle to obtain a presidential pardon for his crimes, most of which he never served time for.* This was at the same time that the Immigration and Naturalization Service (INS) was considering deporting Factor back to England to face the massive mail fraud charges brought against him decades earlier.

Faced with a noisy Touhy threatening to expose the entire Vegas-California enterprise, Jake Factor hired Korshak to prepare a countersuit.[5] But with so much riding on the outcome, a decision was quickly reached that Touhy had to be dealt with in a way much more permanent than a time-consuming lawsuit. Thus, on December 16, 1959, just three weeks after his emancipation, Roger Touhy was murdered with five shotgun blasts, while Jake Factor dined at the Outfit's Singapore Restaurant in Chicago. The *Chicago Daily News* reported two days later, "Police have been informed that the tough-talking Touhy had given Humphreys . . . this ultimatum: 'Cut me in or you'll be in trouble. I'll talk!" On his deathbed, the former gangster whispered, "I've been expecting it. The bastards never forget." Not long after, Factor sold Curly Humphreys four hundred shares of First National Life Insurance stock at $20 a share, then bought them back after a few more months for $125 per share. Curly netted a tidy $42,000 profit. Insiders concluded this was a gift to Curly for arranging Touhy's murder.

Factor was questioned under oath by suspicious IRS agents in Los Angeles, and he explained that he had suddenly decided, after twenty-seven years, to pay Humphreys for assisting in the release of his "kidnapped" son, Jerome, not the recent slaying of his nemesis.[6]

---

*In the late forties, Factor served six years in prison for mail fraud involving the sale of other people's whiskey receipts in the Midwest, but he never stood trial for the thousands he bilked in the United Kingdom, not to mention the railroading of Touhy.

With Touhy removed, Factor was free to lobby for his presidential pardon and to fight the INS deportation threat. Showing great audacity, Factor had none other than Al Hart attest to his rehabilitation. The FBI interviewed Hart on July 6, 1960, and he informed the Bureau that "[Factor] is endeavoring to live down the past." Hart added that Factor contributed to many charities and that he would "highly recommend him for a pardon." Even Estes Kefauver wrote a letter on Factor's behalf. Also backing Factor's pardon were Korshak pals California governor Pat Brown and Republican senator Thomas Kuchel.[7] The effort dragged on for two more years before a decision was reached.

Interestingly, while Factor was trying to burnish his image with the feds, he was simultaneously involved with Jimmy Hoffa in a Florida land deal that would, years later, see Hoffa eventually imprisoned. In May 1960, according to the sworn testimony of a witness, Factor lent $125,000 to a partner in Florida's Sun Valley housing development, later found to have diverted $1.7 million from its Teamsters Pension Fund loan to the partners' own bank accounts. But this transaction was not discovered until 1964, allowing Factor more time to once again escape extradition.[8]

With Jack Kennedy now occupying the Oval Office, the country was in the midst of Robert Kennedy's stewardship of the Department of Justice. For years, Korshak's relationship with G-men had been polite in the extreme; however, after Robert Kennedy declared war on the underworld, Korshak became irritated by the nuisance it was becoming. In the summer of 1961, Korshak informed a Chicago FBI agent, "I believe your organization has forfeited all right to talk to me." He explained that he believed the FBI was opening an investigation of him.[9] Korshak also likely learned that the Nevada Gaming Control Board was inquiring about him to the Chicago Crime Commission. In a letter to the CCC, the Control Board's chief investigator, Robert Moore, had asked Director Virgil Peterson for information about recent Las Vegas arrivals from Chicago. In addition to Korshak, the other names on the list were Joseph and Rocco Fischetti, Frank Ferraro, Gus Alex, Louis Kanne, Murray Humphreys, John Drew, Tony Accardo, and Sam Giancana.[10]

Whereas the Supermob and their mob associates felt beleaguered in Chicago, they continued to enjoy virtual immunity in sunny California, where Korshak was now Hollywood royalty, reporting earnings of $500,000 per year. That figure was fallacious, since he often demanded payment in cash and confided to friends that his income was $2 million plus. His FBI case officer called him "possibly the highest-paid lawyer in the world." Amazingly, on his 1961 home insurance policy Korshak claimed to be "semi-retired." Among his circle of friends, Korshak was beginning to get the reputation of a mensch, freely giving money to those in a jam, and spending lavishly on gifts that the more cynical observers could assume were a tad shy of meeting the altruistic ideal. In 1961, for example, he purchased one thousand seats for friends and business contacts for the first heavyweight fight ever held in Vegas.

Korshak's labor-mediating prowess was now being spoken of, if in hushed tones, in boardrooms from coast to coast. As his stature rose in the eyes of big business, he became the go-to man for entrepreneurs in even the most unconventional professions. One of Sid Korshak's labor "consultancies" in 1961 was widely believed by authorities to have included his brother Marshall in a bribery scheme aimed at one of Chicago's fastest-rising stars, Hugh Hefner, the chairman of Playboy Inc. At the time, the thirty-five-year-old Hefner presided over an empire built around his monthly magazine, *Playboy*, which was itself built on the attributes of the stomach-stapled, airbrushed Playmates that appeared in the magazine's gatefold. Complementing the magazine at the time were four "key clubs" in Chicago, Miami, New Orleans, and St. Louis, which, by 1961, were grossing a combined $4.5 million per year. In the flagship Chicago club on 116 E. Walton Street in the posh Near North district, Hef's bunnies mingled with "keyholders," many of whom represented the upper echelons of the Chicago Outfit and Supermob.

Of course, it was impossible for a successful Chicago club to avoid the fingerprints of the smothering Chicago underworld, and the Playboy Club was no exception. Among the 106,000 Chicago keyholders were Sam Giancana, Joseph Di Varco, Gus Zapas, and the Buccieri brothers; Outfit bosses were bestowed exclusive Number One Keys, which allowed them to date the otherwise off-limits "Bunnies" and to drink on a free tab. Slot king, and Humphreys's crony, Eddie Vogel dated "Bunny Mother" Peg Strak.

As with most other Near North businesses, the Playboy Club had to make accommodations with the countless semilegit enterprises within the all-encompassing grasp of the Chicago Outfit. In addition to the army of hoods cavorting at the new jazz-inflected boîte, the mob's business arm controlled the club's numerous concessions—bartenders, waiters, coat checkers, parking valets, jukeboxes—so vital to the new enterprise. The intersections started with Hef's liquor license, which had to be approved by the Outfit-controlled First Ward Headquarters, where John D'Arco and Pat Marcy reigned supreme. It was said that much of the club's cutlery was supplied by businesses owned by Al Capone's brother, Ralph, while other furnishings had their origin in the gang's distribution warehouses. Local bands that supplied the requisite cool-jazz backdrop were booked either by James Petrillo's musicians union or by Jules Stein's MCA.

Victor Lownes III, who oversaw the Playboy clubs, explained the obvious: "If the mob runs the only laundry service in town, what are we supposed to do? Let our members sit at tables covered with filthy linen?"[11]

Coordinating the gang's feeding frenzy was the club's general manager, Tony Roma (of later restaurant fame), who was married to Josephine Costello, daughter of Capone bootlegger Joseph Costello. Roma was also an intermediary for certain Teamsters Pension Fund loans. One IRS agent noted his "associations with organized crime figures in Canada," while another stated, "I think it's more accurate to say Roma's a trusted courier, probably of money and messages, for the likes of [Meyer] Lansky."[12] Chicago crime historian Ovid Demaris described how Roma operated the Chicago Playboy Club: "One of Roma's first acts as general manager of the Chicago Playboy Club was to award the garbage collection to Willie 'Potatoes' Daddano's West Suburban Scavenger Service . . . Attendant Service Corporation, a [Ross] Prio–[Joseph] DiVarco enterprise, was already parking playboy cars, checking playboy hats and handing playboy towels in the restroom. Other playboys were drinking [Joe] Fusco beers and liquors, eating [James] Allegretti meat, and smoking [Eddie] Vogel cigarettes."[13]

Eddie Vogel's girlfriend, "Bunny Mother" Peg Strak, became Roma's executive secretary when Roma was promoted to operations manager of Playboy Clubs International Inc., which oversaw the empire of sixty-three thousand international keyholders.

When Hefner and Lownes began planning in 1960 for an inevitable club in Manhattan, they ran into a stubborn State Liquor Authority (SLA), which was known for withholding the requisite liquor license without a "gratuity" being offered to its chairman, Martin Epstein. After having purchased a six-story former art gallery on pricey Fifty-ninth Street, east of Fifth Avenue, not far from Sid Korshak's office at the Carlyle, Playboy waited for the license. But by the fall of 1961, with thousands of keys in advance of a December 8, 1961, scheduled opening, the document had yet to arrive.

According to the Chicago Crime Commission, Playboy simultaneously contacted the Korshaks for advice, noting, "Sidney and Marshall Korshak had been approached by Playboy as to how to obtain a New York liquor license."[14] Hefner was well acquainted with the talents of the Korshak brothers. Previously, when his fledgling magazine faced an obscenity charge due to a nude model draped in an American flag, Sidney recommended that Hef engage Marshall, who quickly had the case quashed.

Now, in regard to the license, a Capone hood named Ralph Berger* showed up at Playboy's Chicago office to inform Hefner and Lownes that he could break the stalemate. According to the FBI, Berger, who lived in the Seneca and frequented the Korshak brothers' office at 134 N. LaSalle, had been instructed by the Korshaks to make the overture. For years, Marshall had been an official of Windy City Liquor distributors, and the FBI stated, "Berger was the contact man between Korshak and . . . the chairman of the Illinois Liquor Control Board." Korshak also developed associations with New York's SLA. In fact, he and Berger had previously performed the same "service" for New York's Gaslight Club.[15]

Playboy agreed to pay Berger $5,000 to represent them to the New York authorities, and when his fee did not arrive promptly, Berger, according to his later testimony, called Marshall Korshak, who made it happen. Epstein arranged for Hefner and Lownes to meet with him at the SLA office in New York. When they arrived at the building, they saw a protester outside with a placard that read THE STATE LIQUOR AUTHORITY IS CROOKED AND CORRUPT. Lownes later said, "By the time we came out, I felt like joining him." At the meeting, SLA chairman Epstein asked for $50,000 for the license. And there was more: in subsequent meetings, Playboy was informed that the New York Republican state chairman and aide to Governor Nelson Rockefeller, L. Judson Morhouse, wanted $100,000 plus the lucrative concessions in all the Playboy clubs' gift shops in exchange for his help.

After protracted negotiations throughout the fall of 1961, Epstein eventually settled for $25,000, and Morhouse, $18,000. When the officials were finally placated, the precious certificate arrived just hours before the December 8 opening. However, the fix became unraveled during a grand jury proceeding looking into corruption at the SLA. Eventually, Berger was charged with conspiracy to bribe Epstein and received one year in prison. Epstein was considered too old (seventy-five) and infirm to be charged. Morhouse was also convicted but saw his prison sentence commuted due to his poor health. No one at Playboy was charged; neither were the Korshaks, despite their being named in the testimony.[16]

*In 1935 Berger had been indicted with another Capone hood for attempting to fence $235,000 in bonds stolen from a mail truck. In 1952, when Berger's office was raided, Paul "Needle Nose" Labriola, a friend of Sidney Korshak's, and Accardo attorney Abraham Teitelbaum were arrested there (their garroted bodies were found together in the trunk of a car in 1954). Later, Berger fronted for the Outfit by running the Latin Quarter nightclub, where he was charged with bilking customers out of hundreds of thousands of dollars.

The FBI summarized, "If Berger was able to exert any influence with certain members of the State Liquor Authority [SLA] . . . he undoubtedly would do so as a representative of the Korshaks and not in his own right. It was believed that any conniving Berger might do with the New York SLA or with the Illinois State Liquor Control Board would be done on behalf of and under the instructions of the Korshak brothers."[17]

Despite the embarrassment, Hefner was obviously satisfied with the performance of Sid Korshak; years later, Hefner would again engage the services of Korshak, who, for a $50,000 fee, attempted in vain to settle a film copyright case with Universal Studios, which was run by his old friend Lew Wasserman.

Success followed success for Korshak. Typically, his triumphs were unknown to the public at large, who were nonetheless affected by them in ways large and small. In Los Angeles, he staved off labor strikes at area racetracks, where the Teamster-dominated culinary workers could bring an operation to its knees. When Hollywood Park Racetrack was hit with a work stoppage by the Pari-Mutuel Clerk Union in 1960, Korshak's Hillcrest friend and Hollywood Park Racing Association president Mervyn LeRoy enlisted Korshak to address the stalemate that twenty-eight previous lawyers couldn't resolve. Betsy Duncan Hammes, one of Johnny Rosselli's lady friends, recently recalled how it occurred: "Mervyn LeRoy called me and asked me to call Sidney and ask him to call the Hollywood Park strike off," said Hammes. "So I called Sid, and he said, 'Don't worry, you can go on Monday.' "[18] As promised, the Fixer settled it in forty-eight hours, somehow convincing the strikers to accept another sweetheart contract. In December 1960, Korshak settled his first labor dispute for Santa Anita Race Track in Arcadia, when employees threatened a walkout. According to an FBI source, Korshak received "interest in the racetrack" as his fee.[19]

One Korshak power play with Chicago racetrack labor would have repercussions over the next two decades. By 1960, Ben Lindheimer was the acknowledged sachem of Chicago-area racing, owning the two thoroughbred tracks Arlington Park and Washington Park under the banner of Chicago Thoroughbred Enterprises (CTE). Lindheimer was a well-known reformer and outspoken opponent of the Chicago Outfit's attempts to infiltrate his operation. Exacerbating the bad blood was the fact that Lindheimer was an assimilated German Jew with an inbred dislike of Russians like Korshak. Nonetheless, he could do little about the mob-connected unions that plied their trades in the parking lots and elsewhere (or the fact that Jake Arvey owned six thousand shares of stock in Arlington),[20] but he drew the line at allowing convicted hoods onto the racing grounds; one of Sid Korshak's Outfit mentors, Jake Guzik, was barred for life from Lindheimer's CTE tracks.

However, on Sunday morning, June 5, 1960, when the Korshak-represented mutuel clerks threatened a strike at Washington Park, an extremely ill Lindheimer was forced to deal with the devil: he immediately called Korshak to ask that he avert the work action. But this time Korshak took the union's side against the antimob track owner and allowed them to walk off the job. That same night, Ben Lindheimer died of a heart attack. His stepdaughter Marge Lindheimer Everett, who inherited her stepfather's empire, blamed Korshak for her father's death and fired him after she took over. "We'd never had a strike before, never," Everett later said. "I think it killed him."[21] After later moving to Beverly Hills (a move believed to be influenced by the similar relocation of her great childhood friend, Nancy Davis Reagan), Marge Everett told the Bistro's Kurt Niklas about what she believed Korshak had done: "He killed my father by refusing to call off the strike. All Korshak had to do was pick up the telephone, but he didn't. As far as I'm concerned, it was the same as murder."[22] It would be the beginning of a lifelong feud between Marge Everett and Sid Korshak.[23]

Another sports venue became part of Korshak lore when he made certain that an important new L.A. sports franchise got off to a smooth start. Soon after his election, Governor Pat Brown, Korshak's pal in the statehouse, pledged to sell thirty-six acres in L.A.'s Chavez Ravine tract to the city in furtherance of the plans of Walter O'Malley, who had just relocated his Brooklyn Dodgers to the West Coast. O'Malley was determined to build his dream baseball stadium, and that enterprise hung on the upcoming referendum known as Prop B. Just prior to the vote, on June 1, 1958, the Dodgers aired a live, five-hour "Dodgerthon" from the airport as the Dodger team plane arrived from the East. Helping O'Malley extol the virtues of Prop B were numerous celebrity associates of Korshak/Ziffren/Brown, including Dean Martin and Jerry Lewis, Ronald Reagan, and Debbie Reynolds. Two days later, the referendum narrowly passed (351,683–325,898) and was immediately appealed (all the way up to the Supreme Court) on the grounds that the city's granting of the land use did not follow a "public purpose" clause in the federal government sale to the city. When the high court finally dismissed the appeal on October 19, 1959, the state began evicting squatters who lived in the ravine, and ground was broken for Dodger Stadium.[24]

By the time of the April 10, 1962, opening day, O'Malley had, not surprisingly, engaged Sid Korshak as his $100,000-per-year labor consultant, responsible for keeping the cars parked, the lights on, and the food service employees behind the concession stands. When it came to parking, Korshak had a special influence, as that concession was awarded to a Nevada corporation, Concessionaire Affiliated Parking Inc., of which Korshak was a 12½ percent owner with Beldon Katleman, owner of Las Vegas' El Rancho Vegas Casino.[25] Affiliated, which had contracts at Dulles Airport outside Washington and the Seattle World's Fair, had been given the contract when O'Malley was threatened with an opening-day strike by the first company he had hired. With Affiliated, O'Malley was able to cut a typical Korshak sweetheart contract, wherein the parking-lot attendants received one third of what the original workers had demanded.

O'Malley explained that he hired Korshak to resolve the strike threat since it was not good business to open a stadium without the proper workers and he thought it was the right thing to do to settle it quickly. O'Malley told Sy Hersh in 1976, "We did what any ordinary businessman would do. [Korshak] had the reputation as having the best experience in this area. He provided us a little insulation . . . As far as we're concerned, he does a good job. And unless he's been convicted of a crime, we're not going to do anything."[26] After Korshak and Katleman were awarded the contract, they celebrated with a quick tour of Europe, according to the FBI.[27] (Five years later, when the new baseball players union met with team owners at Chicago's Drake Hotel, O'Malley held a private meeting with his fellow owners, in which he trumpeted a man who could counsel them on how to deal with the upstart players union. With that, O'Malley left the meeting and returned with Korshak, who had been waiting outside. For the next four hours, Korshak advised the owners on how to deal with the union. Korshak went on to become good friends with Dodgers manager Tommy Lasorda, who lunched with him at the Bistro.)[28]

Upon his return from Europe, Korshak negotiated a quick deal that would pay huge dividends. According to court documents, Joe Glaser, owner of Associated Booking Company (ABC), then the nation's third-largest theatrical agency, assigned all of the "voting rights, dominion and control" of his majority stock in the concern to Korshak and himself. The agreement meant that Korshak, who through the 1960s had seemed merely to be the agency's legal counsel, would assume complete control over the company upon Mr. Glaser's death.[29]

Since the thirties and forties, ABC had specialized in representing important black musicians such as Louis Armstrong and Duke Ellington. Under

Korshak's regime, ABC would add Creedence Clearwater Revival and Barbra Streisand to its talent roster. Freddie Bell was one of the longest-running ABC acts, coming to Vegas from Philly in 1954. Bell carved out a legendary career with his lounge band, The Bellboys, opening for Don Rickles for ten years, and writing the revised lyrics to the song "Hound Dog," which Elvis Presley heard in Vegas and used for his hit recording.

"I was the token white guy with ABC, with them for nineteen years," Bell recently recalled. "When Joe died in 1969, I left." Bell has distinct memories of both Korshak and Glaser: "Sid and Joe were very close—they built the La Concha Motel next to the Riviera. But I thought Sid was the power behind the throne, mostly involved in the money end. Joe was a loud-talking tough guy from Chicago, and Sid was just the opposite. It's hard to talk about Sidney because he was so quiet. Nobody really knew the man."[30]

Korshak's association with ABC was also advantageous for his Chicago mob patrons, who used it to acquire talent, not only for their Vegas holdings, but also for events on their home turf. In the late fall of 1962, when Sam Giancana held a monthlong gambling party—actually a skim operation—at his suburban Villa Venice Restaurant, he called on Korshak to supply some of the talent. Giancana asked Korshak to pressure Moe Dalitz at the Desert Inn to release Debbie Reynold's husband, singer Eddie Fisher, to him for the stint. As usual, Korshak's intercession with Dalitz was successful, and Fisher joined Frank Sinatra, Dean Martin, Sammy Davis Jr., and Jimmy Durante for the November-December gig.[31] However, as seen with the Dinah Shore faux pas, Curly Humphreys, as heard by the eavesdropping feds, once again called Korshak to put him in his place.

"Anything you want to do for yourself, Sidney, is okay," Humphreys dictated, "but we made you and we want you to take care of us first. When Chicago calls, we come first." (The FBI noted that Korshak attended Reynolds's opening at the mob's Riviera in January 1963.) Years later, boss Accardo told Vegas functionary Tony Spilotro, "Korshak sometimes forgets who he works for, who brought him up."[32]

Sidney Korshak—Double Agent

What Humphreys and Accardo may have suspected, but could not know for sure, was that Korshak was playing a most dangerous game in his efforts to assure his own legal immunity. According to a recently released FBI document, it is now clear that Korshak had been having secret meetings with Clark County (Las Vegas) sheriff Ralph Lamb, to whom he was feeding a measured dose of intelligence on his Chicago bosses, with the knowledge that Lamb would, in turn, act as conduit to the FBI. A 1962 Las Vegas FBI

Field Office memo stated, "[Sheriff Lamb] furnished the following information which should not be disseminated outside the Bureau nor should any indication be given to anyone outside the Bureau that Sidney Korshak has been talking to Sheriff Lamb, inasmuch as he furnished the information on a very confidential basis." In one report, describing a Lamb-Korshak conversation at the Riviera on July 22, 1962, Korshak advised Lamb that a recent letter regarding Sam Giancana's movements in Las Vegas, which Lamb's office had sent to the Chicago Police Department, had made its way immediately into the hands of Giancana—Korshak knew because Giancana had showed it to him. Korshak warned Lamb not to trust the Chicago PD. Korshak also tipped to Lamb that Moe Dalitz was building a home in Acapulco, Mexico. The memo went on to say:

> Korshak was interested in the overall gambling situation as it pertains to Nevada and would like to prevent any individuals of hoodlum status from gaining a foothold in Las Vegas, and would probably like to see those already established be forced to leave Nevada.
>
> Lamb stated that at no time in his contacts with Korshak has Korshak endeavored to obtain any favors from him or obtain any information regarding Sheriff's Office activities from him. Sheriff Lamb was also of the impression that Korshak possibly furnished him this information so that it could be furnished to the FBI, since on his last contact with Korshak, Korshak had inquired of Lamb as to his association with the FBI in Las Vegas. Sheriff Lamb told Korshak on that occasion that he worked closely with the FBI and that the FBI could have any information in possession of the Sheriff's office, or any assistance whatsoever. Korshak again told Lamb that he felt that the cooperation between the Sheriff's Office and the FBI was the way law enforcement should be handled . . . Korshak classified [DELETED] as a "punk" and told Lamb that he should not tolerate any type of interference from ["Peanuts"] Danolfo or anyone connected with the Strip hotels.[33]

Apparently, the Lamb-Korshak relationship continued for years. Five years later, when Lamb barred Rosselli from Vegas for all but one day per month, Korshak told a friend that he could "square it with Lamb," but chose not to bother.[34] In actuality, Rosselli was himself becoming increasingly skeptical of Sidney Korshak's true loyalties.

The Korshak-Lamb connection was not the only evidence of a Korshak relationship with the Bureau. Eli Schulman, owner of Eli's Steakhouse, one of Korshak's favorite Chicago eateries, once told a mutual friend that Korshak had secretly ratted out L.A. mobster Mickey Cohen, who had also been friends with Guzik in Chicago and Dalitz in Cleveland, to the FBI in 1951.[35] "Mickey was becoming an all-around pain in the ass, setting up crap games [in L.A.] just to rob the players," said a Schulman friend, who asked not to be named. Cohen spent the next four years at the federal prison on McNeil Island.*

> *The Italians think of Korshak as a sort of god and expect him to work miracles, and someday when he fails them, there is going to be a real problem.*
>
> —FBI INFORMANT[36]

According to an FBI informant planted inside the Outfit, Korshak's private dance with the feds was not the only action that threatened his relationship with the Outfit. In a telephone interview, the source told his FBI contact that Korshak "set up a racetrack and Korshak took $250,000 that was not his and was caught. As a result of this, a contract to kill Korshak went out, but Korshak was able to stop it and consequently paid back the money. Because of this Korshak always carries a gun and it would appear that he is somewhat apprehensive of the Chicago hoodlums."[37] Still another informant added, "Sidney Korshak has turned out to be a rat and has broken away from LCN (La Cosa Nostra) influence."[38]

Korshak's closeness to Accardo may likely have been his salvation, but even Accardo, who was known to bludgeon victims to death with baseball bats, had finite patience when it came to traitors. All things considered, the foregoing Korshak covert activities may better explain the intense security at Korshak's Bel-Air manse.

At the time of the Walter O'Malley affair, the senior staff of the *Los Angeles Times* was finally becoming interested in Sid Korshak and the influx of curious Midwesterners to their city. In the early sixties, the *Times* boasted a tough-as-nails investigative unit housed in the paper's city desk and run by managing editor and ex-marine Frank McCulloch, who had recently come to the paper from his post as *Time* magazine's L.A. Bureau chief. McCulloch, one of the greatest journalists of the twentieth century, was often referred to as "a journalist's journalist," and author David Halberstam called him "a legend."[39]

---

*A 1958 FBI report discloses that Korshak's unlisted phone number (Rand 6-2038) was in Mickey Cohen's address book.

Until this time, the paper's philosophy had been dictated by its founder, Norman Chandler, with an assist from his wife, Buff. "It was an instrument of the Republican Party, and an acknowledged one," McCulloch said recently. "The City Hall reporter at that time was a Republican lobbyist. That's how bad it was. Norman and Buffy paid very little attention to the newspaper as a totality. Norman published it, but he saw it as a business enterprise."[40] It was also well-known that Chandler had reached a beneficial arrangement with labor fixer Sidney Korshak. Journalist and three-time Pulitzer Prize winner Knut Royce, who would later investigate both Korshak and the Pritzkers, recently said of the Chandler-Korshak connection, "Sid kept unions out of the *L.A. Times* for Norman Chandler."[41]

However, after the Chandlers' son Otis took over, he made a bold move toward serious journalism, hiring McCulloch to forge a team of serious reporters. Unquestionably, the unit's crack reporters were Gene Blake and Jack Tobin. In 1961, Blake had written a searing five-part exposé of the red-baiting John Birch Society. The controversial series cost the paper advertisers and over fifteen thousand subscribers. Tobin, another ex-marine, had earned his stripes as the country's leading investigative sports journalist. "Tobin and Blake were a great team," McCulloch remembered. "Jack was a sports reporter first. I used to use him as a stringer when I was at Time-Life. He was very quiet. The best records man I've ever known. I became real impressed with him." Ed Guthman, former investigative reporter, press secretary to Attorney General Robert Kennedy, and later national editor of the *Los Angeles Times*, has a similar opinion of Tobin. "Jack Tobin was a great investigative reporter—great with records," said Guthman. "The police and the FBI used to go to *him* for help."[42]

McCulloch recently spoke of his team's coverage of the Supermob: "After we covered the strike at Dodger Stadium, Korshak wanted to sue me. One of the movie people called me—I think it was Lew Wasserman—and said, 'What are you doing this to old Sid for?' He said, 'I'm telling you as a friend, Frank. I wouldn't pursue this any further. There could be legal ramifications *and more*.' I'll never forget that part." (This would not be the first time that Korshak's corporate friends would try to derail bad publicity for Sidney.)

Then the newsman devised a brilliant tactic to deal with the Fixer, as Korshak was now referred to. "It was suggested that we subpoena one of the bosses in Chicago, and Korshak would lose interest in going to court rather rapidly," McCulloch remembered. "And we did serve one of them; I think it was Giancana. We preempted Korshak and we never heard from him again. That's when he donated money to Dorothy Chandler, the publisher's wife."[43]

McCulloch was referring to a typical Korshak damage-control gambit, aimed at defusing any local coverage of his activities. In 1961, Dorothy Buffum "Buff" Chandler, of the Chandler family that owned the Times-Mirror newspapers, had become the company's vice president for corporate and community relations. In that position, she waged a tenacious battle to realize a dream: the construction of a world-class music center. Envisioned as a privately fostered, but not-for-profit, partnership with the County of Los Angeles, the center site was donated by the county, which raised an additional $14 million using mortgage revenue bonds. Los Angeles rabbi Ed Feinstein remembered Chandler's quest: "She had a problem in 1962. It was her great dream to see a cultural center constructed downtown, giving Los Angeles a cultural gravity it had never possessed. She wanted something much more important. She wanted to bring the city together."[44]

More concerned with filling coffers than with the source of the donations, Buff courted political opponents such as Paul Ziffren and Sid Korshak. Publisher Otis Chandler, Buff's son, recently admitted, "My mother would court the devil for contributions. Anybody who'd give her some dough."[45] Chandler told the understandably press-shy Korshak that his name *would never appear* in the *Times* if he would cough up a contribution. Korshak quickly obliged and sent a $50,000 check to Buff's building fund; he likely considered the donation to be a business investment, and a continuation of a relationship he had fostered for years. Back in 1958, Korshak was observed meeting with the *Times* managing editor L. D. Hotchkiss. Allegedly they were discussing the political future of Congressman Richard Rogers of California.[46] However, Hotchkiss was infamous for his refusal to run stories that reflected poorly on the city, to the extent of killing important stories about organized crime.[47] Korshak's friendship with Hotchkiss had guaranteed his continued anonymity during that previous regime.

The Korshak–Buff Chandler arrangement did not, however, proceed as smoothly as the previous one with Hotchkiss. According to the FBI, although Affiliated was granted the parking concession at the pavilion, Korshak's check was returned because of what Chandler's own reporters were turning up about Korshak's bedfellows.

By 1962, McCulloch had become curious about the aberrant real estate transactions that were a fundamental part of California's recent history. In the spring of 1962, McCulloch pulled aside Jack Tobin and pointed out the window. "One day, almost as a joke, I asked him, 'Who the hell owns the Santa Monica Mountains?'" recalled McCulloch. "He took me literally and went and found the Teamster connection." The more they mulled it over, McCulloch and Tobin began to realize that this prime Los Angeles real estate tract, as yet undeveloped, was an invitation to the kind of corruption that the state seemed to cultivate.[48]

Tobin and Blake treaded the same path blazed by Robert Goe, Lester Velie, and Art White (albeit with just one specific locale in mind) straight to the Los Angeles County Recorder's Office. After painstaking research, the duo concluded that the Chicago real estate investments in California were ongoing. As noted in their first article on the subject, Tobin and Blake quickly learned that the Chicago-based Teamsters Pension Fund had loaned over $30 million to out-of-state businessmen like Chicago's Pritzkers, Detroit's Ben Weingart, and Texas's Clint Murchison. Hoffa admitted to the reporters that the fund had earmarked some $4 million for the Pritzkers and their Hyatt enterprise, and that he had personally approved the $6.7 million Murchison loan to develop Trousdale Estates, an exclusive gated community at the top of Beverly Hills that housed Korshak's close friend Dinah Shore, Hillcrest regular Groucho Marx, and later, Elvis Presley.

Another Trousdale purchaser was Richard Nixon, who paid $35,000 for his lot at 410 Martin Lane, far below the listed price of $104,250 ($750,000 in 2004 dollars).[49] The favor was not surprising, given Nixon's cozy relationship with the Teamsters. In the 1960 election, the Teamsters not only endorsed Nixon, but Hoffa also personally coordinated a $1 million contribution to the Nixon campaign from the Teamsters and various mob bosses including Louisiana's Carlos Marcello.[50] As Tom Zander, retired Chicago crime investigator for the Department of Labor, recently said, "Anybody who wanted to pay for it had a connection to Nixon. The locals gave massive amounts of untraced money to Nixon. They got away with murder."[51] Interestingly, it now appears that Nixon hid much of his lucre in the same offshore bank haven, Castle Bank, favored by Moe Dalitz, Abe Pritzker, and the architects of the Las Vegas casino skim.[52]

The loan to Weingart, who had bought so much confiscated Japanese property from Bazelon's OAP, was for a $1.1 million influx into a laundry company he shared with Midwestern trucking magnate James (Jake) Gottlieb, who also owned Las Vegas' Dunes Hotel, itself the recipient of a $4 million Teamsters Pension Fund loan.[53]

Other red-flag names that began showing up in the transactions included Moe Dalitz and "consultant" Sidney Korshak, who controlled labor at Santa Anita Race Track, another site that was determined to have received a large fund loan. Thus, like so many had done before, McCulloch, Tobin, and Blake began corresponding with Virgil Peterson for background info on the loan-happy Midwestern transplants, especially Korshak, the Pritzkers,

Gottlieb, and Stanford Clinton. Simultaneously, L.A. chief of police William Parker asked Peterson for the Korshak file.[54]

Coincidentally, while the *Times'* research was ongoing, publisher Otis Chandler threw a cocktail party attended by none other than Robert Kennedy, who nearly spit out his drink when he was informed of the latest finds by Tobin. "He got red-faced and violent," Frank McCulloch recalled. "His voice rose. He said, 'You'd better lay off that!'" The following day, when Ed Guthman explained to McCulloch that Kennedy had already im-paneled a federal grand jury to investigate Hoffa, McCulloch grasped the national implications of the California real estate rat's nest they were ex-posing. McCulloch's immediate superior, Frank Haven, tried to warn him off the story, saying, "Once you get to the point where you can get a guy to talk, then either you or he or both are going to end up in a lime pit some-where."[55] McCulloch explained that the initial reason for the nervousness was another potential revenue loss like the paper had experienced after the Birch series. Editor Nick Williams also attempted to halt the Teamster se-ries. "Poor Nick Williams was put in the middle," said McCulloch. "He told me, 'Oh, let's drop this stuff, Frank. It's dull; nobody reads it.' I told him he'd have to order me."

Instead of backing off, McCulloch ordered Tobin and Blake to double their efforts. Of course, any scrutiny of Hoffa's California interests would lead to Sid Korshak, which in turn would inevitably track to Ziffren, Bazelon, Arvey, Hart, and the entire seamy underbelly of the Los Angeles economy. For a year, the series continued, inching inexorably toward the Ziffren-Arvey nexus. "There were twenty-seven stories in the series, and the Chandlers were upset all along," said McCulloch. Suddenly, word came from above—as in Otis Chandler—that the series had to be dropped. "Frank, you're killing me. Don't run any more of those pieces," ordered Chandler's underling Williams. McCulloch finally caved. "Nick was getting pressure from above," remembered McCulloch. "So we ended it."

"Obviously some pressure was put on the *Times* and they buckled," said Ed Guthman. "Tobin left the paper over that issue."[56]

McCulloch also left the paper soon thereafter. Gene Blake was effectively stopped from going further when he was dispatched to the *Times'* London bureau, a good fifty-four hundred miles from the L.A. County records files. Tobin went to *Sports Illustrated*, where he was an award-winning discloser of corruption in sports. Connie Carlson, investigator for the California at-torney general, was a friend and colleague of Tobin's, sharing his interest in the Chicago underworld's usurping of the state. Recently, Carlson remem-bered, "Jack Tobin became very disenchanted with the *Times* because there was no follow-up on his discoveries. It was disappointing for a number of the reporters at the *Times*, because under Otis Chandler they had formed a very formidable investigative unit. They were going full bore on everything. And suddenly it all came to a halt."[57] Frank McCulloch returned to his former home at *Time* magazine, where he ran its Saigon office. "I left for a combination of reasons," McCulloch said. "In addition to the problems with the series, Nick wanted me to start a Sunday magazine, and I didn't want to do that—I had left a magazine to come to the paper. Then I got a call from Henry Luce, who said to me, 'Handle that mess in Southeast Asia.' The guy who succeeded me, Frank Haven, hated that corruption stuff. He only wanted to cover City Hall and run wire stories."

Although potential financial woes were the implied reasons for the crackdown, Otis Chandler may have had additional motivations for muzzling his reporters. "It turned out that the paper's holding company, Chandler Securities, owned property that had Teamster money in it," McCulloch said recently. "And they were pretty sure we were going to reach that, which we did, and we ran a story on it."[58] Tobin and Blake had also found that Chandler was a large stockholder in Korshak's Santa Anita Race Track, a long-suspected venue for cleaning mob money. But there was more: the reporters' next scheduled story was to focus on another Los Angeles company, Walt's Auto Parks, which had received Teamster money that also appeared to have been laundered for the mob. This sleazy company, which operated parking lots throughout downtown Los Angeles, counted none other than Otis Chandler as one of its heaviest investors.[59]

Although Chandler declined Korshak's check, others continued to feast at his trough; in November 1962, Korshak underwrote dinner costs for group attending a charity event benefiting the Cardinal Stritch School of Medicine at Loyola University, where both Korshak brothers were trustees. Sid's brother Marshall was host for the bash.[60] Two years later, on November 24, 1964, Sidney, who had himself received an honorary doctorate from Loyola, again showed his support for the Stritch School, this time underwriting the entire cost ($50,000) for the first annual Sword of Loyola Awards Dinner and Benefit. With comedians Allen & Rossi and the Chicago Symphony performing at the Hilton Hotel venue, the dinner raised over $250,000. The Sword prize paid tribute to people who "exhibit a high degree of courage, dedication, and service." Seated at the head table with Sidney was the prize's first recipient, J. Edgar Hoover.[61]

Like Marshall, Sidney gave extensively to numerous Jewish causes. Friend Leo Geffner recently observed, "Sidney was a very strong supporter of

Israel—he contributed a lot of money. Sidney never hid his Jewishness, never tried to assimilate."[62] The largesse was not only emblematic of the Korshaks' lifelong charitable works, but also of the brothers' great love and respect for each other. "Marshall and Sidney were so close it was unbelievable," said one friend of both, who asked that his name not be used. "They were on the phone with each other four or five times a day. And they were so proud of each other. Marshall was proud of Sidney because of his accomplishments and the connections that he had. And Sidney was proud of Marshall because of his public life—he was straight as an arrow. He was the only major Chicago politician who didn't have his hand in the till."[63]

Eventually, the opening of the Music Center for the Performing Arts went off without a hitch on December 6, 1964, becoming the home of the Los Angeles Philharmonic and fountainhead for all of Southern California's performing arts.* Lew Wasserman was enlisted by Dorothy to be president of the Center Theatre Group, which supported the Center's drama program; Wasserman, in turn, brought in Paul Ziffren as counsel to the group. In her nine-year campaign, Buff raised $20 million in private donations, earning her the prestigious cover of *Time* magazine.

Vegas II

> *Korshak is acting as a front man to work out a deal in Las Vegas for Chicago hoodlums to invest in Las Vegas gambling casinos.*
>
> —JANUARY 16, 1961, FBI TELETYPE[64]

In February of 1962, the FBI noted that Sam Giancana was making rumblings about expanding the gang's share of the Nevada nest egg. Giancana functionary "Lou Brady" (Louis P. Coticchia) was utilizing Sidney Korshak to arrange financing of an $11 million casino-hotel in Reno. On wiretaps, Giancana was heard suggesting, "Korshak would expend his best efforts should he be made a partner in this deal and given five or ten points [interest]."[65] The FBI summarized that Johnny Rosselli was heard talking to Giancana to the effect: "Negotiations are in progress in Las Vegas for the Chicago organization to obtain a tighter grip on Las Vegas hotels and casinos, and negotiations are being made through Sidney Korshak."[66] Simultaneously,

---

*The complex, completed in 1967, includes the 3,197-seat Dorothy Chandler Pavilion, which hosted the Academy Awards for the next four decades, the 750-seat Mark Taper Forum, and the Ahmanson Theatre, which offers flexible seating for 1,600 to 2,007.

Giancana wanted to make a grab for Jake Factor's interest in Las Vegas' Stardust, and whether "Mooney" knew it or not, he could not have chosen a better time to plan a hostile takeover.

By the summer of 1962, Jake Factor was in full image-remake, if not life-remake, mode. His epiphany was understandable given two recent events that had to have shaken him to his core: the Immigration and Naturalization Service (INS) was unrelenting in its threat to deport him back to England, where he would likely have spent the rest of his life in prison, and the Chicago Outfit had threatened to end his life immediately if he didn't sell the Stardust back to their consortium with Moe Dalitz. After months of negotiations coordinated by Sid Korshak, Factor sold his interest in the Stardust to Moe Dalitz's Desert Inn Group, which was in fact a partnership of the Chicago and Cleveland crime syndicates. When the deal was finalized in August, the $14 million price tag prompted both the U.S. Department of Justice and the Nevada State Gaming Commission to investigate the hotel's true ownership.

By this time, Bobby Kennedy had authorized the planting of illegal bugs (microphones) in seven of the Strip's hotels, including Moe Dalitz's Desert

In 1960, *GI Blues* costars Elvis Presley and Juliet Prowse visit with the Desert Inn's Moe Dalitz and Wilbur Clark. (Left to right) Dalitz, Presley, Prowse, Wilbur and Toni Clark, Cecil Simmons, and Joe Franks behind Clark (Wilbur Clark Collection, UNLV Special Collections)

Dalitz in Vegas, undated (Cleveland State University, Special Collections)

Inn executive suite. Six months after Factor had unloaded the Stardust, the feds eavesdropped while Korshak and Dalitz discussed the various sales Korshak had brokered in the past, and the Factor sale in particular.

"I scared the shit out of him [Factor] from day one about what was going to happen," Korshak boasted to Dalitz. "I think that was the one reason he finally agreed to give us the option to purchase."

Korshak emphasized the point by telling how, when Curly Humphreys had recently instructed Korshak to send Factor back to Chicago for a meeting, Factor became unstrung.

"He said, 'Well, I've got to run now, but I'll talk to you in about a half hour,' and that was the last I saw of him. He caught the afternoon plane," Korshak informed Dalitz. At this point both Dalitz and Korshak burst into laughter, with Korshak adding, "So this is consistent with what I was saying—he is frightened to death and that is how we were able to make this fucking deal." The Bureau also knew that Korshak had taken Rosselli to meet with Factor at the Beverly Hills Friars Club for a conference, wherein "Factor looked worried."[67]

The discussion then turned to Bobby Kennedy's war on the underworld, ironic since Bobby would soon be listening to the tape of this conversation.

"Bobby has been trying for six months to catch someone either in Las Vegas or Los Angeles who is carrying money," said Korshak. To fight this onslaught, he advised, all concerned should plead the Fifth Amendment when questioned under oath. As one of Korshak's closest Hollywood friends, Bob Evans, summarized, "Sidney's first commandment was, the greatest insurance policy for continued breathing is continued silence."

"Moe, I have preached this all over the country," Korshak counseled Dalitz. "Do not answer anything. I have testified before grand juries in New York and Chicago, and at that time I could do it because then I was dealing with certain people. I tell you now, Moe, if I am called before any grand jury, I will take the Fifth Amendment, and I am a lawyer. I will give my name and address, and from that point on I will answer no questions. They can disbar me, but I will take the Fifth. *Now I have to take the Fifth because I am operating in a different atmosphere.*"[68] (Author's italics.)

The wise counsel was no surprise to one of Korshak's oldest friends in the Chicago legal fraternity. The lawyer, who asked not to be named, had also met Dalitz, who shared a personal story with him. "During the war, it was Sidney, who I had not met at that point, who recommended me for OCS," Dalitz had said. "I'll never forget it." The source added, "As a result, Dalitz didn't go to the bathroom without checking with Sidney."[69]

The conversation was also revealing on another front, as Korshak related

SIDNEY R. KORSHAK
"DOB: 6-6-1907"

Korshak in Vegas (FBI)

how close he had become to Sam Giancana, and how the two had dined together recently. Korshak then told Dalitz to let him know if there was any message he wanted delivered to the Chicago boss.

As for Factor's INS problem, apparently the character references by Al Hart and the others had failed to impress the feds. Thus, Factor decided to go over their heads, this time with the legal assistance of Abe Pritzker's partner Stanford Clinton. Somehow, Factor was able to persuade Attorney General Bobby Kennedy to bring him to Washington to discuss the INS case. Factor later told the press that during their chat, Bobby Kennedy slyly brought up the fact that he needed donations to help secure the release of 1,113 Cuban Brigade soldiers captured by Castro's forces after the disastrous April 1961 Bay of Pigs invasion. Reports had been circulating for months that Kennedy was placing threatening calls to business leaders with tax or other pending legal matters, practically extorting the funds from them. In conversations monitored by the FBI, it was clear that even the underworld was impressed by Bobby Kennedy's mastering of the "velvet hammer" extortion approach. On one occasion, the agents reported that Giancana aide Chuckie English "pointed out that the attorney general raising money for the Cuba invaders makes Chicago's syndicate look like amateurs."

After a number of meetings with "the Barber" in December 1962, Bobby Kennedy recommended to his brother that Factor be pardoned—this despite what his own wiretaps were telling him about Factor's continuing relationship with the mob at the Stardust. Bobby's decision became clearer when Factor told reporters that he'd contributed $25,000 to Kennedy's "Tractors for Cuba" fund.*

---

*It was reported that Factor's payoff to RFK was an Outfit practical joke: the money came from the skim the gang was taking from Las Vegas casinos.

President Kennedy granted Jake's pardon on Christmas Eve, 1962, the same night the prisoners landed in Miami, and just one week after the INS announced its decision to deport Factor.[70] But soon after, Bobby began to have misgivings about what he had done. Jack Clarke, who worked in the investigative police unit of Chicago's Mayor Daley, recently recalled what happened next. "Bobby Kennedy called me and asked if there would be any problem if Jake Factor were pardoned," said Clarke. "When I explained the details of Factor's Outfit background—Capone, Humphreys, the Sands, et cetera—Bobby went, 'Holy shit!' He then explained that he had already approved the pardon." Clarke added that Bobby's dealings with the Factor case were not atypical: "RFK didn't know what he was doing in the Justice Department. He had no idea of the subtleties, the histories of these people." Clarke, however, was unaware of Factor's little donation.

Eventually settling in Los Angeles, the much traveled Factor took particular interest in the welfare of underprivileged black youth in the Los Angeles district known as Watts. In the 1960s, after bestowing a $1 million endowment (allegedly through the Joseph P. Kennedy Foundation) on a Watts youth center, a *Los Angeles Times* reporter brought up his ties with the Outfit. Factor broke into tears, asking, "How much does a man have to do to bury his past?"

Jake Factor was not the only Supermob associate having travails during 1962. Lew Wasserman and Jules Stein saw the unrelenting antitrust nuisance reach the breaking point that year. For decades the Department of Justice had hinted at a crackdown on the runaway MCA juggernaut. Until now, authorities had failed to rein in the company whose books were such a closely guarded secret that even Wall Street was unable to assign a credit rating. Now, thanks to a persistent DOJ prosecutor named Leonard Posner, it looked as if something was actually going to happen.

Throughout the winter of 1962, a grand jury took testimony from actors, producers, and clients who had any dealings with what was now referred to as The Octopus. During the proceedings, MCA, with Paul Ziffren acting in the capacity of MCA "house counsel," intimidated actors such as Joseph Cotten and Betty Grable from testifying and obtained leaks from the testimony of those who did.[71] Those who dared to testify, such as Eddie Fisher, Paul Newman, Audrey Hepburn, and Carroll Baker, gave measured responses that betrayed their fears over losing work if they offended the Octopus.

By far the most anticipated testimony was that of the man who'd granted the blanket waiver to MCA, former SAG president Ronald Reagan. On

February 5, 1962, Reagan appeared before the grand jury, but his testimony wasn't unsealed until 1984, in response to a Freedom of Information Act request by David Robb, then a reporter for *Daily Variety* (later the chief labor and legal correspondent for the *Hollywood Reporter*).

Reagan's appearance was most notable for his staggeringly—some might say impossibly—bad memory. Most shocking, he claimed no memory of the MCA blanket waiver, arguably one of the most important SAG decisions in its history. The befuddled federal antitrust division attorney who conducted the questioning, John Fricano, attempted in vain to refresh him.

"This was a very important matter which Screen Actors Guild was taking up and it was the most important point of the guild," Fricano reminded the actor. The nonplussed Reagan asked when the action was taken. Fricano replied, "July 1952."

"Well, maybe the fact that I married in March of 1952 and went on a honeymoon had something to do with my being a little bit hazy," answered Reagan.

"Do you recall whether or not you participated in the negotiations held by MCA and SAG with respect to the blanket waiver in July of 1952?" asked Fricano.

"No, I think I have already told you I don't recall that. I don't recall," insisted the future U.S. president.

Fricano then attempted to plumb the details of the 1954 waiver extension, with the same lack of success.

"I don't honestly recall," Reagan answered. "You know something? You keep saying [1954] in the summer. I think maybe one of the reasons I don't recall was because I feel that in the summer [of 1954] I was up in Glacier Park making a cowboy picture."

When Reagan lied in denying he had been a producer while serving as SAG president, the interrogators were so convinced of his perjury that they began impounding his tax returns for 1952–55.

On June 17, 1962, DOJ's lead MCA prosecutor, Leonard Posner, filed a 150-page brief that predicted a criminal indictment against MCA was but a week away. Posner had found an "honest and trustworthy" source who testified that Reagan had granted the MCA waiver in exchange for the job on *GE Theater*.[72] Among the infractions cited by Posner, in furtherance of a continued violation of the Sherman Anti-Trust Act:

- Monopolization of the trade in name talent.
- Monopolization of the production of filmed TV programs.

- Conspiracy with SAG regarding the blanket waiver and the above monopolies.
- Restraint of trade (including packaging "tie-ins," extortion for services not rendered, blackballing independent producers, discrimination, and predatory practices).

Lew Wasserman then flew to Washington to plea/negotiate with Attorney General Robert Kennedy, who dropped all the criminal indictments despite the illegal blanket-waiver deal and MCA's twenty-five-year history of violating the Sherman Anti-Trust Act. Leonard Posner's case against MCA would never be heard in court. As part of the agreement, MCA vacated its artist agency work in favor of its more lucrative production wing, which immediately scooped up Universal Studios and Decca Records. MCA-Universal quickly became the biggest film producer in the entertainment industry, while the agency business was sold to former MCA employees who formed Artists Agency Group, which continued to deal almost exclusively with MCA.

Two months after he quit his job with DOJ, Posner died of a heart attack. The brilliant lawyer was described as "bitter" by friends and "disappointed" that his superiors didn't pursue the MCA case. If Posner was suspicious of his boss's inaction, he had good reason, for a potential conflict of interest loomed not far in the background: not only had Bobby Kennedy assigned Jules Stein's son-in-law, William vanden Heuvel, as his adviser on the MCA matter, but one of MCA's lead attorneys on the case was Hy Raskin of Chicago, one of the Kennedy family's most trusted advisers during the 1960 campaign.[73] Within a year of the agency bust-up, Wasserman established himself as one of the Democratic Party's chief contributors. Ed Weisl Sr., who arranged MCA's purchase of Paramount's library and ran interference for Wasserman during the DOJ investigation, suggested that Wasserman throw a fund-raiser for West Coast high rollers to gather support for John F. Kennedy's 1964 reelection campaign. Wasserman happily agreed to cohost the June 7, 1963, $1,000-a-plate dinner with Sid Korshak's great friend and client Eugene Klein.* Afterward, aided by United Artists

---

*Klein, the owner of America's first conglomerate, National General Corporation (which owned a theater chain and the San Diego Chargers football team), told author Dan Moldea, "I hired Sidney Korshak for National General as a labor negotiator. He was terrific. He got things done. I paid him a retainer, fifty thousand dollars a year. Whenever we had any labor problems, I picked up the phone and called Sidney. Whatever he did, it was done. He and I were as close as brothers." (Moldea, *Interference*, 160)

chairman Arthur Krim and Paul Ziffren, Wasserman came up with a gimmick called the President's Club, which gave businessmen increased access to the president in exchange for sustained contributions to his campaign coffers. For a $1,000 contribution, club members received a gold-engraved membership card, invitations to cabinet briefings, and an annual club dinner. But what was most prized was the increased purchase that accompanied such access to JFK.[74] Years later, when Richard Nixon became aware of all the Hollywood Jewish money going to the Democrats, he demanded an IRS workup on them. "Can't we investigate some of the cocksuckers?" Nixon can be heard saying on the White House tapes.[75]

The success of Wasserman's President's Club made the former Justice Department foe a hero to the Kennedy administration. And if Bobby Kennedy's interest in MCA wasn't completely erased by Wasserman's gambit, it would be on November 22, 1963, when his brother was gunned down in Dallas, after which Bobby's interest in all ongoing cases vanished as he retreated into virtual catatonia.

After the MCA breakup, Reagan formally became a Republican (which he had long been in spirit) and entered into a production partnership with MCA. The company soon found him more work as the host of the television series *Death Valley Days*, while staking him for a career in politics.

As Wasserman exercised his influence on the national stage, Sid Korshak did likewise on the state level. In 1984, the staff of the New Jersey Gaming Commission concluded in a report, "It is quite evident that over the years [Korshak] has made good contacts with very powerful politicians . . . Korshak's list of past and present associates reads like a *Who's Who* of prominent southern Californians." By the early sixties, Korshak's business style was well-known for its unconventionality—million-dollar deals were cut in swank restaurants, hotels, or in Korshak's mansion. The same modus applied to his political machinations. At one of his famous home business brunches in 1962, Korshak mediated internal Democratic Party squabbles between Paul Ziffren and Eugene Wyman, Ziffren's successor as California Democratic National Committeeman. The difficulties included differing strategies employed in the Brown-Nixon gubernatorial contest by Jesse "Big Daddy" Unruh, Speaker of the California Assembly, who had been accused of hiring ten thousand precinct workers to elect Pat Brown over Richard Nixon.[76] Even Brown was upset with Unruh, telling his aide at one point, "Do you know that *Unruh* is the German word for unrest? It's where the English word for unruly comes from. Appropriate, isn't it?"[77]

With Ziffren, Wyman, and Unruh now breaking bread at Sidney's Chalon breakfast nook, the Fixer worked his usual magic. "Over coffee, Sidney finally said to Paul, 'You know, we Democrats have a hard time in the state,'" one source told the *New York Times*. "'We shouldn't be taking each other on in public. If you've got a complaint, you should go and talk to Jesse. If you can't get satisfaction, you come to me or Gene before spouting off to the press.'" The confidential source noted, "There was no threat, nothing but sweetness. But, my God, from that day on Paul Ziffren never said another unkind thing about Jesse Unruh." Indeed, Ziffren agreed with Korshak's wisdom, later saying, "It was more important to elect Pat Brown than to have fights."[78]

The resultant truce was pivotal in that year's gubernatorial election victory (by 297,000 votes out of 6 million cast) of Pat Brown over Richard Nixon, who had stooped to new lows in election fraud and red-baiting in his attempt to defeat Brown. During the campaign, Nixon's team (which included many who would later execute the Watergate break-in) formed the phony Committee for the Preservation of the Democratic Party in California, which mailed nine hundred thousand postcards attacking the "left-wing minority" who had hijacked the party and the California Democratic Council (CDC). By this time, the Brown-Ziffren alliance had been resuscitated after Brown appointed Ziffren to head up the CDC. Nixon's ploy was just an updated version of the Knowland charges that had failed in 1958. Nixon also ordered the doctoring of photos in such a way as to depict Brown consorting with known Communist leaders. The Democrats sued, and after protracted hearings, the case was settled in 1964 for a reported $500,000. During the litigation it was determined that Nixon was personally involved in the shenanigans.[79] Writing for the *Nation*, Carey McWilliams summed up Nixon's ethos, saying, "As in 1952, the faceless, amoral Nixon is still on the make, still fighting Communism, still full of tricks, haunted by, as always, the lack of self-knowledge."[80]

The new year 1963 saw Sid Korshak maintaining the same hectic pace he had the previous year. His FBI file noted that he attended Debbie Reynolds's Vegas opening at the Riviera in January. Sid's wife, Bee, continued her globe-trotting; in April, she journeyed to Madrid with her two sons and actress Cyd Charisse, wife of Sid's old Chicago pal Tony Martin. When they returned, the Korshaks hosted Tony and Cyd at the Riviera in Vegas on the occasion of the Martins' fifteenth wedding anniversary. The Kirk Douglases and Vincente Minnellis also attended.[81] Gus Alex's wife, Marianne, continued her close friendship with Bee, while Sidney remained pals with Gus. When Marianne sought to divorce Alex, whose way of life proved too much for her, the Korshaks counseled them. When the love-struck Gussie initially balked at the separation, Sidney convinced him to grant Marianne the divorce. Alex licked his wounds at Korshak's beachfront Malibu rental, availing himself of Sid's Cadillac while there.[82] Bee Korshak eventually brought Marianne out to L.A., where she helped her get a job as Dinah Shore's fashion adviser on her nationwide television show. Marianne Ryan Alex eventually married Shore's producer, Fred Tatasciore.

On April 15, Korshak was spotted trying to enter Al Hart's Del Mar Racetrack with Johnny Rosselli, but they were turned away because Rosselli was barred from the premises.[83] During that same week, an old flame of Johnny's, Judy Campbell, contacted Sid on the advice of Sam Giancana. At the time, Campbell was sleeping with both President Kennedy and Giancana and was under constant FBI surveillance, or, in her opinion, harassment. A number of grand juries were impaneled to look into both Giancana and Rosselli, and Campbell feared testifying before them. Sam told her that Korshak "should be able to take care of things for you. Any more problems, just give me a call."[84] Korshak asked her to fly to Vegas, where he was obviously busy with the Martin festivities. In her autobiography, *My Story*, Campbell described Korshak: "Sid is tall, with a long face, large soft nose, and small eyes. Everything about him is deliberate, relentless . . . No hurry. It can always be done—that kind of attitude. No one was going to stop him. No one was going to say anything unpleasant. No one was going to change his mind . . . I was never afraid of Sam, but Sid frightened me. I could feel the power he wielded as he sat there watching me . . . I had as much chance of staring him down as I would have had with a lizard."[85]

Back in Beverly Hills on the nineteenth, the two met again at the Riviera's second-floor reservation office on Wilshire, and later that day at Korshak's evening hangout, the Polo Lounge in the Beverly Hills Hotel. At the meetings, Korshak assured Campbell she would not have to testify. In the coming weeks, Campbell was stunned by her good fortune. "Someone worked a miracle," she wrote. "I didn't have to appear before the Grand Jury."

There are also anecdotal reports of Korshak's intervention with another JFK paramour, actress Marilyn Monroe. Although the details of the contact are unknown, a number of Hollywood insiders heard the rumors. Milt Ebbins, Peter Lawford's longtime manager, was among those who recently spoke of it. "I had heard that Marilyn went to Sidney for some representation," Ebbins recalled, "but for what exactly I never knew."[86] There are numerous ways Korshak could have been drawn into the Monroe maelstrom.

In addition to being friends with Monroe's confidant (and Kennedy in-law) Peter Lawford, Korshak was close with Giancana and Rosselli, who were well-known friends of Monroe's,[87] Giancana having partied with her and Sinatra at the mob hangout Cal-Neva Lodge just one week before her fatal overdose on August 4, 1962.[88] (Over the years, Sinatra, Joe Kennedy, and Sam Giancana had owned a piece of the hotel-casino, which straddled the California-Nevada border on the north shore of Lake Tahoe.)[89]

Monroe's and Campbell's boyfriend President Kennedy was meanwhile beginning to attend Democratic Party fund-raisers in anticipation of the next year's presidential race. On June 7, 1963, Kennedy had a fund-raiser in Los Angeles, which was attended by Korshak associates Al Hart and Eugene Wyman; Korshak clients in attendance included Donna Reed and Dean Martin.[90]

All the while, Korshak's comings and goings were being watched, not only by the likes of Jack Tobin and Robert Goe, but also by the FBI. Los Angeles FBI agent Mike Wacks was one of those monitoring the elusive power broker. "Sidney was one of our primary targets here in L.A. because we felt that he controlled a lot of the local Teamster business," Wacks recalled. "He had a great say and gave an awful lot of advice to the Chicago mob on how to run the Teamster pension funds. We knew this from a lot of different sources. Over the years, we followed Sidney because our boss was really interested in getting him. He would put us on him for a day or two just to see what he was up to. He knew he was being followed but he didn't care. He just didn't care. He just said, 'Hey, these are my clients and that's what I do.' He was like Teflon, he could never get charged. He was amazing. He was one sharp cookie. Nobody ever ratted him out, and he never got caught on a wire. It's just amazing."

CHAPTER 12

Bistro Days

DESPITE THE APPALLING lack of encouragement from Washington, agents from all federal departments continued on their own initiative to watch over Korshak and the Supermob. One such agent was Andrew Furfaro, who, at the time, headed up the Western Division's elite, and undisclosed, Organized Crime Unit of the Internal Revenue Service. "We were IRS, but we weren't," Furfaro clarified recently. "It was a Treasury intelligence unit that blended between the Justice Department and the IRS. We could pull any tax return anywhere in the country. We had subpoena power. We had the ability to start grand juries. We wrote the subpoenas, pocket subpoenas, for the grand juries and served them as well."[1] (Furfaro would eventually run the IRS's Operation Snowball, the first major investigation of illegal contributions from corporations to politicians, focusing on thirty-one companies in Los Angeles alone.[2] "It was the first political investigation in the country," said Furfaro. "We had every major corporation in the country under investigation. This is the thing that changed laws. They had to change the audit laws.")*

Working under the IRS's Gabe Dennis, Furfaro was told to go to school on the most insidious forms of white-collar corruption, California-style. While the politically vulnerable elected authorities played cat and mouse with local crime gangs, Furfaro's IRS unit knew that these prosecutions represented little more than putting on a show for the voters. Gabe Dennis was

---

*Snowball was killed soon after President Nixon's 1969 inauguration by Attorney General John Mitchell. Mitchell explained his action by saying merely that the businessmen had promised never to do it again (Messick, *Politics of Prosecution*, 91). IRS agent Cesar Cantu added that the investigation had been extremely sensitive because of all the local Los Angeles politicians involved, and that the IRS later destroyed all of its records related to Snowball (Andrew, *Power to Destroy*, 142).

prescient enough to deduce that the more insidious corruption practiced by the seemingly immune Supermob dwarfed that of the Mickey Cohens and Jack Dragnas of the world. Thus, Dennis knew exactly how to bring his charges up to speed. "I was sent to live with Jim Hamilton of the LAPD," said Furfaro. "He became my tutor, and we set up crime files on just about everybody." Hamilton, of course, was one of the earliest sentinels to become aware of the Western intrusion of the Supermob through his investigations of Ziffren, Greenberg, and the Hayward Hotel nexus. Furfaro also developed a close working relationship with Connie Carlson, the Supermob watcher in the state Attorney General's Office.

In short time, Furfaro became intrigued with the transplanted Chicagoans who seemed to be the new power brokers in California. He tracked players like Al Hart, Paul Ziffren, Sid Korshak, and even the Western investments of patriarch Jake Arvey. Operating on a shoestring, Dennis, Furfaro, and the rest of their small unit tracked the Supermob up and down the West Coast and into the Nevada casinos.

In 1963, Furfaro's band was in the midst of "following the money" when they became aware of Sidney Korshak. While investigating an L.A. bookie named Benny Ginsburg, Furfaro stumbled onto the "Chicago connection" and Korshak specifically. "I served Ginsburg with a subpoena, but his doctor, Dr. Elliott Korday, said he had too bad a heart to appear before the grand jury," Furfaro remembered. While checking out Ginsburg, the team learned that his bets were being "covered" in Las Vegas. "The L.A. bookie layoff bets were handled in Vegas, because the locals couldn't cover it," added Furfaro.

When the trail led them to Vegas, the IRS unit stumbled into the rat's nest of skimming and money laundering that was Las Vegas in midcentury. "We learned right away that the Vegas authorities couldn't be trusted, so we covered it out of L.A.," said Furfaro. "Vegas became a 'suburb' of L.A. because the FBI wasn't doing it. We knew that Hoover was with Al Hart in Del Mar, so we just said, 'The hell with the Bureau. We'll cover it.' By 1962, we controlled Vegas with a team of one hundred and fifty guys from the ATF and IRS," recalled Furfaro. "We sat at every table in every hotel. We did a count. This has never been written about."

The investigation quickly focused on Jake Factor's Stardust and a close friend of Sid Korshak's named Mal Clarke. "The Stardust's bad-ledger book was the way they got the money out. The Stardust was writing off bad debts for guys who never even went there. This was the way to hide the skim by saying they lost it to a gambler who didn't pay off his marker. Technically, a guy supposedly goes to the count room and gets twenty-five grand. They put the marker in the cage, but the guy never comes back and pays off his marker. Mal Clarke was one of the names they used for the fake-debt write-offs. And he never even went to Vegas. He didn't even know where Vegas was."

The background check of Mal Clarke opened up the proverbial can of worms. Clarke was a Chicago racketeer associated with none other than Korshak's pal Charlie Gioe.[3] Early in his career, he was the front owner for Tony Accardo of Gioe's Clark Street bookie joint, where Sid's brother Bernie had also worked.[4] He was also an investor in Vegas' Sands Hotel, which had been financed by a consortium that included Al Hart's former partner Joe Fusco.[5] Sidney Korshak, in fact, admitted to authorities that he had known Clarke, a fellow part-time inhabitant of Palm Springs (and a frequent guest at Korshak's condo), for twenty-five years, sponsored Clarke into the Beverly Hills Friars Club, and helped his son Malcolm Jr. gain admission to Loyola of Chicago, where the Korshak brothers were trustees. Clarke paid Korshak's brother Bernard $250 a month to run the cigar shop in the front of Clarke's Chicago bookie joint.[6]

But what drew the investigation into sharper focus was the IRS unit's scrutiny of Clarke's tax filings, which showed that he was receiving a substantial paycheck from a notorious Chicago business for which he performed no discernible service.

"We traced Clarke back to Duncan Parking Meters in Chicago," said Furfaro. "He was getting twenty-five thousand dollars a year from Duncan as their meter representative in Mexico—but there were no parking meters in Mexico!"

The Duncan Parking Meter Company was well-known to Chicago authorities. The firm was ostensibly owned by Jerome Robinson, whom the *Chicago Tribune* referred to as "somewhat of a mystery." Robinson, locally described as connected to the Chicago Outfit, lived at Chicago's Carlyle, where he was a neighbor of Abe Pritzker's and Henry Crown's brother Irving's. In January 1963, Robinson had been convicted of perjury in a New York grand jury investigation of his supposed bribery in the sale of parking meters to New York City, for which he received a suspended sentence.[7] Robinson was well acquainted with the Korshak brothers; Marshall Korshak would obtain tickets for Robinson and his family to attend a 1980 Washington, D.C., reception for Pope John Paul II.

According to an FBI informant, Sidney Korshak had "muscled out" the original ownership of Chicago's Duncan Parking Meter Company, thus allowing his good friend Jerry Robinson to take over. Robinson then bought a house in Beverly Hills, while Korshak's Chicago friends actually ran the company. In an interview with the FBI, Korshak admitted to being the "legal counsel" for Duncan. The FBI report concluded that Duncan "was controlled by the Outfit, specifically Gus Alex . . . and Sidney Korshak." The Bureau was also told that Robinson often visited Korshak in his Palm Springs condo.[8]

Furfaro concluded that Clarke was being paid by Duncan for the use of his name and likely his address in Palm Springs, from where the money was being funneled to Mexico, and from there to offshore Caribbean banks. "Duncan Parking Meters was the conduit," said Furfaro, "but I don't think the old man [Jerome Robinson] necessarily knew about it."

Sid Korshak's name not only surfaced because of his connection to Clarke and Duncan, but also through his direct linkage to the original Benny Ginsburg investigation in Los Angeles. Furfaro ran the numbers in the gambling sachem's phone records and determined that one number belonged to Korshak. Furfaro described what happened next: "So Clarence Turner and I went to Korshak's home in Bel-Air, and his valet came out and told us not to park in the driveway because the grease was getting on it. When we got into the house, it was not a normal house—it was an office. It had about ten card tables set up all around the house. This was a meetinghouse. Korshak made reference to 'holding labor meetings' at the house. Initially, he was appalled by us; we were a nuisance. 'I've been interrogated by experts,' he said. 'Who do you guys think you are?' "

Eventually, Korshak relaxed and spoke casually with the agents. "He talked about his brother more than himself," remembered Furfaro. The agents served Korshak with the grand jury subpoena, and he dutifully appeared downtown to answer more questions. What follows are highlights of Furfaro and Turner's report of the interview, dated October 23, 1963:

• "The interview was quite cordial and informal, and in most instances Mr. Korshak volunteered information without being asked."

• Korshak talked freely about his close friendship with Jake Arvey, and about Arvey's son, Irwin. Jake was "very ill" and had lost "3/4 of his stomach," but Jake was still alive and kicking political asses at this [Furfaro's] writing.

• Korshak was the "first person to be subpoenaed by the Kefauver committee to testify from Chicago," but "he was not asked to testify."

• He admitted that "he is a member of the Friars Club, but he is not proud of, nor does he go near the place. That the Friars Club is a 'cesspool.' That the members are not a social and charitable fraternity but a collection of gamblers who wager on anything if the odds are right. That he suggested that they seal up the Friars." This was a prescient observation, since, at the time—and for the next five years—the Beverly Hills Friars Club harbored a scam wherein many of Korshak's friends, including Harry Karl and Tony Martin, were being cheated out of many thousands of dollars each in rigged poker games, courtesy of a peephole drilled into the wall that allowed the cheats to pick up their "pigeon's" hands.* The fix, which netted in the low millions, was run by Maurice Friedman, a real estate mogul and former owner of Las Vegas' New Frontier Hotel; George Emerson Seach; and Ben Teitelbaum. The inclusion of Teitelbaum's name in the scheme had to have been vexing for Karl, since Teitelbaum was Sid Korshak's partner in Affiliated Parking.

• In reference to the McClellan Committee: "Robert Kennedy and Pierre Salinger appeared in his [Korshak's] office, and questioned him about sweetheart contracts between unions and management. He appeared before the committee for one hour, and Kennedy questioned him again, and then thanked him for appearing."

• Korshak said that "he represents racetracks in the Chicago area. Mervyn LeRoy called him one day before the expected strike at Hollywood Park and asked him to help. He went to Hollywood Park, and met with twenty-eight attorneys from other racetracks, and union officials for the employees. The other attorneys resented his presence, but he was able to settle the strike for which he received a three-year contract. He maintained that this wasn't a sweetheart contract but that he merely brought union and management into accord through some of his contacts."

• Korshak admitted that he "was the legal counsel for the Duncan Parking Meter Company." He also admitted to his long and close friendship with Mal Clarke.

• He named some close friends (Dinah Shore, Cyd Charisse, Kirk Douglas, Debbie Reynolds, Harry Karl, etc.) and said "he uses his influence to get employment for his friends at the Riviera Hotel in Las Vegas. That he would rather not say anymore about Las Vegas."

Only when the agents brought up the Benny Ginsburg case did Korshak bristle. "Mr. Korshak became extremely angry at this point," the report states.[9] Furfaro said that the only result of all this hard work was a lawsuit—against the IRS. "When we busted Ginsburg, we were sued out of Chicago," Furfaro pointed out. "I was sure Korshak was behind it. The suit dragged on for years and was eventually thrown out."

---

*Among those cheated were Harry Karl ($80,000), Tony Martin ($10,000), Zeppo Marx ($6,000), agent Kurt Frings ($25,000), Ted Briskin ($200,000), and actor Phil Silvers (undisclosed amount). Others lost even more.

The Bistro

The L.A. grand jury investigation was just another one of countless bullets dodged by Korshak in his career, and his grand lifestyle was, typically, unaffected. In fact, it only seemed to become grander, if that was possible.

In the fall of 1963, Korshak was most often seen at a new upscale restaurant with French décor in the heart of Beverly Hills. Opening for business on November 1, 1963, the chic Beverly Hills eatery called The Bistro was at 246 N. Canon Drive, in the Beverly Hills business district. Korshak was an original investor (8 percent, or seven shares) when it was incorporated three months earlier. The restaurant was the brainchild of Oscar-winning director Billy Wilder* and local maître d' extraordinaire Kurt Niklas. Niklas was a thirty-seven-year-old German Jew who had barely escaped Hitler's holocaust, then coming to America, where for years he was the maître d' at Romanoff's Restaurant on Rodeo Drive, a magnet for Hollywood elite. When Romanoff's closed on New Year's Eve, 1962, Wilder, a Romanoff's regular, persuaded Niklas to open his own place. After Niklas obtained a thirteen-year lease for the Canon Drive storefront, he went back to Wilder. Niklas later recalled, "I went to see him and within twenty-four hours he had checks in the mail for ninety thousand dollars."[10] The sixty shareholders put up $3,000 each. The resultant $180,000 was deposited in Al Hart's bank—Hart was also among the original shareholders.[11]

For Bistro investor Sidney Korshak, the appeal of the place was obvious. In Chicago and New York, Korshak conducted his business in upscale eateries like the Ambassador East's Pump Room and the Café Carlyle. A creature of habit, Korshak liked to keep things simple, positioning himself in the center of activity, and usually within walking distance of his closest associates. The Bistro was at most a three-block stroll from them all: Paul Ziffren's and Harvey Silbert's law offices, both on Wilshire, Al Hart's flagship bank at Wilshire and Roxbury, Wasserman and Stein's MCA offices on Burton Way, and the two places Sidney used when he needed clerical assistance, the Associated Booking office on Brighton Way, and the Riviera Hotel booking office, also on Wilshire (#9571).

Korshak had known Niklas since 1956, having been introduced by a Las Vegas scion and associate of Mickey Cohen's, Moe Morton, at a party Morton hosted at Romanoff's.[12] Korshak quickly upped his investment to twelve

---

*Wilder had garnered a staggering six Academy Awards and helmed such hits as *The Lost Weekend, Sunset Boulevard, Stalag 17, The Seven Year Itch, Some Like It Hot*, and *The Apartment*.

Site of Sid Korshak's "secret" office on Wilshire Boulevard (author photo)

The Bistro (Marc Wanamaker/Bison Archives)

shares, and by 1974, twenty-one shares, second only to Niklas (135). Besides Korshak, the investing partnership represented a who's who of the Hollywood "in crowd": Al Hart, Greg Bautzer, Jack Lemmon, Jack Benny, Dean Martin, Tony Curtis, Jack Warner, Robert Stack, Otto Preminger, Swifty Lazar, Frank Sinatra, and Doris (Mrs. Jules) Stein.

Wilder suggested the French motif after a film he was shooting at the time, *Irma la Douce*. When completed, the cozy café seated about ninety, with an upstairs room reserved for private parties. An early contribution of Korshak's was the retaining of Richard Gulley as the Bistro's "public relations consultant." Gulley, an old friend of Bugsy Siegel's, first gained work, a "walk around job," at Warner Brothers courtesy of a Siegel phone call to a Warners executive. In addition to his PR work for the Bistro, Gulley performed the same service for the Riviera in Vegas, again enlisted by Korshak. Over the years, Gulley's chief function seemed to be "girl procurer" for male celebrities and their studio executive counterparts.

The night before the Bistro's public grand opening on November 1, Niklas hosted a private opening-night black-tie dinner party for the restaurant's stockholders and their guests. Promptly at eight P.M., stars such as Dean

Martin, Jack Lemmon, Polly Bergen, Louis Jourdan, and Korshak pal Tony Curtis joined studio moguls such as Walter Mirisch and Jack Warner. Sid Korshak's close friends such as Paul Ziffren, Alfred Bloomingdale, and Beldon Katleman joined the festivities. "It was a happening," Niklas wrote. As for the Fixer, who was not known as a great partyer, he was his typical low-key self. "Sidney Korshak spent most of the party in the shadows, avoiding photographers," Niklas wrote. Interestingly, Niklas noted, "Sammy Davis, Jr. was conspicuously absent."[13]

After its November debut, the Bistro's regulars included Ronald Reagan, Paul Ziffren, Pat Brown, Lew Wasserman, Gray Davis, the Kennedys, Gregory Peck, Kirk and Anne Douglas, and Donna Reed—all friends and/or clients of Korshak's. Predictably, countless Hollywood movie deals and labor issues were concluded with handshakes across the Bistro's tables, while the VIP upstairs realm was the setting for the infamous scene in the 1975 movie *Shampoo*, wherein Julie Christie introduced Warren Beatty to oral pleasures available *under* the Bistro's tables.

Without doubt, the most coveted table was Table Three, in the corner just off to the left of the entrance. A profile of the restaurant in the *Los Angeles Times* noted, "At the end of the row is the 'lawyers' table. It's the only downstairs table with a phone. Frequenters are Greg Bautzer, Gene Wyman, and Sidney Korshak."[14] At the request of a Howard Hughes girl procurer named Walter Kane, Niklas installed a telephone on the table. Director Alfred Hitchcock had his own opinion of those who commandeered the precious table. He told Niklas, "On an abstract level, the corner table is a metaphor for narcissism, the driving force that propels the cult of celebrity." Niklas agreed, adding, "The need to have the number one table is a territorial imperative, which can turn otherwise civil men and women into barbarians."[15]

However, both the table and the Hughes phone were soon appropriated by one of Howard's mortal enemies. The truth was that it was Sidney's table, much as Table One in Chicago's Pump Room had become his domain, and when it came to his table, Korshak betrayed a prickly thin skin on occasion, especially when it involved old rivalries. Once, when Korshak's attendance had not been anticipated, he arrived to discover that Hughes's aide Walter Kane was back sitting at his table, using the phone.

"Who the hell's at my table?" Korshak asked Niklas. When told it was an associate of the man who'd betrayed him in the RKO affair, Korshak turned on his heels and was not seen in the Bistro for a year.[16]

Kurt Niklas understood Sidney's protective attitude toward the table. "The corner table at the Bistro was his office," Niklas wrote in his autobiography. "He was in the restaurant so often that people would call and ask,

The Bistro interior (Marc Wanamaker/Bison Archives)

The Reagans at the Bistro with owner Kurt Niklas (second from left) (Mimi Niklas)

'Is the Korshak table available today?' He held court there like an errant pope."

Korshak's daily routine was known to many. "He often ate alone at noon every day at the Bistro," said Hollywood AP columnist James Bacon.[17] Casper Morcelli, who came to California after selling papers in Philadelphia for Moe Annenberg, became the Bistro's headwaiter from opening day until 1993. He recently recalled Sidney's modus operandi at the restaurant:

> Sidney always came in by himself, early in the morning, before we opened the place. Sidney was well dressed. I never saw him with a tie askew. There was a jacket code there, so most of the patrons were well dressed.
>
> He'd do his paperwork, or meet with the boss [Niklas], and then the people would start coming in to meet with him. I saw him every day of the week except Sundays. He didn't come for dinner much. He sat at the corner table almost every day.[18]

Original Bistro maître d' Jimmy Murphy, who later opened his own popular restaurant, Jimmy's Tavern, well remembered Korshak's dietary regime. "He ate very simply," Murphy said. "In the daytime he drank iced tea. He'd eat a Bistro hamburger, or some grilled fish—very simple. Later in the day he'd have a bullshot or a martini or a glass of wine—he wasn't a big drinker. He always dressed immaculately, with silk shirts, and so on."[19]

Both Morcelli and Murphy have nothing but good memories of Korshak. "I loved him," Morcelli said. "He was very generous. He was so soft, yet so tough at the same time. He was just fantastic. He'd come up to me and say, 'How ya doin', Cas? Everything okay? The family okay?' He was there for anybody, even a busboy. He'd help anybody." Murphy's recollection was equally effusive: "He was always a gentleman and respected the help. He was a good tipper. At Christmastime he would give me a bundle of dollar bills. He'd take care of the chef and the others as well. He would always ask me, 'Jimmy, are you having any problems? How's the family?' I liked him a lot."

On one level, Korshak enjoyed the camaraderie afforded by the restaurant. "His Bistro table was like a movie set," said friend Leo Geffner. "He knew all the movie stars. The starlets would all come by and kiss his cheek."[20] Hennie Burke, the current owner of Duke's Coffee Shop on the Sunset Strip, has been a social acquaintance of the Korshaks' for decades. "I knew Sid from the old days," Burke said. "We all traveled in the same circle with Pat Brown and the rest. I still play tennis regularly with Anne [Mrs. Kirk] Douglas and Bee Korshak over at Janet Leigh's house. We all used to go over to the Bistro after playing, and Sid would always be sitting at his table. He'd immediately send over a bottle of champagne for the girls." Burke's memory of Korshak echoes those of Murphy and Morcelli, and she sounded wistful in her description of him. "He was the most wonderful man—almost like an angel," she recently said with a tinge of emotion. "He was powerful, but he treated all his friends like family, which means he'd do anything for you."[21]

Timothy Applegate, longtime counsel for Korshak client Hilton Hotels, recently remembered having dinner with Korshak at his table: "I met him once for lunch and once for dinner at the Bistro. When I met him for dinner, Greg Bautzer was just getting up and leaving. Sidney sat down and said, 'I would have introduced you but you don't want to know that asshole anyway. He's got the biggest ego in Los Angeles.' I replied that I previously had been told that he had 'the biggest ego in the Western United States.' "[22]

What was most consequential about Korshak's Bistro days, however, were the business deals that were struck there—both face-to-face and over the phone. Niklas, Murphy, and Morcelli all remember Korshak's furtive conversations on the Table Three phone that soon came to comprise two lines, and the meetings with such corporate titans and political lions as Al

Hart, Lew Wasserman, Paul Ziffren, Pat Brown, and Gray Davis. There were also confabs with "Dodgers people" such as Walter O'Malley and team manager Tommy Lasorda. Niklas wrote, "I personally knew two-dozen businessmen who paid him twenty to fifty thousand dollars a year for 'protection' from labor unions."

Often, Korshak's business benefited both his legit clients and his Chicago patrons simultaneously. Such was the case in 1963, when Korshak helped Lew Wasserman and the underworld, both of whom were facing exposure by one of America's best-known talents, and one of organized crime's most vocal opponents, composer and television pioneer Steve Allen. The Chicago native and creator of the late-night-talk-show genre became an outspoken anticrime activist in 1954, when he chanced upon a photograph of a man who had been severely beaten after speaking out against the installation of pinball machines in a store that was situated near a neighborhood school. Allen, under the threat of advertiser desertion, produced a two-hour documentary on labor corruption for New York's WNBT, from where his *Tonight Show* originated. After the show aired, one of the interviewees, labor columnist Victor Reisel, was blinded by an acid-thrower, and Allen endured slashed tires on his car and stink bombs set off in his theater. Then there came physical threats. One anonymous caller referred to the Riesel attack and told Allen, "Lay off, pal, or you're next."

But the hoods totally misread Allen, who was only emboldened by the threats. Over the years, Allen continued to take every opportunity to sound the clarion call against not only the underworld, but its Supermob enablers. Allen made frequent trips to Chicago, where he spoke at benefits for the Chicago Crime Commission, and his Van Nuys office contained over forty binders labeled "Organized Crime," holding thousands of notes and newspaper clippings.

But the entertainer's stance had a powerful impact on his career. "I was blackballed in many lucrative establishments," Allen recalled shortly before his death in 2000. "I was only invited to play Vegas twice in my entire career." This alone deprived Allen of millions of dollars from a venue he would have owned if given the opportunity.

In 1963, Allen was hosting the syndicated late-night *Steve Allen Show* when he received a call from Sidney Korshak. "I was asked to take it easy on Sidney's friends," Allen recalled. Not long after politely refusing Korshak's request, Allen felt the power of the underworld-Supermob collusion once again. "We had a terrible time booking many A-list guests for the show," Allen explained. It was clear to Allen that Korshak, in connivance with the Stein-Wasserman entertainment megalith, MCA, had chosen to deprive the

Steve Allen Show of its talent roster, which at the time represented most of Hollywood's top stars. (A subversion by Korshak would have served two purposes since Korshak was also good friends with Allen's late-night competition at NBC, Johnny Carson.)

Despite the talent embargo, Allen concocted a wonderful program with his staple ensemble of brilliant ad-libbers such as Louie Nye, Don Knotts, Bill Dana, and Tom Poston, as well as quirky personalities like madman Gypsy Boots, and then unknown Frank Zappa, who appeared as a performance artist, bashing an old car with a sledgehammer. But Allen's 1963 run-in with Korshak would not be his last encounter with gangster intimidation.[23]

When Korshak's clients were unable to appear at Bistro Table Three, business was handled on his personal table phone. His Windy City pal Irv Kupcinet remembered Korshak's MO. "He could turn more tricks with a telephone call than anyone I knew," Kup said in 1997. At the Bistro, Jimmy Murphy remembered that some of Korshak's business dealings seemed to be more sensitive than others. "Sidney would get a call, then go outside to use the pay phone," said Murphy. Jimmy "the Weasel" Fratianno was among many who witnessed Korshak carrying a bagful of coins should he need to call his Chicago handlers, for whom he always used the pay phone in the lobby. It was widely accepted that Korshak used the untraceable pay phone to converse with Humphreys or Alex.

In later years, Korshak was seen being driven to even more secure locations for making phone contact.[24] The L.A. police spied Korshak entering a Beverly Hills phone booth with a bag of coins, and making a series of calls. One of Korshak's favorite secure phones was located inside the legendary Drucker's Barber Shop on Beverly, just north of Wilshire.[25] Like others, Hilton Corporation counsel E. Timothy Applegate, who was the liaison between the company and Korshak for many years, heard the stories of Sidney's clandestine forays to Drucker's. "I was later told by a union guy that once a week Korshak would go down to Drucker's Barber Shop and meet with local mobsters," said Applegate.[26]

Proprietor Harry Drucker had come to Beverly Hills from New York in the 1940s, the move financed by his pal Bugsy Siegel.[27] In New York, Drucker was Siegel's and Frank Costello's barber in Arnold Kirkeby's Waldorf-Astoria, where Joe Kennedy was occasionally seen accompanying Costello for a trim. When Bugsy moved to Beverly Hills, he took Drucker with him. As a favor, Drucker also set up the barbershop at Vegas' Tropicana Hotel, which was partially financed by Costello.[28]

Beverly Hills native Don Wolfe, whose stepfather Jeffrey Bernerd coproduced Alfred Hitchcock's early films (*The Lady Vanishes* and *The 39 Steps*), was a Drucker's regular and has vivid memories of the popular tonsorial parlor: "The shop was upstairs, above Jerry Rothschild's Men's Shop, where Bugsy got his suits and jackets. Drucker's had a reception desk on the first floor, and you had to be buzzed in to go up to the barbershop. I later learned that it was because Drucker's was also a bookie joint." Wolfe recalled that Drucker's possessed one amenity that significantly added to the attractiveness of the shop. "There was a glassed-in barber chair with a phone in it," said Wolfe. "Bugsy got his hair cut there almost every other day it seemed. I saw Bugsy there often using that phone. Drucker told me that Bugsy used that phone because he suspected his phone was tapped. When they moved the barbershop to Wilshire, they moved the glassed-in booth as well." Over many visits, Wolfe saw other notables using Drucker's secure hotline, including Ronald Reagan, Elvis Presley, and Earl Warren.[29] Johnny Rosselli was also known to be a fan of both Drucker's haircuts and his enclosed booth.

Not all sensitive Bistro conversations were conducted by phone or at Table Three. On occasions, Korshak's business was taken outside. "He was a very low-key guy for a very powerful man," said Jimmy Murphy. "Sometimes he would go to the little bench we had outside for a very private conversation." Casper Morcelli also remembered how Korshak liked to take frequent strolls in the tony Beverly Hills neighborhood: "He used to walk a lot after lunch—he knew the whole of Beverly Hills." Longtime NBC investigative producer Ira Silverman saw the walks as part of a long tradition of hoods who preferred to discuss business where they couldn't be watched. "Sidney would take a walk, much like the boys in New York do," opined Silverman.[30]

One of Korshak's most frequent lunch companions was Andy Anderson, head of the Western Conference of Teamsters. Anderson had started working for the Teamsters in 1954 and rose in the hierarchy, slowly becoming the man Korshak associated with and with whom he finalized legal issues after Hoffa was sent to jail. "We'd negotiate with Sidney on the parking lot at the baseball stadium, the racetracks, the liquor industry, the breweries, the food industry, the motion picture industry," said Anderson.

Anderson and Korshak first met in the 1960s, when Anderson was called upon to negotiate a Teamster warehouse contract with discount-shoe magnate Harry Karl, who brought Korshak along as his counsel. "Sidney would talk, but he was careful of what he said," Anderson remembered. "He was careful of who he sat with when he had lunch. I noticed—he didn't have to tell me—I could see it." The friendship grew over years of doing business together. "When I was the director of the Teamsters in the Western Conference, I even hired one of his sons to do some work for us," Anderson recalled.[31]

Most importantly, Korshak introduced Anderson to Lew Wasserman, and the threesome often met secretly at Korshak's home to nip labor problems in the bud before a strike could ever rear its head. The trio celebrated their friendship with an annual lunch at The Cove, in the Ambassador Hotel.[32] "The Teamsters never struck Lew," Anderson declared. "And it was because of Sidney."

F. C. Duke Zeller, who wrote *Devil's Pact: Inside the World of the Teamsters Union* based on his experiences working as government liaison and personal adviser to four Teamster presidents over fourteen years, recently said, "Virtually every Teamster leader on the West Coast, in the Western Conference, answered to Sidney Korshak. Everything and everybody went through him out in Los Angeles."[33] Andy Anderson disagreed with the analysis. "Sidney's and my acquaintance progressed to an equal and cordial working relationship," Anderson stated.[34] I definitely came to attention when he called me, but he never asked me to do anything untoward and was of assistance to me many times. Sid always watched out for me—in the sense that he would say, 'If there's somebody you're confused about, tell me and I'll let you know.' And he used to do this, but he never told me what I had to do; he told me what *not* to do.[35]

Occasionally, Korshak's dining partners fell into categories far below those of the typical Beverly Hills habitué. Jimmy "the "Weasel" Fratianno has written of meeting Korshak at Table Three; Johnny Rosselli and Moe Dalitz also broke bread on occasion with Korshak. "I saw Sid and JR [Rosselli] together many times," said Rosselli's goddaughter, actress Nancy Czar. "They were either at Chasen's or the Bistro. They knew each other from Chicago."[36]

Gianni Russo, who had been delivering messages from the Eastern bosses (e.g., Costello, Accardo, and Marcello) to Korshak at Chicago's Pump Room, now did the same at the Bistro. "There were about four key guys in this country, and Sid was one of them," recalled Russo. "He was connected to everybody. I used to sit at his table at the Bistro and never paid a dime. He would never conduct business in his house. None of those guys ever did. Nobody could understand it—I was a young kid then, delivering these messages—I don't even know what they were. But Sid was an amazing man. A lot of times we'd have to sit and wait, so we'd have coffee and talk, and he became like a mentor to me. He just felt I was a nice kid and didn't know what I was doing around these people. He was usually drinking Jack Daniel's or Scotch."

Korshak at a Paul Ziffren soirée (Dominick Dunne)

Like everyone else, Russo was impressed with Korshak's impeccable appearance. "Sid was a gentleman and a great dresser," said Russo. "He taught me how to dress. I used to wear the gold chains—what they call the wopsicle." And just as he had displayed his interest in watches to Shecky Greene in Vegas, Korshak expressed it again to Russo. "Pick one good watch," Korshak said. "Forget everything else." When it came to appearances, the Fixer emulated the dashing Wasserman, one of whose favorite expressions was "Dress British, think Yiddish." Korshak's sartorial expertise was fully appreciated by the young gofer. "It was because of Sid that I cut out that New York gangster bullshit," Russo said.[*,37] Leo Geffner was also impressed with Korshak's attention to sartorial detail. "Sidney was always impeccably dressed—the best suits," said Geffner. "I never saw him without a tie unless he was home, and even the sport shirts he wore at home would have been the three-hundred-dollar kind."[38]

Jimmy Murphy recalled some of the less than savory associates who met with Sidney at the Bistro: "He also met with some strange, shady-looking people at the Bistro. Sometimes they would go to the private room upstairs for lunch. Sometimes people just dropped off envelopes for him. There's no record of that, that's for sure." In his Bistro lunches with Korshak, Anderson recalled sometimes being joined "by these characters. Sidney would introduce me, and he'd say about me, 'He's okay, we can talk in front of him.' Then, after they left, he'd say, 'You never met them.' "[39]

Regardless of the rubric, when a deal was eventually consummated,

---

*Dick Brenneman, who lunched with Korshak in 1976, recalled a similar Korshak nod to the importance of appearance, when Korshak proudly displayed a dazzling diamond on the little finger of his left hand. "Absolutely flawless, and the finest color," Korshak puffed. "It cost me sixty thousand, but I could sell it today for twice that."

Korshak's bills were discreetly mailed from his brother Marshall's Chicago law office. Often he would get paid in cash or with barter—like new cars.

The Untouchable: Invulnerability in Sidney's Fortress

Local FBI man Mike Wacks recently recalled how he became aware not only of Korshak's Bistro companions, but also how Sidney represented virtual immunity from prosecution. "Supposedly, we never had enough PC [probable cause] to wire up the Bistro," said Wacks. "Korshak was real easy to pick up over at that restaurant because he would hold court there. If we weren't doing anything, we'd go over there and see who he was having lunch with. He had the same corner booth. He had a certain time. And it was always there for him. As a matter of fact, when we were in there one time, he was using the phone on the corner table and I said, 'God, I can't believe we couldn't get PC for this thing.' We couldn't. And this is one of the primary booths in the place. I can't even recall the exact guys who came in to see him, but they were righteous guys from Chicago, they were made members of the Mafia. It wouldn't be unusual for Sidney to meet with those guys or be seen with them, but he was Teflon. The police would identify these guys and they would go to Korshak, and Korshak would more or less tell them to pound sand—it was his business. He got away with it. Nobody ever questioned it. I mean, we questioned it, but we never could get anything going."[40]

Among other obstacles was Korshak's professional status. It seems that when Jake Arvey advised his wards to obtain law degrees, he was well aware of the ancillary benefits that particular sheepskin provided. Not only could their legal knowledge force the feds to play by the rules, which they often ignored, but with all their conversations with hoods protected by the attorney-client privilege, damning evidence was more deeply hidden than the proverbial needle in a haystack.

Chicago FBI agent Bill Roemer was one of many who understood the challenge represented in investigating Korshak and his ilk. "There was an FBI control file kept on Korshak: No. 92-789, the prefix designated racketeering and the last number was assigned sequentially," Roemer said in 1997. "To my knowledge, we never went out and conducted any real investigation on Korshak. We just never investigated lawyers in those days. The FBI was made up predominately of lawyers."[41]

Fran Marracco, who succeeded Roemer in the Bureau's Chicago Field Office, echoed his predecessor: "You can't run an OC [organized crime] case without running into cops and politicians. It is very hard to bring cases against them. So many people's jobs depended on them that you're not going to find witnesses. Nobody wants to torpedo their career."[42]

The sensitivity was no less apparent in Korshak's West Coast dominion, where A. O. Richards, an FBI agent from 1947 to 1977, hit the same Korshak brick wall in L.A. "He was almost an untouchable," Richards agreed. "You couldn't go after him, he was too well protected. Who would *dare* wiretap Korshak?"[43] Some law enforcement professionals chalked up the inactivity to innocent bureaucratic difficulties. G. Robert Blakey, at the time an attorney in Bobby Kennedy's organized crime section of the Justice Department, said, "The legal problem of doing a direct investigation of a lawyer is a nightmare. A crooked lawyer in our society is almost beyond reach, the way it is organized today."[44] Chicago-based U.S. attorney in the organized crime division David Schippers recently explained, "You need accountants to go through books. The FBI didn't have accountants. It was a matter of evolving. It took a long time for the FBI to adjust to it. It took the government a long time. It started in the thirties with gangsters, bank robbers. Officials were reacting to murders, violence. Then during the war, we're chasing spies. After that came Kefauver and then the rackets hearings. Then somewhere along the line you understand that politicians are in on this too. There are sweetheart deals here."[45]

RFK's Department of Justice colleague, Adam Walinsky, as noted, wrote off the official inaction to being merely a case of "investigative evolution";[46] however, others weren't so forgiving of the feds' performance in relation to the Supermob. One senior FBI official in Los Angeles, who requested anonymity, cut to the chase, saying, "I think the Bureau was a little bit afraid of investigating Korshak because he had so many connections, and he was connected with so many top people out here in the movie industry. I think they were kind of afraid that if the word got out we were working a 92 case on him [organized crime investigation], all hell would break loose. It was the same way with Sinatra. I personally opened a 92 case on Sinatra. We just started to do a little bit on that and then the Bureau said to close the case."

Chicago's Fran Marracco agreed: "The Korshaks had connections in Washington. We were often cut off from pursuing them by headquarters. The U.S. Attorney's Office would just stall everything. They didn't mind if we went after some small-time local *paisans*. You're better off busting a bookie." As to exactly why headquarters would derail investigations of the Supermob, many point to J. Edgar Hoover's known friendship with the likes of Al Hart, the Korshaks, and other questionable operators. Attorney

General Bobby Kennedy was likely torn because of his own family's relationship with the Korshaks in Chicago and Los Angeles.

Often, local FBI field agents took it upon themselves to monitor people like Korshak. Once, when Mike Wacks heard through an authorized wiretap of Allen Dorfman that Korshak, Dorfman, and Andy Anderson were to have lunch at the Bistro the next day, Wacks planned an eyeball surveillance. Posing as an insurance salesman, Wacks landed Table Four and overheard Korshak ask of Andy Anderson, "Have you got the money for Lou [phonetic]? I'm going to have dinner with him tonight." Anderson then handed Korshak a large envelope, which he immediately stashed in his inside coat pocket. Wacks was of the strong opinion that "Lou" was in fact Lew Wasserman, and that Anderson and Korshak were just doing business as usual, preventing Teamster strikes at Wasserman's Universal Studios.[47] According to Wacks's memo memorializing the surveillance, Allen Dorfman showed up soon thereafter to join the party.[48]

There remained other agencies that could have pursued the Supermob, such as the newly established Organized Crime Strike Force. This group of regional Justice Department investigators was formed in 1966, but had a checkered history over the next two decades—again with little support from its Washington overseers. Marvin Rudnick, an attorney in the Los Angeles Strike Force from 1980 to 1989, recently described the workings of the unit: "The way this thing worked was that the Strike Force was made up of lawyers who specialized in complex litigation. Cases would be presented to us by the FBI, IRS, ATF, et cetera. And we would represent them in court. We wouldn't start our own investigations."[49]

But the Strike Force was likewise impotent in the face of Supermob associates like Sidney Korshak. L.A. FBI man Mike Wacks, who often turned such leads over to the Strike Force, recently described the problem: "The Strike Force was very reluctant because Korshak was an attorney. It was very hard back then to get wiretaps against attorneys. It was almost like an act of God. That would have been a wealth of information."[50] L.A. Strike Force attorney Rudnick was also frustrated over the lack of official interest in Korshak et al. "There were no projects on Korshak that I'm aware of, and I'm a little surprised at that," Rudnick said. "We should have dealt with him, but we would have only dealt with him if the FBI dealt with him. To me, Korshak would have been the best target in town for organized crime prosecutors. I've been in L.A. for twenty-five years, and I've never seen where anybody has tried to take down that level of criminal. They took down the L.A. 'family' which was locally important, but that was it."

The situation was mirrored in the Strike Force's Chicago headquarters.

David Schippers, who headed the Chicago Strike Force in the 1960s, remembered the obstacles. "Korshak was never on our radar because Teamster stuff was being handled out of Washington," Schippers said in 2004. "We were more interested in the Italian connections. So Korshak skated. He certainly had friends in Washington. When I first started with the Strike Force under Bobby Kennedy, I asked him, "What about Korshak?" He said, 'We're handling it out here [in D.C.].' But Korshak had political ties everywhere, and he was nonpartisan."[51] Fellow Chicago Strike Force member Peter Vaira agreed, saying, "The U.S. attorneys and the Strike Force were told to stay with the traditional gunslingers because the white-collar guys had political power."[52]

One could reasonably assume that the Labor Department would have had a serious interest in Korshak's Teamster (and other union) machinations. However, such was not the case. Chicago-based crime investigator for the Labor Department Tom Zander described his department's inaction: "We were told by the Washington office not to go after Korshak. 'You can't do that. That's it,' we were told. He must have had a connection in Washington, because such a thing wouldn't have been possible without it. He had contacts in the Illinois judiciary, federal, state—you name it."[53]

Things were no different for IRS investigators. Former IRS Western Region organized crime investigator Andrew Furfaro recalled, "We got zero support from headquarters. The local agents took it upon themselves to follow these guys, and we did. We sent our reports up the chain, but nothing ever happened. I'm sure political connections had a lot to do with it."[54]

With the federal elite showing little interest in Korshak, it was left to the state agencies to work his case. But they were similarly hamstrung, with no one really expecting local district attorneys to move against the Korshaks of the world. As Peter Vaira explained, "Most of the time, the local DAs don't touch those cases—you get elected with fires, rapes, and murders." Connie Carlson, an investigator for the California State Attorney General's Office, was personally interested in the white-collar types like Korshak, Hart, and Ziffren. However, despite great leads and legwork, and after many years on the job, Carlson's tenure ended in frustration. "There was not enough manpower to prosecute these men," Carlson said. "The FBI wouldn't share their information with us, so we just hoped the IRS would get them."[55]

John Van DeKamp, L.A. district attorney from 1975 to 1983, and the state attorney general from 1983 to 1991, recently admitted his lack of interest in Korshak. "I don't remember any open investigations of Korshak, but his name just kept cropping up in all these labor settlements," Van DeKamp said. "I do not remember Korshak ever being a target of our office. The intel guys might have been interested, but it never got up to me, so they never made a case. There were rumors, and he was a mysterious figure." Interestingly, Van DeKamp readily admitted his friendship with Korshak pal Paul Ziffren: "When I first ran for Congress in 1969, I was told that I should talk to Paul Ziffren, who gave me a little money to run. We were friendly over the years until he passed away."[56]

It has been alleged that Van DeKamp's friendships with the former Chicagoans and his concern with the political sensitivity of his office may have played a role in the scuttling of worthy cases. James Grodin, an organized crime investigator in Van DeKamp's office, was, like Carlson on the state level, frustrated by the lack of movement on the Chicago crowd. He was equally disturbed by what he saw as a wholesale trashing of good leads. "John Van DeKamp purged a lot of the DA's files," Grodin recently said. "I was warned in advance, so I copied some of mine before they were trashed. One night they came in with a dolly and carted off the file cabinets. Other DA's were even worse, and really did a number on the office's files."[57]

With Beverly Hills and the Bistro, Korshak had re-created not only a Lawndale-like, close-knit environment, but an establishment that mirrored his Chicago Pump Room "office." Korshak's daily appearances at the Bistro became so predictable that any absence became a cause of concern for owner Kurt Niklas. Once when Korshak failed to show for a few days, Niklas asked him, "Sid, where you been?"

"Sicily," Korshak replied.

Niklas then had the temerity to push the subject. "What the hell were you doing in Sicily?"

"Don't ask stupid questions!" was Korshak's terse answer.[58]

Just two days after the Bistro's gala November 1 opening, Korshak's world began to be rocked by a series of tragedies. On November 3, Sidney and Marshall lost their eighty-year-old mother, Rebecca, who had been living in Chicago's kosher nursing home, Alshore House.[59] Not three weeks later, the Korshaks and most other Americans mourned the death of President Kennedy, gunned down in Dallas on November 22. Kennedy's assassination was likely more painful to the Korshaks than most due to the family's personal acquaintance with the Kennedy clan. But November held still one more misfortune for Sid Korshak: on November 30, Karyn Kupcinet, the troubled daughter of Irv Kupcinet, Korshak's longtime Pump Room companion, was found dead at age twenty-two in Los Angeles, where she was pursuing a career as an actress, and it is all but a given that Korshak had opened some doors for the aspiring movie star with his powerful studio friends.

Throughout much of her young life, Karyn had been obsessed with her body image, and her weight typified the yo-yo fluctuations that go hand in hand with diet-pill abuse. Although the coroner ruled the death a murder by strangulation, some have found errors in his work and believe the death to have been a suicide by overdose, especially when a recent ditching by her boyfriend is taken into account.

Ever the loyal friend, Sid Korshak hastened over to the morgue and identified the body, said Louis Spear, circulation manager for Kup's *Sun-Times*. "When Kup's daughter was killed, I had lunch with Sidney and the Beverly Hills police chief," recalled Korshak friend Leo Geffner. "He was pushing and urging them to conduct the investigation. Sidney offered to help out any way he could. He even offered to put up reward money."[60] According to Kup's son Jerry, Korshak even offered to send his Chicago mob associates to L.A. to help find Karyn's alleged killer, if one in fact ever existed. Other sources noted that Sid later prevailed upon the local police to suspend the investigation, reasoning that it might dredge up information about her drug-abusing lifestyle that would be hurtful to Kup, who was said to have been suicidal himself over the loss of his beloved daughter.[61]

Although the year's final insult to Korshak's world did not involve him directly, few doubt that he counseled the victim, and it is known that his Supermob compadre Al Hart played a hands-on role in the affair.

On Sunday, December 8, Frank Sinatra's nineteen-year-old son, Frank Jr., was kidnapped at gunpoint in his Harrah's Lodge hotel room in Lake Tahoe, Nevada, where he was performing. The three young, bumbling kidnappers contacted Sinatra the next day and delivered their demand for $250,000 in ransom.[62]

According to concert promoter and celebrity photographer Ron Joy, who dated Frank's daughter Nancy in the sixties, Sid Korshak advised a distraught Frank senior to contact everyone's favorite banker, Al Hart, who had a penchant for laying his hands on quick cash.[63] All day Monday and into the night, Hart oversaw the counting and photographing of $250,000 (minus $15 for a briefcase to carry it in).[64] On Tuesday, Hart met Sinatra and the FBI at Korshak's Bistro at two in the afternoon, and after downing a stiff Black Jack, Sinatra proceeded to LAX for the payoff. On Wednesday, Junior was released in Bel-Air, and by Thursday the kidnappers were in jail.

The next day, Sinatra was back at the Bistro for his forty-eighth birthday. After everyone sang "Happy Birthday," Sinatra told Niklas, "I'm just glad it's over with. Gimme a shot of Black Jack."[65]

CHAPTER 13

"He Could Never Walk Away from Those People"

Our state has become the favorite investment area of the veiled finance committee of organized crime.

—1967 STATEMENT BY THOMAS C. LYNCH,
CALIFORNIA ATTORNEY GENERAL[1]

B Y THE MIDSIXTIES, the illegal bugs and wiretaps first installed under the Kennedy administration were beginning to bear fruit, especially in Las Vegas and the Supermob's Chicago homeland. The Bureau was finally starting to trace the movement of the Las Vegas skim through the underworld's key outposts, while learning the nuts and bolts of their extortion and racketeering games. In addition, Accardo, Giancana, Hoffa, and Korshak's key Outfit connection Humphreys were under constant physical surveillance and scrutiny, not only by the FBI, but by the IRS. Accardo, after receiving counsel from Humphreys and Korshak, barely escaped a 1960 conviction for income tax evasion; when Korshak entered Cedars of Lebanon Hospital in L.A. for a serious hernia operation, the feds listened from Chicago as Gussie Alex called to offer his sympathies.[2] Korshak's Teamster ally Jimmy Hoffa was taking a particularly good beating in the courts, first indicted for receiving kickbacks from Teamster clients, then for jury tampering in the kickback trial. Giancana, who was pondering his second federal grand jury appearance in two years, called Sidney for advice from his suburban Armory Lounge headquarters on April 26, 1965.[3] According to a Korshak friend who was also a Bureau informant, Korshak said that he tried to make a deal with the prosecutors "whereby Giancana can answer a few innocuous questions that would not hurt anybody" and result in Giancana's release from prison on his contempt of court charges (the Korshak ploy failed, however).[4]

From the perspective of Sidney Korshak and the Supermob, the most seminal events were those surrounding Mooney Giancana and Curly Humphreys, the two men with the most long-standing and direct Outfit links to Korshak. Both bosses were withering under the nonstop harassment of Bobby Kennedy's Justice Department. For Giancana, the Bureau had devised "lockstep" surveillance, following him everywhere in plain sight, hoping to make the volatile boss crack. Finally, in the spring of 1965, the feds formulated a brilliant plan: they brought him before a grand jury and gave him immunity. The tactic made it impossible for Mooney to plead the Fifth and required him to testify against the Outfit or be imprisoned for contempt. After much soul-searching, Giancana chose the latter, going away for a year. After he was released, Giancana went to Mexico for the next eight years, banished by Accardo, never again to retake the Chicago underworld throne.

If the removal of Giancana loosened the reins on Korshak et al., what happened next all but severed them. Sixty-five-year-old Curly Humphreys was ill, weakened from heart disease and therefore considered, like Giancana, vulnerable to federal pressure. Thus, one month after Giancana went off to prison, the gang's architect of labor racketeering was arrested for failing to appear before the grand jury—he had been lying low at his Norman, Oklahoma, retreat. After posting bail, Humphreys was able to stall for five more months before being rearrested, after putting up a mild struggle, on Thanksgiving Day, 1965. That night, after posting $45,000 bail, the rapidly aging genius of the Chicago Outfit suffered a fatal heart attack while pushing a vacuum in his luxury fifty-first-floor apartment in the Marina Twin Towers, overlooking the Chicago River. (Eight months prior, Korshak and Humphreys had been observed having breakfast together in Chicago. According to the FBI, "During the meeting, Humphreys and Korshak [were] visited by several local judges and politicians who happened to be having breakfast at the same restaurant. Korshak informed Humphreys that he made $800,000 in his law practice last year.")[5]

The death of Humphreys and the virtual death of Giancana were seen as giving Korshak a much larger degree of independence from those who had been overheard upbraiding him on the phone to Las Vegas. One of Korshak's oldest Chicago friends summed up what the events of 1965 meant to the Outfit's fair-haired boy: "Humphreys may have had a hold on Sidney, but after he passed on, he was succeeded by two of Sidney's closest friends—Gussie Alex, who would do anything for Sidney, and Joe Accardo, who loved Sid like a brother. So Sidney was really on his own."[6]

Nonetheless, according to Andy Anderson, Korshak continued to pay homage to his original Chicago underworld patrons. "On Christmas Eve or Christmas Day, he'd have to go to Chicago to see the boys," Anderson said. "I always understood it was something he had to do, to go meet with the boys, as a way of expressing his loyalty. If he had said, 'No, I have something else to do'—well, that would not have been what they expected of him.'"[7]

But practically speaking, Korshak was now two giant steps closer to becoming free of his Chicago overseers. Now the Outfit treated Korshak as an equal, a rare trusted adviser as comfortable on the inside of underworld confabs as on the outside. Although some contended that a degree of subservience still existed, most insiders believed that Sidney, using his hard-earned cachet, was happy to foster the perception of his mob-based power. It seemed to many that Korshak fully grasped the concept that perception is often as good as reality, especially in Beverly Hills. The misinterpretation of Korshak as a full-time mob employee was shared by a large segment of the corporate world, which valued Korshak's uncanny ability to solve intractable problems, whether the mob's or anyone else's.

Korshak's stature continued to rise in the film capital, and he now counted many of the acting elite among his best friends. In 1965, Korshak, as an honorary chairman of the Beverly Hills B'nai B'rith, fêted his pal actor Kirk Douglas (né Issur Danielovitch Demsky) as that organization's Man of the Year. Other notable chairmen with Korshak were his friends Al Hart, Pat Brown, Conrad Hilton, Tony Martin, Stanley Mosk, Pierre Salinger, Sargent Shriver, Billy Wilder, Eugene Wyman, and Frank Sinatra.

Douglas has recounted how he often attended barbecues at Korshak's mansion, where he encountered the likes of actor-cum-mob-wannabe George Raft. Douglas, a resident of Palm Springs, was curious about Sidney's mob friends and asked to meet them, but Korshak refused. "Frankly, I felt that he was extremely considerate of me, protective, and felt that it would be better for me not to," Douglas later wrote. "He knew that whatever he did was watched. And if he took me someplace for a meeting—many of them were living in Palm Springs at the time—it would just give the government a record of the visit.[8] Douglas also described how he had sailed around Sicily in 1967 with Bee Korshak and Dinah Shore aboard Ralph Stolkin's luxury yacht. Douglas was in Italy filming the mafia movie *The Brotherhood*. After the movie opened, Korshak told Douglas that the real underworld bosses were impressed with the picture. "They felt it captured the spirit of their organization," Douglas wrote in his autobiography, *The Ragman's Son*. "They particularly liked my portrayal of a Mafia don. They wanted to meet me."

Douglas added that at one point, Korshak's famous loyalty came to the forefront. "Korshak said that he would like to do me a favor and sell me, at a very reasonable price, four points in the Riviera." Although it was obvious how much money he would have made, Douglas and his wife were wary of whom they might have been getting into business with and declined the generous offer. "We never regretted it," Douglas wrote.

The Douglas friendship eventually drew the Korshaks into becoming Palm Springs residents, after Kirk's wife, Anne, persuaded the Korshaks to purchase a six-bedroom house next door to the Douglases, at 535 Via Lola, one of the most exclusive streets in the Springs.* "My husband and I were staying with Frank Sinatra when Kirk and Anne Douglas showed us a house that was for sale on their street," Bee said years later. "Sidney wasn't looking to buy a house, but they convinced us."[9] Pulling the deed, the FBI learned that Sidney had purchased the home on August 4, 1976, from Mrs. Polly Kahn for $220,000 in cash, then immediately placed the property in Bee's name. The Bureau also sought to learn if neighboring homes were suitable for surveillance of Korshak.[10]

When not in use by the Korshaks, the house was rented to friends such as the Johnny Carsons. After four years' residency on Via Lola, the Korshaks sold the abode for $800,000.

In February 1966, Korshak left his desert retreat in Palm Springs for his desert office in Las Vegas to insert himself in an intractable labor dispute that was aggravating tourists and costing the city millions. The action originated in the wee morning hours of August 1, 1965, when Vegas casinogoers emerged from the pits to find themselves stranded after the five major local cab companies had been struck at midnight by their two-hundred-plus Teamster drivers over wages and pensions. For the next seven months companies hired scabs, who were met with Molotov cocktails, fistfights, slashed tires, and overturned vehicles.[11] After months had gone by with the Teamsters not being accommodated by the owners, an FBI informant reported that Korshak contacted his secret friend Clark County sheriff Ralph Lamb and threatened to bring in outside strikebreakers. The source believed that "this was a maneuver by Korshak to bring pressure to get the strike settled." On March 2, 1966, the FBI learned that Sidney Korshak came to Vegas on February 27 and 28 and told an informant that "he had settled the taxi cab strike." The Bureau added, "It should be noted that the cab strike was reputedly settled on March 1."[12]

---

*The Douglases first purchased property in Palm Springs in the late fifties. Property records show that the home was actually owned by Kirk's production arm, Brynaprod, which according to the FBI was "organized under the laws of Switzerland."

Korshak's name appeared nowhere in the press, and the exact nature of his involvement never came to light.

Chicago Meets Chicano

In the spring of 1966, Korshak was called upon to mediate with an unlikely labor entity, California's migrant workforce. At the time, Cesar Chavez, the thirty-nine-year-old leader of the nascent United Farm Workers, was bringing his band of Mexican-American laborers (known as Chicanos) into an alliance with Filipino farmworkers in Delano, California, where one of Sid Korshak's clients, Schenley Industries, faced a shutdown of its grape fields by the strikers. The UFW chose Schenley as its main target because its well-known "label" products, which included S&W Canned Foods, made it easy to boycott nationwide. Schenley had been founded and owned by Lewis Rosenstiel, a former New York bootlegger often linked with Frank Costello, Meyer Lansky, and Korshak associates Sam Giancana and Al Hart. After Prohibition, Rosenstiel had built up Schenley into the leading U.S. distillery, netting $49 million a year by the midforties.[13]

Chavez, who hailed from Arizona, was one of hundreds of thousands of migrants who made the annual trek to California for the grape, lettuce, and citrus harvests. At the time of the founding of the UFW, migrant workers, with an average life span of just forty-nine years, were being paid ninety cents per hour (28 percent below the minimum wage for the rest of the nation) for their backbreaking work. Other conditions were even more deplorable: child labor was rampant; farms lacked portable toilets; workers drank from a common beer can in the field; they paid two dollars or more per day for unheated, racially segregated, mosquito-infested metal shacks with no indoor plumbing or cooking facilities. Not surprisingly, many workers were injured or died in easily preventable accidents.

By the fall of 1965, the Filipinos of Delano had had enough, and with the support of Chavez's new UFW, some thirty farms were struck, with several thousand workers leaving the fields. Korshak's client Schenley, one of the biggest growers in Delano, initially reacted by treating the strikers like mere pests, spraying them with agricultural poisons. Like Schenley, Korshak's pal Governor Pat Brown also declined to support their movement and, despite the workers' requests that he meet with them the following spring, he instead went to the Palm Springs home of Korshak's and Giancana's good friend Frank Sinatra to celebrate Easter.[14]

To call attention to their plight, which came to be known as La Causa, Chavez organized a march to the state capital of Sacramento, 240 miles away. Seventy strikers left Delano by foot on March 17, 1966, led by Chavez, but before they reached Sacramento twenty-five days later, two events shaped their fortunes. Once again, those events linked the names Kennedy and Korshak.[15]

At the time of the strike, Robert Kennedy, now the junior senator from New York, was assigned to the less-than-prestigious Migratory Labor Subcommittee of the Labor Committee. Persuaded to visit Chavez in Delano before the march commenced, Kennedy was taken, not only with the migrants' horrid situation, but also with Chavez personally. Chavez and Kennedy would remain friends and mutual inspirations until Kennedy's death just two years away. Paul Schrade, leader of the United Auto Workers and a Robert Kennedy campaign aide, vividly remembered the day the two met. "When we held the meeting in a school gym, Bobby looked at me and I could just tell that a fire had been lit," said Schrade. "Afterwards, he went out and walked the picket line with Chavez."[16] Kennedy's biographer Arthur Schlesinger wrote, "By the end of the day, Kennedy had embraced Chavez and La Causa."[17] Over the next few weeks, the Kennedy-Chavez alliance helped swell the ranks of marchers to over five thousand.

However, Rosensteil had already decided against settling. Since the Delano properties were only a small part of his conglomerate, he instructed Korshak to sell Schenley's Delano properties outright. But Korshak informed him that there was word that Herman "Blackie" Leavitt's Bartenders' Union Local 249 was set to boycott the Schenley brand.* "Sidney called Rosensteil in Florida and was persuaded by him to settle," said Korshak friend and fellow labor attorney Leo Geffner.[18] Rosensteil then gave Korshak the go-ahead to settle the strike.[19]

On April 5, as the protesters approached Modesto, 163 miles from Delano, Chavez was told that there was a telephone call for him. When the aide was instructed to take a message, Chavez was informed that the caller wished to speak to Chavez immediately.

"The guy said that he wants to talk to you, because he wants to sign a contract. He says he's from Schenley," the aide told Chavez.

"Oh, the hell with him! I've heard that story before," a road-weary Chavez shot back.

---

*In 1968, Leavitt was sent to Las Vegas to head the drive to organize the casino dealers. During the organizing drive, Leavitt was in constant contact with Sidney Korshak, who, acting as labor consultant for the Sahara, Desert Inn, and Silver Slipper, gave Leavitt advice on how to thwart the elections. In fact, the union lost the certification vote at all three hotels. Shortly thereafter, Leavitt purchased a large ranch in San Diego County. According to a source, the money came from the payoff to Leavitt to throw the election. (Peter F. Vaira and Douglas P. Roller, Attorneys in Charge, Cleveland Strike Force, 1978 Report for the Carter White House)

Five minutes later, the phone rang again.

"Cesar, he's got to talk to you!" Chavez was told. Finally, Chavez took the phone and spoke with a man he had never heard of before.

"Hello, this is Sidney Korshak," the caller said. "I want to talk to you about recognizing the union and signing a contract."

"Oh, yeah? What else is new?" answered the feisty Chicano, hanging up on a man who was rarely hung up on.

Seconds later, the phone rang again. This time Chavez took it; it was the same voice on the other end.

"No, no, look, I'm serious," Korshak said.

"How serious are you?" Chavez asked.

"You want me to prove it? Come down to Stockton." Chavez replied that he could not.

"Okay. If you can't, then forget it," Korshak replied. In his autobiography, *Cesar Chavez: Autobiography of La Causa*, Chavez described what happened next: "After I asked a lot of questions, [Korshak] finally convinced me and gave me the address to meet him in Beverly Hills the next day. I got a hold of my people, had a meeting, and took a vote to see if they'd let me go to negotiate. Then I took off with Chris Hartmire, who drove while I fell asleep in the back seat. We didn't leave until about one in the morning, I guess, but we got to Beverly Hills in time."[20]

Chavez aide Leroy Chatfield recalled that on the drive to Korshak's mansion, AFL-CIO representative Bill Kircher schooled Chavez as to Korshak's connections. "Soon, Cesar began referring to Sidney as the Fixer," said Chatfield. "By the time he arrived in Bel-Air, he knew Korshak was connected, and he had great confidence that he could resolve the problem. And he did."[21] In a recent interview, Wayne "Chris" Hartmire, an aide to Chavez from 1961 to 1989, remembered, "It was a big, beautiful home, and Korshak was very gracious. We had heard that Korshak represented all sorts of people, if you know what I mean—I am glad I got out of that house alive. But he was a friendly host—offered us drinks and munchies. It was pretty clear that he had come to resolve this thing and that he had the authority to resolve this thing. We were there for only an hour or so. It was kind of an out-of-body experience for me; an evening I won't forget."[22]

Chavez picked up the story in his autobiography:

Korshak had Bill Kircher (AFL-CIO representative) and the Teamsters there. He had this huge house and all these drinks and food laid out. But Bill wouldn't be caught in the same room as the Teamsters. They had an argument, and I just said, "To hell with it!" I went over to the table and started playing pool. They argued for about an hour. Finally Korshak said, "Damn it, look. You should be making love to me, I'm the company, I'm ready to sign a contract, and you guys can't get together! You get together, and when you do make up your minds who's going to sign it, then I'll deal with you." "I'm leaving!" I told him at that point. "There's no reason for me being here. You sign a contract with whomever you want, but the boycott stays on!" And I started to walk out. "Wait a minute!" he said. "We're going to sign with a union." "No, talk to me about my Union, not the AFL-CIO or the Teamsters." Then the Teamsters came on very strong and supported our position. Apparently somebody was pushing to have the AFL-CIO sign a contract. The fellow in charge of the Federation in Los Angeles came and tried to sweet talk me into signing with AWOC and I said, "No! You must be kidding. You're trying to tell me to give you a contract, when we fought for it, bled for it, and sweat for it. You must be out of your mind!" So he got mad, and he said, "Well, if you don't give us a contract, we'll just destroy your Union." Finally, Bill and I hit on a compromise. I didn't care if I was helping him to save face as long as I had the contract. "We sign it ourselves, it's our contract," I said. "It means a lot to the workers. But I'll let you witness the contract if you want to." So Bill witnessed it. The preliminary agreement was not even a full page. It was only about three-quarters full.[23]

"The next day, Cesar and I drove back and caught up with the march," remembered Hartmire. "They held up a rally so Cesar could announce the resolution. There were many cheers because it was the first great victory." The walk to Sacramento was thus called off with thirty miles to go, as protesters cheered and tore up their anti-Schenley placards.

The Korshak-Chavez settlement was hailed as "historic" and "monumental." In fact, the Bel-Air agreement was but a letter of intent, and specifics were to be worked out over the next month. Korshak told then *New York Times* reporter Peter Bart that those details would be easy to resolve. "We are mindful of the plight of the workers," Korshak said.[24] Paul Schrade recalled that the fine points were finally put on the agreement at the Beverly Rodeo Hotel at 360 N. Rodeo Drive in Beverly Hills.* "Korshak, Kircher, and Blackie [Leavitt] were upstairs—I believe talking on the phone with

---

*The hotel has long been a popular spot for assignations of all sorts. It was later immortalized in the movie *Pretty Woman* as the hotel where Richard Gere and Julia Roberts had their suite. The hotel was also a favorite of Jimi Hendrix's, who wrote some of his most famous lyrics there.

Rosensteil—while Cesar and I waited downstairs," said Schrade. Regretfully, Kircher's AFL-CIO refused to play ball with the Teamsters as a matter of principle, due to long-standing turf disputes. Had they been less petulant, the UFW might have averted the next ten years of strife with the Teamsters. One participant in the Rodeo Hotel meeting observed, "Sidney Korshak was there and he could have tied up all the loose ends."

Nonetheless, the UFW was elated with Korshak's performance. Thanks to the Fixer, a grassroots, farm-labor union had, for the first time in American history, gained recognition by a U.S. corporation. The Schenley agreement recognized the UFW, gave the workers an immediate wage increase of thirty-five cents an hour, and added credit union privileges. Behind the scenes, rumors swirled as to why Schenley capitulated. Some claimed that it was the potential of a bartenders' boycott, but most interestingly, it was whispered that Robert Kennedy personally influenced Schenley to sign. Given the various linkages between the Kennedys and the Korshaks, it is possible that the two got together on the terms of the deal. (In addition to the previously stated connections, Bobby's father, Joseph Kennedy, himself a former bootlegger and then distributor of Haig & Haig Whiskey, knew Schenley's Rosensteil well, not only from New York, but from Palm Beach, Florida, where both were winter residents.)[25] After the boycott was settled, Pat Brown belatedly offered his support for Chavez.[26]

With the Schenley agreement in hand, there was optimism that Korshak could resolve the situation with all the state's growers if they would enlist him as Schenley had done. Korshak was referred to as "the Disney of the bargaining table, there was so much magic in his touch."[27] Dan Swinton, the labor reporter for the *Los Angeles Herald-Examiner,* who described Korshak as "a man who seldom stops long enough in one place to get a wrinkle in his suit," wrote at the time that "Korshak may be the man to move mountains. He may turn out to be the hole card that Cesar Chavez and his followers didn't know they had—and it could win the pot of gold." Swinton added that Korshak showed "sincere emotion—that he felt deep sympathy for the needs and objectives of farm workers."[28]

What neither Chavez nor his workers could know was that Korshak and his Outfit associates had a history of helping unions get recognized, only to then take them over from within to put the sweetheart-contract game into play. It was the old gambit perfected by Humphreys with the IATSE takeover and repeated throughout the forties and fifties. A decade later, Chavez would see the other shoe drop.

*　*　*

Korshak's 1966 U.S. passport application (State Department records)

On September 6, 1966, Sid Korshak, Al Hart, Harry Karl, and Harvey Silbert sponsored a $100-per-plate dinner at the Beverly Hilton Hotel in honor of John "Jake the Barber" Factor, celebrating his proclamation as the Humanitarian of the Year by the World Jewish Congress.[29] That fall, according to passport records, the Korshaks celebrated another successful year with a six-week tour of England, France, and Italy. The only bump in the road that year was the Nevada Resort Association's dropping of Korshak as its labor counsel because the contracts he had negotiated were "overgenerous."[30]

Reagan Ascending

By this time, Korshak's Bistro table neighbor Ronald Reagan, who was now a Republican (having switched after Bobby Kennedy's investigation of MCA), had attracted the support of some of California's most influential and conservative Republicans. Over a year after Reagan delivered a seminal nationwide speech on behalf of Republican presidential candidate Barry Goldwater on October 27, 1964, these men coalesced into Reagan's "Kitchen Cabinet" and together devised the financing and political strategy necessary to propel their man, and their interests, to the front of the political stage. The founder of the Kitchen Cabinet was wealthy Los Angeles Ford dealer Holmes P. Tuttle. He was joined by Joseph Coors, president of Coors Brewing Co; A. C. Rubel, chairman of Union Oil; Henry Salvatori, oil developer; Justin Dart, of Dart-Kraft and Rexall Drugstores; Leonard Firestone, of Firestone Tire and Rubber; Alfred Bloomingdale, whose Diner's Club employed the services of Sid Korshak; Paul Ziffren's friend and future law partner William French Smith; and Taft Schrieber, the VP of MCA.

The Cabinet, which met weekly at the Bistro[31] and in other private clubs in Los Angeles and San Francisco, first hired California consulting firm

Spencer-Roberts & Associates to supervise the selling of Reagan.* Bill Roberts, the co-owner of the spinmeisters, candidly described the challenge: "We had to overcome three things—Reagan's inexperience, the actor bit, and his lack of knowledge of state government."[32] In the age of televised charisma, lack of knowledge was trumped by telegenic veneer. And Ronald Reagan, the movies' quintessential "good guy," had magnetism to spare. (Korshak, who thought Reagan was not yet ready for the post, bet a Hillcrest member $5,000 against $6,000 that Reagan would lose to Korshak's other pal Pat Brown.)[33]

But regardless of the gubernatorial election outcome, the Supermob was covered, having long-standing ties to both candidates. In fact, Stein and Wasserman's MCA supported both in this election. Producer Henry Denker recalled that Wasserman, like Korshak, supported Brown, while Stein not only backed Reagan, but was also his chief personal fund-raiser, and Stein's VP Taft Schreiber was the campaign manager.

"That was Stein's idea," Denker remembered recently. "Taft was the Republican and Lew was the Democrat. That way they had both camps covered and they gave equally to both sides, and everybody knew that."[34] Denker elaborated on the arrangement: "MCA was divided into two groups. There was a Democratic group and a Republican group. They always wanted to have a hand in the White House, no matter which party was there. When Reagan was doing the *General Electric* show, somebody came up with the idea that he would promote GE to the plants, make visits. These appearances were very successful. They saw how the workers loved him, and somebody at MCA said, 'Hey, he could be governor of the state.' In show business you go with what's working—that's an old maxim. When Taft died in 1976, Reagan was taken over by Wasserman."[35]

On November 6, 1966, Democrat-turned-Republican Ronald Reagan became governor of California, defeating incumbent Republican-turned-Democrat Pat Brown by one million votes. Ironically, the predominantly Democratic state had fared so well financially under Brown that the erstwhile blue-collar Democrats became more fiscally conservative and shifted to the traditional Republican anti-big-government and antitax philosophies.†

---

*According to Bistro owner Kurt Niklas, the Kitchen Cabinet met in private in the upstairs Terrace Room.
†Although the state was exploding with a half million new residents per year, Brown managed the budget skillfully. Among his accomplishments: he built the state's freeway system and aqueducts that brought water to the San Joaquin Valley and L.A.; he came up with California's master plan for education and funded the UC, Cal State, and community college systems so well that there was a place there for every high school graduate; and he shepherded the state's first antismog legislation through the legislature.

Governor Ronald Reagan (Library of Congress)

Becoming governor did not seem to affect Reagan's penchant for dissembling. Before his inauguration, Reagan was required to undergo a comprehensive background check by the FBI, since he would have access to UC's nuclear research data. On the FBI form, Reagan lied about his membership in left-wing ("commie") organizations in the forties. When he filed the report with the Atomic Energy Commission, Hoover let the lie stand, even though he knew better.

The FBI boss had a good reason for not outing Ronnie: as governor, Reagan continued his secret commie informant role with the Bureau. In 1998, after a seventeen-year legal battle with the FBI, the *San Francisco Chronicle* received two hundred thousand pages detailing the sordid history of Reagan and the FBI.* Among other revelations, it was learned that Governor Reagan offered to employ "psychological warfare" and other methods to rid the liberal UC Berkeley campus not only of its free speech activists, but of its president, Clark Kerr, who Reagan and Hoover had decided was "too liberal."

In 1966, Kerr had been president of the university for eight years, and Hoover and Reagan feared commies would plant spies on the campus, then the largest research university and a key defense contractor. As a candidate, Reagan had pledged to remove Kerr, and Hoover took the unprecedented step of offering the Bureau's services to the candidate. Now with Governor Reagan's complicity, the Bureau began compiling "dirty secrets" files on the university's six-thousand-member faculty. After his January 1967 swearing-in, Reagan was burned in effigy at Berkeley when his plans to slash the

---

*The FBI appealed the case in five courts, all of which ruled against it. The futile stonewalling cost the Bureau $1.9 million in legal fees and processing costs. The ultimate release is believed to be among the largest single FOIA releases in U.S. history.

school's budget were leaked. On January 16, Reagan had a secret meeting with the FBI and asked for subversive data on Kerr, whom he blamed for the budget leaks. On January 20, Reagan attended the university's first Board of Regents meeting wherein Kerr was fired by a 14–8 vote (13 were needed).[36]

Reagan's new position likewise failed to diminish his conflicted relationship with MCA. One month after his election, Reagan sold 236 of his 290 acres in Malibu Canyon to Fox for $1.9 million—$8,178 an acre—even though Fox's experts appraised the craggy, useless terrain at $944,000. Reagan had purchased the parcel for $225 an acre twelve years earlier. William French Smith, Reagan's attorney (and Paul Ziffren's friend and future law partner at Gibson, Dunn and Crutcher), oversaw the sale for the Reagan Trust, which had been set up by MCA's Stein and Schreiber. (Later, as president, Reagan would appoint Smith his attorney general.)

"I could not have run for office unless I sold the ranch," Reagan admitted to biographer Lou Cannon. When queried about the sale fourteen years later, Fox real estate unit president Judith Frank said there were no records that would indicate why Fox made such a poor purchase. "Maybe management decided they owed Reagan a favor," she said. "Who knows? Who cares?" At the time, the Zanuck family, a prominent supporter of Reagan's political career, controlled Fox.

With Jules Stein acting as trustee for Reagan on the deal, Reagan used the remaining fifty-four acres as collateral on a down payment for other land he wanted worth $346,950 in Riverside, with the proviso that he had to buy back the fifty-four acres if the purchaser could not sell it within a year. When this actually happened, Stein came to Reagan's rescue and purchased the property for $165,000. Stein also set Reagan up with Oppenheimer Industries, a Kansas City–based cattle-breeding facility that Stein owned and used as a tax dodge. When Reagan's tax records were leaked to the press, they showed that he had used Oppenheimer to avoid paying state taxes.[37] A top California State official who investigated the case said in 1976, "We came away with the feeling that Twentieth Century-Fox was a pawn in the deal. We figured that Reagan's gang had actually put up the money." The official concluded that the purpose of the bailout was to bolster Reagan's finances so that he would be free to run for president after his gubernatorial term expired. In fact, Fox appears to have been in collusion with Stein's MCA in its effort to boost Reagan's political future.

Soon after the 1966 sale, MCA's Universal Studios hired Fox's Richard Zanuck as its new president, and one year after the sale, Reagan appointed former Fox executive assistant to the president Harry Sokolov to the chairmanship of the State Parks and Recreation Board. One year later, Governor

Reagan signed a controversial tax bill that gave Fox and other studios a tax break that saved Fox $250,000 per year. In 1974, Reagan's last year in office, the circle was completed when the state bought Fox's 236 acres back for use as parkland.

While Reagan settled in to the California statehouse, another Korshak associate, Jimmy Hoffa, was getting ready to inhabit "the big house," having just about exhausted his appeals for convictions in the Florida kickback scheme and subsequent jury tampering. With two concurrent thirteen-year sentences facing him, Hoffa made some last-minute pension-fund loan decisions, one of which went against the advice of Sid Korshak.

In 1966, Hoffa and Allen Dorfman were asked to approve a $20 million pension-fund loan to hotel magnate Jay Sarno for the building of Las Vegas' most garish paean to gambling yet, the seven-hundred-room Caesars Palace Hotel and Casino.* But Sid Korshak worried that the loan would only add to Hoffa's woes. According to the FBI, Korshak "advised Hoffa not to make any loans from the Central States, Southeast, and Southwest Areas Pension Fund to the operators of Caesar's Palace in Las Vegas . . . that he, Hoffa, already had made too many loans to Las Vegas gambling interests . . . that if the Teamsters membership ever found out about Hoffa's handling and misuse of the pension funds, he, Hoffa, would never get out of jail."[38] Obviously Korshak knew what the Bureau knew—that the Caesars grand strategy had long been in the planning and that its putative owner would be just another in a long series of front men used by the Chicago Outfit and its partners. An informant later told the FBI that the deal to cut up the Caesars skim was arrived at in October of 1965 at a Palm Springs house rented by two Las Vegas showgirls. In what came to be known as the Palm Springs Apalachin,† mob bosses from around the country, including Joe Accardo, Longy Zwillman, and Jimmy Alo, had arrived to work out the details.

One witness recently recalled sitting with Korshak and Abe Teitelbaum in the penthouse suite of Morris Schenker's Dunes Hotel, where they assuaged

---

*Caesars later expanded to twenty-five hundred rooms and featured Romanesque fountains; the eight-hundred-seat Circus Maximus Theatre, patterned after the Roman Colosseum; numerous marble and concrete-over-chicken-wire replicas of classic Roman sculptures, frescoes, and murals; and an Olympic-size pool formed out of eight thousand pieces of Italian marble.
†In the most infamous underworld conclave ever held, some eighty national bosses met in Apalachin, New York, on November 14, 1957.

Schenker's fears of competition from Caesars, which was going up directly across the Strip from the Dunes. (Schenker, a Russian-Jewish immigrant to St. Louis, was Hoffa's longtime attorney and a man, like Korshak, under lifelong scrutiny by authorities.)

After Hoffa proceeded with the Caesars loan, Korshak nonetheless became its labor adviser. But eventually he was able to convince the Chicago Outfit to significantly lower its profile in Sin City. And they were able to do it at the great expense of an old Korshak foe, aviation pioneer Howard Hughes.

Howard's End—Hughes in Vegas

> I'm not a paranoid deranged millionaire. Goddamnit, I'm a billionaire.
>
> —HOWARD HUGHES

The prosecution of Hoffa and the oppressive Vegas wiretaps were fully appreciated by not only Korshak's Supermob, but by the underworld alike. In Florida, Vincent "Jimmy Blue Eyes" Alo advised his Las Vegas partner Meyer Lansky to sell out. "Let's take the money and have a quiet life," Alo said to his lifelong friend. Sid Korshak's Chicago partners took a similar tack, but with a critical distinction. In 1967, with Jimmy Hoffa packing for "college" (and Allen Dorfman not far behind), Joe Batters Accardo and Sid Korshak devised a temporary solution to the public relations hit the gangs were taking. They instructed Johnny Rosselli to keep an eye out for squeaky-clean suckers with deep pockets, and then start unloading the gang's holdings, with one key proviso: the Chicago Outfit would manage the casinos.

"Timing is everything" goes the aphorism, and Accardo's timing could not have been more fortuitous. One year earlier, on Thanksgiving Eve, 1966, Korshak's RKO nemesis, Howard Hughes—the "billionaire kook," as he was known to the mob—moved into the penthouse suite of Dalitz's Desert Inn Hotel. Hughes, a total recluse, liked the habitat so much that he refused to leave on checkout day, much to the rancorous objection of the hotel's other pampered high rollers.

"Tell them to go to hell," Hughes ordered his aides after the hotel managers attempted to evict him.

Now, in 1967, Hughes played right into Rosselli's hands when he employed his tried-and-true tactic of buying out an adversary. As fate would have it, Hughes, the sole owner of Hughes Tool Company, had just sold his stock in Trans World Airlines for $546 million and it was burning a hole in his pajama pocket. Thus, the famous agoraphobe felt it easier to buy the

Desert Inn than to move out and instructed his key staff to work out the details. Chicago's good fortune did not end there, for Hughes's right-hand man was Robert Maheu, coincidentally a great and good friend of Rosselli's since the early sixties when they'd tried to help the Kennedy administration murder Cuba's Fidel Castro.

Bob Maheu instinctively turned to his old assassination chum Rosselli to get the ball rolling. "I told Mr. Hughes that I thought I had found a person fitting the background that he had requested me to seek," Maheu later testified in court, "a person who had connections with certain people of perhaps unsavory background." In his autobiography, Maheu admitted, "Johnny smoothed the way." Using the skills that later earned him the sobriquet The Mafia's Kissinger, Rosselli spent three months convincing the disparate partners to agree to the Hughes buyout. From the perspective of Rosselli and his skimming cohorts, there could not exist a better dupe than Hughes. Who better to victimize than a man who would never surface to testify in court? For his diplomatic legerdemain, Rosselli was paid a $50,000 "finder's fee."

Thus, like Wilbur Clark, Hughes became merely the newest pawn in the Vegas underworld's front-man motif. Years later, Maheu told Chicago investigator Jack Clarke, "Johnny told me who to hire to run the casinos and pit crews." Journalist Sergio Lalli divined what had happened when he wrote, "The mob went about its business as usual." Historians Roger Morris and Sally Denton called the sale nothing more than "a classic Las Vegas shell game." And Johnny Rosselli himself told Jimmy Fratianno, "The whole thing was a Syndicate scam . . . We roped Hughes into buying the Desert Inn." Fittingly, Hughes took over on April Fools' Day, 1967, for a purchase price of $13.2 million. It was just one month before Hoffa went off to Lewisburg.

Shortly thereafter, the hoods sold their newest sucker the Frontier ($23 million, April 1967), Sands ($23 million, July 1967), Castaways ($3.3 million, October 1967), Landmark (1969, $17.3 million), Silver Slipper ($5.4 million, April 1968), and Harold's Club in Reno ($10.5 million)—total price tag, $82.5 million. By the time Hughes caught on and pulled up stakes four years later, again on a Thanksgiving Eve, the billionaire had been relieved of yet another $50 million via the skim. Sidney Korshak, known for his thin skin, must have been sporting a Cheshire grin at the prospect of watching his RKO foe being robbed blind during Vegas' "Hughes era." One former Las Vegas intelligence chief was quoted as saying about the continued skimming, "We knew the Mob was somehow involved because the same Mob people who ran the casinos before Hughes bought them ran them right after, and these people would not have run a skim of that magnitude without orders from the top. And we knew that the money had disappeared, but we could never find out where it had gone."[39] In a move that had to bring a collective smile to the faces of the hoods, Hughes hired, of all people, Moe Dalitz to investigate where all his profit was going.

Of course, Sidney Korshak was also involved in the Hughes purchase negotiations—in fact he initiated them, as he admitted to the Securities and Exchange Commission three years later. He further testified that Hughes had also wanted to buy the Stardust, but was prevented from doing so by the Justice Department. According to Korshak, after Hughes had purchased six hotels already, "I guess the Justice Department was afraid he was going to buy all of Nevada."[40]

One month after suckering Hughes, Korshak dealt with another Las Vegas adversary, Edward Nicholas Becker, the former publicity director for Gus Greenbaum at the Riviera, and later private investigator. In the latter role, Becker was making the mistake of crossing Sidney Korshak, who was still busied with protecting his Vegas associates.

At the time, Becker was assisting local crime writer Ed Reid in obtaining interviews and information for his forthcoming book on organized crime, *The Grim Reapers* (1969). Becker had known Reid through a mutual friendship with *Las Vegas Sun* publisher Hank Greenspun, for whom Reid worked. "When my boss Gus Greenbaum got killed at the Riviera, everybody took off," said Becker, "all the owners, everybody, we all left. But I stayed around town and commuted between Las Vegas and Beverly Hills."[41] Becker knew where the bodies were buried not only in Sin City, but also in Louisiana, where he had oil business with another Korshak associate, New Orleans godfather Carlos Marcello.

On May 6, 1967, Reid contacted the FBI in L.A., hoping to trade what he knew for some inside information. As a show of sincerity, Reid met with the FBI three days later and handed over his unfinished manuscript. Unbeknownst to Reid and Becker, Sid Korshak was not happy with their probings and the repercussions of Becker's knowledge for Korshak's friends. The very next day, May 10, an L.A. FBI agent was informed by a source who knew Reid that Sid Korshak had asked him "who Ed Becker was and advised that Becker was trying to shake down some of his [Korshak's] friends for money." Korshak added that Becker supposedly offered to "keep the names of these people out of the book" in exchange for a bribe. "Becker's a no-good shakedown artist," fumed Korshak. Most tellingly, a newly released, unredacted version of the FBI report noted another reason for the Korshak call to the source: Korshak told the source to make certain his, Korshak's, name was deleted from the book. The FBI reported that Korshak's name was removed, but in fact, it was not.[42]

In a document released in 2005, the FBI added some clarification to Korshak's worries. A "well-to-do" source told the L.A. office that he had just spoken with Korshak about the possibility of Korshak's cooperating with Reid. The source said Korshak asked him to come to his ABC Booking office in Beverly Hills, where the two walked out front, so as not to be overheard. Once outside, Korshak confided the same thing he had to Harry Busch outside his Randolph Street office three decades earlier. "Korshak brought up the fact that he could not talk to the writer because it would mean his death," the source reported. "He said he could never walk away from those people [meaning the Italians]."[43]

Ed Becker's first inkling of a rift with Sid Korshak came soon after Reid's book hit the stands. "I'd run into Hank [Greenspun] occasionally, and about the time we'd gotten through the book and the book was published, I had met him one day at one of the restaurants downtown, and he said, 'Well, you certainly pissed off Korshak,' and I said, 'What?' I knew I had problems with him through the hotel, but not personally. And he said, 'Well, we were talking and your name came up, and he said, 'You better tell him to watch out. He isn't long for this world if he keeps up this bullshit.' "*

Korshak's fears about the continued heat being placed on Vegas were soon shown to be well-founded when the FBI leaked their casino wiretaps to a veteran Chicago crime reporter. Although Californians, most of whom were transplants themselves, had little interest in the true histories of the Midwesterners who had virtually hijacked their state, such was not the case back in their land of origin, where organizations like the Chicago Crime Commission, and reporters like Sandy Smith, continued to work their sources.

Smith, by this time the dean of Chicago's crime reporters, had covered the underworld since the early fifties, cultivating sources both high and low. He was about to become the first of a parade of journalists whose careers were jeopardized for daring to take on the Supermob. Early in his career,

---

*Some Kennedy assassination writers have inferred that Korshak's sole purpose in complaining to the source was to prevent Reid from promulgating an alleged threat against President Kennedy made by Marcello in September 1962, which Becker had witnessed and gave to Reid for his book. However, although that may have been the source's intent, there is no evidence that Korshak was worried about any one of his associates (e.g., Marcello) more than another, or that he even knew that the Kennedy allegation was in the manuscript. All of the available evidence indicates that Korshak was infuriated by Becker's alleged blackmailing of Korshak's friends, and by the possibility that his own name might surface in the Reid book.

Smith wrote for the *Chicago Tribune*, where he quickly learned of that paper's noninterest in Sid Korshak. "The *Tribune* never really tangled with him. I don't know what scared the editors about Sidney," Smith recently said. "I know the reporters were never afraid of him. But he was part of the fix that made the mob so strong in Chicago."[44] Smith's experience at the *Trib* corroborates that of a close friend of Korshak's, who once recalled that he often heard Korshak boast about his ability to persuade key *Tribune* officials to take it easy on him in print.[45]

By 1966, Smith was at the *Sun-Times* on the occasion of Marshall Korshak's most recent electoral campaign, this time for the important purse-controlling position of city treasurer. "Emmett Dedmon, the editorial director of the *Sun-Times*, wanted a memo with all of my information on the Korshaks," said Smith. "So I gave him that memo." The damning document not only disclosed Marshall's connection to the Playboy license fix, which Smith had nailed through well-connected sources, but it also detailed brother Sidney's checkered history with the Outfit. "The sources of information I had were telling me exactly what the Korshaks were doing," reported Smith. (An unsigned memo buried in the Chicago Crime Commission files, appearing to be Smith's, advised that organization to also lobby against the Korshak candidacy. The memo, which recalled the Playboy license and the linkage to Charlie Gioe, stated that if Marshall Korshak was elected, "it would be like naming a member of a law firm which has fronted for Syndicate mobsters since 1939—which took their money—because money which went to Sidney must have seeped off to Marshall Korshak . . . Marshall may be OK, but Sidney is the mob mouthpiece—fixer, lawyer, and front man . . . Sidney has awful power over Marshall.")[46]

"And so, after reading my memo, Dedmon still endorsed Marshall Korshak," Smith recalled. "Once the *Sun-Times* endorsed Marshall Korshak,

Marshall Korshak (Chicago Jewish Archives, Spertus Institute)

I wrote a memo to Dedmon afterward that read, 'I'm sorry, you get another boy.' And I walked out. I couldn't do anything else but that. The managing editor, named Dick Tresvant, called me after I walked out and said, 'I'm sorry about this. Somehow we'll get you back.' But I told him it was too late."

Korshak's Republican opponent, Edward Kucharski, challenged Marshall to answer Smith's contentions, but he was simply ignored. When the local CBS TV affiliate sent a crew to put the questions to Korshak at a Democratic rally, an FBI report stated that "Korshak, obviously in discomfort and with a nervous twitch, evaded giving answers and instead called Kucharski a liar and a desperate man. Korshak also appeared at the CBS offices twice and refused to answer questions or be interviewed by Sandy Smith."[47] In the end, Korshak won the election easily.

For years, Smith blamed the Korshaks for his departure from the paper. When an investigator from the Chicago Crime Commission spoke with him thirteen years later, the investigator noted, "Smith stated that his sensitivity towards the Korshaks is still rather high inasmuch as Marshall Korshak was responsible for his leaving the *Sun-Times* and going to Washington."[48]

Indeed, Smith was quickly snatched up by the Washington bureau of Time-Life, where his reporting included a seminal two-part series on organized crime for *Life* magazine, and this time he put his concerns about the Korshaks into print, becoming the second journalist after Lester Velie to do so. The articles, part one of which hit the stands on September 1, 1967, not only excoriated numerous friends of Sidney's, but also dared to detail the relationships between the hoods and the corporate and political upperworld. Among other passages in the piece was the following: "Some of Giancana's lieutenants have their own connections with politicians, officials and important people. Gus Alex has an especially warm relationship with Chicago city treasurer Marshall Korshak, and his brother Sidney Korshak. Sidney is a pal of other leading Chicago gangsters . . . 'A message from him [Sidney],' a prominent mobster was quoted on a witness stand, 'is a message from us.' On Alex's application in 1957 for an apartment in the Lake Shore Drive community he described himself as a $15,000 a year employee of Marshal Korshak, then a state senator."[49]

Smith's articles benefited from assistance given him by a frustrated FBI, which leaked a nine-hundred-page bug and wiretap report on Caesars Palace to Smith. Since the Bureau was embargoed from using the illegal tap evidence, they decided to leak the material in hopes of arousing public disapprobation. Smith's articles stated emphatically that the soon-to-open Caesars, like so many other Las Vegas casinos, was actually owned by a gangster consortium that ultimately answered to the Outfit. In his *Life* series, Smith also named "The Lady in Mink," Ida Devine, as the Outfit's new courier, and even displayed an FBI surveillance photo of her at a train station (the only way she would travel).

Smith's exposé went on to win an award from the Graduate School of Journalism of Columbia University. In two years, Frank McCulloch, having returned from his stint in Saigon, would join Smith at *Life*, where he headed Time-Life News Service's bureau in New York. There he organized an investigative "dream team" consisting of Sandy Smith, Pulitzer Prize winner Denny Walsh, Bill Lambert, and Russ Sackett. The group became a consistent thorn in the side of the Supermob. "This was the best investigative team U.S. journalism ever had," said McCulloch. "Among them they had sixty years of experience that they brought to bear."[50]

Despite the accolades accruing to Smith and his colleagues, the fact remained that the Korshaks were unflappable; the *Life* series did nothing to rattle their rarefied world. In 1967, Sidney managed Chicago mob business interests when he arranged a sweetheart contract for the city's J. P. Seeburg Jukebox Corporation, with which the Outfit had done much business. At the time, the Teamsters were threatening to strike the company, and its owners, Delbert W. Coleman and Herbert Siegel, quickly found the best man to settle the dispute, referred to him by David Bazelon's former assistant at the OAP.

"So we called Jay Pritzker [and asked him], 'Is Korshak the best?'" Siegel said recently.

"Absolutely" was Pritzker's reply.

"So we hired him," said Siegel. "The problem went away immediately. And what he wanted for his fee was a new Cadillac, which was then worth about five thousand dollars. I guess he didn't want there to be any record of it."[51] For Seeburg, Korshak's fee was a bargain: the deal cost Seeburg's two thousand

Del Coleman (Robert Lightfoot)

employees $10 a week in wages each, saving the company $1 million a year. And it was just the beginning of the relationship between Seeburg's Del Coleman, the Harvard-grad son of a tavernkeeper, and Sid Korshak, who negotiated Coleman's 1969 divorce. It was also the beginning of a friendship with Coleman's wife, Jan Amory Coleman, a relationship that was revelatory of another side of the enigmatic Korshak. In a recent interview, Amory (who ultimately divorced Coleman) spoke at length about her friend Sidney Korshak:

I met Sid when I became engaged to Del. I was awfully young at the time, and Sidney went with me and we picked out the ring, and he said to me, "Honey, I'm advising you not to marry him." And I said, "Why?" He said, "It doesn't matter why. Take it from me, don't marry him." I said, "But I'm in love with him." And he said, "I don't care. You're making the biggest mistake of your life." And this was kind of a father image talking to a daughter, concerned.

But I ignored him and went ahead with the wedding, a small wedding in Del's apartment in Chicago. Sid was the best man. For his toast he said, "I told her not to do it." Within days I knew I was going to be depressed, and Sidney of course had predicted it.

We separated eight weeks later, and when Del asked me to give the ring back, he said, "Sid will tell ya to give the ring back. I'm gonna put him on the phone." And poor Sidney gets on the phone and he said, "Listen and listen good. I'm gonna tell him that I told you to give the fucking ring back. But I'm telling you put it in the safe, give it to charity, and don't give it back to that bastard." So I said, "Okay, Sidney." He said, "Now put him on the phone and tell him I told you to give the ring back." And I did it and ended up keeping the ring.

Sid was very private, sort of the ultimate WASP that way, without actually being a WASP. He was discreet and protective of his friends. I think he had more woman friends than men friends. He had a very gruff way of talking in a kind of a diamond-in-the-rough way, but he wasn't tough at all. He was sweet and kind and loving, but I never saw him laugh. Women adored him because he was so masculine. He was a woman's friend, I'm telling you. He flirted, but he was a woman's friend. It was kind of like, "You know I'm here to protect you." I miss him a lot. I thought about him recently when I lost all of my money in the market and I started to go into business—because I'd never worked. Sidney would have just said, "Here's one hundred and fifty million dollars, go have fun in Newport." He wouldn't have gotten me a job, he would have just said, "Here's the money." He was the most generous man.

I miss Sidney every day. There aren't too many men out there that you can say, "I lost my last dime, I can't pay the rent," and they'll just send the check over within seven minutes.

I called him at his house when I owed a phone bill and I couldn't pay. He took care of it right away and he said to me, "Honey, when you marry a rich husband, pay me back." I think he respected the fact that he remembered when he had nothing, so if somebody went through a rough time, he was just always there. Sidney was a kind, kind human being covered up by a little bit of a rough façade.[52]

Amory also recalled that Korshak told her how, when Del was at Harvard, he had been recruited by the mob. "Sidney told me that," said Amory. "It's kinda like CIA recruitment, you know?" Actually, it was not uncommon for organized crime to entice promising young lawyers and business majors right out of Ivy League schools into their world. In any case, Coleman's Seeburg was now part of a long list of Korshak's well-heeled clients, as his career continued to skyrocket.

One of Korshak's most powerful patrons was the founder of the Gulf & Western Corporation, Charles Bluhdorn, for whom Korshak served as personal attorney and labor adviser. The association with the man some called the "Mad Austrian" would have profound international repercussions for Korshak, his friends, and the movie business for the next ten years. His appeal to Korshak was obvious: not unlike Abe Pritzker, Bluhdorn had risen from humble beginnings to build one of America's greatest, and most diversified, conglomerates. Bluhdorn was a man with labor issues and truckloads of disposable income that he couldn't wait to spend—just the sort of man who appreciated the unique talents of a Sid Korshak.

The Mad Austrian

Charles Bluhdorn was what would have to be described as a character. Born in 1926 to Czech parents in Vienna, Austria, Bluhdorn and his family fled to England just before Hitler annexed their homeland. Young Charles was considered such a "hellion" that at age eleven he was sent off to an English boarding school to be disciplined. In 1942, Bluhdorn emigrated to the United States to attend City College and Columbia University in New York, although he never earned a degree. In 1946, after one year in the air force, Charles took work at the Cotton Exchange, earning just $15 a week, and soon after, having discovered that Americans have an immense passion for coffee, decided to become an entrepreneur by importing coffee from South America.

Charles Bluhdorn, "The Mad Austrian" (Corbis/Bettmann)

Not yet satiated, Charles realized there might be even more money in selling and distributing replacement car parts than in importing coffee; during this period just after World War II, Americans were forced to take better care of their cars by replacing defective parts, instead of just relying on trade-ins. Thus, in 1949, Bluhdorn acquired Michigan Bumper, a small auto-parts company that developed fan belts, hubcaps, and oil filters. In a short time, at only thirty years of age, Bluhdorn became a millionaire. In 1956, Bluhdorn purchased a majority interest in the Michigan Plating and Stamping Company, which manufactured rear bumpers for Studebakers. The following year, he merged Michigan Plating and Stamping Company with the Beard and Stone Electric Company of Houston. The acquisition of Beard and Stone Electric Company provided Bluhdorn with an authorized auto-replacement-parts distributor. In 1958, he combined these two companies to form Gulf & Western Corporation, the name suggested by the geographical location of the two merged companies.

Like Pritzker, Bluhdorn began absorbing smaller, disparate companies at a frantic pace. "My wife thinks I'm nuts," Bluhdorn told an interviewer. "But when you're building something, you're spinning a web and tend to become a prisoner in the web." Mrs. Bluhdorn was not the only one critical of the Mad Austrian, whose employees took "great pleasure mimicking his Hitlerian inflections, referring to him as Mein Führer, behind his back." In fact, one executive recalled that every time Bluhdorn lost his temper, "these little white foamy stalagmite, stalactite type things appeared on both sides of his mouth. I thought, 'Does he have rabies?'" Former Paramount Pictures assistant production chief Peter Bart described Bluhdorn as a "dynamic, utterly reckless, Austrian-born wheeler-dealer who had come very far, very fast."[53]

Eventually, Gulf & Western controlled over one hundred other firms, including TV production center Desilu Productions, publisher Simon & Schuster, and clothing lines Kayser-Roth, Catalina, Cole of California, Jonathan Logan, and Oscar de la Renta. In addition, Gulf & Western owned nuclear power and mining interests, racetracks, professional sports teams, insurance companies, farm supplies, and missile parts. Academician Ben Bagdikian noted, "Almost every American buys the company's goods." The company also owned 8 percent of the arable land in the Dominican Republic. Within twenty years, G&W was grossing $5.3 billion annually and ranked sixty-first on the Fortune 500. In 1963, Bluhdorn purchased a thirty-acre estate in Ridgefield, Connecticut, where he quietly provided the community with a motorboat for the police department and a trailer for the scuba team.[54]

By the midsixties, few would have guessed that Bluhdorn was interested in acquiring a company like Paramount Pictures, which, at the time, was close to bankruptcy, with most of its meager profits coming from leasing old films to television. The studio's anticipated blockbusters such as *Circus World* and *The Fall of the Roman Empire* (both 1964) had greatly underperformed at the box office, and *Newsweek* reported that the company "has not been managed to realize its full potential."[55] However, some, such as Paramount's hot-tempered VP Martin S. Davis, saw the company as ripe for a takeover, and they also believed it could be turned around with new blood at the helm and on the board. On March 23, 1966, with Davis's prodding, the thirty-nine-year-old Bluhdorn purchased enough stock to land a position on the company's board of directors; at the time, the average age of Paramount's board members was seventy.

By coincidence, Bluhdorn was enamored of all things Hollywood, especially starlets, so Davis had little trouble in convincing the titan to buy the company outright. Adding to the attractiveness of the deal was Paramount's vast real estate holdings, which Davis predicted would only skyrocket in value. In 1966, Paramount consisted of a 31.8-acre back lot with nineteen soundstages, and the 10.2-acre Sunset Studio. However, Bluhdorn was unable to complete the purchase of Paramount on his own—he needed to gain the approval for the buyout from Paramount's executives and board members. Enter Sid Korshak.

G&W corporate attorney and Wall Street whiz Ed Weisl Sr., a graduate of the University of Chicago, who was chairman of the executive committee of the Paramount board, brought in networking mastermind Sid Korshak (whom he had originally introduced to Bluhdorn) to make the necessary introductions and arrange informal sit-downs as only he could. Since MCA founder Jules Stein sat on Paramount's board, and Korshak and Weisl were both close to Lew Wasserman, the group was soon seen with Bluhdorn at Korshak's Bistro table discussing the possible takeover of Paramount by G&W.[56] On October 19, 1966, Paramount Pictures Corporation finally became a subsidiary of Gulf & Western, purchased for $125 million, with Bluhdorn replacing its aging chairman, Adolph Zukor.* Through Paramount, Bluhdorn also owned Paramount TV Enterprises, which was responsible for *Star Trek, Mannix*, and *Mission: Impossible*.

Within the Paramount executive suites it was impossible to be neutral about Bluhdorn; one either was devoted to or feared him. One production executive said of Bluhdorn, "He was a thug, a terrible person, an absolutely unmitigated awful human being." Film director Don Simpson called Bluhdorn "a mean, despicable, unethical, evil man who lived too long. He had no problem breaking the law. He was a criminal." Even Frank Yablans, Bluhdorn's head of distribution, remarked, "Charlie was a very sinister, Machiavellian kind of guy."[57]

By all accounts, Bluhdorn relished his new role as a movie mogul. As Paramount historian Bernard F. Dick wrote, "There was a special kind of power that comes from owning a studio: the power over those who create mass entertainment."[58] Bluhdorn, however, was struck from the Howard Hughes mold, more interested in visiting sets and getting set up with the starlets. An executive at the studio said, "Bluhdorn bought Paramount 'cause he figured it was an easy way to get laid."[59] Thus, Bluhdorn began casting about for someone to actually micromanage the studio's production. Enter Sid Korshak's sybaritic young protégé Bob Evans.

Since their meeting in the fifties, Korshak and Evans had practically become each other's surrogate father and son. Evans was a regular at Korshak's parties, prompting Hollywood insider Dominick Dunne to observe, "Bob wasn't such an asshole in those days. He was hot stuff, and Sidney adored him, absolutely adored him."[60]

Since his acting career was going nowhere, the permanently suntanned Evans had been buying up literary rights, hoping to become the next Darryl F. Zanuck. At the prodding of his consigliere, Sid Korshak, Evans retained the legal services of Sid's friend Greg Bautzer, who was able to secure the wannabe mogul a three-picture producing deal at Fox.[61] Little did he realize that he would soon be at the helm of a major studio, thanks to Korshak's and Bautzer's intercession with Charlie Bluhdorn.

---

*G&W's takeover of Paramount was parodied in Mel Brooks's 1976 film, *Silent Movie*, in which the voracious conglomerate "Engulf & Devour" attempted to buy out Brooks's "Big Pictures" studio.

As Evans told it, soon after a flattering profile of him by Peter Bart appeared in the *New York Times*, he received a call from Bautzer, who said, "Pack your bags, Bob. We're going to New York."

"I've got plans, Greg," answered Evans.

"Break 'em," ordered Bautzer. "Charlie Bluhdorn, who just bought Paramount, wants to meet you. He read that article about you in Sunday's *New York Times*."[62]

Bluhdorn offered Evans a job in Europe to get his feet wet, then quickly promoted him to studio production chief, answerable only to Bluhdorn and Paramount president Martin Davis. Of course, most inside players in Hollywood merely assumed that Korshak had brought his boy to Bautzer and then to Bluhdorn. The Riviera's Ed Becker is among those who are certain that Korshak even went so far as to approve Evans's appointment with "the boys" in Chicago.

Greg Bautzer's former wife, actress Dana Wynter, recently spoke of her memories of the Evans recruitment: "Bob Evans used to hang around, and I never understood why Greg had faith in him and why Evans thought that he knew what he was doing. One day I said to Greg, 'What do you bother with him for? He's a lightweight.' I told him, 'Greg, I met him and his brother when I first hit New York and they were tailors, making such lightweight stuff.' I said I didn't like Robert Evans, but Greg got him the job." Wynter firmly disputed Evans's version that he was hired after Bluhdorn read Bart's *Times* piece: "Don't you believe it. Greg forced him on Bluhdorn, who was just starstruck. After Greg got him that job, I remember the whole town was falling down laughing."[63]

Steve Blauner, the producer of *Easy Rider* and *Five Easy Pieces*, was among those doing the giggling. "What a joke," Blauner said. "I figured he was fucking Bluhdorn or something."[64] The *New York Times* referred to Evans's hiring as "Bluhdorn's Folly," while the slightly less refined Hollywood rag *Hollywood Close-Up* called it "Bluhdorn's Blowjob." Of course, much of the outrage was explained by the staggering jealousy that pervades the business. In 1969, *Life* magazine summarized the feeling that was endemic in Tinseltown: "Robert Evans is an outrage. He has no more right to be where he is than a burglar. He has no credentials, none of the requirements for membership. Robert Evans has never produced a film, doesn't know about movies, and so why should he be a boss of Paramount with control over 25 pictures a year, costing $100 million, influencing the cultural intake of millions of Americans? He is entirely too good-looking, too rich, too young, too lucky and too damned charming. The playboy peacock of

Paramount. Who the hell does he think he is? If there's anything Hollywood wants out of Robert Evans, it's to see him fail."[65]

Bluhdorn lavished Evans with the gift of Greta Garbo's former sixteen-room manse in Beverly Hills, which included an egg-shaped pool, a barrier made of one-hundred-foot-tall eucalyptus trees and thousands of red-rose bushes. Evans named it Woodland. To cut costs, Evans moved Paramount's executive offices to 202 N. Canon Drive, just steps away from Korshak's Bistro. According to one Bistro employee, he even took an apartment above the restaurant.

Evans brought in Peter Bart as his production assistant, worked long hours, began gearing the studio toward a younger market, and surprised almost everyone when he began to turn the company around. Within two years, Paramount was back on top, producing hits such as *The Odd Couple*, *Rosemary's Baby*, and *True Grit*. Over the next few years, Evans's lordship over Paramount would yield still more negotiating adventures for his mentor, Sid Korshak.

As controversial as the Evans appointment was, it paled in comparison to Bluhdorn's next G&W enlistment. In 1968, a shady New Jersey real estate investor named Philip Levin sold his huge block of stock in MGM Studios and invested the $22 million nest egg in G&W, where Bluhdorn promptly appointed him head of the company's new real estate division, Transnation. Soon thereafter, Sid Korshak, who was by now "house counsel" to G&W, personally arranged a $16 million Teamsters Pension Fund loan to Levin's Transnation for a construction project at Chicago's O'Hare International Airport. For his effort, Korshak received a $150,000 finder's fee.[66] But Bluhdorn's decision to bring in Levin also marked the first in a series of corporate moves that opened up G&W as a conduit for both U.S. and Sicilian Mafia operations.

At this point in his career, Sidney Korshak's big-name clients numbered well over one hundred, an amazing list, considering that Korshak was still practically a one-man operation, with no secretary and no office. Interestingly, Korshak's success in the corporate world was not without the occasional ugly reference to his heritage. One Korshak colleague who preferred not to be named recently spoke of what he witnessed: "Some of the companies resented having to use him because they were anti-Semitic, and there was always that taint of the gangsters, so they said, 'We'll use him if we have to use him. But we don't want to mingle with him too much.' Sid was aware of it—that some people didn't like him or trust him, but he only mingled with the kindred types like Wasserman."

A Partial List of Korshak Clients

Desert Inn
Fremont Hotel
Riviera Hotel
Sahara Hotel
Stardust Hotel
La Concha Motel
Echo Products (CT)
Englander Corp.
Robert Hall Quality Clothes
Goldblatt Brothers Department Stores
Chicago Hotel Association
International Brotherhood of Teamsters
United Steel Workers Union
Restaurant Workers and Bartenders Union
Minnesota Mining & Manufacturing (3M)
Max Factor Cosmetics
General Dynamics
Commonwealth United
Kinney Company
National Video (Ralph Stolkin–owned)
The Grocery Owners Association
Thoroughbred Racing Association
General Dynamics
Gulf & Western
Madison Square Garden
Jim Beam Whiskey of Kentucky (the Kovler family)
Schenley Industries
Bohemian Distributing Company
Seeburg Jukeboxes
Duncan Parking Meters
Los Angeles Dodgers
New York Knicks and Rangers
Atlanta Braves (Coleman, director)
San Diego Chargers

Diners Club
National General
Hyatt Hotels
Hilton Hotels
Parvin-Dohrmann
O'Hare International Airport
Playboy Magazine
Del Mar Racetrack
Hollywood Park Racetrack
Arlington Park Racetrack
Santa Anita Racetrack
Washington Park
Universal Pictures
MCA
Paramount Pictures
Warner Brothers–Seven Arts
Rapid American
White Front Stores (CA)

Although assumed to be grossly understated, since Korshak did so much business in cash and trade, his IRS reported income for the period was as follows:

1965: $ 547,121
1966: $ 620,385
1967: $ 647,591
1968: $ 621,108
1969: $ 1,328,144

West Coast Teamsters leader Andy Anderson was among those who knew that these amounts were just the tip of the Korshak iceberg. "By February of each year, he told me he'd have more than one million dollars in retainers, already paid up," Anderson said. He also picked up on one Korshak financial peculiarity: "Sidney always used new money, usually hundred-dollar bills, fresh from the bank, so the money from the boys couldn't be traced to him."[67]

Sidney closed out a good year by attending another in a series of galas honoring his brother. On December 20, 1967, new city treasurer Marshall Korshak,

Jake Arvey, Richard Daley, Marshall and
Edith Korshak, and R. Sargent Shriver, at
Korshak's naming as 1967 Israel Bond Man
of the Year (*Chicago Tribune*)

chairman of the State of Israel Bonds, was named its Man of the Year. In the
first three years of his chairmanship, the organization raised $21 million,
and although Israel was his main charitable interest, Marshall donated to
literally dozens of other organizations.*

In 1968, Sidney performed a favor for another celebrity friend—actor
Warren Beatty—that was reminiscent of his assist for comedian Alan
King. At the time, Beatty had joined the anti–Vietnam War chorus that
was at a fever pitch after the June 5, 1968, assassination of antiwar presidential candidate Senator Robert Kennedy. All indications pointed to the
upcoming Democratic National Convention in Chicago at the end of August as a potential climactic confrontation with the pro-war party delegates. Beatty wanted to attend the showdown, but was unable to secure a
room in the city's long-sold-out hotels. It was well-known in Los Angeles
that Sid Korshak not only had pull with numerous hotel chains like
Pritzker's Hyatt and Kirkeby's Hilton hotels, but that his influence with
Chicago hoteliers, through the Chicago Hotel Association, was unparal-
leled.

"I called Sidney," said Beatty, and he asked, "Can you find me a room?"

"Where would you like to stay, Warren?" asked Korshak

"The Ambassador East would be nice—but, really, *anywhere.*"

"How many suites would you like?"

"A room, Sidney—I really don't need a suite. A room would be great."

---

*He also raised funds for the Boy Scouts, Girl Scouts, Joint Negro Appeal, St. Jude's
League, United Negro College Fund, United Settlement Fund, Chicago Youth Centers,
United Cerebral Palsy, Roosevelt University, and Fu Jen Catholic University in Taiwan.
His tax records show an average of $3,000 per year donated and divided among over fifty
charities.

Three minutes later, the phone rang. "You have three suites at the Ambassador East," said the Fixer.*,68

Jan Golding Amory tells another Korshak-Beatty war story that occurred after her divorce from Seeburg's Del Coleman. The incident took place at Manhattan's swank La Grenouille restaurant. Amory, then in her midtwenties, was dining with friends when she noticed Sid Korshak waving her over to his (the best) table, where she joined him for lunch. Korshak introduced her to his disheveled, unshaven dining companion.

"Jan Golding, Warren Beatty," said Korshak. According to Amory, sometime during midlunch, Beatty just blurted to Amory out of left field, "Do you want to fuck?" With that, Korshak burst into laughter.

"No, thank you very much, but, no," answered an agape Amory.[69]

As Jan Golding Amory soon learned, Beatty's indelicate pass was part and parcel of the world in which these men lived. She also knew that Sid Korshak had his own reputation in the womanizing department, a propensity greatly facilitated by his great access to the armies of aspiring actresses and dancers in Hollywood and Las Vegas.

---

*The convention did not disappoint the prognosticators. On August 29, five thousand protesters in Grant Park, located across the street from Kirkeby's Hilton Hotel, where many of the delegates were staying, were met by a primed Chicago PD; over a thousand activists were treated for injuries, the result of tear gas, Mace, clubbings, and beatings by Chicago's Finest. At a press conference after the convention, Mayor Richard Daley presaged the verbal eloquence of George W. Bush when he explained, "The policeman isn't there to create disorder, the policeman is there to preserve disorder."

A subsequent investigation (*The Walker Report*) by The National Commission on the Causes and Prevention of Violence rightly determined that the mêlée was the result of a "police riot."

CHAPTER 14

Scenes from Hollywood, Part Two

DURING THE SIXTIES, Sidney Korshak began grabbing attention for something other than his labor-negotiating prowess. It is a truism that, for the male of the species, a prime motivation for the accumulation of power is the attendant benefit of attracting nubile sex partners. And success in vibrant cities like Chicago, Beverly Hills, and Las Vegas avails power brokers of the most nubile of the nubile. In this world, it matters little that one has a beautiful and immensely likable wife, like Bee Korshak, at home raising the kids. What counts is that only a tiny fraction of men are capable of denying their genetic imperative in the face of nonstop temptation. According to people who observed him, Sid Korshak was most definitely not among that fraction. "He liked the girls," pal Irv Kupcinet said euphemistically.

MJ Goldblatt, who worked for a time as the executive secretary to Korshak's Chicago buddy Joel Goldblatt, recalled how "Sidley" (as she disparagingly referred to Korshak) utilized his link to Goldblatt's Department Stores' inventory to lavish women other than Mrs. Korshak. "Sidley bragged about his girlfriends—he had an ego," Goldblatt recounted. "He used to call Joel's office to have us send them gifts—TVs and stereos. I know because I had to do it. He looked me over a few times. He was a womanizer. Joel once told me Sid was actually more of a voyeur."[1]

In Las Vegas, the FBI took note of Korshak's philandering. "He had lots of girlfriends," chuckled former Las Vegas SAC Dean Elson.[2] But it was in Beverly Hills that Korshak was most often seen with beauties other than Bee Korshak, or otherwise on the prowl.

"A girlfriend of mine wanted to sell roses in a restaurant," added movie producer Gray Frederickson (*The Godfather* series, *Apocalypse Now*). "I asked Sidney if he knew of anything, and he said, 'Is she cute?'" In fact, she was a stunner, Korshak was informed. "So he met with her and set her up at one of the biggest hotels in town."[3] The Bistro's Jimmy Murphy saw the parade of Korshak consorts passing through his Canon Drive front doors. "If Sidney was there with a girl, he was well-covered," remembered Murphy. " 'I was just advising her,' Sidney would say." Gianni Russo, who often met Korshak for lunch at the Bistro, agrees: "He always told his wife it was business, because he consulted with a lot of studios."[4] Of course, Korshak was not alone in openly bringing his lady friends to the posh restaurant, where spreading gossip was a no-no. In fact, the only danger in these trysts was the chance arrival of the man's wife. "The Bistro didn't have many hiding places," said Murphy, laughing, "so it was par for the course to have to sneak a girlfriend out through the kitchen when someone's wife showed up."[5]

Not all of Korshak's partners were unknown starlets or flower girls. Inevitably, he was linked to some of the most desired and well-known actresses of the time. Both Johnny Rosselli's girlfriend Betsy Duncan and Korshak's former daughter-in-law Virginia Korshak were among those certain of a Korshak affair with titian-haired actress Rhonda Fleming. Bistro owner Kurt Niklas, Irv Kupcinet, and Virginia Korshak all also witnessed a "long-term affair" with Stella Stevens.[6] Judy Campbell Exner recalled seeing Sidney with Stella at his Riviera Hotel.[7] At the time of the alleged Sidney-Stella affair, Virginia Korshak was dating a well-known television star and attended parties with him at Stevens's home. "He was one of Stella's best friends," Virginia said. "He told me that Stella is being kept, that money is provided to her by Sidney Korshak." Still other sources have linked Korshak to beautiful blond Warner Bros. contract starlet Diane McBain, thirty-four years younger than Sidney, and a ubiquitous face in such sixties television fare as *Surfside Six*, *77 Sunset Strip*, *Maverick*, and *Hawaiian Eye*. But of all the Korshak affairs, the one that stands out as the most valued—and represented what the FBI termed "Korshak's only known weakness"[8]—was that with a flame-haired temptress, thirty-three years his junior, who went by the name Jill St. John.

Jill

With the boosting of her stage mother, Betty Oppenheim, Jill St. John first appeared under the name Jill Oppenheimer as a child actress in the film *Sandy Dreams*. While still not out of her teens, St. John had appeared on over one thousand radio shows. By the early 1960s, St. John, who the studio flaks liked to point out had an alleged 162 IQ, found her niche as a guest star on comedy variety specials, especially those of Bob Hope, who relied on a constant supply of female eye candy for his shows. She had also appeared in a number of forgettable films with Korshak friends such as Frank Sinatra

Jill St. John (Photofest)

(*Come Blow Your Horn*, 1963; *The Oscar*; 1966; and *Tony Rome*, 1967), whom she also dated; Dean Martin (*Who's Been Sleeping in My Bed?*, 1963); Warren Beatty (*The Roman Spring of Mrs. Stone*, 1961); and Peter Lawford (*How I Spent My Summer Vacation*, 1967; and *The Oscar*, 1966).

One constant in St. John's life was her insatiable attraction to wealthy and powerful men. By 1969, the twenty-nine-year-old actress was already in the midst of her third failed marriage, this one to singer Jack Jones, to whom she had been married less than two years.* Just as he had done thirty years earlier with Dorothy Appleby, Sid Korshak, whom St. John said she met in 1962,[9] "arranged the [divorce] settlement," according to a Hollywood columnist. And, by all accounts, again like *l'affaire* Appleby, Sid Korshak took a special liking to the striking redhead. "I introduced Sidney to Jill St. John," said veteran MCA agent Freddie Fields, "something for which he was always grateful."[10]

"Everyone in this town knew about Sid and Jill," asserted Johnny Rosselli's goddaughter, actress Nancy Czar,[11] and, according to some, Korshak's interest in St. John predated his handling of the Jack Jones divorce. One friend of both Jill's and Jones's, who asked not to be named, said emphatically, "They married Jill off to Jack Jones. Sid not only set Jill up with movie roles, but he set her up with Jack, who was a foil for Sidney, although he probably didn't realize it." The contention rang true with Frederic Sidewater, a Hollywood producer friend of Korshak's (*King Kong, The Bible*). "Sidney told me that when they were in Vegas, Jill and her husband were

---

*She married laundry scion Neil Durban at age seventeen in 1957 (divorced a year later) and Formula One race-car driver (and Woolworth heir) Lance Reventlow in 1960 (divorced three years later).

given separate suites so she and Sidney could get together."[12] The FBI also noted that Korshak often used a "beard" in his assignations with St. John.[13] However, according to the FBI, when Bee went off to Europe with girlfriends, Sidney seized the opportunity to openly spend a couple of weeks "with his paramour" in Aspen, Colorado, or New York's Regency Hotel.[14]

About this time, according to Kurt Niklas, "Korshak had Jill ensconced in an apartment in Beverly Hills, and they dined almost daily at the Bistro. Suffice it to say, their affair was not a well-kept secret."[15] Another St. John friend added, "It was common knowledge that he was keeping her. Sidney was incredibly powerful, generous, and charming. My opinion is that neither one thought this was going to last forever. I think they were both very real. If I was an attractive young lady, I would see nothing wrong with Sidney."

The apartment was just one of many perks to be enjoyed by a Korshak mistress. One of Jill's boyfriends claims that Korshak lavished the actress with ten grand a month in CDs (certificates of deposit). Korshak's Teamster associate Andy Anderson recalled being asked to purchase a hand-carved ivory chess set for Jill when Anderson was in Hong Kong. But St. John's special passion was jewelry; she liked to brag that her engagement ring from her second marriage contained a diamond that stretched "from knuckle to knuckle."[16] Anderson knew of a $50,000 diamond bracelet given to St John. When Jill spied one pricey bauble she wanted, Korshak suddenly cashed in his Bistro stock. Although he had promised Niklas that if he ever got out, he would sell his stock back at the original price of $21,000, he now demanded the current valuation, $70,000.[17]

"Go write me a check for seventy thousand dollars," Sidney ordered Niklas. "Jill saw something she wanted at Van Cleef & Arpels, and I didn't want to lay out pocket money. Besides, you can afford it."[18] (One of Korshak's rules was to always buy with cash, thereby leaving no paper trail.) Others assert that Korshak went so far as to buy Jill a home in Aspen, Colorado. Producer Gray Frederickson came to believe it after what Jill told him years later. "When Sid called, I'd run," she said. "He was paying for the house."[19]

Teamster leader Anderson recalled how one trinket intended for St. John never made it to her. When Sidney was in England, he eyed a convertible Rolls-Royce that he thought Jill would like, so he purchased the car and had it sent over. But the car was sent to Korshak's house by mistake while he was away. His wife, Bee, thought it was for her. According to Anderson, Bee said, "Sidney, you are such a sweet husband!"[20]

Jill and Frank Sinatra (David Sutton, MPTV)

The Korshak–St. John affair was seemingly immune to public embarrassment, and whatever private cost it may have incurred was kept surprisingly discreet for the microscopic showbiz-capital glare—no tabloid exposés or public shouting matches with spouses, etc. The relationship did have a curious sidelight when St. John began being seen on the arm of Dr. Henry Kissinger, the national security adviser to newly installed President Richard Nixon. For years, Kissinger had been close to MCA VP Taft Schreiber, a staunch Republican supporter who introduced Kissinger to the Hollywood party circuit. And like so many Washington pols before him, Kissinger was quickly seduced by the allure (and the starlets) of the film capital. Along the way he became good friends with Korshak pals such as Frank Sinatra, for whom Kissinger threw a number of parties when the singer visited Washington.[21]

While the admitted "secret swinger" Kissinger orchestrated the wholesale obliteration of Vietnamese and Cambodian civilians by day, his nights were spent in the company of a parade of young-enough-to-be-his-daughter consorts.[22] In Washington, the gossip wags devoted much copy to the Tinseltown exploits of Dr. K., who was seen dating unnamed "mystery blondes" as well as known celebs such as Marlo Thomas, and even a Danish star of X-rated flicks named Judy Brown. There were even whispers in the White House that he was enamored of press secretary Ron Ziegler's twenty-seven-year-old researcher, future ABC newsreader Diane Sawyer, a former America's Junior Miss.[23]

But it was Kissinger's relationship with St. John, seventeen years younger, that garnered most of the ink. Jan Amory Cushing, a friend of both Korshak's and Kissinger's, remembered how she first heard of the "affair of state." "Henry told me he said to Jill, 'Look, I would like to invite you to the White House. It's a big dinner, dance, you know, the president will be there.'

And she said, 'That's so kind of you, but I've been to the White House many times. I'll take a pass.' But I think Sidney fixed them up anyway," Amory posited. "Even though Sidney was having the affair with her, he said, 'Go to the White House, it'll be fun.' So she went."[24] One has to give it to St. John, who was able to simultaneously enthrall both one of the country's most powerful public officials and its most furtive power broker. Andy Anderson just rolls his eyes at the thought: "Jill St. John was seeing Kissinger *and* Sidney," he said in wonderment.

Eventually, Kissinger began escorting St. John to Los Angeles parties that included Korshak pals such as Lew Wasserman, Paul Ziffren, and Kirk Douglas, with the actress openly crowing about her relationship with the good doctor. "Jill used to sit in Eli's Steak House [in Chicago] with Sid [Korshak] and Gussie Alex and talk about Kissinger," said Eli's regular Jack Clarke, who witnessed the trio there chatting about it.[25]

During one film shoot, screenwriter Tom Mankiewicz paid a visit to Jill's London apartment, where he overheard the national security adviser speaking with Jill during a critical moment in history. "The phone rang and it was Henry Kissinger, and he was in Paris," Mankiewicz recalled. "Turns out he was actually in the secret negotiations with the Vietnam War at the time, but we didn't know it."[26] In late 1972, Korshak remarked to Kurt Niklas, "Can you believe what Kissinger told Jill? The guy is a prick." Niklas asked for clarification. "I'm talking about the jerk violating his national trust," said Korshak. "The dumb sonuvabitch told Jill that we're going to bomb Hanoi into oblivion—and they complained about Jack Kennedy and Judy Campbell. Keep this under your lid. I don't want Jill getting into trouble." According to Niklas, this revelation occurred one week before American B-52s in fact began bombing Hanoi.[27]

Andy Anderson related that the Nixon-Kissinger carpet-bombing of North Vietnam led to a more intimate kind of Cold War. "Sidney told me that she said to Kissinger that she wouldn't sleep with him anymore unless he ended the Vietnam War," Anderson recalled.[28] Others were dubious of the idea of the bedroom brinkmanship. "I doubted Jill ever slept with him," offered Tom Mankiewicz. "I think it was for show. He went with a friend of mine—Hope Lange—and nothing happened. I think Henry thought he'd look great."

One would suspect that the powerful Kissinger ranked first in the peccadillo pecking order, and that might have been true with most mortals, but not so with Sid Korshak. Los Angeles labor lawyer and Korshak friend Leo Geffner recalled, "Often, when Kissinger invited Jill St. John to the White

House, she would say, 'Sorry, I have an invitation from someone more important.' "*,29

As the Korshak–St. John affair lost momentum years later, friends witnessed the tightrope St. John attempted to walk. "I was at this ski trip in Bear Valley, California, in the early seventies," recalled Missy Chandler, the former wife of *Los Angeles Times* publisher Otis Chandler. "There was a pro-celebrity ski race, and Jill was there, paid to promote it. She was there with [skier] Spider Sabich. She was in the hot tub with Otis and myself and she said, 'Don't you dare tell anybody I'm here, because Sid will find out and I'm creamed.' " According to Missy, Jill was particularly worried that her date with Savitch would appear in the gossip columns of Otis's newspaper.[30]

Photographer and concert producer Ron Joy dated St. John during a period when the actress was making a halfhearted attempt to separate from Korshak. After coming off a five-year relationship with Frank Sinatra's daughter Nancy, Joy met St. John at a Hollywood party, and the two began dating soon thereafter. "We dated for quite a while. At that time, she was a girlfriend of Sidney. Korshak and I were aware of each other, actually, because of Nancy—I had seen him at Frank's house. Anyway, when I met Jill, Sidney hadn't been coming around for a while—I think because he was trying to be a good husband to his wife. He had reformed for about a year. One day after lunch at Jill's house on 1326 Beverly Estate Drive,[†] she said, 'Sidney's coming up. Do you want to stay and meet Sidney?'

" 'No. I want to get out of here,' I told her. But I was slow moving out that day and I didn't get out in time—I had a phone call or something. He was already there by the time I came out of the bedroom. I think he was standing at the time, holding a briefcase."

What happened next left an indelible impression on Joy, unaccustomed to power on the level of a Sid Korshak.

"He didn't introduce himself or anything," remembered Joy. "He just said, 'So, you're the guy who was fucking Nancy Sinatra.' That was his

---

*Years after the Kissinger–St. John relationship faded, the presidential adviser's son, David Kissinger, obtained a job as a staff reporter (1990–92) for *Daily Variety*, prompting rumors of a little assist from Sid Korshak. (Former Paramount executive Peter Bart, friend and assistant to Korshak's protégé Paramount production chief Bob Evans, had just become senior editor at the magazine. Such an intercession for David is made more plausible given that in the 1970s, Bart had watched over Korshak's son Harry as a favor to Sidney when the novice filmmaker had tried his hand at producing a Paramount movie.) In 2001, David Kissinger was chosen as president of Lew Wasserman's Universal Television Productions.

†Well-placed sources claim that Korshak bought the Beverly Estate home for Jill.

comment. Then he turned to Jill and said, 'Here, this is for you.' And, boom, the briefcase opens and cash falls in her lap—tightly bundled hundred-dollar bills. I would assume—and I didn't count it, obviously—that it was half a million dollars to over a million. He dumped this money right in front of me. He wasn't trying to hide anything, that's for sure. This was her present."

Joy said Korshak gave him a look that said, "She's back with me now," and Jill merely smiled at the young photographer in agreement. "I was out. I knew it," Joy added. "I'd been around her for a long time and I was smart like a fox. I said, 'Jill, I guess this is the end. Thank you for a fabulous time.' I felt bad for about ten days or so—physically sick. But I had a great relationship with her. Jill was just great."[31]

The Korshak–St. John affair ended, according to an FBI source, after the actress gave the Fixer an ultimatum to either move in with her, or else. But Korshak refused to leave Bee, and so it ended. The source described Korshak as "melancholy" after the breakup.[32]

Perhaps the most troubling aspect of Korshak's infidelity was his utter lack of discretion. One of Bee's friends described him as "just a bastard" because he would even bring his mistresses to his family parties.[33] Virginia Korshak remembered one particular embarrassment. "Bee told me that Rhonda Fleming's husband called her up, after thirteen years of marriage, and let it be known Sidney was having an affair with his wife. Bee even said to me that 'Sidney would deny it if I caught him in bed. He'd say I was seeing things, it's not the truth.' "[34]

For those unaccustomed to living in such rarefied air, the question always arises as to how the cuckolded spouse copes with such regular public humiliation, a lifestyle that often saw Bee escorted to parties by family friends, such as Ambassador John Gavin, when Sid was off doing his thing. Those who knew Bee Korshak said that Sidney offered her such a great life in every other respect that the trade-off was tacitly accepted. "All the traveling to Europe with Dinah Shore and Barbara Sinatra. If she broke up with Sidney, she wouldn't have that life," said one acquaintance.[35] Former daughter-in-law Virginia Korshak opined, "I honestly think that Sidney made it up to her. He must have said, 'If you can put up with these things, you get a sixty-carat emerald.' I think Bee liked that. I mean, Bee liked the Norell gowns." She may also have liked that the giving of a long leash was mutual. "Sid was a permissive guy and let her do her thing as well," explained one family friend. "She liked tennis pros," said another.

Inevitably, the situation led Bee to consider her options. "I knew about his wife because one of my partners knew her very well and said she was quite dismayed that she had married Sidney," said former Riviera PR man Ed Becker.[36] "Bee had thought of leaving," said MJ Goldblatt. "She packed her bags more than once. But she had two kids. 'Let him walk,' she told me. 'Why should I leave?' " During one tense period in 1965, "Korshak spoke at length about his problems with his wife and his paramour, actress Jill St. John," the FBI summarized. "He is looking for another house for St. John to live in."[37]

MJ Goldblatt detected another interesting aspect of the Korshaks' relationship." I thought Sid was jealous over how everyone loved Bee," Goldblatt said recently. "She was a trophy for Sid and he knew it." Indeed, poking around Beverly Hills even for the briefest time, one elicits a constant refrain of "Bee is the nicest person you could want to meet." Her fan club is legion, and loyal to a fault.

Sidney's dalliances, in a city where such things seem de rigueur, did nothing to diminish the Korshaks' popularity among the celebrity set. Symbolic of their growing purchase in the film community was an event chronicled by *Los Angeles Times* "Party Line" columnist Doris Lilly. The occasion was an anniversary party thrown for Bee and Sidney by Kirk and Anne Douglas. The fifty or so partyers took over the Douglases' toddler son Michael's playhouse to enjoy an original musical comedy based on the Korshaks' life, written by award-winning Broadway and Hollywood composer Sammy Cahn, arguably the greatest popular songwriter of his time, and a frequent contributor to the catalog of Korshak's pal Frank Sinatra.* As reported by Lilly, the guests included "Dinah Shore with Dick Martin, Ellie and David Janssen, Cyd Charisse and Tony Martin, Polly Bergen and Freddie Fields, Kitty and Mervyn LeRoy, Fran and Ray Stark, Greg Bautzer and model Nancy Curfman, Harry Karl and Debbie Reynolds, Bobby Evans, Charles Evans, Ingrid and Jerry Orbach, and maestro Sammy Cahn with his very best girl, Dee Hawks."[38]

During this period of high living, a number of Korshak's most well-heeled Beverly Hills pals were approached by Korshak with a proposal to constuct a getaway co-op South of the Border. Little did they realize that Korshak, typically, had a secret agenda buried in his Acapulco retreat blueprint—an agenda that also accommodated his superbosses in the underworld.

---

*Among his hundreds of classic compositions were "High Hopes," "All the Way," "My Kind of Town," "Call Me Irresponsible," "Come Fly with Me," "Teach Me Tonight," "Time After Time," and "Ain't That a Kick in the Head."

CHAPTER 15

"A Sunny Place for Shady People"

THE YEAR 1968 saw Sid Korshak once again building a consortium with a grand vision, but, like his RKO experience, this one fell short of its goals. The labyrinthine concept, to build a tower of private condos, came via the man who'd introduced Korshak to Kurt Niklas years earlier, Moe Morton, an entrepreneur with a checkered background, to say the least.

After moving to L.A. from Chicago in the forties, when the Supermob made its inroads into California real estate and entertainment, Morris "Moe" Morton became a well-known San Diego bookie associate of L.A. mobster Mickey Cohen and a long-term friend of both Meyer Lansky's and Bugsy Siegel's. For a time, he was barred from Hollywood Park Racetrack, while his brother Jack was permanently barred from all California tracks after it was learned that he was running a book operation at Al Hart's Del Mar facility, obviously with Hart's blessing.[1] (In those days, "on track" bookies were a common convenience that allowed large wagers and wins away from the IRS's prying eyes.) Moe was once imprisoned for defrauding the Carnation Milk Company out of $250,000[2] and was also known to be a courier for the Las Vegas skim, which he moved through Mexico.[3] It is believed that this skim smuggling was linked to the Mal Clarke/Mexican-parking-meter money laundering (see chapter 12).

Morton also had a residence in Acapulco, the home of his American wife, Helen, who'd grown up in Mexico, where her father was employed as an engineer. Helen, in turn, had gone to grammar and high school with the former president of Mexico Miguel Alemán Valdés, whose corrupt regime's links to Meyer Lansky would give Morton the idea in 1966 to build a retreat for hoods, where they could relax, make deals, and otherwise go on the lam from their pursuers in the United States. Of course, one of Morton's silent investors in the condo construction would be Lansky, and as for the requisite "owners of record," Moe turned to his Bistro buddy Sid Korshak to reel them in.

The Acapulco Towers (author photo)

According to confidential sources, the prequel to the new scheme occurred when Meyer Lansky helped elect Alemán the president of Mexico in 1947 by advising him and paying for his campaign. Lansky's quid pro quo was essentially "You become president of Mexico and the first thing you do is make sure that they do not try to legalize gambling in Mexico." Lansky was merely trying to assure the success of the nascent Las Vegas, where he was bankrolling Bugsy Siegel, among others. Mexican politicians were notoriously corrupted; during Aleman's term, there was a national lottery scandal (1947–49), when Mexican senators were openly bought by mob money. Such massive corruption was tolerated because at least some of the payoffs were rechanneled into local investments. One prominent Acapulco businessman said in 2005, "The Alemán family holds a tremendous fortune; he stole a lot of money, but he did a lot for the country."

Alemán supposedly took millions from Lansky in bribes and lived up to his end of the no-casino bargain. Regretfully for Alemán, Mexican law dictated just one six-year term in office for the President, so to ensure his continued power, Alemán created the powerful President of Tourism position for himself—with no term limit. Over the next few decades, the bribing of Mexican politicians almost put Chicago to shame, and Alemán was said to wield so much behind-the-scenes power that he virtually appointed his presidential successors. Locals alleged that Alemán "owned Acapulco" in the 1960s.*

With Alemán's and Lansky's blessing, Morton began work on his relatively

---

*One source attesting to the Lansky-Alemán bribe is a well-known Mexican-American entertainer who was a frequent guest on Alemán's yacht, where he heard the former president brag about the relationship with Lansky. The entertainer relayed the information to the IRS's John Daley in L.A. and the LAPD's Frank Hronek, who corroborated the relationship.

modest "hotel," bringing in two Mexican investors, a Mexican manager named Porfiro Ybarra, and L.A. contractor Brewster Stevens. The new corporation was christened Satin (or Satan, depending on whom one believes), named after a deceased Morton dog. Morton bought the land for $110,000 and brought in Beverly Hills real estate developer (and owner of Kahlúa Liqueur) Jules Berman, who put up an additional $400,000. And as per Mexican custom, a good portion of the money ended up lining the pockets of corrupt local pols. When U.S. investigators conducted interviews two years later, they interviewed hotel staff who told them, "On numerous occasions, various types of Mexican officials came to the hotel, and instead of conforming with business practices and standards in Mexico, Mr. Morton would choose to bribe those officials in their official capacity."[4] At the time, it was illegal for aliens to own land in Mexico, so to guarantee a waiver of the statute, certain pols were typically taken care of.[5]

The property was located in the hills overlooking Acapulco Bay, where Morton first instructed Stevens to build a warehouse so that Morton could store construction items—doorknobs, appliances, silverware, and other furnishings—smuggled from the United States and transshipped on his own fifty-one-foot yacht.[6] During the hotel's construction, Morton freely boasted to Stevens, his son James, and others that he was the skim "bagman" for the Outfit in Las Vegas and was close with many other hoods.[7] "In no way did Mr. Morton try to be secretive about the fact," investigators were told.[8] The real estate agent who sold Morton the property said recently that he had no doubt that Morton would make such a revelation. "Moe was a well-known blowhard," the agent said.[9]

What Stevens couldn't know were the ultimate origins of his paychecks. Agents of the Illinois Bureau of Investigation later testified that Morton, as an "associate of big name mobsters and courier for transfer about the country of money skimmed off the top of Las Vegas gambling income, [who] formed a Mexican corporation to buy the land, got American businessmen to put up the money, then squeezed them out at 50 cents on the dollar." According to the investigators, Meyer Lansky, Sam (Momo) Giancana, and Sidney Korshak "were around the edges of the transaction."[10] This echoed what Johnny Rosselli told his goddaughter, Nancy Czar: "The Acapulco Towers was built with Vegas skim money."[11]

Before the condos opened, Morton had a disagreement with one investor and bought him out, as noted, for fifty cents on the dollar; the other investor, Jules Berman, who argued with Morton over the wisdom of bribing the local officials, was thrown bodily out of the hotel. Morton then turned to Korshak, described the operation, and invited Korshak to put together one of his famous investment groups and join the action. Korshak, who already maintained a villa on Pichilingue Beach near Acapulco, liked what he heard. Thus, in 1968, Korshak and Morton formed a new corporation named Simo, for Sidney and Moe.

By October 1968, Korshak had convinced ten friends to invest $50,000 each for what most believed to be a private time-share, although it is highly unlikely that Korshak apprised his L.A. pals of the hoodlum connection. There were a number of familiar faces among the investment group: Al Hart and a banking partner, Alfred Lushing; Delbert Coleman; Greg Bautzer and Eugene Wyman; Gulf's Philip Levin; actress Donna Reed and her husband, Tony Owen; Eugene Klein, the owner of the San Diego Chargers; and brothers Nathan and Gerald Herzfeld, owners of Yonkers Raceway in New York.

Korshak later told the SEC about his investors: "These were all people who had visited from time to time in Acapulco. This is a place that was probably built for condominiums, and we all felt that if we bought this thing, that maybe we would each take a condominium. It is only twenty apartments . . . We had a fifty percent interest."[12]

One of the most interesting of the new names was Philip J. Levin, the same Levin who had recently become a major investor in Bluhdorn's Gulf & Western and ran that company's real estate arm, Transnation. But Levin was anything but a mild-mannered real estate speculator and corporate executive. The son of a minor loan shark, Levin was a Rutgers Law School graduate who lived in Bethel, New Jersey, and had made over $100 million as president of Philip J. Levin Affiliated Companies, which comprised thirty corporations and real estate holdings in California and Florida. Much of the land he had sold in Florida was to "syndicate figures."[13]

Phone records revealed that in one month, someone in Levin's home had over thirty-five phone conversations with someone in the home of Angelo "Gyp" DeCarlo, a lieutenant in the Genovese crime family, one of the top five Mafia families in the country.*,[14] Other calls were traced from Levin to DeCarlo's partner Sam "the Plumber" DeCavalcante. (Levin later testified that his son Adam was gabbing with DeCarlo's son, Lee—but he was never asked about the DeCavalcante calls.) Federal investigators were certain that Levin's fast rise in real estate was financed by Meyer Lansky, and that Levin figured prominently in both DeCarlo's and Lansky's operations.

Levin later testified that he first met Morton in February 1967 when Levin

---

*Korshak friend Murray Chotiner would later arrange DeCarlo's presidential pardon from Richard Nixon.

spent a week in Acapulco with Twentieth Century-Fox mogul Darryl F. Zanuck.[15] Levin said he met Korshak there around the same time. "He had a house there and I visited it one night and met him for the first time," Levin testified. "[Al] Hart acted as negotiator for the hotel. And on the advice of Korshak I entered into the venture." Levin said Korshak and Hart approached him with an offer to purchase a 5 percent interest in the hotel for $50,000.

When completed, the Acapulco Towers was a far cry from the opulent Kirkeby-owned Hilton at the base of the mountain. Jack Clarke, who later traveled to Acapulco to investigate the ownership of the condos, recently described the layout: "It was toward a mountain, and this is about a half a mile or a mile from the Hilton, which is on the main strip. You go up the side of a mountain—I found out later I drove right by the place, didn't even know it was there. Then I came back and I see a tiny sign, ACAPULCO TOWERS, and sure enough, there it was."[16] Clarke described a gray, seven-story building, comprising fourteen three-bedroom apartments and seven with one bedroom, a swimming pool, and a garden. As another investigator put it, "Hardly a place to get lost in the lobby."

Once the doors opened, the Towers welcomed its celebrity owners and their friends. Manager Ybarra said, "There was a steady stream of Hollywood personalities coming to the hotel as soon as it was open." The place was empty for the majority of the year, but when it did function, it played host to many of Korshak's best Hollywood friends, such as Tony Curtis, Tony Martin and Cyd Charisse, Kirk Douglas, MGM honcho Kirk Kerkorian, and, of course, Robert Evans. Reservation cards retrieved later showed that Marshall Korshak was also a regular guest at the hotel. Co-owner Eugene Klein told author Dan Moldea, "We used to go down there. We used to bring our own food. We swam in the pool. We cooked hot dogs and hamburgers. It's not even a real hotel. It's an apartment hotel. We spent three, four days in the sun. And then we went home."[17] Ybarra later told investigators, "It was never really operated like a hotel. It was in essence just a private club."[18]

Hollywood gossip maven Joyce Haber described a week of partying in Acapulco, in which guests such as Gene Klein, Eugene Wyman, the Korshaks, actress Merle Oberon, actor Noël Coward, CBS honcho William Paley, and MCA's Milton Rackmil bounced between the home of host Miguel Alemán and Moe Morton's Acapulco Towers.[19]

Haber's and Klein's bucolic descriptions, however, are far from the complete story of the Acapulco Towers. An investigation two years later found that during the "off-season," the hotel became a meeting place/hideout for some of the most notorious organized crime bosses of the era, including

Meyer Lansky, Sam "Momo" Giancana, and a host of underworld heavy hitters from Canada. They used the place for relaxation, to make deals, and go on the lam when things were hot across the border. Alberto Batani, one of the original Mexican investors in Satin, told investigators, "There were several people who didn't like newspaper publicity and who would like to, in essence, hide out at the Towers."[20]

Batani and others reported seeing Morton entertaining Sam "Momo" Giancana on Morton's yacht in Acapulco Bay, a craft that Morton later sold to another Moe—Dalitz. Giancana was living in Mexico at this point, having been banished from Chicago by Accardo. Interestingly, Morton's company also went by the name Meymo, which could be seen as a contraction of Meyer and Momo. Likewise, Meyer Lansky was seen there "numerous times" with his "associate and confidant" Hyman Siegel. Moe Dalitz was also a frequent guest.

In February 1970, Canadian authorities monitoring the movement of that country's organized crime family, the Cotronis, reported on a virtual underworld convention at the Towers, ostensibly to conduct some business involving Canada's liquor scions, the Bronfman family. They reported that Sid Korshak was there with Meyer Lansky, his attorney Moses Polakoff, and Frank and Vincent Cotroni, Paul Violi, Leo Berkovitch, Raymond Doust, Anthony "Papa" Papalia, Frank Pasquale, Newton Mandell (of Transnation), Del Coleman, Tony Roma, Phil Levin, Irving Ellis, Jimmy Orlando, Pino Catania, and Angelo Bruno. The group's first meeting was held in the Acapulco home of Canadian gangster Leo Berkovitch. Two weeks later, *Playboy*'s Hugh Hefner and offshore investment wizard Bernard Cornfeld were also seen there.[21]

Coincidentally, during one of the off-season bookings, a relative of a Los Angeles investigator in the DA's office, Jim Grodin, witnessed a telling tête-à-tête. "My cousin Sam was in Acapulco with his wife when he met Al Hart on the Acapulco Towers balcony with Lansky," said Grodin. "Hart introduced Sam and his wife to Meyer, and they took a photo together." When Sam relayed this to his cousin, Grodin went back to his office and ran a criminal-history workup on Hart. "I learned that he went to prison in the thirties for some kind of land fraud in San Bernardino," added Grodin. He also learned that many L.A. investigators believed that Lansky was a silent partner in Hart's City National Bank.[22]

During a 1970 investigation of the Towers, the chairman of the Illinois Bureau of Investigation, Alexander MacArthur, appropriated W. Somerset Maugham's description of Monaco when he said of the facility, "This is a sunny place for shady people."[23]

More Fun with Sidney, Delbert, and Phil

Soon after their ill-fated Acapulco partnership began, Korshak, Del Coleman, and Phil Levin initiated another phase of the scheme. This gambit involved a Korshak-orchestrated takeover by Del Coleman of a California company, then manipulating its stock by announcing pending mergers and purchases of a number of Vegas casinos, namely the Riviera and Stardust. They would then swap the inflated stock, make a killing, and end up with the casinos. The plan was made possible after Nevada passed the 1969 Corporate Gaming Act, which allowed publicly traded companies to purchase Vegas casinos. (In 1970, Howard Hughes put his Las Vegas growth spurt on permanent hold, as his Mormon Mafia aides secreted him out the Desert Inn's back door to the Bahamas. In a parting shot, Hughes called Bob Maheu "a no-good, dishonest son of a bitch" who "stole me blind."[24] Although Hughes's company Summa Corp. maintained the investment, Hughes himself became disinterested in Sin City; in addition to being robbed in the casinos, Hughes had grown weary of battling the federal government's antitrust regulators, tired of battling Kerkorian for Vegas land, and paranoid over the military's continual A-bomb tests in the desert outside the city.)

Thanks to the Gaming Act, corporations seized the baton lustily, moving quickly, as one local historian put it, "to purifying the wages of sin." Overnight, upperworld bastions such as Hilton Hotels, MGM, Holiday Inn, The Ramada Inn Corporation, and impresarios such as Steve Wynn began their irreversible push to give Sin City a superficial veneer not unlike that of Disneyland—but at the heart of it all would remain gambling activities shamelessly rigged in the casino owners' favor.

Thus, to take advantage of the new Gaming Act, Korshak et al. decided they needed to go corporate. As they had done with Moe Morton, the Korshak-Coleman-Levin trio devised a plan that involved partnering with another Chicago to Beverly Hills transplant named Albert Parvin. On the surface, Parvin ran a straitlaced corporation, Parvin-Dohrmann (P-D) Inc., which sold kitchen, hotel, and restaurant supplies and furnishings. P-D even maintained a charitable foundation (The Albert Parvin Foundation) that boasted a current Supreme Court associate justice (and former SEC chairman), William O. Douglas, on its board. The public face of the Parvin charity involved large donations to both UCLA medical research and scholarships to Princeton and UCLA for students from third world countries.[25] But other aspects of Parvin drew the interest not only of many in law enforcement, but also of Sid Korshak and others interested in new Supermob business opportunities.

On April 15, 1970, Representative (and future president) Gerald Ford gave an impassioned speech calling for the impeachment of Douglas, in which he described the earliest allegations about the Parvin Foundation and its connections to hoods such as Meyer Lansky partner Bugsy Siegel. "Accounts vary as to whether it was funded with Flamingo Hotel stock," said Ford, "or with a first mortgage on the Flamingo taken under the terms of the sale. At any rate, the foundation was incorporated in New York and Mr. Justice Douglas assisted in setting it up." For his help, Douglas was given a lifetime position on the Parvin Foundation board and by 1968 had been paid over $100,000.*

In fact, Albert Parvin acquired Siegel's Flamingo after Siegel was murdered in 1947, and when he sold it to Morris Lansburgh of Miami Beach in 1960, Meyer Lansky landed a $200,000 finder's fee, and it was assumed Lansky maintained some silent points in the casino.[26] Over the years, Albert Parvin had been accused of being a front man for Lansky, having employed Edward Levinson, who had been identified as Lansky's bagman in Las Vegas.[27] After selling the Flamingo in 1960, P-D purchased the Freemont and Aladdin hotels, and it was reported that Parvin's Vegas interests contributed $28,000 per month to the foundation. But there was more.

Still others have described the Parvin Foundation as a "pass-through" for funds of both the CIA and the underworld. Federal courts and Congress have divulged some of these links over the years, including contentions that at least some of Parvin's altruism may have involved setting up third world tax shelters for U.S. hoodlums.[28] The company also showed special interest in countries where gambling concessions were up for grabs, such as Cuba and the Dominican Republic. In his speech, Ford noted that in 1963 Parvin began donating educational materials to the regime of the newly installed DR president, Juan Bosch, during a time when he was still mulling over who should be granted that country's casino gambling license. However, when the concession was granted to Nevada's Cliff Jones, Parvin disappeared. "When this happened," Ford said, "the further interest of the Albert Parvin Foundation in the Dominican Republic abruptly ceased. I am told that some of the educational-television equipment already delivered was simply abandoned in its original crates."

In Beverly Hills, former Chicagoan Albert Parvin was well-known to former Chicagoan Sidney Korshak, who later testified to being his friend and

---

*Douglas was not the only Chicago-born Supreme Court justice with dubious business interests. Recall that Justice Arthur J. Goldberg was a partner with Ziffren, Drown, and Kirkeby in the San Diego Hotel investment (chapter 5).

fellow Hillcrest member.[29] In fact, Korshak had owned stock in P-D since 1962, when it was called the Starrett Corporation. Parvin was also plugged into the Greg Bautzer nexus: Bautzer's partner Harvey Silbert, who operated the Riviera for Korshak, was also on the Parvin Foundation.[30] Korshak and Silbert were both directors of Cedars-Sinai Hospital.[31]

According to testimony, Parvin expressed to Korshak that he was tired of doing business in Vegas and was looking to get out. He was "weary of all the problems in Las Vegas," as one Korshak account put it. Once again, timing played into the fortunes of the Supermob. Since Vegas' recent passage of the Corporate Gaming Act predicted a corporate takeover of the industry, there appeared to be no way for the hoods to compete with Hughes and the rest— their era seemed to have passed. But if they were able to maintain a presence via the indiscreet P-D operation, the cash flow would remain intact.

The Parvin-as-front theory gained traction in July 1968, when LAPD intel reported that Korshak, Dalitz, Dorfman, Lansky's Wallace Groves, and Mrs. Hoffa (standing in for imprisoned Jimmy) had met at La Costa, ostensibly to discuss the sale of the Stardust to P-D. Initially, Dalitz did not want to sell, but it was believed by law enforcement that he was ordered by Meyer Lansky to do so. For the record, Sid Korshak took the credit. In later SEC testimony, Korshak explained, "I told Mr. Dalitz that I thought in view of the fact that he was sick—he had related that to me—he was undergoing a series of tests, there was trouble with a kidney, I believe the other kidney was beginning to become infected too. Mr. Dalitz was past seventy, that he ought to give serious thought to selling the Stardust."[32]

When Dalitz caved, it would be at least the third time that Korshak took a fee (a whopping $500,000) for helping the Stardust find an owner. Korshak was unabashedly proud of what many believed was an exorbitant fee. "I did an excellent job for the Parvin-Dohrmann Company," Korshak later said. "And my fee was a very inadequate one." He stated he based that assertion on the fact that the total sale price was $45 million.[33]

Lastly, with Harvey Silbert's help, a deal was also quickly negotiated for P-D to purchase the Riviera. Don Winne, a Justice Department attorney assigned to the Strike Force, expressed the Bureau's fears about Korshak's plan in a 1970 memo that stated, "If allowed to escape unscathed, which so far it has, it will allow the Riviera to be allowed to capitalize their skim on the stock market."[34]

In later SEC testimony, Korshak put a benign spin on the notorious Las Vegas hotel turnover rate: "There were half a dozen people talking to me at different times about possible acquisitions in Nevada. They would have been companies I was close to, probably represented. There was a period

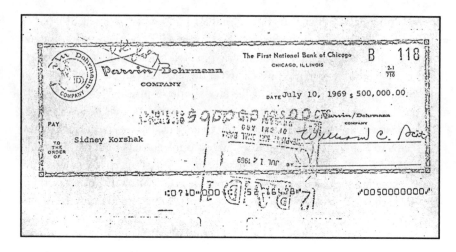

Sid Korshak's paycheck for his help in arranging the 1968 sale of the Stardust to Parvin-Dohrmann (SEC Parvin-Dohrmann Evidence File, Southern District Court of New York)

immediately following Mr. Howard Hughes's acquisitions where everybody became interested in making an acquisition in Nevada . . . Every day someone was interested in selling, buying, everybody—if business was good, I guess they would say it is fine; if business was bad, they would say, 'Why do I need it?' If there was an adverse newspaper story, people would say, 'I don't want it. I am going to get out of here. There is an onus on Vegas.' That might change two days later." Korshak also described how he consulted for G&W, Hilton, and Hyatt regarding Vegas acquisitions.[35]

All that was left was for Korshak and Coleman to buy controlling stock interest in Parvin-Dohrmann, and for that, Coleman had to come up with some serious cash. Thus, in August of 1968, Coleman sold his Seeburg stock to Commonwealth United for $9.6 million.[36] With cash in hand, and while Albert Parvin took off for an extended African safari, Coleman and Korshak went to work. Before raiding Parvin's stock, the duo made certain their plan was foolproof by eliciting advance interest in Parvin with numerous money managers, including a new offshore company that specialized in investing the monies of millionaires at such a frantic pace that its collapse was all but inevitable.[37] On October 10, 1968, Coleman and Korshak began talking up the P-D stock to the Swiss-based investment company named Investors Overseas Services (IOS), a bold international mutual-fund investment house that just happened to have two Korshak friends on its board, former California governor Pat Brown and FDR's son James Roosevelt.

IOS was the brainchild of former New Yorker Bernard (Benno) Cornfeld, interestingly, a friend of Korshak's great friend Jill St. John. Because it was based offshore, IOS was free of regulation, and its investments were largely secret, although it was known to speculate in casinos worldwide. By the late sixties IOS managed $2.5 billion; however, chroniclers of the firm concluded that it was "so steeped in financial and intellectual dishonesty and directed so recklessly that it was absurd that it should have been entrusted with so much of other people's money."[38]

Organized crime expert Hank Messick neatly summed up the IOS style: "The company bought stock for anonymous customers from public corporations which ran the casinos, and there was no way to tell if the purchaser was Meyer Lansky or Henry Ford II."[39] Of those investments that were known, IOS held huge blocks of Resorts International and Caesars Palace, and Bernie Cornfeld also shared Lansky's skim courier Sylvain Ferdman. Cornfeld also shared Vicki Morgan with Ronnie Reagan's Kitchen Cabinet member Alfred Bloomingdale.*[40] Lastly, Cornfeld was also known to be a guest at the mob getaway retreat, Acapulco Towers.[41]

Cornfeld divided his time between a sumptuous chalet in Geneva and Douglas Fairbanks's former thirty-five-room mansion, Grayhall, in Beverly Hills. He always had girls around, including Victoria Principal, later of the hit series *Dallas*, who got a London court order against Cornfeld for roughing her up.

IOS's James Roosevelt had a checkered professional career and was usually brought into companies solely for his name recognition. He had worked for Sam Goldwyn in 1938, but failed as a movie producer; he became friends with Chicago's Arthur Greene and invested in Store Properties with the notorious Alex Greenberg, Paul Ziffren, and Sam Genis; in the early fifties, he ran unsuccessfully for mayor of Los Angeles and then governor of California. It was Roosevelt who brought Pat Brown to the IOS board.[42]

Since his 1966 gubernatorial loss to Reagan, Brown had been a partner at the prestigious L.A. law firm of Ball, Hunt, Hart, Brown, and Baerwitz. Once aboard Cornfeld's IOS, Brown in turn brought in his California treasurer of the Democratic Party, attorney Barry Sterling, as president of IOS

---

*Bloomingdale, who had a fetish for taping his trysts with Morgan, died of cancer in 1982. One year later, Morgan was beaten to death with a baseball bat. Three days later, Robert Steinberg, a prominent Beverly Hills attorney, said that he had received three videotapes that depicted orgies whose participants included Vicki Morgan and several other women, Bloomingdale, two high-level members of the Reagan administration, and a congressman. The tapes were reported stolen and have never surfaced.

Financial Holdings.[43] Board member Dr. Pierre Rinfret made note of Brown's self-interest when he attempted to use the IOS to gain work for his law firm in other countries, such as Argentina. Over the objections of other IOS board members such as Rinfret, Brown also helped bring controversial financier Robert Vesco aboard IOS.[44] Before he was finished, Vesco transferred about $500 million from the IOS fund into his personal accounts. He ultimately absconded and has been a fugitive from American justice ever since.*

On October 11, 1968, Parvin signed the agreement to purchase the Stardust, pending approval of a license by the Gaming Commission, which meant that control of the company would not officially pass into Coleman's hands until the license was granted sometime in January 1969.

On November 5, 1968, the nation went to the polls, electing "law and order" candidate Richard Nixon by a slim .7 percent of the vote over Democratic incumbent vice president Hubert Humphrey. At the time of the vote, a key issue was whether the opposing North and South Vietnamese would attend the scheduled Paris Peace Talks, a discussion that it was hoped would shorten a conflict that had already taken over thirty-eight thousand American and over one million Vietnamese lives. What the voters could not know at the time was that Nixon's camp had orchestrated events in such a way as to guarantee that the U.S. allies of the South Vietnamese delegation would decline to participate in the talks. That failure to appear guaranteed Nixon's electoral victory and prolonged the war by another five years and an additional 20,763 U.S. lives. Nixon's fix was known as the October Surprise, and the successful ploy would be revisited by Ronald Reagan's campaign trust

---

*Vesco, the undisputed king of the fugitive financiers, fled to Costa Rica in 1973 to avoid standing trial for the IOS theft. Shortly before Vesco left, he delivered $200,000 in illegal campaign contributions to Richard Nixon's reelection campaign. The money was stuffed in a suitcase and handed over to campaign treasurer Maurice Stans, who ended up paying a $5,000 fine for "nonwillful violation" of campaign-finance laws. Vesco was indicted in absentia. He was indicted yet again in 1989 on drug-smuggling charges. From Costa Rica, Vesco hopscotched to the Bahamas, Antigua, Nicaragua, and, finally, Cuba, where he has lived for the past two decades and, since 1995, been domiciled in a Cuban jail. Vesco was convicted in connection with an alleged scheme to defraud Cuba's pharmaceutical industry. Also arrested by the Cubans was Vesco's partner and houseguest Donald Nixon, nephew of the former president. Nixon was allowed to return to the United States, but Vesco went to the slammer. He gets out in 2009, when he'll be seventy-four. Vesco's Cuban wife, Lidia, was convicted on lesser charges and in 2005 was scheduled for release, but it has yet to occur.

twelve years later.* After the inauguration, according to Howard Hughes aide Robert Maheu, Hughes quickly sent Nixon an envelope containing $100,000 in cash. Congressional investigators such as Terry Lenzner believed the cash was given to guarantee Hughes favorable government treatment for his casino and airline businesses. At the time, Hughes needed federal approval for his desired takeover of Air West, and the payoff to Nixon guaranteed it.† All told, over the years, Hughes had given Nixon at least $505,000 that is known.[45] As Hughes told Maheu, "Bob, remember that there is no person in the world that I can't either buy or destroy."[46]

On January 10, 1969, with everything in place, Coleman purchased 300,000 shares of Parvin-Dohrmann stock via five different brokers for $35 a share;[47] Acapulco Towers partner Phil Levin bought 9 percent of Parvin's stock (129,000 shares), while Sidney Korshak purchased 10,000. Sidney also tipped off his brother and other friends to Parvin, as the stock was about to explode. Among those who took the advice, to the tune of a thousand shares apiece, were Marshall, Jill St. John, Eddie Torres (the manager of the Riviera), New York's Herzfeld brothers, and Harold Butler, president of Denny's Restaurants in California. Lesser investors were Korshak's Teamsters Pension Fund trustee liaison Donald Peters, William Bartholomay, president of the Atlanta Braves baseball team (in which Coleman was a stockholder), and Charlie Finley, owner of the Oakland Athletics baseball team. St. John later said she was first told of the Parvin investment when she and her soon-to-be-ex-husband, Jack Jones, dined with Sid and Bee Korshak and Coleman in October 1968 at New York's La Grenouille, a Korshak favorite.[48]

At corporate headquarters, Korshak began to dominate Parvin-Dohrmann, to the extent that he attended board meetings from which the president of the company, William Scott, was excluded. "Coleman did not make a move without clearing it with Sid Korshak," a chairman of another

---

*In 1996, the author investigated this affair for Irish author Anthony Summers in furtherance of research for Summers's Nixon biography, *The Arrogance of Power* (Viking, 2000). Among the many interviews I conducted was the first-ever on-the-record conversation (2-11-96) with the key intermediary in the affair, Anna Chennault. Her information was corroborated by numerous other interviews and documents. (See Summers, 297–308.)

†Hughes made certain that the previous Air West ownership would sell to him by convincing friends to temporarily dump their shares (over eighty-six thousand) to depress the company's stock. (Maheu and Hack, *Next to Hughes*, 229.)

company was quoted as saying. In addition, this businessman indicated, "When it came to a deal point, Del Coleman would excuse himself and call Korshak." Korshak even hired a new director for the company, Sol Cantor of New York.[49]

Korshak and Coleman next sold 143,000 Parvin shares to Cornfeld's IOS and other investment firms, then took $4 million from that sale and reinvested it in Parvin stock to create a false appearance of investor interest—the stock rose from $68 to $150.[50]

After the Stardust deal was consummated in February 1969, Korshak and Coleman sprung a trap on Denny's president Harold Butler when they convinced him to merge with P-D. Within the agreement, Denny's was to purchase the Parvin-Dohrmann stock of Korshak and his friends for $150 a share. Soon, Korshak's friends began selling their shares of the company at the falsely inflated high rates. Marshall Korshak admitted parlaying his initial $35,000 investment into a $125,000 sale, for a fast $90,000 profit.[51] What he didn't offer was that he was vacationing at the mob-frequented La Costa Resort when his brother Sidney had called to invite him into the investment group.[52]

On May 5, 1969, before Sidney could sell off his ten thousand shares (for a profit of $1.1 million in less than a year), the SEC and American Stock Exchange, alarmed at the rapid rise in the price of the stock, intervened and halted trading, causing a devastating effect on the Parvin-Dohrmann stock. In addition, the SEC began to investigate Parvin-Dohrmann stockholders such as Jill St. John, Marshall Korshak, and fifteen other defendants. Korshak went into "fixer" mode and enlisted the help of Washington lawyer Nathan M. Voloshen, an old friend of the Speaker of the House, John W. McCormack. Korshak friend and D.C. power attorney Edward Bennett Williams had told him that Voloshen had the requisite congressional contacts. Korshak later said, "It was a matter of common knowledge that Mr. Voloshen was known around Washington."[53] Korshak wanted Voloshen to bring pressure on the SEC to relax its trading restriction on Parvin-Dohrmann.

According to lobbyist Robert Winter-Berger, McCormack was illegally renting Voloshen a portion of his rent-free Speaker's office for $2,500 a month. From this point of influence, Voloshen and Dr. Martin Sweig, chief administrative aide to McCormack, were essentially providing "access" for a fee; and even the most notorious criminals were able to buy influence, among them Mafia gambling expert Salvatore Granello; Manuel Bello, a close associate of New England Mafia boss Raymond Patriarca; and New York labor racketeer Jack McCarthy.[54] Interestingly, Voloshen was getting these crime syndicate contacts through New York labor racketeer George

Scalise,[55] who'd risen to prominence with the assistance of Sid Korshak (see chapter 3).

Korshak later testified that Voloshen initially wanted $150,000 for his efforts, but that Korshak talked him down: "I stated to Mr. Voloshen that there was a possibility of getting him some future business from Mr. Coleman." Korshak then revealed a bit of his secret negotiating style: "I have had conversations like this with lawyers many, many times, saying to them, 'Don't worry about your initial fee, there may be other work. You may find yourself being used again,' and so forth. It is part of bargaining with a lawyer on the possibility of a reduction of a fee."[56]

The day after the stock sales were suspended—and the day after Korshak made his call—mountains were moved for Del Coleman. "With amazing speed," wrote lobbyist Robert Winter-Berger, "Speaker John McCormack set up a meeting for eleven o'clock the next morning, May 6, in the office of [SEC chairman] Hamer Budge." And one week later, the trading ban was indeed lifted, albeit temporarily.[57] Throughout the summer of 1969, as the SEC investigated the labyrinthine world of Korshak, Coleman, and Parvin, the stock valuations for Parvin-Dohrmann were in free fall.

Lurking in the shadows was Korshak nemesis Howard Hughes, hoping to buy the beleaguered Parvin-Dohrmann. Unbeknownst to Korshak and Coleman, on June 6, 1969, Hughes wrote a memo to aide Robert Maheu that read:

Bob—
I would be ecstatic at the prospect of purchasing Parvin . . . Do you think this could really be accomplished? I just assumed that the critics of monopoly would rule it out.

If this could be accomplished, I think it would be a ten strike and might change all of my plans.

Please reply. Most urgent,

Howard[58]

The Hughes purchase never materialized.

While Sid Korshak anticipated the SEC's inquiry, at least a couple of gratifying occurrences improved both his personal and business life. His youngest son, Stuart, received his BA from Yale, graduating magna cum laude. (In

1975, he would receive his law degree from UC Davis and take a position in the firm of his father's pals Eugene Wyman and Greg Bautzer.)

Sidney's oldest son, Harry, after returning from a Far East stint in the Peace Corps, took up with Virginia Berman, the free-spirited stepdaughter of recently deceased legendary film producer Pando S. Berman.* "Harry brought acid back from Indonesia and turned the whole world on— including me," said Virginia. She recalled that the couple's hippie lifestyle did not go over well with the Korshaks, especially Bee. "[Bee spoke] so poorly of her son Harry, and I would think, 'Boy, if she's saying that about her blood, what the hell is she saying about me?'" Virginia, however, passed muster with Sidney, who seemed to appreciate her feisty nature. "Sidney did not scare me or intimidate me, and I think that's why he liked me," Virginia remembered. "Also, I was the niece of Sidney Buchman, the blacklisted screenwriter who worked for Harry Cohn, Sidney's great friend. So I was okay."†

According to Virginia, when the couple married in 1968 and moved into a $275 apartment in "the slums of Beverly Hills," Korshak did his best to improve the living situation. "He had a top decorator come in and decorate it for eighty thousand dollars—wallpaper, chandeliers, but tastefully done," recalled Virginia. "Great apartment; had an upstairs and downstairs." When Harry and Virginia adopted a daughter, Katie, in 1970, Sidney bought them a proper home that had formerly belonged to jazz legend (and fellow Chicagoan) Mel Tormé.

Harry and Virginia divorced after four and a half years, with Virginia taking custody of Katie. Still, the Korshaks continued to support their ex-daughter-in-law and new granddaughter, even persuading Virginia to not move away with a new boyfriend. But everything changed when Virginia suffered a debilitating brain aneurysm in March 1976, two months after her thirtieth birthday, and endured subsequent surgery. After a few years of trying to raise Katie despite her illness, Sid and Bee showed up with "papers," adopting Katie at age twelve and raising her as their own daughter. "I didn't have it in me to fight," said Virginia. "My mother was the one who was fighting." Sadly, as the years progressed, Virginia's contact with her daughter decreased until it faded away altogether.[59]

* * *

---

*Among the numerous credits of the Thalberg Award winner: *Citizen Kane, Room Service, Top Hat, The Hunchback of Notre Dame, The Brothers Karamazov, Butterfield 8, The Prize, Sweet Bird of Youth*, and *Jailhouse Rock*.
†Buchman's credits include *Lost Horizon, Mr. Smith Goes to Washington*, and *Cleopatra*.

After the June 6, 1969, death of his Associated Booking Company (ABC) partner, Joe Glaser, Korshak assumed control over ABC and thus became the sole user of its office on 9477 Brighton Way in Beverly Hills, an office with an unmarked door, where he tended to the occasional clerical necessities. Korshak was listed as the executor of Glaser's probate, filed in Los Angeles, while the conservator was designated as Mary Oppenheim, then a partner in Sidney and Marshall Korshak's Chicago firm. The attorney for the L.A. estate was Paul Ziffren's attorney, Isaac Pacht. Glaser's probate listed his net worth at $3 million, with numerous investments in companies represented by Sidney, such as Hyatt Hotels and the Parvin-Dohrmann Company. In Glaser's will, Sidney's sons Harry and Stuart received savings bonds valued at $11,000 each.[60]

Producer Jerry Tokofsky, who often had to meet with Korshak at the Brighton Way office, recalled that more than musical acts were booked out of Korshak's ABC operation. "Every Friday, a parade of beautiful women would ride the elevator up to ABC's office," Tokofsky said. "Sidney would be slouched behind the desk, where he'd give each woman a packet of money. That embarrassed me, since I knew about two thirds of them." According to Tokofsky, the women weren't singers, but hookers, living on stipends from Korshak.*[61] Sidney's daughter-in-law Virginia (Harry's wife) also got a glimpse of the girl action when she was dating Korshak's son. "I saw Sidney in the presence of girlfriends of mine, up at my home, bringing out wads and wads of money," Virginia said. "It was in my house; one was an actress who's no longer with us, who used to turn tricks for George Raft. Sidney was getting them work with men—as prostitutes."[62]

That summer, Korshak successfully mediated—via the sweetheart deal—strike threats by Las Vegas Teamsters, which comprised front-desk clerks and switchboard operators. As per his custom, Korshak negotiated a deal for the Riviera in which the employees ended up with a substandard contract. The Nevada Resort Association, which represented other hotels, held out and got better terms.[63]

On the negative side, two minor nuisances appeared in the form of seminal investigative books by Ovid Demaris and Ed Reid. Demaris's study of

---

*An FBI memo notes another alleged Korshak side venture: "Korshak had a strong-room built at the home of [DELETED] in West Los Angeles. The purpose of this room, according to the police source, was for storing furs and jewelry but could also be used for the storage of papers and records" (FBI memo, DELETED to SAC L.A., 7-30-76, #90-183-172). Interestingly, Mike Brodkin, one of the Chicago Outfit's regular attorneys from the firm Bieber & Brodkin, once told a friend, "I bought a fur coat from Korshak's wife. I complained to Sidney because it was a piece of shit" (confidential int.).

Chicago corruption, *Captive City,* was the first book to call attention, albeit in passing, to the Bazelon-Ziffren-Greenberg real estate partnerships. Reid's *Grim Reapers* was a state-by-state explication of the hidden partnerships between the organized crime syndicate and the business world. Reid paid particular attention to political corruption in Chicago, California, and Las Vegas, where he named both the owners of record and the secret investors in the casinos. Although the books were met with critical acclaim, they failed to inspire official action, especially in "law and order" President Nixon's Department of Justice, run by Attorney General John Mitchell.

Whereas Korshak and the Supermob had succeeded in crafting an invulnerable world for themselves, their original underworld facilitators were in the early stages of their endgame. The proverbial "nail in the coffin" was the passage of the Organized Crime Control Act of 1970, the most important aspect of which was a section entitled Racketeer Influenced and Corrupt Organizations, or RICO, crafted largely by one of Bobby Kennedy's Justice Department subordinates, G. Robert Blakey. Now the feds would be able to indict not only entire crime organizations by showing a pattern of criminal activity over ten years, but also anyone who could be shown to be involved in said organization. Such associations would not be easy to prove, but at least it was now possible to make war on the "organized" part of organized crime.

Combined with the Omnibus Crime Control and Safe Streets Act of 1968, Title III of which sanctioned court-approved wiretaps, RICO would eventually decimate criminal organizations in every major city. (During the next decade, over twenty Mafia bosses were indicted and most were convicted.) The FBI heard one New York mob boss complain, "Under RICO, no matter who the fuck we are, if we're together, they'll get every fuckin' one of us." Interestingly, the first prosecutor to successfully navigate the intricacies of RICO was an Italian U.S. attorney in New York City named Rudolph Giuliani, who worked tirelessly for years to create the templates for the first RICO convictions.

Nonetheless, the likes of Korshak, Ziffren, Hart, Bazelon, and the rest were deemed off-limits, despite the mass of FBI data and local intelligence reports such as a recent LAPD memo that noted Detroit mob boss Anthony Giacalone's stay at Korshak's villa at La Costa.

Throughout the summer of 1969, Sid Korshak began to tire in his role as the go-to man regarding the Acapulco Towers. "You know, the problem here is that all the partners keep calling me," he complained to Phil Levin. "I don't know anything about it. Al Hart is the fellow that is in charge of it, but they all bother me." Korshak then asked Levin if Transnation would be interested in buying the hotel outright if Korshak could convince his L.A. consortium and Moe Morton to sell for their original purchase price. "Fine," said Levin. "It is a million-dollar deal."[64]

Korshak was able to convince the partners to sell, and on September 9, 1969, the Acapulco Towers investors signed a contract to release the condo to Levin's G&W spin-off, Transnation, for $1 million. But that was not the only Transnation transaction consummated on September 9. Since the spring of 1969, Chicago Thoroughbred Enterprise (CTE) president Marge Everett had been seeking a buyer for her debt-ridden operation. By coincidence, Chicago native Ed Weisl Sr., the same Gulf & Western counsel who had assisted in the Paramount purchase, was also a director of CTE.[65] Soon, Everett was steered to Gulf's Transnation as a potential buyer. Everett, like her father a staunch anticrime activist, had no idea that her nemesis Sidney Korshak was behind Transnation's Levin, nor was she aware of Levin's own questionable connections. After Levin succeeded in hooking Transnation, he spent the summer buying up shares of CTE for himself and his wife, Janice.

When the Levins stopped buying on September 9, they owned 79,200 shares, or 30 percent of the company, and on September 22, Transnation bought another 42 percent. Transnation also bought huge blocks of Santa Anita, Hialeah, and Hollywood Park racetracks in Southern California. The buying spree continued as Transnation also bought the Madison Square Garden Corporation and, with Korshak's help, obtained a $16 million Teamster loan for the construction of a thousand-room hotel near Chicago's O'Hare International Airport. Although Gulf officials admitted to the *New York Times* that they paid Korshak a $150,000 finder's fee, no paper record of it was maintained in their files. (Five years later, Korshak would become the G&W's $50,000-per-year labor consultant, which Bluhdorn engineered by firing Theodore Kheel, whom columnist Jack Newfield called "the best labor attorney in the city." Soon after Korshak's hiring, G&W's Washington Park and Arlington Park tracks were granted more racing days by the Illinois Racing Board: increased from 50 to 67, and 84 to 109, respectively.[66]

Still unaware that Korshak was in the shadows, Marge Everett received $21 million for her stock in CTE and was given a $50,000-per-year job as an executive.

On September 15, 1969, less than a week after these deals were consummated, a long-overdue profile of Korshak appeared in the *Los Angeles*

Times, entitled SIDNEY KORSHAK: THE MAN WHO MAKES THINGS HAPPEN. In the piece, written by staff writer Paul Steiger, Korshak was portrayed as a shadowy power broker, about whom nothing illegal could be proven, despite his obvious relationships with the Capone gang. Ed Guthman, then national editor of the paper, recently spoke of how the article came about.

"I had first heard of Korshak when I came to L.A. in 1965," Guthman said in 2004. "It was understood whom he represented, and that when he came into a room, his wishes were carried out. When the Dodgers bought the new stadium, Korshak said, 'This is the way it's going to be'—and it was. He had incredible power. And I don't know any place else where somebody had that kind of power. And I don't know why he had it here, but he sure as hell had it."[67]

For his part, Paul Steiger, now the managing editor of the *Wall Street Journal*, became aware of Korshak through his coverage of the ongoing Parvin-stock roller-coaster ride and the SEC investigation. Steiger traveled to Chicago and Washington over four months in his effort to "background" his subject. "The public record on him was enormously slim," Steiger said.[68] Guthman summarized the Korshak research, saying, "The reporter [Steiger] never found his name on a public record: no property, no civil suits, no nothing."

Nonetheless, Steiger soon learned that the *private* accounts of Korshak were ubiquitous. "I discovered that he was everywhere," he remembered. "When Walter O'Malley had parking problems at Dodger Stadium, there was Korshak to work out a deal with the Teamsters; he was involved with the casinos in Vegas; he was a mob lawyer in Chicago." Then, just as Frank McCulloch had experienced when he dared to surface Korshak's role in the 1962 Dodger Stadium episode, Sidney's good friends weighed in, trying to apply the velvet hammer.

"I got a call from Gene Wyman," recalled Steiger, "who said, 'I understand that you're doing a story on my good friend Sidney Korshak. I just want you to know that this guy is the subject of a lot of false and malicious rumors—he's really a sweetheart of a guy. Why don't you come over to the Hillcrest Country Club and we'll have lunch and I'll tell you about him?' Here I am a kid reporter who's never been to Hillcrest, and my head was spinning with all these retired stars and power brokers who were there. I said, 'I'd really love to talk to Mr. Korshak.' He said, 'Well, as soon as we get a better sense of what questions you want to ask him—he doesn't really give interviews—I might be able to prevail upon him, depending.'"

Declining the Hillcrest offer, Steiger soon learned of another Korshak interloper: "All of a sudden I become aware of the fact, I think from a senior editor, that Lew Wasserman called Otis [Chandler] and said, 'This brat you have in the business section has been asking slanderous questions about Sidney Korshak. Yeah, there's this history in Chicago, but he's an important guy in the community . . .' and so on. Now, Wasserman calling is pretty heady stuff." The last person to try to instill fear in Steiger was the Dodgers' Walter O'Malley, who literally yelled at the young reporter on the phone, "You don't know what you're dealing with here, kid!"

Korshak never responded to Steiger's requests for an interview. "I never met or heard from Korshak," Steiger said. West Coast Teamster boss and Korshak associate Andy Anderson remembered how reporters used to ask him to intercede with Sidney. "They'd come to me and say, 'Andy, we've got some money to give you if you can make a connection for us.' I said, 'You want me to make a connection with Sidney?' 'Yeah.' I said, 'I won't do it. You guys are big boys, you go call him up, and if he wants to be interviewed, he'll tell you.' He would never give an interview to anybody on the *L.A. Times* or anywhere else."[69]

Steiger forged ahead and wrote an article that assiduously avoided outright accusations. "When Paul wrote the story," remembered Guthman, "the lawyers looked at it and the publisher looked at it, and they determined that we didn't really have the stuff to back up what we *believed* to be the case. I just remember the frustration that they had that there was nothing. Of course, when we did it, he was still alive." Guthman was alluding to the fact that Korshak's FBI files were then unobtainable.

Steiger actually believed there was much more to the Korshak story, but could not say so in print. In 2004, with Korshak now gone and his FBI file open, Steiger felt free to say what he couldn't write in 1969. "He was a mobbed-up bad guy, involved with La Costa, Vegas—" he concluded in a recent interview. "Sweetheart contracts were wrong. He used the glamour of Hollywood and the panache of his connections to front for some bad people. I have no doubt that he was involved in illegal and criminal-minded stuff in the Parvin case. That case was pretty well made. It's certainly plausible that there was some conning going on, letting his reputation precede him. But he was not averse to going across the line, but how often and to what extent, I don't know."

Before his story appeared, Steiger considered any number of ways it might be received by Los Angelenos, but afterward, he was shocked by a reaction he could not have anticipated. "I got three calls after the piece ran from people who wanted to know if I could give them his address or phone number because they wanted him to represent them," said a bemused Steiger. "Everybody thought it was an advertisement," Korshak boasted to one associate.

Steiger's piece left Korshak shaken but not stirred. "Sidney was very upset about the articles over Parvin because the bad publicity had an impact on those investments," said friend and fellow attorney Leo Geffner. "He thought he got a raw deal on that lawsuit, that the SEC was prejudiced because of the *L.A. Times* article."[70] According to one source, Korshak made certain it never happened again.

Not long after the Steiger profile appeared, *Los Angeles Times* matriarch Buff Chandler showed up at the Bistro in her ongoing effort to coax contributions from the well-heeled clientele for her Los Angeles Music Center. According to a companion who accompanied her, when Chandler approached Korshak, he made it known that he did not appreciate the recent exposé. "She approached Sidney at the Bistro one day when he was lunching there with [Teamsters president] Frank Fitzsimmons," said the companion. "He took out his checkbook and told her he'd give her $25,000 on the spot on one condition: his name would never appear in the *Los Angeles Times* again. Buff agreed, and he handed over the check."[71] Unlike his previous attempt to buy anonymity from the paper, this time Korshak's payout did the trick; the check was not returned, and the paper never published another article about the Fixer in his lifetime.

On October 16, 1969, one month after Steiger's article, the SEC issued a press release detailing a multiple-count charge against Coleman, Korshak, et al. The complaint maintained that Coleman had filed false and misleading reports with the SEC and the American Stock Exchange, concealed the true identity of the participants in his takeover group as well as the dates on which some of them had joined the group, and withheld the circumstances surrounding the fact that some were able to buy the shares at a deflated price. In addition, numerous Parvin-Dohrmann press releases were distributed that were false or misleading, with the cumulative effect being to manipulate the price of P-D stock.

With regard to the insider tips given to Korshak's pals, the SEC added that the defendants sought to "manipulate the market price of shares of Parvin-Dohrmann and then engage in a fraudulent plan to confer a substantial benefit upon certain Parvin-Dohrmann shares in the form of a payment of a cash premium for their Parvin-Dohrmann shares at the same time that the uninformed public shareholders of Parvin-Dohrmann were to receive a stock package of shares of Denny's Restaurants, Inc., worth substantially less."

As the days progressed, the news got worse for Coleman and Korshak, with baseball commissioner Bowie Kuhn simultaneously opening an inquiry into the Parvin stock holdings of team owners Bartholomay and Finley. Lastly, a Parvin-Dohrmann stockholder, Dr. David Gardner of New Mexico, filed suit against Coleman, Korshak, and six other P-D officers, charging them with illegal stock manipulations. Dr. Gardner sought $100 million in damages.[72] (Meanwhile, in 1969, Justice Douglas quietly resigned from the Albert Parvin Foundation, explaining that it was "too heavy a workload" for him.)

It only took two weeks for Del Coleman to knuckle under and settle with the SEC, agreeing (1) not to merge with Denny's or anyone else, (2) to testify about Korshak and others, and (3) to divulge Korshak's $500,000 finder's fee to other stockholders.[73] The decision would eventually add Coleman to the growing list of Korshak's sworn enemies such as Howard Hughes and Marge Everett. Coleman's former partner at Seeburg, Herbert Siegel, recalled running into Korshak at the posh New York restaurant "21." "If your ex-partner isn't careful," Korshak intoned, "he's going to be wearing cement shoes."[74]

CHAPTER 16

Coming Under Attack

GOVERNOR REAGAN FACED a political embarrassment. As 1970 began, his state was mired in a strike by racetrack employees demanding a $4-a-day raise in a desire for parity with employees of Eastern tracks like Belmont Park in New York. The work stoppage, which was costing California $300,000 a day in tax revenue, had started the previous December 2 and by mid-January 1970 had become a serious financial issue, with $2 million already lost at Santa Anita alone. That track, the main one affected, missed its December 26 opening day and feared that the entire season, which was to end in April, would be a washout.

Sid Korshak, who represented the track owners through their Federation of California Racing Associations, told the press that his clients were firm in their position. "I am the chief negotiator for the tracks," Korshak pronounced. "There is no question in my mind that their offer of a $2-a-day raise is the last and final one, even if it means no season at all this year."[1] His counterpart, Leo Geffner, attorney for the striking AFL-CIO Service Employees International Union, began meeting informally with Korshak. "There have been a number of informal meetings," Geffner told the press, "including one held this past Tuesday at the Bistro Restaurant with only Korshak and myself."[2] In fact, for a two-week period, Korshak arranged for all the negotiators to take suites at the Beverly Hills Hotel, where they worked over breakfasts, lunches, and dinners in the Polo Lounge.

Geffner recently recalled not only the strike, but also the labor prowess of his longtime friendly opposition, Sid Korshak:

> I met Sidney in 1961 during my first negotiations with the Building Services Employees Union, which represented the pari-mutuel clerks, ticket sellers, ushers. Sid represented the tracks and I represented the Unions. The Building Services Union's president came out of Chicago and was

very close to Sidney. The tracks wanted Sidney not because he was a particularly skillful negotiator, but because he knew all these people and he had the best entrée to them. They wouldn't strike because of their friendship with Sidney.

Sidney always felt that he was representing management, but he was very pro-union. He never had an inkling to break a union. His whole style was that you compromise to get an agreement and avoid a strike. Sidney could get the best deal because the union leaders were friends of his. Sidney got in trouble with the ownership sometimes because he didn't always tell them what he had agreed to. He just felt it was more important to get the strike settled. Once they went ballistic and had to call emergency meetings. They had to agree to it, but they were furious at him.[3]

With the crisis beginning to nip at the governor's heels, a decision was made to make a personal, and private, overture to Korshak. Accounts differ as to whether Kitchen Cabinet member (and Korshak client) Diners Club president Alfred Bloomingdale suggested the gambit to Nancy Reagan, or Nancy brought the idea to Bloomingdale, but a close Reagan aide was soon sent to call on the Fixer. ("When Mrs. Reagan told Alfred to go to Sidney Korshak if he had to, I nearly fell over," said the factotum.)

The Reagan emissary met clandestinely with Korshak at the Riviera's booking office on Wilshire "in a room with no windows, no name on the door, no listed address." After imploring Korshak to work some sort of compromise as a personal favor to Reagan, Korshak gave his pronouncement.

"If that's what he wants, then the employees will return to work Monday morning," a smiling Korshak decreed, but on one condition. "I just want the governor and his wife to know who did them a favor."[4]

On Monday morning, as Korshak promised, the twenty-eight-day-old strike ended and the tracks opened. Bloomingdale's aide said, "I'll be damned if the union pickets didn't suddenly disappear and the deadlock that had gripped both sides for twenty-eight days didn't miraculously melt away, and lo and behold, if it wasn't post time exactly when Sidney Korshak said it would be."

"I just heard he had union connections," Mrs. Reagan later told reporters. "I've still never seen any proof that he's a mob lawyer. And neither has Ron."[5] The Bloomingdale aide said, "I don't know if Korshak ever collected on that favor because I never asked. But since then I've always thought of Nancy Reagan as the female version of the Godfather because she's certainly a woman who knows how to get things done without leaving any fingerprints."[6] Thanks to Korshak, Californians now started referring to Reagan as a "great labor peacemaker."

Although the California tracks were back to normal, the Illinois race venues controlled by CTE and its new parent, Transnation, were soon to enter a period of turmoil. The problems started when Korshak pal Phil Levin fired Marge Everett from her "golden parachute" management position on March 4, 1970. Over the last few months of the new relationship, Everett and Transnation fought bitterly over finances and other managerial decisions, with one CTE officer referring to the opinionated Everett as "a bitch."[7] That is the well-known version of the story, but according to one Everett confidant, there was more. "Right after they made the deal to buy CTE, Marge met with Bluhdorn [of Transnation's parent, Gulf & Western] in New York," said the friend. "And Bluhdorn said, 'I got some bad news for you. These guys really don't want to be in business with you.' She said, 'What do you mean?' He explained that they, meaning the mob, had used Transnation to get the tracks. Even Bluhdorn had been used in the scheme. He told Everett that he had been threatened after the purchase and said that he was warned, 'You spin this off, you motherfucker, or we'll kill you.' "

Lest Bluhdorn doubted their seriousness, Phil Levin let him have it. "Levin told him, 'The people I deal with don't fool around.' Adding salt to the wound, Bluhdorn said that her enemy Sidney Korshak was involved in throwing her out of Arlington Park. Then Bluhdorn tells her, 'These guys are buying out Gulf & Western's interest, spinning off to a company called Recrion.' "[8] Recrion, it turned out, was the new corporate name of Parvin-Dohrmann, which had adopted the moniker to avoid the stigma attached to Parvin's SEC indictments.* If the source is correct, then a new picture emerges of the Korshak-Levin grand scheme: the original intent of the Parvin takeover was for Levin and Korshak to end up with not only four or more Vegas casinos, but control of Chicago racing, and a getaway retreat in Acapulco to boot. It is unknown how much of the enterprise would have involved silent investors from Levin's and Korshak's underworld connections, but it is hard to imagine that some form of tribute could have been avoided.

After her dismissal, Marge Everett promptly sued Levin, pointing out his

---

*By May 1970, Parvin/Recrion stock had plummeted to $12.50, and the company was forced to sell the Aladdin (once the Tallyho) for $6 million. By the end of 1973 it had reduced its debt to $37 million.

Jack Clarke (Courtesy Jack Clarke)

purchase of 79,200 shares for himself at $32 the previous summer, knowing that Transnation was going to make the CTE purchase at $46. Everett settled with Transnation when they awarded her 5 percent of Hollywood Park Race Track.[9] (She eventually purchased another 64,000 shares to become the track's largest shareholder.) But Everett's need for vengeance was unsatiated. She brought in Chicago überdetective Jack Clarke to investigate Levin to try to have CTE's racing license revoked. What follows is Clarke's own description of his investigation:

> I had been retained by Marjorie Everett to take over the security at Arlington Park.
>
> After she was fired, I got a phone call from her, and she said, "I want to investigate these people. They have broken their word with me." Her husband, Webb Everett, was still alive at the time. He was a terrific guy and he had warned her against it, but, as always, she knew it all. The idea being that she could expose them so they couldn't get a license. So I started to do an investigation of Phil Levin.
>
> I went to New Jersey and found out that Phil Levin, the shopping-center king, had been caught on a federal wiretap with the two top hoods [DeCarlo and DeCavalcante] in New Jersey.
>
> After New Jersey I found out that Levin spent a lot of time in Acapulco. So I went to Acapulco. When I went down there and checked into the Hilton, which was owned by the ex–president of Mexico, Miguel Alemán and Arnold Kirkeby, by sheer coincidence, I ended up with the room next door to Meyer Lansky and his attorney Moses Polakoff. They're in the next room. [Lansky in Room 993, Polakoff in 994.] So I'm on the wall listening to their conversation, and of course I didn't get most of it because they spoke Yiddish.

Now along comes the *federales* and they go through the room and they're questioning Lansky and Polakoff.

I wanted to see where he would go next. Lansky said to them, "Let me make a couple of phone calls and we can get the fuck out of here and figure out where we're gonna go."

They got their bags, they got everything, and they're driving. I followed them and it was the strangest thing; they made a left turn on a road and went up the road. I did the same thing. It was toward a mountain, and this is about a half a mile or a mile from the Hilton, which is on the main strip. This is off the strip, but you go off the side of a mountain and you get up there and all of a sudden they disappeared. I found out later I drove right by the place, didn't even know it was there. Then I came back and I see a tiny sign, ACAPULCO TOWERS, and sure enough, there's their Jeep. They had moved from the Hilton to the Acapulco Towers.

I see all these people meeting at the Acapulco Towers and at the pool and so on. And it's the Canadian Mafia, and Lansky was meeting with them. I literally burglarized the Acapulco Towers and found papers, and the registry, which showed quite a few people from Chicago being there. I did a background on them and they were all connected people—Jews and Italians.

So I called a Mexican *federale* and laid the story on him, that these two guys in room so and so in the Acapulco Towers had a collection of artifacts in their room—like historic relics and things, without permission of the government, which is a big deal in Mexico. It was a lie, but I knew it would get their attention.

And then all of a sudden, Lansky disappears. I get the tip that he's left Acapulco. The maître d' of the Acapulco Towers and I became good friends. He literally told me that when Lansky had to get out of town—Moe Morton called and said, "We got to get this guy out of town and we can't let anybody know"—he'd say, "No problem." He went over to the airport and spoke to his friends at the airport, who all loved him because he provided them with rooms sometimes. They said, "Sure, we'll put him on a plane." He personally drove Lansky out to the airport with Moe Morton or someone from the hotel and put him on a plane to Florida unmanifested.

Within a half hour I found out that he was in fact gone and on a plane to Miami. And then I found out that about an hour into his flight he was put on the manifest in Acapulco. So I made a call to the DEA in Florida there and told them he'd be coming in and he was carrying drugs—another lie.

I came back and gave my report to Marge Everett. So then she went to

Governor Ogilvie and said, "We got these guys tied in with mobsters. Guys from the northwest side, mostly Jews." These were bookmakers, gamblers, shady guys. The report leads to the investigation of Arlington Park by the Illinois Board of Investigations [IBI].

So they come up with an idea that I take [IBI investigator] Dick Gliebe and two other agents to Mexico and take them through everything I did. On that trip I found out where the corporate record-keeping was—in an open room—so we went in there and made copies of all the documents of who went there all the time, and there's Sidney Korshak, his brother Marshall. They all owned a piece of the Acapulco Towers. It was Moe Morton, Sidney Korshak, and eight others. That's what the papers stated—those were the original incorporators. They had two Mexican fronts, because you always had a Mexican have and buy property there.

We brought back the documents and got all the names in the documents, and of course, Lansky's name is in there and Polakoff's name, and some other interesting characters.

Sidney Korshak became aware of Clarke's sniffing around, as Clarke later found out when he was asked by Marshall, "Why doesn't my brother want me to talk to you?"

The period of upheaval for the Korshaks was made more pronounced by recent events within the family: on September 17, 1970, brother Bernard Korshak died, and one year later, in September of 1971, brother Ted Korshak passed away, after years of battling drug demons. All that remained of the Korshak nuclear family were Sidney and Marshall, and by all accounts they cherished every moment they were able to spend together.

Bringing the Mob to Paramount

While Levin and Korshak were expanding Charlie Bluhdorn's investments in Acapulco and Chicago, the Mad Austrian himself was busy making his own controversial business deals. Although he was awaiting the SEC's pronouncement, Bluhdorn boldly continued to make inroads with organized crime as if he were immune to prosecution. The New Jersey hoods already had hooks into Gulf & Western via Phil Levin and Sid Korshak, but the Italian Mafia would soon join the G&W party, thanks to a stock swap made in the spring of 1970 by Charlie Bluhdorn. This time, Paramount Pictures would serve as host for the mob infestation.

That spring, Paramount production executive Peter Bart saw an obvious early manifestation of the tawdry alliance. "When I was a young executive at Paramount, I noticed a sudden change in the type of people frequenting the lot," Bart wrote in 2000. "The diners in the commissary looked like a casting call for *The Godfather*."[10] What Bart was witnessing was the effect of a new partnership between Bluhdorn and his mysterious Italian alter ego, Michele "the Shark" Sindona. Like Bluhdorn, Sindona was a high-flying, conglomerate-building businessman and student of Machiavelli (the subject of his thesis at the University of Messina). By the time he met Bluhdorn, Sindona had vast holdings in pharmaceuticals, textiles, publishing, metals, real estate, etc.

Michele Eugenio Sindona was born in Sicily on May 8, 1920. After World War II, Sindona forged his first alliance with the Sicilian Mafia in his desire to expand his lemon-exporting business; the mafiosi had a vise grip on all goods imported or exported from the island. In 1946, Sindona left Sicily for Milan, where he worked for a business consultancy and accounting firm, from where he continued to correspond with numerous Mafia clients, and where it was widely believed that he himself became a "made" Mafia member.[11] In 1957, Sindona was approached by the Gambino crime family and their Sicilian cousins, the Inzerillos: the Mafia wanted Sindona to launder monies garnered through the heroin drug-trafficking pipeline between Italy and the United States; the laundering was accomplished through Sindona's Milan currency brokerage, Moneyrex. Shortly after the accommodation was reached, Sindona purchased his first bank, an undertaking that would soon render him an adviser to the Vatican Bank in Rome. His advice became so crucial to the Vatican that he became known as St. Peter's Banker.

Sindona was also a pioneer in the use of *anstalten*, a term denoting a Swiss- or Liechtenstein-based corporation with only one stockholder, and a powerful financial tool, especially if an individual wishes to remain anonymous while moving his money around. Investigative author RT Naylor wrote, "In the postwar period, Sindona, a pioneer in the use of the Liechtenstein *anstalten,* allegedly put his financial skills to work channeling CIA money to the church and the Christian Democratic Party, and laundering and reinvesting heroin profits for the Mafia."[12]

In 1964, Sindona was inducted into the secret Masonic lodge known as Propaganda Due, or P-2, a shadowy clique that contained members of some of the most powerful corporations in Italy and counted a number of cardinals among its supporters. It has been referred to as "a parallel state" and the "secret power behind Italy."

Sindona also offered advice to Roberto Calvi regarding international expansion for his own institution, the Banco Ambrosiano. Calvi established shell companies in Panama that on paper looked to be controlled by the Vatican Bank. According to *Fortune* journalists Shawn Tully and Marta Dorion, Calvi "lent $1.3 billion to shell companies, which used the money to manipulate the stock of Banco Ambrosiano to push up its price and to buy big stakes in other companies." Calvi had to borrow almost $600 million from 120 foreign banks so he could lend the $1.3 billion to the shell companies.

Throughout the 1960s, Sindona continued to purchase banks, launder money for the Mafia—his network of banks and offshore companies were a convenient vehicle for the laundering of dirty money earned from heroin traffic and other mob-connected businesses—and to forge closer financial links with the Vatican. Interestingly, during this period he was represented in the United States by the law firm Mudge, Rose, Guthrie and Alexander, where both Richard Nixon and his future attorney general John Mitchell were partners.[13] By 1964, Sindona directed over five hundred companies in Italy, England, France, Switzerland, and the United States. In 1968, Sindona developed a new plan that would allow the Vatican money to be hidden in offshore investments. He eventually invested the Church's money in weapons manufacturing and even a pharmaceutical firm that produced birth control pills. In 1969, the Vatican honored Sindona as a "man of confidence."[14]

Around the time that he purchased the Brown Paper and Plywood Company of New Hampshire, Sindona appeared on Bluhdorn's radar, himself a commodities magnate. In January 1968, Sindona was in Milan when he received a telephone call from Bluhdorn in New York, asking for a meeting next morning at the Grand Hotel in Rome. Bluhdorn indicated that he had an interesting deal to propose. In just one hour the following day, Sindona sold the Brown Company to Bluhdorn for $15.5 million in cash.

In the spring of 1970, Bluhdorn again became enmeshed in negotiations with Sindona, successfully effecting a stock swap that provided Società Generale Immobiliare (SGI), Sindona's real estate investment company, half of the Paramount lot, and Bluhdorn a seat on Immobiliare's board of directors.* Gulf & Western also purchased 15 million shares of SGI and listed them on its books at one and one-half times their market value. Sindona, in turn, purchased a Hollywood holding company at double its assessed value from Bluhdorn's conglomerate. The Securities and Exchange

---

*Ironically, one of SGI's properties was the Watergate Complex, events at which would later precipitate the downfall of Richard Nixon, whose law firm represented SGI and Sindona in the United States.

Commission, already adjudicating Gulf's connection to Parvin-Dohrmann, quickly charged Sindona and Bluhdorn with violating securities law by trading worthless stock back and forth to create a false market. Sindona and Bluhdorn agreed to halt all trading, and the SEC therefore decided to drop all charges.[15]

Throughout this period, Peter Bart's journalistic instincts were unrestrained, as he took copious notes on what he was seeing and hearing at Paramount, including details of a secret Bluhdorn confab with Fidel Castro in an attempt to persuade him to launch a global sugar cartel with him, and a Bluhdorn plan to use Sindona's dirty European money for a limitless G&W expansion.[16] When Sid Korshak became aware of Bart's note taking, he stepped in, as only he could.

"Peter, do you know what's the best insurance policy in the world that absolutely guarantees continued breathing?" Korshak asked. "It's silence." In his book *Who Killed Hollywood?* Bart described his reaction to the rare, and valued, Korshak advice. "How often did one receive advice from the man who was arguably the word's best fixer?" Bart pondered. "I realized that the single most prudent thing I could do with my notes was not simply to discard them but to incinerate them. They were quite accurate; they were also quite dangerous . . . It would be fascinating to re-create precisely who did what to whom . . . It would be great to have a record. On the other hand, I have felt a sense of security over the years, knowing that I took out Sidney Korshak's recommended insurance policy."[17]

Before the IBI (Illinois Board of Investigation) and SEC hearings commenced, Sid Korshak's pal Irv Kupcinet revealed in his column that Korshak was going to file a libel suit against Len O'Connor of Channel 5 (Chicago) for saying that he was involved in $500,000 in "hanky-panky" concerning the O'Hare Airport hotel deal.[18] When the IBI convened their hearings that spring, investigators Richard Gliebe, Thomas Schupp, and Edward Wolf testified as to what they and Jack Clarke had found in New Jersey and Acapulco, including the fact that Meyer Lansky had gone to Morton, Korshak, and Levin's Acapulco Towers for "many meetings." Morton himself refused to come to Illinois from California to testify.[19] As noted previously, Levin explained that it was his son who was making all the calls to the home of the Jersey mafioso DeCarlo.

Coincidentally, on the same day Levin testified in Illinois, June 23, 1971, his partner Sid Korshak was doing the same in Washington for the SEC Parvin probe. In Korshak's three days of testimony, transcribed in 463 pages, it is clear that his interrogators knew nothing of the hoodlum conventions at the Acapulco Towers. While in Illinois, the IBI was in the dark about the stock fraud shenanigans of Parvin-Dohrmann, in which Levin was a major shareholder.

In Washington, Korshak rolled out the big ammunition: D.C. power attorney Edward Bennett Williams (whom Korshak also hired for St. John), and Frank Rothman of Greg Bautzer's firm and former head of MGM (1982–86). "He was not an admitted California lawyer," Rothman later said of his friend Korshak, "and he referred a considerable amount of legal business to me."*

Williams first refused to allow Korshak to testify if the SEC wouldn't guarantee them a copy of the transcript. In his opening remarks, Patrick K. Leisure, the attorney for plaintiff Denny's Restaurants, criticized Korshak and Coleman over their alleged associations in the Acapulco deal. Rothman then derailed the commission by showing that Leisure had been a partner in a law firm that represented Korshak's group in the sale of Acapulco Towers to Transnation, and since Coleman and Korshak were involved in both Acapulco and the pending Parvin action, Leisure was "conflicted out." SEC attorney William Sullivan said, "This raises in my mind the propriety of the attorneys who represented several of their now adversaries, whether they should put themselves into a position where they are attacking their former clients based upon the same transaction."[20]

When Korshak finally testified, he merely described how he'd brought the other partners into the Parvin investment with no intent to defraud Denny's

---

*Rothman was a 1951 USC Law School graduate and one of the nation's most respected and well-known trial attorneys, held in great esteem by judges and business executives across the country. The National Law Journal called Rothman a "legendary litigator" and included him several times on its list of the country's one hundred most influential lawyers. Rothman's clients included Warner Brothers, Walt Disney, Paramount Pictures, and Twentieth Century-Fox, as well as the NFL, NBA, NHL, and PGA. He was perhaps best known for defending the NFL in a 1986 antitrust case filed by the now defunct United States Football League, in which a jury found the NFL guilty of violating one count of antitrust law—but awarded only one dollar rather than the $1 billion in damages sought by the USFL. He also handled a case that invalidated an NBA rule preventing players from entering the league before their college class graduated.

Rothman was especially beloved at USC Law, where he maintained close personal friendships and advised the school's administration as a member and chairman of the school's Board of Councilors; his USC legacy is perpetuated by the Frank Rothman Scholarship Program, established in 2002 by the Rothman family with support from his colleagues, friends, and business associates. Rothman passed away in 2000 at the age of seventy-three.

or the majority of Parvin investors. An example of Korshak's overweening confidence was when he was asked, "What did you know about hotel operations in Las Vegas?"

"Very little" was Korshak's patently absurd answer.[21]

In questioning Korshak about his Stardust commission, the government was able to show that all he did to earn his huge fee was introduce Coleman to Morris (Moe) Dalitz, the owner of the Stardust, and make about twenty telephone calls.[22] When his turn came, Del Coleman was accompanied to Washington by his close friend Nevada governor Paul Laxalt. Despite the obvious conflict, Laxalt also accepted a free round-trip to Switzerland from Coleman, even while the SEC was investigating Coleman's Las Vegas casino purchases.* Coleman also testified to Korshak's minimal work and his unreported $500,000 fee—a fact that attracted the attention of the IRS, it would later be learned.

The SEC case was settled with a consent decree that cost Korshak most of his potential profit and required him and Coleman to cut their ties with Parvin-Dohrmann. The SEC determined Korshak's profits to be unlawful and placed the funds in escrow with a court trustee who would reimburse aggrieved stockholders. No criminal charges were filed.[23]

Paul Steiger, the author of the *Los Angeles Times* Korshak profile, and presently managing editor of the *Wall Street Journal*, recently offered his opinion of the seemingly mild judgment: "The resolution was a typical SEC injunction. It's the way they did business in those days. There were very rare criminal prosecutions. It was fairly significant that the SEC would bring a case to that level of conclusion. That was as tough as it got in those days."[24]

The punishment was, however, more severe for the investors' go-betweens. In 1971, lobbyist Voloshen (who died soon thereafter) was fined $10,000, his cohort Sweig went to prison for influence peddling, and Mc-Cormack did not seek another term.[25]

Not long after, Korshak and Coleman had a permanent falling-out. "Del betrayed Sidney," said Coleman's ex, Jan Amory. "Del did the ultimate thing that a mob close friend would never do—he gave an interview to a writer in which he implied that Sid was having a romance with Jill. It was despicable to Sidney that he would open his trap, and it also hurt Bernice." There was little doubt in Amory's mind how Del knew about Jill: apparently Sid shared the actress with Del. "We were married for a swift eight weeks in

---

*Shortly thereafter, Coleman arranged for Laxalt to obtain the interest-free, collateral-free loan from the First National Bank of Chicago that built Laxalt's dream Ormsby House casino. (Denton and Morris, *Money and the Power*, 317)

1971," remembered Amory. "I was pretty young and married Del against Sid's advice. I soon understood why he was against it. We were on our honeymoon in Miami, and Del said he was in a meeting, so I went out. But I came back to the suite early and caught him in bed with—are you ready for this?—Jill St. John. I filed for the divorce the next morning."*,26

At about the same time, in the IBI hearings, Phil Levin agreed to sell his 129,000 shares of Parvin stock, as the board seemingly overlooked a mountain of mob-related evidence and granted Transnation and Levin the coveted racing license. "I don't want to put anybody out of business or in business," Illinois Racing Commission chairman Alexander MacArthur said on August 10. "You're getting pretty close to playing God then."27 The Republican-controlled board's decision sparked a controversy, given the evidence gathered in Acapulco, and turned into a firestorm when it was discovered what occurred less than two weeks after the hearings. On the advice and guidance of Sid Korshak, Levin made a $100,000 "contribution" to a number of prominent Republicans on August 30. When the payments were investigated a year later, Levin testified that Korshak had advised him as to who exactly should receive the funds, and that Levin's aide subsequently delivered twelve checks to Korshak's office for disbursement. One likely painful payout was a $25,000 gift to GOP county chairman Edmund Kucharski, who had opposed Sid's brother Marshall over the Playboy license affair.28

In the payoff probe, Levin of course testified that these were just political contributions. But even in the unlikely event that that was true, the payments still were illegal, since Illinois law prohibited political contributions from any business that held a liquor license.29 It would all be a moot point when, on August 2, 1971, just weeks after the probe, sixty-two-year-old Phil Levin died of a heart attack in his Pierre Hotel apartment in New York.30 The next day, a New Jersey cop called Jack Clarke with the news. "Well, you finally killed the bastard," the cop said.

Moe Morton was arrested in Mexico after the hearings, and his loyal friend Ybarra worked hard to keep him in local prisons where he could be protected from inmates by friendly guards. After a few weeks, Morton scurried back to California, never to return South of the Border. Two years

---

*Amory said the vitriol between Korshak and Coleman was so profound that when Coleman suffered a stroke years later, some believed that Korshak had sent him a dose of poisoned cocaine, which Coleman ingested just before the crippling event.

A casual Sid Korshak,
mid-1960s
(Dominick Dunne)

later, Transnation sold the Illinois racetracks, which were victims of mis-management.

In California, where Marge Everett now possessed enough stock to put her on the board of Hollywood Park, Sid Korshak lobbied in vain with his pal Eugene Wyman, the racetrack's counsel (and also an Acapulco Towers investor), to keep Everett off the board.[31] Years later at the Bistro, a choking Everett was saved by a deft use of the Heimlich maneuver by actor-Ambassador John Gavin, a Bistro regular. Owner Kurt Niklas wrote, "The next day Korshak [who wrongly assumed that a Bistro waiter had saved Everett] came storming through the restaurant doors like a bull entering at a *corrida.*

" 'I want that bastard fired!'

" 'What bastard?' I asked.

" 'The waiter who saved that bitch's life!'

" 'It's already done,' I lied. 'I fired him yesterday.' "[32]

A smiling Korshak assumed his place at Table Three, never the wiser according to Niklas. When Everett's name was innocently mentioned by a guest at a Korshak holiday bash, Korshak said, "Don't spoil our dinner by talking about that bitch!"[33]

Niklas asked Korshak what was the problem between him and Everett. Korshak answered, "Acapulco Towers. She was the bitch who had a private investigator snooping in my business."[34]

Three years later, the racing board continued its beneficent treatment of G&W's Illinois racing enterprise when it granted the company an additional thirty-seven lucrative days of racing at its Korshak-represented tracks.

CHAPTER 17

From Hoffa to Hollywood

IN 1971, SIDNEY KORSHAK'S focus quickly turned right back to Washington, where the Nixon White House, as part of Richard Nixon's long-standing ties to the Teamsters, strategized over what to do about Jimmy Hoffa. Apparently, Korshak was among those with a suggestion.

At the time, Nixon was under pressure from many corners to offer executive clemency to Hoffa, imprisoned since 1967 on the jury-tampering and pension-fund kickback convictions. Without presidential intervention, Hoffa was likely to serve out his two concurrent thirteen-year terms; the parole board had rejected Hoffa's parole application three times previously, after expressing concern that Hoffa's wife and son were still on the Teamsters' payroll with salaries totaling nearly $100,000 a year, while Hoffa had received a $1.7 million lump-sum retirement settlement. However, both the rank and file, and the interim Teamster boss, Frank Fitzsimmons, who counted Nixon as a close friend, had been lobbying for Hoffa's release. Other influential constituents such as Ronald Reagan, World War II hero Audie Murphy, and California senator George Murphy all lobbied Nixon on Hoffa's behalf, hoping to obtain either Teamster business or pension-fund financing for pet projects. At the time, Murphy was working for D'Alton Smith, the son-in-law of Korshak associate New Orleans Mafia boss Carlos Marcello. Often Murphy and Smith stayed at Moe Dalitz's Desert Inn while brainstorming the Hoffa issue. On other occasions they met at the same Beverly Rodeo Hotel in Beverly Hills where Korshak negotiated the Schenley labor peace with Chavez's farmworkers.[1]

In prison, a confident Hoffa told his son, "My association with the mobs has hurt me, no doubt about it. It gave Bobby Kennedy the handle to immobilize me, put me in jail—uproot me from my union work. But I'm coming back."[2] Aware of the work of his fellows on the outside, Hoffa felt certain that an early parole was inevitable. Nixon may have been leaning toward such a move, since he felt he owed Hoffa for the million-dollar contribution he had made to Nixon's candidacy in 1960. However, Nixon was finally convinced by the promise of another fat check, this one from none other than the Supermob's underworld partners in Chicago and Las Vegas. According to some, Sidney Korshak was one of the key behind-the-scenes negotiators— understandable given his power in Vegas and his connections to such Nixon intimates as Murray Chotiner and Henry Kissinger.

By early 1971, the Korshak allegations were reverberating across the country. In Washington, F. C. Duke Zeller, who served as communications director, government liaison, and personal adviser to four Teamster presidents, was among those who learned of Korshak's intercession. "I certainly heard that [Korshak] was involved in the negotiating or at least involved in the process," Zeller said recently. "Fitzsimmons had used several people to get to the Nixon White House, and Korshak was one of them. Korshak apparently had intervened on Fitzsimmons's behalf with [Nixon aide Chuck] Colson. I heard about it early on in direct conversations with Fitzsimmons, so there was never any doubt in my mind that Korshak intervened with the Nixon White House to execute that Hoffa deal."[3]

Also in Washington, an investigator for syndicated columnist Jack Anderson was told of Sidney's broker role by D.C. political-gossip maven *Washington Post* reporter Maxine Cheshire. "Maxine told Jack Anderson the Hoffa pardon was organized by Korshak using Jill St. John to work Kissinger in order to get to Nixon," said the source, who wished to remain anonymous.

In Chicago, investigator Jack Clarke also picked up evidence of the Sidney connection. "I conned Marshall Korshak into a conversation at Eli's [Steakhouse]," said Clarke. "He told me and a number of other people that his brother Sidney had intervened with the Nixon administration. Hart was involved in that too—the money came from Vegas and Chicago and was being held in one of Hart's banks where the IRS couldn't get to it." Clarke also heard the story from Audie Murphy. "Audie Murphy was my best friend. He told me he was asked by Sidney Korshak to go see Nixon in the White House. Senator George Murphy and Nixon had been good to Audie, and he was told to go to the White House and cop a plea for Hoffa. Korshak talked to Murphy about it in the office of Senator George Murphy, and they got Audie to go talk to Nixon."[4]

In Las Vegas, where production was ongoing on *Diamonds Are Forever*, screenwriter Tom Mankiewicz, who saw Korshak often during the shoot, also heard the rumor. "If memory serves me right, it was Sidney who negotiated Hoffa's release with Nixon," Mankiewicz said in 2003.[5]

Mob messenger boy/actor/singer Gianni Russo said the Korshak-Hoffa story was known from New York to L.A. "I knew the Korshak talks were going on because there were some messages about it that were going back and forth," Russo recalled recently. "There was a lot of problems coming out of that for a lot of people."[6]

The main problem was that during Hoffa's absence, both the mob and the Supermob had grown to like Frank Fitzsimmons (and his partner Dorfman) more than Jimmy Hoffa, who only used the mob loans to help strengthen the Teamsters; he was never considered "one of ours" by the hoods. (Hoffa would later become a government informant against Fitzsimmons.) Before going away in 1967, Hoffa had said to his board about Dorfman, "When this man speaks, he speaks for me." He made similar statements about Frank Fitzsimmons. Now the duo surpassed their iconic colleague in his appeasement of the underworld. Under Fitzsimmons and Dorfman, Moe Dalitz was loaned $27 million to expand La Costa; Frank Ragano, Santo Trafficante's lawyer, received $11 million in a Florida real estate deal; Irving Davidson, Carlos Marcello's D.C. lobbyist, received $7 million for a California land purchase; and in addition to Caesars, the fund was tapped to construct the skim-friendly Landmark, Four Queens, Aladdin, Lodestar, Plaza Towers, and Circus Circus.

All told, the pension fund controlled by Allen Dorfman had loaned over $500 million in Nevada, 63 percent of the fund's total assets, and most of it went to the hoods' favored casinos. But, perhaps most important, Fitzsimmons had decentralized Teamster power, which benefited local mob bosses, who could now easily outmuscle small union fiefdoms without having to bargain with an all-powerful president.

Thus all agreed that any Hoffa release would be conditional, mandating that he not assume a political role in the affairs of the Teamsters for at least eight years. According to White House tapes released in 2001, Nixon informed Henry Kissinger on December 8, 1971, "What we're talking about, in the greatest of confidence, is we're going to give Hoffa an amnesty, *but we're going to do it for a reason.*" (Italics added.) Nixon then whispered about "some private things" Fitzsimmons had done for Nixon's cause "that were very helpful." It is now taken as fact that Nixon was referring to another promised "contribution" when the 1972 campaign rolled around.

"It's all set for the Nixon administration to spring Jimmy Hoffa," Walter Sheridan told Clark Mollenhoff. As the man who'd worked closest with Bobby Kennedy in putting Hoffa away, Sheridan was frustrated. "I'm told Murray Chotiner is handling it with the Las Vegas mob."[7]

It was a busy year for Korshak's good friend (and Richard Nixon's mentor) Murray Chotiner. According to Jeff Morgan and Gene Ayers of the *Oakland Tribune*, Chotiner was also putting out Teamster fires in Beverly Hills, where a fund borrower had come under indictment for fraud. The affair started with an $11 million 1969 fund loan for a development named Beverly Ridge Estates, a similar undertaking to the misbegotten Trousdale Estates investment in Beverly Hills a decade earlier. In this case the loan went to Leonard Bursten, a Milwaukee attorney who had founded the Miami National Bank, which was used by Lansky and others to launder money and have it transferred to Swiss accounts. Bursten, a political protégé of Joe McCarthy's, had also distributed anti-Catholic literature for Nixon's 1960 campaign versus JFK, most likely under the direction of Chotiner. When the Teamsters tried to foreclose on the bankrupt Beverly Ridge partnership, Bursten attempted to conceal $500,000 of the total from the IRS. (When Bursten pled guilty and was sentenced to fifteen years in 1972, the punishment was reduced to probation and the record was expunged after Chotiner supposedly interceded with the U.S. attorney in L.A. who was handling the case.)[8]

On December 23, 1971, Sheridan's fears were realized, when Nixon in fact granted Hoffa's early parole.* It was later learned that money had been pouring into various Nixon slush funds from Teamster coffers for just that purpose. It was also reported that the money would guarantee that Nixon-Mitchell would take it easy on investigations of pension-fund loans. According to newly released FBI documents, the first payoff came in 1970, via Korshak's underling at the pension fund, Allen Dorfman. The file stated,

---

*Hoffa's wasn't the only release bought from Nixon by the mob. As president, Nixon pardoned Phil Levin's pal Angelo "Gyp" DeCarlo, described by the FBI as a "methodical gangland executioner." Supposedly terminally ill, DeCarlo was freed after serving less than two years of a twelve-year sentence for extortion. Soon afterward, *Newsweek* reported the mobster was not too ill to be "back at his old rackets, boasting that his connections with [singer Frank] Sinatra freed him."

In FBI files released after Sinatra's 1998 death, a memo of May 24, 1973, describes Sinatra as "a close friend of Angelo DeCarlo of long standing." It adds that in April 1972, DeCarlo asked singer Frankie Valli (when he was performing at the Atlanta Federal Penitentiary) to contact Sinatra and have him intercede with Agnew for DeCarlo's release. Eventually, the memo continues, Sinatra "allegedly turned over $100,000 cash to [Nixon campaign finance chairman] Maurice Stans as an unrecorded contribution." Vice-presidential aide Peter Maletesta "allegedly contacted former Presidential Counsel John Dean and got him to make the necessary arrangements to forward the request [for a presidential pardon] to the Justice Department." Sinatra is said to have then made a $50,000 contribution to the president's campaign fund. And, the memo reports, "DeCarlo's release followed."

"Dorfman and another individual (not identified) had a private meeting with [Attorney General] John Mitchell. Dorfman gave $300,000 to Mitchell and obtained a receipt. The money was paid to obtain the release of James R. Hoffa from jail."[9]

The next big payback came less than a month after five men linked to the White House were nabbed breaking into the Democratic National Committee headquarters housed in the Watergate Complex. The venue itself was riddled with Supermob connections, bizarre coincidences, and laughable ironies:

• The residential portion of the Watergate served as home to the nation's most influential jurist below the Supreme Court—Chief Judge David L. Bazelon of the U.S. Court of Appeals for the District of Columbia Circuit, friend of both Paul Ziffren and Howard Hughes's enemy Sid Korshak. One year after the break-in, Bazelon would make a critical ruling on the Watergate prosecution, and in 1975 Bazelon and his wife returned home from Christmas vacation to discover their own Watergate break-in: $16,000 worth of jewelry was missing from their apartment.

• The Watergate Complex was owned by none other than Michele Sindona's Società Generale Immobiliare (SGI), and owned in part by the Vatican. SGI, linked to Charlie Bluhdorn's Gulf & Western and Bob Evans's Paramount Pictures, had bought the ten-acre site from Washington Gas for $7 million.

• In what the *Washington Post* called "a delicious irony for the father of the Watergate," the first Bush administration tapped SGI in 1989 to demolish the new U.S. embassy in Moscow because it was infested with electronic bugs.

• The first known Watergate break-in was a 1969 residential burglary in which jewelry and a papal medal were stolen from the apartment belonging to Nixon's secretary Rosemary Woods, later accused of erasing eighteen and a half minutes of incriminating evidence from one of the president's secret tapes, in which he discussed covering up his own break-in at the Watergate. (Dozens of White House staffers and fully one quarter of the cabinet lived at the complex, including Attorney General John Mitchell, Commerce Secretary Maurice Stans, and Transportation Secretary John Volpe; the residence was nicknamed Administration Arms, and White House West.[10]

At least one purpose of the June 17, 1972, break-in appeared to have been Nixon's worries over what the Democrats may have sussed out about the payoffs given by Howard Hughes to Vice President Nixon in the fifties and President Nixon in 1968. Nixon had reason to worry: in 1972, at the time of the break-in, the new head of the Democratic National Committee was one Lawrence O'Brien, Hughes's former D.C. lobbyist, who had a good likelihood of knowing about the bribes.

On July 17, 1972, Frank Fitzsimmons and the Teamsters executive board met at La Costa Country Club, and for the first time in its history the Teamsters pledged that its huge membership would support a Republican presidential campaign. It was estimated that more than $250,000 would be collected for the campaign from Teamster officials alone.

Over the coming months, as Nixon became frantic to provide hush money to the burglars, he suggested to aide John Dean (in a conversation being recorded by Nixon), "You could get a million dollars. You could get it in cash. I know where it could be gotten." When Dean observed that money laundering "is the type of thing Mafia people can do," Nixon calmly answered, "Maybe it takes a gang to do that."

Soon thereafter, just as Nixon predicted, over $1 million was funneled to the White House from sources that were the known domain of Sidney Korshak: the Teamsters Pension Fund and Las Vegas. FBI "Hoffa" documents released to the *Detroit Free Press* in 2002 point out that informants reported:

• Jay Sarno, the owner of Circus Circus, delivered $300,000 to Allen Dorfman at his Chicago home in August of 1972.[11]
• That same month, Hoffa said "he was aware of certain Las Vegas casino people who had made large cash contributions to the Nixon campaign."
• On January 6, 1973, $500,000 was given to Nixon aide Charles Colson, or a designee, in Las Vegas (Colson later denied this to reporters).[12] On that same day, Fitzsimmons retrieved the money from Dorfman's home. Two years earlier, in an internal memo marked SECRET, Colson had reported that "substantial sums of money, perhaps a quarter of a million dollars, available for any . . . purpose we would direct" could be generated by "arrang[ing] to have James Hoffa released from prison." Attorney Colson told D.C. attorney Richard Bergen, "I am going to get the Teamster account in several months."[13] In fact, Fitzsimmons later transferred Teamsters legal business to a law firm where Colson would eventually work. Colson, who did prison time for his involvement in the Watergate affair and who now runs a prison ministry, maintained that there was no connection between the commuted Hoffa sentence and the change in Teamsters legal business. Soon after the Teamster money was received by the Nixon camp, John Mitchell indeed

scuttled investigations into the Teamsters Pension Fund loans and rescinded the taps on Accardo and friends.

• On February 8, 1973, Fitzsimmons met with numerous California mobsters* near Palm Springs at Indian Wells Country Club (coincidentally the winter home of Chicago boss Tony Accardo) during the Bob Hope Desert Classic golf tournament. The topic of discussion was a new Teamsters prepaid health plan, expected to generate a possible $1 billion in annual business, and real estate transactions in Orange and San Diego counties involving more than $40 million in commercial property—all financed by Teamsters Pension Fund loans.

In the next days, the meetings shifted to Rancho La Costa, where Fitzsimmons met with Chicago's Vegas enforcers Anthony Spilotro and Marshall Caifano, Outfit boss Tony Accardo, and an unnamed Justice Department informant. The motley crew discussed the prepaid health plan, under which a Los Angeles physician named Dr. Bruce Frome would provide West Coast Teamsters with medical care. Monthly medical fees for each member would be paid by the central-states fund from the millions of dollars contributed into it by employers. But most important, it was agreed that 7 percent of take would go to the California underworld, with 3 percent kicked back to a shell company called People's Industrial Consultants, run by the Chicago Outfit. FBI wiretaps revealed that Accardo's underboss Lou Rosanova had set up a Beverly Hills office of People's Industrial Consultants to handle the kickbacks to be paid under the health plan. The office was located at 9777 Wilshire Boulevard, two blocks from Korshak's Riviera office (#9571). The wiretaps at the shell company picked up a conversation between Dr. Frome and Raymond de Derosa, identified by the California authorities as a muscleman for California mafioso Peter Milano, who operated out of the consulting company's offices.[14]

On the morning of February 13, 1973, Fitzsimmons drove to El Toro Marine Air Station and joined Nixon on board Air Force One for the flight to Washington. According to mob sources located by author William Balsamo, Fitzsimmons told Nixon on the flight, "We're prepared to pay for the request I put on the table. You'll never have to worry about where the next dollar will come from. We're going to give you one million dollars up front, Mr. President, and there'll be more that'll follow to make sure you are never wanting."[15] Just days later, the Justice Department shut down the FBI's court-authorized wiretaps.

---

*Among them, Sam Sciortino, Peter H. Milano, and Joe Lamandri.

In May 1973, Korshak's Beverly Hills friend Murray Chotiner publicly took credit for arranging Hoffa's early parole. Chotiner bragged, "I did it, I make no apologies for it, and frankly I'm proud of it!" But when Chotiner was charged by the *Manchester Union Leader* of April 27, 1973, with also having funneled $875,000 to the Nixon campaign from Teamster officials and Las Vegas gambling interests, Chotiner typically responded with an attack of his own: "Unless there is an immediate retraction, I plan to sue or take whatever action the law allows against whoever is responsible for this horrible libel." Unwilling to take on the expense of a multimillion-dollar lawsuit, the paper retracted the story.

Observing from Chicago, Labor Department organized crime investigator Tom Zander saw what was happening but could do nothing about it. "Anybody who wanted to pay for it had a connection to Nixon," Zander said recently. "The locals gave massive amounts of untraced money to Nixon. They got away with murder." An FBI agent told *Los Angeles Times* reporters Jack Nelson and Bill Hazlett, "This whole thing of the Teamsters and the mob and the White House is one of the scariest things I've ever seen. It has demoralized the Bureau. We don't know what to expect out of the Justice Department."

Any Korshak participation in the Hoffa-Nixon financial arrangements was juggled with Korshak's own monetary negotiations with the feds. After following up on the SEC's Parvin revelations, the IRS's scrutiny of the sixty-five-year-old Korshak's tax statements resulted in a September 7, 1972, charge that Korshak was guilty of tax evasion and fraud. The agency alleged that between 1963 and 1970 the Fixer had, among other things:

• Only reported $4.4 million of his $5 million taxable income.
• Taken improper deductions for expenses to the tune of $428,056.
• Failed to pay gift taxes on such items as $115,000 in stocks to his sons, and $10,000 to Jill St. John.

Among the details in the charge were the notations that in 1969 Korshak had given each of his sons $20,000 in shares of Al Hart's City National Bank, and that he claimed an average of $16,000 per year in deductions for his Chalon Road mansion, which he claimed as his office. The IRS examiner auditing Korshak's taxes concluded that Korshak's actions were "intentional and substantial." All told, according to the IRS, Korshak owed over $677,000 in back taxes, plus $247,000 in penalties.[16]

Within months, the IRS turned on Sidney's sixty-three-year-old brother, Marshall, who was at the time the city collector for Chicago, a $23,000-a-year job. The feds were focused on the years 1967 through 1970, when Marshall's reported earnings had averaged $155,000 per year, a fraction of his older brother's income, but almost five times his own city pay. The IRS said in a press release that it was interested in Korshak's stock holdings in sixty companies and alleged contributions to an astonishing forty-seven charities.[17] Official sources said that the IRS mostly wanted to determine if Korshak was acting as a "nominee" for others in all the stock holdings—a number of local pols, including former governor Otto Kerner (for whom Korshak had served as revenue director), had recently been convicted in a bribery scandal involving horse-racing stocks, and it was believed that illegal investments were now being fronted by nominees. The IRS wanted to see Korshak's brokerage statements to make the case.

Appearing under a summons at the IRS offices on February 6, 1973, Korshak failed to bring his stock records as ordered and instead pleaded immunity under the Fifth Amendment.[18] Within days, Marshall traveled to Los Angeles, probably to confer with his big brother.[19] Meanwhile, the IRS went to court and obtained an April 18 deadline for Korshak to produce the records. In a headline reading KORSHAK: TALK OR RESIGN, the *Sun-Times* editorialized that "ethics laws and rules require that public officials be open and aboveboard about their financial affairs . . . If Korshak persists in his refusal to discuss his financial affairs candidly and openly with federal income tax officials, he should resign his public job or be removed by Mayor Daley."[20] A *Chicago Today* editorial called Korshak's recalcitrance "striking."[21]

A defiant Korshak appeared for the appointed court show-up empty-handed, again invoking the Fifth. Korshak's attorney, Harvey Silets, contended that the records might incriminate his client, and that the IRS actually wanted the records not for a civil IRS case, but for a possible criminal probe.[22] IRS attorney Michael Sheehy told the court that Korshak had admitted the same to him, but that he was most concerned that the records might be used in a criminal case against his brother.[23]

In August 1973, six months after the IRS probe began, it ended suddenly when word came down from Washington that the agency had in fact been pursuing a criminal investigation, which allowed Korshak to invoke the Fifth and to refuse to deliver his records unless he was charged with a crime.[24] The matter of Sidney's taxes was litigated over the next year and was settled just before the case went to trial in 1974, with the IRS dropping all the fraud charges against Korshak and agreeing to allow him to pay only $179,244, 20 percent of the initial demand.

Interestingly, the period was marked by tax problems not only for the Korshaks, but also for Al Capone's former personal attorney Abraham Teitelbaum, the man who'd introduced Sidney to the world of organized crime legal representation and mentored him in the labor-negotiating game. In the years since his recruitment of Korshak, Teitelbaum's star had risen and fallen precipitously. After Capone, Teitelbaum drew a suspicious $125,000-per-year salary from the Outfit-controlled Chicago Restaurant Association, represented bosses like Joey "Doves" Aiuppa, and repeatedly pleaded the Fifth Amendment before the McClellan Committee. In the sixties, the IRS hit Teitelbaum with a bill for over half a million in back taxes, forcing him into bankruptcy, and a divorce from his wife.

In December 1972, Teitelbaum was convicted for real estate fraud and sent to serve a one-to-ten-year sentence at California's State Prison in Chino. In desperation, according to a close family friend, Teitelbaum had him make a call to the protégé he had advised for three decades, Sidney Korshak, hoping he would come see Teitelbaum and employ his famous talents as the Fixer and make the conviction just go away. He located his high-flying recruitee, then living in Chalon Road luxury, and made his request. However, the voice on the other end of the phone was cold and dismissive.

"I won't go anywhere near that place," Korshak said. "I wouldn't go visit him. I won't help him, and as far as I'm concerned, his days are over. I don't want anything to do with Abe Teitelbaum."[25]

It is not known what turned Korshak against Teitelbaum, although it might be assumed that he was still bristling over Teitelbaum's $50,000 fee in Vegas in 1964. Also, Teitelbaum had famously had a falling-out with Korshak's great friend Chicago boss Tony Accardo, in 1953, prompting two Accardo enforcers to threaten to push Teitelbaum out of his office window.[26] After his brief prison stint, Teitelbaum stayed in California, where he lived in the $2.50-per-night Burton Way Hotel, sharing a kitchen with twenty other forlorn men. Teitelbaum died in 1980.[27]

Making Movies with Charlie, Bobby, Cubby—and Sidney

The advent of 1971 saw Sid Korshak navigating the safer waters of his labor consultancy forte. At the time, Paramount's production chief, Robert Evans, was attempting to package a film project based on Mario Puzo's wildly successful novel *The Godfather*, for which Evans owned the movie rights. Three years earlier, as Evans tells it, he gave Puzo $12,500 to pay off gambling debts in exchange for a then unpublished 150-page manuscript entitled *The Mafia*. When Puzo's retitled book *The Godfather* took off, Paramount began assembling the film version in earnest. However, the director, Coppola, was part of the new breed of film auteurs who were keen on creating paradigms at odds with executives such as Bob Evans, who were tied to the old traditions. As "New Hollywood" chronicler Peter Biskind aptly put it, "The casting of *The Godfather* was a battle between the Old Hollywood approach of Evans and the new Hollywood ideas of Coppola."[28]

When considering the key role of Mafia scion Michael Corleone, Coppola's first choice was a young Bobby De Niro, who tested beautifully, but was considered too much of an unknown by the suits. The director's second choice was a diminutive young New York actor named Al Pacino, but this selection was also greeted with disapprobation, especially by Evans, who referred to Pacino as "that little dwarf." Like De Niro, Pacino tested well for the part, but Evans wouldn't accept him; Evans wanted the film to be anchored by a studio stalwart such as Warren Beatty or Jack Nicholson. However, when Coppola went on a European vacation, Pacino's *The Panic in Needle Park* opened and immediately convinced Evans that Coppola was right about the young thespian. But by the time Evans warmed up to Pacino, the actor had already signed with MGM to film *The Gang That Couldn't Shoot Straight*.[29] And MGM's new owner, a Bluhdorn-like wheeler-dealer named Kirk Kerkorian, was not about to sell him to the competition.

The Avis of Vegas

Kerkor "Kirk" Kerkorian was born on June 6, 1917, in Fresno, California, the son of an Armenian grocer. Like Howard Hughes, Kerkorian became enamored of aviation, creating a charter flight service that carried gamblers like himself to Las Vegas. A stock swap with the Studebaker car company was the initial link in a chain of events that included Kerkorian's buying back the company and taking it public. The business would develop into Trans International Airlines (TIA), the object of Kerkorian's first great financial triumph. A former high-stakes gambler (said to have bet $50,000 at a craps table in one night), Kerkorian also shared Hughes's reputation as a womanizer, later being linked with actresses Priscilla Presley and Yvette Mimieux before his divorce from his second wife, Jean, and with Cary Grant's widow, Barbara, in the years since.

Much like Wasserman, Kerkorian was more interested in power accumulation than the actual business itself. As Richard Lacayo wrote in *Time*, "For him it has always been the deal, not the business . . . Deal making seems to satisfy the gambler in Kerkorian, a man more at home in Las Vegas than in Hollywood."

Kerkorian, however, was not without his own associations with underworld denizens, especially after a 1961 New York wiretap implied that he was making payments to the mob. A 1970 investigation in New York State revealed the nine-year-old recording of Kerkorian promising to send a $21,300 check to Charlie "the Blade" Tourine—a known enforcer for the Genovese crime family. When Tourine called Kerkorian, he used the code phrase "George Raft is calling." On this occasion, Kerkorian told Tourine that he (Kerkorian) would write a check to himself, endorse it, and have it sent to "George Raft" at New York's Warwick Hotel. Kerkorian said he did the payment this way so as to avoid Tourine's endorsement signature on the back, since, as Kerkorian said, "The heat was on."[30]

The same year that *The Godfather* went into production (1971), New York businessman Harold Roth testified before the New York State Joint Legislative Committee on Crime that Tourine had introduced Kerkorian to Roth twelve years earlier, with Tourine calling Kerkorian "a very good friend of mine." At the time, Tourine was hoping to have Roth help finance Kerkorian's purchase of an $8 million DC-8 jet. Kerkorian later told a friend that he indeed knew Tourine, whom he referred to as Charlie White. Kerkorian explained that he was simply paying a gambling debt and was not involved in organized crime. A 1971 *Forbes* interview, in which Kerkorian asserted his innocence, was his last press interview to date.

In 1969, Kerkorian sold his TIA stock for more than $100 million and, as per his custom, reinvested the profit right into his next brainstorm—Las Vegas. Thanks to the same Corporate Gaming Act of 1969 that gave other publicly traded companies a Vegas foothold, Kerkorian announced that he would be opening what was then the largest hotel in the world (1,512 rooms), the International (now the Las Vegas Hilton), on Paradise Road. Kerkorian had already purchased the Flamingo in 1967 as a training ground for the new colossus, from a group that included Meyer Lansky. At the same time, Kerkorian asked Korshak pal Greg Bautzer to call MGM to discuss a possible sale of the studio. In this pre-*Godfather*, preblockbuster era, big studios were in decline. Some say *Easy Rider*, which was shot for $300,000 and grossed $30 million, started the trend toward less expensive "youth market" movies. Kerkorian believed it to be a cycle that would reverse, and the time was right to buy cheap. A year later, Hughes asked Bautzer to do the same for him.

The International was less than a spectacular success, and mounting debts forced Kerkorian to sell controlling interest to Hilton Hotels with the proviso he would not build a competing hotel in Las Vegas. All the while, Kerkorian was buying huge blocks of stock in troubled MGM, and by 1971 he had succeeded where Korshak partner Phil Levin had failed and now controlled MGM. And he had one more big announcement: he would—again—build the world's largest resort hotel (2,084 rooms), again on Paradise Road in Las Vegas. This time, he would have to do it behind the corporate veil of MGM in order to comply with his Hilton contract.

Kerkorian thought to use the association with the MGM film *Grand Hotel* to construct the new hotel, which assumed the name The MGM Grand. Kerkorian purchased the land from Realty Holdings, which was controlled by Merv Adelson, Irwin Molasky, and Korshak's great friend Moe Dalitz. "I don't see anything wrong with buying a piece of vacant property from these people," Kerkorian said. "What's wrong with Moe?"[31]

Such was the setting when Paramount asked MGM to sell its Pacino contract to them, allowing the actor to become "Michael Corleone." Evans first called MGM's president, Jim Aubrey, who had been introduced to owner Kerkorian by the ever-present Greg Bautzer. "With the emotion of an IRS investigator," Evans wrote in his autobiography, "he turned me down." The way Bob Evans saw it, he had no choice but to call his consigliere, Sidney Korshak.[32]

As recounted in his memoir, *The Kid Stays in the Picture*, Evans, who was in New York at the time, placed a call to Korshak at his New York "office" in the Carlyle Hotel.

"I need your help."

"Yeah?"

"There's an actor I want for the lead in *The Godfather*."

"Yeah?"

"I can't get him."

"Yeah?"

"If I lose him, Coppola's gonna have my ass."

"Yeah?"

Evans advised Korshak of his out-of-hand rejection by MGM's Aubrey, a revelation that elicited a nonstop recitation of "Yeah"s from Korshak.

"Is there anything you can do about it?"

"Yeah."

"Really?"

"The actor, what's his name?"

"Pacino . . . Al Pacino."

"Who?"

"Al Pacino."

"Hold it, will ya? Let me get a pencil. Spell it."

"Capital *A*, little *l*—that's his first name. Capital *P*, little *a*, *c-i-n-o*."

"Who the fuck is he?"

"Don't rub it in, will ya, Sidney. That's who the motherfucker wants."

As Evans tells it, twenty minutes after his call to Korshak, an enraged Jim Aubrey called Evans.

"You no-good motherfucker, cocksucker. I'll get you for this," Aubrey screamed.

"What are you talking about?"

"You know fuckin' well what I'm talking about."

"Honestly, I don't."

"The midget's yours; you got him."

That was Aubrey's final statement before slamming the phone down on a befuddled Evans, who immediately called his mentor Korshak. The Fixer advised the producer that he had merely placed a call to Aubrey's boss, Kirk Kerkorian, and made the request. When Kerkorian balked, Korshak introduced his Teamster connections into the negotiations.

"Oh, I asked him if he wanted to finish building his hotel," Korshak told Evans.

"He didn't answer . . . He never heard of the schmuck either. He got a pencil, asked me to spell it—'Capital *A*, punk *l*, capital *P*, punk *a*, *c-i-n-o*.' Then he says, 'Who the fuck is he?' 'How the fuck do I know? All I know, Bobby wants him.'"

Interestingly, after Pacino was released from the MGM picture, his replacement was Bobby De Niro, who had previously tested so well for Pacino's Michael Corleone role.

Kirk Kerkorian stands in front of his under-construction Vegas hotel, the International, 1969 (UNLV Special Collections)

Al Pacino in *The Godfather* (Photofest)

On April 15, 1972, Kerkorian broke ground for the MGM Grand (now Caesars Entertainment's Bally's) and opened the hotel on December 5, 1973, earning him the moniker Father of the Mega-Resort. The movie-nostalgia-based hotel boasted a twenty-five-floor tower with "walls of glass," and Rhett Butler and Lara suites. For the grand opening, Korshak friend Dean Martin appeared in the Celebrity Lounge. Many viewed with suspicion the fact that the hotel was completed just one day before a new code came into effect that would have mandated fire-suppression sprinklers be installed. Seven years later, eighty-seven MGM Grand guests and employees were killed and hundreds injured in a horrific fire that would likely have been minimized by the sprinklers. The tragedy is still referred to as the worst disaster in Las Vegas history.

Although Kerkorian has typically been seen as second to Howard Hughes in the Vegas mogul sweepstakes, the reverse was true. "He's the second deep pocket who brought legitimate capital to town. [But] he's also the first person to come here and build as a hands-on operator," University of Nevada, Las Vegas, History Department chairman Hal Rothman said. "Howard Hughes doesn't count because he didn't build." Rothman added that Kerkorian is no longer "the Avis of Vegas." Casino expert Bill Thompson pointed out that Hughes did not bring in the massive capital infusions that were ultimately successful in squeezing out the mob: "Kerkorian rescued us from Hughes. By making properties so big, he took them out of the reach of the Mafia. They were too big and too expensive."*

---

*Kerkorian continued to expand at an astounding pace. In 1986, he sold the MGM lot to Adelson's Lorimar Productions. In 2000, he masterminded a $6.4 billion buyout of Wynn's Mirage Resorts, at the time the biggest merger in gaming industry history; on September 13, 2004, Kerkorian sold his film division, Metro-Goldwyn-Mayer Inc., to

As *The Godfather* proceeded into production with Pacino and the rest of the cast now assembled, Evans et al. faced their next hurdle, this time with antagonists even more intransigent than Kerkorian: the Italian Anti-Defamation League and the Mafia. Mario Puzo had already warned Coppola, "Francis, when you work on this, the real Mafia guys are gonna come. Don't let them in."[33] Coppola knew what Puzo was saying. "I remember when I was a kid—they're like vampires," Coppola said. "Once you invite them over the door, then you're theirs."

As expected, the production felt the backlash, first in Los Angeles, where the famous Paramount gates were blown off their hinges by pro-Italian protesters. On their New York set, the moviemakers were stopped before they could start, while Evans received anonymous phone calls at his Sherry Netherland suite in which his son Josh's life was threatened. The voice on the other end warned, "If you want your son to live longer than two weeks, get out of town." The thought of his newborn son, Josh (with actress Ali MacGraw), being killed prompted another Evans call to Korshak for rescue.

According to Evans, what opened up New York "like a World's Fair" was a phone call to the Mafia from Korshak. Suddenly, according to Bob Evans, everyone cooperated, "the garbagemen, the longshoremen, the Teamsters." New security people even showed up. Evans later wrote, "One call from Korshak, suddenly, threats turned into smiles and doors, once closed, opened with an embrace." In a 1997 interview Evans concluded, "*The Godfather* would not have been made without Korshak. He saved Pacino, the locations, and, possibly, my son."[34] Producer Al Ruddy remembered that Evans still couldn't relax. "Evans hid out on the whole fuckin' movie," Ruddy said. "He went to Bermuda with Ali."

Footnote cont'd

Sony for $2.9 billion, netting him more than $1.7 billion. *Variety*'s Peter Bart wrote that Kerkorian was not only a victim of bad luck, but that he was "out of place in Hollywood . . . He had no real passion for the business . . . [and] never really understood the potential of the ancillary markets" (*Variety*, 4-25-05). In February 2005, with his Sony deal in hand, Kerkorian laid out $8.7 billion for the purchase of Mandalay Inc., creating a twenty-eight-casino company that will employ more than seventy-five thousand, include seventy-four thousand rooms on the Strip, and control about 40 percent of its slots and about 44 percent of its table games. Among other properties, the merger gave Kerkorian control of the (new) MGM Grand, New York–New York, Bellagio, Mirage, Treasure Island, Monte Carlo, Mandalay Bay, Luxor, Excalibur, and Circus Circus.

Although a career of buying and selling companies in the entertainment and leisure industries has made Kerkorian a billionaire, he remains unaffected in person. Longtime friend General Alexander M. Haig Jr. said, "For a billionaire, he's almost meek . . . I've never heard him raise his voice. It seems like he would just as soon have his actions speak for him."

A lawyer friend of Korshak's who had been referred a number of hoodlum clients by Korshak told Los Angeles DA investigator Jim Grodin that Korshak was well compensated for his efforts, supposedly receiving a piece of the movie's gross profits.*

But even Korshak could not predict that an upstart mafioso would exert his own *Godfather*-type power play in a bid to start a sixth New York crime family. Production assistant Dean Tavoularis has spoken of how the Italian Anti-Defamation League, which was run by mafioso Joe Colombo of the Profaci crime family, had his unions and supporters shut down the production in New York. The traditional five families were already disturbed by Colombo's affiliation with the League and his love affair with the press, a cardinal sin in the eyes of the traditional Mustache Petes. The problem's resolution came from an unlikely source.

At the time, Las Vegas singer and occasional Mafia messenger boy Gianni Russo was desperate to get a major role in the movie and had auditioned in vain weeks earlier. When he heard about the Paramount gate destruction and the intrusion by Colombo, Russo, a Brooklyn native and now a captain of the Italian Anti-Defamation League in Vegas, saw his golden opportunity. He took the first plane to New York and went directly to the Gulf & Western building, somehow finagling a meeting with Bluhdorn and producer Al Ruddy. He convinced Bluhdorn that he had influence with Colombo and would broker a peace if he was given a plum role in the movie. The trouble was, Russo had never even met Colombo, but he knew his son and some of his underlings.

With Bluhdorn's blessing, Russo visited Colombo in his Brooklyn office

---

*Others suggest that Korshak was honored by the inclusion of the *Godfather* movie character "Tom Hagen," the non-Italian consigliere to the Corleones. In the film, Hagen, much like the rumored Korshak intervention for Sinatra with Columbia's Harry Cohn, met with the president of "Woltz International Pictures" to get an up-and-coming Italian entertainer named "Johnny Fontaine" a role in an upcoming career-making war movie. The famous horse-head scene that followed was supposedly inspired by Korshak's alleged tactic. In the film, the threat was successful for the Corleones—Fontaine landed the part he wanted and became a big star, just as Sinatra had succeeded with *From Here to Eternity*.

Also like Korshak, Hagen was offered the vice presidency of a Vegas casino, when toward the end of the second film Michael tells Hagen he can take his "wife, family, and mistress and move them all to Las Vegas." Lastly, just as Korshak briefly ran afoul of his Chicago bosses with the booking of Dinah Shore into the competition's Vegas lounge, Hagen was similarly reprimanded for misplacing his loyalties, with Michael Corleone once warning Hagen that he was "not a wartime consigliere." Neither the fictitious Hagen nor Korshak was ever so careless again.

and convinced him to meet with Bluhdorn and the rest, where he could demand some script changes and Defamation League black-tie fund-raisers at
every local premiere of the movie. "He bought the idea and loved it," Russo
said. All Russo wanted in return was one of three coveted roles in the movie:
Corleone's sons Michael or Sonny, or the wayward son-in-law, Carlo. Again,
Colombo agreed.

The next morning, Russo, Colombo, and his entourage sat across the
table from the G&W suits on the thirty-third floor of the Gulf building.
Also there were the film's producers Al Ruddy, Gray Frederickson, Fred
Roos, and their lawyers. "They were as white as ghosts," Russo said of the
executives. "They did not know what they were about to hear or if they were
all gonna get thrown out a window."[35]

In short time, it was agreed that Colombo could see the script, and he
turned to an underling and said, "Butter, read it." After some give-and-take,
the producers agreed to remove all anti-Italian references, such as *Mafia* (the
term never appears in the movie). They also agreed to the black-tie events,
but, as the group started to rise and shake hands, Russo worried about his
reward for brokering the deal. "I leaned over to Joe Sr.," recalled Russo,
"and I say, 'What about me?'"

With that, Colombo raised his hands, and everyone sat back down like puppets on a string. "What about my boy here? What are we gonna do for him?"
the boss asked. The producers said that the first two roles were spoken for, but
they had not yet gotten to the part of Carlo, Don Corleone's son-in-law.

"You're gonna get to Carlo right now," Russo ordered.

"Oh, yes, please," added Colombo. "Gianni is playing Carlo."

No one present was about to argue, and Russo got the part. However,
when filming commenced, Marlon Brando, playing the lead role of patriarch
Don Corleone, informed Coppola that he would not perform with the unknown Russo. When Russo heard, he put his arm around Brando and walked
him to a back room, where they could speak privately—"because I didn't
want to embarrass the guy in front of the other actors," Russo later said.

"Let me tell you something, okay?" Russo told the acting icon. "This is
my fucking break in life and you or nobody else is gonna fuck it up. Do you
understand what I'm tellin' you? I don't give a fuck who you are, I'm staying
in this fucking movie." To which Brando responded meekly, "That was brilliant, great acting." As Russo wrote in his autobiography, "That was the end
of the story."[36]

Russo was not the only "connected" person to appear in the movie. "All
the extras in the wedding scene were Colombo hoods," producer Gray
Frederickson recently said.[37] Predictably, some of the actors were infatuated

by the hoods—but not Coppola, who remarked, "I never wanted to know them. I never started hanging out with the big one, like Jimmy Caan." When asked who "the big one" was, Coppola said he believed it was Carmine Persico.[38] G&W reneged on the black-tie events after Colombo was shot on the league's dais during a June 28, 1971, rally, soon after the New York filming wrapped. (The assassination attempt, which ironically occurred right in front of the G&W building, left Colombo in a vegetative state until his death on May 23, 1978.)

When the film was screened for a party of Hollywood insiders at a Malibu estate, television icon and antimob crusader Steve Allen somehow made the guest list. "There was the usual crowd there," Allen said in 1997, "but there were also a few swarthy Vegas boys who had 'organized crime' written all over them. After the movie, my wife Jayne made a remark about gangsters that caused one producer, who was friendly with the mob, to get in her face. 'You have no idea what you're talking about, lady,' this character told her." Allen said he intervened before the face-off got ugly, and soon thereafter, he and Jayne made their exit.

"The next morning, while I'm just waking up," Allen said, "our housekeeper came banging on our bedroom door."

"Mr. Allen! Mr. Allen!" called the frantic woman. The entertainer rushed out and followed his housekeeper to the front porch, where, in a scene reminiscent of the movie he had just seen, he found an enormous severed leg and shoulder of a horse. Allen knew the name of the producer who had the set-to with Jayne and, in a show of defiance, had the carcass delivered to his home. (The producer, whom Allen identified to this writer, was a close friend of Johnny Rosselli's, who Allen believed also attended the screening.)[39]

On March 14, 1972, the night before the gala New York premiere of *The Godfather*, Bob Evans put out still another fire for his precious film; this time the quixotic star, Marlon Brando, had decided to skip his own premiere. A frantic Evans reached his good friend Dr. Henry Kissinger, who was dealing not only with a Washington snowstorm, but a setback at the Paris Peace Talks with the North Vietnamese, who were threatening to walk out. Incredibly, Evans convinced Kissinger to come to New York and stand in for Brando. When Evans informed Korshak, in town with Bernice for the event, the Fixer was not impressed.

"You sure it's all right?" Korshak asked. When Evans asked why there might be a problem, Korshak explained, "It ain't no ordinary film. That's why. It's about the boys—the organization. It's a hot ticket." When Evans demanded to know exactly what the problem was, Korshak said tersely, "Nothing and everything."

At the postpremiere party at the St. Regis Hotel, Evans strolled over to Sidney and Bee's table and told Bee, "Without the big man, none of this could have happened. Join our table, will you?" An unsmiling Korshak said, "No." When Evans again demanded an explanation, Korshak's fuse was lit.

"And give the press a fuckin' field day?" Korshak asked.

"Come on, Sidney, it's your night too," Evans persisted.

At that, Korshak grabbed Evans's arm "like a vise" and fixed him with "the Look" he had mastered forty years earlier on the mean streets of the Outfit's West Chicago domain. "Don't ever bring me and Kissinger together in public. *Ever!* Now go back to your table, spend some time with your wife, schmuck."[40]

The Godfather netted $86.2 million in its first run domestically, going a long way toward both reinvigorating Paramount Pictures and justifying Evans's hiring to the disbelievers. Francis Ford Coppola quickly used his new clout (and his profit share of the movie as collateral) to secure a $700,000 loan from Al Hart's City National Bank of Beverly Hills so that he could help finance the film *American Graffiti* for his friend director George Lucas. However, before he actually took the money, Sid Korshak talked Coppola out of it, explaining that if *Graffiti* flopped, Coppola's children would suffer by losing their future royalties from *The Godfather*.[41]

Coppola's profits, however, are far less interesting, and less ironic, than those of the Sicilian industrialist who had been brought into the Paramount ownership structure two years earlier. It will never be known how much profit was funneled by Michele Sindona from the iconic Mafia movie to the real Mafia, but it is a certainty that some was. However, Sindona's star had reached its apogee and was soon to start a steep descent into eventual burnout. It was a complicated drama, with the following highlights:

• In 1972, Sindona bought a 21 percent interest in New York's Franklin National Bank, which collapsed two years later, leading to Sindona's conviction for massive bank fraud and to a chain reaction in Italy that saw Immobiliare stocks crash and the Vatican Bank, or IOR (Istituto per le Opere di Religione), which Sindona had tied to Immobiliare, lose $30 million. In addition, much of the $1.3 billion invested in the Bahamian shell companies simply vanished when the IOR stock collapsed. The IOR eventually acknowledged "moral involvement" with Sindona and Calvi and was forced to pay back $241 million to the creditors involved with Banco Ambrosiano.

• In 1974, after Sindona was indicted in Milan for bank fraud, he retained the law firm of Nixon's former attorney general John Mitchell to represent him in fighting the extradition from the United States. However, he was found guilty in absentia on twenty-three counts of misappropriating funds and sentenced to three and a half years in prison.

• On August 6, 1978, Pope Paul VI died after fifteen years in the papacy. Three weeks later Pope John Paul I assumed the papal throne. On September 28, Cardinal Jean Villot, the former Vatican secretary of state, was asked to stay on temporarily and begin an investigation into the financial dealings of the IOR. Later that night the pope was found dead, allegedly due to natural causes. He had been pope for only thirty-three days.

• On July 11, 1979, Italian magistrate Giorgio Ambrosoli, who had been compiling evidence against Sindona for five years, was shot to death, as were two other prosecutors. Enrico Cuccia, an Italian banker who had met with Sindona in New York three months earlier, testified that Sindona had told him that "he wanted everyone who had done him harm killed, in particular Giorgio Ambrosoli."

• In February 1980, Sindona went to trial on charges stemming from the collapse of the Franklin National Bank. Soon after, on March 27, 1980, he was found guilty of sixty-five counts, including fraud, conspiracy, perjury, false bank statements, and misappropriations of bank funds, and sentenced to three twenty-five-year terms and one twenty-four-year term.

• The Vatican bank scandal was effectively swept under the carpet in 1982. However, in Sicily, Sindona and sixty-five mafiosi were indicted for smuggling $600 million worth of heroin a year.

• On March 18, 1986, Sindona was sentenced in Milan to life for the murder of Ambrosoli. Two days later he died of cyanide poisoning—a favorite Mafia method to silence prisoners who know too much.[42]

Eighteen years after *The Godfather* premiered, *The Godfather Part III* was released, which drew heavily on the actual history of the Sindona-Immobiliare-Vatican bank scandals and the cross-pollination of the Sicilian and New York Mafias. It went so far as to use the name Immobiliare and to suggest that the pope had been murdered because of his intent to clean house. The film's closing credits include the following: "Dedicated to Charlie Bluhdorn, who inspired it."*

*   *   *

---

*On December 20, 1990, *The Godfather Part III* premiered in Beverly Hills, and the Immobiliare reference was not lost on insiders such as Peter Bart, who noted that Charlie Bluhdorn had tried numerous times over the years to persuade Francis Coppola to direct a second sequel of *The Godfather*. Bart wrote that Bluhdorn unfortunately never once

Before 1972 ended, Charlie Bluhdorn had still one more face-off with the Mafia. At the time, Italian producer Dino DeLaurentiis had just completed filming *The Valachi Papers*, about the infamous Mafia turncoat Joseph Valachi. According to DeLaurentiis's assistant to the producer, Fred Sidewater, the film was another that proceeded only with the sage counsel of Sid Korshak:

> We had three production assistants working as drivers who were really the greatest gofers around, and they were running around the lots and using their cars to run errands. Well, I got into the office and was told the Teamsters were shutting down the studio because we were using non-Teamster-affiliated drivers.
>
> I said, "Korshak can help," and I asked him and he said, "Don't let those kids drive anymore," and I said I couldn't join the Teamsters 'cause it would have changed my independent position and I'd get in trouble with all the other guilds. So finally he told me to go meet these three Teamster guys in Culver City Park and stand near a phone booth and talk to the guys standing next to it and answer the phone when it rings. I did what he said, and I told them that we weren't taking business away from them and that we couldn't afford to pay for a driver. Then the phone rang and it was Sidney. "Let me speak to one of the guys," he said—I think it was Andy Anderson. Anyway, I spoke to the guy after he got off the phone and he said, "Look, just don't let them do anything that Teamsters guys would be doing."[43]

Hoping to corner the market on mob cinema, Paramount was set to distribute *The Valachi Papers*—Paramount had distributed DeLaurentiis's films since 1955. However, at the last moment, Bluhdorn called the producer in a panic and pulled out of the deal after the Mafia had threatened to bomb the Gulf & Western building if he proceeded. DeLaurentiis then took the film to Warner Brothers, which was interested, but begged off after hearing of the threat to Bluhdorn. To save the film, DeLaurentiis went to Miami and met with Meyer Lansky's right-hand man, Vincent "Jimmy Blue Eyes" Alo, who promised to have the mob back off if DeLaurentiis would set one of Alo's Mafia friends up in Hollywood, which DeLaurentiis readily admitted

---

Footnote cont'd
sat down with Coppola to discuss his knowledge of Sindona, the assassination of Pope John Paul I, and other shadowy figures that he had met. Bart believed that if Bluhdorn had taken these steps, this might have prompted an earlier start to the production of *The Godfather III*, avoiding the sixteen-year gap between parts II and III. (Bart, *Who Killed Hollywood?*, 112–21)

he did.* From that point on, DeLaurentiis was dogged by rumors of his own Mafia connections, stories that alleged that he laundered mob money to finance his extravagant foreign-financed films.[44] Fuel for that fire also came from the fact that DeLaurentiis was a longtime friend of Michele Sindona's, who had personally approved a $1 million loan from his Franklin Bank for DeLaurentiis's move to New York and into his new offices on the fiftieth floor of Bluhdorn's Gulf & Western building.[45]

The King of Cool Meets the Fixer

Helping his ward Evans with *The Godfather* production was but the first of two favors that the Fixer performed for the young Paramount chief that year. However, the second series of intercessions had little to do with business, and much to do with Bob Evans's third sinking marriage.

While wrapping *The Godfather* in early 1972, forty-one-year-old Evans was weakly attempting to navigate the stormy waters of marriage number three, this one to actress/model Ali MacGraw, eight years his junior. After marrying the beautiful former Wellesley art history major in 1969, Evans cast her in the blockbuster Paramount film *Love Story*. But MacGraw, now the hottest young actress in America, was soon to learn that Evans's workaholic lifestyle was not the stuff of a good marriage. (Evans spent one night in January 1971 in Hollywood meeting with Coppola instead of with Ali in New York when she gave birth to their son Joshua.[46] In 1972, when Ali picked up a serious case of adult mumps while the two were in Europe, Evans flew back to the United States to put out more fires on *The Godfather*, leaving her with a strange French doctor in Antibes.)

In early 1972, Evans strongly suggested that Ali costar with macho actor Steve "the King of Cool" McQueen in a movie to be entitled *The Getaway*. Ali, who had met McQueen briefly once before, resisted—the sexual tension between the two was an affair waiting to happen. Ali later said that after the first meeting, "I had to leave the room to compose myself. He walked into my life as Mr. Humble, no ego, one of the guys. Steve was this very original, principled guy who didn't seem to be part of the system, and I loved that. He was clever, demure, exciting, and had all the answers. I bought that act in the first second. We had this electrifying, obsessive attraction." Ali knew that if she accepted the role, she and McQueen would become lovers, and her floundering marriage to Evans would be over.[47]

---

*The man DeLaurentiis set up was Dino Conte, an alleged associate of Alo's and also the Lucchese and Colombo crime families, who went on to produce *48 HRS*, *Another 48 HRS*, and *Conan the Barbarian*. (*Wall Street Journal*, 7-13-90)

But Evans prevailed, MacGraw moved to El Paso to start the picture, and the sparks between the two actors flew immediately. According to Paramount's distribution chief Frank Yablans, Evans intentionally torpedoed the marriage. "Evans pushed them together," Yablans said. "He didn't give a shit. It didn't matter to him. He's a very strange man. He couldn't be married, couldn't live a normal, sane life. He drove her out."[48]

By July 1972, as the Evans-MacGraw union was crumbling, Henry Kissinger offered to go to Texas for Evans to attempt to broker a peace between the two sides—hopefully with more success that he was seeing in his efforts with the warring Vietnamese factions. However, Evans declined the offer, citing Kissinger's more pressing concerns.[49] Eventually, Sid Korshak was brought into the fray for the first of many Evans-MacGraw minidramas. The occasion was a marital breakdown at one of Evans's and Korshak's favorite getaways, The Hotel Du Cap on the French Riviera. For this impasse, Evans called Sidney in Bel-Air, and his friend hopped a jet for the six-thousand-mile marriage-counseling trip. "On to the rock flew Sidney Korshak," Evans wrote, "my consigliere, for one purpose and one purpose only—to keep my rocky marriage from falling into the sea. Each day Sidney would sit with Ali for hours, trying to persuade her to make the marriage work." Korshak's attempt at damage control temporarily forestalled the inevitable.[50]

When Evans learned of the MacGraw-McQueen affair, he again called on Korshak. According to Bistro owner Kurt Niklas, who overheard the conversation, Evans met with his mentor in the restaurant's private room upstairs and informed him that he wanted his rival McQueen murdered. "Just calm down, Bobby," Korshak said. Over the next few minutes, Korshak succeeded in cooling off Evans, who left the restaurant. "He hadn't been gone ten minutes," Niklas wrote, "when McQueen arrived, asking for Korshak." Now, not only Niklas but the entire wait staff strained to eavesdrop on the confab. According to one good source, McQueen had met Korshak years earlier, an occasion that supposedly left McQueen shaken. In a recent interview, the source related, "It was at a New York post-movie-premiere party for one of McQueen's movies. Korshak happened to be there as well. McQueen was drunk—he was known to have a 'short guy' chip on his shoulder. Anyway, Korshak turns from the bar and spills McQueen's drink. So McQueen winds up to punch Sidney, who he didn't know, and Sidney puts up one finger and says, 'Wait, you may be a big star, but if you lay one finger on me, I will have your fucking eyes ripped out.' McQueen either was told or realized who Sidney was and left his own premiere party."

Perhaps with this memory in mind, an obsequious McQueen, known far and wide as a macho figure, appeared before Korshak at his Bistro lair.

"Mr. Korshak, please—I don't want any problems, but he's threatening to kill me," McQueen implored.

"Nobody's gonna get killed, unless things keep going sour," Korshak assured him.

"But I'm talking about my life!" persisted McQueen.

"Just shut up and listen to me," Korshak demanded. Then the two began speaking in hushed tones that Niklas et al. were unable to divine. Finally, Korshak spoke up:

"You do as I say, and nobody's gonna get hurt."

A "sheepish" McQueen then left, only to continue the affair with Mac-Graw soon thereafter.[51]

MacGraw moved in with McQueen, and after marrying him in 1973, sought to obtain custody of her son with Evans, Joshua. Evans relented on that, but drew the line when the new couple informed him that they were legally changing the toddler's name to Josh McQueen. McQueen sealed his fate when he had the temerity to call up Evans and criticize the sybarite's lifestyle.

"Your butler's a homosexual," said McQueen. "Your surroundings, the way you live, is not the environment that's right for Joshua . . . I intend to change his name to McQueen . . . have full control." Of course, McQueen had a good point; Evans was well-known to engulf Woodland in hedonism of all sorts. Lastly, McQueen added, his attorney was drawing up custody papers.

"Good. Take your best shot, motherfucker," railed Evans. "One of us, pal, only one of us is going to come out in one piece."

Slamming down the phone, Evans called his go-to man, Father Sidney, who offered the solution. At Korshak's direction, Evans hired a particular attorney, who, within two weeks, compiled a dossier on McQueen that, according to Evans, was almost one foot thick. When the file was shown to McQueen and his attorney, they crumbled. Not only was McQueen prevented from renaming the child, he was forced to eat more crow when he agreed to only refer to Joshua's father as "Mister Evans."[*,52]

A final post-*Godfather* favor for Evans was not quite as successful. When his contract with Paramount was up for renegotiation, Evans told Korshak that, since he had elevated Paramount from ninth to first in studio profits, he felt he should make mogul money.

---

*MacGraw and McQueen divorced in 1978.

Bob Evans (left) with Mia Farrow and
Roman Polanski, 1968 (Photofest)

"I'll take care of it and quick," Korshak told Evans. "You're gonna get gross." Bluhdorn, however, would hear none of it. The best Korshak could obtain for Evans was a one-film-per-year independent production deal that would see him share any profits fifty-fifty with Paramount. Evans took the deal and formed Robert Evans Productions, but later lamented, "Korshak was a negotiator, not an entertainment attorney."[53]

Evans went on to produce a number of successful films, such as *Marathon Man* (1976) and *Urban Cowboy* (1980). But perhaps his greatest post-*Godfather* triumph was a film laden with Supermob irony, *Chinatown* (1974). Directed by a brilliant Polish pederast named Roman Polanski, the same man who helmed Paramount's *Rosemary's Baby*, the film thinly fictionalizes William Mulholland's "Rape of Owens Valley" (see chapter 4). Since the savage murder of Polanski's pregnant actress wife Sharon Tate and four of her jet-set pals by Charles Manson's "family" on August 9, 1969, Polanski had begun indulging his predilection for having sex with children, thirteen- to fifteen-year-old girls preferably, as a way to assuage his grief.* The sickness would eventually bring him before Korshak's great friend Judge Laurence Rittenband. In the film *Chinatown*, which also included a Polanski nod to sexual perversion, the character Hollis Mulwray subbed for William Mulholland. It is not known if Evans was aware of the similarities between the California land and water grabs of Mulholland/Mulwray and those of Korshak's Supermob associates Greenberg/Ziffren/Bazelon.

---

*One Polanski friend said, "He told me that after his wife and baby were killed, he changed. He started having sex with young people because he couldn't bear to be with regular women. Regular women wanted commitment from him, and he felt he would be betraying Sharon if he got involved with another woman. So he went after these young girls. That way there was no commitment." (Kiernan, *Roman Polanski Story*, 229)

Chinatown marked the high point of Evans's career, which was soon to succumb to a cocaine-fueled hedonism that was extreme even by Hollywood standards.

The Man with the Golden Touch

Korshak's casting prowess was again evidenced in the spring of 1971—just one month after *The Godfather* went into production—when Korshak's great friend producer Cubby Broccoli was casting a new film, and Korshak had an idea as to who should get the lead.

Albert Romolo "Cubby" Broccoli was born in 1909, the son of immigrants from Calabria, Italy. The Broccolis were in the vegetable business, with one of Cubby's uncles actually having brought the first broccoli seeds into the United States in the 1870s. In 1933, after years of toiling in the vegetable business, Cubby visited his cousin (and ex-husband of blond movie goddess Thelma Todd) Pat DeCicco, a Hollywood agent and starlet gofer for Howard Hughes, and decided to get into the movie business.* "Pat had brass balls and was very charming," said friend Tom Mankiewicz, screenwriting son of director Joseph Mankiewicz. "He'd take guests to Hughes's island in the Bahamas— the island would always be filled with Pat and his people."[54] Coincidentally, on his first flight to L.A., Broccoli sat next to Korshak pal Jake "the Barber" Factor.[55] After working on the Howard Hughes film *The Outlaw* (and becoming close to Hughes), Broccoli moved to England, where he entered into a producing partnership with Harry Saltzman, and in the late 1950s they bought the screen rights to the James Bond novels of MCA client Ian Fleming, producing the first Bond movie, *Dr. No*, for $1 million in 1962.[†56]

In the interim, Broccoli relocated to Beverly Hills, where he nourished his friendships with Sid Korshak, Lew Wasserman, Greg Bautzer, Mike Romanoff, and others in their circle.

"Cubby Broccoli and Sidney were like brothers," said a Korshak family friend. "They had lunch together at the Bistro all the time."[57] Tom Mankiewicz recently said, "Cubby and Sidney's relationship was amazing."

In early 1971, Broccoli was prepping the seventh film in his Bond franchise, *Diamonds Are Forever*, a roman à clef parody of his friend Howard Hughes. By this time, Hughes was a debilitated billionaire hermit, recently

---

*DeCicco was married for a time to millionaire fashion designer Gloria Vanderbilt, later the mother of CNN's Anderson Cooper. Among others DeCicco brought to Hughes was Elizabeth Taylor. (Deitrich and Thomas, *Howard*, 275)

†The seventeen Bond films Broccoli was associated with were reported to have earned $1 billion worldwide by the time of his death in 1996.

Cubby and Dana Broccoli, 1993 (private collection)

relocated to the Bahamas after being holed up for two years in the Desert Inn, which he'd purchased from Moe Dalitz. Insiders knew that the white-collar tycoons would soon be squeezing the mob out of its own creation. In Broccoli's version, the Hughes character was named Willard Whyte, owner of the Whyte House casino, and a pawn in a nefarious scheme to build a massive superlaser out of thousands of smuggled diamonds. Assisting Bond in saving both Whyte and the planet Earth was a beautiful diamond smuggler (rehabilitated by Bond, of course) named Tiffany Case.

The film production would inevitably unite friends Broccoli and Korshak, since much of the story would be filmed in Korshak's Las Vegas dominion, with key scenes shot in his Riviera Casino. In the *Encyclopedia of Fantastic Film and Television*, buried way down the *Diamonds Are Forever* credits, is this entry: "Legal advisor (Las Vegas): Sidney Korshak (uncredited)." But Korshak did much more than guarantee the cooperation of Vegas Teamsters—it appears he once again assisted the casting department.

Journalist Peter Evans first broke the story of Korshak's intervention, writing, "In Los Angeles, attorney Sidney Korshak, who was helping Broccoli set up location deals in Las Vegas, asked whether a small role could be arranged for actress Jill St. John, a close friend of his. She had been up for various Bond heroines before but never with success."[58] According to the film's then twenty-eight-year-old screenwriter, Tom Mankiewicz, Jill was given a small supporting role, with Natalie Wood's sister Lana set for the lead role of Tiffany Case. "At some point Jill was going to play Plenty O'Toole, a lot smaller part than Lana would have played," Mankiewicz recalled. "And then she was mysteriously bumped up." Wood recently remembered her casting, saying, "I was contacted by my agent, who said, 'They want you to be in the Bond film.' I was considered for the lead role. I don't know how

Jill St. John with Sean Connery in *Diamonds Are Forever* (Photofest)

things got flipped around. I know that Jill was being considered for Plenty O'Toole, but it was supposed to be the exact opposite."*,59

For the young Mankiewicz, the shoot was an eye-opener. "We were up at Sidney's 'house,' the Riviera, which Eddie Torres was running," he remembered. "It was one of the last mob-run hotels in Vegas. Korshak, Jill St. John, Sean Connery, and others stayed at the Riviera, while the crew stayed at the Happy Times Motel."

Five years after the film's release, when Pat DeCicco suffered a stroke and fell into a coma in Cubby's Beverly Hills home, Cubby was frantic to get him to his New York doctor. When no planes were found on short notice, Broccoli called Korshak, who knew that pal Frank Sinatra had millionaire Fabergé perfume-company chief—and airplane owner—George Barrie as a guest at his Palm Springs home. Korshak called Sinatra and obtained the Barrie jet, which whisked DeCicco off to New York, a rescue that revived him from his coma long enough to get his affairs in order.[60]

As the summer of 1972 wound down, Korshak's confidence was soaring. According to a top FBI source, in August 1972, Korshak made a $22-per-share offer to purchase one hundred thousand shares of Kerkorian's MGM, a failed bid that would have given him controlling interest in the company.[61]

---

*Other interesting casting included singer/actor Jimmy Dean as Whyte/Hughes, an ironic choice given that Dean was at the time performing in Hughes's Desert Inn. And when Sean Connery initially passed on reprising the Bond role, the part was given to Korshak friend John Gavin, who was forced to withdraw when Connery signed on after having been given a record-breaking $1.25 million fee, all of which he donated to his charity.

CHAPTER 18

From Dutch Sandwiches to Dutch Reagan

As KORSHAK APPROACHED what is retirement age for most Americans, he continued brokering labor peace at his regular pace. Slowly, however, his financial success became a point of criticism among those who regularly paid his exorbitant fees in exchange for little more than a few phone calls. "Sidney was not cheap on his fees," remembered friend and colleague Leo Geffner. "My tongue used to hang out, seeing him make in five minutes what I made in an hour. Most lawyers charged by the hour, but his flat fee: 'Fifty thousand.' It may take just one or two short lunches at the Bistro. And he never carried a yellow pad like most lawyers. He wrote everything down on an envelope, if you can believe that."[1]

Where Were They When Capone Needed Them?

In 1973, soon after attending the February 9 funeral of Ralph Stolkin in Palm Springs with Tony Accardo,[2] Korshak was paid $300,000 for his minor role in facilitating an offshore tax dodge for the Supermob's Charlie Bluhdorn and Lew Wasserman. Three years earlier, Paramount's Bluhdorn had persuaded Wasserman and MCA-Universal to enter into a foreign partnership, Cinema International Corporation (CIC), an unethical masterstroke that allowed the companies to avoid both U.S. antitrust laws and U.S. taxes. Universal and Paramount would later form a distribution partnership called Universal International Pictures (UIP), referred to by Edward Epstein as "a highly profitable off-the-books foreign-based corporation."[3]

The concept, a mirror of the Pritzkers' Castle Bank arrangement in the Bahamas, allowed the merger to pool overseas resources for film distribution, hide its profits in an Amsterdam bank, then use complex "flow-through" subsidiaries to bring the untaxed lucre back into its own U.S. banks. Nicknamed a Dutch Sandwich since the client's money was hidden between a sham corporation based in Amsterdam and a sham trust in Curaçao (Dutch

Antilles), the scheme allowed the customers' income to be brought into the United States disguised as untaxable "loans" from the Caribbean bank. One banker working for Curaçao's Credit Lyonais Nederland Bank admitted to *Time* magazine that he had no qualms about helping U.S. companies and individuals dodge taxes. "Many of your largest corporations, many of your movie stars, do much the same thing here," the banker said. "We wouldn't want to handle criminal money, of course. But if it's just a matter of taxes, that is of no concern to us."[4] The banker might have had a hard time convincing Al Capone's family that tax evasion and criminality were not the same thing.

MCA executive George Smith openly admitted that vast profits accrued from the setup. "I would say that, on the average, one hundred to two hundred million tax dollars were deferred every year," Smith said. "Generally, we put it in a bank and got interest." Paramount's new COO, Frank Yablans, stated frankly, "It was a brilliant tax dodge."[5] The intricate construct became a template for Hollywood conglomerates that would outlive its creators.* It would also herald a new era, one where tax lawyers eclipsed all others in importance in the film business. These facilitators favored creative accounting measures such as EBIDTA (earnings before interest, depreciation, taxes, and amortization), which, by allowing the studios to postpone the reporting of losses, gave a false impression of earnings to potential investors.

Soon, numerous high-rises appeared on the West Hollywood skyline, housing the lawyers that run the town to this day. The towers themselves were often financed using the Dutch Sandwich.

Assisting Hollywood's assault on the IRS were the likes of Senator Thomas Kuchel, the minority whip on the Appropriations Committee (and a partner at Wyman, Bautzer), who introduced legislation that would allow producers to understate their taxable gross income by 20 percent—the legislation was also lobbied for hard by the likes of Governor Ronald Reagan. Lew Wasserman, with his extensive ties in Washington, worked overtime to see the enactment of the 1971 Revenue Act, which allowed the film and television industry to define their product (films and television programs) as equipment and machinery, thus becoming eligible for a traditional 7 percent tax write-off for industry that had begun in 1962. The March 1972 issue of

---

*The tax dodge courtesy was also offered to millionaire movie stars, who have since become incorporated in the Netherlands and receive their income as tax-free loans. With Wasserman viewed as the most adept at the offshore schemes, many top actors had still one more huge incentive for signing up with MCA.

Variety reported that "97% of [MCA's] profit increase last year is directly attributable to the new tax rules." Universal and the other studios quickly joined Disney in a suit aimed at recovering back credits dating to 1962, a successful effort that saw them receive another windfall totaling almost $400 million.[6] The credit was then raised to 10 percent, and the benefits multiplied. In addition, one clause in the legislation allowed movie investors to reap an astounding 100 percent indefinite tax deferment on half of all profits from exported films.[7]

Wasserman, Korshak, Kuchel, and Reagan were not the only actors working to feather Hollywood's nest. Also looking out for the financial health of the movie moguls was Jack Valenti, head of the Motion Picture Association of America (MPAA). Valenti was a former Houston, Texas, adman and special assistant to President Lyndon Johnson, who was brought to the White House after the assassination of President Kennedy in November of 1963. In 1965, Wasserman and attorney Ed Weisl Sr. (the man who had assisted Korshak in working out the details of Bluhdorn's purchase of Paramount and was also a director the Chicago Thoroughbred Enterprises *and* was a longtime friend of Johnson's) obtained LBJ's permission to headhunt Valenti and bring him to Hollywood (Valenti had earlier recommended to Johnson that Wasserman be named secretary of commerce, which Johnson proposed, but Wasserman declined).

A flamboyant attention seeker, Valenti took to Hollywood as if he were born there and for the next four decades would lobby hard in Washington for legislation that enabled the movie moguls to enjoy tax benefits (thanks to what was essentially protectionist lawmaking) unavailable to the average hardworking American. Valenti's view was that anyone involved in what he believed to be the precious film business was entitled to special financial treatment. And Wasserman's MCA-Universal profited more than any other; as one studio head put it, "The MPAA wagged to Lew's desires."[8]

In the years that followed, another key player in offshore tax schemes was Peter Hoffman, a brilliant attorney who had in 1974–75 clerked for none other than Paul Ziffren's great friend U.S. district court judge—and former tax attorney—David Bazelon. Hoffman became a specialist in the Dutch Sandwich, using it to become the architect and CEO of Carolco Pictures, a major independent player that, as a result of creative offshore financing, was able to finance such hits as the *Rambo* pictures, *Terminator 2: Judgment Day, Total Recall, Cliffhanger,* and *Basic Instinct.* (In a December 1996 indictment for tax evasion and filing a false income tax return, the Justice Department charged that Hoffman treated income of more than $400,000 as "sham loans" to avoid paying taxes. In its trial brief, the government charged that Hoffman had created a "deferred compensation scheme" to obtain more than $1 million in tax-free income. Simultaneously, the IRS audited Carolco partners Andy Vajna and Mario Kassar and returned a $109.7 million tax assessment against them. The bulk of the claim focused on earnings by the partners' offshore companies that were set up in tax-haven countries such as the Netherlands Antilles—i.e., the Dutch Sandwich. In 1998, Hoffman pled guilty to one count of filing a false tax return and paid a puny $5,000 fine. Carolco had already closed shop.[9] Under the banner of C-2 Productions, Kassar would resurface as the producer of such films as *Terminator 3* and *The Kingdom of Heaven*.

In 2002, Paramount exec turned *Variety* editor Peter Bart described Hoffman's legacy: "Peter Hoffman, a lawyer-turned-producer, earned a certain renown years ago for creating such an arcane legalistic lexicon that no normal mortal could understand what he said. Now many lawyers have emulated the Hoffman model."[10]

The new focus on international profits also had a chilling effect on the artistic merit of the movies that were now deemed most desirable by the new multinational studios; gone were the days when the major suppliers released the likes of *To Kill a Mockingbird* and *On the Waterfront*. In their place were now cartoonish action movies whose minimal dialogue required no translation in order to appeal to the lowest-common-denominator audience in many countries simultaneously. For astute observers, this effect represented the most insidious legacy of the Korshak-Wasserman international design, a trend that regretfully continues to the present day.

In 1973, CIC was having problems convincing MGM to join its offshore party—MGM was demanding that its television productions be included in the operation, an idea that was not part of the original plan. The impasse forced Paramount attorney Art Barron to do what so many had done before: "I got out my Korshak number. I said, 'Sidney, this is where we're at.' He said, 'Hold your ground.'"

Just as he had done for Bob Evans with the Pacino casting, Korshak once again called MGM owner Kirk Kerkorian, who was still struggling to pay for the construction on the MGM Grand in Las Vegas; Korshak knew the pending deal with CIC would give him enough cash for the project. According to Barron, within thirty minutes Kerkorian had taken MGM's demand off the table. Soon thereafter, Barron received a piece of SIDNEY KORSHAK, COUNSELOR-AT-LAW stationery that stated simply, "Fees—$50,000." Although a shock to Barron, who typically paid hourly fees to attorneys, the bill was paid on orders of Lew Wasserman.[11]

In the following days, Kerkorian and Korshak worked out the fine points at the Bistro, where the deal was soon inked on October 25, 1973.[12] For bringing aboard Kerkorian, an addition valued at $17 million to CIC, Korshak billed CIC another $250,000.[13] Like Wasserman, Charles Bluhdorn had no problem with the fee. "Mr. Korshak was very close to Wasserman and Kerkorian and played a key role as a go-between," Bluhdorn later told Sy Hersh. "It was a very, very tough negotiation that would have been broken down without him."[14] However, MCA senior executive Berle Adams bristled at the oft-heard suggestion that Korshak was responsible for the formation of CIC. "Sidney had nothing to do with it," Adams said recently. "I was there—it was all Bluhdorn's doing."[15]

A world away from Dutch Sandwiches and heady CIC negotiations, UFW leader Cesar Chavez was locked in mortal combat with his Teamster rival for the hearts and minds of Northern California's migrant farmworkers. As he had in 1966, Chavez would once again enter the domain of Sidney Korshak, not because of Korshak's work for farmers like Schenley, but because of his long-standing allegiance to the Teamsters.

Since the Schenley settlement, the UFW had engaged in a series of strikes and boycotts against growers (most notably of lettuce and table grapes) who refused to allow Chavez's organization to recruit workers into its fold. In 1973, grape growers began signing sweetheart contracts with the Teamsters, even though the workers had, for the most part, never asked for Teamster representation. "[The growers] knew the Teamsters would let them off easier than Cesar would," said one veteran labor activist. "And instead of telling the growers to go to hell, the Teamsters accepted their invitation. It was a straight steal on the part of the Teamsters. They had been in the farm industry for thirty or forty years and they hadn't done a thing for these people. Then, after Chavez knocks his brains out for them, they tried to take it all from him."[16]

The move sparked violent confrontations between Teamster goons and migrant workers, resulting in injuries, deaths, and thousands of arrests for the Chicanos. In response, Chavez called for a nationwide boycott of table grapes. According to a nationwide Louis Harris poll, at one point some seventeen million Americans were boycotting grapes.

What seemed to imply the presence of Sidney Korshak was that the Teamster enforcers were ostensibly working at the behest of Western Teamster boss Andy Anderson, who, in turn, was understood to be a functionary of Sid Korshak. (The thugs came to be known as Anderson's Raiders, a bit of wordplay based on a band of Confederate Civil War rogues that went by the same name.) As Duke Zeller, the former adviser to four Teamsters national presidents, recently said, "Virtually every Teamster leader on the West Coast, in the Western Conference, answered to Sidney Korshak. Everything really went through Korshak, who by all accounts was very astute and very bright. He knew what he was doing and knew how to play the game, certainly with the Teamsters." Mafioso Jimmy Fratianno told Teamster leader Jackie Presser that he knew Korshak had orchestrated the attacks. "[Frank] Fitzsimmons heard that Andy got a payoff from the farmers in the Delano area," Fratianno said. "They wanted Chavez out of there. Andy and Jack Goldberger [of the San Francisco Teamsters] got Sid Korshak to work it out."[17]

The struggles played out for five more years. In 1978, newly elected DA John Van DeKamp was given a prognostication of the soon-to-be settlement, an eventuality that again conjured the Korshak name. "It's one of the most interesting Korshak stories that I remember," Van DeKamp said recently. "It involved [Herman] Blackie Leavitt, the international vice president of Bartenders' Union [Local 249] and a Las Vegas organizer. I didn't know him well—he had a checkered reputation. Blackie made an appointment to see me when I was DA. He came into my office in a sort of hush-hush way. He said, 'I want to tell you something. I want you to know that Sidney Korshak is going to be the intermediary between the Teamsters and the Farm Workers. I am going to tell you that in three months there is going to be a settlement between them that gets the Teamsters out of competition with the Farm Workers.'"[18] Three months hence, Van DeKamp joined the ranks of those who marveled at the effect Korshak had on labor imbroglios when the two unions resolved the issue with an agreement giving the UFW sole right to organize farmworkers.

However, membership in the UFW later fell, in part due to disputes between Chavez and his followers, some of whom accused him of nepotism. (On April 23, 1993, Chavez died peacefully in his sleep at the modest home of a retired San Luis, Arizona, farmworker while defending the UFW against a multimillion-dollar lawsuit brought by a large vegetable grower. Since his death, the plight of the farmworkers has again reverted to the pre-UFW conditions, largely because of the massive influx of undocumented alien workers, which now make up 90 percent of the force.)

* * *

In 1973, after attending the February funeral of Ralph Stolkin in San Diego,[19] Sid Korshak dabbled in a bit of nepotism, landing his son Harry a producer's job at Paramount. Harry (who some friends say was named after Harry Karl, not Sidney's father, Harry Korshak) had shown an early interest in the entertainment biz, appearing as an actor in episodes of the long-running television series *The Donna Reed Show*. Of course, Donna Reed and her husband were close friends of the Korshaks' and likely gave the nod to young Harry's TV debut.*

Nine years afterward, Paramount production executive Peter Bart was paid an unannounced visit by Harry's father, who had shown up to help accelerate his grown son's fledgling movie career, this time as a producer. Korshak informed Bart of a project that Bart had never heard of, surprising given Bart's position at the studio. For this film—a thriller entitled *Hit!*—Harry was to be the producer, and the project was to begin immediately. Bart remembered Korshak saying, "Peter, my son has not produced anything before. I would be greatly in your debt if you kept an eye on him. He doesn't have your savvy." Bob Evans's right-hand man had no choice but to offer his assistance. "When Sidney Korshak asked a favor," Bart later wrote, "it wasn't smart to decline, especially when it was such a reasonable one."[20] According to Bart, right after his decree, Korshak borrowed Bart's phone and placed a call on a direct line to the most powerful man in the industry, Lew Wasserman (Jules Stein had resigned from MCA on June 5, 1973, making Wasserman the new chairman). The call raised the possibility that Korshak was asking Lew to donate some MCA talent to his son's endeavor (which eventually starred Billy Dee Williams and Richard Pryor).†

As it happened, Gray Frederickson, the coproducer of *The Godfather,* got the call to watch over Harry Korshak. Three years earlier, Korshak had prevailed upon Frederickson to hire Harry as a PA (production assistant) on the Paramount feature *Little Fauss and Big Halsy,* starring Robert Redford. Frederickson recently recalled getting the call from Sidney, who said, "We're sending Harry as a PA on the film." Now, during the start-up of the *Hit!* shoot, Frederickson said an incident took place that hinted that Daddy Korshak was also shepherding the film from afar. "This was a low-budget film and we were using nonunion drivers to cut costs," recalled Frederickson.

---

*Harry played "Steve" in episode #7.16, "Overture in A-flat," which aired December 31, 1964.

†*Hit!* opened on September 18, 1973, and told the story of a federal agent whose daughter dies of a heroin overdose, and his determination to destroy the drug ring that supplied her. The ambitious action flick received some good, but overall mixed, reviews.

"On the first night of the shoot in D.C., the Teamsters showed up to demand work. This would have killed us financially, but they could have shut us down if we refused to hire them. Harry just said, 'I'll call Daddy.' "[21] According to Frederickson, the Teamster contingent returned to the set soon thereafter, only this time their demeanor spoke volumes to the seasoned producer about the power of Sidney Korshak. "The Teamsters showed up and offered anything we needed for free," said a still awed Frederickson. "That's when it hit me."

In the end, Frederickson paid dearly for all his help with Harry's producing bow—young Korshak began an affair with Frederickson's socialite wife, Tori, the half sister of Mrs. Conrad Hilton. The recently divorced Harry ended up marrying Tori and went on to produce just two more, inconsequential, films, *Sheila Levine Is Dead and Living in New York* (1975) and *Gable and Lombard* (1976).

On October 1, 1973, soon after the *Hit!* premiere, Sidney hosted at his home the seventy-eighth-birthday party for George Raft.[22]

Eleven days later, the attention of Supermob watchers turned to Washington, where, on October 12, Judge Bazelon, chief of Washington's U.S. Court of Appeals, upheld Judge John Sirica's U.S. district court ruling, thereby forcing President Nixon to hand over the incriminating White House tapes to the Watergate special prosecutor, which he did on November 26, leading to his eventual resignation on August 8, 1974.

Twenty-three hundred miles away, Sid Korshak made a ruling in his own Supermob jurisdiction—Beverly Hills—the result of an altercation on a typical Beverly Hills late afternoon in the spring of 1974, as Bistro owner Kurt Niklas was preparing to make the transition from the lunch crowd to the dinner arrivals.

On this particular evening, one lunchtime party refused to leave in time for the dinner setup—an occasional problem for restaurateurs. But what made this case exceptional was that the party was headed by the charming but dangerous Chicago mafioso Johnny Rosselli, a man Niklas called "the asp" for his deadly stare. "Johnny Rosselli came in regularly in the afternoons," said former Bistro maître d' Jimmy Murphy. "He started coming in there about 1965."[23] Bistro headwaiter Casper Morcelli said of Rosselli, "He was nice to us for the most part, but he was a rough guy."[24]

Niklas said that Rosselli began getting habitually drunk and stiffing the bar, opting instead to fold the check into a paper airplane, floating it back to Niklas and barking, "Give this fucking check to your Jew friend Korshak!"

Johnny Rosselli walking to his June 24, 1975, Senate testimony (Corbis/Bettmann)

Niklas said that he merely ate the loss, without telling anyone, especially Korshak.[25] Actress and Rosselli "goddaughter" Nancy Czar explained Rosselli's behavior recently, saying, "JR [Rosselli] was pissed at Sid—he thought Sid was taking over his territory."[26] Jimmy Murphy said Czar knew what she was talking about, as she and Rosselli were constant companions. "Rosselli used to date these beautiful women, like eighteen-year-old Nancy Czar, who was with him a lot," said Murphy. "He was taking good care of her, and she dined with him often at the Bistro."*

But, Czar's beliefs notwithstanding, there was another element to Rosselli's fury at Korshak, for he was among those who suspected Korshak of playing both sides of the law—which, in fact, he was. When he was imprisoned on the Friars Club scam, Rosselli had told a fellow inmate that Korshak was an FBI informant; Rosselli's key reason, also noted by others, was "that he had had never been prosecuted by the Federal Government."[27]

Czar was with Rosselli on the evening in question, as was Bugsy Siegel's pal Allen Smiley and mob attorney Jimmy Cantillon. "We got there before the dinner hour," remembered Czar, "when JR and Kurt, who he called 'the Nazi,' got into it." Murphy described how the situation evolved before a full house of patrons: "There was a section near the service bar where people could sit and have drinks. But by six or seven they had to vacate those tables because we needed them for dinner. One night Rosselli was there with a few friends who had a lot to drink, and he just said, 'No, I'm not leaving.'"

---

*Czar had an interesting career herself, appearing in a number of Elvis Presley movies, including *Girl Happy* (1965) and *Spinout* (1966), and becoming a B-movie queen in such low-budget classics as Ray Dennis Steckler's *Wild Guitar,* playing opposite the legendary Arch Hall Jr.

Finally, Kurt came over and said, 'Look, you're leaving, I need this table.' As he was approaching the door, he turned to Kurt and called him an SOB. Out of nowhere, Kurt threw him a punch and hit him square on the jaw, knocking him through two doors. His head of white hair was all over his face. Rosselli got up, looked at Kurt, and said, 'This place is history!' " According to Niklas, the threat was much more frightening, with Rosselli, the man with the deadly stare, yelling back, "You're a fucking dead man, Kurt!"

It suddenly dawned on the Bistro owner just how imprudent his punch had been. "He was the real thing and his threats scared me shitless," Niklas later wrote. Morcelli saw the fear in Niklas's face. "Kurt was worried because Johnny was nuts," Morcelli recalled.

Of course, there was only one man to approach with a problem of this magnitude—Korshak. "If Rosselli was the asp, Korshak was the asp-eater," said Niklas. "The one thing Sidney Roy Korshak was reputed to be able to do better than anyone else in the world was to talk privately to Johnny's boss, the legendary Chicago godfather, Sam Giancana."[28] What Niklas couldn't know was that Giancana was still living in "exile" in Mexico, having been banished by the Outfit's capo, Joe Batters Accardo. But that mattered little, since Korshak was even closer to Accardo. As Chicago FBI man from the seventies Pete Wacks recently noted, "In the seventies, Korshak made monthly visits to his suite at the Drake, where he met with Accardo and the others."[29]

On hearing of Niklas's careless cuffing of Rosselli, Korshak exclaimed, "Are you nuts? Check into a hotel and call me in the morning." When Niklas called back as instructed the next day, Korshak was at his minimalist best.

"Everything's okay," Korshak assured him.

"Are you sure?" demanded an unconvinced Niklas.

"Goddammit, what did I just say?" answered an irate Korshak. "Johnny's not going to do a fucking thing. Got it?" With that, Korshak hung up.

"Kurt's call to Sidney saved the day," Murphy said. "It was the last time we saw Rosselli." Niklas was more effusive: "I know Korshak saved my life."[30] Months after the dustup, Niklas finally told Korshak that Rosselli had regularly made anti-Semitic remarks about him. "How come you never told me that?" Korshak asked. "I didn't want to cause any problems," Niklas answered.

Korshak's display of power illustrated that, although he was increasingly more "legit," he still maintained a powerful connection to old Chicago. Significantly, a 1974 FBI memo stated, "Korshak is undoubtedly best contact any LCN [La Cosa Nostra] anywhere has and conducts activity constantly for all LCN families, being in constant contact with [Gus] Alex whose assignment it is to 'handle him.' "[31] On January 15 of that year, Korshak was observed meeting with Joe Batters Accardo in Palm Springs. According to an FBI informant, "The meeting concerned a liquor salesman union meetings [sic]. [Source] advised that election of officers to replace two who have recently died is to be held in future in New York. Korshak wanted to discuss with Accardo background of two candidates whom he is recommending . . . Korshak visited Accardo during the day and returned to Los Angeles in late afternoon."[32]

Korshak's name next surfaced that summer, albeit briefly, again in relation to his Nevada foe Howard Hughes. The Korshak linkage concerned testimony gathered after what came to be known as the Great Hughes Heist.

At one A.M. on June 5, 1974, four or five burglars entered the fortresslike office of Howard Hughes's holding company, The Summa Corporation, located at 7000 Romaine Street in Hollywood, in what was later concluded to be an inside job. The building contained twenty-five years' worth of handwritten Hughes memos, as well as personal and corporate files, and safes full of cash; it was the nerve center of his empire. In their four-plus hours on the scene, the burglars, who came equipped with acetylene torches, largely ignored the cash-engorged wall safes, more interested in a meticulous reading of the sensitive documents, occasionally remarking, according to the bound security guard's deposition, "Looky here, this is it!"

Interestingly, it was the sixth unsolved burglary of a Hughes office in the last five months. However, until this burglary, no papers had been taken—obviously the thieves were looking for something specific. This time, though, they hit the jackpot, filling up cardboard-box-loads of Hughes's personal files, and anywhere from $60,000 to $300,000, according to differing reports.[33]

There were many possible motives for the heist, including: with the Senate Watergate investigators hounding him, Richard Nixon had ordered the theft to destroy any evidence of the graft he had received from the billionaire over the years (on the very day of the burglary, Donald Nixon was to testify about the Hughes loans to the Senate investigators); or, Hughes himself had ordered it so that any record of the bribes and stock manipulations connected to his recent buyout of Air West would be beyond the reach of a Senate subpoena. FBI reports show that the Bureau was certain that the break-in was related either to Watergate or organized crime in Las Vegas. One Bureau report suggested that organized crime desired to steal Hughes's intel reports into the Mafia's stealing from his casinos "to maintain organized crime status in Nevada."[34] The CIA even entered the investigation, the result of their secret alliance with Hughes (Project Jennifer) to raise a sunken Russian submarine from the floor of the Pacific.* Like the FBI, the CIA also concluded that the affair had its genesis in a world very familiar to Sid Korshak. One CIA memo, based on a "fairly reliable source," stated, "The burglary in question was committed by five individuals from the Midwest and was mob sponsored . . . The contents are said to be highly explosive from a political view and, thus, considered both important and valuable to Hughes and others as well . . . Source believes [the material] is still being held in the Los Angeles area."[35]

Two weeks after the theft, according to later court testimony, a petty thief named Donald Ray Woolbright supposedly admitted to a witness that he held the stolen papers. Woolbright said he had been given them by "a man from St. Louis," adding that the papers, not the money, were the whole objective of the burglars, and that after the papers were lifted, they were spirited to Las Vegas.[36]

Vegas, the mob, the Midwest, Hughes—they all intersected the world of Sidney Korshak, whose name was first openly injected into the mystery when Woolbright showed the documents to Korshak pal Greg Bautzer and later to Korshak's nephew L.A. attorney Maynard Davis, hoping to fence them to Korshak. A witness who accompanied Woolbright testified that Bautzer expressed some interest in the papers, and Davis placed a call to "Uncle Sidney," who was supposedly out of town at the time. Davis then advised Woolbright, "If I were you, I'd drop it. You're playing with dynamite."

According to an LAPD report of August 25, 1976, Hughes's security chief Ralph Winte, who had earlier assisted the Watergate burglars in a Las Vegas burglary, said he had "received information that there were possibly two attorneys involved, Sidney Korshak and [Hoffa's St. Louis lawyer] Morris Schenker . . . if a sale [of the Hughes papers] was made, it would be through these attorneys." Schenker denied involvement, while Korshak, typically, refused comment.[37]

Although Woolbright was eventually charged in the crime, he profited from two hung juries in 1977 and 1978, leaving the break-in forever unsolved. Although the Senate Watergate Committee originally wrote a forty-page

---

*The Soviet ballistic-missile submarine (SSB) *K-129* sank off Hawaii on April 11, 1968, probably due to a missile malfunction, and was later located by the CIA in 16,500 feet of water. Hughes's contribution to the partnership was the *Glomar Explorer*, a sixty-three-thousand-ton deep-sea salvage vessel built specifically for the top-secret operation. The ship was built under the cover story that she was a deep-sea mining vessel, ostensibly intended to recover manganese nodules from the ocean floor. Half of the sub was eventually raised, and the bodies of the Soviet sailors recovered inside were buried at sea.

report that stated that the motive for the Watergate break-in was the Nixon-Hughes bribery, that document was suppressed at the last minute. Committee chairman Senator Sam Ervin said, "Too many guilty bystanders would have been hurt."[38] Committee member Lowell Weicker added, "Everybody was feeding at the same trough."*

On April 5, 1976, Hughes died at age seventy aboard a plane en route to Houston, ostensibly of kidney failure. However, his dehydration, malnutrition, and the shards of broken hypodermic needles buried in his thin arms suggested other factors to many. In the ensuing years, over forty wills and four hundred claimants surfaced to vie for part of Hughes's $2 billion estate, which was eventually settled with twenty-two cousins in 1983.† One year after Hughes's death, author Michael Drosnin was allowed to see and photograph the explosive papers purloined from the Romaine office, which filled three steamer trunks and numbered some ten thousand pages. The documents, which became the basis for his 1985 book, *Citizen Hughes,* in fact showed that Hughes had bought countless U.S. politicians, lock, stock, and barrel.

In 1974, Jerry Brown, the thirty-six-year-old San Francisco–born son of Korshak pal, and former governor, Pat Brown, made his own bid for the governor's mansion. Although Jerry's political beliefs were complex at best, one aspect was a given: his potential for success would be predicated on a continued relationship with Supermob powers.

In his youth, Jerry began to display a more complex understanding of government's social contract than his father. Not only was he skeptical of the "backroom deal" style of his Democratic Party, Brown was, like Ronald Reagan, equally dismayed with exaggerated New Deal handouts and the concomitant explosion in the size of government. Young Jerry was actually naïve enough to believe that individual responsibility and altruism could overcome all the ills that infected the American system. California historians Kotkin and Grabowicz wrote, "Brown's revulsion against the consumption-oriented, materialistic world of his father at first drove him away from politics."[39] Indeed,

---

*Among the many recipients of Hughes's money over the years (in addition to Nixon) were Lawrence O'Brien, Senator Joseph Montoya (who was a member of the Senate Watergate Committee), Bobby Kennedy, President Lyndon Johnson, and Vice President Hubert Humphrey.

†The U.S. Supreme Court ruled that Hughes Aircraft was owned by the Howard Hughes Medical Institute, which sold it to General Motors in 1985 for $5 billion. The court rejected suits brought by the states of California and Texas, which claimed they were owed inheritance tax on the Hughes estate.

Brown spent four years in a Spartan Jesuit seminary before gaining a degree from Yale Law School in 1964. (Years later he would spend two years working with Mother Teresa in India.)

After a brief stint on the Los Angeles Community College Board, Brown ran for statewide office, becoming secretary of state in 1970. Almost immediately after assuming office, Brown admitted to confidants that his ultimate goals were, as Reagan's had been, not only the governorship, but the U.S. presidency. And in a state where media savvy and access to deep-pocket donors were more important than experience, anything was possible. When the 1974 contest rolled around, Reagan chose not to run again for governor in order to focus on his White House aspirations, prompting Brown to throw his hat in the gubernatorial ring, opposing a weak Republican candidate, state controller Houston Flournoy.

Although Brown had some philosophical differences with the world in which his father operated, he was also well aware that he could never afford the cost of a campaign without going to the same gentry and Supermob that had supported his father. When Brown enlisted electronics mogul Richard Silberman, the son of a Russian-Jewish immigrant junkman, as his chief fund-raiser, it quickly became apparent that the same Chicago money that had transformed California in the forties would continue to play a key role in the seventies. (Silberman would be convicted in a 1991 FBI drug-ring money-laundering scheme.) Thus, with a brilliant media campaign, massive contributions from the likes of Lew Wasserman, Jake "the Barber" Factor,[40] and later Sidney Korshak, Brown defeated Flournoy by 175,000 votes. When he would run for reelection, his association with Korshak especially would become a major point of criticism and even mockery.

Predictably, Governor Brown's terms were typified by seeming contradictions. On the one hand, he clung to his Jesuit training and refused the trappings of his office—canceling a raise for himself, refusing to ride in limousines, and failing to occupy the ultramodern, new governor's mansion, which he referred to as the "Taj Mahal." With his chief of staff, Gray Davis, whom some referred to as having been mentored by his Bistro lunch companion Sid Korshak, Brown adopted some standard liberal positions, such as vetoing the death penalty (overridden), favoring the right to choose abortion, strengthening environmental regulation and conservation, and protecting the rights of migrant workers. Brown's populist style proved popular with voters, and by 1976 his approval rating was 80 percent. Brown attempted to cash in on this popularity with a last-minute run at the Democratic presidential nomination, but he started too late, and Georgia's Jimmy Carter took control of the presidential national stage.

Curiously, Brown soon evolved into what Kotkin labeled a "born-again capitalist," courting not only Asian businesses, but also American titans such as Bank of America, ARCO Oil, the Irvine Corporation, Pacific Lighting, Kaiser Steel, Warner Brothers Records, and even some subsidiaries of the Howard Hughes empire. Brown even infuriated his environmentalist base when he championed the refining of Indonesian liquefied natural gas at a facility located on a pristine section of central-California coastline; and the company involved was represented by father Pat Brown's law firm. The overtures led one crestfallen Brown aide to say of his boss, "He's gone to the corporations because that's where Jerry thinks the power is at."

Reagan's New Teammate

Jerry Brown was not the only California pol to recognize the importance of maintaining good relations with former residents of 134 N. LaSalle Street. Brown's gubernatorial predecessor, Ronald Reagan, who had eyed the White House for years, chose as his 1976 presidential campaign chairman a man who maintained intimate associations with numerous individuals who once kicked up their heels at the infamous Chicago address. Although he was already friendly with 134's Sid Korshak, Reagan reached out for more support from those connected to the Chicago seat of Supermob power.

Fifty-three-year-old Senator Paul Dominque Laxalt (R-Nevada) had first met Reagan in 1964 when the two worked on the presidential campaign of Senator Barry Goldwater, himself no stranger to the Vegas gambling venues controlled by the mob and Supermob. The two men went on to become best friends when both became new governors of neighboring states (Laxalt in Nevada) in 1966. Chief among Laxalt's campaign policy planks was his defense of those in the state's casino industry; his mantra on the stump was a denunciation of the feds, whom he accused of harassing the good men purveying Las Vegas gambling. It was therefore little surprise that his staunchest supporters became those with the most to lose from the "harassment."

The first inklings of Laxalt's curious coterie surfaced that year, when he chose as his fund-raising chief one Ruby Kolod, a former member of Moe Dalitz's Mayfield Road Gang and Cleveland Syndicate (see chapter 9) and Dalitz's partner in the Desert Inn. Just one year before his fund-raising assignment, Kolod had been convicted in a murder-extortion plot in Denver, Colorado—his appeal was pending during the 1966 campaign.[41] Others who were close to Laxalt were Moe Dalitz, Sid Korshak, Allen Dorfman, Lefty Rosenthal, and Hoffa's attorney Morris Schenker.

When Laxalt's term expired in 1971, he turned to real estate speculation as his next venture, despite that his net worth was only just over $100,000. Laxalt's chief goal was to construct a first-class, multimillion-dollar casino-hotel in Carson City, to be named the Ormsby House. The proposal called for a 237-room "gambling palace" to be built on seven acres directly across from the state capitol; a secret part of the proposal was that Laxalt invest none of his own money in the project (although he ended up contributing just over $900). Although initial loans were secured from Nevada banks, Laxalt was well short of his financial goal. Thus, according to Las Vegas FBI agent Joe Yablonsky, Laxalt chose, as so many had before, to meet with the Fixer, Sid Korshak, who brought along Del Coleman for the strategy session. But before Korshak agreed to help, he wanted a couple political favors up front: Laxalt proceeded to accompany Del Coleman to Washington for his ongoing SEC Parvin testimony (see chapter 16), and to write a letter to President Nixon on behalf of Jimmy Hoffa's pending early parole. Laxalt's January 26, 1971, letter to "Dear President Dick" extolled the virtues of both Hoffa and "Al Dorfman, with whom I've worked closely the past few years." Laxalt laid it on thick, writing that "Hoffa and Dorfman and their activities here have been aboveboard at all times, and they have made a material contribution to the state."

Laxalt was soon jetting off to Switzerland with Del Coleman on Coleman's dime before visiting the First National Bank of Chicago, where they met with VP Robert Heymann, personal banker to Korshak pals Coleman and Joel Goldblatt—both had been set up with Heymann by Korshak, who was close friends with Heymann's father, Walter, also a VP of the bank. As promised, Heymann gave Laxalt a nonsecured $1 million loan, followed by three more loans totaling $8.3 million. The FBI said that the Outfit was "instrumental in the loans."[42]

"It was astonishing," the FBI's Joe Yablonsky would say later, "but while governor, Laxalt had a meeting with Dorfman, Korshak, and Coleman and then wrote a letter to President Nixon extolling the virtues of Jimmy Hoffa, and Korshak arranges his Chicago loan right after that. It was pretty blatant. Laxalt began to emerge in my mind as a tool of organized crime."[43] In a secretly recorded conversation made a decade later, Laxalt's former sister-in-law said that her husband, Peter, who was also a partner in the Ormsby venture, accompanied his brother Paul to Palm Springs for the meeting, and that he told her "every hood in the nation was there."[44]

Not surprisingly, the largest individual investor in Ormsby House was another Korshak neighbor from 134 N. LaSalle, Hoffa pal Bernard Nemerov, also an investor in and operator of Korshak's Riviera. Nemerov chipped in some $550,000 to Laxalt's casino, but according to Las Vegas FBI special agent Joe Yablonsky (1980–84), Nemerov had reason to know it was a sound investment. "Nemerov was there to get the skim out," Yablonsky said.[45]

More Ties to the Outfit Are Severed

As Sid Korshak's favored California pols such as Reagan and Brown continued their ascendance, his own independence from the Chicago bosses became complete with the June 18, 1975, murder of Sam "Mooney" Giancana in the basement of his Chicago home. A year before Johnny Rosselli met a similar fate, Mooney had placed himself in an impossible position, and thus, to those on the inside, the clipping of the sixty-seven-year-old former boss came as no surprise. Almost a year earlier, Giancana had been booted out of his Mexican exile by local authorities and handed over to the Chicago FBI. Thereafter, he attempted to lie low in his small suburban house, making the occasional trip to Santa Monica to squire his current love interest, Carolyn Morris, a former wife of Broadway composer Alan Jay Lerner, and also a former roommate of actress Lauren Bacall.[46]

This seeming serenity did nothing, however, to mollify Joe Batters Accardo and his current street boss, Joey "Doves" Aiuppa, who had two major disputes with the aging don: Giancana continued to ignore Accardo's demands that Chicago be cut in on the vast profits he had accrued in Mexico (the result of offshore gambling operations with Hy Larner),[47] and the fear that Giancana, who was extremely ill, would likely testify before the Senate in the coming weeks, as per a subpoena.* It was well-known that Giancana would do anything to avoid going to prison again, especially in his frail condition. Thus it was decided that, for the good of all, he had to go. Recent interviews with a close personal friend of Aiuppa's driver Dominic "Butch" Blasi (previously Giancana's driver) indicate that Blasi late in life admitted to the shooting, as so ordered by Accardo.

On July 30, less than six weeks after Mooney's whacking, former Teamster boss and Korshak associate Jimmy Hoffa disappeared forever. His fate, like Giancana's, was sealed when he refused to toe the line of the new Teamster powers—in this case, President Frank Fitzsimmons, who had, during Hoffa's incarceration, forged real Mafia alliances with the likes of East Coast bosses

---

*Giancana had recently undergone two problematic gallbladder surgeries and was simultaneously called to testify before a Senate committee looking into the Castro assassination plots of the early sixties that linked both the CIA and the Chicago Outfit.

Tony Provenzano of New York and Russell Bufalino of Pennsylvania. Not only had Hoffa recently declared his desire to retake the union, ahead of the timetable implicit in his early parole, but he had also, like Giancana, given signals that he would "sing" to the feds, in this case, the FBI. Both the feds and outside Hoffa experts came to believe that Provenzano and Bufalino used a trusted Detroit mobster named Anthony Giacalone to lure Hoffa to his fatal encounter. The FBI called Giacalone's propensity for violence in Detroit "legendary."[48]

As with the Giancana rubout, insiders developed their own rumors about Hoffa's disappearance, and oftentimes their whispers included the name Korshak. Just days after the Hoffa disappearance, Korshak's partner in the Bistro, Kurt Niklas, asked Sidney, "What do you think happened to Hoffa?" According to Niklas, Korshak threw him a "steely glance" and warned, "He's dead, and don't ever mention his name again."[49] Of course, it was weeks before the press and authorities came to the same conclusion.

Similarly, Las Vegas investigator Ed Becker noticed a curiosity surrounding Korshak and Hoffa's snatching: "After the disappearance of Hoffa, Korshak and Dorfman took off for Europe. They were conveniently not in Chicago. So it was interesting."[50]

What Niklas and Becker likely didn't know was just how well Korshak was plugged in to the very man whom the Bureau and other Hoffa experts would later suspect of enticing Hoffa to his doom. According to an LAPD Intelligence report, none other than Anthony Giacalone was not only a friend of Sid Korshak's, but had stayed at his La Costa condo in 1969.[51]

Whatever Korshak's level of knowledge regarding Hoffa's fate, it seemed to give him little comfort after returning from his European getaway with Dorfman. "Korshak started traveling with a bodyguard after Hoffa disappeared," said a Labor Department investigator who had followed Korshak's career for nearly twenty years. "Lew Wasserman beefed up security at his home around the same time."[52]

With Hoffa gone, the mob's infiltration of the Teamsters was virtually unchecked. Consequently, by the spring of 1976, L.A. mafioso Jimmy "the Weasel" Fratianno cooked up another scam involving the union's health plan, and when the rip-off did not proceed as quickly as he wished, the Weasel brought Sid Korshak into the fray.

At the time, Fratianno, one of the most feared mob hitmen, was attempting to sell Andy Anderson's West Coast Teamsters a questionable dental plan, which, like the health plan involving People's Industrial Consultants, would see massive skims to the underworld. "I've got to make some money," Fratianno had said to his San Francisco Teamster ally Rudy Tham, the head of freight checkers Local 856, the city's second-largest Teamster union. It was Tham's membership roster that Fratianno hoped to use as foils in the plan. Fratianno explained the operation to Johnny Rosselli: "You pick the dentist and the union gives him a contract to do all the dental work for the members of the locals signed up and their families. Dorfman's company, Amalgamated Insurance Agency, processes all medical claims and author- izes payment, which means he controls the whole thing. So now we can play some games. Number one, the dentists kick back to certain people so many dollars for each member signed up; and number two, Dorfman can submit phony claims and nobody's the wiser. It's a sweet setup, believe me."[53]

A frustrated Fratianno waited for months for Anderson to rubber-stamp the plan, eventually turning to Cleveland Teamster boss Jackie Presser for advice.

"Go see Sid Korshak," Presser said. "Andy's his man. You believe me, Jimmy. This Korshak can take care of the whole thing with one phone call . . . This's the smoothest sonovabitch in the business. There's nothing he can't fix."

Per custom, Sidney met the Weasel at his Bistro corner table, escorted him outside to the bench Korshak reserved for sensitive negotiations, and heard the pitch.

After a few minutes, Korshak merely said, "I'll talk to Andy and get it straightened out . . . Jimmy, I'll do the best I can, believe me. But, please, don't call me on the telephone.' "[54]

When more weeks went by with no movement, Fratianno took up the matter with Korshak's Chicago patrons, meeting first with street boss Joey "Doves" Aiuppa. Fratianno was thereupon told what so many had been in- structed before: that he should have no contact with Korshak. "The less you see him the better," Doves said. "We don't want to put any heat on the guy." Then he summed up Korshak's life, as interpreted by the Chicago bosses: "Let me explain something, Jimmy. Sid's a traveling man. He's in every- body's country, but he's our man, been our man his whole life. So, you know, it makes no difference where he hangs his hat. Get my meaning?"

When Fratianno started to argue, Aiuppa started laughing. "Jimmy, you're not listening. He's got a permit. We gave him one. Understand? Don't put any heat on Sid. We've spent a lot of time keeping this guy clean. He can't be seen in public with guys like us. We have our own ways of contact- ing him and it's worked pretty good for a long time."

But Fratianno was too hot to heed the warning. He went right back to the

Bistro and, in an attempt at intimidation, showed up with mob tough guy Mike Rizzitello. Again they sat on the little bench outside the restaurant, as Korshak explained that he didn't actually control Anderson, and that Anderson was not returning calls.

"Then the guy's going to get hurt," Jimmy warned. "I told you last time, Sid, I don't want no stories. As far as I'm concerned, that's bullshit. You know this fucking Andy better than I know my own brother."

"Jimmy, I don't want to argue with you," answered an unfazed Korshak. "I'll talk to him again. What else can I do?'

"Look, we don't want to take this into our own hands," said the imploding mobster. "We're not asking for the moon. All we want's for him to give Rudy what he's entitled to. And by Christ, Rudy's going to get it, one way or another."[55]

Continued inaction pushed Fratianno to the next level. When an answer from Korshak was not forthcoming in the following weeks, a dead fish was deposited in Korshak's mailbox, a transgression that was quickly reported back to Joe Batters Accardo. Now, the Weasel was ordered back to Chicago to explain himself to Korshak's closest friend in the Outfit, boss Accardo.

Joey Aiuppa opened the meeting, telling Jimmy, "I told you last time, we don't allow nobody in the family to talk to this guy. We don't want no fucking heat on him." After hearing the Weasel's denials that he had put the dead fish in Korshak's mailbox, the boss uttered his pronouncement: "Jimmy, Sid's been with Gussie over thirty years and Gussie's with us. Sid's a good provider for our family and we don't want nobody to fuck with him. I appreciate your problem, but we don't want him seen with nobody. We don't want nobody muscling this guy. I can't make it no plainer than that. He's off-limits. That's it, Jimmy."

Fratianno made one last foray into the West Coast Teamster scam, this time going directly to Andy Anderson at the Teamsters headquarters in Burlingame, California—once again with the menacing Mike "Rizzo" by his side. Once alone with Anderson in his office, Rizzo closed the door behind them. A few menacing words later, and Anderson caved.

"All right, Jimmy," Anderson said, "tell Rudy to call me and we'll straighten it out."

"Andy, you do it," warned Fratianno. "We don't want to come back here a second time."

In short time, Fratianno and Tham got their dental plan, but the victory was short-lived. Like Henry Hill, of *GoodFellas* (1990) fame, Fratianno became a government witness in 1977 when he was confronted with a raft of charges by the government, and the simultaneous realization that the Los

Angeles mob had ordered him killed. In 1978, Fratianno was sentenced to two concurrent five-year sentences, the result of a plea bargain to testify and go into witness protection, where he spent the next ten years. His matter-of-fact accounts of Mafia "hits" and operations helped convict more than two dozen members of the Mafia around the country during the 1970s and 1980s. In one 1980 trial that led to the racketeering convictions of five Mafia figures, Fratianno admitted that he had committed five murders and partici-pated in six. He later admitted to four more hits. He was dropped from the witness protection in 1987 after the Justice Department said further pay-ments might make the program appear like a "pension fund for aging mob-sters." In retirement, Fratianno was the subject of two books, *The Last Mafioso* (1981) and *Vengeance Is Mine* (1987), both of which he claimed never to have read, and appeared on several television talk shows. Aladena "Jimmy the Weasel" Fratianno, the former mob boss who turned govern-ment witness, died in his sleep in July 1993, at age seventy-nine in an undis-closed U.S. city, where he was living under an assumed name.[56]

In 1980, a federal jury convicted Tham for embezzlement of union funds.

> *Korshak has been very active in this sort of investment [real estate and private industry] and since he carries considerable weight in de-termining where Chicago funds are invested it now appears some of the Chicago Family's surplus is in the film industry.*
>
> —1977 FBI MEMO[57]

Korshak ended 1975 with another show of film business acumen, this time involving the planned remake of the classic 1933 movie *King Kong*. His ac-tions amplified the FBI's growing interest in the Chicago Outfit's latest infil-tration into the movie business.

In 1975, according to *King Kong* chronicler Bruce Bahrenburg, "Para-mount was looking for another 'big' picture in the same league as their re-cent blockbuster, *The Godfather* and the forthcoming *The Great Gatsby*."[58] When the *Kong* project was announced in the trades that year, Lew Wasser-man's Universal Pictures sued the new film's director Dino DeLaurentiis for $25 million, claiming Universal alone held the rights to the remake of the original 1933 RKO production. Universal simultaneously filed suit against RKO, which had sold the rights to DeLaurentiis, after it had supposedly al-ready done the same to Universal.

DeLaurentiis then countersued Universal for $90 million, and the legal morass became more entangled with each successive day. "The legal issues surrounding the copyright to Kong," Bahrenburg wrote, "are as puzzling as a maze in a formal British garden."[59] With the lawsuits casting a shadow over the film, Paramount nonetheless went ahead in early January 1976 with principal photography, making it imperative that the legal issues be resolved. Although the courts had failed to bring about a deal, there was, of course, one man who was famous for just that, and given Sidney Korshak's great connections at both Paramount and Universal, he was the natural choice to mediate the dispute. Or as DeLaurentiis later said, "The only way to get through to Lew is to talk to Sidney."[60]

With DeLaurentiis's office located on Canon Drive, just a few steps from Korshak's Bistro, it was merely a matter of walking up the street to enlist Sidney. According to a source close to the production, a luncheon was arranged at Korshak's Bel-Air home between executives of Paramount and Universal (MCA).* "Sidney was the court," said the source. "In a couple hours, a deal was arrived at that made everybody happy. Sidney had done more over his lunch hour than dozens of high-priced attorneys had done in eight months." The source, a producer at Universal, added that Korshak was paid a $30,000 fee for his two-hour business lunch.[61] DeLaurentiis himself would later corroborate the fee.

There may have been a hidden agenda at play that explained both Korshak's and DeLaurentiis's desire to get the movie going. In a recently released memo describing a tip from an undisclosed source, the Los Angeles FBI Field Office noted:

[Source] indicated that Korshak was bringing in laundered money, skim money, mob money from the Chicago–Las Vegas areas for the purpose of producing a revival of the classic film *King Kong*, which is a joint venture between Paramount Studios, a subsidiary corporation of Gulf & Western, Universal Studios, which is a subsidiary of MCA, and [deleted][†] of Rome, Italy. According to [source], Korshak is alleged to be handling $12 million in illicit funds gathered through skimming in Las Vegas and Syndicate money in Chicago . . . [Source] further points out that Korshak is also handling "laundered" money controlled by mob interests in Chicago and Las Vegas in the production of a second movie in production now at United Artists, which is being produced by Joseph Levine, entitled *A Bridge Too Far*.

---

*DeLaurentiis's biographers, while acknowledging Korshak's role, claim that the meeting took place over dinner at Bluhdorn's office. (Kezich and Levantesi, *Dino*, 218)
†The deleted producer is most definitely Dino DeLaurentiis.

It is [source's] understanding that *King Kong* has been budgeted at 25 million dollars and that at the rate of production expenditures thus far, it will exceed 25 million dollars. [Source] offered that the excessive costs of the production would add to the concealment of illicit funds, in his judgment.*,62

Variety later reported that Universal agreed to allow Paramount to make the film, with Universal maintaining the rights to a future remake. "I am very pleased," DeLaurentiis told the press, "and would like to thank MCA's Lew Wasserman and Sid Sheinberg for their understanding and generosity in making such accommodations possible." And as per custom, Sid Korshak's name never surfaced in connection with the resolution.

Despite the coverage given to the *Kong* settlement by the fourth estate, the press nonetheless avoided addressing the "elephant in the room": Why did Universal cave so quickly, and with no equivalent benefit? Some have posited that DeLaurentiis's production of Universal's *The Brink's Job* in 1978 (another film that required Korshak's intervention with the Teamsters) was the quid pro quo.† However, the word among insiders was that Korshak had decreed that DeLaurentiis give Universal a percentage of the *Kong* profits.63 DeLaurentiis's assistant to the producer Fred Sidewater said, "The settlement cost Dino five million dollars." Sidewater also clarified that the unpublicized subtext to all the arguing was marketing rights. "The reason for all the fights was that they wanted to put the ride in Universal's theme park after all the success with the *Jaws* ride. We gave them the merchandising rights as a compromise."64 Although panned by critics, the $24 million movie made $46 million in profits. But Universal's *King Kong* thrill ride,

---

*Interestingly, the agency source of the above memo is deleted, which usually implies CIA. The memo contains fifty-two more pages, currently withheld for review by that other agency. One guess is that it involves CIA investigations of laundered Mafia money coming from Italy.

†*The Brink's Job* was based on a true story that occurred in 1950. The period piece was shot in the North End of Boston, which was at the time dominated by Italians and Irish, and problems first arose when residents refused to take their TV antennas down, even for a few hours—television antennas did not exist in 1950. Universal production chief Ned Tanen called Lew Wasserman, who in turn called the Fixer. Two hours later, Tanen received a call from the unit producer. "You want to see something funny? You ought to see these 280-pound Italian women climbing up on their roofs, tromping around in their black skirts and work boots, ripping out their TV aerials." As Tanen later noted, "Now there's nothing dishonest about that. But Lew had called his good friend Sidney, and they had got it done." The film received an Oscar for set decoration—although it is doubtful that Korshak ever received a statuette. (Sharp, *Mr. and Mrs. Hollywood*, 351–53)

which operated for over two decades, undoubtedly made more profit than Dino's movie.

According to Korshak friend and Hilton Hotel general counsel E. Timothy Applegate, Korshak's performances regarding Valachi and *Kong* ingratiated him with the producer. "While eating at the Bistro, Sidney told me how Dino DeLaurentiis thought the sun rose and set on him," recalled Applegate. "He told me how he had helped Dino with *King Kong*, and that Dino later gave him a new Ferrari for his help. Sidney, who was over seventy at the time, said, 'What the hell am I going to do with that?' "[65]

In 2005, Universal finally began production on its *Kong* remake, with Oscar-winning *Lord of the Rings* director Peter Jackson at the helm.

Sid Korshak's latest triumph added still more luster to an already vaunted reputation. Toward the end of 1975, actor David Janssen's wife, Dani Greco Janssen, was inspired to further refine Joyce Haber's demarcation of Korshak's "A-list" to include an exclusive subset that she called The Big Six, consisting of the Korshaks, the Ziffrens, and the Wassermans.[66] In March 1976, Korshak exerted his power in Las Vegas again, this time in another broadside against his foe Howard Hughes's Summa Corporation. On this occasion, Korshak orchestrated a seventeen-day strike by the Hotel and Restaurant Employees and Bartenders International Union against a group of casinos and hotels, six of which were owned by Summa. Typically, none of the hotels or casinos that employed Korshak's services were affected.[67]

On May 4, 1976, Korshak renewed his passport, falsely writing on the form that his "permanent residence" was 69 W. Washington Street in Chicago—which was actually his brother's law office—and advising that he planned to travel throughout England, France, and Italy for two months in the summer of 1976.*

---

*Just above his signature, the form reads, "False statements made knowingly and willfully in passport applications or other supporting documents are punishable by fine and/or imprisonment under the provisions of 18 USC 1001."

CHAPTER 19

Airing Dirty Laundry and Laundering Dirty Money

LESTER VELIE, ROBERT GOE, Art White, Sandy Smith, Frank McCulloch, Jack Tobin, and Paul Steiger had all taken their best shots at Sid Korshak. Now the gauntlet would be passed to a red-hot firebrand of a journalist who was certain to find any dirt that was there to be found. It was inevitable that the two would be pitted against one another: Sidney Korshak, the immovable object, and Seymour Hersh, the irresistible force.

Sidney and Seymour

Hersh, at just thirty-nine years old, had already established himself as one of the most respected and most persistent investigative reporters of his time. Born and raised in Sid Korshak's Chicago, "Sy" Hersh entered the journalistic fray as a police reporter for the Chicago City News Bureau and later worked for the national wire services, before a sabbatical in 1968, when he was the press secretary for Senator Eugene McCarthy's antiwar presidential bid. Hersh's investigative talents first gained national prominence in November 1969, when he broke the story of the My Lai massacre in Vietnam, earning him a Pulitzer Prize for international reporting as well as several other prestigious awards.*

---

*By just 1976, Hersh had amassed the following accolades: The George Polk Award, Worth Bingham Prize, Sigma Delta Chi Distinguished Service Award, and Pulitzer Prize for international reporting, all 1970, all for stories on the My Lai massacre; *My Lai Four* was named one of the best nonfiction books of the year by *Time*, 1970; Front Page Award, Scripps-Howard Service Award, and George Polk Award, all 1973, all for stories on bombing in Cambodia; Sidney Hillman Award and George Polk Award, both 1974, both for stories on CIA domestic spying; John Peter Zenger Freedom of the Press Award and Drew Pearson Prize, both 1975, for stories on CIA involvement in Chile.

Hersh parlayed that acclaim into a full-time reporting job at the *New York Times*, where he quickly delivered another bombshell with the disclosure of the CIA's massive illegal domestic mail-opening scheme known as MH/ CHAOS. By 1976, Hersh had earned the enviable position of being able to name his assignment at the most prestigious paper in America. During a rare lull in his frenetic activity, Hersh began sounding out colleagues for ideas about how on earth he could top his own reputation with his next exposé.

"I got to know Peter Adelman and Adam Walinsky because they were doing the same things for Bobby [Kennedy] that I did for McCarthy," Hersh said in a recent rare interview, "writing speeches and being a press guy. So I was looking for things to do and somehow I bumped into Adam and he said, 'If you want the great story of all time, I'll give it to you. Two words: Sidney Korshak.' "[1]

New Yorker Adam Walinsky, the same age as Hersh, was at the time an associate in the firm of Kronish, Lieb, Weiner & Hellman. In 1963 he had gone to the U.S. Department of Justice under Attorney General Robert F. Kennedy, where he worked on the drafting and passage of the Immigration Reform Act of 1965, the Civil Rights Act of 1964, the Economic Opportunity Act of 1964, and matters of crime and national security, later becoming Kennedy's legislative assistant.

"What I got to hear about Korshak was from Walter Sheridan," Walinsky remembered. "Sheridan was the guy who told me a lot of stuff about the rackets, and Korshak was obviously a really major figure. We talked about that and the information that had come out in the committee's investigations of organized crime. The one thing I said to Sy is that you don't want to import today's sensibility and bring it back thirty years, because to actually go after a guy like Korshak back in those days would be a much bigger deal than it would be today. He was a really serious player and he was a guy who could pick up the phone and call the publisher of the *Times* and all of that."[2]

Hersh said that Walinsky sent him to meet with Sheridan, who in turn gave him the background on the murky world of labor rackets, sweetheart deals, and Sid Korshak's central role in them. Sheridan advised Hersh to pay a visit to Berkeley, California, to learn more from freelance journalist Jeff Gerth, with whom Sheridan had floated an unsuccessful 1973 book proposal on the Korshak crowd. Gerth was currently defending himself in the largest libel lawsuit ever brought before a U.S. court, brought against him and others by a group headed by the Supermob's Moe Dalitz, Korshak's closest pal in Vegas. Just a year earlier, Gerth had teamed with fellow freelancer

Lowell Bergman* in writing "La Costa: The Hundred-Million-Dollar Resort with Criminal Clientele," for the March 1975 edition of *Penthouse*. The piece exposed the resort, owned by Dalitz, Roen, Adelson, and Molasky, or DRAM, as a mob-friendly, upscale version of the Acapulco Towers right here in the United States. As *Penthouse*'s lawyer Roy Grutman wrote, the allegations were hardly news, but nonetheless, this time DRAM fought back with a $630 million libel suit that would drag on for an astounding ten years.[3]

"I just liked him right away," Hersh said of Gerth, "and I said, 'Come work with me.' He said okay.'" For the next six months, with Gerth credited as researcher, the duo would plumb sources from coast to coast in their attempt to unravel the Korshak mystery. It was a massive undertaking, one of the biggest ever for the *Times*, and certain to be a front-page multipart account.

Armed with a $30,000 budget, the new partners made an initial research trip to Reno, Nevada, where they learned what it meant to "dig up" a story. "We met this retired FBI guy in Reno," Hersh recalled, "and we went out to his cabin somewhere, and there he had this great document—later it was unfortunately stolen. It was about a 250-page FBI dossier on Korshak that was incredible. We published the gist of it; we leaned on it a lot. He gave us that document, but I remember we had to go out to his farm and dig it up, literally."

From there, the pair moved on to Jack Tobin, who gave them his LAPD sources. In Chicago, they read a clipping of how Korshak had sided with Joel Goldblatt's ex in a divorce proceeding. "We figured Goldblatt might be mad," said Hersh, "so we found him, remarried to a younger wife, living in the Near North on Lake Shore Drive." Another Goldblatt ex, MJ Goldblatt, remembered that Joel began receiving calls from Korshak friends before Hersh arrived in Chicago. "Don Maxwell of the *Tribune* warned Joel not to give the interview to Hersh, but he did it anyway," said MJ.[4]

When Hersh and Gerth arrived at the Goldblatt abode, they found a man bursting to talk. "He was very wealthy, and very angry," remembered Hersh. "He made us promise to protect him and he dumped everything on us." Goldblatt told them, among other things, that he had seen Korshak's compromising photos of Estes Kefauver back in the early fifties. However, Goldblatt remained an unnamed source when the story ran.

---

*Bergman would go on to become one of the country's top investigative journalists, immortalized in the 1999 film *The Insider*, in which Bergman was portrayed by Al Pacino. The story recounted Bergman's attempts to have CBS's *60 Minutes* air his report on tobacco executive Jeffrey Wigand, portrayed in the film by Russell Crowe. The film garnered seven Academy Award nominations and won numerous other accolades.

The assignment was not without the occasional reminders of Sid Korshak's long reach. Near the top of the list is this one, as recounted by Hersh: "Best story I can tell you: I'm into the story about six months, or four months. I'm living in New York, my wife's in med school, when we get a call from the district attorney of L.A., John Van DeKamp. He says, 'Get to a pay phone.' 'What do you mean?' I say. 'Just get to a pay phone.' So I leave my kids—I'm making hamburgers for my kids, seven and five [years old]—and go down to the corner candy store, I call him collect. He says, 'Korshak has all of your phone records and all of your expense accounts from inside the *Times*.'" A former *Times* employee who wished to remain anonymous explained that L.A. District Attorney's Office investigator Frank Hronek later told the pair how Korshak had done it. "One of Hronek's sources said that Korshak got the records from one of Korshak's contacts in the *Times* payroll department," said the insider. "The *Times* later did an investigation and found him—it was a guy from Chicago, but they chose not to prosecute him.[5] Thus alerted, the reporters began submitting phony expenses and proceeded onward.

Before the story ran, *Times* executives began getting letters from the Wyman, Bautzer law firm, written by Greg Bautzer. "Your man's been going around saying terrible things about my client," said one. "You're calling him names, he's never been found guilty of anything." Hersh called them "standard, good lawyer letters."

Of course, Hersh attempted to speak with Korshak during the research phase, but was unsuccessful. Jan Amory, Del Coleman's ex-wife, remembered historian Arthur Schlesinger trying to broker an interview when all the parties were dining at the same New York restaurant. "I remember Schlesinger saying to me, 'Would you introduce Sidney to Seymour Hersh? I know you're having lunch with Sidney at the Grenouille, and Hersh is dying to meet him.' I said, 'You mean he's never met him?' And he said, 'No, and he just wants to come over to the table.' And I said, 'No, I'm not going to compromise Sidney like that, I'm not doing it.' I just thought it was too tacky."[6]

Although Hersh and Gerth wrote that Korshak declined to be interviewed for the piece, the true story was far more interesting, and sinister. "I called Korshak one day, and he took the call," Hersh vividly remembered. "This was late [in the process]. I was in West L.A. and called from a pay phone. I said, 'Mr. Korshak, I am here.' He said, 'I won't see you.' Then he said, 'Mr. Hersh, let me ask you a question'—I'll never forget it as long as I live—'What are you doing? You're an expert in mass murder, you write about crimes where people are dead and there are bodies all over. Why are you writing about me? You write about murder.' He kept on talking about murder. 'Blood running in the ditches, and murders.' He just kept saying, 'You write about mass murder. Why are you interested in me? I'm just a businessman, and you write all these terrible things. Go back to your mass murderers. Go back to the blood and the killings and gore, that's what you write about. Not about me.' It was very interesting what he did. He just kept talking about murders and blood. He never said a word that was threatening, but the whole context was 'murder, murder, blood, murder'—you couldn't finish the conversation without realizing that . . . it set me on edge, as it should've. It was pretty chilling. His whole message to me was very subliminal, or so I thought—maybe that's the way he talked to everybody. That was the extent of contact with him." Tom Zander, the Chicago-based crime investigator for the Labor Department, insisted that Korshak's veiled threat was not uncommon. "That's the way he talked," said Zander. "He was not beyond anything, believe me."[7]

Internally, the story proved a world-class headache for the *Times* and its publisher, Arthur Ochs "Punch" Sulzberger, who constantly rode Hersh's back for sourcing and accuracy. At least two top *Times* executives voted to scuttle the series altogether.[8] With Ziffren and Bautzer making their presence known, Sulzberger enlisted an army of attorneys to vet the first draft. Later, Hersh learned of another reason for Sulzberger's sensitivity. "[Executive Editor] Abe Rosenthal told me that Korshak knew Punch," Hersh said. "They used to go to the movies together. Charlie Bluhdorn used to show private screenings at his house and Punch would go with Sidney once in a while."

Interestingly, on the eve of the series' scheduled May 1976 debut, a Teamsters strike hit the paper. Hersh wondered if Sidney was sending another subliminal message. When the front-page "above-the-fold" series finally opened, three hundred interviews later, on Sunday, June 27, Hersh noted that Korshak's hometown paper didn't even mention it. "The *L.A. Times* didn't touch it," said Hersh. (Apparently, Korshak's $25,000 contribution to the *Los Angeles Times*' Buff Chandler in 1969 still counted.) "But Pacifica [Radio] ran it twenty-four hours a day," Hersh added. "They read it aloud. They read it around the clock."

The opening salvo was entitled THE CONTRASTING LIVES OF SIDNEY R. KORSHAK: SUCCESSFUL CALIFORNIA LAWYER IS CALLED LINK BETWEEN CRIME AND BIG BUSINESS. The hard-hitting broadside included allegations of fixed judges, blackmailed senators, labor racketeering, Teamsters Pension Fund abuses, tax dodging, etc. Although many of the charges were unproven, the sheer extent of them made it seem as though the 1969 *Los Angeles Times* article had been circumspect in the extreme.

In Chicago, on the very night part one hit the newsstands, the sixty-nine-year-old Korshak was rushed to Michael Reese Medical Center after a flare-up of diverticulitis, or inflammation of the colon caused by too much low-fiber food. He was reported in fair condition.[9] Although one might conclude that stress from the Hersh affair had brought it on, it may have been just coincidental, since most internists now believe that stress plays no role in the illness. (Three years earlier, Korshak had spent four days in L.A.'s Cedars of Lebanon Hospital with a stomach inflammation that saw his white-blood-cell count soar to twenty thousand, over twice the norm, due to a bleeding ulcer. The incident left Korshak depressed and telling a friend that he "might as well be dead" if he couldn't eat and drink what he wanted.) "Sidney had a lot of stomach problems," said friend Leo Geffner. "He had to watch what he ate. He was very careful not to eat spicy or rich foods."[10]

Unbeknownst to Geffner and Korshak was that while Korshak recuperated at Michael Reese, the FBI watched all his phone records and attempted to monitor his visitors.[11]

The Fallout

As might be expected, the *Times*' Korshak series provoked reaction and fallout of all manner. Even before the series concluded, Greg Bautzer fired off a telegram to the *Times* complaining that he had been taken out of context in the first installment. Bautzer said that he never meant to imply that Sidney might have had early ties to the Outfit. "I never knew Mr. Korshak in Chicago," wrote Bautzer, who claimed that he told Hersh, "If he had represented these men, and it was conceivable that he did, I was unaware of it; that during all of my association with, knowledge and observation of Mr. Korshak while he has been residing in California, I found him to be a lawyer possessed of intelligence, integrity and loyalty."[12]

The series also drew the attention of Hersh's fellow journalists (except in Korshak's adopted hometown, where the *Los Angeles Times* did not even acknowledge the articles). Predictably, Korshak friends such as Irv Kupcinet and Joyce Haber excoriated the Pulitzer-winning writer, labeling his work nothing less than character assassination. Most surprising was the response of respected New York columnist Nat Hentoff, who wrote that Hersh had "set out to get Sidney Korshak . . . Tom Jefferson may not have had this mouthpiece [Korshak] precisely in mind when he envisioned the democratic populace two centuries hence, but he could not have excluded him even from the Bill of Rights." Hentoff, a respected civil libertarian, went so far as to call for the prosecution of federal officials who had leaked government documents to Hersh.[13]

Other peers, such as Denny Walsh of the *Sacramento Bee*, supported Hersh's work, even though it was long on inference and short on hard proof of Korshak criminal activity. "Men like Korshak deserve all the publicity they can get," Walsh told *New West*. "Sy Hersh did a public service by getting all the information on Korshak in print."[14] Many seemed to think that Hersh was employing the same strategy that had led to his Pulitzer-winning My Lai revelations and his series on CIA abuses, which had begun with unfocused scattershot allegations that eventually prompted key witnesses to come forward with the complete stories. "This is exactly the strategy that paid off in Sy's CIA series," said Frank McCulloch. "I have the utmost respect for Sy and the *Times*. I hope he keeps on digging."[15]

Regarding the provocative Kefauver blackmail story, a number of Kefauver's senior staff, such as Organized Crime Committee counsel Downey Rice and investigator George Martin, wrote letters to Sulzberger, Hersh, and the U.S. Senate, protesting what they believed were gross inaccuracies in the Kefauver story. Senator Thomas McIntyre (D-New Hampshire) inserted a scathing letter from Rice and Martin into the *Congressional Record*, which stated in part that Hersh's "sole objective seems to be to disparage, distort, denigrate, and defame."[16] Historian William Howard Moore of the University of Wyoming was among those who seized on minor errors in the piece (such as the date and reasons for the Kefauver Committee's postponement of Chicago public hearings) to say that Hersh was therefore also wrong about Korshak's blackmailing of Kefauver.[17] Six years later, Moore expounded on this in an article in the journal *Public Historian*.[18] Most of the protesters assumed that Hersh's source for the allegation was an underworld type. They never learned that it was in fact Joel Goldblatt, one of the most respected businessmen in Chicago.

In response, Sulzberger not only wrote letters in defense of Hersh, but printed an editorial on July 1, in which he stated that the articles "clearly demonstrated" that there was "a great deal of evidence—much of it already in the hands of federal agencies—that would have warranted an indictment" of Korshak. Sulzberger ended by saying, "Mr. Korshak is surely one of the people who have been involved in building links between organized crime, labor unions and corporations. His career . . . strongly indicates that major reforms are needed in the administration of criminal justice and corporate law."[19]

Among the more suspicious of the postpublication occurrences was the discovery that all the voluminous work files compiled by Hersh and Gerth turned up missing from the *Times* storage facility—files that might have insulated them from potential legal actions. "We were all very upset at the time. There were huge files, they were excellent," said Hersh, who believed the files were accidentally lost during a *Times* storage relocation. "Jeff has his doubts, but they were really moving, and there were renovations, and they disappeared during the moving. I think it was just stupidity."

Hersh gained a rare glimpse into Korshak's personal moral code when he received a postpublication call from one of the Fixer's nieces. As best Hersh remembered it, this is what the niece related to him:

> You missed the real story. Let me tell you about my uncle Sid: When I was about twelve or thirteen, we used to go to seders . . . Sidney would drive the kids. We'd all go for Passover seder and he would run the seder. Once, in the early sixties, I was in the backseat with one of Sidney's sons, who was about twelve or thirteen. I remember everyone was scared of Sidney. We were playing in the back of the Cadillac, and I went, "Eenie-meenie-miney-moe, catch a nigger by his toe." And Sidney stops the car and turns around and slapped me across the face. It's one of those things you never forget. Uncle Sidney said, "Don't ever talk about them that way. If you don't talk about them that way, they won't talk about us that way." So then, hours later, in the middle of the seder, there's a phone call, and Sidney's sister was very nervous because she was scared of Sidney. Uncle Sidney took the phone at the front of table and says, "Good. You got the goy, good."

Hersh later investigated the incident, learning that a sanitary-district official, a reformer in Stickney Township in Illinois, had been assassinated. Hersh concluded that Sidney had fingered him. "Couldn't get closer than that," Hersh said about the *goy*'s murder. "After he had just given his niece a lesson in racial manners."

Incredibly, there was no discernible effect from the Hersh charges on Korshak's thriving business practice, with the stories only giving a momentary pause to some clients. Hilton Hotels made a cursory investigation to determine if they should sever their relationship with Korshak. E. Timothy Applegate, Hilton's longtime general counsel and Korshak's liaison at the company, was the man in charge of such things. "I am very suspicious of second- and thirdhand information, and so much of that series was based on it," Applegate said recently. "A prosecutor would say that there was no case there. But I went to Frank Johnson, a former reporter for the Reno newspaper, who had been chairman of the Nevada Gaming Control Board; he was a very upstanding guy without a crooked bone in his body. Frank knew a lot of FBI people in Vegas and he made his inquiries on Korshak and came back to me and said, 'There's no basis for doing anything.' I also called another board chairman, Phil Hannifin, and asked if we should be concerned. He said no."[20]

Likewise, the bombastic series failed to generate any real law enforcement interest in Korshak's doings. Two former Justice Department organized crime specialists told the press that they had explained their inaction to Hersh. "We don't have a shred of evidence against Mr. Korshak," they claimed to have said. "Otherwise, we'd have prosecuted him."[21] Another Justice official tried to explain the problem this way: "If you're going to take on the Sid Korshaks, you're going to have to commit one hell of a lot to it. Maybe if we committed the whole federal Strike Force to it, we might be able to nail the guy. But there are four or five guys who are equally as important [in organized crime], so what are you going to do?"[22]

Marvin Rudnick, at the time an assistant state's attorney in St. Petersburg, Florida, was among those who shook their heads in awe—but he had his own theory, one that he shared with Johnny Rosselli, and which jibes with what is now known about Korshak's secret meetings with Las Vegas sheriff Ralph Lamb. "After Hersh laid it all out, nothing happened," Rudnick recently said. "It's hard to believe that Korshak survived all those years of scrutiny without there having been some alternate explanation. So there were only two possibilities: either Korshak was paying somebody off, or he was an informant. I lean towards the latter, because it's hard to believe that the entire FBI was manipulated by corrupt people. Who would be a better informant than Korshak? If you're involved in crime at a high level, there's an FBI agent who's going to try to get you to turn and make his career."[23] And, as noted, years earlier, Korshak had not only been "flipping" for Ralph Lamb, but had fingered Mickey Cohen to the feds.

For the most part, Korshak gave the impression that the Hersh series, which would have devastated most people, merely rolled off his back. Hollywood screenwriter Tom Mankiewicz, who saw Sidney in the aftermath, remembered, "One day in Beverly Hills when Seymour Hersh was doing these articles, I ran into Sidney and I said, 'Boy, they are really raking you over the coals in the *Times*, aren't they?' He said, 'If any of that were true, Tom, I'd be in jail, wouldn't I?'"[24] He was similarly dismissive with Del Coleman's ex, Jan Amory, telling her, "Honey, I put that up on my bulletin board. He ain't got nothing on me." Amory recently elaborated on Korshak's unfazed demeanor. "He didn't get depressed then or ever," Amory recalled. "But he was unhappy to be attacked by this guy—and the lies—and he vowed to fight it the rest of his life. On the other hand, he never said anything that would lead me to believe that he was telling me the whole story or none of the story."[25]

There were, however, occasions when Korshak's bravado faltered. Hilton Hotels president Barron Hilton, a longtime Korshak client and pal, later recalled how Korshak "was quite depressed with the adverse publicity he had received," and that Hilton subsequently wrote Korshak "a note of sympathy."[26] According to "Marty," a close friend of Marshall Korshak's, the *Times* series did indeed affect brother Sidney. "I used to enjoy stopping by to see Marshall in his law office," said the friend. "And one day while I was sitting there, Marshall was very upset because Seymour Hersh was doing his series about Sidney. I told Marshall, 'Don't worry. It doesn't mean anything. It will all be used to paper birdcages.' Marshall said, 'You got to tell Sidney.' 'What?' 'You got to tell Sidney he's got nothing to worry about.' Now I can't believe this, but he dialed Sidney in Beverly Hills, or wherever he was hanging out, and said, 'Sidney, my friend Marty here knows everything there is to know about the media. And he says that you got nothing to worry about by the series in the *New York Times*.' Then he said to me, 'Sidney wants to talk to you.' Now I can't believe this—here is Sidney, who an outsider would think would be the most confident man in the world, never lacking in confidence, Sidney is going to talk to *me* to have his confidence built up. This gives you an insight to the psychology. I get on the phone—what the hell am I going to say? Run for the hills? So I told him, 'Sidney, you got nothing to worry about. It's a nothing. It's a nothing.' He said, 'Oh, God, Marty, I'm so happy to hear that. That's really reassuring.' "[27]

Marty added that the most devastating quote in the series was the infamous Willie Bioff testimony of 1943, reported by Velie in 1950, in which he referred to Korshak as "our man in Hollywood."

"That was the magic sentence," said Marty. "But for every person that turned away from Sidney for that quote, fifteen admired him. That quote is what made Sidney." Supermob patriarch Jake Arvey weighed in on this subject, telling the *Chicago Sun-Times*, "It was a lie in 1950 and it's a lie today. The article was written by a man who wanted to smear Sidney Korshak, who is a friend of mine, as was his father. We are social friends, and he has never controlled me, and I have never controlled him."[28]

In Beverly Hills, the Korshaks' friends rallied around the beleaguered couple, paying close attention to Bee, who seemed more upset about the Hersh articles than her husband. On July 3, just days after the series ran, Sid and Bee attended Lew and Edie Wasserman's fortieth wedding anniversary party, wherein Edie took Bee aside to ask, "How are you doing, honey?" As

Wasserman friend and "surrogate daughter" Wendy Goldberg explained, "Edie will go to any length to protect her friends. She will fight for you to the end."[29] Also at the gathering, Lew took Sidney aside and consoled his friend, making a point of being seen embracing Korshak as he got up to leave.[30] Two months later, during a Democratic fund-raiser at the Wassermans' attended by the likes of U.S. senators Alan Cranston and John Tunney, billionaire Armand Hammer, producer Norman Lear, DNC national chairman Robert Strauss, Representative Andrew Young of Georgia, and studio honchos Barry Diller (Paramount) and David Begelman (Columbia), Lew personally introduced Sidney to presidential candidate Jimmy Carter. The Democratic front-runner later told W magazine that he had met Wasserman while still governor of Georgia, and that Wasserman's friends played a key role in his campaign. "When [Wasserman] let his friends know he had confidence in me, it was extremely helpful," Carter said.[31]

Korshak soon went back to business as usual: in 1976, the FBI received information that Korshak had made arrangements for excessive union featherbedding on the set of Paramount's recent production of The Great Gatsby, filmed in Newport, Rhode Island.[32] While the investigation yielded no charges, one possible reason is that the Bureau was more focused on simultaneous allegations about Korshak on the West Coast.

In 1976, Korshak was believed to have been involved in labor racketeering regarding the luxury liner Queen Mary, berthed in Long Beach, California. After receiving a windfall from its share of the Tidelands Oil agreement with the State of California, Long Beach had purchased the ship from the Cunard Line in 1967 for $3.4 million for use as a tourist attraction. When the ship's renovation budget skyrocketed from a predicted $8 million to $80 million, a city audit disclosed numerous questionable expenditures, including huge fees to none other than the ubiquitous Sidney Korshak.

When the FBI joined the investigation, it developed "numerous sources" that cited corruption of appointed and elected Long Beach officials; the Bureau believed that State Lands Commission members were being "paid off in the form of political contributions to continue their support of the Queen Mary project."[33] According to the FBI, Korshak had been paid $25,000 to $35,000 to help his and Reagan's friend Alfred Bloomingdale (president of Diners Club) secure a labor contract with the mob-infested Hotel and Restaurant Culinary Union, which would be cheaper, thanks to sweetheart contracts, than siding with the Marine Cooks and Stewards Union. In addition to Diners Club, long-standing Korshak client Hyatt, which was slated to operate a four-hundred-room hotel on board, was to join Diners as the principal commercial lessees of the Queen Mary.

According to an informant who participated in the Korshak dealings, meetings on the *Queen Mary* issue were held in Korshak's ABC Booking office, which one FBI witness described as "very elaborate, but poorly illuminated . . . Korshak's desk contained a pile of telephone messages which had obviously gone unanswered by Korshak for some period of time." Other meetings took place at the Chalon home, which the witness described as "very pretentious."[34] One FBI report noted, "Payoffs were made by unidentified representatives of Diner's Inc. to Sidney R Korshak to insure labor peace and guarantee 'sweetheart' contracts."[35] Sources reported that Korshak flew to Las Vegas, where he received his payment.[36]

Despite a two-year RICO investigation, Korshak emerged unscathed as usual.[37]

In St. Petersburg, Florida, new assistant state's attorney Marvin Rudnick clipped the Hersh series out of the paper and attached it to the side of his refrigerator, where it remained for over a decade, when the exposé would become an inspiration for Rudnick's own investigation of the machinations of Korshak's pal at MCA, Lew Wasserman.[38] Meanwhile in southern Florida, grislier business was afoot.

On August 7, 1976, Johnny Rosselli's chainsawed, decomposed corpse was found in a fifty-five-gallon oil drum floating in the Florida Keys. He had recently been testifying for the Senate about the Chicago mob's ties to the Castro assassination plots of the Kennedy administration. In Hollywood, insiders saw the triple murders of Giancana, Rosselli, and Hoffa as a watershed time for Korshak.

That Korshak's social circle and client base did not exactly rise up in faux disapprobation over the Hersh charges may well have been due to the fact that so many of them, also with tainted Chicago roots, dared not risk having their own dirty laundry be given a public airing. But that was not to be the case, as the *Times* quickly followed up with a business-section report on the Hyatt Hotel chain, owned by Korshak's former Supermob neighbors at 134 N. LaSalle Street the Pritzker family. On August 29, 1976, in an article entitled HYATT'S KINGDOM OF ROOMS, by *Times* L.A. Bureau chief Robert Lindsey, the paper described not only the sixty-five hotels controlled by the company, but also its "asset management" approach, and, most important, its dealings with the Teamsters Pension Fund and Sidney Korshak. In a sidebar entitled HYATT, KORSHAK, LAS VEGAS AND THE TEAMSTERS, Lindsey pointed out that Korshak had told the SEC in 1970 that he worked for the Pritzkers, drawing the inference that he likely arranged their Vegas Teamster loans.[39]

Two weeks later, the *Times* received a four-paragraph letter from Hyatt chairman Jay Pritzker that pointed out what he believed were sundry discrepancies, and closed with the following:

> The brief accompanying article was unfair to Sidney Korshak and to Hyatt. The headline leads the reader to assume that there is some relationship among the four, while none exists in fact. Mr. Korshak was not involved in any way with Hyatt's acquisition of hotels in Nevada or in any other of the negotiations with the Teamsters Union or its pension fund.
>
> /Signed/
> Jay Pritzker[40]

The Pritzker Paper Trail

It wasn't just the Teamster connections that put fear into the hearts of those connected to Korshak. Like Parvin-Dohrmann, Bernie Cornfeld's IOS, and the Bluhdorn-Sindona nexus, many of their closeted skeletons involved tax evasion via offshore shelters. Many of those with creative tax strategies were, again, connected to Sid Korshak's clients and former LaSalle neighbors the Pritzkers.

By the midseventies, the Pritzker empire was awash in profit, the most recent success coming from Nevada casino investments. Between 1959 and 1975, the Pritzkers had obtained $54.4 million in Teamster loans for their hotels, undoubtedly (although impossible to prove) with the aid of Korshak. When they cast their sights on gambling lucre, they again turned to Korshak. As Korshak himself told the SEC back in 1970, "It is possible that Hyatt Hotels talked to me about the possibility of making an acquisition in Nevada." Thus, in 1972, under their Elsinore banner, the Pritzkers joined the Vegas party when they bought the Four Queens in "Glitter Gulch" and King's Castle with Teamsters Pension Fund loans (obtained at a 4 percent discount, saving Hyatt $8 million).[41] In return, the Teamsters bought $30 million in Hyatt stock. Sources reported that Donald Pritzker had met with Korshak friend and client Moe Dalitz in Honolulu on May 14, 1972, to discuss the Four Queens loan.[42]

Castle Bank

It was around this time, the early seventies, that IRS agents like Andy Fur-faro noticed that the Pritzkers' billion-dollar Hyatt chain was paying no taxes. It turned out that the Pritzkers were the largest depositors in one of the most notorious offshore tax havens ever devised, The Castle Bank of the Bahamas, which was nothing less than an intersection of the Supermob, known gangsters, pop stars, a U.S. president, and the covert branch of the CIA—all of whom had good reason to hide their money from Uncle Sam.

Bahamian and Cayman Islands banks have long been valued by those wish-ing to hide their money because those nations absolutely refuse to cooperate with U.S. law enforcement. Bank expert and author Penny Lernoux wrote of the main advantage of the Caribbean banks: "Relying on a strict code of banking secrecy that makes Swiss banks look like blabbermouths, hundreds of banks have set up operations in the Caribbean."[43] To further guarantee its clients' anonymity, Castle had arranged for Miami National Bank, which was controlled by Lansky associates, to accept the deposits, then transfer the de-posit list to Castle with no names attached—only code numbers.

Agent Furfaro was among those frustrated by the government's inability to follow the money trail. "The money was getting out of the country through Western Union," Furfaro recently said. "But we weren't allowed to follow it. And the foreign banks wouldn't let us in. We had reports that money was also being shipped in railroad cars and containers placed on ships. There was so much money that they would just weigh it instead of count it."[44] A 1979 Ford Foundation study on offshore banking concluded that the "flow of criminal and tax evasion money" into the Bahamas alone was "up to $20 billion annually."[45] Indeed, the statistics are incredible: one Caribbean bank for every six hundred residents.

Castle, merely a variation of Hollywood's Dutch Sandwich, was the brainchild of longtime CIA "front organization" mastermind Paul Helli-well, who had come up through the ranks to become a senior officer in the CIA's predecessor, the Office of Strategic Services (OSS). As the Cold War intensified, the CIA, in its zealous desire to defeat Communism, relied on people like Helliwell to set up "brass plate" operations that allowed the CIA to launder funds to be used for propping up heroin-dealing—but anticommunist—warlords and dictators.[46]

In 1964, Helliwell joined forces with Morris Kleinman of Moe Dalitz's Mayfield Road Gang, Pritzker Chicago tax attorney (and Hyatt board mem-ber) Burton Kanter, and Pritzker law firm partner (and Teamsters Pension Fund trustee) Stanford Clinton to establish the Castle Bank, where foreign-ers could set up trust accounts that were the key to both personal and commercial tax avoidance: since the trusts were, for U.S. tax purposes, foreign citizens, they owed no taxes to the U.S. government. The added beauty of the Castle setup was that the actual deposits never had to be delivered to the bank, which was a fake depository for money that the client could use anywhere in the world.

In the midseventies, as the result of a narcotics-trafficking prosecution, the IRS mounted Operation Tradewinds (later Project Haven), an all-out investigation of Castle, referring to the probe as potentially the single biggest tax-evasion case in U.S. history. Despite the inability to serve warrants in the Bahamas, wily IRS agent Richard Jaffe and detective Sybil Kennedy obtained a list of the bank's depositors,* which included the Pritzkers, Detroit land developer Arnold Aronoff, *Playboy*'s Hugh Hefner, *Penthouse*'s Robert Guccione, rock band Creedence Clearwater Revival, Korshak pal and actor Tony Curtis, and the Mayfield's Moe Dalitz, Morris Kleinman, and Sam Tucker. Other Castle memos included a list of Vegas racketeers such as the Stardust's Yale Cohen (an associate of the Outfit's Anthony Spilotro), Nicholas "Peanuts" Donolfo (a Giancana underling), and Jimmy "the Weasel" Fratianno, who were all doing business with Castle.[47] It is not certain how many of these investors may have been directed to Castle by Sid Korshak, but one longtime friend of Hefner's recently stated that the *Playboy* sachem, for one, mentioned that Sidney had tipped him to the bank.[48]

Given all the Pritzker associates involved in the management of Castle, it came as no surprise when Pulitzer Prize–winning journalist Knut Royce determined in 1982 that the Pritzkers were in fact the bank's largest depositors.[49] A September 1972 IRS statement noted, "An informant [F. Eugene Poe, a former VP and director of Castle Bank] with access to the records of Castle Trust has stated that the Pritzker family of Chicago, through their Hyatt Corporation, received their initial backing from organized crime."[50]

Castle Bank was not the only shady partnership entered into by Kanter and the Pritzkers. In the 1970s, Kanter and Pritzker were also involved in a massive kickback scheme with two executives from the real estate wing of Prudential Insurance Company, which controlled $20 billion in properties across America.[51] In a complex setup that took prosecutors over twenty years to unravel, Kanter and the Pritzkers devised a scheme wherein contractors paid them and the Prudential executives under the table in exchange for lucrative Prudential business.[52]

---

*The story of how they obtained the precious document is a drama in and of itself, best described in Alan Block's *Masters of Paradise* and Penny Lernoux's *In Banks We Trust*.

The Castle Bank saga was but a pointed reminder that while agents like Andy Furfaro were allowed to pursue the mob in Vegas, and years earlier the FBI had resorted to illegal wiretaps to learn about the mob's skim operation, the government tacitly declared the offshore tax dodges of the former residents of 134 N. LaSalle (Kanter, Pritzker, etc.) and the similar schemes by the likes of Korshak's friends at MCA to be off-limits. It is also worth noting that the tax losses sustained due to Supermob scams (estimated in the billions) dwarfed those of the regular mobsters, who, like Capone, were regularly carted off to prison.

The Presidential Offshore Pension Fund

Although it did not appear on the purloined master list obtained by Jaffe and Kennedy, one U.S. president's name had been observed on another Castle list by a Castle executive working undercover for the IRS. "One of the first names I saw," bank officer Norman Casper said in 1997, "was the name of Richard Nixon." Although Nixon's name was deleted from the master list, a Castle Bank transfer slip bore the name "N&R," who had transferred over $11 million to Cosmos Bank, a Zurich, Switzerland, *Privatbank*. Casper was told by a Castle source that the initials stood for "Nixon and Rebozo." (Millionaire businessman/banker Charles "Bebe" Rebozo was a longtime confidant and adviser of Nixon's; he was also the bagman for the Hughes cash transfers to Nixon.) A Swiss hotelier is on record as saying Nixon and Rebozo visited Zurich at least once a year.[53]

In separate investigations, both New York district attorney Robert Morgenthau and Herschel Clesner, chief counsel of the House Commerce and Monetary Affairs Subcommittee, concluded that Nixon had money in both the Castle and Cosmos banks. Lastly, Maurice Stans, Nixon's reelection finance chief, admitted in 1997 that Rebozo had in fact set up a trust fund for Nixon's family. He also donated $19 million to Nixon's presidential library.[54]

Unfortunate Sons

Kanter also offered his tax consulting services to Berkeley-based jazz label Fantasy Records, the recording home of such giants as Thelonious Monk, Miles Davis, John Coltrane, and Chet Baker, among others. Founded in 1949, Fantasy was purchased in 1967 by Saul Zaentz, a New Jerseyite of Russian-Polish extraction. When Zaentz expanded the company to include rock and roll, he hit the jackpot almost immediately with the signing of "swamp rock" kings Creedence Clearwater Revival (CCR), who went on to record eight successive gold singles, such as "Proud Mary," "Green River," and "Fortunate Son." Kanter and Zaentz convinced CCR that they had an airtight shelter for the band's millions: Castle Bank. Thus, for most of the seventies, CCR's royalties, some of which financed Zaentz's production of the 1975 Oscar-winning film *One Flew Over the Cuckoo's Nest*, made the circuitous Supermob journey before actually arriving in the band's bank accounts.*

In their book, *The Cheating of America*, Lewis and Allison described the scheme: "Kanter and his partners then designed a complex scheme that involved shifting income from the film through various foreign entities and trusts in twenty-six separate steps before it was repatriated to the United States. The money was funneled through companies with names like Zwaluw N.V., Leeuwirik N.V., Nellthrope Cayman, Campobello Panamanian, and Inversiones Mixtas. Payments back and forth were disguised as loans, investments in other films, or repayments of loans, until what was income for whom was thoroughly confused."[55] During one year of the tax dodge, CCR paid not one cent in taxes on $2.5 million in income.

After CCR disbanded in October 1972, they attempted in vain throughout the 1970s to have their Castle Bank trusts converted into individual accounts elsewhere. After Castle broke up in 1977, the IRS went after CCR for unpaid taxes, and the band turned right around and sued Kanter for malpractice, claiming that Kanter not only lied about the airtight tax shelter, but also misappropriated millions of the band's money.[56] Filed by CCR founder and songwriter John Fogerty, the original suit was against Burt Kanter; Edward J. Arnold, an Oakland accountant; and Barrie D. Engel, an Oakland attorney. They were charged with professional malpractice, fraud, and breach of fiduciary duty. The suit asked for $10 million in damages. In 1983 a jury in San Francisco Superior Court ruled in favor of Fogerty and his band. John Fogerty was awarded $4.1 million, and the rest of his bandmates received approximately $1.5 million each.[57]

The bad publicity surrounding Castle resulted in its losing its Bahamian license before moving to Panama, where it finally dissolved in 1977.[58] Kanter, Helliwell, Pritzker, and the other bank officers, in no small thanks to IRS commissioner Donald Alexander (appointed by President Nixon) and the CIA, escaped indictments. That the Cincinnati law firm of Dinsmore, Shohl, Coates, and Deupree was among those making deposits in Castle when Commissioner Alexander was a senior partner was not lost on observers of the ill-fated probe.[59] Alexander often made his opposition to offshore investigations known: he removed the question about foreign bank

---

*Zaentz later produced films such as *Amadeus* (1984) and *The English Patient* (1996).

investments from IRS Form 1040 and canceled Operation Tradewinds, even though it had reclaimed some $52.5 million in tax penalties.

When Kanter was eventually investigated, Alexander's IRS gave 90 percent of its Castle Bank file to Kanter and his defense team; one congressman said that the file "provided those under investigation with a blueprint on how to elude prosecution."[60] Incredibly, Kanter was given the material after filing a routine request under the Freedom of Information Act, prompting an embarrassed IRS official to term the mistake a "royal screwup." Furthermore, a federal judge in Cleveland ruled that the Castle account-holder list had been illegally obtained and couldn't be used as evidence in criminal cases.[61] Lastly, the CIA's general counsel John J. Greaney intervened and demanded that the Department of Justice and IRS end the probe—it seemed that the CIA had also used Castle Bank to launder money in furtherance of its clandestine operations, and it feared that an investigation would jeopardize national security, not to mention its own congressional free ride.[62]

Using seed money from Chicago investors including the Pritzkers and Hugh Hefner, Kanter next became the legal adviser to Charles Dolan's nascent Cablevision System, which went on to become the largest privately held cable television company in the United States.* Saul Zaentz was charged by the IRS with sending all the profits from *Cuckoo's Nest* offshore (at least $38 million), only to have them returned as phony, untaxable loans.[63] It is believed he settled with the IRS in 1990 by paying the government $14 or $15 million.[64] Donald Alexander quit as IRS commissioner and went into private practice, where he was an expert on offshore tax havens.[65]

As will be seen, however, the federal government was far from finished with both Kanter and the Pritzkers.

Bill Allison of the Center for Public Integrity noted that the IRS conservatively estimates that tax avoidance and evasion will cost the Treasury nearly $2 trillion over the next decade, much of it due to the offshore tax dodges of banks and entertainment conglomerates. Citicorp alone deposits $1.3 billion overseas annually, helping it avoid some $399 million in taxes. Thanks to federal tax lawyers recruited from the staff of the House Ways and Means Committee, Supermob associates lobbied for arcane tax loopholes that allowed them to make inexpensive sham overseas investments, such as in a sewer system in Germany, in order to claim massive tax write-offs. One

---

*Dolan also founded the short-lived satellite HDTV service VOOM, which folded in April 2005 after sustaining losses of over $661 million.

of the most favored foreign schemes is the "lease in, lease out," or LILO option,* which has been a boon for U.S. banks such as Wachovia. In 2004, Bob McIntyre, the director of the Institute on Taxation and Economic Policy, told *Frontline* correspondent Hedrick Smith how Wachovia used the LILO gambit: "Well, Wachovia, amazingly, in 2002, even though it reported four billion dollars in profits, reported that it didn't pay any taxes and, in fact, got a tax rebate from the government of about one hundred and sixty million dollars . . . they saved three billion dollars in taxes over the last three years from leasing."[66]

In addition, according to the IRS's most recent statistics, there were 101 returns filed by millionaires who paid absolutely nothing in federal income taxes.[67]

---

*Simply stated, LILO is a tax-dodging loophole that allows corporations to make minuscule overseas leasings in exchange for massive domestic tax credits.

CHAPTER 20

Pursued by the Fourth Estate

O N JULY 11, 1976, less than two weeks after the Hersh exposé appeared, Supermob friends and families convened in Southern California to witness the fourth marriage of their favorite crooner, Frank Sinatra. Notable among the elite guests was Ronald Reagan, who interrupted his presidential campaign to attend Sinatra's wedding at Outfit wire-service boss Moe Annenberg's son Walter's Sunnylands estate in Rancho Mirage. With Bee Korshak serving as matron of honor to bride Barbara Marx, other attendees included Korshak pals such as Gregory Peck, Kirk Douglas, and the disgraced former vice president of the United States, Spiro Agnew.[1]

The newest Mrs. Sinatra, Barbara Blakeley Oliver Marx Sinatra, was a friend of the Korshaks' from Las Vegas, where she was a chorus girl at Sid's Riviera Hotel. According to Sinatra's daughter Tina, Korshak "knew Dad's new bride better than any of us."[2] When Sinatra and Marx met in 1972, Barbara was married to Marx brother Zeppo, an inveterate gambler whom she met at the Riv and had married in 1959 (recall that the Marx Brothers were part owners of the land on which the Riv was built). The marriage to Zeppo brought Barbara to his home just across the seventeenth fairway from Sinatra's bachelor pad at Palm Springs' Tamarisk Golf Course. Soon, she was recruited into the spirited tennis matches at the Sinatra court, where she joined in doubles contests with the likes of Bee Korshak, Dinah Shore, and others.* The marriage to Zeppo, who was much older—and, more important, in a financial free fall—was doomed; after Barbara divorced Zeppo and moved in with "The Chairman," Zeppo told his brother Groucho's son Arthur Marx, "She left me with a deck of cards and an old Sinatra album."[3] However, the relationship with the volatile Sinatra was anything

---

*Bee contributed her dessert recipes to both Barbara's and Dinah's celebrity cookbooks (*The Sinatra Celebrity Cookbook*, and *Someone's in the Kitchen With Dinah*).

The Reagans attending Sinatra's July 11, 1976, marriage to Barbara Marx, where Bee Korshak was matron of honor (David Sutton, MPTV)

but smooth sailing, and during the stormy courtship the Korshaks often consoled Barbara.

The protective Sinatra clan was suspicious of Marx, and daughter Tina wrote that her fears were only assuaged when she spoke with Sidney Korshak after the ceremony.* In her autobiography, Tina recalled how, when she was sitting by the pool with Kirk Douglas, she was approached by "a tall, reedy, silver-haired man . . . It was Sidney Korshak, the legendary (and absolutely charming) attorney who'd cut his teeth with Al Capone, a man who could fix the bitterest labor dispute."[4] Taking a seat next to Kirk and Tina, Korshak produced a black Flair pen from his breast pocket and told Tina, "Keep this as a memento—it just saved you a *lot* of money and aggravation." Korshak explained that he had been asked to represent Barbara and convinced her to sign a prenuptial agreement. (Twelve years after the marriage ceremony, Barbara convinced Frank to rescind the agreement, giving her 50 percent of everything Frank earned during their marriage. "It would be as though the prenup had never existed," wrote Tina, "—as though Sidney Korshak's Flair pen had vanished into a parallel universe.")[5]

---

*Daughter Tina alleged that Marx later confided to a friend, "This time, I married for money." (Sinatra, *My Father's Daughter,* 159)

Bee Korshak, interior decorator, undated (Dominick Dunne)

Soon after Barbara settled in, the new couple enlisted interior decorator Bee Korshak to redo their Palm Springs eighteen-bedroom, twenty-three-bath compound, where over the years there had been a constant flow of guests, including President Kennedy, who had once used the Sinatra guest room during his 1960 presidential campaign. "It was almost a hotel at times," Bee later said. "Frank liked having people around him." Among other changes, Bee tried in vain to diminish the ubiquitousness of Frank's favorite color: "I couldn't quite get the orange out of him," she lamented years later.*,6

As the years progressed, the Korshaks and Sinatras were regularly seen in each others' company: Bee and Barbara often shopped together and even traveled to Monaco for Princess Grace's annual Red Cross benefit, and to Senegal to christen a new medical dispensary and church on behalf of the World Mercy Fund, a favorite Frank Sinatra charity.7 And the spotlight-dodging Sidney even showed up backstage at the Universal Amphitheater for a 1980 Frank Sinatra concert.8

Nineteen seventy-seven saw the opening of Kurt Niklas's Bistro Gardens just down the street from the Bistro, at 176 N. Canon. Bistro maître d'

---

*Together, Barbara and Bee renamed rooms after Frank's recordings: Frank's office was now "My Way"; the projection room, "Send in the Clowns"; the guesthouses, "High Hopes" and "Young at Heart"; the quarters where JFK trysted with his lady friends, "The Tender Trap"; and the main building became "The House I Live In." For Frank's projection room, Korshak removed the old gold draperies and busy carpet. "We redid it very simply," said Korshak, "with a lot of off-white textured fabrics and furniture from J. Robert Scott." With architect Ted Grenzbach, Korshak added travertine floors for Barbara's new master suite, a Jacuzzi and exercise room, renovated the well-used projection room, and purchased new lawn and pool furniture.

Jimmy Murphy remembered the reasoning behind Niklas's seeming desire to go into competition with himself. "Kurt always wanted an outdoor garden," said Murphy, "and the space wasn't there at the old Bistro, which was very formal, whereas the Bistro Gardens was casual dining for a younger group of people. But Kurt shot himself in the foot when he opened the Bistro Gardens—he spread himself too thin." Nonetheless, the Gardens became the home to Irving "Swifty" Lazar's soon-to-be-famous Oscar parties. And although Sidney Korshak was no longer a stockholder in the Bistro, he continued to hold court at the original restaurant as well as putting in regular appearances at the Gardens.* (The location now boasts the celebrity-friendly Spago Restaurant.)

That spring, the buzz at both the Bistro and the Bistro Gardens—and every other Beverly Hills hot spot—was the March 11, 1977, handcuff arrest of Bob Evans's producer friend Roman Polanski in the lobby of the Beverly Wilshire on six counts of child molestation—offenses that carried a maximum fifty-year prison sentence.† It was not unnoticed that the judge who was assigned the case, Laurence J. Rittenband, was the great friend of Bob Evans's consigliere, Sidney Korshak.

According to then thirteen-year-old Samantha Geimer, the forty-four-year-old Polanski had lured her to the Mulholland Drive home of actor Jack Nicholson, who had appeared in Evans-Polanski's *Chinatown*, under the pretense of introducing her to Nicholson and taking photos of her for the French edition of *Vogue* magazine. Of course, Polanski knew that Nicholson was off skiing in Colorado at the time. Geimer reported that Polanski drugged her into unconsciousness before raping her in every conceivable manner—she awoke with Polanski's head between her legs. Amazingly, Polanski admitted to all, including the police, that he had had sex with Geimer, whom he knew to be thirteen—they only differed over whether the tryst was consensual. According to LAPD detective Phil Vanatter, Polanski hadn't a clue regarding the immorality of having sex with children. "He'd screwed plenty of girls younger than this one, he said," Vanatter recalled, "and nobody gave a damn."[9] In France, according to his biographer, Polanski's "reputation as a seducer of pubescent girls was legendary."[10]

When the pretrial hearings got under way, Rittenband, who normally was

---

*At this time, the Bistro's treasurer was Jerry Orbach, and among its sixty-one stockholders were Jack Benny, Harris Katleman, Beldon Katleman, Doris Stein, and Jack Warner.

†Polanski was charged with furnishing quaaludes to a minor, child molestation, unlawful sexual intercourse, rape by use of drugs, oral copulation, and sodomy.

a harsh judge, was excoriated in the press for what seemed to be the preferential treatment he was affording Polanski, who was allowed to go to the South Pacific to work on DeLaurentiis's next film, *Hurricane.* "The man has a right to make a living," Rittenband answered his critics. The judge next gave Polanski a ninety-day stay before having to submit to a court-appointed psychiatric workup. The *Hollywood Reporter* wondered if Rittenband was "going soft in the head." Others wondered if he had succumbed to industry pressure from the likes of his and Evans's pal Sid Korshak. *Santa Monica Evening Outlook* court reporter Dick Brenneman, who was then meeting regularly with Rittenband—once in Korshak's company—in order to write a profile of him, had no doubt about Korshak's input into the Polanski affair, noting that the two dined together at least twice a week. "I am morally certain Rittenband had asked [Korshak] to advise him on Polanski," Brenneman later wrote. "Korshak was the judge's best friend, a lawyer renowned for his political media savvy. Besides, Korshak's specialty was advice."[11]

Rittenband, however, reverted back to his normal hard-edged style when he received reports that Polanski was cavorting in Europe with fifteen-year-old wannabe actress Nastassja Kinski. "How can I believe this remorse stuff," Rittenband told a reporter, "when the son of a bitch was playing around in Europe with a fifteen-year-old at the same time he was about to go on trial here for raping a thirteen-year-old?" Word leaked to the press that Rittenband was going to throw the book at the director. Thus, on the day before his January 30, 1978, sentencing, Polanski fled to Paris, where he spent his first night making love to another fifteen-year-old.[12] He has been a fugitive from the United States ever since, although the Academy of Motion Picture Arts and Sciences had no qualms about honoring him with a Best Director honor in 2002 for *The Pianist.**

In July 1977, Sy Hersh and Jeff Gerth took aim at another Supermob figure, Charlie Bluhdorn. In a *New York Times* three-part series, the duo cited over seventy-five sources that pointed out a litany of Gulf & Western transgressions, many of which were the focus of still another SEC probe. Among the numerous questionable G&W activities described were:

---

*As promised, Polanski made Kinski a star when he cast her as Tess in the film *Tess* (1979), which told the tale of an innocent young servant girl entrapped by a lecherous older man. In 1989, the fifty-six-year-old Polanski married twenty-three-year-old actress Emmanuelle Seigner.

- Millions in profit hidden from stockholders.
- Unreported use of company resources for the private use of senior company officials, including Bluhdorn.
- The moving of all Paramount Pictures files from the New York office the day before an IRS audit.
- The creation of a Canadian subsidiary that allowed G&W to dodge U.S. taxes much the same way as MCA-Universal was doing in Amsterdam.[13]

It would later be disclosed that the SEC also alleged that Gulf & Western and the mob-linked Resorts International Corporation had inflated the value of real estate properties in the Bahamas. The SEC filed formal fraud charges in 1979, stating that Gulf & Western held undisclosed profits for sugar revenues from the Dominican Republic and occasionally took part in stock transfers to make losses look like profits. That year, *Forbes* magazine referred to Gulf's accounting as a "$400 million credibility gap." In addition, the SEC charged Bluhdorn with an outrageous scheme to turn Blake Edwards's *Darling Lili* (1970) into a profitable film.[14] According to Gulf scholar Bernard Dick, Bluhdorn exchanged the rights for the $20 million bomb to a British firm, Commonwealth United Entertainment, for $31.2 million in Commonwealth debentures and a $10 million promissory note. As Dick summarized, "When Commonwealth suffered a financial crisis, rather than acknowledge the loss, Gulf & Western substituted income from other transactions and continued to carry the debentures on the books at $31.2 million, even though their market value was only one percent of that amount."[15]

In 1981, after a four-year SEC investigation, Gulf & Western settled with the feds by agreeing to fund a $39 million economic and social development fund in the Dominican Republic;[16] however, it never denied or admitted to the allegations, but, like a chastised child, promised to clean up its act and never to do it again.[17]

One month after the newest Hersh disclosures, the Supermob experienced the beginning of a cascade of losses among its ranks, and the first earthly exit could not have been more significant. On August 26, 1977, patriarch Jake Arvey died at Chicago's Weiss Memorial Hospital. Over twelve hundred mourners showed for the funeral of the man who had dispensed countless patronage jobs over the years. However, few seemed to grasp the national influence he had exerted through protégés from Bazelon in the East, to Ziffren and Korshak in the West. His probate listed an estate valued at $1.75 million,[18] although it was likely the tip of the iceberg, with pricey California property having already likely been bequeathed to his heirs. (Interestingly, Arvey's son Howard currently maintains a valuable mountaintop estate overlooking Santa Barbara.)

Arvey's passing prompted the local press to seek a statement from a favorite Arvey ward, Marshall Korshak, who said, "What can I tell you? Can I tell you that he never felt the kind of power he had? Can I tell you that nobody in the history of the Democratic Party did what Arvey did? Can I tell you that the party was his life? He lived and breathed it. And no one left it with more friends, no one left it loved by more people."[19] Twenty-five years later, the *Chicago Jewish News* would rank Arvey number three on its list of "Chicago's Top 100 Jews of the 20th Century," behind Philip Klutznick, downtown developer and international president of B'nai B'rith and president of the World Jewish Congress, and Julius Rosenwald, president and chairman of the board of Sears Roebuck and an extraordinary philanthropist.*,[20]

Not long after, Marshall Korshak made his own symbolic exit—from the political stage. After over four decades in public life, Marshall had had enough and decided to step down from his current post of city collector, which he had held since 1971. Although his career had afforded him great rewards—with no small thanks to his brother's investment advice—it had come at a price. Not only had he been pursued publicly by the IRS and the SEC, Marshall had also garnered a fair degree of local negative publicity in recent years:

• 1972—Korshak was named in an investigation that claimed that as city treasurer he owned stock in Metropolitan Bank and Trust Company, in which $1 million in city funds had coincidentally been deposited, thereby boosting Korshak's stock. The investment was perceived as a severe conflict of interest.[21]

• 1973—A federal grand jury subpoenaed Marshall Korshak and nine others in an investigation of whether precinct captains had falsified their addresses to make it appear that they lived within their districts. The predominantly white captains had addresses showing that they supposedly lived in predominantly black precincts. This practice is known as plantation politics.[22]

• 1974—The Illinois state's attorney Bernard Carey investigated Marshall Korshak and Mayor Daley's son Michael Daley for their roles in the

---

*Klutznick also played a large part in the creation and development of the state of Israel and was the backstage contact responsible for the Soviets allowing Jews to leave the country.

contract negotiations between three major car-rental agencies and Chicago-O'Hare Airport. Korshak, who was city treasurer at the time, was alleged to have been representing Hertz Rental Agency, while Daley was representing Avis. It was claimed that the city was slighted by 2–3 percent of what the rental agencies should have been paying to operate at O'Hare. Due to Korshak's position as a city employee, Carey thought there was a "clear conflict of interest."[23] The probe was soon bumped up to a federal investigation. City Corporation Counsel Richard Curry, who also had a hand in the negotiations, came forward to say Korshak had no involvement in the contracts or negotiations. Marshall Korshak also went to the press stating that he had no part in the negotiations or the preparation of the contracts. However, it was noted that Richard Curry was the cousin of Mayor Daley.[24] In a round of political hardball, Korshak and Curry came forward to denounce Alderman William Singer's allegations that the men had violated public trust with regard to the car-rental airport contracts. Both Korshak and Curry called Singer a liar and reaffirmed there was no wrongdoing and that the city had made a good deal with the rental agencies.[25]

• 1974—Reporters probed into whether Chicago was being cheated out of $3 million in cigarette tax revenue, claiming that the Department of Revenue director Marshall Korshak and his sixty department inspectors were doing little to arrest those responsible for selling cigarettes without the state tax stamp.[26] The day after the exposé ran, Marshall Korshak's team of inspectors seized vending machines selling unstamped packs of cigarettes and promised to audit three cigarette wholesalers.[27]

After Marshall's declaration that he was leaving the public arena to concentrate on his law practice, brother Sidney led a group of Marshall's friends and relatives in hosting a farewell luncheon at the Bismarck Hotel. One friend who was there recalled how Sidney took the opportunity to point out what he considered to be a lack of respect shown his brother in recent years by Chicago's Democratic bigwigs. "After a number of little comments and remarks and humorous little sayings," remembered the attendee, "Sidney rose from this long table of probably like twenty-four people in attendance and said, 'I am very happy that my brother will be leaving City Hall. My brother and I are very close; we talk on the phone just about every day. And every day, my brother tells me that he saw Mayor Daley in the lobby of City Hall and the mayor said, "Hi, Marsh." Or he saw Mayor Daley going out the exit of City Hall and the mayor just brushed him off and said nothing to him. Or he was walking down LaSalle Street and the mayor smiled at him. I am so tired of having my brother's days shaped by whether

Mayor Daley smiled at him or didn't smile at him. I am relieved that now he'll be leaving city government and never again will I have to receive one of those phone calls.' "28

A few years earlier, a local politician had expounded on the same theme: "Daley really shortchanged him. Daley made him run for the Sanitary District trustee, but that was a dead end, and Korshak was very disappointed. Daley was very ungenerous to him in awarding patronage and so on."29 Korshak made a brief return to politics in 1979, when Mayor Jane Byrne appointed him to the Chicago Police Board, a nine-member commission whose purpose was to study the feasibility of legalized gambling.30 But controversy continued to follow Korshak. In 1983 he became executive director of the late Sam Rosen's estate, for which he and two other lawyers split $70,000 in fees. At the same time, Mayor Byrne's administration approved a $900,000 bond for the Rosen estate to be used to rebuild Sam's Liquors, which was dubbed The World's Largest Wine Cellar. Korshak denied using his influence at City Hall to push the industrial revenue bond through the city bureaucracy for his client.31

Nonetheless, in retirement, Korshak continued to receive accolades, much as he had since the early sixties. In 1989, Marshall received the Torch of Learning Award from The American Friends of the Hebrew University of Jerusalem.32 In 1990, at Korshak's eightieth-birthday celebration, *Chicago Sun-Times* columnist Steve Neal praised him as one of the best politicians ever to have served the city of Chicago.33

The anecdotes shared around the dais at Marshall's farewell bash were anything but ancient history. One of the many common memories held by the Korshak brothers was about to be revisited in the person of Hugh Hefner, whom the brothers had helped with his liquor license difficulties in 1961. In March 1978, Hefner and Playboy were being sued by Lew Wasserman, who claimed that Hefner had obtained numerous videotape copies of Universal films for his vaunted private library. Although Hefner retained licensed attorneys to handle the suit, he decided to recruit Sidney Korshak, still unlicensed in California, to intercede with his good friend Wasserman.

As Hefner described in testimony five years later, Korshak demanded, and received on March 16, 1978, his standard $50,000 retainer in return for placing a call to a man he was ordinarily speaking with twice a day anyway. But money was no object for Hefner, who was hoping to avoid bad publicity surrounding the films, which certainly appeared to be stolen property. Some have opined that Hefner had read of Korshak's close relationship with Wasserman in Hersh's 1976 *New York Times* series, but Hefner denied it; he did admit to being aware of Paul Steiger's 1969 Korshak profile in the *Los Angeles Times*.[34] In actuality, it is inconceivable that Hefner was unaware of the friendship between Wasserman and Hefner's fellow Chicagoan Sid Korshak.

However, this time Korshak either lost his magic touch or pulled a classic "sweetheart" deal and never even called Wasserman, preferring instead to just abscond with Hefner's money. After being forced to return the films to Universal, Hefner called Korshak "remarkably unsuccessful."

On April 9, 1978, the Korshaks attended a $1,000-per-plate private fund-raising dinner for Governor Jerry Brown, held at the home of Lew Wasserman, taking Teamster chief Andy Anderson and his wife as their guests.[35] Also at the dinner was another Curly Humphreys protégé, the former head of Chicago's mob-saturated Bartenders Union, Edward T. Hanley, who now presided over the oft-investigated Culinary Workers Teamsters Union, which worked closely with Korshak. Korshak played a vital role in the event, which raised $50,000, by pulling one hundred invitee names from his personal address book—Joyce Haber's "A-list."[36] Republicans later charged that Brown accepted an additional $50,000 contribution from the Culinary Workers.[37] When Peter F. Vaira and Douglas P. Roller, attorneys in charge of the Cleveland Strike Force, wrote a briefing paper for the White House in 1978, they noted the following about Hanley: "Edward Hanley was elected president of HRE [Culinary] International in 1973 on the power and influence of Aiuppa and the Chicago mob . . . Ed Hanley represents the classic example of an organized crime take-over of a major labor union. Since his election, Hanley has moved to solidify his power, both in terms of the local Union officials and elements of organized crime. Likewise, the HRE [Culinary Union] under Hanley's guidance has moved to insure support in the appropriate government circles by carefully selected and generous political campaign contributions . . . Many of the persons placed on the payrolls as organizers are organized crime figures or friends of Hanley, mostly from Chicago."*

*According to Vaira's report, "Hanley was born in Chicago on January 21, 1932. His associates include Joey Aiuppa, organized crime boss of Chicago, and organized crime figures John Delasandro and Rich Conboys. Hanley's brother-in-law is Frank James Calabrese, burglar and loanshark collector. Hanley was handpicked for his current position by Joey Aiuppa. Hanley started his union career in 1957 as Business Agent for Bartenders Local 450 in Cicero, Illinois, and held a similar post in Local 278 of the Chicago Bartenders union, both of which are tightly controlled by Aiuppa. In 1962 Hanley became president of the Culinary Workers Chicago Joint Executive Board, which is also under the control of organized crime. He became International President in 1973."

Supermob observers like Jack Tobin found it curious that Brown shortly thereafter appointed Hanley's brother-in-law, Ted Hansen, to be the director of the Fifty-second District of the California Agricultural Association, which named the concessionaires at all the state's racetracks and county fairs. One woman who ran a concession at the fair—coincidentally held at Del Mar, formerly owned by Al Hart—told reporter, and Supermob watcher for the *Santa Monica Evening Outlook*, Dick Brenneman that she personally skimmed $17,000 per day, which was sent to Joe Batters Accardo's Palm Springs home.[38]

Brown's links to the Culinary Workers went even further: one of Brown's key advisers, future U.S. circuit court judge Stephen Reinhardt (sponsored by Paul Ziffren), had been on an $833 monthly retainer from the Culinary Workers International from 1974 to 1976, when Hanley was president, and in that position had personally negotiated a $2 million Teamster loan for Hoffa's attorney—and Korshak's St. Louis alter ego—Morris Schenker for the purpose of building a resort in Murrieta Hot Springs, near Riverside, California (Schenker was already the owner of the Teamster-funded Las Vegas' Dunes Hotel and Casino). The *Los Angeles Herald-Examiner*, in noting the Reinhardt-Schenker loan, wrote, "Schenker is viewed by law enforcement officials as a major figure in organized crime."[39]

This was far from the first hint of Brown's coziness with questionable supporters. In 1976, Governor Brown was observed meeting and traveling with Herman "Blackie" Leavitt, head of the Chicago Outfit–infiltrated Hotel and Restaurant Employees and Bartenders International Union (HREU). On February 4, 1976, Leavitt and Brown attended HREU's executive board meeting at D'Amico's Restaurant in Palm Springs; D'Amico was a known close associate of alleged Chicago organized crime subject Frank Buccieri.

Washington Post columnist Jules Witcover noted Brown's strategy sessions for the 1976 run were held at Paul Ziffren's home at 23920 Malibu Road,[40] while other observers, especially those in the L.A. District Attorney's Office, began noticing Korshak's growing association with Brown's chief of staff, future governor Gray Davis.* It was said that Korshak appealed to Davis

---

*Davis had begun at the local level, but the horizon expanded quickly for the future governor. At home in Los Angeles, he worked on the mayoral campaign of the late Tom Bradley, then spent six years as the appointed chief of staff to Governor Jerry Brown. Davis won his first elected position in 1982 as a representative to the California State Assembly, from the Beverly Hills district of Los Angeles County. For eight years, between 1986 and 1994, Davis was state controller of California and chaired the California Council on Criminal Justice. As the state controller, Davis exposed fraud in California's medical welfare system and helped reduce a runaway budget deficit.

because of his influence with Teamsters such as Hanley, who attended Wasserman's fund-raiser. DA investigator Frank Hronek went so far as to describe Korshak as Davis's mentor, telling his son Steve, "Gray Davis was a protégé of Korshak's."[41] Fellow DA investigator Jim Grodin recently agreed, saying, "I saw Gray and Sid together at the Bistro a number of times."[42] NBC crack investigative reporter Brian Ross (now with ABC), who would soon expose many of these relationships on national television, remarked, "Gray Davis and Korshak admired each other's style."[43]

Just three weeks after the 1978 Brown fête, California attorney general Evelle Younger, himself a Republican gubernatorial hopeful, released the eighty-six-page *First Report of California's Organized Crime Control Commission*, which gave the names, photographs, and home addresses of the state's ninety-two leading organized crime figures. Based on nine months of work, the report was billed as the most comprehensive study of organized crime ever conducted in the state. Among those included in the sensational list was none other than Governor Brown's good friend the "well-known Los Angeles labor lawyer, Sidney R. Korshak." The report called Korshak "the key link between organized crime and big business." Next to Korshak's smiling driver's-license photo was the following summary: "His name has been linked with organized crime for more than 30 years, and he has been the subject of several organized crime investigations. A U.S. Justice Department official has described Korshak as a 'senior adviser' to organized crime groups in CA, CHI, LV and New York."

Also on the list were Korshak's great friends boss Joe Accardo, who had a home in the desert, and Moe Dalitz, who the report stated came to Las Vegas and "began investing and supervising organized crime investments in

Korshak depicted in the 1978 Report of the California Commission on Organized Crime (California Commission on Organized Crime)

hotel and gambling business" before his La Costa, California, investment. The report also called attention to Dalitz's involvement in a partnership that had invested between $10 million and $13 million in the state's San Joaquin Valley wine vineyards. However, Korshak's and Dalitz's names stood out in the report's list, which otherwise read like a page from the Rome phone book, with all the other politically connected, Russian-pedigreed Supermob associates, aside from Korshak and Dalitz, assiduously avoided. (It should be noted, however, that a second "secret" list was released only to law enforcement officials. That list has never surfaced.) It likewise made no mention of the hundreds of millions in mob lucre that had been invested in the state or the massive offshore tax dodges of the movie studios.

"The best thing that could happen is that these persons would leave California," Younger said at the news conference heralding the report's release. Also at the press conference, commission chairman James Glavis noted, "California does not yet have someone sitting as its godfather. Despite popular conceptions to the contrary, organized crime doesn't require a top dog to go about its business . . . There doesn't need to be a godfather if there's a functioning board of directors." Insiders might have called that an apt description of the Supermob.

The report also noted the vast illegal profits that funneled back to Chicago and elsewhere, which the commission estimated at $6.8 billion per year. The report broke down the dirty profits thus:

- $4.8 billion worth of gambling, which "provides the greatest amount of gross revenue to syndicated organized crime."
- $1.3 billion in income from loan-sharking, which is usually closely linked to gambling operations.
- $500 million worth of crime-related securities thefts and investment frauds (generally known as white-collar crime).
- $200 million worth of income from pornography, which is used to support other activities, such as prostitution and drug trafficking.[44]

The *Los Angeles Herald-Examiner* weighed in editorially on May 3, 1978, with the header IS LOS ANGELES BECOMING A CRIME CAPITAL? The article, which noted Younger's likely political motivation for the report, added, "No doubt he believes that there are votes in looking like a tough-jawed crime-fighter. And he may be right. But whatever his motivation in so closely identifying himself with this report—and perhaps timing its release—the report was long overdue. Perhaps it's not too late for Los Angeles to wake up to what's happening in its own backyard." E. Timothy Applegate, Korshak's liaison at Hilton Hotels, felt it necessary to make a few cursory calls to see if there was any truth to the Korshak allegations. "When Evelle Younger listed Sidney in his crime report, I talked to Frank Johnson [chairman of the Nevada Gaming Commission] and one of the Vegas FBI guys, and they laughed at it," Applegate recently said. "They said Evelle was grandstanding for votes and he didn't have anything other than news articles."[45]

A few days later, the man himself, Sidney Korshak, gave a once-in-a-lifetime interview to enterprising *Herald-Examiner* reporter Mike Qualls. "He can put up or shut up," Korshak said of Younger, whom he challenged to either back up the damning allegations or retract them. "I've never been cited, let alone indicted, for anything," Korshak declared. "I've never been called before any bar association. As far as I know, there's never been a complaint against me of any kind . . . What am I charged with? What part of this [organized crime] am I supposed to be?"

Korshak then pointed out that he had donated $3,000 to Younger's political campaigns in 1970 and 1971, and that, amazingly, as recently as three weeks prior to the report's release, he was asked to contribute to Younger's gubernatorial campaign and to serve on his campaign committee. "I read the letter and threw it away, because I don't serve on any committees," Korshak said.* For good measure, Korshak added that he now wanted his $3,000 contribution back. "I don't understand how Younger can fail to return that to me by messenger," said Korshak. "But, so far, I haven't received it. If I'm the kind of person he says I am—and I'm not—then I don't think he would want it on his record that he took money from me."

Korshak then echoed the *Herald* editorial, charging that the report was "pure, simple, unadulterated politics . . . Here's [a] man who has been attorney general eight years . . . and he never has come up with one indictment against any of the people he speaks about. I guess Younger saw his ratings slipping, because the report was released simultaneously with a poll showing [former police chief Ed] Davis forging ahead of him.† I imagine he thought he would revitalize his campaign with this type of sensationalism."

Then, in a rare display of vulnerability, Korshak said, "The damage this has caused me is irreparable, because what can I do to combat it?" Korshak

---

*Younger's aides confirmed that Korshak had received the letter, signed by campaign chairman Charles Bakaly, but explained it had been sent out in error after volunteers handling the solicitation mailing had been ordered to drop Korshak's name from their list.

†Davis was a law-and-order candidate whose views were seen as resonating with the electorate.

ended the interview by saying, "Someday I hope I have a confrontation with Younger, and I can ask him, 'Why me? What was your purpose?' "[46]

The canny Korshak was correct in his assessment of Younger's controversial history, and especially accurate in his reference to the AG's limp prosecutorial record. In 1970, the year before he had taken office, there had been thirty-one organized crime prosecutions, but in the seven years following, Younger had overseen none. Thus, it was widely perceived that the report was a feint, aimed, just as Korshak said, at getting votes. In fact, Younger's "soft on crime" history led some to believe he had a personal interest in giving hoods a free ride in California. In his previous post as L.A. district attorney, Younger had quashed a subpoena for his files on Moe Morton when Morton had filed a civil suit against Hollywood Park for barring him from the track (all other agencies—L.A. police, L.A. sheriff, and U.S. marshal—had promptly delivered their files). However, insiders had a good guess as to why Younger might be sensitive about Morton. A decade earlier, a Los Angeles superior court judge had to recuse himself from a hearing involving Morton when it was revealed that he had met Morton—thanks to an introduction by Younger at Sid Korshak and Moe Morton's notorious Acapulco Towers, where, according to a former L.A. FBI agent, Younger had received a briefcase containing $50,000, delivered by messenger from Sam Giancana, then living in Mexico.[47] Interestingly, in February 1969, Younger had been among a group on Marvin Whitman's private plane to Mexico, where it was suspected that he had stayed at Morton's Acapulco Towers. Among the other thirty-four passengers were Paul and Micki Ziffren, and Al and Viola Hart.[48]

But there was more. In 1967, when the FBI had busted the Beverly Hills Friars Club card-cheating scheme orchestrated by Maurice Friedman, DA Younger had failed to cooperate with the Bureau, prompting FBI agent Wayne Hill, who investigated the case, to remark, "There was an attempt [by Younger's office] to put pressure on us to pull in our horns." In fact, in 1967, Younger had written a letter on Friedman's behalf to the Nevada Gaming Commission to help him obtain a gambling license for Vegas' Frontier Hotel and Casino, where he fronted for the Detroit Mafia. Friedman later bragged about how he had bribed someone in the DA's office with $2,000 for the letter. Worse still, soon afterward, Younger was Friedman's personal guest at the Frontier.

Thus it came as no surprise when Younger and his AG office were frozen out of an ongoing federal probe into possible political corruption in California. It was rumored that federal authorities were holding Younger at arm's length due to his acceptance of Korshak's $3,000 contribution to his election.[49]

The entire series of accusations made Korshak a virtual behind-the-scenes campaign issue, with the Democrats hitting Younger for his ties to Korshak's partner Morton, and the Republicans excoriating Brown for his association with the Korshak-influenced Culinary Workers Union.

Ira Silverman had heard enough. As NBC News' top investigative producer, Silverman decided it was time for a major broadcast network to follow up on the tireless work of the print journalists who had been dogging Korshak and friends over the decades. Silverman convinced his superiors at *NBC Nightly News* and his on-air reporting partner Brian Ross to pursue not only Korshak, but also the murky history of organized crime's link to the movie business. "Ira Silverman was the main guy—he moved heaven and earth for that show," Ross recently recalled.[50] At the time, Ross was the hottest, and arguably the most talented, reporter at the major networks. He had joined NBC News as a correspondent in 1976, and soon after, his five-part series on the Teamsters won both the 1976 Sigma Delta Chi Award and a National Headliner Award. In 1977, he had won a National Headliner Award for a five-part study of organized crime in the United States.

After weeks of investigation, the duo parceled the story, to be called "The Mob and the Movies," into three segments. Part one dealt with Teamster extortion of the studios on films such as Dino DeLaurentiis's *The Brink's Job*, in which Korshak had played such a key role (see chapter 18). Ross and Silverman named the Mafia bosses who were the focus of a Boston grand jury probe into the scheme and also interviewed both DeLaurentiis, who said the payoffs to the Teamsters cost the production an extra $1 million, and the overprotective head of the Motion Picture Association of America (MPAA), Jack Valenti, who warned Ross about the dangers of singling out his precious movie business for corruption charges. For his part, DA John Van DeKamp assured Ross that he was looking into movie corruption.

Part two of the series focused squarely on Korshak, whom Ross introduced as "the most powerful man in Hollywood . . . [and] believed by law enforcement to be the senior adviser to organized crime bosses, looking out for the mob's interests in Nevada and California." They were drawn to Korshak after learning that his friend Lew Wasserman's Universal Studios was the only major in town to have never suffered a labor walkout "because they had Korshak."

"We had this great stakeout for two weeks at the Bistro's Table Three," Ross recently recalled. He and Silverman utilized every technique available to observe their mark: helicopter flyovers of the Chalon manse, off-the-record sources, surveillance cameras across from the Bistro, and even a courtroom sketch artist who drew Sidney from the next table. Ross elaborated:

> We did some long stakeouts at the Bistro, which served as his office. At the corner table he had this trunk line of phones—a four- or five-line phone, right there, like an office phone. When we went into the Bistro with a sketch artist from NBC, he sort of became afraid. He started showing up in a zoot suit.
>
> We had a van across the street and saw him coming out the front door with Andy Anderson, who was picking lint off of Korshak's jacket. The body language was one of subservience. The maître d' told Sidney about the camera crew outside and he tried to hide behind a screen and look out for us saying, "Where are they?"
>
> We saw Gregory Peck there with Sidney. Peck was trying to get labor support for [son] Cary Peck to run for Congress. It was an incredible scene. Everyone came and paid homage to him.

Ross and Silverman's hidden cameras trailed Korshak as he walked between the Bistro and DeLaurentiis's office, steps away on Canon, or to his "secret office" at the Riviera's headquarters two blocks away on Wilshire. DeLaurentiis's assistant Fred Sidewater remembered the occasion: "Sid actually came to my office a few times, using the door that connected from the street. One time Brian Ross used a hidden camera and snapped a picture of him talking to Swifty Lazar on the street, then walking into my office, trying to expose him."[51] Korshak's walks rang familiar with Silverman. "Sidney would 'take a walk,' much like the boys in New York do," remembered Silverman. "We got footage of him coming out of the Riviera office with George Raft."

The investigators' sources provided them with Wasserman's phone logs, which evidenced the closeness of the relationship between Korshak and the strike-immune studio boss. "The logs showed that Lew Wasserman began and ended every day with phone calls to Korshak," said Ross, "with numerous phone calls in between. Every day." With the Ross-Silverman work on the Korshak-Wasserman–*King Kong* negotiations tightly held, there was great surprise when they received advice from an NBC talent, who was not then even part of *Nightly News*. In a recent e-mail correspondence, Silverman wrote at length about the working climate:

> In my years [as an investigative reporter], there were very few outright threats. The pressure was usually much more subtle. An intermediary

would come to you with a strong suggestion not to do such and such a story. You would be told, "Let somebody else do this story." That kind of thing. In working the Korshak-Wasserman connection, a federal agent I was talking with at the time predicted that an attempt would be made to get me to back off. "You're going to get a visit," the agent said.

Sure enough, Brian and I did get a visit. The visitor, a very prominent person, said, in a very pointed way, "If you're working Lew, you better be right." I said, "If we're working anybody, we better be right." And then I asked this person if his visit had been prompted by a call from Wasserman. He said it wasn't Wasserman, but someone very close to Wasserman.

No threat. Just a visit. But, the message had been delivered just as the federal agent, a veteran of organized crime investigations in L.A., said it would be.[52]

In a recent interview, Ross was less circumspect about the identity of the well-known visitor: "I remember Tom Brokaw, who was on the *Today* show then, came to Ira and me and said, 'Well, I just advise you to be careful.' I don't know what that meant, but he had obviously gotten a call from Wasserman. Brokaw had worked in Burbank as a local anchorman and knew the Wassermans. They were socially and politically powerful people. It was not that we were dealing with Korshak but with Wasserman, and people were very protective of Wasserman. MCA supplied a lot of product to NBC." Whether or not Brokaw carried a message from Wasserman's quarter or was merely voicing personal concern over the importance of journalistic accuracy cannot be known. But the power of Lew Wasserman was undeniable.

Ross next confronted DeLaurentiis, who, with his power attorney Richard Ben-Veniste at his side just off-camera, emphatically denied Korshak's role in the *King Kong* production détente. Then Ross advised him that NBC had obtained Wasserman's testimony from one of the *Kong* lawsuits, wherein Wasserman described the powwow with Dino at Sidney's home. As aired nationally, DeLaurentiis is seen taking a long pause, then finally fessing up, "Oh, I remember now."

"That was a great moment," Ross remembered with a laugh. "You can see the man thinking to himself, 'What do I do?'" DeLaurentiis later told NBC about the $30,000 payment to Korshak, but not the new Ferrari.

The segment closed with a classic, cameras-rolling ambush of Korshak on the street outside the Riviera's office. Ross continually pointed the microphone in Korshak's face, asking for an interview, while Korshak's path changed directions a number of times in an attempt to shake off his pursuer.

ROSS: "Can we talk with you for just a minute?"

KORSHAK: "No, you can't!"

ROSS: "We just want to ask a couple questions."

KORSHAK: "Will you quit pestering me?"

ROSS: "We're not pestering you, we just want to ask—"

KORSHAK (Aggressively Jabbing His Hand Toward Ross): "You're not going to ask me any questions. Now, good-bye."[53]

With that, Korshak walked away. "He was like an old man with a lisp, not intimidating," said Ross. "He was a scared old man. As far as we knew, this had never happened to him before. He probably imagined a thousand things we could be asking about that we weren't even aware of."

The final episode described how many producers tried to persuade their guild to join the Teamsters, essentially capitulating because the entire industry was "swimming in a pool of corruption" anyway. Pro-Teamster producer John Mantley noted, "The Teamsters can stop this industry tomorrow." In closing, Ross reported how Columbia chief David Begelman had recently pleaded no contest to a charge of stealing $40,000 from his own studio—for which he was rewarded with the producing gig for the film version of the Broadway musical *Annie*. "So far," Ross narrated with no small amount of sarcasm, "there are few signs that Hollywood is ready to clean up its act."

What neither Ross nor the gullible pro-Teamster producers were aware of was that the FBI had a high-level Teamster informant who told them the true purpose of the organizing drive: "Source indicated that organized crime wanted the producers guild to join the Teamsters Union as it would be possible from then on to exert pressure through Teamster leaders and connections to launder funds through film production."[54]

After the show aired on December 13, 14, and 15, 1978, Ross heard from one of the many law enforcement officials who traditionally gave Korshak's ilk a pass. "The Los Angeles DA, John Van DeKamp, inquired as to whether we should be prosecuted for obtaining Wasserman's phone logs," Ross recalled. As to Van DeKamp's own probe into shady Hollywood, like other Los Angeles DAs, his office made a few "show busts" that focused only on the mob's connection to pornographers, steering clear of the major studios' links to the Teamsters, the curious studio associations with the likes of Michele Sindona and Dino Conte, Universal's offshore tax "avoidance" schemes engineered by Korshak, or showbiz investments by Eastern crime bosses. In Boston, a federal grand jury found that the Universal production had paid local bosses Ralph Lamatina and Joseph "Joe Shoes" Cammoratta for their help in persuading North End residents to "cooperate" with the crew of *The Brink's Job*, yet their studio Supermob contacts remained predictably untouched.[55]

Of course, the program had zero effect on Korshak's legal status or lifestyle, although he displayed some concern over another possible effect of the reports. "Sidney was very angry over the Brian Ross program," said lawyer friend Leo Geffner, "mostly because his grandchildren were watching television. That was his main concern. The rest he sort of shrugged off."[56]

The NBC-Universal love affair that had started in the fifties (see chapter 10) was consummated when the two entities merged in May 2004, becoming NBC-Universal (a subsidiary of GE), the fifth-largest media conglomerate on the planet.* It was thus virtually assured that NBC would never bother Universal again.

NBC's absolution of Universal did not, however, extend to Sid Korshak. Six months after the "Mob and the Movies" series, Ross and Silverman went right back at Korshak, with a one-parter on Korshak's most recent adventures with Hollywood Park racetrack, tied to his twenty-year feud with Marge Everett, now a board member of the track. The situation was notable because Korshak had previously represented the track in labor talks, until Everett fired him in 1973. Now, according to Ross's sources, Korshak, whose client the Service Employees Union had called strikes against the track to protest the installation of new betting computers, was actually trying to pave the way for an organized crime takeover of the facility. When "The Hollywood Park Story" aired on June 19, 1979, Ross noted, "Korshak was believed to represent Chicago mob interests on the West Coast."

Of course, the vitriol between Everett and Korshak virtually guaranteed little movement in the talks. "Marge can't stand the sight of Sid," said one racetrack insider.[57] With the impasse ongoing, Korshak tried unsuccessfully to force a total shutdown of the track. Just then, Governor Brown played into Korshak's hands by trying to close the track down himself, claiming it was unsafe since so many critical employees were on strike—Brown told Ross he only wanted to shut the track down to show he was "pro-labor." Brown had hoped his new appointment of Korshak friend Gray Davis to the state Racing Board would lead to the desired shutdown. Davis's motion, however, was outvoted 3–2. Board chairman Charles Chatfield told Ross that Brown was under extreme pressure to go along with the shutdown, and that Korshak was behind it. Chatfield added, "We heard from both sides that

---

*The top four in order are Time Warner (which owns WB television), Disney (ABC), Viacom (CBS), and NewsCorp (Fox).

Mr. Korshak was involved . . . He was the man behind the scenes directing the negotiations." Marge Everett told Ross, "I think he [Brown] was under tremendous pressure from Sidney Korshak." When asked if she saw the hand of Sidney Korshak behind Brown's decision, Everett responded, "Not only do I see the hand, I see the total image of Sidney Korshak." Brown made a general denial of the allegation.

Eventually, Leo Geffner replaced Korshak and the strike ended. However, there was one curious footnote: in April 1979, not long after siding with Korshak at Hollywood Park, Brown traveled to New Hampshire, where he was entered in the state's presidential primary versus Georgia's Jimmy Carter, and where Korshak's Service Employees Union had dispatched campaign workers and cars to assist Brown's effort.[58]

Unbeknownst to Ross and Silverman, as they were readying their report in May, Korshak was a topic of discussion among Teamsters insurance man Allen Dorfman, Chicago Outfit boss Joey "the Clown" Lombardo, the Outfit's Vegas enforcer Tony Spilotro, and two other associates in a conversation secretly taped by the FBI. Dorfman was discussing the problems they were having with West Coast Teamsters leader Andy Anderson.

DORFMAN: "You know, he's absolutely an eighteen-carat cunt, but he belongs lock, stock, and barrel to Sidney."
LOMBARDO: "All right."
DORFMAN: "That I can tell ya."
LOMBARDO: "How old is Sidney?"
DORFMAN: "Ah, Sidney is seventy . . ."
LOMBARDO: "Sidney Korshak. Well, if Sidney dies, who's got Anthony Anderson? Nobody?"
DORFMAN: "Nobody. Nobody, he belongs to him lock, stock, and barrel."[59]

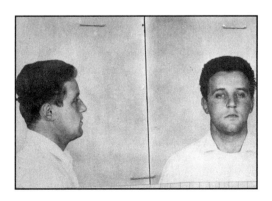

Anthony Spilotro (Chicago Crime Commission)

The highly decorated Ross, who has covered all manner of corruption and scandal, recently gave his summation of Sid Korshak, opining, "A guy like Korshak is essential for that bridge between polite society and criminal society. He's the one who can bridge that, one way or the other. Neither side quite knows what he's doing. It was a dangerous game for him, but that's where his place was."

Brian Ross went on to spend eighteen years at NBC News, serving as chief investigative correspondent for the newsmagazine *Dateline NBC*. Along with producing partner Ira Silverman, Ross's work has been show-cased throughout the years on *NBC Nightly News*. Ross joined ABC News as chief investigative correspondent in July 1994, where he has reported extensively for *20/20, Primetime Thursday, Nightline, World News Tonight with Peter Jennings*, and *Good Morning America*. Over the years, Ross has scooped his peers on countless major stories and has won virtually every media journalism award possible. Thirty years on, Ira Silverman is still producing hard-hitting segments for NBC News and is a contributor to the *New Yorker* magazine. For his work in television news, he has received two Emmy Awards, the George Foster Peabody Award, the Columbia Dupont Award, the George Polk Award, and the Overseas Press Club Award.*

Instead of prompting more law enforcement attention to the Supermob, Ross and Silverman's critiques inspired thirty-one-year-old syndicated cartoonist Garry Trudeau to fix his acid-penned talent on the Brown-Korshak affair. After originating as a feature in Trudeau's Yale school paper, his satiric *Doonesbury* comic strip started its national circulation in 1970 in twenty-eight newspapers and by 1979 was seen in over five hundred. *Time* magazine said of Trudeau, "Neither radicals nor reactionaries are safe from his artillery. Stuffed shirts of Oxford broadcloth or frayed denim receive the

---

*Among Ross and Silverman's many groundbreaking disclosures: Wal-Mart's use of child labor in Bangladesh; Colombian drug-cartel links to Israeli mercenaries; Iraq's attempted purchase of nuclear "triggers" in 1990; and ABSCAM, BCCI, and Russian Mafia scandals. Ross was the first reporter to name Mohamed Atta and describe him as the ringleader of the World Trade Center and Pentagon attacks. He was also the first to report on Zacarias Moussaoui's role in the attacks and his questioning by the FBI prior to September 11. Ross's *Primetime Thursday* story about the hijacking of United Airlines Flight 93 featured the first airing of transmissions between the plane's cockpit and air traffic controllers. Among Ross's awards: three 2003 National Headliners Awards; three 2003 CINE Golden Eagle awards; the 2003 Gerald Loeb Award for business investigation; a 2002 Emmy for Outstanding Investigative Journalism; a 2002 IRE award for Investigative Reporting; a George Polk Award; and a 2002 Gracie Allen Award.

same impudent deflation. Yet Trudeau attacks with such gentle humor that even hard-nosed presidential aides can occasionally be heard chuckling over the daily White House news summary—when it includes a *Doonesbury*."

In fact, Trudeau was often ahead of his time in taking on powerful, and seemingly untouchable, hooligans. As New York columnist David Rossie wrote, "Almost alone he has pointed up the hypocrisy that has attended the canonization of Henry Kissinger."[60] (Thirty years later, the former secretary of state—and former squire to Jill St. John—is now widely perceived as a prime architect of the genocide the United States perpetrated in Southeast Asia.) Trudeau's incisive takes on pomposity and political fraud earned him a Pulitzer Prize in 1974.

Throughout July and August 1979, Trudeau's strip featured Duane Delacourt, Brown's fictitious "secretary of symbolism," as he attempted to control the spin on the Brown-Korshak relationship, with special attention to Korshak's $1,000 donation to the 1974 war chest and the Hollywood Park story covered by Ross and Silverman. The July 18 episode depicted Ross as "Roland Hedley, Jr." saying to the camera, "But ABC News has learned that Brown was seen lunching at The Bistro, Korshak's restaurant, the day he moved to close the track. Brown was said to have had the duck." Another rendition showed a Brown associate named "Gray," an obvious reference to Gray Davis, calling Korshak a "local lowlife, an alumnus from the Capone mob." In still another, the Brown character questioned, "What's an 'undisputed mobster' anyway? Isn't that just a tired cliché?" Pressured, Trudeau's Brown said, "Okay, so I may have run into him [Korshak] a few times at Lew Wasserman's parties . . . Lew Wasserman. He's a movie mogul. He has to deal with Korshak to get his movies made."

At least seven California and Nevada newspapers refused to carry part or

Garry Trudeau's July 11, 1979, *Doonesbury*. One of his many strips from the summer of 1979 lampooning the Brown-Korshak relationship (© GB Trudeau. Reprinted with Permission of Universal Press Syndicate)

all of the eleven-part series on Brown and Korshak, citing the potentially libelous and unsubstantiated information—the papers were legally responsible for Trudeau's assertions. It was not the first time that Trudeau's occasionally incendiary strip had been pulled; previous episodes on Elizabeth Taylor, homosexuality, and premarital sex had been deleted around the country. What made this exceptional was that in this case, the censoring papers were primarily in Korshak's two areas of influence, California and Nevada. The *Los Angeles Times* refused to run the cartoon because they thought its contents were "unsubstantiated and possibly defamatory." The paper inserted in its place a parody strip entitled *Gonesbury*, which depicted Trudeau being asked by his lawyer, "Do you have any proof?"—to which Trudeau responds, "Hell, I don't need any proof. This is just a cartoon." The *San Francisco Chronicle* inserted the following panel in place of the popular strip: "Yesterday's and today's episodes of *Doonesbury*, as well as certain others in the current sequence, will not be published in *The Chronicle*. These episodes are being omitted because they contain allegations that could be extremely libelous against a private citizen. *The Chronicle* regrets this necessary action and assures its readers that *Doonesbury* will remain a regular *Chronicle* feature."[61]

In response to the brouhaha, Trudeau said, "I fully respect the right of a subscribing newspaper to choose not to publish [*Doonesbury*]."*,[62] Most papers, however, carried the panels without incident; interestingly, their lawyers had come to a different conclusion from those on the West Coast. Even the *Chicago Tribune* carried the controversial serial, although that decision infuriated Korshak's pal Irv Kupcinet over at the *Sun-Times*; Kup labeled the pieces "deprecatory and libelous" and quoted from *Gonesbury* instead.[63]

Brown claimed that he was "flattered" by Trudeau's attention, even though the series was "false and libelous." He called the stories "a great coup for Gray Davis because not many chiefs of staff have made nationally syndicated cartoons." As expected, Sid Korshak was unavailable for comment. (Brown was not the only pol tainted by a donation from Sid Korshak. In 1980, Chicago reform mayor Jane Byrne was ridiculed in the press for accepting a $2,000 donation from Korshak, in addition to $5,000 from the Outfit's committeeman friend John D'Arco, $3,000 from three Tony Accardo–controlled unions, $2,000 from the Outfit's front man at Duncan Parking Meters, Jerome Robinson, and $5,000 from the Pritzkers. The $1.5

---

*In 1980, Trudeau married Jane Pauley, Tom Brokaw's NBC *Today* show cohost. In 1984, Trudeau took on Korshak pal Ronald Reagan with his New York musical *Rap Master Ronnie*.

million fund drew the reprobation of *Tribune* columnist Bob Wiedrich, who wrote, "Not only is it business as usual at City Hall, the mobsters and the fixers and the ripoff artists have gained an even firmer foothold under the Byrne administration. If you were the reform mayor of Chicago, would you accept $2,000 from Sidney Korshak, the Los Angeles lawyer who has served as the Mafia's errand boy for so many years he looks like the Godfather?")[64]

Whereas Trudeau's take on the Brown-Korshak-Hanley web was primarily for giggles, behind the scenes Hanley and Korshak's mob connections were the focus of an investigation with deadly serious implications. Although there was little chance that their superiors would ever authorize indictments of Supermob bosses such as Korshak, intrepid FBI agents continued to dissect the periphery of their world in the hopes of winning at least minor victories. So it was that in 1979, the FBI "turned" insurance salesman Joseph Hauser, who had been convicted with Nixon's attorney general Richard Kleindienst for swindling the Teamsters Pension Fund by trading kickbacks for Teamster insurance contracts.* Once embraced by the Teamsters, Hauser's insurance business swelled to over $180 million in premiums, much of which he siphoned off for personal gain.

For the next few years after his conviction, Hauser agreed to wear a wire, in what was ultimately a successful, if dangerous, effort to entrap mobsters, especially the tried-and-true Italian versions such as New Orleans's Carlos Marcello. (The sting was known as BRILAB.) Hauser's lack of success in bringing down non-Italian Supermobsters like Korshak was not for lack of trying. Throughout his period of cooperation, and in later congressional testimony, Hauser described Korshak as having been set up in California by Tony "Joe Batters" Accardo, and how Korshak's Hotel Union pals Ed Hanley and Herman "Blackie" Leavitt were likewise "handpicked by Tony Accardo." Hauser added that Hanley, whom he witnessed in constant close coordination with Korshak, extorted L.A. restaurants such as Nicky Blair's, which was bombed for not paying up.[65]

* * *

---

*In November 1977, Kliendienst, whom Hauser had paid $250,000 to set him up with the Teamsters, was sued by the State of Arizona for his role in the swindle. He and two others eventually agreed to settle the case and pay $150,000. However, Kleindienst's troubles weren't over yet, because the Arizona State Bar then looked into the matter, recommending in March 1981 that Kleindienst be suspended from practicing law in Arizona for a year. Although he was acquitted of perjury before the bar in October, the earlier recommendations were followed through and he was suspended in 1983, forcing him to quit the Tucson law firm where he worked. He was later readmitted to the Arizona bar.

In Los Angeles, Paul Ziffren, who spent the period in his typically low-key, celebrity-tax-lawyer role, weathered an internecine feud that saw him leave his partnership with his brothers Lester and Leo at Ziffren and Ziffren (housed coincidentally in the Kirkeby Center on Wilshire Boulevard). However, he was not orphaned for long, thanks to an invitation from Ronald Reagan's personal lawyer, William French Smith, to join his legal powerhouse, Gibson, Dunn, and Crutcher. "Paul and I used to be on the political debating circuit together," Smith told the *Los Angeles Times*. "This goes back to the Eisenhower campaigns. We debated on radio, on TV, all around. It was during that period I developed a high respect for his talents."[66] Simultaneously, Ziffren and travel company chairman Peter V. Ueberroth were named by the U.S. Olympic Committee as permanent chairman and president–general manager, respectively, of the Los Angeles Olympic Organizing Committee for the 1984 Olympic Games.

Meanwhile, Korshak's thirty-two-year-old son, Stuart, was welcomed into another very fraternal L.A. legal convergence, Wyman, Bautzer, Christianson, and Silbert. Stuart, an associate at that company, must have felt like family, as he was welcomed into a firm that boasted the likes of Greg Bautzer, Eugene Wyman, Harvey Silbert, Frank Rothman, Senator Thomas Kuchel, and Stanley Zax, all of whom figured so prominently in the successes of his father and others such as Lew Wasserman and Howard Hughes.

As for Stuart's parents, Sid and Bee were continually seen on the Beverly Hills social pages throughout the period. In July 1981, Sid gave away actor David Janssen's widow, Dani Greco, in marriage to director Hal Needham; sixteen months earlier, Korshak had handled David Janssen's funeral arrangements.[67] Taking place on the Universal western set, the marriage

Sid and Bee on the town, 1985 (private collection)

ceremony was attended by, among others, Paul and Mickey Ziffren, George and Jolene Schlatter, Rod and Alana Stewart, Suzanne Pleshette, and Tina Sinatra.[68]

In August 1979, sources within the Department of Justice Organized Crime Strike Force leaked that it had informants and "other information" that the Riviera Hotel was still "controlled by the Chicago Mafia through Mr. Korshak and eastern Mafia figures" linked to Meyer Lansky.[69] However, not the Strike Force probe, the California Crime Commission report, the NBC reports, or even *Doonesbury* had any derailing effect on Korshak and the Supermob, especially since the group's invulnerability was about to be cast in stone when their fair-haired boy Ronnie Reagan assumed the U.S. presidency the following year, naming Ziffren's partner William French Smith as his attorney general.

As for Korshak, he continued in his fixer role as successful as ever. In the fall of 1979, when Wasserman's Universal Pictures was filming its John Belushi–Dan Aykroyd movie *The Blues Brothers* in Chicago, there were few who doubted that the name Korshak would lurk somewhere in the shadows. As expected, when the production-location scouts ran into snags, Sidney came to the rescue.

The movie's climactic scene called for a massive SWAT team to take on "Jake and Ellwood Blues" in Daley Square, where the glass-walled lobby of the Cook County Center was to be rammed by the "Bluesmobile." When the Cook County Board refused the request, director John Landis turned to Wasserman's savior, Sidney Korshak, who was also known to the film's producer, Bernie Brillstein. According to Landis, Korshak asked, "What do you need?" After Landis described the problem, Korshak answered, "Let me see what I can do." According to Landis, "Suddenly, all the doors were open." The city's chief administrator at the time, Paul McGrath, was stunned by the acquiescence. "Doing things like that was absolutely unheard of," McGrath said in 2005.[70] Keeping things in the family, Marshall Korshak's daughter Margie handled the PR for the movie.*

---

*Margie Korshak Associates, to this day a Chicago PR powerhouse, specializes in film and theatrical work, handling many of the city's entertainment-related accounts. Margie also shares many of her uncle Sidney's former clients and associations, such as Chicago's Hyatt-Regency, Arlington Park Racetrack, the Sherman House Hotel, and the Michael Reese Hospital. She readily admits to being a frequenter of the La Costa Resort. (*Today's Chicago Woman*, November 1989)

As the year drew to a close, the Supermob suffered one more loss among its ranks. In December 1979, Al Hart died at age seventy-five. His *Los Angeles Times* obit was headlined ALFRED HART: PHILANTHROPIST.

Sid Korshak continued to be observed hobnobbing with Oval Office residents, both past and present. In addition to his recent sightings with White House aspirants Jerry Brown, Jimmy Carter, and Ronald Reagan, Korshak attended a February 1980, Frank Sinatra–hosted, $1,500-per-plate benefit dinner for a local hospital in Palm Springs with former president Gerald Ford. The Department of Justice noted that, although he could have chosen to dine with the president, Sinatra instead chose another power player's company: "Of all the people Sinatra could have sat with during the party, Sinatra chose to sit with Sidney Korshak and his wife." And as with the Jerry Brown fund-raiser two years earlier, Ed Hanley, of the corrupt Culinary Union, was also in attendance as one of the only two guests to receive comp tickets to the benefit.[71]

CHAPTER 21

The True Untouchables

U.S. WARNED MOB MIGHT ELECT A PRESIDENT IN 1980.
—HEADLINE FROM A 1969 NEWSPAPER ARTICLE[1]

IN 1980, SIXTY-NINE-year-old Ronald Reagan made his second run at the U.S. presidency, using his tried-and-true anticommunist polemic, and attacking incumbent Jimmy Carter for a "weak" foreign policy. With the man he called his "best friend," Senator Paul Laxalt, as campaign manager, Reagan was especially critical of Carter's handling of the Iranian hostage crisis, in which revolutionaries had held sixty-six U.S. citizens and diplomats at the U.S. embassy in Tehran since November 4, 1979. (In later years, rumors surfaced that Reagan had reprised Nixon's 1968 "October Surprise" tactic to ensure his victory—this time the candidate's team was said to have secretly met with Iranians and promised to supply them with weapons if they would just wait until Reagan was elected to release the hostages.)*,[2]

---

*Although some accusations were fallacious, enough had teeth to make the contention more than a possibility. A 1981 congressional probe into the Reagan campaign's theft of White House briefing books on the eve of a presidential debate disclosed that the Republicans had set up an espionage network that gathered intelligence on the Carter campaign and the president's efforts to liberate the hostages. Reagan's CIA director William Casey could never provide proof of where he was during the alleged 1980 meetings with Iranian revolutionaries in Madrid.

   Claude Angeli, chief editor for *Le Canard enchaîné*, a French newspaper, and David Andelman, a former *New York Times* and CBS News reporter, gave damning testimony to a congressional probe of the affair. Angeli told the task force that French intelligence officials, who refused to go on the record, claimed that their organization provided "cover" for meetings between the Reagan camp and Iranian officials on October 18 and 19, 1980. Andelman, who ghostwrote the autobiography of Alexandre de Marenches, the former head of French intelligence, testified that "de Marenches acknowledged

Supermob watchers took note that the first major union to endorse Reagan was the two-million-member, and highly corrupted, Teamsters. It turned out that there was good reason to be suspicious of the endorsement. Allen Friedman, uncle of Teamster Cleveland boss and future national president Jackie Presser, later wrote that he had given Reagan aide, and his future attorney general Ed Meese, a suitcase full of money for the campaign war chest, the payment made at the behest of Jackie's father, Bill Presser, the often-convicted former Cleveland Teamster head.[3] In his autobiography, Friedman wrote, "[Presser] had a suitcase that he said was full of money. He told me to take it to Edwin Meese for Ronald Reagan. This I did, meeting both Meese and another man only long enough to pass on the case, explaining who sent it."[4]

The problem was that any alliance with the likes of the Pressers was fraught with corruption traps. An FBI report noted that Cleveland Mafia underboss Angelo Lonardo was heard in a wiretap saying that after Jackie Presser's eventual ascension to the union's presidency, his status in the Teamsters was in fact a boost for the mob. The report summarized, "They felt it was better to have someone in office that they knew, and besides, it would add prestige to the Cleveland family to be in control of the head of the Teamsters."[5] Interim Teamster boss Roy Williams, himself under the umbrella of the Chicago Outfit via its subsidiary in Kansas City, later said that Presser told him of his long-standing alliance with the Cleveland Mafia: "He told me that the mob was split in Cleveland, and he's afraid he picked the wrong side."[*6] Practically at the same time that Reagan's team received Presser's cash-filled briefcase, Jimmy "the Weasel" Fratianno, as part of his witness protection deal, was telling a federal grand jury that Presser told him that he took his orders from James Licavoli, the boss of the Cleveland Mafia.

Soon thereafter, at a meeting at La Costa, the Teamster board voted for the Reagan endorsement.

In addition to his traditional anticommunism themes, Reagan campaigned on his anti-FDR and anti-LBJ platform—against both New Deal

Footnote cont'd

setting up a meeting in Paris between Casey and some Iranians in late October 1980." By the time Andelman dropped his bombshell, the House task force had already interviewed de Marenches, who denied any knowledge of such meetings. Unable to reach de Marenches for further questioning after Andelman made his claim, the task force decided to take the French clandestine services veteran at his previous word.

In 1991, while playing golf with George Bush in Palm Springs, Reagan himself let slip that he had "tried some things the other way" to free the hostages, but added that "some of these things are still classified." (See note 2 to this chapter.)

*Williams once said that every major Teamster local had "some connection with organized crime" and that Jackie Presser was as controlled by the mob "as I was."

and Great Society federal assistance programs—as he insisted that, in essence, if the rich got richer, the spoils would "trickle down" to the masses.

"How do you tell the Polish one at a cockfight?"
"He's the one with the duck."
"How do you tell the Italian one?"
"He's the one who bets on the duck."
"How do you know the Mafia is there?"
"The duck wins."
—JOKE TOLD ON THE CAMPAIGN TRAIL BY RONALD REAGAN*

On November 4, Reagan-Bush trounced Carter-Mondale with a 489–49 electoral college majority. (In the subsequent 1984 contest, the Reagan-Bush ticket easily outdistanced the Democratic ticket of Mondale-Ferraro with nearly 60 percent of the popular vote and an electoral margin of 525 to 13.)

On December 12, 1980, Paul Ziffren's law partner—and Reagan's attorney general–elect—William French Smith attended Sinatra's sixty-fifth birthday bash in Palm Springs, also attended by Sid Korshak.[7] Two weeks after the Sinatra gala, advance copies of Jimmy Fratianno's biography by Ovid Demaris (*The Last Mafioso*) began to circulate, describing in vivid detail the organized crime connections of Sinatra, Korshak, and Reagan Teamster ally Jackie Presser, among others.[8]

Despite heavy interest in Hollywood, Demaris told the press his book's film potential was being sabotaged by the likes of Frank Sinatra and Sidney Korshak, noting that the pair were "killing me in this town." He told Chicago's Channel Two that Bob Evans had been "eager" to buy the book, but that Korshak had stopped it. Referring to Hollywood, Demaris added, "Sinatra's very powerful in this town. He has friends, he makes phone calls. And Korshak is tight with heads of studios. A lot of people in this city are afraid of him." On cue, Irv Kupcinet rose to Korshak's and Sinatra's defense, noting that Evans told him his alleged interest was a total fabrication, "which is how some critics have described the book," Kup added.[9]

LAXALT TO HAVE A KEY ROLE IN REAGAN'S WASHINGTON
—*NEW YORK TIMES*, NOVEMBER 28, 1980

Within minutes of Reagan's January 20, 1981, inauguration, the Americans held hostage in Iran were released, after 444 days in captivity. As president,

---

*The joke was told to Senator Gordon Humphrey (R-New Hampshire) on February 16, 1980.

Ronald Reagan moved quickly, despite the revelations of Fratianno, to repay the Teamsters by appointing Jackie Presser as senior adviser to his economic affairs transition group, prompting outgoing attorney general Benjamin Civiletti to remark that he could not fathom "how anyone trying to develop a new government could conceive of making this [Presser] selection." The icing on the cake was Reagan's appointment of William French Smith as attorney general, and Paul Laxalt as the new chairman of the Republican National Committee, nominations that were met with a degree of disbelief in law enforcement circles.* Allen Friedman later wrote, "[Under Carter] we didn't dominate White House labor policy as we had under Nixon and as we were about to under Ronald Reagan."[10]

Once installed, Reagan decreed massive budget cuts at the Justice Department, reductions that meant, according to the FBI, that "no new undercover operations would be authorized in fiscal 1982 against organized crime or White Collar crime." As painstakingly recounted by Dan Moldea in his books *Interference* and *Dark Victory*, Reagan weakened the Organized Crime Strike Force, a prelude to its complete destruction in 1989.[11] With supporting legislation introduced by Senator Laxalt, new attorney general Smith set to reshuffling the Department of Justice staff so as to shift priorities to "street crime." Interestingly, D.C. U.S. Circuit Court judge David Bazelon claimed that Reagan's self-proclaimed war on organized crime was actually *too tough*, and that his measures would jeopardize the targets' civil liberties.[12]

Sidney's "Son" Takes a Fall

All the while that Reagan had been beating up on Jimmy Carter on the campaign trail, Carter's DEA was fixing its sights on Korshak's protégé Bob Evans, whose drug problems were known throughout the film community. On Memorial Day weekend, 1980, Bob Evans and his brother Charles were busted in a DEA sting for attempting to purchase five ounces of pure pharmaceutical cocaine, and Charles's attorney forbade Bob from bringing in Korshak: "He's too highly profiled" was the dictum.[13] Reluctantly, Evans agreed, but going along with his brother's advisers would widely be perceived as one of the most nonsensical things Evans would ever do.

---

*Bistro owner Kurt Niklas was even more shocked soon after the election to see Smith seated at a table next to Meyer Lansky. Headwaiter Casper Morcelli told Niklas, "They seemed to know each other. I mean they acknowledged each other when they sat down." (Niklas, *Corner Table*, 410)

According to various Korshak acquaintances, the Fixer had been distraught over Evans's lifestyle for years. "Sidney was like a godfather to him. I think he was trying to set him on the straight path," said Jan Amory. "I think Sidney liked the glamour and the girls at Bobby's, but Sidney was not into any of the drugs or any of that stuff. He would have two whiskeys and that would be it." Johnny Rosselli's goddaughter Nancy Czar recalled that Korshak had been running the gauntlet for Evans with his employers. "Sid saved Bobby Evans's ass," Czar said. "Bobby had a coke problem, and it was because of Sidney that he was allowed to stay on the Paramount lot. I saw Bobby sitting with Sidney at the Bistro, saying, 'Yes, yes, yes,' as Sidney was advising him." One friend, who wished to remain anonymous, recalled that during this period Korshak had told his wayward friend, "You don't come around. You're not a good man; you're not good to your family. What kind of a Jewish man are you, drinking and putting this stuff up your nose? Promise me you'll never do it again." To which Evans was alleged to have said, "I promise. I promise. I promise."

Despite his failure to call in Korshak, word traveled fast, and Evans's mentor was soon calling his wayward sybarite.

"I hear you're in trouble," said Korshak. "What's going on?"

"Nothing's wrong," Evans lied.

"If I find out different, I'll break your head" came Korshak's retort.

Evans was next summoned to Bluhdorn's Connecticut estate, where he was practically ordered by the Mad Austrian to enlist Korshak.

"You dumb idiot," Bluhdorn bellowed just inches from Evans's nose. "Korshak could settle this sitting on the toilet."

In California, Evans's Hollywood crowd was equally dumbfounded. "You didn't bring in Korshak?" asked a dumbfounded Greg Bautzer. "I'm not hearing right. Do you know who his closest friend is? A top guy at the DEA. They go back more than thirty years. Went to college together, schmuck."

According to Evans, Bautzer was not yet finished with his rant. He told Evans a typical Korshakian tale wherein two well-known performing brothers were busted for cocaine possession the previous year right in the middle of their show in Anaheim. From jail, one of the brothers made his only allowed phone call—to Korshak. "Twenty minutes later he was out and the big man hardly knew him," said Bautzer. "And *you* didn't call him?" An incredulous Bautzer, who feared his prestige would be tarnished because he had brought Evans to Bluhdorn years earlier, sighed in disbelief, "And you're the guy who made Paramount number one."

But Evans was committed to his brother's legal strategy, which in fact gained him a mild sentence. Instead of receiving a possible one-year prison term, Evans was put on probation and ordered to pay a $5,000 fine and produce a thirty-second antidrug public service announcement (PSA) film, which came to be entitled "Get High on Yourself," a pre–"We Are the World" chorus of ninety-three celebrities trying to sing in tune.[14] But the video nonetheless garnered White House backing from new first lady Nancy Reagan and convinced the NBC brass to devote an entire week to antidrug programming.* However, the man who was now known as Bob "Cocaine" Evans had done irreparable harm to both his career and social life. As he wrote in his autobiography, "Gone now were the sacred embrace of Kissinger, Korshak, and Bluhdorn, three of the five fingers that made my life singular. Never to return again."[15] Bluhdorn and Korshak had left of their own volition; Evans purposely cut off Kissinger so as to not cause him embarrassment.†

Four months after Reagan's inauguration, the man who had done so much to create his career—and bail him out financially—passed away. On April 28, 1981, two days after his eighty-fifth birthday, MCA founder Jules Stein died of a heart attack following gallbladder surgery. Stein's eighty-six-page will provided for his $200 million estate to be divided among his wife, his children and grandchildren, and his Jules C. Stein Eye Institute, endowed at UCLA. Among the honorary pallbearers were President Ronald Reagan (unable to attend), Lew Wasserman, Alfred Bloomingdale, Irving Lazar, and James C. Petrillo.

Just a week after Reagan's January 1981 inauguration, Jeff Gerth and Lowell Bergman decided that they had thrown enough good money after bad and chose to extricate themselves from the costly La Costa–*Penthouse* fracas, which was still four years away from a resolution. On January 28, after a prearranged bargain, the duo wrote a conciliatory letter to the La Costa partners, extolling the charitable works of the DRAM group. Supermob watchers especially perceived the last paragraph to be overly obsequious

---

*Not long after, Evans received a call from NBC's Brian Ross, who wanted his comment regarding his being named in the recent cocaine bust of car manufacturer John DeLorean. A bewildered Evans hung up and contacted an attorney, who called Tom Brokaw and his fellows at the network, demanding they kill the story, which was about to go out; it turned out that the offender was *Richard* Evans.
†Evans's legal difficulties were not over. He later came under suspicion when Roy Radin, an investor in Evans's *Cotton Club* movie, was murdered in 1983, amidst a haze of massive cocaine purchases and thefts. When the case came to trial in 1989, Evans, under the guidance of his attorney Robert Shapiro, took the Fifth Amendment and refused to testify. (See Wick, *Bad Company*)

(writer Dan Moldea called it "groveling"). It read, in part, "In summary, we feel it right to acknowledge the positive information we have received about you in recent years and, accordingly, to express regret for any negative implication or unwarranted harm that you believe may have befallen you as a result of the *Penthouse* article."[16] *Penthouse* attorney Roy Grutman wrote that the departure of Gerth and Bergman "created a huge hole in the *Penthouse* defense."[17] In March 1985, after ten years and $14 million in legal fees, both sides agreed to walk away from the suit.*

The next Supermob entity to take its place on the investigative hot seat was the Pritzker dynasty. Prompted by the July 1981 collapse of the Kansas City Hyatt Hotel's skywalk, which killed 114 people, journalist Knut Royce, then working for the *Kansas City Times*, delivered an exhaustive report on the complete history of the notoriously secretive family. Over three installments on March 8, 9, and 10, 1982, Royce exposed much more about the labyrinthine Pritzker business dealings to the light of day than the *New York Times* had done in 1976. Among the many disclosures were:

- The SEC had recently completed a two-year investigation of the Pritzkers' $54 million in loans from the Teamsters Pension Fund, beginning in 1959, for the purchase of casinos in Las Vegas and Lake Tahoe. The investigation ended with the findings that Hyatt from 1969 to 1978 had made inadequate public disclosures to stockholders about transactions between the corporation and the Pritzker family and between the corporation and the pension fund. Hyatt agreed to a consent decree, which forced the Pritzkers to make a full disclosure to the stockholders without admitting or denying any of the allegations. The Pritzkers reacted by arranging a private takeover of the Hyatt Corp., thus eliminating future requirements for filing with the SEC.

- During the SEC's investigation of Hyatt, they'd looked into Melville Marx, who was instrumental in the purchase of two Hyatt Nevada casinos.

---

*When the case finally came to a first trial in 1985, it was assigned to Judge Kenneth Gale, who, incredibly, was the former attorney for *Penthouse*'s star witness, Jimmy Fratianno. Gale made absurd rulings and pronouncements, such as declaring, "Everyone knows there's no such thing as organized crime in California." On the other hand, DRAM's star witness, San Diego sheriff John Duffy, lied in declaring that La Costa was not mobbed up, although Gale refused to let Grutman present the proof; Grutman unearthed a previous Duffy grand jury declaration that La Costa was indeed a mob planning headquarters. When the jury nonetheless found for *Penthouse*, which was owned by Robert Guccione, Gale overturned the ruling. However, when a new trial was set, the chief judge of the State Superior Court of California removed Gale without explanation (Grutman, and Thomas, *Lawyers and Thieves*, 141–54). Fratianno later said, "I won that fuckin' case for Guccione." (Zuckerman, *Vengeance Is Mine*, 360)

Royce learned that he was also the director and a partner at Hollywood Park racetrack, where Korshak had acted as a labor lawyer during the recent strike at the track.

- A first-ever listing of the numerous Pritzker holdings (see appendix B).
- A thorough discussion of the allegations of the Pritzkers' ties to the Chicago Outfit, including a quote from an informant saying, "The Pritzker family of Chicago through their Hyatt Corp. initially received their backing from organized crime."
- The revelation of the Pritzkers' offshore tax-dodging setup in the Bahamas' Castle Bank, as directed by their attorney Burt Kanter.

"Jay Pritzker almost bought the paper after the first installment," said Royce.[18] Royce was fortunate that the purchase didn't transpire, as the series earned Royce the second of his three Pulitzers.

The Curse of Korshak I

One month after the Royce series, the Pritzker name was in the news again, this time through its linkages to *Playboy*'s Hugh Hefner and—again—Sid Korshak.

On April 7, 1982, Hefner was denied a New Jersey gaming license for his Atlantic City Playboy Casino, a partnership with the Pritzkers (under their Elsinore banner), who had a 45 percent stake in the venture. The Hefner-Pritzker team benefited Hefner because the Pritzkers had ready access to the Teamsters Pension Fund through Korshak, while the Pritzkers hoped to trade on the *Playboy* cachet. The team bought a $1.8 million site on the Atlantic City boardwalk, but it was on the corner and at the end of a street, almost unnoticeable to the public except from farther down the street. Since the $135 million, five-hundred-room hotel-casino had opened a year before the license denial, it was operating on a temporary permit while the gaming board held hearings to determine the owners' fitness for a permanent license.

Although interested in the Pritzkers' long ties to the Teamsters Pension Fund, the New Jersey Casino Control Commission's hearings were hampered by the nonappearance of pension-fund assets chief Alvin Baron and fund adviser Allen Dorfman, who'd worked so closely with Korshak, Hoffa, and the Chicago Outfit. The commission had wanted to grill them over their contacts with Pritzkers for past loans, since both Baron and Dorfman had previously been convicted for taking kickbacks for loans; both had also dealt with Pritzkers.[19] Outfit associate Mike Corbitt (see chapter 6) was among those who knew of the Dorfman connection to the Pritzkers. "It was common knowledge," Corbitt wrote in his autobiography, "that most of the

Pritzkers' financial backing at that time came from the Teamsters, meaning Pension Fund manager Allen Dorfman."[20] However, without appearances by fund associates, the Pritzkers were able to successfully deny the accusation that they had, like so many others, provided kickbacks for their loans.

On January 11, 1982, Hefner was questioned under oath by the New Jersey Casino Control Commission, which expressed most concern about Hefner's supposed bribe of New York's State Liquor Authority (SLA) board members in 1961 (see chapter 11) and Sid Korshak's $50,000 bilking of Hefner in 1978 over MCA's film library. New Jersey deputy attorney general James F. Flanagan III described Hefner's $50,000 as a payment to Korshak to "whisper in Lew Wasserman's ear." Hefner said he regretted the entire Korshak-MCA matter, but he thought there had been "nothing inappropriate" about it.

Although the Control Commission located the six-thousand-word transcript of the 1961 SLA grand jury proceeding, in which, after obtaining immunity, Hefner admitted bribing the SLA, it appeared to have never linked the Korshak brothers to *that* affair. Without the relevant FBI and Chicago Crime Commission files, the board failed to make the connection, an oversight that became moot when the board denied the Playboy license with just the evidence in hand.

Although three of the five commissioners voted to grant Hefner and Playboy Enterprises Inc. a gaming license, the law required approval of four of the members (Elsinore/Pritzker had already been approved unanimously). The commission found that Hefner was "unsuitable for licensure and association with a licensed New Jersey casino." Commissioner Carl Zeitz cited the SLA bribery as a chief factor in the denial, while commissioner Martin Danziger quoted not only the bribery, but also regulatory offenses in the United Kingdom, an SEC investigation, and Playboy's "organized crime ties" as his reasons for the rebuke.[21]

Hefner immediately pulled up stakes in Atlantic City, receiving $45.4 million in a note at 10 percent interest from Pritzker-Elsinore, due in installments over the next six years, plus $5.6 million in management fees. As Playboy chronicler Russell Miller wrote, "Unquestionably, Playboy had arrived at its darkest hour . . . Instead of the 'significant profits' promised by Hefner in November, Playboy Enterprises, Inc., reported a loss of $51,681,000 [for fiscal 1982]."[22] The losses prompted Hefner to reach out to Abe Pritzker for some help with his cash flow. "[Hefner] wanted to borrow money," Abe Pritzker said in 1985. "I offered some, but as compensation I wanted an option on part of his magazine. He didn't want that. In Atlantic City, let's say we're kissed out."[23]

However, the buyout of Playboy's share weighed down Pritzker/Elsinore, which now operated the casino under the name the Atlantis Casino-Hotel. (In 1985, Elsinore disclosed that it might not meet interest payments to creditors, including Playboy Enterprises. Eventually, Elsinore filed for bankruptcy protection from its creditors and the Atlantis Casino closed in 1989, the only Atlantic City casino to have failed.)

The Pritzkers next figured in the background of an event that had major repercussions for the continued survival not only of Sid Korshak, but of others within the Supermob. The trouble began in December 1982, when Korshak's Teamsters Pension Fund contact Allen Dorfman was convicted along with Teamster president Roy Williams for bribing U.S. senator Howard Cannon of Nevada in return for Cannon's influence on pending pro-Teamster legislation.[24] Dorfman's sentence could have landed him a maximum fifty-five-year sentence, but even before the sentence could be pronounced, Dorfman was indicted with four others on January 11, 1983, on kickback and other charges related to Ed Hanley's Hotel and Restaurant Employees Union. Although the indictment did not charge Korshak, it described him as the man Dorfman had gone to in order to influence Hanley.[25] Many assumed Korshak's own indictment was imminent. However, the key witness was about to disappear.

On January 19, just eight days after Dorfman's indictment, he was murdered in the parking lot of the Pritzkers' Hyatt Hotel in Lincolnwood, Illinois, a Chicago suburb.[26] At the time, Dorfman was rumored to be cutting a Joe Hauser–like deal with the FBI regarding their investigation (known as PENDORF) into the Teamster fund kickbacks to the mob; and Dorfman knew infinitely more about the inner workings of the Teamsters Pension Fund irregularities.

"There was real fear among the Chicago Outfit that Dorfman was ready to talk to save himself," said then president of the Chicago Crime Commission Patrick Healy. "And if Dorfman had decided to talk, he could have done some serious damage. They knew that he was not prepared to spend the rest of his life in jail."[27] A source close to both Dorfman and Korshak recently stated his belief that Korshak was well aware of Dorfman's impending demise. "I was told that Dorfman had been drinking too much at La Costa," said the source, "blabbing about knowing what happened to Hoffa. Korshak told someone that Dorfman wasn't long for this world. I know he had to be concerned that Dorfman was a time bomb."

At least one "connected" individual believed that even the location of the murder was not a coincidence. During the run-up to the murder, slot king Hy Larner's partner Mike Corbitt, who doubled as the director of security for the Chicago Hyatt, had been putting up visiting Outfit-connected Panamanian generals at the same Lincolnwood Hyatt. "We received a tip—I don't know who the tip came from," Corbitt said. "I was told to go to the Hyatt in Lincolnwood, a little town outside of Chicago, and get the generals out of that fucking hotel."[28] It was the same hotel where Dorfman would be killed.

Seven days after the Dorfman hit, the FBI contacted Korshak in L.A., but he "refused to discuss the Dorfman matter with agents."[29] On April 27 and 28, 1983, Joe Hauser, the "flipped" witness with considerable information about the Dorfman-Korshak-Hanley world, gave the explosive details to a Senate subcommittee investigating links between Hanley's Hotel Union and organized crime. When that same body subpoenaed Korshak, his lawyer informed them that he would merely invoke the Fifth; he was never called.

As for Ed Hanley, he wisely declined to go the Hauser-Dorfman route, and during his 1984 testimony before the same subcommittee, he asserted his Fifth Amendment right against self-incrimination thirty-six times. In 1995, a court-appointed monitor began to review the business practices and mob infiltration of Hanley's union, a proceeding that led to the removal of both Hanley and his son, Thomas Hanley, who was the union's director of organization. However, instead of being indicted, Hanley was fêted by the Cook County Democratic Association on June 17, 1997, at a $125-per-person fund-raising dinner. "The very fact that Hanley is being used as the lure to bring money into this event indicates how pervasive the stranglehold of organized crime is on our everyday lives," said former Cook County Police organized crime specialist John Flood. The monitor's final report accused Hanley of a wide range of corruption, and he was forced to resign in 1998 due to the allegations. However, he swung criminal and civil immunities deals with the Department of Justice, infuriating agents who had worked the case, and secured a $267,000 annual pension, more than his annual salary of $250,000. Hanley died in an auto accident on January 7, 2000, at age sixty-seven.[30]

Allen Dorfman was not the only Supermob associate to shed his mortal coil in early 1983. On January 19, 1983, Charlie Bluhdorn, age fifty-six, died of a heart attack while in flight from a business trip in the Dominican Republic. He had a small private funeral at St. Mary's Church, which was attended by the former secretary of state Henry Kissinger. In addition to his vast conglomerate, Bluhdorn left his visible mark in Manhattan, where his Gulf & Western building became a prominent feature of the New York City skyline, reaching heights of forty-two stories just off the southwest corner of Central Park, at Columbus Circle.[31]

The Fourth Estate Stays on the Supermob Trail

It seemed that once a journalist was bitten by the Supermob bug, there was little chance it could be shaken off. Over the decades, the same handful of investigators continued to try to call attention to what was happening in the country's shadow power structure. Such was the case with Frank McCulloch, who had covered the well-connected players for both the *Los Angeles Times* and *Life* magazine, then briefly taking a job away from the national news deadlines. One night in 1975, he told his wife, "I'm going to die of boredom, but I can't bring myself to ask *Time* magazine or the *Los Angeles Times* for a job." Fate stepped in almost immediately, when the very next morning McCulloch received a call from C. K. McClatchy, editor of his family's five West Coast *Bee* newspapers, with an offer.[32] McCulloch thus became the executive editor of all the papers, reuniting him with crack corruption and organized crime reporter, Pulitzer-winning Denny Walsh. The duo churned out hard-hitting reports that gained not only attention, but their share of lawsuits, all of which they successfully defended. Not surprisingly, the largest action came courtesy of the Supermob. Although Paul Laxalt's 1983 $250 million libel suit was not as large as Dalitz's filing against *Penthouse*, it certainly got the attention of the *Bee* staff.

Laxalt's lawsuit was instigated by Walsh's November 1, 1983, story in the flagship *Sacramento Bee*, which cited IRS and Gaming Control Board sources for their conclusion that Laxalt's Ormsby House Casino, which he owned from 1971 to 1976, was skimming the wagers—a full 20 percent of the profits—and diverting the lucre back to the Chicago mob via its subordinates in the Milwaukee Mafia. The article also ticked off the numerous hoods who seemed to be overly friendly toward Laxalt. The contentions were especially worrisome to Laxalt because he was lining up support for a possible run at the presidency in 1988.

Refusing to be intimidated, the McClatchy newspapers countersued, and toward the end of an exhausting three-and-a-half-year process, the name of Sidney Korshak was finally brought to the forefront. "When Laxalt sued, we deposed Korshak," remembered McCulloch, "and it was settled just before Korshak was called."[33] Former *Bee* reporter Dick Brenneman heard a similar account. "I was told that it was settled on the day before the FBI was to turn over its Korshak files to the defense," said Brenneman.[34] "Laxalt still considered himself a presidential candidate," added McCulloch.

The suits were thus dropped in June 1987, with the paper paying Laxalt's legal fees and issuing a carefully worded statement to the effect that their pretrial investigation failed to prove that the skim allegations were known to

Laxalt—of course, their job was not to prove it, but to make the case for it in order that officialdom might follow up. Immediately after the dismissal, McCulloch told the press, "We have not retracted, we have not apologized, and we have not paid any damages. Regardless of what the senator may say to further his efforts in his campaign, we are not backing away from anything we say in the news story."[35] Today, McCulloch has no reservations about his paper's essential conclusions. "Paul Laxalt had Chicago money in his Carson City casino, and he was being totally skimmed," he said recently.

Walsh pointed out that the revelations were instrumental in Laxalt's ultimate decision not to seek the Oval Office in 1988, this despite Reagan's touting him for the job in a March 3, 1986, $1,000-a-plate dinner held in Laxalt's honor.* "The story sank Laxalt's attempts to become president," Walsh said proudly.[36] However, the Supermob, as usual, emerged largely unscathed. IRS agent Laurence A. Rooker later testified that he resigned his post back in 1973 when his superiors made it clear they were not going to pursue what they were learning about the Ormsby House a decade before the Walsh article. Rooker said that the case was solid and "the only logical explanation [for dropping it] was the fact that there was a political figure involved in the case."[37]

Rooker was thus inducted into the ranks of those frustrated over the decades with the staggering lack of interest in prosecuting the Supermob. Even Frank McCulloch still sometimes feels exasperated. "I must say at this distance, I sometimes wonder whether all the money that was spent to defend the libel suits that I created, and all the energy that went into it, whether it was a good trade-off or not," McCulloch said in 2004. "I'm not so sure now. I'll bet you that very few people remember the stories per se. They remember the libel suits, but I don't think they remember the stories."[†,38]

---

*At the gala, Reagan said, in part, "As most of you know, Paul [Laxalt] and I were elected governors of our respective states at about the same time. They say we started even. I had California, with one of the biggest economies of the nation. Paul had Nevada and Howard Hughes . . . There were those who said a straight shooter like Paul could never make it in Washington. But sure enough, Paul has disposed of problems here just as [easily] as he disposed of them in Nevada. He had the best possible training for Washington—as a rancher and a herder: they have exactly the same sort of disposal problems that we have." Reagan then added the following endorsement: "Look to the son of the high mountains and peasant herders, to the son of the Sierra and the immigrant Basque family. Look to a man, to a friend, to an American who gave himself so that others might live in freedom."

*In 1985, McCulloch retired at age sixty-five—for one week. He was immediately recruited to work at the *San Francisco Examiner* until his final retirement in 1991.

And the frustrations spilled over into the television industry as well. One year after Walsh's 1983 piece on Laxalt, California investigative reporter Lowell Bergman, then working as a producer for CBS's *60 Minutes*, joined the anti-Laxalt journalistic klatch when he produced an episode that focused on Laxalt's ties not only to Dalitz, but also to the Wassermans (recall that Lew's wife, Edie, had her own ancient history with Dalitz). However, just days before the piece was to air, Bergman was stunned to discover that *60 Minutes* executive producer Don Hewitt had just dined with his good friends the Wassermans (with whom he often stayed when in California) and had also discussed the story with GOP fund-raiser Pete Peterson, all of whom dissuaded him from airing the exposé. According to Bergman, it wasn't just Hewitt's bowing to his friends that derailed the investigation, but the fear that President Reagan, who was in the midst of deregulating the broadcast industry, might bring the hammer down on the network. "It was the first episode in my career in which I became aware of self-censorship," Bergman said.[39]

To many observers, the sad fact remained that only God could intervene in the high-flying affairs of the untouchables from Chicago. Three years after the death of philanthropist Jules Stein and five years after the passing of philanthropist Al Hart, Jake "the Barber" Factor, the man who had used Hart as an INS character reference to avoid spending his life in a British prison, died of natural causes in January 1984 in Beverly Hills. Not surprisingly, his *Los Angeles Times* obituary headline read JOHN FACTOR, NOTED PHILANTHROPIST, DIES AFTER LONG ILLNESS.[40]

Like so many other Supermob associates, Factor had learned that the quickest way to rewrite one's CV was to move to L.A. and give away some money, as he had been doing in the downtrodden Watts district. Former California mob investigator Connie Carlson, who had followed the Supermob doings for

Jake Factor, philanthropist (Library of Congress)

years, recently said about Factor, "To the end, he was trying to acquire more social status. He tried to get a diplomatic passport—he didn't need one, he just wanted it for social status."[41]

Next it was L.A. labor expert David Robb's turn to take on the untouchables. As a staff reporter for *Daily Variety*, Robb began looking into the history of President Reagan's relationship with MCA, Wasserman, et al. Robb, a dogged pursuer of the paper trail, was able to obtain over six thousand pages of unsorted Department of Justice documents about Reagan, MCA, and the Screen Actors Guild through the Freedom of Information Act.[42] His resultant April 18, 1984, *Variety* article explained previously untold details of Reagan's relationship with MCA, including the infamous waiver granted by SAG, and culminating with Reagan's previously undisclosed testimony before the 1962 federal grand jury. But, like every other Supermob exposé, Robb's fell on deaf federal ears. No U.S. agency was about to look into the conflicted affairs of the president whose appointees headed those agencies.

The journalistic gauntlet next fell to thirty-four-year-old, Washington-based investigative journalist Dan Moldea, a similarly indefatigable investigator of all things Mafia since his landmark 1978 work on Jimmy Hoffa and the mob (*The Hoffa Wars*), and a mob murder case in his Ohio hometown, a case in which Moldea elicited confessions from three of the conspirators (*The Hunting of Cain*).*

Looking for a third book project in 1984, Moldea was drawn to the world of the Supermob after reading both the Hersh 1976 series on Korshak and a subsequent August 17, 1980, *Los Angeles Times* article by William Knoedelseder on Reagan's curious history with MCA. With a $5,000 grant from Washington's liberal think tank The Institute for Policy Studies, where he was a visiting fellow, Moldea made a preliminary trip to Los Angeles, where he was introduced to Jack Tobin.

"You have to go after Sidney Korshak," Tobin told him. "He's where Reagan's connections to MCA, as well as to the underworld, will begin and end."[43]

---

*Moldea's work has also appeared in, among other publications, the *Los Angeles Times*, the *Washington Post*, the *London Observer*, *Playboy*, the *Boston Globe*, the *Atlanta Constitution*, the *Montreal Star*, *Regardie's*, *Editor & Publisher*, and the *Nation*. In addition, he has done freelance work with *NBC Nightly News*, National Public Radio, the *Detroit Free Press*, and syndicated columnist Jack Anderson. His book reviews have appeared in the *Washington Post Book World*. Also, he is a former contributing editor for Washington Crime News Service, which includes such law enforcement publications as *Crime Control Digest* and *Organized Crime Digest*.

Moldea next sought out Dave Robb, who gave Moldea unlimited access to his document cache, marking the beginning of a lifelong friendship. After securing a book deal with Viking, Moldea went into his "bat mode," working almost around the clock for the next year. He soon concluded that he would have to work primarily from the documentary record. "They were at the height of their power," Moldea recently said. "I couldn't get anyone to talk to me. The book is mostly based on documents." Out of 127 people contacted, only 20 would go on the record; some superstar actors actually broke down crying at the thought that their recollections might get back to Wasserman and Korshak. Nonetheless, Moldea followed in the Supermob's footsteps as best he could in his effort to understand their synergy.

"I went to the Bistro and asked, 'Where did Reagan sit?'" Moldea remembered. "Right next to Korshak" came the answer from a waiter.

The resulting book, a 382-page critique entitled *Dark Victory: Ronald Reagan, MCA, and the Mob*, was the most courageous, and well-researched, indictment of a sitting president and his power base in history. The book was critically well received and sold a respectable thirty-five thousand copies, despite being next to impossible to find in bookstores. Despite the depth and import of the research, the national media, so many of whom were tied to MCA product, ignored the book altogether. "I couldn't get on TV," said Moldea. "The book caused me great political problems." Not the least of Moldea's difficulties originated within his own Institute for Policy Studies, whose directors forced him to resign; Jules Stein's daughter was a coveted IPS contributor, whom they could not afford to offend. In addition, Lew Wasserman was planning to throw a Hollywood fund-raiser for IPS.

Hilton in Atlantic City: The Curse of Korshak II

On February 28, 1985, Hilton Hotels became the second Atlantic City casino wannabe after Hyatt to suffer a major setback due to their long association with Sid Korshak. The company applied for a license at about the same time as Hefner-Pritzker, but was turned down by a 2–2 vote (with one abstention) just three months before the planned May 1985 opening of the $270 million hotel-casino.

According to Barron Hilton, his company had employed Marshall's firm since the 1940s in its dealings with the Chicago Hotel Association, which his brother Sidney represented in labor "negotiations" with the Chicago Outfit. Former Hilton general counsel E. Timothy Applegate remembered that Marshall had other creative methods for squeezing the golden Hilton goose. As noted previously, Marshall's close relationship with the Cook County tax assessor appeared to play a role in the frequent tax audits Hilton received, a nuisance that conveniently led to more work—and more fees—for Marshall.[44]

Since 1971, Hilton's period of greatest expansion, Sidney Korshak had been on retainer to Hilton Hotels as its labor consultant. However, the origins of Sidney's hiring by Hilton was foggy; Barron Hilton, Conrad's son, ventured that it occurred at the recommendation of Hilton's then general counsel, Stanley Zax, whose mother was a friend of Sidney's. According to one Hilton employee, Zax referred to Korshak as "Uncle Sidney." When gaming board investigators spoke with Sidney in his brother's Chicago office, he said he was recommended to Barron Hilton by Patrick Hoy, a VP at Henry Crown's General Dynamics Corporation. Korshak believed both Zax and Hoy went to bat for him, adding that Zax was likely returning favors, since Marshall had secured Zax a job with a local law firm, and Sidney had helped Zax land work with National General Insurance. When the investigators interviewed Henry Crown, he said that Conrad Hilton would likely not approve of Sidney's hiring. "Connie's rolling in his grave over Hilton's retention of Sidney Korshak," Crown said, laughing. He added cryptically that he had recently met up with Korshak at the Beverly Hills Friars Club under "shady circumstances," feeling that he was "set up."

Barron Hilton also said he knew of Sidney's Las Vegas reputation, where he arranged sweetheart contracts for his Riviera Hotel. "I have got to say this about Sidney," Hilton later testified. "He told me, 'Whatever you do, don't give the union people even a pencil, give them nothing.' "[45]

According to records that Korshak provided to Hilton in 1983, Hilton had paid Sidney $612,000 over the years, and $366,000 to his brother's firm, where the work was actually done. The New Jersey Casino Control Commission noted that Sidney's fees seemed exorbitant "for the few identifiable legal services" he rendered. However, Hilton general counsel E. Timothy Applegate and his superiors believed that the Korshak brothers' fees were a bargain, considering all the successful work they had rendered over the years, including the successful defenses in all of the eighty-plus Equal Employment Opportunity Commission (EEOC) appeals cases, largely handled in Marshall's office by Don Peters. According to Applegate, Sidney, now a multimillionaire, was not even remotely interested in his own cut of the fees, telling Applegate, "Look, I don't need the money, and I enjoy having a class company like Hilton as a client."[46] Interestingly, Hilton was Korshak's adversary in Las Vegas, where they refused to join his rogue hotel association. That decision cost Hilton millions when they were subsequently forced to close down due to a strike by Ed Hanley's Hotel Workers Union.

The Hilton-Korshak relationship went smoothly until Hilton's expensive gamble in Atlantic City. Hilton had invested so much in the venture because it had come to realize the vast profits to be made in the casino game; its two Las Vegas locations, the Las Vegas Hilton and the Flamingo Hilton, accounted for 45 percent of the company's total profit ($70 million by 1988).[47] The Atlantic City venture, with 614 rooms—with a possible expansion to 2,000 rooms—represented the largest undertaking in the history of the company, which had started out as partnership with Kirkeby and assorted underworld luminaries.

During the requisite hearings before Jersey gaming officials, Hilton began to realize that its association with the Fixer could be devastating. As noted, the company had previously checked out Korshak after the Hersh *New York Times* series and came away satisfied. Barron Hilton testified that he sympathized with Korshak after the 1976 series hit: "I frankly felt kind of sorry for the individual because I felt he had some special talent and still do, as far as doing a job in labor relations. I think the man, [and] his office, has done an outstanding job for our company." However, the gaming board wasn't buying and continually berated Hilton for still associating with Korshak.

Under intense questioning by division director Thomas O'Brien and other commission members, Hilton finally caved, saying, "I wish to hell we would have never hired him, because I can see it's a very distinct problem here in the minds of you gentlemen about this fellow's integrity. I'm sorry we ever had this problem occur."

Under a constant battering, the company relented and decided to sever its long relationship with Korshak, not only because of the board's objections, but also Sidney's recent refusal to cooperate with the congressional panel looking into the union corruption under Ed Hanley. Applegate was assigned the unenviable job of delivering the bad news. "At about the same time as Barron's testimony, Sidney was subpoenaed by a congressional committee on corruption in the hotel industry," Applegate recently recalled, "and when he said he'd plead the Fifth Amendment, that was the last straw for Hilton. I called Sidney [to fire him], and he was very unhappy, saying that we were kowtowing to 'those pricks.' I asked for his Hilton work files to give to the board, and he said, 'To hell with them. I would do it for Hilton, but not for those people.'" Korshak eventually delivered approximately twenty linear feet of work files to Hilton, and when they were perused by Hilton's New Jersey law firm, it was reported that "all legal services provided to Hilton Hotels by the Sidney R. Korshak law firm were performed exclusively by

Donald F. Peters, Jr., Esq., and David Mendelsohn, Esq."*,48 During their interview with Mendelsohn, New Jersey gaming officials also learned that 90 percent of the work done for the Chicago Hotel Association over the years had, in fact, also been performed by Mendelsohn, pursuant to an arrangement worked out with Korshak, who disdained the nuts-and-bolts work.49 Gaming commissioner Carl Zeitz wanted to know whether Korshak "ever did a lick of legal work for the company," and Applegate responded, "I don't know."

Applegate followed up with a condolence letter to Korshak on March 30, 1984, thanking Korshak for his understanding. "We very much regret this situation," Applegate wrote. "We feel however, that we cannot risk jeopardizing in any way the huge investment we have committed in Atlantic City." Applegate added, "My own inquiries and reading of the public press have never revealed to me any reason to consider terminating our relationship." However, he observed, gaming officials "appear to believe that you have questionable associations and have made an issue of your retention by Hilton." Applegate also acknowledged the quality of Korshak's work over the years for Hilton:

> I appreciate very much your understanding the action we feel we're forced to take in dissolving the long-standing relationship between you and Hilton Hotels Corporation . . .
>
> You know that it has always been my opinion that we would have had to pay far more elsewhere for the services of comparable quality over the past twelve years, and I certainly don't question your entitlement to the full annual fee for 1984. You can also rest assured that you continue to be held in huge esteem and affection by those of us at Hilton who have had the pleasure of having you as a friend and advisor.
>
> Sincerely, Tim

However, the New Jersey officials were not impressed with Hilton's too-little-too-late action. One commissioner remarked that Hilton "apparently

---

*Mendelsohn's daughter Carol moved to Hollywood in 1980, where she became the executive producer of *Melrose Place* and *CSI*, the most successful dramatic television series in history. The *New York Times* wrote, "Her father's connections helped open some doors." (*New York Times*, 10-19-03)

didn't get religion until it was pounding on the pearly gates of licensure." The Casino Control Commission called Applegate's post-Hersh investigation of Korshak "perfunctory."[50]

The Korshak connection was a major but not the only reason for the official problems with the Hilton application. Commissioner Carl Zeitz pointed out that in 1975 the Las Vegas Hilton had cashed $100,000 in checks for the Aladdin Hotel's general counsel Sorkis Webbe, "which we know were kick-back payments on the Aladdin hotel-casino construction financed by the Teamsters." Webbe, a St. Louis associate of Morris Schenker's, was later convicted and sentenced to prison for concealing the kickbacks on his tax returns, and federal prosecutors charged that the checks, totaling over $1 million, were "laundered" at the Hilton. And there was the matter of Hilton's casino division VP Henry Lewin, who had been indicted in 1979 for comps given to Jimmy Fratianno's Teamsters boss pal Rudy Tham.

Thus, on February 28, 1985, two years into construction, the commission rejected Hilton's bid. In its decision, the gaming commission called Korshak "a key actor in organized crime's unholy alliance with corrupt union officials and its pernicious efforts to frustrate the rights of working men and women by infecting legitimate unions, to rob their members' future by stealing the benefits they have earned in the past from honest labor." At the conclusion of the hearings, New Jersey gaming commissioner Joel R. Jacobson said, "In my judgment, the . . . relationship of the Hilton Hotels Corporation with Sidney Korshak is the fatal link upon which I primarily based the conclusion that this applicant has not established its suitability for licensure in New Jersey."

When Hilton's testimony was released to the press months later, his rebuke of Korshak prompted a rare display of acrimony from the famously unflappable Fixer. On November 29, 1985, Korshak fired off a vitriolic letter to his former friend Barron Hilton. The letter in its entirety stated:

> Dear Sir:
> I find it extremely difficult to address you in any other fashion.
>
> I read with interest your disparaging remarks about me to the New Jersey Gaming Commission. When did you discover that I was unworthy of being an attorney or that I was associated with characters that shocked your most decent sensibilities?
>
> I have in my possession a number of letters from your staff attorneys extolling my virtues as an attorney and telling me how happy

the hotels were with my representation of your corporation. Those letters were also sent to your office for your personal perusal. I am sending them to you again today.

Was I in a sorry plight when I met you in New York and worked out a deal with Charlie Bluhdorn of Gulf & Western, giving you their airport hotel and the Arlington Hotel to manage without you investing one penny, despite your offer to pay Gulf & Western $10,000,000 for one-half investment in these hotels? If you recall, I never billed you for my services in these matters. My fee would ordinarily be a very high one. Do you remember calling me in Las Vegas at 6 one morning while you were with Kirk Kerkorian and Frank Rothman for me to ask the unions not to strike you, namely Dick Thomas of the Teamsters and Bob Fox of the Engineers? As you well know, there was no fee involved.

You have caused me irreparable harm, and as long as I live I will never forget that. When did I become a shady character? I imagine when you were having difficulty getting a license in Atlantic City.

Very Truly Yours,
Sidney R. Korshak

Korshak's anguish was, uncharacteristically, conveyed to his Hollywood pals. Paramount president Frank Yablans said, "What Barron did pained Sidney so."[51]

In retrospect, Tim Applegate believed Korshak was only part of Hilton's problem. "Sidney was the ostensible reason for the denial, although lying behind that was a general feeling that we were arrogant as hell—and there was some truth to that," Applegate said recently. "When we showed up for the first hearing, Christ, we showed up in five limousines. And Barron has a way of seeing the world revolve around him. He didn't want to be bothered with having us prep him for his testimony: 'I already know it all,' he'd say. Barron claimed to have approved all the attorneys hired, when in fact I hired over one hundred, and I doubt he even met two of them."

And there may even have been other hidden agendas, in Applegate's view. "At the time, Barron and I were highly suspicious that some competitor had done us in," said Applegate. "We knew that there were a lot of suspicious people operating casinos back there that didn't want us in. Initially, New Jersey was practically begging us to come in. There was a Democratic administration in place, and our attorneys were very friendly with the governor. But we backed off for a year due to a nationwide recession. In the meantime, the Republicans took over, and our attorneys had no rapport with them."

Applegate was not alone in his suspicions. When Hilton's bid was officially declined, knowledgeable people pointed out the quixotic nature of the decision; the same board had recently voted 3–2 in favor of a license for Resorts International, over the objections of gaming enforcement staff members who believed Resorts had bribed the head of a foreign government, the Bahamian prime minister.

Less than a month after it denied Hilton a gaming license, the Casino Control Commission agreed to reopen its hearing into Hilton's qualifications for a license, but on April 27, Hilton announced that it had accepted an offer of $325 million from Donald Trump for the nearly finished complex on which Hilton had spent about $308 million. Trump would later belittle Barron Hilton in his book *Trump: The Art of the Deal*, calling him a member of "The Lucky Sperm Club," and bragging about how he'd pressured Hilton into a bargain deal.[52] However, Trump paid Hilton more than Hilton had spent in its costs and had to borrow every cent for the purchase, for which he managed to overcome his great humility in naming it Trump's Castle.

Ironically, Trump was quickly granted a license, although his attorney was Roy Cohn, who had been indicted four times—Korshak was never indicted. Cohn would later be disbarred, after racking up an appalling list of alleged misdeeds, including being accused of ordering a luxury yacht set ablaze to collect on a $200,000 insurance policy, as well as committing the federal crimes of fraud, conspiracy, and corporate manipulations. Though he was acquitted of all charges in 1986 (the same year he was disbarred for borrowing $109,000 from a client and never repaying), he died mere weeks later on August 2 from the AIDS he was diagnosed with in 1984.[53]

Years later, when Trump ran into a close friend of Korshak's, he said, "Oh, Sidney Korshak. Great guy—if it wasn't for him, I never would have gotten Trump's Castle." Trump's crowing, as usual, was premature: his Atlantic City investment has been a steady money loser ever since.[54]

Tim Applegate, like every other executive besides Barron, was forced to resign from Hilton in order to salvage the precious application. But Applegate, who said he was given "a platinum parachute," was not bitter. "Barron felt very badly about it and gave me everything he could to ease the pain," remembered Applegate. But the experience had one bizarre twist remaining. "Barron dropped his application anyway," said a still quizzical Applegate. " 'To hell with them,' he said. I thought, 'Barron, why didn't you say that three months ago?' " Another executive who was forced to re-sign ran into Applegate months later and gave him a message. "Korshak told him that I was really a stand-up guy, and that if I needed any help in L.A., to let him know," said Applegate. "And I thought to myself that's probably the last thing I need. Knowing him, he probably would have got-ten me located with one of the studios. I was later told by a union guy that once a week Korshak would go down to Drucker's Barbershop and meet with local mobsters."

After some years in private practice, Applegate landed another coun-selor's position with a national corporation. Hilton finally got its Atlantic City license in 1991, taking over Steve Wynn's Golden Nugget and renaming it the Atlantic City Hilton—but they would sell that off in short time, and the property continues to shift ownership. At the time of Hilton's purchase of the Golden Nugget, Frank J. Dodd, a new member of the Casino Control Commission, noted, "It was a major blunder to deny a casino license to Hilton [in 1985]. The industry has since fallen on hard times in Atlantic City; the decision sent out a hostile signal to investors about how arbitrary and unreasonable New Jersey gambling officials could be. I don't think I would have denied them a license. That was a major turning point in the his-tory of Atlantic City. It sent out a bad signal."[55]

On June 9, 1984, Jackie Presser, the Teamster boss who had been instru-mental in Reagan's election, decided Sidney had become too hot, the last straw being Sidney's parasitic connection to a $60,000 organizing fee that the International Brotherhood of Teamsters sent to the West Coast once a month for two years to organize dockworkers. By 1983, the International had poured $1.2 million into the endeavor, Korshak's cut being an exorbi-tant $800,000. Despite the huge retainer, Korshak hadn't handled any cases, and the dockworker organizing effort had brought in all of about two hun-dred new Teamsters. "That's nothing for all that money," said Presser.

Most disturbing was an FBI report from a high-level Teamster informant (unnamed, but likely Presser) that Korshak had enlisted his son Stuart's law firm, Wyman, Bautzer, Rothman, Kuchel, and Silbert, of Century City to funnel the lion's share of the money."[56] Regarding the firm's money launder-ing: ". . . one of the many ways of accomplishing this is through the over-charging of legal fees and taking the overcharges and laundering those funds through West Germany. Source further advised that he does not know how or why the funds are passed through West Germany or where the funds go from that point, but did advise that it may be only a coincidence, however,

Lorimar Productions in Hollywood, California, receives funding from some source in West Germany."[57]

It is not known how or if the FBI resolved this sensitive raw intelligence.

The Teamster leadership wasn't the only entity with the impression that Korshak had outlived his usefulness. Presser, who had since turned FBI informant, told his government contacts that the New York and Chicago families "are concerned about his image and want Korshak to 'phase out.' "*,[58] Senior Teamster adviser Duke Zeller added that Presser's hatred of Korshak was the by-product of Presser's siding with the Cleveland hoods over Korshak's pals in Chicago. "[Presser] wanted Korshak out of the Teamsters," Zeller stated. "His ouster was part of the deal Jackie made with his mob friends to secure his election as Teamster president."[59]

Presser was also known to have been obsessed with Korshak's influence in the Reagan White House, believing Korshak was responsible for his recent fall from grace with officialdom. The FBI seemed to agree: in a 1981 memo, the Bureau noted that "Korshak was a strong contributor to President-elect Ronald Reagan's campaign, and possibly Korshak will push to have Reagan's support for [Roy] Williams for the presidency of the IBT at the upcoming IBT National Convention to be held in Las Vegas in June 1981."[60] (Williams was, in fact, elected and became the first labor leader invited to the White House to consult with President Reagan.) In another FBI report, it was noted that Korshak was actively negotiating with the leaders of the Boston Mafia to convince them that their support of a different Teamster presidential choice—deleted in the document, but likely Presser—"would go contrary to the desires of the Chicago mob."[61]

According to Presser, Korshak also used America's best singer as his liaison to Reagan. "It's that damn Sinatra and his ties to Nancy, I know it is!" Presser screamed to Duke Zeller. According to Zeller, Presser said that he "always felt that Korshak was dealing with the White House and had some sort of revolving-door status there. Jackie was both jealous of it and feared it."[62] In a recent conversation, Zeller added, "Jackie was very respectful of Korshak and also was somewhat frightened of him. And he always blamed Korshak. He said he thought that Sidney had poisoned Reagan on him."

---

*Presser had been set to be indicted in 1984 in a union "ghost employee" scam, but the indictment was dropped when the FBI revealed that Presser had been a key informant for years. On November 10, 1987, as a result of a ten-year Labor Department civil suit, the court ruled that it would be supervising the pension fund for the next twenty years. Eighteen former trustees of the fund, including Jackie Presser, had to pay fines for their roles in bilking the fund. Presser would eventually be indicted for embezzlement and racketeering, but died three days before his July 12, 1988, trial was to start.

Hollywood Teamster leader Marty Bacow agreed that Korshak was merely coasting on his reputation. "Korshak bullshitted around a lot of people," Bacow believed. "Everybody believed he has these Mob guys behind him and all of this. Well, they're all away now. There is nothing left of them. When his name came up in my conversations, I said, 'Don't tell me about Sidney Korshak. He couldn't make a move without getting permission. He was an order taker.' And that was the end of it."[63] Paramount Pictures president Frank Yablans noted recently that, as Korshak's reputation began to take a hit, even his closest friends, such as Lew Wasserman, began to put some distance between themselves and the aging Fixer. Yablans said recently that the deaths of Sidney's Chicago patrons were crucial to the sea change. "After they were gone," Yablans said, "Sidney started to lose his power. He still had influence in Chicago and Vegas, but he lost it in Hollywood. In Chicago and Vegas, people respected him for what he'd done. But not in Hollywood— Hollywood only respects you for what you can do." Perhaps the hardest pill to swallow was the loss of Wasserman, for whom Korshak had done so much to keep his studio strike-free. Yablans said that Korshak's "old school" style just "brought Lew too much heat." Yablans added, "At the end of his life, Sidney was very bitter about Lew, bitter about everything . . . Not because he regretted the life he lived, [but] because he couldn't *live* the life anymore."[64]

Whereas Korshak's prestige was in decline in 1984, his friend Paul Ziffren was enjoying the kind of public lionizing afforded only a few of the Chicago expatriates. On July 28, the games of the XXIII Olympiad opened in Los Angeles, due in large part to the work of Ziffren, the founding secretary of the L.A. Olympic Organizing Committee, which was the only bidder for the games. After serious economic problems caused by the 1976 Olympics in Montreal, the 1984 Olympic Games saw, for the first time ever, corporate sponsors for the event, with forty-three companies licensed to sell "official" Olympic products. The corporate sponsorships caused the 1984 Olympic Games to be the first Olympics to turn a profit ($225 million) since 1932.*

---

*The only negatives associated with the 1984 games were the boycotts of nations allied with the Soviets, who passed up the games in retaliation for the U.S. boycott of the 1980 Olympic Games in Moscow. Along with the Soviet Union, East Germany, and Cuba, fourteen other countries boycotted the games. Though these countries boycotted, China participated in the games for the first time since 1932, joining 140 other countries. Notable among the approximately sixty-seven hundred athletes, Mary Lou Retton of the United States received perfect scores in her final two events, becoming the first American woman to win an individual gold medal in gymnastics.

In some circles, Ziffren was practically deified when the final tallies came in for what were the most financially successful games in history:

- The games provided over seventy-four thousand new jobs for city workers.
- They brought an amazing $3.3 billion into the local economy.
- The engineers laid miles of fiber-optic cable under the city, making L.A. the first U.S. city with that added infrastructure, and giving it a huge advantage in the booming communications market.
- With the massive $225 million surplus, the Amateur Athletic Foundation was endowed, housing the largest sports library in North America. In 1988, that library was named The Paul Ziffren Sports Research Center.

Nineteen eighty-five saw another Sandy Smith–style casualty in the journalism ranks. Just as Smith had sacrificed his *Chicago Tribune* job over that paper's perceived coddling of the brothers Korshak, Dick Brenneman would do likewise at the *Sacramento Bee*, where he had diligently been preparing his own Korshak investigation. Brenneman was drawn to the world of Sid Korshak when he met Korshak and Judge Rittenband while covering the Polanski trial for the *Santa Monica Evening Outlook*. Over lunch at the Hillcrest, as Brenneman remembered, Korshak mostly complained about finding good household help.[65] For years thereafter, Brenneman tracked down both the paper and the people that might shed light on Korshak's power.

"[LAPD lieutenant] Marion Phillips and Jack Tobin gave me introductions to scores of sources," recalled Brenneman, "and I dropped their names to countless others in the years that followed." Like many before him, Brenneman began securing Supermob files from the Chicago Crime Commission and various federal agencies such as the Department of Labor, where he learned that the agency held a sixteen-inch-thick printout on Korshak's labor activities (that file has since been destroyed). During his research, Brenneman spoke with many of Phillips's and Tobin's best sources, insiders who described the strange bedfellows that appeared to link prominent California pols to Korshak and ultimately to the bank accounts of the Chicago Outfit bosses. However, after years of exhaustive work, Brenneman's editors refused to green-light an article in 1985. The decision staggered the diligent and meticulous Brenneman, who felt compelled to do what Smith had done years earlier. "I quit the *Bee* after they killed my Korshak story," said Brenneman.[66] At present, Brenneman is the managing editor of the *Berkeley Daily Planet*.

* * *

On November 21, 1985, the *Chicago Sun-Times* interviewed Abe Pritzker in advance of his upcoming (January 6) ninetieth birthday.[67] AT 90, PRITZKER STILL FEELS LIKE A MILLION ran the headline. Just ten weeks later, on February 8, 1986, Abe Pritzker died at Chicago's Michael Reese Hospital. To the astonishment of those unfamiliar with the world of offshore tax havens, Pritzker's survivors had the audacity to claim only $3,000 in taxable assets. In contrast, the IRS asserted that they underestimated their estate by a mere $97 million, and owed $53.2 million in back taxes. The case was settled for $9.5 million, thanks to the efforts of their tax lawyer Burton Kanter.

In April 1986, the President's Commission on Organized Crime delivered its final report, entitled *The Impact: Organized Crime Today*, to President Ronald Reagan. Although the investigation ostensibly looked hard into labor corruption, the final document suspiciously neglected to mention Reagan friend Sid Korshak. This despite hearing damning Korshak testimony from the likes of Jimmy Fratianno, who told how Aiuppa had upbraided him for contacting Korshak, and current Teamster president Roy Williams, who informed the commissioners that Korshak was "a member" of the mob and controlled Andy Anderson for them.[68] Fratianno went so far as to tell the commission that Korshak "practically runs the Mafia industry."[69]

In fact, over half of the eighteen commissioners filed supplemental views or dissenting opinions on the report, charging that too many "dark places" had been ignored. "Poor management of time, money, and staff has resulted in the commission's leaving important issues unexamined," one wrote. "The true history of the commission . . . is a saga of missed opportunity." When asked by writer Dan Moldea why Korshak's name had not appeared in the final report, one commissioner replied, "That's a sensitive area. Korshak did come up in a couple of interviews and in one of the staff reports. But there was dissension about him throughout the life of the commission . . . Several of us wanted to highlight him, particularly since he played such an important role in the Hilton hearings in Atlantic City. But it was just not meant to be. There were forces that didn't want Korshak touched. So the commission just rounded up the usual suspects."

Another commissioner, who also preferred to go unnamed, recently added, "In many executive sessions that we had—not testimony, but meetings of the committee—there was a lot of talk about Korshak and of doing a separate investigation just on Korshak. We were known as the Gang of Five because we were the people dissenting to a lot of things the committee was doing. We didn't make a lot of friends with that." One final commissioner went further, citing a nine-hour meeting prior to the release of the final report. "Leaving Korshak out of the final report was no accident. A conscious decision was made to leave out any reference to him, and we were told about it at that meeting. It was too late to do anything about it. We [the commissioners] really never had a chance to see the final version of the report before it was released. I felt there was pressure to keep Korshak out. And where that pressure came from, well, your guess is as good as mine."[70]

Although it was now clear to all that Korshak would never be made to explain his six-decade dance with the Chicago Outfit, there was at least one personal repercussion from the onslaught to his reputation that had begun with Sy Hersh's revelations: Korshak began to distrust many of his lesser acquaintances, becoming even more careful, and retreating still further from the spotlight, if such a thing was possible. According to Bistro owner Kurt Niklas, the Korshaks' annual Christmas-bash guest list was slashed from four hundred to a mere twenty-four trusted dinner guests.[71]

For Korshak, his once legendary "fixing" was all but a memory, save for the occasional sage advice given to an old friend. Such was the case after a man went on a violent rampage in Gianni Russo's State Street Club in Las Vegas on October 30, 1988. After a broken-bottle brawl, Russo, who for many years had delivered messages from back East to Korshak at the Bistro, shot and killed the madman, who had threatened to murder a waitress. Within three days, Korshak had heard about the incident and called Russo.

"Are you okay?" Korshak asked.

"Yeah," replied Russo.

"Here is what I want you to do. I want you to jump on a plane, and go to L.A."

"When?" Russo asked.

"Now. There are two guys I want you to go see. Robert Shapiro at Twentieth Century Tower and Alan Smiley."

At the time, Shapiro, the future defender of O. J. Simpson, was a partner at Bushkin, Gaims, Gaines and Jonas, while Smiley was best known as the pal of Bugsy Siegel, who was with him when he was murdered in 1947. Russo went to the Las Vegas airport, where Korshak had a prepaid ticket waiting. Upon arriving in L.A., Russo proceeded directly to Shapiro's office as instructed by Korshak. Shapiro told Russo, "Sidney is very worried." However, after Russo explained the details, Shapiro concluded that the DA would rule it justifiable homicide. Shapiro gave him his home number and said, "Just call me if you need anything."

From there, Russo went to Smiley's penthouse apartment on Doheney Drive, where Smiley asked the same questions as Shapiro. He then said that he had been worried that the killing was drug-related. "That's why I told Sidney to have you come and see me today," explained Smiley. "If you need anything, you know where to find me."[72]

Russo concluded that the intervention was just a case of Korshak looking out for an old friend. "They just needed to check everything out," Russo said. "Sidney was just being overprotective. Steve Wynn* called me that night and said, 'Did you go?' I said, 'Yeah. How the fuck did you know?' He said, 'Sidney called me.' "[73]

As predicted, no charges were filed. The Vegas DA indeed called it justifiable homicide.

One Last Attempt at an MCA Probe

While Korshak's history was being whitewashed in Washington, Wasserman's was about to be similarly glossed in the Golden State. In the interim since he'd first affixed the 1976 Hersh articles to his St. Petersburg, Florida, refrigerator, U.S. Attorney Marvin Rudnick had relocated to the L.A. Strike Force, where he was able to exercise his interest in the likes of Korshak and Wasserman. It was a period of some concern for the Supermob's entertainment wing; over a dozen grand juries were impaneled across the country to delve into corruption in the record business—MCA Music was among those under close scrutiny; on February 14, 1986, Ross and Silverman aired a piece on NBC *Nightly News* that pointed out the mob's relationship with the industry, again with MCA implications.[74] Soon, Rudnick would jump into the fray fully loaded.

At the center of the allegations was Sal "the Swindler" Pisello, a New York pizza and ice cream distributor, who had no experience in the music business, but had nonetheless had a strong business relationship with MCA since 1983. In fact, Pisello was a street hood in the Gambino family, who smuggled heroin into the country inside frozen fish and bragged about the executions he had carried out.

Among other things, Pisello had arranged for MCA to purchase the catalog belonging to Chicago's Chess Records, which featured black artists like Chuck Berry, Etta James, Muddy Waters, and The Dells. MCA also used Pisello to sell off its "cutouts"—otherwise nonsellable older recordings.

---

*Wynn was then the owner of the downtown Golden Nugget and soon to open the $630 million Mirage on the Strip. He later opened Treasure Island and the Bellagio. In 2005, Wynn finished construction on the most expensive Strip hotel ever, the $2.7 billion Wynn Las Vegas on the grounds of Moe Dalitz's (and later Howard Hughes's) former Desert Inn.

Legitimate distributors who refused to purchase the musical junk because the promised sweeteners (good records) were not included were routinely roughed up by Pisello's enforcers. Over the years, numerous Eastern crime families had feasted at the trough of cutout records supplied by MCA through Pisello. MCA lost as much as $3 million on these deals, while Pisello made at least $600,000. Unwitting MCA employees were startled at how Pisello was received when he visited MCA headquarters. According to *Los Angeles Times* reporter Bill Knoedelseder, who covered Pisello's connection to MCA, "He had the run of the place."[75]

Pisello was just one of many embarrassments nipping at MCA's heels. According to U.S. Attorney Carolyn Henneman, New York mobster and convicted tax cheat Edward Sciandra had been directing "hundreds of thousands of dollars" of MCA's Universal division film processing to a company "in return for ten percent in cash under the table."[76]

With the blessing of L.A. Strike Force chief David Margolis, Rudnick subpoenaed four top MCA executives, who quickly advised that they would plead the Fifth before the L.A. grand jury. Simultaneously, Strike Force member Richard Stavin was spearheading a second, but overlapping, investigation of MCA's VP and chief of Universal's $100 million home-video distribution wing, Eugene F. Giaquinto, a former New Yorker. According to FBI wiretaps placed at MCA headquarters, Giaquinto was continuing to send Universal's videographic business to a mob-infiltrated Pennsylvania firm, North Star Graphics, even though it had been caught bilking Universal out of hundreds of thousands of dollars back in 1981.

One wiretap had Giaquinto telling the Mafia contact at North Star to stop the bilking or he would have his New York boyhood pal John Gotti read him the riot act. The taps also revealed that Giaquinto enlisted Gotti-Gambino soldiers to come to L.A. to put a stop to production of a biopic of Meyer Lansky that *Godfather* star James Caan wanted to make with the Genovese mob, with whom Caan was quite friendly—Giaquinto had dreams of making his own Lansky-approved film. However, neither film was ever made.[77] Giaquinto was fired from MCA when the probe was made public, but he was never indicted.

The wiretaps also revealed the possibility that mob money was being laundered through at least four motion picture productions, but that the mob worried whether Wasserman's successor at MCA would be someone with whom they could continue to conduct business as they had with Giaquinto. Stavin told CBS's *60 Minutes* in 1989 that the tapped conversations "are quite clear that Giaquinto was the Mafia's man within MCA."[78] In

April 1988, Pisello was convicted of tax evasion on $400,000 in unreported MCA income and sentenced to four years in prison. Rudnick and Stavin hoped that this would be just the beginning of a probe that would determine why MCA would be in business with this crowd. In fact, it was the end of the investigation—a typical "show bust" that saw the low-level Italian connection collared, while the Supermob enablers skated.

What happened was that in May 1988, according to one high-level source within MCA, Giaquinto went into action. "He went ballistic," said the source. Giaquinto then said, "I'm calling [Attorney General Ed] Meese and getting this thing stopped right now."[79] William Dwyer II, an attorney who represented three MCA executives who had been fired for cooperating with Rudnick, said, "There was [talk] about how Ed Meese wanted certain actions taken because Nancy Reagan had a friend in high places in the entertainment industry."[80] In another interview, Dwyer concluded, "Something was rotten somewhere. My clients had cooperated fully with Rudnick's investigation. Since he had his stripes taken away, we haven't given the government any further cooperation—and the government hasn't asked us for any."

Dwyer may have found the government's seeming ennui surprising, but he may not have if he had been aware of what was occurring in the Supermob's radarproof world. On May 19, 1986, within three months after the grand jury investigation began, Lew Wasserman became the largest individual contributor to the Ronald Reagan Presidential Foundation, donating $517,969 for the construction of the Reagan library, according to documents obtained from the California secretary of state's office. Most suspiciously, Wasserman had been coordinating the library fund-raising effort with none other than Ed Meese.

MCA then enlisted the legal services of power attorney William Hundley, who not only was a partner in the law firm of MCA board member Robert Strauss, but also had headed the original Strike Force, set up by Bobby Kennedy, when he'd worked for the attorney general in the Kennedy administration. In short time, Hundley met with Rudnick's new L.A. Strike Force chief, John Newcomer, who in turn ordered Rudnick to end his probe into MCA's affairs. When he refused, he was fired in July 1989. Richard Stavin had resigned just two months earlier, disgusted that his department refused to indict MCA executives he had been building a case against. That same year, Bill Knoedelseder quit his *Los Angeles Times* job, not long after being ordered to curtail his MCA coverage. At the time, the paper's publisher was Tom Johnson, a former LBJ aide, who had obtained his *Times* position thanks to Lew Wasserman's kind intercession with the Chandler family.

In a recent interview, Rudnick summarized his feelings about the termination of the probe: "One week they were going to give me an award for getting the Pisello tax evasion convictions, but as soon as I tried to turn Pisello against the people who paid him off [MCA], they just snuffed it out. They called me a loose cannon. They pushed me out of my job and my career all because they wanted to stop something. What was it? They said it was because MCA was complaining about me. But it was because Wasserman was the connection between Korshak and the higher-ups in Washington. Wasserman was known for his political connections. You have to ask yourself, 'Is someone getting paid off somewhere?' "[81]

Future probes into MCA were rendered all but impossible when it was discovered that many evidence volumes of both the FBI and Strike Force's MCA probes had disappeared. Among other explosive investigations that were shelved was Stavin's interest in MCA employee Robert Nichols, who traveled the world for the company, allegedly tracking down counterfeit operations. However, Nichols was also simultaneously working for the same Reagan administration operatives who were illegally selling weapons to rogue nations in order to fund the Nicaraguan contra movement. The suspicion was that Reagan's close pals at MCA were assisting in the worldwide movement of the illicit monies. "MCA could pay for Nichols to travel, visit certain countries, and act as a bagman to deliver money to foreign nations," Stavin recently conjectured.[82]

Rudnick and Stavin were never able to determine how and why the mob had gotten its hooks so deeply into MCA in the first place. However, Rudnick remained curious about a cryptic, unsigned letter he had received from Pisello's and Giaquinto's New York stomping grounds on September 24, 1986. It stated:

To whom it may concern:

Wasserman wanted his daughter's boyfriend murdered
Sal Pisello committed the murder
Wasserman is now indebted to Sal Pisello.
Wasserman gives orders to [Irving] Azoff to allow Sal to move around freely
To keep Azoff quiet, Wasserman bought Azoff's company.[83]

Irving Azoff, the head of MCA Music, owned three outside companies, for which Wasserman had paid $30 million in stock options—six to ten times the value of the companies.

Regarding the unsigned note, Marvin Rudnick recently spoke of an allegation he would have tracked had he been allowed to stay on: "The rumor was that Wasserman had somebody murdered by the Chicago Outfit. New York [the Gambinos] heard about it, and then Wasserman paid Pisello to keep it quiet."[84]

CHAPTER 22

Legacies

THE SUPERMOB WAS NOW well into the inevitable era of passings and transitions, the parade of Russian Ashkenazim into eternity having already begun with the deaths of notables such as Greenberg, Arvey, Pritzker, Hart, and Factor. They were joined on October 26, 1987, by Greg Bautzer, who suffered a fatal heart attack while brushing his teeth. His service boasted such honorary pallbearers as Lew Wasserman, Frank Sinatra, Pat Brown, Tony Martin, and Ambassador John Gavin. Also attending was Sid Korshak, who threw a champagne and caviar wake and memorial lunch afterward at the Bistro Gardens.[1]

Korshak had recently sold his Chalon Road manse (which had long ago been folded into the Korshak Family Trust) to James Lacher, chief lieutenant for Jack Kent Cooke, the man who invented cable television in 1964 and went on to own a number of major league sports franchises;*[2] he was also friends with both Pat Brown and Ronald Reagan. The L.A. Recorder's Office records reveal that Lacher bought the home, which was assessed at $2.1 million, for Cooke's organization, which sold it in 1992 (today the home would cost north of $6 million). Sid and Bee purchased a one-story rancher for $900,000 at 808 North Hillcrest Road in Beverly Hills, just north of Sunset, and across the street from great friends the Cubby Broccolis. Korshak told friends that he preferred Beverly Hills because its flat terrain afforded him the ability to continue his constitutional strolls.†[3]

---

*Among them, the Toronto Maple Leafs, L.A. Kings, L.A. Lakers, and Washington Senators.

†Despite the fact that they abandoned the Chalon house in the eighties, every Christmas until 2003, a two-pound box of gourmet peanut brittle arrived there anonymously, addressed to the Korshaks. The new owners, however, enjoyed it and were dismayed when the package recently stopped arriving.

In Washington, outgoing president Ronald Reagan redressed the surviving Japanese World War II internees whose confiscated properties had given such a financial boost to Greenberg, Ziffren, Bazelon, and the many other Midwesterners who'd descended on Southern California in the 1940s. On August 10, 1988, Reagan signed HR 442, paying $20,000 to the sixty thousand Japanese survivors of the camps—a tiny fraction of what the commercial property alone was worth—and bestowing a $1.2 billion education fund. Reagan's letter of apology stated in part, "Internment of Japanese-Americans was just that: a mistake . . . For here we admit a wrong."

Five years earlier, the congressionally created bipartisan Commission on Wartime Relocation and Internment of Civilians had reviewed the wartime measures by hearing more than 750 testimonies and studying copious archival records. The commission's definitive report, *Personal Justice Denied*, found that there had been no military necessity for the unequal treatment of the ethnic Japanese, and that the causes of the incarceration were rooted in "race prejudice, war hysteria and a failure of political leadership." Regarding the "Magic Cables" that predicted spies among the nisei, Special Counsel Angus Macbeth noted in an addendum to the report that the cables did not justify the mass internment of Japanese Americans.

Morris Schenker, perhaps the Supermob associate to have come the closest to a conviction, died of heart disease on August 9, 1989. Six months earlier, the St. Louis attorney who'd defended Jimmy Hoffa and many of the hoods called before Kefauver and gone on to own the Dunes Hotel and Casino, had been indicted on two counts of having defrauded the IRS out of hundreds of thousands of dollars. The man whom *Life* magazine once called "The Lawyer to the Mob" had been in bankruptcy since 1984, after he was found to have defaulted on nearly $55 million in Teamster loans. Like so many of his peers, Schenker helped raise millions for charity, especially for children's causes. Under his photo accompanying his *St. Louis Post-Dispatch* obituary was the legend MORRIS A. SCHENKER . . . BUSINESSMAN, PHILANTHROPIST.[4]

Three weeks later, on August 31, 1989, Moe Dalitz died, and his *Los Angeles Times* obit typified the contradictions implicit in Supermob membership: CIVIC LEADER, PHILANTHROPIST WAS ALSO ALLEGED UNDERWORLD BOSS. Las Vegas advertising executive and longtime Dalitz friend Marydean Martin said of Dalitz, "Moe was always such a gentleman. He gave back to the community. When the Maude Frazier Building [at UNLV] was built, it had no furniture. He bought all the furniture and didn't want anybody to know about it. He was that kind of person." Regarding the scrutiny that arose at regular intervals, Martin said, "Moe almost never complained, but he was feeling down. He said, 'I'll bet your grandpa drank whiskey,' and I said that he did. 'I'm the guy who made the whiskey, and I'm considered the bad guy. When does the time ever come that you're forgiven?' It was one of the very few times he ever said anything about it." Former Stardust Hotel general manager Herb Tobman, who knew Dalitz well, said, "As far as I'm concerned, he was a great man . . . Moe's charity is legendary around this town. There has never been a greater influence on this city."

Dalitz had been named Humanitarian of the Year by the American Cancer Research Center and Hospital in 1976, two years before the California Organized Crime Control Commission named him one of that state's top criminals, referring to him as "one of the architects of the skimming process." In 1982, Dalitz received the Torch of Liberty Award from the Anti-Defamation League of B'nai B'rith, and in 1979 he set up the Moe Dalitz Charitable Remainder Unitrust, a million-dollar fund to be divided upon his death. When Dalitz died, fourteen nonprofit organizations split $1.3 million. *Las Vegas Review-Journal* columnist John L. Smith wrote, "His contributions to the growth of Las Vegas are priceless."[5]

Also dying that year was Ronald Reagan's lifelong nemesis, the "Evil Empire" controlled by the USSR. In January 1990, the Soviet-backed Communist Party ceased to exist in Poland after years of struggling with Lech Walesa's Solidarity Party. On February 7, 1990, the Central Committee of the Soviet Communist Party voted to give up its monopoly of power, and within a month former Soviet states such as Ukraine and the Baltics began declaring their independence.

Almost immediately, former President Reagan's sycophants attempted to hijack history by giving their boy much of the credit for the fall of Soviet Communism—it was deemed too much of a stretch to call him a philanthropist. Since his days of implicating fellow actors in the forties, Reagan's hatred of all things Communist was agreed by all; in 1983, his stance famously saw him enlist Donald Rumsfeld to hand-deliver a letter of support to Iraq's Saddam Hussein in his anticommunist purges,* and his "tough on commies" history was further burnished when he visited Berlin in 1987, exhorting Soviet leader Mikhail Gorbachev to "tear down this wall," a remark that was followed two years later by the wall's actually coming down. Reagan's anticommunist obsession also saw him support the overthrow of the

*Although Reagan had referred to Soviet leaders as criminals, liars, and cheaters in his first press conference, Hussein may have thought the same thing about Reagan two years later when it was learned that the United States was simultaneously secretly supplying weapons to the Iraqi mullahs who opposed Hussein.

democratically elected Communist government of Nicaragua, encourage legislation that opposed Nelson Mandela's pro-Communist African National Congress, and provide support and training to Usama bin Laden in Afghanistan.*

But those positions and his support for out-of-control military spending actually had precious little to do with the end of the Soviet empire. The real heroes were the likes of Gorbachev, whose courageous moves toward a more open society (perestroika and glasnost) encouraged the breakaway republics; Pope John Paul II, whose bold support of Walesa played a key role in the breakup; and Russian dissident Andrey Sakharov, the physicist who fathered the Soviet H-bomb, whose outspoken and eloquent opposition to the Soviets' human rights abuses led to his being stripped of all his awards (including the 1975 Nobel Peace Prize) and sent into exile in Gorky in 1980—until Gorbachev freed him in 1986. Sadly, Sakharov died one year before the breakup of the Soviet Union.

Confronted with these arguments, Reagan's apologists fall back on the logic that at least he bankrupted the USSR by forcing it into a costly military buildup. However, the CIA's final revised estimates of Soviet military expenditures concluded that they were in fact more or less constant throughout the seventies and eighties—Reagan's spending spree had no reciprocal effect. In February 1994, Gorbachev discussed Reagan's weapons spending with the *Atlantic Monthly*, saying unequivocally, "These were unnecessary and wasteful expenditures that we were not going to match." Aleksandr Yakolev, the Soviet ambassador to Canada, insisted that Reagan's vaunted "Star Wars was exploited by [Soviet] hard-liners to complicate Gorbachev's attempt to end the Cold War." And even if the Soviets had chosen to waste more money on arms, it would likely have had no connection to its breakup; other regimes such as North Korea, Israel, and Taiwan spend disproportionate amounts on the military, but show no signs of coming apart.[6]

George Kennan, the two-time Pulitzer winner and former U.S. ambassador to the Soviet Union, wrote, "The suggestion that any administration had the power to influence decisively the course of a tremendous domestic political upheaval in another country on another side of the globe is simply childish."[7] In fact, had Reagan's positions not encouraged Soviet hard-liners to clamp down on freedom movements, the regime would most likely have collapsed years before it actually did. Again Kennan: "The general effect of Cold War extremism was to delay rather than hasten the great change that

---

*On the other hand, Reagan routinely tolerated totalitarian military regimes such as those in Guatemala, El Salvador, and Chile, just so long as they weren't Communist.

overtook the Soviet Union at the end of the 1980s." He pointed out that, for even many Communist Party members, the collapse of the Soviet system became inevitable as far back as the death of Stalin in 1953.

The next Supermob associate to join the earthly exodus was Paul Ziffren, who died on May 31, 1991, at age seventy-seven. The *Los Angeles Times* headlined THE QUIET MOVER AND SHAKER: THE LATE PAUL ZIFFREN WAS A HARDWORKING PATRIOT FOR LOS ANGELES and referred to him as "a soft-spoken civic leader."[8] On June 3, over five hundred mourners attended his funeral at Hillside Memorial Park, including then state controller Gray Davis, Pat and Jerry Brown, Lew Wasserman, Robert Wagner, and Bob Newhart. Charlton Heston delivered one of the three eulogies, quoting from Shakespeare and the Old Testament. One of Ziffren's many protégés, U.S. district court judge Stephen Reinhardt, who had been on retainer from Ed Hanley's Culinary Workers Union and had negotiated Morris Schenker's Teamster loan, said Ziffren "almost single-handedly led California Democrats out of generations of oblivion and turned this previously Republican stronghold into a two-party state." Gray Davis added, "Paul was a peacemaker. He could find consensus where the rest of us couldn't see it . . . Paul Ziffren was the glue that held together sometimes-warring factions. I hope God gives us another Paul Ziffren."[9]

The praise heaped on Ziffren was predictable, and in many cases warranted. However, one must question how valid such plaudits are in a city infamous for allowing transplants to reinvent themselves, no questions asked, and white-collar crime to flourish. In 1960, Supermob gadfly Lester Velie wrote a more suitable epitaph: "Paul Ziffren broke no law as a business associate of underworld fronts. Yet such associations raise a vexing problem for our society. When gangster profits flow, via fronts, into legitimate business,

Paul Ziffren (private collection)

what share of the responsibility must be borne by men like Paul Ziffren, lawyer for and business associate of such fronts?"[10] Connie Carlson, the unflinching former white-collar-crime investigator for the California Attorney General's Office, recently added a question with just a touch of sarcasm: "Isn't it interesting how all these 'civil libertarians' ended up with the confiscated Japanese land?"[11]

Paul Ziffren's legacy is perhaps most visible in the accomplishments of his son, Hollywood überattorney Kenneth "the Pope of Hollywood" Ziffren. Born in Chicago in 1940, Ziffren was the editor in chief of the UCLA *Law Review* before clerking for Chief Justice Earl Warren. He next became a cofounder of the powerhouse firm Ziffren, Brittenham, Branca, Fischer, Gilbert-Lurie, Stiffelman & Cook, which represents the elite of the Hollywood elite, among them Bruce Willis, Tom Hanks, Sandra Bullock, Aerosmith, Michael Jackson, DreamWorks, Jay Leno, Eddie Murphy, and Harrison Ford; producers Marvin Davis, Stephen J. Cannell, James Brooks (*The Simpsons*); Miramax founders Bob and Harvey Weinstein; and Interscope Communications.* At one time, Ziffren represented the producers of fully one third of all prime-time television series. In 1995, he served as outside counsel to Turner Broadcasting in its acquisition of Metro-Goldwyn-Mayer–United Artists and subsequently brokered the 1996 sale of MGM Inc. to Kirk Kerkorian. He also worked with Microsoft Corp., helping it to form its MSNBC cable channel and interactive joint venture with NBC Studios. "He is so preeminent, it's hard to imagine his star rising any further," said one prominent L.A. attorney. "Everyone wants Ken Ziffren." Another said, "He's the top dog."[12]

In his counsel to major stars, Ken Ziffren is seen as pioneering the "unsigned contract," wherein an elite actor never signs a film contract, a strategy that allows them to pull out of agreement at any time or make last-minute demands of a film producer.

Representing studios, producers, and talent has landed Ziffren in the same sort of hot water that plagued Wasserman's MCA: conflict of interest. Ziffren's firm was sued in 1992 by *Simon & Simon* producer Philip DeGuere Jr., who claimed the company conspired with CBS to defraud him of almost $1 million. In a description some would say fits Paul Ziffren and the rest of the Supermob, UCLA legal ethics professor Carrie Menkel-Meadow said, "Entertainment lawyers generally behave like they are outside the rules, and

---

*When Melanie Cook joined the firm in 2004, she brought her impressive client base into Ziffren et al., including Keanu Reeves, Barry Sonnenfeld, Scott Rudin, Sam Mendes, Christina Ricci, Tim Burton, Mimi Leder, Julie Taymor, Paul Attanasio, Nancy Meyers, and Robin Wright Penn.

they are quite nervous when you say what the rules are." However, Menkel-Meadow added, unlike DeGuere, most clients are afraid to sue the likes of Ken Ziffren, for fear that they'll "never work in this town again."[13] Larry Sackey, attorney for another Ziffren plaintiff, added, "There are a lot of people who have been harmed who are afraid to bring this issue up."[14]

Ken Ziffren is on the board of directors of Al Hart's City National Bank of Beverly Hills.

Nineteen ninety-two saw still more close Korshak friends in the headlines. In April of that year, as Jerry Brown kicked off a strong grassroots presidential bid, Gussie Alex, one of Korshak's oldest Outfit pals, and an early liaison to the inner sanctum of Joe Batters Accardo, was sentenced to fifteen years for extortion, at age seventy-six. One month later, on May 27, 1992, the man himself, Antonino "Joe Batters" Accardo, died at age eighty-six in Chicago. He was buried in the Queen of Heaven Cemetery in suburban Hillside, flanked on either side by the remains of his key aides Paul "the Waiter" Ricca and Sam Battaglia.

That fall, CBS aired *Sinatra*, a five-hour miniseries produced by Frank's daughter Tina. After the telecast, Tina was puzzled by the lack of feedback from Frank's inner circle, among them the Korshaks. "The mystery was solved at the Korshaks' Thanksgiving fest," Tina later wrote, "where Tommy and [actress] Suzanne Pleshette Gallagher were annual participants. Suzanne made some casual comment about the miniseries, to which Katie Korshak, Bee and Sidney's granddaughter whom they raised, replied, 'Oh, we didn't watch it. Auntie Barbara didn't want us to see it.' "[15]

On February 19, 1993, liberal court icon David Bazelon died in Washington. As the *Chicago Tribune* headlined, Bazelon had helped "shape the insanity

Sid and Bee, 1993 (private collection)

defense," creating a legacy of activism for the legal rights of the mentally handicapped, the Bazelon Center for Mental Health Law being the most visible symbol. Like Stein, Factor, Dalitz, and countless other Supermob associates, Bazelon's second life virtually erased any memory of his questionable land deals with the likes of Pritzker, Ziffren, Alex Louis Greenberg, and others.

At the Korshaks' fiftieth wedding anniversary party in August 1993, Bob Evans read a chapter on his consigliere from his forthcoming book, *The Kid Stays in the Picture*. All the Korshak regulars—the Broccolis, Wassermans, Tony Martins, and Dinah Shore*—were entertained by Evans's tales of the man he called The Myth.[16] The subsequent 1994 release of the autobiography, which avoided any mention of Korshak's long-standing relationship with the Outfit, reawoke journalist David Robb's interest in writing about Korshak. "When Evans's book came out and gave a bullshit story about who Sid Korshak was, I decided to write a story about who Sid Korshak *really* was," Robb recalled. Then working for the *Hollywood Reporter*, Robb soon experienced the sort of melodrama that always surrounded those attempting to interview Korshak's inner circle. "You'd be in a restaurant with them; whenever people would talk about Sid, they'd lower their voice when they mentioned his name." One family member who spoke to Robb decried the theory of him being ruled by the mob. "Sidney wasn't ruled by anybody but God," the relative said.

Ultimately, Robb sought out Korshak himself to hear his side of "the myth" legends. "I followed him around," remembered Robb. "I parked on Hillcrest and waited for him to come out—Bee was driving. I lost him on the street, then the car stopped at a mailbox. Just like a scene from a movie, I screeched up in front of him and parked in front of his car. 'Are you Sid Korshak?' Click, click, click—I snapped some pictures of him."

Robb said that Korshak looked at him as if he were a hit man, fifty years overdue, not surprising given what is now known about Korshak's furtive meetings with Sheriff Ralph Lamb and others. "When I said I was a reporter, he seemed relieved," said Robb. "I said, 'I'm doing a story about Bob Evans's book. Would you give me an interview?' Then came the classic Sid Korshak: 'Yeah, just call Bob's office and set it up.' Of course, when I called, nothing happened. Sid's specialty was 'Always say yes even when you mean no.' What do you lose by saying yes?"

---

*At the time, Shore was battling cancer, which would claim her soon thereafter. On February 24, 1994, two days after dining with Sid and Bee, Frances Rose "Dinah" Shore passed away in her Beverly Hills home at age seventy-six. (Kupcinet, *Chicago Sun-Times*, 2-25-94)

Korshak, captured on a Beverly Hills street in 1994 by labor reporter turned paparazzo David Robb (David Robb)

On August 19, Robb's story appeared, entitled EVANS PAINTS PICTURE OF KORSHAK AS "THE CONSIGLIERE." Initially, the piece described Evans's recounting of Korshak's power in the movie business, but then added much more about Korshak's Chicago Outfit connections, labor racketeering, Hoffa, and his naming by countless witnesses as the mob's man in Hollywood— something Evans has always denied. Like most other reporters who reported Korshak's history, Robb soon learned that Sidney's pals placed calls to his boss. Robb recently recalled, "After the story came out, [Greg] Bautzer told my editor, 'Dave Robb better be careful about what he says about Sid Korshak. If I ever see him, I'm going to punch him in the nose.' "[17]

With so many of its clientele—and owners—either dying or growing too old to hobnob, the Bistro closed its doors for the last time in November 1994.* "Its time had come and gone," owner Kurt Niklas wrote. "The days of evening gowns and jewels and black ties had almost become a memory." Niklas also had no energy to compete with the new hot spots such as Le Dome and L'Orangerie.

---

*The location now houses Mastro's Steakhouse.

As Sid Korshak's days also grew short, he remained no less of a sphinx, with opinions at odds as to his physical condition. Peter Bart had one impression: "In Sidney's final days, he still put on his dark suit every morning, walked into his den, and watched television," wrote Bart.[18] Kurt Niklas called him senile, and VP-turned-writer Dominick Dunne is firm that he saw a failing Korshak in a fragile state. "The last time I saw Sidney was at Freddie and Janet DeCordova's twenty-fifth wedding anniversary party at Chasen's," Dunne said. "I hadn't seen him in quite a few years. He was in a wheelchair and his voice was weak and raspy—I was shocked. He said to me, 'I am so proud of you. I read everything you write.' That was so nice coming from someone who they said was such a tough guy. But then again, he was always nice to me."[19]

But veteran television producer and close Korshak pal George Schlatter had a different take on Korshak's waning days. "We would go to breakfast with Sidney and Bernice and his granddaughter to Jerry's Deli on Sunday mornings," remembered Schlatter. "And he would pick up the paper and they'd walk around and it was great to see him. He was still a dynamic force field of energy. The last conversation I had with Sidney, he was on it. Not vague or anything. Colorful as it would be to see this powerful man reduced to whatever . . . the guy I saw was not that."[20] Another close friend agreed, saying that Dunne may have been confused with eighty-five-year-old Cubby Broccoli, who was wheelchair-bound after suffering a stroke after eight hours of cardiac surgery in July 1984; he also suffered permanent speech problems. "I saw Sidney just a week before his death and he appeared fine," said the friend, "dashing across the room at the Bistro Gardens. 'How's everything, buddy?' he said to me."[21] (Korshak's nuclear family, who could obviously clarify the situation, typically did not respond to requests for interviews.)

Former Korshak daughter-in-law Virginia Korshak remembered one aspect of the Korshaks' health regimen that likely remained in place until the end: his reliance on his personal physician, Dr. Rex Kennamer, a Beverly Hills cardiac internist who was also the longtime doctor to Frank Sinatra, Lew Wasserman, and countless other Hollywood elite.* "If Sidney needed

---

*At a Kennamer family reunion in Alabama in 1978, Rex Kennamer described his career thus: "Uniquely there are few MDs who have cared for more famous people than I have. I have run the gamut from the most famous of movie stars, politicians, writers, financiers, Pulitzer Prize winners, and Nobel Prize winners . . . I have been labeled one of America's superdoctors, and almost invariably I will be on the list of doctors that doctors themselves would go to as their physician." In 1997, the Wasserman Foundation Chair in Clinical Electrophysiology at Cedars-Sinai Medical Center was dedicated in honor of Kennamer. (*Variety,* 11-14-97)

something, he would call Rex, any time of the day or night," remembered Virginia. "They [Sid and Bee] were like little puppets. Every Sunday, Rex Kennamer would give Sidney and Bee vitamin B$_{12}$ shots."[22]

Whatever the truth of Korshak's health, he was without question too weak to endure the news he received on January 19, 1996, the day his beloved brother Marshall Korshak, age eighty-five, died at Chicago's Northwestern Memorial Hospital. Hailed by the *Chicago Tribune* as a "great political leader," Marshall's obituary made no reference to his infamous brother in Beverly Hills, but instead made a point of mentioning his friendship with the likes of the Kennedys, and that he was survived by Edith, his wife of sixty-one years, and two daughters.[23]

The very next day, less than twenty-four hours after getting the news, the Fixer himself died suddenly at home at age eighty-eight of "a cerebrovascular incident caused by generalized arteriosclerosis," from which he had suffered for the last ten years, according to his death certificate. It was Saturday, January 20, 1996. Considering brother Marshall's coincidental passing in Chicago one day before Sidney's, one wag offered, "It seemed natural that Sidney, eighty-eight, might have dispatched Marshall, eighty-five, to size up the next world for him, perhaps to set up negotiations for him with higher powers about safe passage into the hereafter." The same writer noted the legendary reticence of friends to talk on the record about the Fixer—even after his death. "I heard Sidney died," explained one jittery associate. "I didn't hear he was buried."[24]

In their official death notice, the family not only listed Bee, but referred to Sidney as "the devoted brother of Marshall . . . [and the] loving father of Harry, Stuart, and Kate." Of course, Kate was his granddaughter by Harry, whom Sid and Bee came to call their own daughter.

And the newspapers finally felt free to get it right. The *New York Times* headlined SIDNEY KORSHAK, 88, DIES; FABLED FIXER FOR THE CHICAGO MOB. And the *Los Angeles Times*: SIDNEY KORSHAK, ALLEGED MAFIA LIAISON TO HOLLYWOOD, DIES AT 88.*

Among the 150 in attendance at Korshak's private service at the Jewish Hillside Memorial Park were Barbara Sinatra, Robert Evans, Dani Janssen, Niki Bautzer, Tony Martin and Cyd Charisse, Angie Dickinson, Suzanne Pleshette, and Rona Barrett. "There were quite a few eulogies at his funeral," remembered the Bistro's Jimmy Murphy. "But Robert Evans was the guy that just wouldn't get off. He kept going on, and on, and on. He seemed

---

*Despite the headline, Korshak was still relatively below the radar for most Americans. Within days of Korshak's passing, Dave Robb knocked out a book proposal on him, but had no luck selling it. "The publishers said, 'Who's Sid Korshak?'" Robb remembered.

Korshak's final resting place,
Hillside Memorial Park
(author photo)

like he was on something. Finally somebody had to grab him and say, 'Look, Robert, we have to move on here.' "[25] After the service, Evans said, "There wasn't a day in thirty years we didn't spend an hour on the phone together. He treated me with the same respect from when I was a wannabe actor to when I ran Paramount. In life and in memory, he was the quintessential example of a friendship treasured."[26]

At Hillside, Korshak's remains joined (or would soon be joined by) those of many of his closest associates: Eugene Wyman, Paul Ziffren, Lew Wasserman, Taft Schreiber, Harvey Silbert, Mickey Cohen, Stanley Mosk, and David Janssen. However, even in death, only Sid Korshak succeeded in maintaining his invisibility. When the Hillside office was asked in 2005 to locate his crypt, it discovered that his entry had been deleted from their four-inch-thick directory—virtually all its other luminary "residents," such as Jack Benny, Moe Howard, Milton Berle, Al Jolson, and Eddie Cantor, were easily located in the book, but not the Myth. "That's odd," said the cemetery manager. "Everyone else seems to be here." Finally a nine-year-old document was retrieved that indicated the location of the simple crypt, located not far from friends such as Dinah Shore and Max Factor.

The complex dichotomy that was Sidney Korshak can be seen in the variant summaries of his life from those who knew him and those who pursued him. "They were two of the greatest men I've ever known," reflected Marshall's daughter Margie Gerson about her father and Sidney. "I adored them both. They were very different brothers, but yet they adored each other."[27] Paul Ziffren's son Kenneth said, "I knew Sidney well. Charming guy. You never felt fear around him."[28] Cousin Leslie Korshak told the *Los Angeles Times*, "He had a tremendous amount of power, and he understood the power of anonymity. He wore power the way the average guy wears a sweat suit. There's rich having money in the bank and there's rich knowing that you can get your hands on unlimited amounts of money just by asking, And he was both."[29] Gianni Russo said wistfully, "He was a mentor to me—to all of them—to the day he died. People would call him at home for advice. I know that for sure. And he liked being in it."[30] Paramount chief Frank Yablans said, "Sidney was in the mob, but the way a Jew was in the mob. They wanted him to handle Hollywood, the Teamsters, Las Vegas—but not to kill people in Hollywood."[31] Producer-friend George Schlatter opined, "The boys needed a lawyer. Sidney was a lawyer. And he came in and he handled things as a lawyer. Sidney did what lawyers do. There was never any threat of Sidney being disbarred. Everybody wanted to know Sidney and nobody did. A lot of people thought they did. Sidney was a very loud man in a very quiet way. He was a legend, and the legend was bigger than the man. Sidney built a hell of a reputation because he was very effective and very successful. The mob didn't 'make' Sidney Korshak. How would they make him?"[32] Nancy Czar concluded, "Everybody thought Sidney was backed up by the mob in Chicago, but it was a total illusion. He played it for all it was worth." Marty Bacow, a leading Teamster official in Hollywood, summed up Sidney Korshak's true power source, saying, "He couldn't make a move without getting permission [from the Chicago mob]. He was an order taker. And that was the end of it . . . Everybody *thought* he had power, so he had power."[33]

Among the many others who registered their opinions were:

• Jimmy "the Weasel" Fratianno, who described Korshak's life thus: "He made millions for Chicago . . . he's really burrowed in. He calls himself a labor relations expert, but he's really a fixer."

• Bob Evans: "He was known as the Myth, from the [Palm Springs] Racquet Club to the '21' Club in New York. Many said they knew [Korshak], but few actually did. One thing was for sure, he was one powerful motherfucker."

• A 1965 FBI informant: "He is one of the biggest guys in the country today who has a pipeline right to the government in Washington."

• United Artists executive Max Youngstein: "The few times I worked with Sidney Korshak, I knew what he was doing, I knew who he was doing it with, but somehow he carried it off with a kind of grace. He could never do anything in a straight line, but he could always handle the curves. He was like some fat guy who turns out to be the best dancer in the world."

Not surprisingly, Korshak's law enforcement and journalistic opponents had a different view:

• Network reporter Brian Ross takes Schlatter's point about Sidney's "legend" status, saying, "I think ninety-five percent of what organized crime does is based on their reputation. They don't have to reprove it every time. You would never know how much was a con and how much was real."

• Chicago FBI man Bill Roemer, who, over his thirty-year career, tried repeatedly to trip Korshak up, remembered Korshak as "the primary link between big business and organized crime."[34]

• G. Robert Blakey, who was a senior Justice Department Organized Crime attorney, said, "His life was one of living in a minefield and never stepping on anything."

• Los Angeles FBI agent Mike Wacks remembered, "The younger agents coming in and the people who worked OC viewed him as an old fossil or something that really didn't have any clout. But he did. He had clout all the way until his death. He was active until the day he died. He's an amazing character."[35]

• Connie Carlson, of the Attorney General's Office in California, concluded, "I subscribe to the theory that he was created by the mob. He may have done other things along the way, but he never escaped his relationship with the mob. He could settle in any kind of labor dispute. That's where you see the mob influence. And it wasn't L.A., it was the Beverly Hills crowd— movie people and lawyers—and Korshak was the king of the pen in Beverly Hills." Carlson, like so many of her peers, was ultimately frustrated that the Supermob could never be brought to justice. "I got as far away from L.A. as I could and not be in northern Mexico," she said recently. "Everyone who was involved in these investigations tried to get as far away as we could to forget about it."

• The famously terse Sy Hersh said, "He was the godfather. There's no question, he ordered people hit."[36]

Sidney Korshak said of himself during an FBI interview, most likely in reference to his infamous friends, "I won't back away from anyone or repudiate anybody."[37]

Whatever he was, most agree on one point: he could not exist today. Korshak came up at a unique moment in American history, when the Chicago Outfit held a stranglehold over a huge segment of U.S. labor. Donald Cressey, consultant to the President's Commission on Violence, summarized the era by saying, "The penetration of business and government by organized crime had been so complete that it was no longer possible to differentiate 'underworld' gangsters from 'upperworld' businessmen and government officials."[38] Thus, Korshak was a necessary link for corporate sachems who wished to guarantee their stockholders' investments. "I don't think you could do that today," said former *Los Angeles Times* national editor Ed Guthman, "and

I don't think anybody replaced him. If they tried, it didn't work."[39] Screenwriter-friend Tom Mankiewicz agreed, saying, "With the changing of our culture, I'm not sure a guy like Sidney could exist today."[40]

As one might expect, Korshak's estate was hidden behind one of those impenetrable family trusts, preferred by many of the upper class, including the Supermob. Thus a tally of his full worth is impossible, but it is known that he had vast investments around the country, if not the world. His personal property alone (homes, artwork, cars, etc.) was assumed to be worth many millions.

Korshak's elder son, Harry, a former producer for Paramount, is now an architect married to the half sister of Mrs. Conrad Hilton Jr., and living in Egypt and Palm Beach, Florida; Korshak's younger son, Stuart, is a successful California attorney, specializing in (what else) labor collective bargaining. One professional bio said of Stuart Korshak, "He specializes in creative and proactive labor management programs where he is generally successful in having the clients' unions work cooperatively with the client to resolve their mutual concerns instead of engaging in litigation or confrontation."* In 1999, Stuart Korshak negotiated a historic settlement between California liquor wholesalers and their twenty-two hundred Teamster employees and helped settle a major dispute between fourteen San Francisco hotels and the infamous Hotel and Restaurant Employees Union. Obviously, the acorn stayed near the tree.

There is no information in his father's FBI file as to whether the Bureau is investigating the allegations of Stuart's firm's alleged money laundering via West Germany.

One week after Korshak's death, the Bistro Gardens announced its closing, coinciding with the retirement of Kurt Niklas.[41] The era was fading fast, as Pat Brown died of a heart attack one month later, on February 16, 1996, in Beverly Hills. On June 26, 1996, eighty-seven-year-old Cubby Broccoli joined his friends in the afterlife. On May 14, 1998, "The Chairman" himself, Frank Sinatra, died in his Beverly Hills home. Holding vigil in the Sinatra home on

---

*His firm, Korshak, Kracoff, Kong and Sugano, has represented clients that would have made Sidney proud, among them Fairmont Hotels of San Francisco, Seagram's, Southern Wine and Spirits of Nevada, Chicago Wines, the Los Angeles Dodgers, Los Angeles Hotel Council, Pacific Gas & Electric, and Union Bank.

Foothills Drive were Steve and Eydie Lawrence, George and Jolene Schlatter, and Bee Korshak.[42]

The Supermob's Chicago contingent was similarly unraveling. Burt Kanter, the man who had devised so many tax dodges for the Pritzkers and other cadre associates, died of cancer on October 31, 2001, while awaiting sentencing on a finding that he had defrauded the IRS.

In 1994, after spending years unraveling the Kanter-Pritzker Prudential insurance kickback scheme, the IRS had finally brought the case to trial. It took the judge five years to rule, due to the complexity of the case, that the companies created under Prudential were merely tax-avoidance vehicles. Judge Couvillion concluded that Kanter and associates had devised a scheme of kickbacks to avoid paying taxes to the federal government.[43] (By his own admission, Kanter had paid no taxes between 1979 and 1990, although he was audited for each of those years.)

In December 1999, the special trial judge for the U.S. Tax Court delivered a three-hundred-plus-page decision against Kanter, which stated in a section entitled "Kanter's Fraud," "In our view, what we have here, purely and simply, is a concerted effort by experienced tax lawyer . . . to defeat and evade the payment and to cover up their illegal acts so that the corporations, Prudential and Travelers, and the Federal Government would be unable to discover them . . . Kanter created a complex money laundering scheme made up of sham corporations and entities . . . to receive, distribute, and conceal his income, as well as [the other defendants'] income."

After more years of legal stalls, it appeared that Kanter was about to "go away," when the grim reaper intervened. *Variety* announced his passing with a blindly hagiographic obituary, calling the 71-year-old an "art patron, preeminent tax attorney and movie finance innovator." No mention was made of his mountain of legal woes stemming from his lifelong quest to evade taxes for himself and his clients through offshore dodges such as Castle Bank.*

As for the Pritzkers, over the last quarter century the family business had partnered with the infamous Bank of Credit and Commerce International (BCCI) in developing Hyatt hotels in Saudi Arabia.[44] BCCI, a Pakistani-based bank, was known for laundering drug-cartel money, providing financial havens for terrorist organizations, helping corporations dodge taxes through an impenetrable web of holding companies, and falsifying bank records to throw off regulators. BCCI's founder, Agha Abedi, once boldly

---

*Through the offshore-bank gambit and the questionable use of tax shelters, Kanter provided cofinancing for such films as *One Flew Over the Cuckoo's Nest*, *The Longest Yard*, *Papillon*, *Urban Cowboy*, *The Pedestrian*, and *The Rocky Horror Picture Show*.

informed a BCCI executive, "The only laws that are permanent are the laws of nature. Everything else is flexible. We can always work in and around the law."[45] Former CIA director Robert Gates referred to BCCI as "the Bank of Crooks and Criminals."

By 2001, the Pritzker family's holdings would be worth over $15 billion and included not only the Hyatt chain of hotels but a share in Royal Caribbean Cruises, as well as a credit-reporting company, TransUnion, and numerous other lucrative enterprises. Over the years, hundreds of companies have been bought and sold by the dynasty.

On December 11, 2001, the Pritzkers agreed to pay the U.S. government a record fine of $460 million for the collapse of the Superior Bank of New York. It is widely believed that the cause of the bank failure was the fraudulent sales of junk bonds. The massive settlement allowed the Pritzkers to escape from having the actual charges aired publicly, and as the Pritzkers said, they hoped the agreement would also prevent their reputation from being further tarnished.[46] Penny Pritzker dealt with the collapse of the bank, saying, "My family is not going to litigate with the federal government at a time like this," referring to the September 11, 2001, terrorist attacks.[47]

In 2003, Abe Pritzker's granddaughter nineteen-year-old actress Liesel Pritzker (*Air Force One*) and her brother, Matthew, sued their father, Robert, for $6 billion for "looting" their trust fund. The siblings alleged that their father had wrongly emptied their funds, worth roughly $2 billion, in the mid-1990s when he was having postdivorce squabbles with their mother. In April 2004, the judge instructed the plaintiffs to refile after granting them access to the family's sealed financial records, a motion that unearthed a secret family deal cut after Liesel's uncle Jay Pritzker's death in 1999, a plan that would have broken up the fortune into eleven shares valued at $1.4 billion each. In early 2005, rather than expose the complicated Pritzker offshore shelters to the light of day, the Pritzker family put the final touches on a private settlement agreement that would pay the two youngest grandchildren of A. N. Pritzker in the neighborhood of $500 million each to drop all litigation against the Chicago clan. Now Liesel can afford to be a producer as well as an actress.

Like so many of the Supermob who increased their wealth with offshore tax dodges, the Pritzkers attempted to balance their reputation with philanthropy, the clique's way of saying that they'd rather choose where their money goes than allowing the IRS to do it. To that end, the Pritzkers have donated more than $500 million to institutions and charities, not only in Chicago but around the country. On June 5, 2002, they donated $30 million to the University of Chicago to celebrate the anniversary of the 1902 founding of the law firm by Nicholas Pritzker.[48] But the philanthropy failed to mute the long-overdue reappraisals of the clan. "The Pritzkers have had a pristine and exceptionally respected reputation in Chicago and throughout the nation and the world," said Craig Aronoff, cofounder and principal of the Family Business Consulting Group. "All that's gone on has presented the family in a different light, one that is not as flattering."[49]

On June 3, 2002, weeks after suffering a stroke, Lew Wasserman died at his Beverly Hills home at age eighty-nine. THE HOLLYWOOD MOGUL AND KING-MAKER DIES AT 89 ran the *Los Angeles Times* headline the next day. Former president Bill Clinton, whose candidacy had been aided by Wasserman's fund-raising efforts, remarked at Wasserman's memorial tribute six weeks later, "He was one of the smartest men I ever met, and in more than intellectual ways. He just came across as someone who understood what life was all about and was pulling for people to have good lives." Recalling the Clinton fund-raisers at the Wasserman home, he added, "Lew helped me become president, and he helped me stay president. He helped me become a better president, and he never asked for anything."* Steven Spielberg, whose career was nurtured by Wasserman, said, "For decades he was the chief justice of the film industry—fair, tough-minded, and innovative. I feel that all of us have lost our benevolent godfather."†,[50]

As a philanthropist, Wasserman had donated much to the $40 million Edie and Lew Wasserman Eye Research Center, part of the Jules Stein Eye Institute complex at UCLA.

When documentary filmmaker Barry Avrich began work in 2004 on a profile of Wasserman,** Universal Pictures refused to cooperate, and Lew's grandson Casey Wasserman confirmed that the family had asked Universal not to assist the filmmaker. "It is a family policy to turn down all requests regarding my grandfather without exception," young Wasserman said. "We have not or will not participate in any historical portrayal of his life in any form."[51] Casey Wasserman, who runs the Wasserman Media Group, which spans five firms working in production, management, music, and marketing

---

*In 1995, Clinton awarded Wasserman the Presidential Medal of Freedom, the country's highest civilian honor.
†In addition to preventing Spielberg from being fired from his first Universal assignment, Wasserman released such Spielberg hits as *Jaws, Jurassic Park, E.T. the Extra-Terrestrial*, and *Schindler's List*.
**The Last Mogul: Life and Times of Lew Wasserman.*

as well as owning the Los Angeles Avengers of the Arena Football League, had recently married Ken Ziffren's daughter Laura, the senior VP of Fox Music.

In recent years, Lew Wasserman had overseen the November 1989 selling of MCA/Universal to the Japanese version of Gulf & Western, Matsushita Electric, for $6.13 billion. It was the beginning of an era of massive corporate takeovers and conglomerate-building, and the initial players in the feeding frenzy were the Japanese, whose strong yen was facilitating massive U.S. buyouts, such as Sony's $4.7 billion purchase of Columbia Pictures two months earlier. It later came out that Wasserman had obtained a secret $350 million fee—tax-free—from Matsushita for his MCA shares, an arrangement that saved him $100 million.[52] When the Japanese economy experienced its own "correction" in the nineties, Matsushita sold MCA/Universal to Seagram heir Edgar Bronfman in April 1995 for $5.7 billion; the Canadian Ashkenazic Bronfmans made their fortune during Prohibition by illegally shipping their whiskey across the U.S. border (by truck and underground pipelines) into the organizations of Abner "Longy" Zwillman and Frank Costello.[53]

Five years later, the company would change hands yet again, this time coming under the umbrella of the French multinational Vivendi. Most recently, in April 2004, Vivendi merged with NBC's parent company, GE, to form NBC-Universal. The resulting media giant now boasts television networks NBC, Telemundo, USA Network, Sci-Fi Channel, Bravo, Trio, CNBC, and MSNBC (jointly owned with Microsoft); film studio Universal Pictures; television production studios Universal Television and NBC Studios; a stations group comprising twenty-nine NBC and Telemundo television stations; and interests in five theme parks including Universal Studios Hollywood and Universal Orlando. NBC was a fitting home for the company that it had sought to protect from the probings of Brian Ross and Ira Silverman in 1978.

Like Korshak, Wasserman is universally perceived as a man unique to his era, a time when a patriarchal movie studio system made possible the ascent of the solitary visionary. With today's multinational studios run by stock-conscious boards, the emergence of another Lew is highly unlikely. "There won't be anyone like Lew Wasserman again because these companies are too big," Robert Daly, former head of Warner Brothers, said in 2002. "It was an industry town and totally controlled by the studios and the networks. He was the number one guy at the networks and the number one guy in Washington for the industry." Haim Saban, owner of the *Power Rangers* franchise, added, "We are no longer led by patriarchs. One father figure could have more influence than the whole of [media conglomerate] AOL Time Warner in the Hollywood of Wasserman."[54]

Sid Korshak's Lawndale pal and frequent Pump Room Table One companion, ninety-one-year-old Irv "Mr. Chicago" Kupcinet, died on November 10, 2003, having filed his most recent *Sun-Times* column just a week earlier. Also the son of Russian Jewish immigrants, Kup had amassed fifteen Emmy Awards for his late-night television show, and one Peabody Award for his column. A tireless supporter of Jewish charities, Kup spent much of his adult life in a grief-laden shadow after the 1963 murder of his daughter, Karyn.

On June 5, 2004, Ronald Reagan died of pneumonia and complications from Alzheimer's disease. He was ninety-three. His grieving widow oversaw a weeklong bicoastal media orgy that eclipsed the funerals of John F. Kennedy, Martin Luther King Jr., Robert Kennedy, and Abraham Lincoln. His admirers eulogized him for his supposed role in the defeat of Communism, while his critics continued to question whether he had ever been anything more than an actor, taking direction from others.

The Final Word

Their apologists assert that no proof can be found of Supermob lawbreaking. Pointedly, Sid Korshak was never convicted of so much as a parking violation. But the truth is Korshak and company constantly bent, folded, mutilated, and—yes—broke the law. In their continual aiding and abetting of traditional mob enterprises, such as Korshak's advising of the skim masters in Vegas, and cutting secret Teamster sweetheart contracts, or committing white-collar offenses such as stock fraud, Lew Wasserman's MCA collusions with Ronald Reagan, and Paul Ziffren's and David Bazelon's assistance in fronting for the Outfit's California investments, a case could be made that the Supermob violated the RICO racketeering statutes by operating an ongoing criminal enterprise.

Without doubt, Sid Korshak played the most dangerous game of all his fellows, staying in continuous contact with hoodlums who *were* on law enforcement's radar, while negotiating that tightrope by the judicious parceling out of information to the FBI. But thanks to early canny decisions to align itself with key judges and politicians—both local and national—the Supermob rendered its members untouchable. Furthermore, many well-intentioned investigators were frustrated by legal restraints: thanks to their law degrees, the protégés Jake Arvey inspired shielded their nonstop RICO violations behind the "attorney-client" privilege. And by paying just enough to the IRS and relocating to mob-friendly California, where residents' pre-histories are historically erased, the Supermob further insulated itself from prosecution.

Technical lawbreaking aside, what is perhaps most disturbing is the ethi-cally bankrupt philosophy that saw the Supermob and its commercial enter-prises dodge billions in taxes using offshore shelters in places like the Bahamas and the Netherlands. In that sense, their actions can be viewed as nonpatriotic, if not anti-American. After acquiring the land of Japanese in-ternees at the same time that the Nazis were similarly victimizing their own kin in Europe, the Supermob associates assuaged their consciences by do-nating a small fraction of their lucre to Jewish hospitals and other Jewish causes. Whereas Joe Six-pack had to pay his fair share to the nation's infra-structure, the Supermob declared that it alone could choose where its money would be allocated.

What they left behind is a legacy, or a dirty secret, that is virtually taboo for polite discussion, for it implies a country that has evolved into a plutoc-racy that allows a certain segment to be perpetually above the law and supremely entitled. What the lawyers from Lawndale pioneered has now vir-tually been codified in arcane tax laws and lobbying and PAC loopholes, cre-ating a society within a society. The Supermob's invention has now become a part of the American fabric, where, ironically, the most unpatriotic Amer-icans are given free rein to ridicule the country's tax collectors while the less privileged fight their overseas oil wars.

Perhaps the most cogent characterization of the Supermob and its legacy came from Jimmy Fratianno, the lifelong hood who bumped up against his insulated counterparts regularly, although their immunity failed to transfer to him. In his authorized biography, *The Last Mafioso*, Fratianno discussed with Johnny Rosselli a cadre he obviously envied:

> You've got to give the Jews credit. They started out as fronts for the Italians, and now they've got millions they made through Italians. They were smart and declared some of that money to the government. See, a Jew makes a million, he declares two, three hundred grand. A fucking Italian makes a million, he declares ten grand. The Jews in Cleveland—Dalitz, Kleinman, Rhody—they were running all them gambling joints and they tell the Ital-ians they've got to put so much money aside for taxes. That's how guys like Dalitz got wealthy and respectable. That's why they can invest in Vegas.
>
> Now look at the Italians. They stash their money. They can't invest it without going through fucking fronts. Them Italians in Cleveland made

millions and what good is it? They live like peasants. Everything's under the table. Even when they die, their heirs got to hide the money.[55]

It is a stark contrast to the fortunes of the descendants of the Supermob. Kenneth Ziffren, Stuart Korshak, Casey Wasserman and Laura Ziffren Wasserman, and the numerous Pritzker and Hilton heirs are all revered as legitimate movers and shakers in twenty-first-century America. Their ascendance is an unintentional nod to the Gabrielino Indians, who inhabited Beverly Hills for centuries before the Russians and Europeans invoked Manifest Destiny, and who also traditionally passed their power and authority on to their sons.[56] The offshore dodges so brilliantly concocted by many of the new titans' parents are now also de facto legitimized, should the new generation ever wish to avail themselves. And should they choose to do so, they would likely receive as little scrutiny from the city's newspaper of record as did their parents. Interestingly, by 2005, Southern Californians were referring to the paper as the *Chicago Los Angeles Times*, in sarcastic reference to the *Chicago Tribune*'s purchase of the L.A. paper in 2000. However, few appreciated that the moniker was long overdue, given the *Times*' anemic coverage of Chicago's Supermob over the previous sixty years.

Acknowledgments

As with any book of this scope, *Supermob* owes its existence in no small degree to the work of predecessors, in this case a dedicated group of gadfly
journalists who for decades strove to call attention to the vaporous world of
Sid Korshak and company. Among those deserving special kudos for their
exceptional reportage are: Lester Velie, Jack Anderson, Ovid Demaris, Ed
Reid, Art White, Robert Goe, Jack Tobin, Sandy Smith, W. Scott Malone,
Dan "The Bat" Moldea, Dick Brenneman, Dennis McDougal, Ira Silverman, Sy Hersh, Jeff Gerth, Denny Walsh, Dave Robb, Alan Block, and Constance Weaver, every survivor of which helped guide me through the
quagmire, often digging out long-stored-away files for my use. In this regard, special thanks go to Moldea, McDougal, and Robb, who unselfishly
loaned me their voluminous files.

Additional colleagues who made meaningful contributions include Jim
Grady, Bill Thomas, David Ashenfelter, Don Barlett, Tony and Robbyn
Summers, Connie Bruck, Carol Felsenthal, and Julie Payne. A very busy
Garry Trudeau made time to dig out his old Korshak file and send it to me,
and the iconic network investigative producer Ira Silverman took me into
his confidence during numerous lunches at D.C.'s Woodside Deli.

Once again, I was fortunate to benefit from the graphic expertise of a
great friend, Steve Parke of What?design. Regrettably, the reader will never
know the extent of Steve's brilliant and subtle touch in rescuing many dam-
aged photographs.

Invaluable institutional help came from many quarters: At the Library of
Congress's Legislative Archives, Matt Fulghum and Bill Davis always responded promptly to my many requests; likewise, Steve Tilley, Martha Wagner Murphy, Marty McGann, and Fred Romanski opened many new files at
the National Archives in College Park, Maryland; Jeanette Callaway and
Lee Lyons gathered reams of documents (and trusted me with the keys

to the legendary storage basement) at the Chicago Crime Commission, a national treasure of organized crime history; Joe Eagan, Doug Adolphsen, and the staff of Baltimore's Enoch Pratt Library were, as always, cheerfully helpful; at the Spertus Institute in the Chicago Jewish Archives, reference librarian Dan Sharon and director Joy Kingsolver made countless great research suggestions; Doug Moe, columnist for the *Capital Times* of Madison, Wisconsin, provided details of Korshak's undergraduate years, as did David Null of the University of Wisconsin Alumni Association; Norman Schwartz of the Chicago Jewish Historical Society contributed files and interview suggestions; Chris Driggs of the Nevada state archives conducted file searches on key Las Vegas players; and Gloria Ralph McKissic of the FBI's Freedom of Information section helped deliver on my numerous requests for file openings.

We gypsy journalists are often at the mercy of friends made on the road, kindred spirits who open local doors for us, introduce us around, feed us, and sometimes offer their guest rooms. In Vegas, Ed Becker, Hal Rothman, Eve and Ted Quillin, and John Neeland were among the most gracious. In Chicago, I was welcomed by informed friends such as Jim Agnew, Andy Kolis, Bob McDonnell and Antoinette Giancana, Roy Suzuki, Joe Marchetti, Julius Draznin, Jim Johnsen, Michael Glass and Marie Beckman, and Rich and Judy Lynn Samuels. As always, great friend Jack Clarke made time to give countless suggestions, even while dealing with serious health issues.

In Los Angeles, the friendship and encouragement of Jeff Silberman, Steve Molton and Pamela Galvin, Bob Harris, John Leekley, and Lynn Hendee made the City of Angels feel like it actually deserves its nickname. In Pioneertown, Pappy & Harriett's provided a great space to kick up my heels, tie up my horse (right), while staring at desert stars and pondering the cosmic relationship between Sid Korshak and Gram Parsons.

Other pals hither and yon who were always available included Laurence Leamer, Captain Alberto Miller, Dan Smith, Steve and Janet Nugent, Kevin Perkins, John and Ellen Bollinger, and the late Mike Corbitt. The Russo extended and nuclear families are a constant source of love, support, and lasagna.

Freelancers such as myself, accustomed to occasional periods of professional inactivity (aka poverty), have a habit of never turning down work, often taking on multiple projects in anticipation of future periods of drought. As fate would have it, when this daunting project began in early 2003, I simultaneously found myself pulled in six directions at once: writing this book, reporting and/or cowriting two ninety-minute investigative news documentaries, cowriting a book with goodfella Henry Hill, developing a complex motion picture script, and writing a book proposal for actor Vin

Diesel. Each of these projects was so appealing that I decided to do them all—obviously I would need some help. Thus, for the first time, I reached out to the local schools to see if anyone wanted to help with the smothering workload. It was a delegating move that initially frightened me, but it turned out to have been something I should have done years ago.

Before the first intern came aboard, I was already receiving documents and guidance from Beverly Hills native Sara Stanfill. Sara's insider knowledge of the social connections of the Hollywood power elite was crucial to starting this book research with the proper mind-set. The first student intern to come to my rescue was Towson University's Justin Smulison, whose energy, wit, and intelligence were priceless. Justin brought aboard three of his journalism classmates, Rachel Kneppar, Jason DuPont, and Chris Blackmon, to help transcribe over 150 interviews. Their work was meticulous and timely.

From the University of Maryland came the invaluable assistance of Claire Patterson, Jason Rivlin, and Frank "Nitti" Butcher. Claire took on the thankless task of reading and creating database summaries of the thousands of records and news articles I was obtaining (some twenty crates of material). After Claire's graduation, Jason completed the databasing chores (and some house- and dog-sitting), before Nitti showed up to make frequent trips to the Library of Congress, where he surveyed ancient newspaper microfilm and photo holdings. When time came to archive the material, Jonathan Scott Fuqua, a local friend and writing colleague of renown, introduced me to Emily Moy and Zack Wilson, two of his standout creative writing students at Baltimore's Carver School, a magnet high school for the city's best students. Emily and Zack went file by file to create an Excel spreadsheet that was critical to sourcing. To all of these volunteer assistants, I give a huge thanks. This book, and the other projects completed during this hectic period, would have been impossible without them. I hope I can open some doors for you in the future.

No investigative book could exist without the cooperation of knowledgeable people who agree to give interviews, even those who speak only on background. I appreciate my interviewees' faith that I would not take their quotes out of context, or, in some cases, betray their anonymity. I hope they are happy with the final result.

Thanks again to Noah Lukeman, who worked hard to find a home for *Supermob*, and, as a literary agent who truly cares about his authors, negotiated a sterling contract. At Bloomsbury, I am beholden to publisher Karen Rinaldi for showing continued faith in my work; managing editor Greg Villepique; copy editor Steven Boldt; indexer Judith Hancock; Panio

Gianopoulos, who contributed an informed and brilliant line edit; as well as Amanda Katz and Yelena Gitlin, both of whom I want to thank in advance for turning *Supermob* into a best-selling, prize-winning epic with the global impact of *The Da Vinci Code* and the Bible combined.

Supplying the all-important background music this time around were Brian Wilson, Count Basie, Richie Furay, Kate Bush, Django Reinhardt, Mark O'Connor's Hot Swing Trio, Donald Fagen, Stevie Wonder, Dan Hicks, Shirley Horn, Matt Bianco, and Dean Martin.

Deepest thanks of all go to Scout and Mrs. Teasdale, steadfast companions I was honored to know.

Finally, a very special thanks goes to anyone I've forgotten. I hope you'll understand—I'm really exhausted.

Appendix A: Supermob Investments

Following is a partial list of properties taken over by Korshak's Chicago friends, often with underworld financial partners such as Arthur Greene (fronting for Guzik and Capone) and Alex Greenberg (fronting for Frank Nitti), and often associating with one of Korshak's oldest friends, Paul Ziffren. The record searches were largely undertaken by Robert Goe and Art White (see text). This list does not include the hundreds of properties taken from German owners and the Japanese nisei who were interned during World War II. Nor does it include the many thousands of acres of undeveloped land in Southern California obtained by the Chicago group.

California

Al Hart's City National Bank of Beverly Hills
Bel-Air Hotel, Los Angeles
Beverly Wilshire Hotel, Beverly Hills
Hyatt House (Sunset Strip), West Hollywood
Hilton Hotel, Beverly Hills
Hilton Hotel, Los Angeles
Sunset Towers, Los Angeles
Plaza Hotel, Los Angeles
San Diego Hotel
U. S. Grant Hotel, San Diego
Manor House, San Diego
Del Mar Hotel, San Diego
Morris Hotel, Los Angeles
California Hotel, Los Angeles
Asbury Apartments, Los Angeles
Wyvernwood Apartments, Los Angeles
Hotel Hayward, Los Angeles
Rosslyn Hotel, Los Angeles
Lafayette Hotel, Long Beach
Wilton Hotel, Long Beach
Clark Hotel, Los Angeles
Breakers Hotel, Long Beach
Ocean House, Santa Monica
Normandie Club, Gardena
Buena Park Motel, Los Angeles
Hollywood Hotel, Los Angeles
Melody Lane Restaurants, Los Angeles

Clock Restaurants, Los Angeles
Garden Land Company, Los Angeles (consisting of over 3,000 acres in West L.A.)
Sand and Sea Club, Los Angeles
Emery Ranch, Buena Park
Spreckles Building, Los Angeles
Broadway Arcade Building, Los Angeles
Los Angeles Warehouse, Los Angeles
Lakewood Rancho Land Company, Orange County
Northrop Building, Beverly Hills
Brighton Building Annex, Beverly Hills
Normandie Hotel, Los Angeles
Davies Warehouse, Los Angeles
Arrowhead Springs Hotel, San Bernardino
Entire block on E Street, San Bernardino
Padre Hotel, Bakersfield
Sands Hotel, Bakersfield
Hacienda Motels, Bakersfield
Californian Hotel, Fresno
Taft Hotel, Taft
El Camino Hotel, King City
Fairmont Hotel, San Francisco
Pickwick Hotel, San Francisco
Bright-Holland Ranch, Lassen County (300,000 acres)
Hotel Senator, Sacramento
Hacienda Motel, Indio

Nevada

(In addition to the Chicago underworld's well-known Las Vegas holdings in The Flamingo, Stardust, Desert Inn, Riviera, and Tropicana)

Mapes Hotel, Reno
Riverside Hotel, Reno
El Rancho Hotel and Casino, Las Vegas
Sands Hotel and Casino, Las Vegas
Gay Nineties Hotel, Las Vegas
Las Vegas Club, Las Vegas
Frontier Club, Las Vegas
La Rue's, Las Vegas

Colorado

Tabor Building

Chicago

Conrad Hilton (later Stevens, and still later The Hilton)
Drake Hotel
Palmer House
Seneca Hotel and Suites
Blackstone Hotel
Congree Hotel
Borg-Warner Building

DuSable Hotel
New Pershing Hotel
Sherman Hotel
Vernon Country Club
State and Madison Building
Edmund Theaters
Ken Theaters
Westminster Building

Hotels and Properties Elsewhere

Nacional Hotel and Casino, Havana, Cuba
Warwick Hotel, Philadelphia
Willard Hotel, Washington, D.C.
Warwick Hotel, NYC
Gotham Hotel, NYC
Hampshire House, NYC
Hilton Hotel, NYC
Sherry Netherland Hotel, NYC
Deshler-Wallich-Hilton, Columbus, OH
Neil House, Columbus, OH
Hollenden Hotel, Cleveland
Roadside Hotel, Lansing, MI
Mississippi Valley Trust Building, St. Louis
General Mills Building, Minneapolis
Meridian Hill Hotel, Washington, D.C.
Carver Hotel, Washington, D.C.
David Janis Hall, Washington, D.C.
Aquila Court Building, Omaha
Park Shelton, Detroit
Spencer Hotel, Marion, IN
Bel-Air Hotel, Belleair, FL
El Panama Hotel and Casino, Republic of Panama

Sources

1. County grantee-grantor records in California, Arizona, Colorado, Iowa, Illinois, and Ohio.
2. Probate records in California, Arizona, Colorado, Iowa, Illinois, and Ohio.
3. Kefauver Committee reports.
4. Chicago Crime Commission files.
5. Archives of *New York Daily News, Chicago Daily News,* and *Chicago Tribune.*
6. Dun & Bradstreet reports.
7. LAPD Intelligence Division files.
8. California State Corporation Commission.
9. California Secretary of State records.
10. Reports of the 1952 "Chelf Committee," U.S. House of Representatives, Committee on the Judiciary.

Appendix B: Pritzker Holdings

Following is a partial list of Pritzker holding companies (as of 1982), subsidiaries, affiliates, plus corporations in which the Pritzkers own large shares of voting power, compiled by Knut Royce for the *Kansas City Times* (3-8-82) from filings with the Securities and Exchange Commission, Standard & Poor's, and the New Jersey Division of Gaming Enforcement.* Subsidiaries of subsidiaries are indented.

HG Inc.

(HG Inc., according to New Jersey gaming division documents, is a holding company for all the common stock of the Hyatt Corp. and of several subsidiaries.)

Hyatt Corp.

HCB Corp.

   W.P. Equities

   Stamford Equities Corp.

Refco-Properties Inc.

   Hyatt Development Corp.

Hyatt Minneapolis Corp.

Hyatt Greenville Corp.

Oasis Development Corp.

Hyatt Columbus Corp.

BRC Corp.

Hyatt Milwaukee Corp.

Hyatt San Diego Corp.

Rosemont Purchasing Co.

Hyatt Crystal City Corp.

West Palm Hotel Inc.

Hyatt Flint Corp.

Hyatt Long Beach Corp.

FMG Inc.

   Hyatt Management Corp. of New York Inc.

   Texas Facility Management Inc.

   Florida Facility Management Inc.

   Facility Management Inc. of Maryland

---

*Data concerning voting power and subsidiaries may have changed since the filings with Standard & Poor's, the SEC, and the New Jersey Division of Gaming Enforcement.

Facility Management Inc. of Illinois
Facility Management Inc. of California
Facility Management Inc. of Southern California
Hyatt Management Corp.
HT-Operating Corp.
HMC Management Corp.
Facility Enterprises Inc.
HCG Corp.
HCN Corp.
HCQ Corp.
HCV Corp.
HT-Boston Inc.
HT-Nami Inc.
HT-Houston North Belt Inc.
Hyatt Galleria Inc.
Hyatt Resorts Management Corp.
Refco Marine Services Inc.
Two-Two-Three Corp.

Hyatt Corp.

(Source: New Jersey Gaming Division)
California Hyatt Corp.
Hyatt Wilshire Corp.
Edgewater Hyatt Corp.
Hyatt Del Monte Corp.
S.C. Hyatt Corp.
Hyatt Des Moines Corp.
Thruway Hyatt Corp.
Hyatt Furnishings Corp.
Riviera Hyatt Corp.
Hyatt Hotels Corp.
Hyatt Hotels Corp. of Maryland
Northridge Industries Inc.
Tradewinds Hyatt Lodge-Fresno Inc.
Tradewinds Restaurant-Fresno Inc.
Two-Two-One Corp.
Two-Two-Four Corp.
Two-Three-Six Corp.
Beef N'Barrel–Palo Alto Inc.
LTT Properties
JTD Corp.
HCC Corp.
Dallas Regency Corp.
Hyatt Tahoe Management Corp.
Hyatt Regency Corp.
Regency Houston Corp.
Tudor California Corp.
HC Airlease Inc.
Hyatt on Wells Corp.

Marmon Group Inc.

(Source: Standard & Poor's)

 American Safety Equipment Corp.
 Cerro Copper Products Co.
 Cerro Copper Tube Co.
 Cerro Sales Corp.
 Cerro International S.A.
 Cerro Mining Co. of Canada Ltd.
 Fetterolf Coal & Construction Inc.
  M.F. Fetterolf Coal Co. Inc.
  M.F. Land Co. Inc.
 RegO Group Inc.
  RegO Co.
 Marmon Co.
 Marmon Group Ltd.
 Marmon Group Inc. (Michigan)
  Marmon-Keystone Corp.
  Marmon Group of Canada Inc.
 Hammond Corp.
 Behring Corp. (66%)

RegO Group

(89.6% owned)

(Source: Standard & Poor's)

 4201 W. Peterson Corp. Co.

GL Corp.

(GL Corp., according to Standard & Poor's, is the parent company of Marmon Group Inc.)

(Source: 1979 filing with SEC)

 Accutronics Inc.
 Accutronics, Wisconsin, Inc.
 Amarillo Gear Co.
 Ankh Insurance Co.
 Bay Meadows Inc.
 Bintwerp Inc.
 Boca Housing Inc.
 Boykin Enterprises Inc.
 Broward Estates Inc.
 The Communities Group Inc. of Broward County
 Downtown Management Co.
 Film Properties Inc.
 Gibbs Manufacturing & Research Corp.
 Halmac Inc.
 Hammond Corp.
 Hammond Organ Corp.
 Hammond Organ Western Export Corp.
 Hammond Service Centers Inc.
 James Foundry Corp.

Keystone Pipe & Supply Co.

Keystone Tubular Service Corp.

K. Ueda Co. Inc.

L.A. Downtown Inc.

Lakeview Inc.

La Salle Travel Inc.

La Salle Traventures Inc.

Lockhart Manufacturing Co. Inc.

Long-Airdox Construction Co.

Mainlands Construction Co.

Margate Development Co. Inc.

Marmon Automotive International Co.

Marmon Insurance Agency Inc.

The McCall Publishing Co.

Miles Metal Co.

Movie Development and Finance Inc.

Movie Service Functions Inc.

Movie Service Functions Inc. II

Órganos Hammond de México S.A. de C.V.

Oxford Tile Co.

Penn Aluminum International Inc.

Penn Brass & Copper Co.

Refco-Cambridge Inc.

Refco Consolidated Inc.

Refco Del Ray Inc.

Refco Enterprises Ltd.

Refco-Equities Inc.

Refco-General Inc.

Refco-Holdings Ltd.

Refco Indianapolis Corp.

Refco Investments Inc.

Refco-Louisiana Inc.

Refco-Louisville Corp.

Refco-Montreal Inc.

Refco–New Orleans Inc.

Refco–Poydras Plaza Inc.

Refco-Properties Inc.

Rio Mar Associates Inc.

Rue Royale Corp.

Select Communities Realty Inc.

Tarpon Construction Co. Inc.

Tex-Apt. Inc.

Tubular Service Corp.

Wells Lamont Corp.

Willow Creek Construction Corp.

Woodmont Construction Co.

Woodmont Development Co.

Woodmont Management Co.

Workwall Inc.

Alpha Mining Inc.

Anderson Copper and Brass Co.

Cerro CATV Devices Inc.
Cerro Coal Trading Co.
Cerro Copper & Brass Co.
Cerro Corp.
Cerro de Pasco Corp.
Cerro Gas & Oil Corp.
Cerro-Marmon Corp.
Cerro Mineral Exploration Co. Inc.
Cerro Purchasing Corp.
Cerro Sales Corp.
Cerro Wire and Cable Corp.
CJI Inc.
Colony West Country Club Inc.
Compañía Industrial del Centro, S.A.
The Country Club at Tarpon Lake Villages Inc.
G.M. & W. Coal Company Inc.
Golvest Corp.
The Housing Group
International Industrial Services Inc.
International Services Inc.
July Investment Corp.
M.F. Land Co. Inc.
Leadership Cable Systems of Palm Beach Inc.
Leadership Communities Inc.
Leadership Homes
Leadership Homes of West Florida Inc.
Leadership Housing Inc.
Leadership Housing Systems Inc.
Leadership Housing Systems of Florida Inc.
Leadership of Hawaii Inc.
Leadership Realty & Management Inc.
Leadership Title Agency Inc.
LHI Recreation Co.
LHS Management Corp.
Mainlands Realty Inc.
Maui Land Investors Inc.
Orangeburg Plastics Co.
Richmar Development Corp.
Richmar Inc.
Rockbestos Cables International Inc.
Somerset County Coal Corp.
South Canal Utilities Inc.
Stereo Tape Club of America
James M. Stott Coal Co.
Tamarac Utilities Inc.
Tarpon Lake Corp.
T.U.I. Inc.
Westcliff Escrow Co.
Woodlands Construction Corp.
Communities Title Co.

Salem Corp.

(Refco Consolidated, controlled by the Pritzker family, owned 22.8 percent of the common stock, and the Birdsboro Corp., controlled by Pennsylvania Engineering Co. and the Posner family, owned 22.2 percent.) (Source: Standard & Poor's)

Herr-Voss Corp.
Wilputte Corp.
Industrial Resources Inc.
Industrial Contracting of Fairmont Inc.
Mountaineer Resources Inc.
Salem Construction Co.
West Virginia Electric Corp.
Salem Industries Canada Ltd.
Salem Engineering (Australia) Pty. Ltd.
Salem Engineering Co. Ltd.
Salem Herr-Voss Co. Ltd.
Coaltek Corp.
A.L. Lee Corp.
Salem S.A.
Salem Furnace Co.

Affiliates (50% owned or noted)

ForSalem S.p.A.
Nippon-Herr Co. Ltd.
Finnsalem Oy (40%)
Salem-Dowson & Dobson (Pty.) Ltd.

Altamil Corp.

(GL Corp., controlled by the Pritzker family, held 34.3 percent of the voting power while J.P.K. Fontaine owned 18.5 percent.)

American Box Co.
Fontaine Truck Equipment Co.
Aluminum Forge Co.
Transall Truck Equipment Co.
Basca Martinville Corp.
Superlock Manufacturing Inc.

Playboy-Elsinore Associates
Sources

1. Reid, *The Grim Reapers*, Chicago chapter.
2. Demaris, *Boardwalk Jungle*. Chapter 24.
3. Block, *Masters of Paradise*.
4. *Kansas City Times*, 3-8–10-82.
5. Truell & Gurwin, *False Profits*.
6. Lewis and Allison, *Cheating of America*. "Haven's Gate" chapter.
7. Jack Clarke int.
8. *New York Times*, 12-11-01.
9. "Shattered Dynasty," *Vanity Fair*, May 2003.

10. "Hyatt's Kingdom of Rooms," "Hyatt, Korshak, Las Vegas and the Teamsters," and "Letters," *New York Times*, 8-29-76, sec. 3, p. 1.
11. "The Castle Bank of Nassau Story."
12. *Chicago Tribune*, 11-1-01.
13. Chicago Crime Commission, Arthur Greene file, memo from Virgil W. Peterson, 8-26-58.
14. Chicago Crime Commission, Arthur Greene file, pages 65–98 from McKesson to Peterson, Business Investigation Summaries.
15. To file from William K. Lambie Jr., Associate Director, 11-18-81.
16. Memo concerning Pritzker, Pritzker and Clinton on 134 N. LaSalle Street, from the Chicago Crime Commission documents from Virgil Peterson, 6-23-60.
17. *Chicago Tribune*, 2-19-57.
18. Letter to James S. Hamilton from Virgil Peterson on the Pritzker family, 01-17-57.
19. Hamilton sent a report of one page on Abram Pritzker to Peterson, 1-9-57.
20. Letter to Virgil Peterson from James Hamilton, 5-14-56.
21. Letter to Peterson from Hamilton, 2-28-55.
22. Chicago Crime Commission report by Dixon on a labor matter, 9-24-44.
23. "Business Diary: The Donald Trumps Pritzkers with Lawsuit," *Crain's Chicago Business*.
24. Jon Anderson, "Pritzker on Pritzker, a Mogul Talks About His Family Dynasty," *Chicago Tribune*, 11-24-85.
25. "At 90, Pritzker Still Feels like a Million," *Chicago Sun-Times*, 11-21-85.
26. "Do the Pritzkers Have McCall's on Block?" *Chicago Tribune*, 10-8-85.
27. "Pritzkers, Patricof Explore Bid for UPI," *Chicago Tribune*, 9-30-85.
28. "Bottom Line: A Pro Manager for McCormick," *Chicago Tribune*, 9-18-85.
29. *Chicago Tribune*, 9-16-85.
30. "Pritzker Fears Another Braniff Bankruptcy," *Chicago Sun-Times*, 11-29-84.
31. "Pritzkers Ponder Sale of Stake in Levitz After Bid Is Thwarted," *Chicago Tribune*, 8-14-84.
32. "Braniff Talking Merger," *Chicago Sun-Times*, 8-8-84.
33. "Pritzker to Buy Miami Furniture Chain," *Chicago Sun-Times*, 6-30-84.
34. "College of Hard Knocks, B. Pritzker, President," *Chicago Tribune*, 3-23-86.
35. "A. N. Pritzker, Pioneer," *Chicago Sun-Times*, 2-11-86.
36. "Levitz Investors Sue Pritzker," *Chicago Sun-Times*, 6-08-84.
37. *Chicago Tribune*, 6-02-84.
38. "New Offer for Eastern?" *Chicago Tribune*, 4-24-86.
39. "Pritzkers Buy Hungarian Firm," *Chicago Tribune*, 8-19-89.
40. "Libertyville Twp. to Buy Open-Space Land Rights," *Chicago Sun-Times*, 11-6-87.
41. "Pritzkers to Buy Stake in Sugar Firm," *Chicago Sun-Times*, 9-20-87.
42. "Pritzker Family Trying to Sell McCall to Seatrain Lines Inc," *Chicago Tribune*, 10-11-86.
43. "Pritzkers Plan to Go into Brokerage," *Chicago Tribune*, 10-02-86.
44. "Lawyer Tells Court of Hired-Gun Plot," *Chicago Sun-Times*, 7-15-86.
45. " 'Marvin, You Left Me for Dead,' " *Chicago Sun-Times*, 7-15-86.
46. "Hefner Denied Casino License in New Jersey," *Chicago Sun-Times*, 9-08-82.
47. Chicago Crime Commission, letter from Patrick F. Healey to Bob Samsot, 3-15-82.
48. "Looping Chicagoland . . . ," *Chicago Tribune*, 2-10-83.
49. "Attorney Probed on Home Thefts," *Chicago Sun-Times*, 6-20-82.
50. "Out to Trump the Pritzkers," *Chicago Tribune*, 7-29-93.
51. "Byrne Political Fund Rises to $1.5 million. Carter Fête, 'Clout' Figures Fed Kitty," *Chicago Tribune*, 3-5-80.
52. "IRS v. CIA: Big Tax Investigation Was Quietly Scuttled by Intelligence Agency: Bahamian Bank's Hundreds of U.S. Account Holders Go Unchecked as a Result," *Wall Street Journal*, 4-18-80.
53. "Elsinore Corp. Teams in Two Joint Ventures," *Las Vegas Sun*, 7-4-80.
54. "Pritzkers May Make Marmon All-Private," *Chicago Tribune*, 6-11-80.
55. Letter from William Lambie Jr. about the Pritzker family, 5-21-80.

56. "Pritzkers Reject Saudi's Offer," *Chicago Tribune*, 4-4-81.

57. "Hyatt International Merger Extends Pritzker Control," *Chicago Sun-Times*, 3-24-81.

58. "Pritzker May Help Revive Steel Mill," *Chicago Tribune*, 3-15-81.

59. "Four Snub Hearings on Playboy Casino," *Chicago Tribune*, 3-08-82.

60. "Pritzker Denies Payoff for Teamster Loans," *Chicago Tribune*, 2-24-82.

61. William K. Lambie file on Abe Pritzker.

62. "Teamster Fund Tie May Affect Pritzker Bid," *Chicago Tribune*, 12-16-81.

63. "8-Month Probe of Hyatt Chain by SEC Revealed," *Chicago Tribune*, 9-16-77.

64. "Pritzkers Eye Hyatt Sweep," *Chicago Tribune*, 6-27-78.

65. "4 Attorneys Indicted on Tax-Fraud Charge," *Chicago Sun-Times*, 3-5-76.

66. "Hyatt Shakeup: Pritzker Ousts 2, Scandal Hinted," *Chicago News*, 9-01-77.

67. Letter to Virgil Peterson from the Chicago Crime Commission's Robert Goe.

68. Chicago Crime Commission, report on Louis Hiller.

69. Corbitt, *Double Deal*, 216–17.

70. Letter from the Chicago Crime Commission to Frank McCulloch, 5-8-62.

71. Chicago Crime Commission, Unidentified letter (possibly a copy, the first page elsewhere) beginning "Rado was business manager . . ."

72. Chicago Crime Commission, memo on Pritzkers, 6-23-60.

73. Letter from *Los Angeles Times*, 5-2-62.

74. Chicago Crime Commission, letter to Peterson, 6-9-55.

75. Chicago Crime Commission, document headed "Frank McCulloch," 8–9.

76. Chicago Crime Commission memo, 11-13-47.

77. "Saudi Bids for Hyatt International," *Chicago Tribune*, 7-20-78.

78. "Saudi Firm Bids for Hyatt Intl.," *Sunday Times*, 7-20-78.

79. "Airport Hotel Foe Switches Sides," *Los Angeles Times*, 8-29-62.

80. *Los Angeles Times*, 5-17-62.

81. *Chicago Tribune*, 6-14-78.

82. "Jack Pritzker, 75, Dies," *Chicago Tribune*, 10-31-79.

83. "Jack N. Pritzker Dies," *Chicago Sun-Times*, 10-31-79.

84. "Pritzkers in Big for Sandburg," *Chicago Tribune*, 2-5-79.

85. "$300,000 Question in Teamsters Hotel Deal," *Los Angeles Times*, 7-6-62.

86. "Oversight Hearings into the Operations of the IRS (Operation Tradewinds, Project Haven, and Narcotics Traffickers Tax Program)," *Hearings Before a Subcommittee of the Committee on Government Operations*, House of Representatives, 94th Cong., 1st sess., October 6, November 4 and 11, 1975 (Washington, DC: U.S. Government Printing Office, 1976).

87. Lernoux, *In Banks We Trust*.

88. Graham Nixon, *The Castle Bank of Nassau Story* (Internet).

Appendix C: Ziffren-Greenberg-Genis Documents

Cash Disbursements

LEA CARTWRIGHT - J.R.GREI

Cks. signed by Pearl Edelman - now his wife.

Ck.				
139	Arthur A. Elrod (L.R.Horwits & Assoc.)	2-29-46	1,049.61
171	Schultz & Schwartz - Atty.	6- 6-46	10,000.00
190	" " " "	7- 6-46	10,000.00
191	Swiftsure Beer Service	7-16-46	15,000.00
203	" " "	7-31-46	55,000.00
214	" " "	8-31-46	50,000.00
267	" " "	9-28-46	50,000.00
246	Arthur Elrod Campaign Fund	10-28-46	1,000.00
252	Swiftsure Beer Service	10-31-46	50,000.00
293	" " "	11-27-46	50,000.00
272	" " "	12-26-46	50,000.00
298	Edward J. Fleming & Chas. H. Albers Trustees Chicago City Railway Co.	2-26-47	120,441.05
367	Paul Ziffren (cashed Calif)	6-25-47	10,000.00
388	Irving Greenberg	7-31-47	25,000.00
433	Samuel P. Rosenfeld	10-15-47	4,305.66
473	Swiftsure Beer Serv.	12-11-47	37,387.22
509	Irving Greenberg (dec'd in 1950)	2- 6-48	60,000.00
521	Fred Evans	2-19-48	20.57
525	Swiftsure Beer Service	3- 5-48	22,046.11
836	Charles Keeshin, Inc.	5- 5-48	20,000.00
	Louis E. Nelson, County Collector South Side B. & T. Co.		
28	Joseph C. Engert	6-11-46	69,650.20
31	Swiftsure Beer Service	6-28-46	59,650.20
34	Paul Ziffren - Lawyer	7-26-46	14,945.73
44	Irving Greenfeld - Partner in Seneca		32,063.98

Page from Alex Greenberg's tax return. Note payments to Paul Ziffren and Fred Evans
(Kefauver exhibit from confidential source)

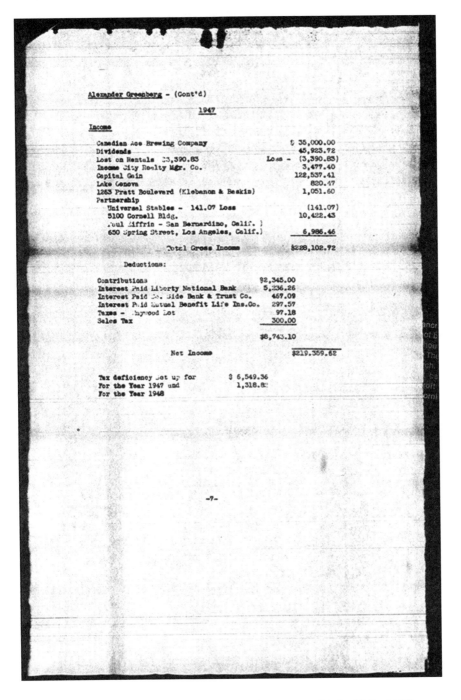

Alexander Greenberg - (Cont'd)

1947

Income

Canadian Ace Brewing Company	$ 35,000.00
Dividends	45,923.72
Loss on Rentals 3,390.83	Loss - (3,390.83)
Income City Realty Mgr. Co.	3,477.40
Capital Gain	122,537.41
Lake Geneva	820.47
1263 Pratt Boulevard (Klebanon & Beskin)	1,051.60
Partnership	
Universal Stables - 141.07 Loss	(141.07)
5100 Cornell Bldg.	10,422.43
Paul Ziffrin - San Bernardino, Calif.)	
650 Spring Street, Los Angeles, Calif.)	6,986.46
Total Gross Income	$228,102.72

Deductions:

Contributions	$2,345.00
Interest Paid Liberty National Bank	5,236.26
Interest Paid So. Side Bank & Trust Co.	467.09
Interest Paid Mutual Benefit Life Ins.Co.	297.57
Taxes - Haywood Lot	97.18
Sales Tax	300.00
	$8,743.10

Net Income	$219,359.62

Tax deficiency set up for	$ 6,549.36
For the Year 1947 and	1,318.82
For the Year 1948	

-7-

Another Greenberg tax-deduction page, showing his "partnership" with Paul Ziffren
(Kefauver exhibit from confidential source)

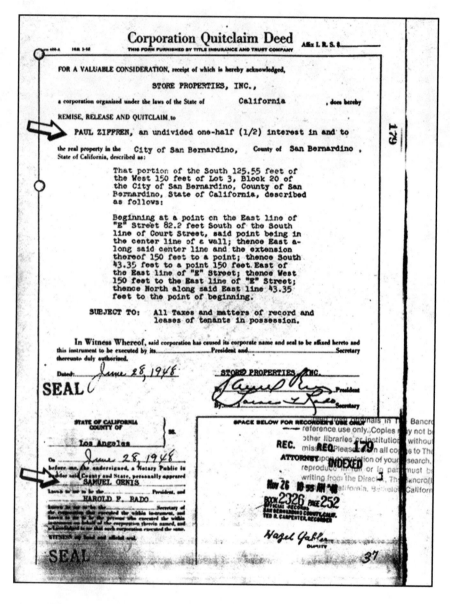

A Paul Ziffren–Sam Genis 1948 real estate partnership (San Bernardino County Recorder's Office records)

Notes

Chapter One

1. "Out Working," *Baltimore Sun*, 4-18-04.
2. Robert Scheer, "The Jews of LA," *Los Angeles Times*, 1-29-78.
`3. Wirth, *Ghetto*, 205.
4. Berkow, *Maxwell Street*, 9.
5. Cited in Fried, *Rise and Fall of the Jewish Gangster*, 90; and in Longstreet, *Chicago*, 423.
6. Cutler, *Jews of Chicago*, 211–12.
7. Int. of Wendell Rawls, 6-17-04.
8. *Sources on early Russian Jews and Lawndale:*

    "Anti-Semitism," article in *Encyclopedia Judaica* (Keter Publishing).

    "Anti-Semitism in the Soviet Union, Its Roots and Consequences" (proceedings of a seminar held in Jerusalem, April 7–8, 1978, Hebrew University, Center for Research and Documentation of East European Jewry), 1979.

    Robert S. Wistrich, *Anti-Semitism: The Longest Hatred* (Pantheon Books, 1992).

    Aronson, Michael, "The Anti-Jewish Pogroms in Russia in 1881," in *Pogroms: Anti-Jewish Violence in Modern Russian History*, ed. John D. Klier and Shlomo Lambroza, 44–61 (Cambridge: Cambridge University, 1992).

    Berkow, *Maxwell Street.*

    Birmingham, *"Our Crowd."*

    Bowden and Kreinberg, *Street Signs Chicago*, especially ch. 9.

    Cahan, Abraham, "The Russian Jew in America," *Atlantic Monthly* 82 (July 1898): 263–87.

    Cutler, *Jews of Chicago.*

    Encyclopedia Judaica.

    Fried, *Rise and Fall of the Jewish Gangster.*

    Hendrick, Burton J., *The Jews in America.*

    Horne, *Class Struggle in Hollywood.*

    Int. with Michael Glass, Chicago historian, 12-22-03.

    Kniesmeyer, J., and D. Brecher, "Beyond the Pale: The History of Jews in Russia" (exhibit, 1995), http://www.friends-partners.org/partners/beyond-the-pale/english/guide-cond.html.

    Kotkin, *Tribes.*

    Lynch, Michael, *Reaction and Revolutions; Russia, 1881–1924.*

    Meites, H. L., *History of the Jews of Chicago.*

    North Lawndale clip files in Chicago Historical Society and Harold Washington Library, especially South Lawndale Community Collection, 1911–52.

    "The Pale of Settlement and the Pogroms of 1881 in Russia" (The Zionist Exposition: Homeward Bound, 1997), Internet, 1-29-99.

Ritter, Leonora, "Nineteenth Century Russia" (Charles Sturt University–Mitchell, 1998), Internet, 1-29-99.

Rogger, Hans, "Conclusion and Overview," in *Pogroms*, ed. Klier and Lambroza, 314–72.

Rosenthal, "This Was North Lawndale."

Sentinel's History of Chicago Jewery (at the Spertus Institute, Chicago).

Thrasher, *Gang.*

Wanklyn, "Geographical Aspects."

Wertheimer, Jack, *Unwelcome Strangers.*

Wiernik, Peter, *History of the Jews in America.*

9. *New York Times*: "Arson Trust Prisoner in Confession Implicates Chicago Adjuster," 5-1-14; "Indict Adjuster for Arson," 7-26-13; "Made Husband Confess: Chicago Woman Tells of Receiving $10,000 to Expose Firebugs," 12-17-13; and "Woman Exposes Firebugs: Confession of Fugitive's Wife Results in 12 Chicago Indictments," 7-29-13.

10. Int. with Judy Lynn Korshak, 6-4-04.

11. Int. of Rich Samuels, 11-24-03.

12. Rakove, *We Don't Want Nobody*, 10.

13. Record of birth: Chicago, State File Number 200223:
Signed by Sidney Korshak, 200 East Chestnut Street Chicago, Ill.
Supporting evidence:
1. New York Life Insurance Company Policy # 17 385 576, dated 08-06-45.
2. Brother's affidavit: Theodore Korshak, 4665 Lake Park Drive, Chicago.
Mother's affidavit: Rebecca Korshak, 5454 South Shore Drive, Chicago.
Fifteenth Census of the U.S., 1930: Illinois, Chicago: 16-884, Sheet 23A, 4-16-30.

14. Hersh, *New York Times*, 6-27-76.

15. FBI HQ Korshak file, Korshak bio, 9-17-63.

16. *Chicago Tribune*, 1-12-29.

17. Marshall Korshak oral history, 6-4-82, for the Chicago Jewish Historical Society; in the Spertus Institute, Chicago.

18. Moe, Doug. "Crime-Linked Attorney Was Student at UW," *Capital Times*, 6-29-76.

19. Doug Moe, "More Secretive Than the CIA," *Capital Times*, 12-31-02.

20. *Chicago Sun-Times*, 1-8-89.

21. Int. of "Zander," 12-8-03.

22. Berkow, *Maxwell Street*, 240.

23. A detailed seven-page biography of the Rosenbergs was located in the papers of Jake Arvey in the Chicago Historical Society (box 20-G, folder 20-4). The unsigned biography appears to have been written by Arvey.

24. Demaris, *Captive City*, 103.

25. Cahan, *Court That Shaped America*, 103–6.

26. Confession quoted in Demaris, *Captive City*, 104–6.

27. Transcript of interview by ABC News for 1997 program "Dangerous World: The Kennedy Years."

28. O'Conner, *Clout*, 224–25.

29. Rakove, *We Don't Want Nobody*, 4.

30. Ibid.

31. Demaris, 107.

32. Ehrenhalt, *Lost City*, 44.

33. Marshall Korshak oral history, 6-4-82.

34. *Chicago Daily News*, 12-11-67.

35. *Arvey biographical resources:*
"Arvey, 80, 'Debuts' with Grandson, 28," *Chicago Sun-Times*, 7-11-75.
Berkow, *Maxwell Street.*
Bruck, *When Hollywood Had a King.*
"Chicago Politician: Arvey Estate Value $1.7 Million," *Chicago Sun-Times*, 6-27-78.
Cohen and Taylor, *American Pharaoh.*

"Col. Jack Arvey: A Master Politician for the Democratic Organization," in *Chicago*, by Charles B. Cleveland.

Demaris, *Captive City*.

Gilbreth and Schultz, "Inside Politics: Still Jake with Arvey's Army," *Chicago News*, 8-11-77.

Kelley, *His Way*.

McDougal, *Last Mogul*.

Moldea, *Dark Victory*.

Mooney, "Jake Arvey: He Delivered Votes," *Chicago Daily News*, 8-26-77.

New York Times, 8-26-77 (obit).

O'Connor, *Clout*.

Plous Jr., "A Last Tribute to Arvey," *Chicago Sun-Times*, 8-27-77.

"Politicians Among 1,200 at Jacob Arvey's Rites," *Tribune*, 8-26-77.

Simon, "Jacob Arvey's Machine Was Fueled by Loyalty," *Sun-Times*, 8-28-77.

36. *Chicago Sun-Times*, 8-28-77.
37. Rakove, *We Don't Want Nobody*, 5.
38. Cohen and Taylor, *American Pharaoh*, 157.
39. "Jake Arvey," Kefauver investigative files, box 64.
40. *Chicago Tribune*, 10-1-64.
41. New Jersey Division of Gaming Enforcement interview report with Sidney Korshak, 10-18-83.
42. Demaris, *Captive City*, 229–32.
43. Lait and Mortimer, *Chicago Confidential*, 241.
44. Int. of Rich Samuels, 11-24-03.
45. Editorial backing Marshall for city treasurer, *Chicago Sun-Times*, 3-30-67.
46. Marshall Korshak oral history, 6-4-82.
47. Confidential int., 1-14-05.
48. FBI HQ Korshak file, 20.
49. Velie in *Collier's*, September 1950.
50. Faulkner, *Requiem for a Nun*, 92.
51. Rakove, *We Don't Want Nobody*, 15.
52. Norman D. Schwartz, "A Look at Highlights of Decalogue Society's 50-Year History: April Meeting Emphasizes Wide Scope of Jewish Law Group's Activities," *Chicago Jewish Historical Society News* 8, no. 4 (June 1985).

Chapter Two

1. Quoted in Robert Scheer, "The Jews of L.A.," *Los Angeles Times*, 1-29-78.
2. Cutler, *Jews of Chicago*, 225–26, 232–33.
3. *Chicago Chronicle*, 1-16-25.
4. Cohen, *Mickey Cohen*, opening epigraph.
5. Int. of Ira Silverman, 3-10-04.
6. Confidential int., 1-14-05.
7. Int. of Fran Marracco, 2-27-04.
8. Int. of Pete Wacks, 5-10-03.
9. Rakove, *We Don't Want Nobody*, 8.
10. Evans, *Kid Stays in the Picture*, 68.
11. Int. of Berle Adams, 3-3-03.
12. Demaris, *Boardwalk Jungle*, 315.
13. Bruck, *When Hollywood Had a King*, 27.
14. "Arvey, 80, 'Debuts' with Grandson, 28," *Chicago Sun-Times*, 7-11-75.
15. *Chicago Tribune*, 8-27-77.
16. *Chicago Tribune*, 5-3-1931.
17. Early Cook County court records, noted by court observer and placed in Korshak file at the Chicago Crime Commission.

18. "Find Maxie Eisen Guilty; Gets Six Months in Jail," *Chicago Tribune*, 09-6-33.
19. Bacon quoted by Nick Toches, *Vanity Fair*, April 1997.
20. Murray, *Legacy of Al Capone*, 158.
21. Select Committee on Improper Activities in the Labor and Management Field, U.S. Senate (McClellan Committee), Second Interim Report, 10-23-59, and Final Report, 3-28-60, pt. 3, 592–674.
22. Bruck, *When Hollywood Had a King*, 166.
23. Velie in *Reader's Digest*, July 1957.
24. Confidential int., 1-30-03.
25. Int. of Roysten Webb, 1-31-04.
26. Confidential int., 5-14-05.
27. Int. of Jim Agnew, 6-04-04. FBI agent Bill Roemer admitted the Postl's bugging to Agnew.
28. Note from Kefauver investigator George S. Robinson, Associate Counsel, U.S. Senate Committee to Investigate Organized Crime, 1950, summarizing letter from Peterson.
29. Wirth, *Ghetto*, 258.
30. Murray, *Legacy of Al Capone*, 34.
31. FBI HQ Korshak file, Korshak bio, 9-17-63, 12.
32. Gioe testimony before Kefauver, 9-9-50.
33. CCC office memo, 6-6-62.
34. FBI int. of Korshak, 9-27-47, CCC file #58-194.
35. Reid, *Grim Reapers*, 180.
36. LAPD confidential report re Paul Kalmanovitz, 12-3-66 (CCC files).
37. *Hart biography sources:* FBI HQ Alfred Hart file, obtained under FOIA; *Los Angeles Times,* 12-31-79 (obit); *Los Angeles Times,* 5-28-74 (Haber column); int. of L.A. DA Office investigator Jim Grodin, 12-8-03; Turner, *Rearview Mirror*, 7, and *Hoover's FBI*, 73; Demaris *Judith Exner*, 51, and *Captive City*, 224; Summers, *Official and Confidential*, 235; and Kate Berry, "City National Grows . . . ," *Los Angeles Business Journal*, 5-12-03.
38. Los Angeles FBI report, 3-29-62 (#92-934-243) (Korshak file).
39. Kupcinet, *Kup*, 151.
40. Ibid., 152.
41. *Chicago Tribune*, 12-10-55.
42. Greenberg testimony to Kefauver, 1-19-51.
43. Kefauver Committee biography of Greenberg, 7.
44. *Chicago Tribune*, 2-26-25.
45. Testimony given in *U.S. v. Campagna, et al.* (Bioff extortion case), Southern District Federal Court of New York.
46. Greenberg testimony to Kefauver, 1-19-51.
47. Kefauver Committee biography of Greenberg, 2.
48. *Chicago Sun-Times*, 10-12-50.
49. McPhaul, *Johnny Torrio*, 277.
50. Kefauver Committee biography of Greenberg, 4.
51. *Chicago Daily News*, 4-9-57.
52. Virgil Peterson, letter to Senator Estes Kefauver, 11-19-53.
53. Virgil Peterson, memo to file, 8-26-58.
54. Demaris, *Captive City*, 224.
55. Virgil Peterson memo re Greenberg and Goe, 8-26-58.
56. W. D. Amis, Kefauver Committee "Greenberg Memo," 11-1-50; also, Russo, *Outfit*, 97–98.
57. Greenberg int. by W. D. Amis, Kefauver Committee staff report, 11-6-50.
58. *Nitti v. Greenberg*, Superior Court of Cook County, 2-14-57, case #57S-2335. The estate was probated in Probate Court of Cook County, file #43P-5267, docket 561.
59. FBI Korshak Correlation Summary, 8-12-68.
Other Greenberg biography sources include:

CCC investigative biography of Greenberg, file #8943, 1-24-49.

Demaris, *Captive City*, 222–25.

"Gang Trail Leads to Graves," *Chicago Daily Tribune*, 12-9-55.

Letter from Robert L. Goe to Mr. Virgil W. Peterson (CCC), 10-1-59.

McDougal, *Last Mogul*, 36–38.

Murray, "The Richest SOB in Hell," in *Legacy of Al Capone*.

Virgil W. Peterson memo, 8-26-58.

60. Ragen's sworn testimony in Kefauver Continental Wire investigative files, box 75.

61. Bruck, *When Hollywood Had a King*, 11.

62. Sharp, *Mr. and Mrs. Hollywood*, 107.

63. Bruck, *When Hollywood Had a King*, 31–32.

64. Russo, *Outfit*, 192.

65. McDougal, *Last Mogul*, 40–41.

66. Bruck, *When Hollywood Had a King*, 32.

67. Demaris, *Captive City*, 125.

68. Moldea, *Dark Victory*, 40.

69. Bruck, *When Hollywood Had a King*, 31.

70. McDougal, *Last Mogul*, 141; Moldea, *Dark Victory*, 14; and Peretti, *Creation of Jazz*, 147–48.

71. Moldea, *Dark Victory*, 22.

72. Bruck, *When Hollywood Had a King*, 30.

73. *Additional Petrillo sources: New York Times* and *Chicago Tribune*, 10-25-84 (Petrillo obits); *Current Biography* (1940), 650–52; *Chicago Tribune*, 3-1-41, 3-4-41, 6-14-40, 8-21-40, and 9-18-40; Jerome Beatty, "Hard-Boiled Maestro," *American Magazine*, October 1940; *PM's Weekly*, 9-8-40; Bruck, *When Hollywood Had a King*, ch. 1, "The Two Caesars"; and Sharp, *Mr. and Mrs. Hollywood*, 397–98.

74. Bruck, *When Hollywood Had a King*, 67–68.

75. McDougal, *Last Mogul*, 57–58.

76. Bruck, *When Hollywood Had a King*, 65.

77. Ibid., 354.

78. Int. of Henry Denker, 8-30-04.

79. Demaris, *Captive City*, 123.

80. *Factor sources:*

Chicago American, 11-12-62, 11-13-62.

Chicago Daily News, 11-12-62, 12-27-62.

Chicago Daily Tribune, 8-11-54, 8-13-54, 11-14-62.

Chicago Tribune, 11-13-62, 12-28-62.

Factor's pardon file at National Archives, College Park, MD.

Johnson, Wicked City, 350–53.

Los Angeles Herald Express, 10-16-61.

Los Angeles Times, 1-24-84 (obit).

Newsweek, 1-7-63.

New York Times, 2-16-67.

Russo, Outfit, 100–104.

Touhy, When Capone's Mob Murdered, passim.

81. Bruck, *When Hollywood Had a King*, 61.

82. Messick, *Beauties and the Beast*, 235.

83. CCC memo in files of Jack Tobin.

84. *U.S. v. Nitti*, Southern District Court of New York, case #114-101, p. 1055.

85. Michael Denning, *The Cultural Front: The Laboring of American Culture in the 20th Century* (New York: Verso, 1996), 375–76.

86. *Chicago Tribune*, 6-13-48.

87. Fox, *Blood and Power*, 148.

88. Gomery, *Shared Pleasures*; and "Barney Balaban," *International Dictionary of Films and Filmmakers, Volume 4: Writers and Production Artists* (St. James Press, 1996).
89. *Chicago Tribune*, 3-31-39.
90. *Dorothy Appleby sources:* Ints. with James Appleby, Jennifer Silberblatt (probate executor), and Craig Robins (probate attorney); *Portland Press Herald*, 9-9-90 (obit); and *Chicago Tribune*, 8-16-26, 5-21-31, 4-2-32, 5-12-32, 6-30-35, 9-11-35, 9-13-35, 9-19-35, 9-22-35, 9-24-35.
91. Int. of Wendell Rawls, 6-17-04.
92. FBI L.A. Field Office, Korshak summary update, 8-12-68.
93. James Doherty, *Chicago Daily Tribune*, 2-3-46.
94. FBI int. of Korshak, 9-27-48, on file at CCC, #58-194.

Chapter Three

1. Niklas, *Corner Table*, 35.
2. *Scalise sources:*
   "Aides Tell How Scalise Ruled Union Treasury," *Chicago Daily Tribune*, 5-4-40.
   Chicago Crime Commission memo, Sidney R. Korshak #70-36, 1-19-76.
   Chicago Crime Commission memo from Virgil W. Peterson, 6-6-62.
   Chicago Daily News, 5-4-40.
   Life magazine, 5-6-40, 34.
   Los Angeles Times, 9-15-69.
   New York Times, 9-15-40, 10-8-40.
   Pegler, various 1940 "Fair Enough" columns, at Hoover Library, West Branch, Iowa.
   Witwer, "Scandal of George Scalise."
3. CCC Peterson memos, 12-14-40, 12-17-40, 12-14-42.
4. Alan Hynd, "The Rise and Fall of Joseph Schenck," *Liberty* magazine, 3-pt. series, June–August 1941.
5. John Bartlow Martin, "Who Killed Estelle Carey?" *Harper's*, June 1944.
6. *Hollywood extortion-case sources:* Int. of Kostelanetz, 4-10-01; other details from Bioff's testimony in *U.S. v. Frank Nitto, et al.*, U.S. District Court for Southern District of N.Y., case #19456-19460, box 5808, Record Group 276, National Archives, New York.
   Also:
   Chicago American, 3-29-50.
   Chicago Tribune, 9-24-47.
   Dunne, *Hollywood Labor Dispute*.
   Fox, *Blood and Power*, 210–15.
   Gage, *Mafia U.S.A.*, 344–56.
   Horne, *Class Struggle in Hollywood*.
   Messick, *Secret File*, 167–83.
   Neilsen and Mailes, *Hollywood's Other Blacklist*.
   Newsweek, 11-10-41, 54–55.
   Rasmussen, "L.A. Then and Now," *Los Angeles Times*, 1-2-00.
   Variety, 8-22-33, 7.
7. *Chicago Daily News*, 3-18-43.
8. Int. of Fran Marracco, 2-27-04.
9. Int. of Tom Zander, 12-8-03.
10. Int. of MJ Goldblatt, 6-6-04.
11. Arthur Engel, "Paul Ziffren: California's Cure for Tired Democratic Blood," *Harper's*, September 1959.
12. Quoted in *U.S. v. Campagna*.
13. Berkow, *Maxwell Street*, 245.
14. Int. of Pete Wacks, 5-10-03.
15. Int. with Author, 5-21-04.

16. See, among others, McDougal, *Last Mogul*, 141.
17. FBI telex, SAC L.A. to director, 10-15-59.
18. *Chicago Tribune*, 6-13-37.
19. Ibid., 5-16-40.
20. FBI memo, Ladd to Rosen, 7-14-52, in FBI Bazelon file.
21. Greenberg tax records in Kefauver Exhibit 70, 11-1-50.
22. Nick Tosches, "The Man Who Kept the Secrets," *Vanity Fair*, April 1997.
23. Velie, *Reader's Digest*, July 1960.
24. Memo from Hoover to attorney general, 7-14-52, Bazelon file.
25. Chelf Committee memo, unsigned, 11-2-51, based on interview with a prominent D.C. attorney friend of Bazelon's.
26. Ibid.
27. *Chicago Tribune*, 11-24-85.
28. CCC memos to file from William Lambie, director, 11-18-81, 11-20-81.
29. FBI HQ Korshak file, Korshak bio, 9-17-63, 19.
30. CCC report of "Dixon," 9-24-44.
31. *Chicago Tribune*, 11-24-85.
32. Ibid.
33. Confidential int., 1-14-05.
34. *Kansas City Times*, 3-9-82.
35. Quoted in Demaris, *Boardwalk Jungle*, 269.
36. Int. of Jack Clarke, 6-30-03.
37. Sandy Smith, *Chicago Tribune*, April 12–14, 1961, 4-4-61.
38. Letter from LAPD intelligence chief Jim Hamilton to CCC, 1-9-57.
39. New Jersey Division of Gaming Enforcement interview report of Sidney Korshak, 10-18-83.
40. From L.A. FBI report, 2-35-63 (92-113-2085), Korshak file.
41. Int. of Sy Hersh, 5-16-03.
42. Int. of MJ Goldblatt, 6-6-04.
43. FBI case file 156-23-26, Korshak-Humphreys labor case.
44. Int. of Brian Ross, 4-19-04.
45. Int. of Sandy Smith, 11-11-03.
46. Int. of E. Timothy Applegate, 4-12-04.
47. Int. of Jack Walsh, 5-13-04.
48. Int. of Pete Wacks, 5-10-03.
49. Int. of Fran Marracco, 2-27-04.
50. Tosches, "Man Who Kept the Secrets."
51. FBI HQ Korshak file, Korshak bio, 9-17-63, 4.

Chapter Four

1. Roemer, *Enforcer*, 171.
2. Rabbi Edward Feinstein, "City of Angels," Rosh Hashanah, 2000, Feinstein Archives.
3. Starr, *Dream Endures*, 185.
4. Robert Scheer, "The Jews of LA," *Los Angeles Times*, 1-29-78.
5. Cleland, *California in Our Time*, 127.
6. Gabler, *Empire of Their Own*, 274.
7. *Sources on Beverly Hills and Hillcrest include:*
   Gabler, *Empire of Their Own*, 263, 274–76, 289.
   McDougal, *Privileged Son*, 128.
   Newmark, *Sixty Years in Southern California*.
   Rachlis, "The Patron Class," *Los Angeles Magazine*, June 2003.

Scheer, "The Jews of L.A.," series in *Los Angeles Times*, January 28, 30, 31, 1978.

Vorspan and Gartner, *History of the Jews of Los Angeles*.

Weddle, *Among the Mansions of Eden*.

8. Niklas, *Corner Table*, 355.

9. Gabler, *Empire of Their Own*, 6.

10. Samish and Thomas, *Secret Boss of California*, 146.

11. Cohen, *Mickey Cohen*, 2–3.

12. Ibid., 94, 96.

13. Ibid., 232–33.

14. McShane, *Life of Raymond Chandler*, 121.

15. Rappleye and Becker, *All American Mafioso*, 54.

16. Int. of Connie Carlson, 10-20-04.

17. *Land grab sources:*

Davis, Margaret Leslie. *Rivers in the Desert: William Mulholland and the Inventing of Los Angeles.*

Hoffman, Abraham. *Vision or Villainy: Origins of the Owens Valley–Los Angeles Water Controversy.* College Station: Texas A&M University Press, 1981.

Hundly, Norris. *The Great Thirst: Californians and Water, 1770s–1990s.* Berkeley: University of California Press, 1992.

Kahrl, William. *Water and Power: The Conflict Over Los Angeles's Water Supply in the Owens Valley.* Berkeley: University of California Press, 1982.

Sanchez, Rene. "Quenching the Thirst of a Century—Los Angeles May Restore River It Diverted Years Ago." *Washington Post*, 6-1-04.

Walton, John. *Western Times and Water Wars: State, Culture, and Rebellion in California.* Berkeley: University of California Press, 1992.

18. Velie, *Readers Digest*, July 1960.

19. From White's unpublished manuscript, "A Benign Machiavelli of the West," quoted in FBI telex, SAC L.A. to director, 10-22-59.

20. McDougal, *Privileged Son*, 194–96.

21. Bowron testimony before Kefauver Committee, 12-13-50.

22. James E. Hamilton, L.A. police chief, Kefauver Testimony, 11-15-50.

23. Bowron testimony.

24. Kefauver Committee testimony of Bowron, 12-13-50; Utley, 2-28-51; and Gould, 2-28-51.

25. Donner, *Protectors of Privilege*, 245–51.

26. Int. of Wanda Goe, 7-25-04.

27. Especially *Government Employee* 3 (June 1960).

28. Especially the 1952 House Judiciary Committee (Frank Chelf Committee) and the FBI's 551-page file on David Bazelon.

29. Knoedelseder, *Stiffed*, 76–77.

30. *Chicago Tribune*, 12-25-47.

31. Chelf memo from Robert Collier, 7-10-52, 82nd-83rd Congress, Judiciary Committee, Subcommittee to Investigate Justice Department, Case Files, Series B, Bazelon File, Box 53, Congressional Legislative Archives, Library of Congress.

32. Arthur A. Engel, "Paul Ziffren: California's Cure for Tired Democratic Blood," *Harper's*, September 1959.

33. McDougal, *Last Mogul*, 141.

34. Int. of Connie Carlson, 10-20-04.

35. LAPD officer's memo, "Hotel Hayward," 10-17-50; also L.A. County Clerk Records Book 31268, p. 159. See also "Chicago Links to Los Angeles Gambling Told," *Chicago Tribune*, 2-28-51.

36. *Biographical information on Evans from:* Murray, *Legacy of Al Capone*, esp. 207–16; Russo, *Outfit*, 61–62, 79, 98, 139, 162, 169, 342–47, 429; Demaris, *Captive City*, 23, 24, 39, 82, 223; and FBI HQ Humphreys file.

37. James E. Hamilton, L.A. police intel chief, Kefauver testimony, 12-13-50.

38. Greenberg testimony quoted in Murray, *Legacy of Al Capone*, 35.

39. Peterson letter to Kefauver, 2-19-53.
40. Demaris, Captive City, 223
41. Peterson letter to Goe; Robinson, counsel, Kefauver Committee, 11-1-50.
42. Kefauver Committee staff interview of Evans by H. P. Kiley, 10-30-50.

Chapter Five

1. *Chicago Tribune*, 8-6-53.
2. Velie, *Reader's Digest*, July 1960.
3. *Chicago Tribune*, 5-16-47; and *New York Times*, 4-25-47, 18.
4. Chelf memo from Stephen Mitchell, 6-15-52, 82nd-83rd Congress, Judiciary Committee, Subcommittee to Investigate Justice Department, Case Files, Series B, Bazelon File, Box 53, Congressional Legislative Archives, Library of Congress.
5. Chelf Committee memo, unsigned, 11-2-51, 82nd-83rd Congress, Judiciary Committee, Subcommittee to Investigate Justice Department, Case Files, Series B, Bazelon File, Box 53, Congressional Legislative Archives, Library of Congress.
6. Telex from Chicago SAC to Hoover (date unreadable). Information on Neil House partnership: Franklin County (OH) Official Records, Deed Books 1358, 1391, 1592. Information on Deshler: Ohio State Corporation Files #215074, 45096.
7. Testimony of H. Richard Niehoff (who attended the meeting with Pritzker) before Chelf Committee, 11-11-52, files of Committee on Judiciary "Chelf " Subcommittee, Gordon Bazelon file.
8. FBI memo, Cleveland office, 9-12-52, Bazelon file.
9. Demaris, *Boardwalk Jungle*, 269.
10. Peterson, *Barbarians*, 266.
11. Airtel, Cincinnati to Hoover 11-8-52, Bazelon file.
12. Memo, Rosen to Ladd, 7-22-52, Bazelon file.
13. Hilton obit in *New York Times*, 1-5-79.
14. Kirkeby citation in *Who Was Who in America*, vol. 4, 1961–68.
15. Kefauver Committee investigative files, Jules Endler, Box 84.
16. Bruck, *When Hollywood Had a King*, 86.
17. Greene & Hilton Partnerships: L.A. County Recorder's Office, Book 21063, p. 304, L.A. County Clerks Files.
18. Lait and Mortimer, *Chicago: Confidential!* 241.
19. FBI HQ Korshak file, Korshak bio, 9-17-63, 10.
20. Kirkeby investments: L.A. County Clerk File #C150504, C78498; and LAPD intel reports: "Hilton Hotels," 3-10-58; "National Cuba Hotel Corporation," 1950; "Kirkeby Inc.," 9-24-57.
21. New Jersey Division of Gaming Enforcement interview report of Marshall Korshak, 10-18-83.
22. Int. of Don Wolfe, 1-5-05.
23. FBI memo from SAC L.A. to director, "Reactivation of the Capone Gang," 7-22-46.
24. Goe-White notes, 3-29-57, based on 1956 LAPD intel report.
25. Nick Tosches, "The Man Who Kept the Secrets," *Vanity Fair*, April 1997.
26. *Chicago Tribune*, 3-5-62; and *Variety*, 3-7-62.
27. Letter from Robert Goe to Virgil Peterson, 10-1-59. Additional information on Store Properties: L.A. County, Clerk's Office, file C-78498; L.A. County Recorder's Office, Records Books 22746, p. 302; 22872, p. 19, 26099, p. 87, 42495, p. 120; and California State Corporation Commission, file LA-126420.
28. Greenberg memo from W. D. Amis to files, 11-1-50, Kefauver Committee.
29. Demaris, *Captive City*, 223.
30. Chelf memo to Robert Collier from Mitchell, 8-6-52, 82nd-83rd Congress, Judiciary Committee, Subcommittee to Investigate Justice Department, Case Files, Series B, Bazelon File, Box 53, Congressional Legislative Archives, Library of Congress.
31. Int. of Andrew Furfaro, 10-20-04.
32. Beck and Williams, *California*, 458–59; and Cleland, *California in Our Time*, 248, 250.

33. Friedrich, *City of Nets*, 102.

34. *Washington Post*, 2-15-42.

35. Quoted in Friedrich, *City of Nets*, 112.

36. Testimony of Earl Warren, U.S. Congress, House Select Committee Investigating National Defense, San Francisco Hearing, 77th Cong., 2d sess., 11009–19.

37. Cray, *Chief Justice*, 430, 478.

38. From the 1989 album *Tokyo Rose*.

39. Joseph Y. Kurihara, quoted in William Minoru Hohri, *Repairing America: An Account of the Movement for Japanese-American Redress* (Pullman: Washington State University Press, 1988).

40. Winifred Ryder, Tolan Committee hearings, 11667; cited in Richard Lawrence Miller, "Confiscations from Japanese-Americans During World War Two," 11-6-01, on the Forfeiture Endangers American Rights Web site.

41. *Other sources on internment:*

Beck and Williams, *California*.

Commission on Wartime Relocation and Internment of Civilians, *Personal Justice Denied: Report of the Commission on Wartime Relocation and Internment of Civilians* (Washington: Government Printing Office, 1982) (SuDocs Y3.W19/10:J98).

Daniels, *Decision to Relocate*.

Kotkin and Grabowicz, *California Inc.*

Ng, *Japanese American Internment*.

Robinson, *By Order of the President*.

U.S. House, Select Committee Investigating National Defense Migration (Tolan Committee): hearings, 77th Cong., 2d sess., 1941–42 (SuDocs Y4.N21/5:M58/pts. 29–31); report, 77 Cong., 2d sess., 1942, H. Rpt. 1911, serial 10668; and report, 77 Cong., 2d sess., 1942, H. Rpt. 2124, serial 10668.

42. Commission, *Personal Justice Denied*, 130.

43. Winifred Ryder, Tolan Committee hearings, 11667; and Tolan Committee, Report 1911, 19.

44. John Tateishi, *And Justice for All: An Oral History of the Japanese American Detention Camps* (New York: Random House, 1984).

45. Sandra C. Taylor, *Jewel of the Desert: Japanese American Internment at Topaz* (Berkeley: University of California Press, 1993).

46. Commission, *Personal Justice Denied*, 132.

47. Ibid., "Instructions to All Persons of Japanese Ancestry," 4-30-42, fig. C; and Taylor, *Jewel of the Desert*.

48. Dorothy Swaine Thomas and Richard S. Nishimoto, *The Spoilage* (Berkeley: University of California Press, 1946).

49. Fletcher Bowron to John H. Tolan, 4-27-42, in Tolan Committee, Report 2124, 40.

50. Kotkin and Grabowicz, *California Inc.*, 206.

51. Ibid.

52. Rakove, *We Don't Want Nobody*, 17, 19.

53. Ibid., 18.

54. Arvey was actually critical to the passing of the UN resolution. When he heard from New York sources that three nations were wavering and might tip the balance against the resolution, he got in touch with Truman, who quickly picked up the phone and made the saving appeals. The bill passed by just two votes more than needed.

55. Berkow, *Maxwell Street*, 259.

56. Kupcinet, *Kup*, 85.

57. *Chicago Tribune*, 8-30-52.

58. *Washington Post*, 12-22-49.

59. FBI memo, Ladd to Rosen, 7-22-52, Bazelon file; and FBI SAC telex, Cleveland to Hoover, 9-12-51.

60. Chelf Committee, 8-7-52, 82nd-83rd Congress, Judiciary Committee, Subcommittee to Investigate Justice Department, Case Files, Series B, Bazelon File, Box 53, Congressional Legislative Archives, Library of Congress.

61. *Chicago Tribune*, 3-7-48.

62. Ziffren letter to Treasury, 4-22-41, NARA RG 131, Foreign Funds Control, Box 795.

63. Memo from Evans to Rosen, 5-29-57, Bazelon file.

64. Demaris, *Captive City*, 221.

65. Weingart holdings culled from numerous files by Robert Goe, including Alien Custodian Book of Vesting Orders; California State Grantee-Grantor Records, Assessors Records; and L.A. City Clerks Records.

66. *Chicago Tribune*, 3-7-48.

67. Quoted in Murray, *Legacy of Al Capone*, 35.

68. Warehouse records: L.A. County Official Records Books 49977, p. 272; 26341, p. 222; 24907, p. 357; and L.A. County Clerk Partnership File F146629.

69. Goe-White notes: Memo re Ziffren and Greene with notes on alien property, 11-5-57.

70. Ridgely Cummings, *Government Employee* 3 (June 1960).

71. L.A. County Grantor-Grantee Records, Book 26241, pp. 184–207; Book 49977, p. 272; and FBI telex, SAC L.A. to director, 10-15-59.

72. Goe-White notes, 3-29-57.

73. Memo from SAC L.A. to Hoover, 4-22-57, Bazelon file.

74. FBI memo from Rosen to Ladd, 7-14-52, 2, Bazelon file.

75. Memo from SAC WFO to Hoover, 5-24-57, Bazelon file.

76. Confidential int., 5-10-04.

77. *Chicago Tribune*, 8-5-49.

78. Peterson memo to file, 8-26-58.

79. Ickes letter to Truman, 9-22-49, Truman Library, OF 41-H Official File, WH Central Files.

80. From White's unpublished manuscript "A Benign Machiavelli of the West," quoted in FBI telex from SAC L.A. to director, 10-22-59.

81. FBI telex from SAC L.A. to director, 3-31-60.

Chapter Six

1. From Joan Didion's first collection of nonfiction, *Slouching Towards Bethlehem* (1968).

2. Korshak-Gioe-Ash: Ash testimony before House of Representatives "Busbey" panel looking into the parole scandal, 80th Cong., 2nd Session, Report No. 2441, hearings September 1947–March 1948. Also, FBI int. of Korshak, 9-27-47, in FBI parole investigation, 9-10-47 (located in FBI Rosselli file); undated FBI int. of Ash; *Chicago American*, 1947 (various); *Chicago Daily Sun*, 9-24-47; and Chicago Police Department report of M. P. Scanlon, September 25, 26, 1947.

3. Levy, *King of Comedy*, 79–83; and Tosches, *Dino*, 157–59.

4. Sharp, *Mr. and Mrs. Hollywood*, 17.

5. Kefauver's tax subpoenas on file in Kefauver Committee holdings, Legislative Archives, Library of Congress, Washington, DC. Especially letter to Snyder, 7-14-50 (Box 21).

6. FBI Chicago report on Korshak and Goldblatts, 11-23-54, report by Howard Carlson.

7. Peterson, *Barbarians in Our Midst*, 259–62.

8. Collins, *Scorpion Tongues*, 167.

9. Miller, *Fishbait*, 350.

10. Fontenay, *Estes Kefauver*, 343; and Collins, *Scorpion Tongues*, 168.

11. Collins, *Scorpion Tongues*, 169.

12. Kupcinet, *Kup*, 151–52.

13. Baker, *Wheeling and Dealing*, 48.

14. Int. of Sy Hersh, 5-15-03.

15. Int. of MJ Goldblatt, 6-6-04.

16. Int. of Sandy Smith, 11-11-03.

17. Memo, 1-5-51.

18. Robinson notes in Kefauver Committee files, Box 21; and Korshak to press in *Chicago Tribune*, 10-27-50.

19. Greenberg testimony to Kefauver, 1-19-51.

20. *Other Kefauver sources:*

Robert S. Allen, "How Congress Scuttled Kefauver," *U.S. Crime* 1, no. 1 (12-7-51).

Anderson and Blumenthal, *Kefauver Story.*

Chicago American, 10-26-50.

Chicago Sun, 10-27-50.

"Estes Kefauver: RIP," *National Review*, 8-27-63.

Fox, *Blood and Power.*

Lundberg, *Rich and the Super Rich.*

Moore, *Kefauver Committee.*

Moore, "Was Estes Kefauver Blackmailed?"

Joseph Nellis, "Legal Aspects of the Kefauver Investigation," *Journal of Criminal Law, Criminology and Political Science*, July-August 1951.

Peterson, *Barbarians in Our Midst.*

W. Scott Stewart, "Kefauverism: A Protest," Patterson Papers, Library of Congress, Manuscript Division.

Swados, *Standing Up for the People.*

Lester Velie, "Rudolph Halley," *Collier's*, 5-19-51.

21. Confidential int., 1-20-03.
22. Nick Toches, "The Man Who Kept the Secrets," *Vanity Fair*, April 1997.
23. Int. of Frank Buccieri, 12-4-03.
24. Int. of Don Wolfe, 1-5-05.
25. *Chicago Tribune*, 8-20-52.
26. Reynolds, *Debbie*, 203.
27. FBI memo from Don Winne to Edward Joyce, deputy chief, DOJ OC and Racketeering Section, 1-27-70 (#94-430-1833), Korshak file.
28. Bruck, *When Hollywood Had a King*, 354.
29. Reid, *Grim Reapers*, 202–4.
30. *Albuquerque Journal*, 3-9-77, 1.
31. Int. of Richard Brenneman (who supplied his Rittenband notes), 12-2-03.
32. See, among others, Andersen, *A Star*, Chs. 6–8.
33. Munn, *Hollywood Connection*, 60–61.
34. *Bautzer sources:* Unpublished Bautzer biography by Hollywood PR man Henry Rogers (Special Collections, Brigham Young University); Maheu and Hack, *Next to Hughes*; *Los Angeles Magazine*, January 1969; *Hollywood Reporter 54th Anniversary Issue*, December 1954; obits in *Hollywood Reporter, Los Angeles Herald-Examiner*, and *Los Angeles Times*, 10-27-87; *Los Angeles Times*, 8-12-91; and int. of ex-wives Dana Wynter (Bautzer), 3-17-03, and Niki Dantine Bautzer, 3-17-04.
35. LAPD confidential report re Paul Kalmanovitz, 12-3-66 (in CCC files).
36. Dietrich, *Howard*, 273.
37. *Hughes sources include:* Garrison, *Howard Hughes in Las Vegas*; Maheu and Hack, *Next to Hughes*; Barlett and Steele, *Empire*; Hack, *Hughes*; Brown and Broeske, *Untold Story of Howard Hughes*; Drosnin, *Citizen Hughes*; Thomas, *Howard Hughes in Hollywood.*
38. CCC, "Jukebox Report of 1954," 168.
39. RKO sources: *Wall Street Journal*, 10-16-52, and passim; *Time*, 10-27-52.
40. Niklas, *Corner Table*, 26.
41. Moldea, *Dark Victory*, 105.
42. *Chicago Tribune*, 1-20-53.
43. *Time*, 8-30-54, 67–68.
44. Lewis, *Mondale*, 99–101; and Cohn, *Sister Kenny*, 239–51.
45. Dietrich, *Howard*, 281–86; DeMaris, *Dirty Business*; Miller, *Breaking of the President*, 350–52.
46. Memo from Ladd to Rosen, 8-12-52, Bazelon File.
47. Chelf memo from Robert Collier, 7-10-52, 82nd–83rd Congress, Judiciary Committee, Subcommittee to Investigate Justice Department, Case Files, Series B, Bazelon File, Box 53, Congressional Legislative Archives, Library of Congress.

48. Chelf memo, Bob Lee to Mr. Collier, 1-2-53.
49. Chelf memo, Nulty to Mitchell, 7-11-52.
50. Chelf memo, Mitchell to Collier, 8-6-52.
51. Chelf memo, Bob Lee to Mr. Collier, 1-2-53.
52. Chelf memo on David Bazelon, from TC Link, 3-31-52.
53. Chelf Committee, letter from Frank Chelf to secretary of treasury, 5-29-52; memo from Robert Collier to Thomas Connor, 7-21-52; and Chelf memo to file from "JCW," 4-8-52.
54. Mollenhoff, *Tentacles of Power*, 6.
55. Letter from AG to Hoover, 8-8-52, Bazelon File.
56. Memo from Evans to Rosen, 5-13-57, Bazelon File.
57. Searches were conducted for the author over many months by senior archivists Fred Romanski, Steven Tilley, and Martha Wagner Murphy.
58. Memo from Sorenson to JFK, 11-22-62.
59. *Sources for Bazelon biography include:* bazelon.org, *Chicago Tribune*, 2-23-93; McDougal, *Last Mogul*, 141; University of Pennsylvania Law School, Biddle Library, Bazelon Papers; Demaris, *Captive City*, 222–23, 225; Moldea, *Dark Victory*, 324; *New York Times*, 2-21-93; Peters and Branch, *Blowing the Whistle*, 26; Powell, *Covert Cadre*, 51; Schrag, *Mind Control*, 103–5, 237–38; Bradlee, *Good Life*, 418; Kilian and Sawislak, *Who Runs Washington?* 46; the 561-page FBI Bazelon File; and the over one thousand pages of Goe-White real estate records, some of which are in the Chicago Crime Commission files, and others in private holdings.
60. Velie, *Reader's Digest*, July 1960, 115.
61. Demaris, *Captive City*, 225.
62. CCC memos, 4-15-58, 6-6-62; and *New York Times*, 4-13-54.
63. LAPD officer's memo, "Hayward Hotel," 10-17-50.
64. Letter from James Hamilton to Virgil Peterson, 10-18-50.
65. Hamilton letter to Peterson, 11-26-56.
66. LAPD Hamilton internal memo, 2-2-54.
67. "Shattered Dynasty," *Vanity Fair*, May 2003; Knut Royce, *Kansas City Times*, March 8-10-82; and "Hyatt's Kingdom of Rooms," *New York Times*, 8-29-76.
68. Corbitt and Giancana, *Double Deal*, 216.
69. Int. of Mike Corbitt, 3-19-03.
70. Lynch letter to Peterson, 7-13-54.
71. *Los Angeles Mirror*, 4-30-54; *Los Angeles Herald*, 4-30-54; *San Diego Evening Tribune*, 5-1-54; and *Los Angeles Times*, 5-1-54.
72. *Chicago Tribune*, 9-4-54.
73. Ibid.
74. L.A. County Grantor-Grantee Records, Book 49977, p. 272.
75. Kate Berry, "City National," *Los Angeles Business Journal*, 5-12-03.
76. FBI report, 9-17-63.
77. Letter from Robert Goe to Virgil Peterson, 1-16-59.
78. CNB corporate history from its Web site, www.cnb.com.
79. Int. of David Nissen, 9-4-04.
80. Int. of Jack Clarke, 1-31-04.
81. Int. of Connie Carlson, 10-20-04.
82. FBI memo from Don Winne to Edward Joyce, deputy chief, DOJ OC and Racketeering Section, 1-27-70 (#94-430-1833), Korshak File.
83. Int. of Ed Becker, 10-11-04.
84. Int. of George Schlatter, 1-20-04.
85. Exner, *My Story*, 50–51.
86. Int. of Milt Ebbins, 1-17-05.
87. Int. of Virginia Korshak, 1-20-04.
88. Int. of Selene Walters, 3-2-05.

89. FBI memo from G. H. Scatterday to Rosen, 10-4-61.
90. Virgil Peterson, *Annals of the American Academy of Political and Social Science* 347 (May 1963): 33.
91. Quoted in Murray, *Legacy of Al Capone*, 36.
92. *Chicago Tribune*, 12-10-55.
93. *Greenberg sources:*
    Chicago Daily Tribune, December 9–13, 1955.
    Death notice, 12-11-1955 (*Tribune*).
    Demaris, *Captive City*, 222–25.
    McDougal, *Last Mogul*, 36–38.
    Murray, *Legacy of Al Capone*, ch 2.
    Nitti v. Greenberg, Superior Court of Cook County, 2-14-57, case #57S-2335. The estate was probated in Probate Court of Cook County, file #43P-5267, docket 561.
94. FBI memo, Gale to De Loach, 10-20-66.
95. FBI report, Chicago, 7-21-54.
96. FBI report, Chicago, 11-28-54.
97. FBI airtel, SAC Las Vegas to director, 4-18-63.
98. FBI HQ Ziffren file; and memo from SAC LA, 4-30-58, 3.
99. Noted in *Los Angeles Times*, 5-25-56.
100. *Chicago Tribune*, 5-31-56.
101. *Chicago Tribune*, 8-20-52.

Chapter Seven

1. Evans, *Kid Stays*, 69.
2. Int. of Tom Mankiewicz, 4-4-03.
3. Int. of George Jacobs, 2-4-04.
4. Confidential int., 7-1-05.
5. Int. of George Schlatter, 1-20-04.
6. Confidential int., 1-30-03.
7. Nick Tosches, "The Man Who Kept the Secrets," *Vanity Fair*, April 1997.
8. Kelley, *His Way*, 243.
9. Kupcinet, *Kup*, 63–64.
10. Messick, *Secret File*, 346.
11. Messick, *Lansky*, 196.
12. Stanley Pen, *Wall Street Journal*, 2-4-70.
13. Int. of Dr. Lewis Yablonsky, 6-22-04.
14. Int. of Leo Geffner, 3-18-05.
15. Douglas, *Ragman's Son*, 404.
16. Yablonsky, *George Raft*, preface.
17. Int. of Fred Sidewater, 10-31-03.
18. Yablonsky, *George Raft*, 208.
19. *Los Angeles Herald Examiner*, 11-29-80.
20. Int. of Betsy Duncan Hammes, 1-4-03.
21. Int. of Jan Amory, 3-5-03.
22. Confidential int., 1-14-05.
23. *New York Times*, 1-22-96 (Korshak obit).
24. Haygood, *In Black and White*, 222.
25. Fishgall, *Gonna Do Great Things*, 109–18.
26. Haygood, *In Black and White*, 261.
27. Ibid., 259–67.
28. Early, *Sammy Davis Jr. Reader*, 109 (quoting *Kim Novak: Reluctant Goddess* by Peter Harry Brown).

29. Int. of Dana Wynter, 3-17-03.
30. Early, *Sammy Davis Jr. Reader*, 109 (quoting Brown, *Kim Novak*).
31. Silber, *Sammy Davis Jr.*, 200.
32. Int. of George Jacobs, 2-4-04.
33. Silber, *Sammy Davis Jr.*, 195–203; and int. of Arthur Silber, 10-19-04.
34. Haygood, *In Black and White*, 270.
35. Robert Lusetich, "U.S. Lawyer Walked Mob Minefield," *Australian*, 2-16-96.
36. Int. of A. O. Richards, 4-29-03.
37. Int. of Mike Wacks, 4-22-03.
38. Bruck, *When Hollywood Had a King*, 171.
39. Int. of John Van DeKamp, 3-31-04.
40. McDougal, *Last Mogul*, 328–29.
41. Bruck, *When Hollywood Had a King*, 62.
42. Int. of Berle Adams, 2-2-03.
43. Ibid., 172.
44. Int. of John Van DeKamp, 3-31-04.
45. Bruck, *When Hollywood Had a King*, 356.
46. Biskind, *Easy Riders*, 142.
47. Evans, *Kid Stays*, 67–68.
48. Ibid., 69–70.
49. *New West*, 9-13-76.

Chapter Eight

1. *Hoffa biography sources:*
   Brill, *Teamsters*.
   Franco, *Hoffa's Man*.
   Friedman and Schwartz, *Power and Greed*.
   Hoffa, *Hoffa*.
   Hoffa, *Trials of Jimmy Hoffa*.
   "Jimmy Hoffa," *World of Criminal Justice*, 2 vols (Gale Group, 2002), reproduced in Biography Resource Center.
   Moldea, *Hoffa Wars*.
   Schlesinger, *Robert Kennedy*.
   Sheridan, *Fall and Rise of Jimmy Hoffa*.
   Sloane, *Hoffa*.
   Zeller, *Devil's Pact*.
2. Int. of Tom Zander, 12-8-03.
3. Quoted in Moldea, *Dark Victory*, 116.
4. Bruck, *When Hollywood Had a King*, 166.
5. Ibid., 359.
6. Int. of Anderson, 11-6-03.
7. Bruck, *When Hollywood Had a King*, 171.
8. Hersh, *New York Times*, 6-28-76.
9. Demaris, 277.
10. CCC, Lambie memo to file, 1-6-82.
11. Int. of Gianni Russo, 4-28-03.
12. *Chicago Sun-Times*, 9-7-55; and *Chicago Daily News*, 12-7-55.
13. FBI Korshak Correlation Summary, 8-12-68.
14. *New York Daily News*, 3-19-56; also, CCC letter from Virgil Peterson to Lester Velie, 1-17-57.
15. Int. of Royston Webb, 1-31-04.

16. Shefferman sources: Lester Velie in *Reader's Digest*, July 1957; Moldea, *Dark Victory*, 118; *Chicago Tribune*, 10-31-57; Korshak, McClellan testimony.

17. Int. of Wendell Rawls, 6-17-04.

18. Hersh, *New York Times*, 6-27-76.

19. Ibid., 6-30-76.

20. Collier and Horowitz, *Kennedys*, 272.

21. Schlesinger, *Robert Kennedy*, 153.

22. Collier and Horowitz, *Kennedys*, 272–73.

23. Int. of Zander, 12-8-03.

24. Salinger memo to RFK, 6-12-57.

25. Hoffa, *Hoffa*, 105.

26. Ibid., 93–94.

27. Friedman and Schwartz, *Power and Greed*, 148–49.

28. Korshak testimony, McClellan Hearings, pt. 16, 6274–91.

29. FBI HQ Korshak file, Korshak bio, 9-17-63, 9; also, Roy Rowan with Sandy Smith, "50 Biggest Mafia Bosses," *Fortune*, November 1986.

30. Confidential int., 1-14-05.

31. Carol Felsenthal, "The Lost World of Kup," *Chicago Magazine*, June 2004.

32. Letter from Lester Velie to CCC's Virgil Peterson, 1-12-57.

33. Demaris, *Boardwalk Jungle*, 273.

34. FBI HQ Korshak file, Korshak bio, 9-17-63, 15–16.

35. From William K. Lambie Jr. re Marshall Korshak and Sidney Korshak, CCC memo, 10-9-79.

36. Int. of George Schlatter, 1-20-04.

37. Shore, *Someone's in the Kitchen*, 7–8.

38. *Chicago Tribune*, 9-9-58.

39. *Los Angeles Times*, 5-10-62.

40. *Los Angeles Times*, 9-15-69.

41. Details of Alex on the lam from numerous FBI field reports in FBI HQ Korshak file, especially Korshak bio, 9-17-63, 15; and FBI HQ Gus Alex file; also, Roemer, *Man Against the Mob*, 32–42.

42. McClellan Hearings, pt. 34, 13118–24.

43. *Chicago Tribune*, 11-19-58.

44. Int of Zander, 12-8-03.

45. Int. of Adam Walinsky, 12-2-03.

46. Nick Tosches, "The Man Who Kept the Secrets," *Vanity Fair*, April 1997.

47. Int. of Jack Clarke, 5-11-01.

48. *Chicago Tribune*, 1-20-96.

49. *Chicago Daily News*, 12-21-67.

50. Confidential int., 1-14-05.

51. For extensive details of the Kennedy-Raskin relationship, see Hersh, *Dark Side of Camelot*.

52. Unsourced 9-20-79 news article by Roy Harvey, in Marshall Korshak's CCC file.

53. Letter from Kenny O'Donnell to James Foley, 10-18-62, JFK Library Central Name File, box 1513.

54. See Abel, *Missile Crisis*, 75–77; and Schlesinger, *Thousand Days*, 806–8.

55. Int. of Connie Carlson, 10-20-04.

56. Int. of Wendell Rawls, 6-17-04.

57. Int. of Philip Manuel, 11-13-03.

58. Schlesinger, *Robert Kennedy*, 282n.

59. McDougal, *Last Mogul*, 279–80.

60. Hersh, *New York Times*, 6-27-76.

61. McDougal, Last Mogul, 281.

62. *Los Angeles Times*, 5-6-81; and Jules Stein Probate, No. P-664540, filed May 1, 1981—see especially 1988 Complete Inheritance List, 6: 8.

63. Confidential LAPD report, 4-29-69.
64. *Chicago Tribune*, 9-1-59.
65. Reynolds, *Debbie*, 206.
66. Ibid., 16.
67. FBI memo from SAC L.A. to director, 1-29-60, in Rosselli FBI file.
68. Dick Lyneis, *Palm Springs Press-Enterprise*, 7-27-76.
69. Kelley, *His Way*, 448–49.
70. Johns, *Palm Springs Confidential*, passim.
71. Deed cited in FBI Korshak Summary, 8-13-63.
72. *Architectural Digest*, December 1998.
73. Niklas, *Corner Table*, 28–29.
74. Int. of Virginia Korshak, 1-20-04.
75. Int. of Ron Joy, 1-19-04.
76. Bruck, *When Hollywood Had a King*, 354–55.
77. Int. of Leo Geffner, 3-18-05.
78. Int. of Gray Frederickson, 2-28-03.
79. Int. of Dick Brenneman, 12-2-03.
80. Tosches, "Man Who Kept the Secrets."
81. Int. of Leo Geffner, 3-18-05.
82. FBI HQ Korshak file, Korshak bio, 9-17-63, 8.

Chapter Nine

1. Int. of George Jacobs, 2-4-04.
2. Int. of Irvin Owen, 2-15-97; and letter from Owen to author.
3. Int. of John Detra, 5-22-01; also "The Capone Connection," *Las Vegas Review-Journal*, 3-21-99.
4. Roemer, *Man Against the Mob*, 88–89.
5. FBI HQ Alfred Hart file, obtained under FOIA.
6. The history of the Flamingo is best told in W. R. Wilkerson's *The Man Who Invented Las Vegas*.
7. Bruck, *When Hollywood Had a King*, 64.
8. Nick Tosches, "The Man Who Kept the Secrets," *Vanity Fair*, April 1997.
9. Surveillance transcript in FBI HQ Morris Dalitz file.
10. Quoted in Lester Velie, "Las Vegas: The Underworld's Secret Jackpot," *Reader's Digest*, 10-8-59.
11. *Los Angeles Times*, 9-1-89 (obit).
12. Confidential int., 12-11-04.
13. J. Richard Davis, *Collier's*, 8-14-49.
14. Sharp, *Mr. and Mrs. Hollywood*, 445–46.
15. Reid and Demaris, *Green Felt Jungle*, 57.
16. Porrello, *Rise and Fall*, 141.
17. Sifakis, *Mafia Encyclopedia*, 96; and Porrello, *Rise and Fall*, 204–5.
18. Porrello, *Rise and Fall*, 132.
19. Gosch and Hammer, *Last Testament of Lucky Luciano*, 167.
20. Ibid., 286.
21. Fried, *Rise and Fall of the Jewish Gangster*, 234; and Lacey, *Little Man*, 96.
    Additional Dalitz sources include: Hopkins and Evans, *First 100*, 120–24; John L. Smith, "Moe Dalitz and the Desert," in Jack E. Sheehan, ed., *The Players: The Men Who Made Las Vegas* (Reno: University of Nevada Press, 1997), 35–47; and Matt Potter, "Mob Scene," *San Diego Reader*, 11-18-99.
22. Roemer, *War of the Godfathers*, 49–50. Although a fictionalized account, Roemer contended in both the book and in interviews with this author that the dramatizations were based on actual events as learned by the Bureau.
23. *Los Angeles Times*, 9-1-89.

24. Reid and Demaris, *Green Felt Jungle*, 58.

25. Ibid., 53–54.

26. Sharp, *Mr. and Mrs. Hollywood*, 199.

27. Reid and Demaris, *Green Felt Jungle*, 58.

28. Int. of Gray Frederickson, 2-28-03.

29. Int. of Ed Becker, 1-1-03.

30. Int. of Luellen Smiley, 3-21-03.

31. FBI airtel, from SAC Las Vegas to director, 5-21-63.

32. FBI airtel, Las Vegas to HQ, 3-18-61.

33. McDougal, *Last Mogul*, 220.

34. Lacey, *Little Man*, 291–92; and Demaris, *Last Mafioso*, 145.

35. Castle Bank list of depositors obtained from confidential source; also, Lacey, *Little Man*, 386.

36. FBI memo from SAC Las Vegas to director, 11-20-64 (in Dalitz FBI file).

37. FBI teletype from SAC Chicago to director, 2-3-65 (#92-177-144), Korshak file.

38. Rothman, *Neon Metropolis*, 19.

39. Memo from DELETED to SAC LA, 11-19-68 (#92-1112-1165), Korshak file.

40. These details and more about the history of the Las Vegas Strip can be accessed at Deanna DeMatteo's fantastic Web site, lvstriphistory.com.

41. Int. of Tom Mankiewicz, 4-4-03.

42. Int. of Sonny King, 8-9-04.

43. FBI Las Vegas report, 3-19-65 (#92-1170-139), Korshak file.

44. Hersh, *New York Times*, 6-28-76.

45. FBI HQ Korshak file, Korshak bio, 9-17-63, 18.

46. Int. of Dean Elson, 5-3-04.

47. FBI airtel, from SAC Las Vegas to director, 4-18-63.

48. Carlson's notes supplied to author by confidential source.

49. Sheridan DOJ memo to files, 3-13-62, cross-filed in Korshak FBI file.

50. FBI memo from Don Winne to Edward Joyce, deputy chief, DOJ OC and Racketeering Section, 1-27-70 (#94-430-1833), Korshak file.

51. FBI airtel, from SAC Las Vegas to director, 4-18-63.

52. Letter from Clark County Sheriff's Office Intelligence Unit to FBI HQ, 4-3-63.

53. Evans, *Kid Stays*, 114.

54. FBI memo from Don Winne to Edward Joyce, deputy chief, DOJ OC and Racketeering Section, 1-27-70 (#94-430-1833), Korshak file.

55. Los Angeles FBI report, 9-25-63 (#92-113-2085), Korshak file.

56. Int. of confidential source, 1-30-03.

57. Bruck, *When Hollywood Had a King*, 205.

58. Int. of Ed Becker, 1-1-03.

59. Bruck, *When Hollywood Had a King*, 204.

60. FBI HQ Korshak file, Korshak bio, 9-17-63, 5–6.

61. Ibid., 11.

62. Ibid., 20

63. Hersh, *New York Times*, 6-30-76.

64. FBI memo of conversation with informant in New York, 10-13-78 (#CG 183-538-139), Korshak file.

65. FBI teletype from SAC LA to director, 1-16-81 (#183-96 7B-11), Korshak file.

66. Rappleye and Becker, *All American Mafioso*, 139.

67. Demaris, *Last Mafioso*, 131.

68. Ibid., 130–31.

69. Chicago FBI report of John Roberts, 8-31-62.

70. Demaris, *Last Mafioso*, 375–76.

71. CCC memos, 4-15-58, 6-6-62; and *New York Times*, 4-13-54.

72. Reid and Demaris, *Green Felt Jungle*, 70–74.

73. *Chicago Tribune*, 9-9-58.

74. Steven Lovelady, "Cleanup of Vegas Fails to Oust Hoodlums," *Wall Street Journal*, 5-25-89.

75. Rappleye and Becker, *All American Mafioso*, 136.

76. FBI Chicago Field Office memo, John Roberts to file, 8-31-62.

77. Ibid. For more on the Rosselli-Baron friendship, see Rappleye and Becker, *All American Mafioso*, passim.

78. Int. of Morton Downey Jr., 8-17-96.

79. Russo, *Outfit*, 375–78, 389–90.

80. Int. of Joe Longmeyer, 4-14-03.

81. Robert Lusetich, "U.S. Lawyer Walked Mob Minefield," *Australian*, 2-16-96.

82. Int. of Shecky Greene, 3-3-03.

83. FBI HQ Korshak file, Korshak bio, 9-17-63, 17–18.

84. Surveillance transcript in FBI HQ Humphreys file.

85. Zeiger, *Frank Costello*, 187–88.

86. Molasky quoted in A. D. Hopkins, "The Developer's Developer," *Las Vegas Review-Journal*, Internet, undated.

    Other Sunrise Hospital sources: Reid and Demaris, *Green Felt Jungle*; Friedman and Schwarz, *Power and Greed*; Denton and Morris, *Money and the Power*; Reid, *Grim Reapers*; Neff, *Mobbed Up*; and Roemer, various titles.

    Miscellaneous Las Vegas sources: Velie, "Las Vegas"; Jane Ann Morrison, "Mob's LV Clout Doubtful," *Las Vegas Review-Journal*, 4-20-97; Rothman, *Devil's Bargains*; Littlejohn, *Real Las Vegas*; Hal Rothman, "A Hard Look at Las Vegas: The Money and the Power and the Rest of Us," *Las Vegas Review-Journal*, 4-22-01.

87. Moldea, *Interference*, 413; Messick, *Lansky*, 225; and "Scandal in the Bahamas," *Life*, 2-3-67.

88. Grutman and Thomas, *Lawyers and Thieves*, 151.

89. Becker was quoted on a recent History Channel special on the history of Las Vegas.

90. Denton and Morris, *Money and the Power*, 232.

91. Brill, *Teamsters*, 238.

92. Ibid., 239.

Chapter Ten

1. McDougal, *Last Mogul*, 82–85.

2. Kotkin and Grabowicz, *California Inc.*, 59.

3. Horne, *Class Struggle*, passim.

4. Ibid., 213.

5. *San Francisco Chronicle*, 6-9-02; also the Web site http://sfgate.com.

6. Kotkin and Grabowicz, *California Inc.*, 60.

7. Reagan, *American Life*, 108–9.

8. *Reagan sources:* Vaughn, *Ronald Reagan*; Edwards, *Early Reagan*; and Earl Gottschalk Jr., *Wall Street Journal*, 10-29-80.

9. Gottschalk, *Wall Street Journal*.

10. Horne, *Class Struggle*, 214.

11. Int. of Selene Walters, 3-2-05.

12. Moldea, *Dark Victory*, 111.

13. The six-thousand-page 1962 DOJ record was first obtained under FOIA in 1984 by David Robb, who was then with *Daily Variety*, and later chief labor and legal correspondent for the *Hollywood Reporter*. Robb graciously supplied the records to the author.

14. Sharp, *Mr. and Mrs. Hollywood*, 80.

15. Dan Moldea, *The Corruption of Ronald Reagan*, http://Moldea.com, p. 2.

16. Int. of Henry Denker, 8-30-04.

17. Moldea, *Dark Victory*, 126.

18. Ibid., 140.
19. Reagan and Hubler, *Where's the Rest of Me?* 317–18.
20. Moldea, *Dark Victory*, 141.
21. McDougal, *Last Mogul*, 262–65; and Moldea, *Dark Victory*, 142–43.
22. FBI HQ Korshak file, Korshak bio, 9-17-63, 22.
23. Confidential int., 4-25-05.
24. For details of Voloshen's relationship with McCormack (and Korshak's with Voloshen), see Winter-Berger, *Washington Pay-Off.*
25. Miller, *Breaking of a President*, 279–90.
26. *Alhambra Post-Advocate*, 2-2-60.
27. Hill, *Dancing Bear*, 169.
28. Cited in *Alhambra Post-Advocate*, 10-18-58; *Los Angeles Times*, 10-19-58; *Los Angeles Herald-Express*, 10-16-58; and others.
29. Montgomery and Johnson, *One Step from the White House*, 393.
30. *Los Angeles Mirror*, 6-8-58.
31. *Los Angeles Mirror-News*, 4-21-59.
32. Lester Velie, *Reader's Digest*, July 1960, 117.
33. Ibid.
34. Int. of Dick Brenneman, 12-2-03.
35. *Hollywood Citizen News*, 1-5-60.
36. Int. of Connie Carlson, 10-29-04.
37. FBI telex, SAC L.A. to director, 2-15-60.
38. *Los Angeles Times*, 6-19-60.
39. *Los Angeles Mirror-News*, 6-22-60.
40. Bruck, *When Hollywood Had a King*, 215–16.
41. FBI memo, SAC L.A. to director, 6-22-60.
42. L.A. FBI Crimdel memo, 9-27-60.
43. FBI telex, SAC L.A. to director, 5-9-60.
44. FBI telex, SAC L.A. to director, 5-10-60.
45. FBI telex, SAC L.A. to director, 10-16-59, Ziffren FBI file.
46. Ridgely Cummings, *Government Employee* 3 (June 1960).
47. L.A. County Grantor-Grantee Records, Book 26241, 184–207; Book 49977, 272; also FBI telex, SAC L.A. to director, 10-15-59.

Chapter Eleven

1. McDougal, *Last Mogul*, 263.
2. Kelley, *His Way*, 286.
3. Denton and Morris, *Money and the Power*, 218, 222.
4. Sandy Smith, "Bob Kennedy's Role in Factor Pardon Is Told," *Chicago Tribune*, 12-28-62.
5. Bruck, *When Hollywood Had a King*, 201.
6. Demaris, *Captive City*, 123–24.
7. Factor file in the Parole Board Records Collection at the National Archives, College Park, MD.
8. *Detroit Free Press*, 6-10-64; and *Washington Post*, 6-10-64.
9. FBI memo, SAC Chicago to director, 4-26-63.
10. Letter from Moore to Peterson, CCC, 2-16-61.
11. Miller, *Bunny*, 84.
12. Quoted in *Overdrive Magazine*, April 1975.
13. DeMaris, *Captive City*, 89.
14. Chicago Crime Commission, memo to file from William K. Lambie Jr., 10-9-79.
15. FBI HQ Korshak file, Korshak bio, 9-17-63, 7.

16. *Sources for Hefner and the SLA bribery:* Miller, *Bunny*, 81–92; Demaris, *Captive City*, 90–91; Byer, *Hefner's Gonna Kill Me*; *New York Post*, 2-7-62; FBI HQ Korshak file; and various files of Chicago Crime Commission.
17. FBI HQ Korshak file.
18. Int. of Betsy Hammes, 1-4-03.
19. FBI HQ Korshak file, 14.
20. *Chicago Tribune*, 4-13-72.
21. "Marge Everett: Sid Korshak Is My Enemy," *Chicago Daily News*, 1-29-72.
22. Niklas, *Corner Table*, 27.
23. Paul McGrath, "Horsing Around with Off-Track Betting," *Chicago Magazine*, November 1973.
24. *Los Angeles Times*, 2-18-59, 5-12-59; and walteromalley.com.
25. FBI L.A. Field Office, Korshak bio, 8-13-63, 9.
26. Hersh, *New York Times*, 6-28-76.
27. FBI HQ Korshak file, 19.
28. FBI teletype, SAC Chicago to director, 8-4-67 (#92-177-160), Korshak file; and *Los Angeles Times*, 6-13-85.
29. Hersh, *New York Times*, 6-27-76.
30. Int. of Freddie Bell, 8-11-04.
31. Re Villa Venice: Russo, *Outfit*, 43–434; Re Korshak and Fisher: FBI airtel, SAC Las Vegas to director, 10-3-62 (#92-143-144); and FBI Las Vegas report, 11-16-64 (#92-084-61), Korshak file.
32. Roemer, *Enforcer*, 172.
33. FBI Las Vegas airtel to director, 7-24-62 (#92-903-86), Korshak file.
34. FBI memo, DELETED to SAC L.A., July 1967 (#166-1048-166), Korshak file.
35. Reid, *Mickey Cohen*, 42, 45; and confidential int. of friend of Eli Schulman, 4-24-05.
36. FBI memo, DELETED to SAC L.A., 6-14-66 (#92-742-66), Korshak file.
37. FBI memo, DELETED to SAC L.A., 12-3-63 (#91-742-138), Korshak file.
38. FBI memo, SAC San Diego to director, 11-25-69 (#92-742-276), Korshak file.
39. For a profile of McCulloch, see Felch and Tevlick, "Unsung Hero," *American Journalism Review*, 6-29-04.
40. Ibid.
41. Int. of Knut Royce, 4-22-03.
42. Int. of Ed Guthman, 1-19-04.
43. Int. of Frank McCulloch, 1-5-05.
44. Rabbi Edward Feinstein Archives, *City of Angels*, Rosh Hashanah, 2000.
45. McDougal, *Last Mogul*, 241.
46. FBI L.A. Field Office, Korshak bio, 8-13-63, 23.
47. See McDougal, *Privileged Son*.
48. Int. of Frank McCulloch, 1-5-05; see also McDougal, *Privileged Son*, 246–49.
49. Ronald Kessler, *Washington Post*, 12-16-73.
50. Moldea, *Hoffa Wars*, 107–8; and Summers and Swan, *Arrogance of Power*, 211–12.
51. Int. of Tom Zander, 12-8-03.
52. Investigated by Summers and Swan, *Arrogance of Power*, 253–59.
53. Tobin and Blake, *Los Angeles Times*, 5-17-62.
54. Letters from McCulloch to Peterson, 5-23-62, 6-6-62; from Tobin to Peterson, 5-2-62; and Parker to Peterson, 5-4-62.
55. McDougal, *Privileged Son*, 246–49.
56. Int. of Ed Guthman, 1-19-04.
57. Int. of Connie Carlson, 10-20-04.
58. Int. of Frank McCulloch, 1-5-05.
59. McDougal, *Privileged Son*, 249.
60. FBI HQ Korshak file, 3.
61. *Chicago Tribune*, 11-25-64.
62. Int. of Leo Geffner, 3-18-05.
63. Confidential int., 1-4-05.

64. FBI teletype, Salt Lake City to L.A., 1-16-61 (#92-143-57).

65. FBI report of John Roberts (Chicago), 8-31-62.

66. FBI airtel, Chicago SAC to director, 12-8-61 (#92-113-636).

67. FBI memo, DELETED to SAC L.A., 4-25-63 (#92-113-2155), Korshak file.

68. FBI teletype, SAC Las Vegas to director, 2-2-63.

69. Confidential int., 1-14-05.

70. Smith, "Bob Kennedy's Role"; also, Touhy, *When Capone's Mob Murdered Roger Touhy*, 252–54.

71. McDougal, *Last Mogul*, 286.

72. Robb DOJ cache.

73. For extensive details of the Kennedy-Raskin relationship, see Hersh, *Dark Side of Camelot*.

74. McDougal, *Last Mogul*, 317–18.

75. Quoted in Andrew, *Power to Destroy*, 214.

76. Mills, *Disorderly House*, 84.

77. Ibid., 86.

78. Hersh, *New York Times*, 6-29-76.

79. Summers and Swan, *Arrogance of Power*, 228–30; also, Miller, *Breaking of a President*, 157–58.

80. McWilliams, *Nation*, 6-2-62.

81. Louella Parsons, *Los Angeles Herald Examiner*, April 15, 24, 1963.

82. Chicago Crime Commission, memo from Virgil W. Peterson, 6-6-62.

83. FBI HQ Korshak file, 18.

84. Exner, *My Story*, 277–81.

85. Ibid.

86. Int. of Milton Ebbins, 1-17-05.

87. Rappleye and Becker, *All American Mafioso*, 209; Summers, *Goddess*, 268 (NAL paperback version); and Giancana and Giancana, *Double Cross*, 311–16.

88. Roemer, *Man Against the Mob*, 175; and Russo, *Outfit*, 431–32.

89. Russo, *Outfit*, 375–78, 389–90.

90. *Chicago Tribune*, 6-8-63.

Chapter Twelve

1. Int. of Andrew Furfaro, 10-20-04.

2. Andrew, *Power to Destroy*, 4–5, 141–42.

3. Reid and Demaris, *Green Felt Jungle*, 77.

4. FBI report of DELETED, 9-11-64 (#161-171-9), Korshak file.

5. Reid, *Grim Reapers*, 254.

6. IRS int. of Sidney Korshak by Furfaro, 10-23-63.

7. *Chicago Tribune*, 1-20-80.

8. FBI HQ Korshak file, Korshak bio, 9-17-63, 11.

9. IRS report of Furfaro and Turner, 10-23-63.

10. Quoted in Zolotow, *Billy Wilder in Hollywood*, 225.

11. Bistro records from California Division of Corporations, file #1922461.A, filed on 8-1-63; and California Department of Alcoholic Beverage Control, lic. #47-3071.

12. Niklas, *Corner Table*, 21, 33.

13. Ibid., 334–35, 339.

14. "The Bistro's Secret of Success," *Los Angeles Times*, 1-30-72.

15. Niklas, *Corner Table*, 10–11.

16. Ibid., 22–26.

17. Int. of James Bacon, 1-14-04.

18. Int. of Casper Morcelli, 2-20-04.

19. Int. of Jimmy Murphy, 2-6-04.

20. Int. of Leo Geffner, 3-18-05.
21. Int. of Hennie Burke, 1-24-04.
22. Int. of Timothy Applegate, 4-12-04.
23. Ints. of Steve Allen, January and February 1997; see also Allen, *Hi-Ho, Steverino!*, 132–48, and Allen, *Ripoff*, passim.
24. Demaris, *Last Mafioso*, 525.
25. Int. of Dick Brenneman, 12-2-03. Brenneman, a former reporter for the *Sacramento Bee,* extensively researched Korshak and located sources who were aware of Korshak's phone habits. "SK's chauffeur used to drive him around L.A. with a bag full of coins to use pay phones," Brenneman said. "He often used the phone belonging to Harry Drucker."
26. Int. of Timothy Applegate, 4-12-04.
27. Rappleye and Becker, *All American Mafioso*, 62.
28. Ibid., 162.
29. Int. of Don Wolfe, 1-5-05.
30. Int. of Ira Silverman, 3-10-04.
31. Int. of Andy Anderson, 11-6-03.
32. Bruck, *When Hollywood Had a King*, 359–60.
33. Int. of Duke Zeller, 4-8-03.
34. E-mail from Andy Anderson, 2-14-05.
35. Int. of Andy Anderson, 11-6-03.
36. Int. of Nancy Czar, 1-25-04.
37. Int. of Gianni Russo, 4-28-03.
38. Int. of Leo Geffner, 3-18-05.
39. Bruck, *When Hollywood Had a King*, 359.
40. Int. of Mike Wacks, 4-22-03.
41. Quoted in *Vanity Fair*, April 1997.
42. Int. of Fran Marracco, 2-27-04.
43. Bruck, *When Hollywood Had a King*, 351–52.
44. Hersh, *New York Times,* 6-30-76.
45. Int. of David Schippers, 5-11-04.
46. Int. of Adam Walinsky, 12-3-03.
47. Bruck, *When Hollywood Had a King*, 390–91.
48. FBI memo of surveillance, 4-26-79 (#183-96-&C-1), in FBI Korshak file.
49. Int. of Marvin Rudnick, 4-2-04.
50. Int. of Mike Wacks, 4-22-03.
51. Int. of David Schippers, 5-11-04.
52. Int. of Peter Vaira, 4-12-04.
53. Int. of Tom Zander, 12-8-03.
54. Int. of Andrew Furfaro, 10-20-04.
55. Int. of Connie Carlson, 10-20-04.
56. Int. of John Van DeKamp, 3-28-04.
57. Int. of James Grodin, 12-8-03.
58. Niklas, *Corner Table*, 19.
59. *Chicago Tribune*, 11-4-63.
60. Int. of Leo Geffner, 3-18-05.
61. Int. of Carol Felsenthal, 7-1-04, author of June 2004 *Chicago Magazine* profile of Kupcinet; see also James Ellroy, "Glamour Jungle," *GQ*, December 1998, 291.
62. Kelley, *His Way*, 329–31.
63. Int. of Ron Joy, 1-19-04.
64. Sinatra, *Frank Sinatra*, 181.
65. Niklas, *Corner Table*, 348.

Chapter Thirteen

1. Quoted in Reid, *Grim Reapers*, 208–9.
2. FBI airtel (Chicago to L.A.) of electronic surveillance (ELSUR), 7-16-64 (#92-149-A-3), Korshak file.
3. FBI Korshak Correlation Summary Report, 8-12-68.
4. FBI memo from DELETED to SAC L.A., 10-19-65 (#92-742-169), Korshak file.
5. FBI teletype from Chicago to director, 3-1-65 (#92-149-47), Korshak file.
6. Confidential int., 1-14-05.
7. Bruck, *When Hollywood Had a King*, 360.
8. Douglas, *Ragman's Son*, 403.
9. Johns, *Palm Springs Confidential*, 82.
10. FBI memo from DELETED to SAC L.A., 3-8-77.
11. Various issues of the *Las Vegas Sun*, August 1965 to March 1966, copied at Library of Congress.
12. FBI radiogram from SAC L.A. to director, Chicago and Las Vegas, 3-2-66, in FBI HQ Korshak file.
13. Summers, *Official and Confidential*, 247–53; also numerous mob biographies, especially Lacey, *Little Man*, 66, 97, 99.
14. *Los Angeles Times*, 4-11-66.
15. Ints. with UFW communications director Marc Grossman, 1-24-05, and Chavez film biographer Rick Tejada-Flores (producer, *The Fight in the Fields*), 1-24-05; various California newspapers from June 1966, especially *Los Angeles Herald-Examiner*, 6-21-66; also, UFW history at Web sites ufw.org and cesarchavezfoundation.org.
16. Int. of Paul Schrade, 1-24-05.
17. Schlesinger, *Robert Kennedy and His Times*, 851.
18. Int. of Leo Geffner, 3-18-05.
19. Dunne, *Delano*, 90–91.
20. Levy, *Cesar Chavez*, 215–17.
21. Int. of Leroy Chatfield, 1-24-05.
22. Int. of Wayne "Chris" Hartmire, 2-7-05.
23. Levy, *Cesar Chavez*, 215–17.
24. Bart, *New York Times*, 4-6-66.
25. Confidential int. with former Rosensteil attorney, 1-24-05.
26. Re Korshak and Chavez: Levy, *Cesar Chavez: Autobiography of La Causa*, 215–17; Griswold del Castillo and Garcia, *Cesar Chavez*, 52–53; Ferriss and Sandoval, *Fight in the Fields*, 121–22; Taylor, *Chavez and the Farm Workers*, 175–76; Dunne, *Delano*, passim.
27. Dan Swinton, *Los Angeles Herald-Examiner*, 5-29-66.
28. Ibid.
29. FBI memo from DELETED to SAC L.A., 9-14-66 (#92-438-63), Korshak file.
30. *Los Angeles Times*, 9-15-69.
31. Niklas, *Corner Table*, 406.
32. Hill, *Dancing Bear*, 214.
33. FBI memo from DELETED to SAC L.A., 11-17-66 (#92-742-214), Korshak file.
34. McDougal, *Last Mogul*, 331.
35. Int. of Henry Denker, 8-30-04.
36. *San Francisco Chronicle*, 6-9-02; also the Web site http://sfgate.com.
37. Jim Drinkhall, *Wall Street Journal*, 8-1-80; Paul Wilner, *Los Angeles Herald-Examiner*, 8-2-80; and Howard Kohn and Lowell Bergman, *Rolling Stone*, 8-26-76.
38. Undated FBI memo cited in Moldea, *Dark Victory*, 227.
39. Drosnin, *Citizen Hughes*, 474.
40. Korshak testimony before the SEC, 6-23-70, 419–20.
41. Int. of Edward Becker, 1-1-03.
42. FBI airtel from SAC L.A. to director, 5-17-67; secondary docs: airtel from SAC L.A. to director, 6-5-67; HSCA outside-contact reports of Ed Reid, 1-1-78, 10-20-78; FBI memo, Rosen to DeLoach, 5-15-67; and HSCA, vol. 11 (Organized Crime), 78–92.

43. FBI L.A. memo of conversation, 12-18-70, Korshak file.
44. Int. of Sandy Smith, 11-11-03.
45. Hersh, *New York Times*, 6-30-76.
46. Unsigned memo in CCC Korshak file, 11-15-66.
47. FBI teletype, SAC Chicago to director, 11-4-66.
48. CCC memo, from William K. Lambie Jr., 10-9-79.
49. Sandy Smith, "The Mob," *Life*, 9-1-67.
50. Felch and Tevlick, "Unsung Hero," *American Journalism Review*, 6-29-04.
51. Bruck, *When Hollywood Had a King*, 165–66.
52. Int. of Jan Amory, 3-5-03.
53. Bart, *Who Killed Hollywood?*, 113.
54. Bluhdorn, "The Gulf and Western Story" (speech before the Newcomen Society, 6-7-73).
55. *Newsweek*, 5-31-65.
56. McDougal, *Last Mogul*, 231, 367.
57. Biskind, *Easy Riders*, 144–45.
58. Dick, *Engulfed*, 102.
59. Biskind, *Easy Rider*, 147.
60. *Vanity Fair*, April 1997.
61. Evans, *Kid Stays*, 98.
62. Ibid., 106.
63. Int. of Dana Wynter, 3-17-03.
64. Biskind, *Easy Rider*, 146.
65. James Mills, *Life*, 3-7-69.
66. Moldea, *Interference*, 466; and Hersh, *New York Times*, 6-29-76.
67. Bruck, *When Hollywood Had a King*, 359.
68. Ibid., 355.
69. George Gurley, "Afternoon of a Golden Girl," *New York Observer*, 10-27-03.

Chapter Fourteen

1. Int. of MJ Goldblatt, 6-6-04.
2. Int. of Dean Elson, 5-3-04.
3. Int. of Gray Frederickson, 2-28-03.
4. Int. of Gianni Russo.
5. Int. of Jimmy Murphy, 2-6-04.
6. Niklas, *Corner Table*, 31; Kup quoted in *Vanity Fair*, April 1997; and int. of Virginia Korshak, 1-20-04.
7. Exner, *My Story*, 278–79.
8. FBI memo, DELETED to SAC L.A., 10-19-65 (#92-742-169), Korshak file.
9. Jill St. John, SEC testimony, 8-21-69, 60.
10. Bruck, *When Hollywood Had a King*, 297.
11. Int. of Nancy Czar, 1-25-04.
12. Int. of Fred Sidewater, 5-6-03.
13. FBI airtel, SAC L.A. to director, 3-4-66 (#92-742-180), Korshak file.
14. FBI memo, DELETED to SAC L.A., 10-19-65 (#92-742-169), Korshak file.
15. Niklas, *Corner Table*, 31.
16. Heymann, *Poor Little Rich Girl*, 283.
17. Ibid., 33–34.
18. Niklas, *Corner Table*, 33–34.
19. Int. of Gray Frederickson, 2-28-03.
20. Ibid.
21. Maxine Cheshire, "Sinatra-Agnew," *Washington Post*, 2-35-72.

22. See especially, Christopher Hitchens, *Trial of Henry Kissinger*.
23. Maxine Cheshire, "Too Many Cooks," *Washington Post*, 9-17-72.
24. Int. of Jan Amory, 3-5-03.
25. Int. of Jack Clarke, 1-31-04.
26. Int. of Tom Mankiewicz, 4-4-03.
27. Niklas, *Corner Table*, 31–32.
28. Bruck, *When Hollywood Had a King*, 297–98.
29. Ibid., 297.
30. Int. of Missy Chandler, 2-27-04.
31. Int. of Ron Joy, 1-19-04.
32. FBI memo, DELETED to SAC L.A., 12-9-71 (#92-742-328), Korshak file.
33. Nick Tosches, "The Man Who Kept the Secrets," *Vanity Fair*, April 1997.
34. Int. of Virginia Korshak, 1-20-04.
35. Confidential int., 1-14-05.
36. Int. of Ed Becker, 1-1-03.
37. FBI memo, DELETED to SAC L.A., 10-12-66 (#92-792-207), Korshak file.
38. Doris Lilly, "Party Line" column, *Los Angeles Times*, undated clipping.

Chapter Fifteen

1. *Los Angeles Times*, 6-24-70.
2. Testimony of Richard F. Gliebe before Illinois Board of Investigation, 7-15-70, 166–68, 183.
3. *Chicago Sun-Times*, 7-16-70.
4. Testimony of Gliebe, 195.
5. *Chicago Today*, 6-24-70.
6. Testimony of Gliebe, 161–63; Robert Glass, "Hint Mob Role in Hotel Sale," *Chicago Today*, 7-15-70; and *Chicago Sunday Times*, 7-16-70.
7. Testimony of Gliebe, 179.
8. Ibid., 183.
9. Confidential int., 2-22-05.
10. Fletcher Wilson, *Chicago Sun-Times*, 7-16-70.
11. Int. of Nancy Czar, 1-25-04.
12. Korshak, SEC testimony, 7-23-70, 425.
13. Messick, *Politics of Prosecution*, 90.
14. Glass, "Hint Mob Role."
15. *Los Angeles Times*, 6-24-70.
16. Int. of Jack Clarke, 1-31-04.
17. Moldea, *Interference*, 222.
18. *Overdrive* magazine, April 1975.
19. Haber, *Los Angeles Times*, January 28, 29, 1969.
20. Testimony of Gliebe, 223.
21. The Canadian reports are included in the personal files of the late IRS "Operation Tradewinds" investigator Sally Woodruff, supplied to author. For more on this operation, read Block, *Masters of Paradise*; see also Messick, *Lansky*, 263–64.
22. Int. of Jim Grodin, 12-8-03.
23. *Chicago Tribune*, 7-15-70.
24. Transcript of Hughes press conference, 1-7-72.
25. *Los Angeles Times*, 5-9-69.
26. Messick, *Lansky*, 152.
27. Moldea, *Interference*, 471.

28. See #17181, U.S. Court of Appeals, 7th Circuit, Additional Appendix, 109–20; *New York Times Index*, "U.S. Intelligence Agency," 1967; and Final Report by the Special Subcommittee on House Res. 920, of the Committee on the Judiciary, House of Representatives, 91st Cong., 2nd sess., 9-17-70, 18–21.

29. Korshak SEC testimony, 287.

30. *Newsweek*, 6-2-69, 7-23-70.

31. Korshak SEC testimony, 288.

32. Ibid., 425.

33. Ibid., 384.

34. Memo from Winne to Edward Joyce, deputy chief, DOJ OC and Racketeering Section, 1-27-70 (#94-430-1823), Korshak file.

35. Korshak SEC testimony, 293, 385.

36. *Wall Street Journal*, 1-7-70.

37. *Fortune*, December 1969, 163.

38. Raw et al., *Do You Sincerely Want to Be Rich?*, 4.

39. Messick, *Lansky*, 248.

40. See Basichis, *Beautiful Bad Girl*; and Milton and Bardach, *Vicki*.

41. The presence of Cornfeld (and mobsters) at the Towers is noted in Canadian intelligence reports in Operation Tradewinds files of investigator Sally Woodruff, supplied to author. For more on this operation, read Block, *Masters of Paradise*; see also Messick, *Lansky*, 263–64.

42. Raw et al., *Do You Sincerely Want to Be Rich?*, 151.

43. Ibid., 242.

44. See Rinfret's Web log, rinfret.com/vesco; also, Herzog, *Vesco*, passim.

45. Drosnin, *Citizen Hughes*, 489.

46. The Lenzner-Maheu revelations appeared in a *60 Minutes* (CBS) interview of 2-27-05; see also Drosnin, *Citizen Hughes*, 5, 304, 489.

47. *Wall Street Journal*, 6-9-69.

48. Jill St. John, SEC testimony, 8-21-69, 30–31.

49. *New York Times*, 6-29-76.

50. *Wall Street Journal*, 6-9-69; and Demaris, *Last Mafioso*, 319.

51. *Chicago Daily News*, 10-17-69; and *Chicago Tribune*, 10-18-69.

52. Sidney Korshak SEC testimony, 371–72.

53. Ibid., 401; also, *Time*, 10-24-69, and numerous *New York Times* articles in 1971.

54. Winter-Berger, *Washington Pay-Off*, 80; Miller, *Breaking of a President*, 284–87.

55. Miller, *Breaking of a President*, 286.

56. Korshak SEC testimony, 356–57, 410.

57. Winter-Berger, *Washington Pay-Off*, 80.

58. Drosnin, *Citizen Hughes*, 19; and Barlett and Steele, *Howard Hughes*, 521.

59. Int. of Virginia Korshak, 1-20-04; see also Sharp, *Mr. and Mrs. Hollywood*, 349–51.

60. Glaser Primary Probate in Cook County (IL) Circuit Court, File #69 P 3458, Docket 160, p. 89; also, L.A. Superior Court Probate, #P552490.

61. Sharp, *Mr. and Mrs. Hollywood*, 348.

62. Int. of Virginia Korshak, 1-20-04.

63. *Los Angeles Times*, 9/15/69.

64. IBI (Illinois Board of Investigation) testimony of Phil Levin, 6-23-70, 71.

65. Bluhdorn testimony before IBI, 7-14-70, 29–32.

66. Jack Newfield, "The Power of Sidney Korshak," *Village Voice*, 3-18-76.

67. Int. of Ed Guthman, 1-19-04.

68. Int. of Paul Steiger, 4-19-04.

69. Int. of Andy Anderson, 11-6-03.

70. Int. of Leo Geffner, 3-18-05.

71. McDougal, *Last Mogul*, 396–97.
72. *Chicago Today*, 10-21-69.
73. *Chicago Sun-Times*, 10-31-69.
74. Bruck, *When Hollywood Had a King*, 353.

Chapter Sixteen

1. *Los Angeles Herald-Examiner*, 12-28-69.
2. *Los Angeles Times*, 1-24-70.
3. Int. of Leo Geffner, 3-18-05.
4. Niklas, *Corner Table*, 29–30.
5. McDougal, *Last Mogul*, 442.
6. Kelley, *Nancy Reagan*, 177–78.
7. Messick, *Politics of Prosecution*, 92–95.
8. Confidential int., 12-18-04.
9. *Los Angeles Times*, 7-10-70.
10. Peter Bart, "On the Trail of Funny Money," *Variety*, 12-11-00.
11. Yallop, *In God's Name*, 308.
12. Naylor, *Hot Money*, passim.
13. Lernoux, *In Banks We Trust*, 180.
14. *Sindona biographical sources:*

    DiFonzo, *St. Peter's Banker*; Robinson, *The Laundrymen*; Williams, *Vatican Exposed*; Yallop, *In God's Name*; Cornwell, *God's Banker*; Tosches, *Power on Earth*; *National Catholic Reporter*, 3-28-86, 3-13-87, 12-24-93, 4-4-86, 1-24-86, 3-4-86, 3-6-87, 4-27-87, 5-15-87, 3-17-89, 11-9-90, 10-4-00; *Wall Street Journal*, 7-7-99, 7-8-99, 7-2-99, 3-19-86, 3-10-89, 6-22-87, 4-27-87, 2-27-87; *New York Times*, 12-18-83, 1-30-86, 11-4-86, 3-23-86 (obit), 3-26-86, 3-22-86, 3-21-86, 3-19-86, 10-17-93, 4-27-89, 3-10-89, 6-9-88, 12-11-87, 7-18-87; *Guardian*, 3-22-01; Associated Press, 10-26-02; Diane Scarponi, *The Herald Sun* (online), 5-16-02; *Variety*, 4-1-99; *Forbes*, 8-16-93; *Euromoney*, October 1998; *Newsweek*, 3-31-86; *Time*, 3-31-86; *New Statesman*, 3-28-86; *American Banker*, 7-3-89; *Canadian Banker*, March 1997.
15. Dick, *Engulfed*, 122–47.
16. Bart, *Who Killed Hollywood?* 114.
17. Ibid., 114–17.
18. *Chicago Sun-Times*, 5-21-70.
19. *Chicago Tribune*, 7-15-70.
20. Korshak SEC testimony, 7-23-70, 129.
21. Ibid., 298.
22. *New York Times*, 6-29-76.
23. *SEC v. Parvin Dohrmann et al.*, Consent Decree, 69 Civ. 4543 (ELP) U.S. District Court, Southern District of New York; also "Final Judgment" and various affidavits of defendants.
24. Int. of Paul Steiger, 4-19-04.
25. *New York Times*, 8-25-71.
26. Int. of Jan Amory, 3-5-03.
27. *Los Angeles Times*, 8-11-70.
28. *Chicago Daily News*, 7-20-71; and *Chicago Sun-Times*, 6-16-71.
29. *Chicago Tribune*, 6-18-71.
30. *Chicago Daily News*, 8-3-71.
31. *Chicago Tribune*, 11-16-71; and *Chicago Daily News*, 1-29-72.
32. Niklas, *Corner Table*, 28.
33. Ibid., 29.
34. Ibid.

Chapter Seventeen

1. Sheridan, *Fall and Rise of Jimmy Hoffa*, 487–521.
2. Velie, *Desperate Bargain*, 133.
3. Int. of Duke Zeller, 4-8-03.
4. Int. of Jack Clarke, 1-31-04.
5. Int. of Tom Mankiewicz, 4-4-03.
6. Int. of Gianni Russo, 4-28-03.
7. Mollenhoff, *Game Plan for Disaster*, 45.
8. Gordon Chaplin, *Washington Post*, 4-2-80; Blumenthal and Yazijian, *Government by Gunplay*, 135; Jeff Gerth, "Nixon and the Miami Connection (Nixon and the Mafia)," *Sundance*, November–December 1972; and Gerth, "Richard M. Nixon and Organized Crime," *Penthouse*, 1974.
9. *Detroit Free Press*, FBI "Hoffa Disappearance" cache, obtained in 2002, and given to the author by *Free Press* reporter David Ashenfelter.
10. Mike Livingston, "Watergate: The Name That Branded More Than a Building," *Washington Business Journal*, 6-14-02.
11. Justice Department memo, Muellenberg to Stewart, 11-26-76, 15.
12. FBI Detroit Field Office internal memo, 3-29-77.
13. Velie, *Desperate Bargain*, 151.
14. Brill, *Teamsters*, 92–93; Miller, *Breaking of a President*, 298–99; and Moldea, *Hoffa Wars*, 317.
15. Balsamo and Carpozi, *Crime Incorporated*, 347.
16. Korshak tax records obtained from U.S. Tax Court, Docket Nos. 4850–72, 4851–72, 2145–71, 4677–71; *Chicago Today*, 9-8-72, 9-9-72, 9-29-72; *Chicago Daily News*, 9-8-72; *Chicago Tribune*, 9-9-72, 10-1-74; and *Chicago Sun-Times*, 9-9-72, 10-1-74; and *Los Angeles Times*, 9-16-72.
17. *U.S. v. Marshall Korshak*, U.S. District Court for Northern District of Illinois, Eastern Division, Docket #73 C 820, filed 4-23-73.
18. *Chicago Sun-Times*, 3-31-73.
19. *Chicago Tribune*, 4-3-73.
20. *Chicago Sun-Times*, 4-20-73.
21. *Chicago Today*, 4-4-73; and *Chicago Tribune*, 4-3-73.
22. *Chicago Daily News*, 4-24-73; and *Chicago Tribune*, 4-25-73.
23. *Chicago Tribune*, 5-18-73.
24. *Chicago Daily News*, 8-13-73; *Chicago Today*, 8-13-73; *Chicago Sun-Times*, 8-14-73; and *Chicago Tribune*, 8-14-73.
25. Confidential int. of close Teitelbaum acquaintance, 5-14-05.
26. Demaris, *Boardwalk Jungle*, 316.
27. Bob Wiedrich, *Chicago Tribune*, 2-28-71.
28. Biskind, *Easy Riders*, 153.
29. "The Godfather Speaks," *Cigar Aficionado*, October 2003; and Biskind, *Easy Riders*, 142–64.
30. Torgerson, *Kerkorian*, 230–31.
31. *Kerkorian biographical sources*:
    Torgerson, *Kerkorian*; *Washington Post*, 9-15-04; *Business Week*, 5-6-91, 74; 4-14-95, 34; 5-15-95, 40; *Car and Driver*, July 1995, 29; *Fortune*, 5-15-95, 44; *Newsweek*, 4-24-95, 46; *New Yorker*, 12-11-95, 44; *Time*, 4-24-95, 54; *Vanity Fair*, February 1996, 88; and Rod Smith, *Las Vegas Review-Journal*, 6-20-04.
32. Evans, *Kid Stays*, 222.
33. "Godfather Speaks," *Cigar Aficionado*.
34. Michael Sragow, "Godfatherhood," *New Yorker*, 3-24-97.
35. Int. of Gianni Russo, 4-28-03; also, Al Ruddy, 2-27-03.
36. Int. of Gianni Russo, 4-28-03; and his unpublished autobiography, "Godfathers, Popes, and Presidents."
37. Int. of Gray Frederickson, 2-28-03.
38. "Godfather Speaks," *Cigar Aficionado*.
39. Interviews of Steve Allen, 1996, 1997.

40. Evans, *Kid Stays*, 3–11.
41. Biskind, *Easy Riders*, 236.
42. See ch. 16, n. 14.
43. Int. of Fred Sidewater, 5-6-03.
44. Kezich and Levantesi, *Dino*, 223–25.
45. Tosches, *Power on Earth*, 178.
46. Evans, *Kid Stays*, 202.
47. Terrill, *Steve McQueen*, 220–30; also, McCoy, *Steve McQueen*.
48. Biskind, *Easy Riders*, 160.
49. *New West*, 9-13-76.
50. Biskind, *Easy Riders*, 239.
51. Niklas, *Corner Table*, 389–90.
52. Evans, *Kid Stays*, 273–74.
53. Ibid., 256.
54. Int. of Tom Mankiewicz, 4-4-03.
55. Broccoli, *When the Snow Melts*, 40.
56. Ibid., passim; and *New York Times*, 6-29-96.
57. Confidential int., 1-14-05.
58. Peter Evans, "Has Time Banked the Fires of Sexy Agent 007?" *Calendar*, 7-25-71.
59. Int. of Lana Wood, 12-19-03.
60. Broccoli, *When the Snow Melts*, 251.
61. FBI memo to SAC L.A., 8-21-72 (#92-1485-13), Korshak file.

Chapter Eighteen

1. Int. of Leo Geffner, 3-18-05.
2. FBI memo, DELETED to SAC L.A., 7-20-73 (#92-1112-1949), FBI People's Industrial Consultant file.
3. Epstein, *Big Picture*, 110.
4. Beaty and Hornik, "A Torrent of Dirty Dollars," *Time*, 12-18-89.
5. Bruck, *When Hollywood Had a King*, 345–48.
6. Puttnam, *Movies and Money*, 212.
7. For more on movie investment tax credits see U.S. Senate, *Hearings Before the Committee on Finance*, 92nd Cong., 1st sess., 1971, 196; also, Richard Warren Lewis, "Gimme Shelter," *New West*, 6-7-76.
8. Brownstein, *Power and the Glitter*, 217.
9. *Variety*, 9-9-97, 9-25-97, and 4-8-98.
10. Bart, *Variety*, 12-22-02.
11. Bruck, *When Hollywood Had a King*, 351.
12. Torgerson, *Kerkorian*, 295; Joyce Haber, *Los Angeles Times*, 10-29-73.
13. McDougal, *Last Mogul*, 368.
14. Hersh, *New York Times*, 6-29-76.
15. Int. of Berle Adams, 3-3-03.
16. Brill, *Teamsters*, 373–74.
17. Demaris, *Last Mafioso*, 373.
18. Int. of John Van DeKamp, 3-31-04.
19. Letter, FBI SAC San Diego to acting director, 2-21-73 (#92-267-292), Korshak file.
20. Bart, *Who Killed Hollywood?*, 116.
21. Int. of Gray Frederickson, 2-28-03.
22. *Los Angeles Herald-Examiner*, 10-2-73.
23. Int. of Jimmy Murphy, 2-6-04.
24. Int. of Casper Morcelli, 2-20-04.
25. Niklas, *Corner Table*, 19.

26. Int. of Nancy Czar, 1-25-04.
27. FBI memo, DELETED to SAC L.A., 7-19-73 (#92-113-3979), Korshak file.
28. Niklas, *Corner Table*, 18.
29. Int. of Pete Wacks, 5-10-03.
30. Niklas, *Corner Table*, 20.
31. FBI teletype, Chicago to director, 1-16-74.
32. FBI airtel, Chicago to director, New York, and L.A., 1-16-74 (#92-267-297), Korshak file.
33. Details of the heist from Barlett and Steele, *Howard Hughes*, 518–49.
34. Drosnin, *Citizen Hughes*, 4–5.
35. CIA memo to FBI director, 8-5-74.
36. Barlett and Steele, *Howard Hughes*, 526.
37. Drosnin, *Citizen Hughes*, 26, 467; and Barlett and Steele, *Howard Hughes*, 527.
38. Drosnin, *Citizen Hughes*, 505.
39. Kotkin and Grabowicz, *California Inc.*, 82.
40. Ibid., 85.
41. *Miami Herald*, 1-25-81.
42. *Laxalt background: Organized Crime Digest* (VA), February 1982; *Miami Herald*, 1-5-81; *Sacramento Bee*, 11-1-83; and Denton and Morris, *Money and the Power*, passim.
43. Denton and Morris, *Money and the Power*, 340.
44. Ibid., 348.
45. Int. of Joe Yablonsky, 5-31-05.
46. Brashler, *Don*, 320, 328, 341–342; and Roemer, *Roemer*, 226.
47. For more on these operations, see Corbitt and Giancana, *Double Deal*.
48. The FBI's suspicions of Giacalone are memorialized in a 349-page file from their "Hoffa Disappearance" investigation, headed by Kurt Muellenberg, released to the *Detroit Free Press* in 2002. The complete report was kindly supplied to the author by the lead reporter on the story, David Ashenfelter. Hoffa expert Dan Moldea independently reached a similar conclusion in his book *Hoffa Wars*.
49. Niklas, *Corner Table*, 21.
50. Int. of Ed Becker, 1-1-03.
51. Report supplied by a confidential source.
52. McDougal, *Last Mogul*, 395.
53. Demaris, *Last Mafioso*, 323.
54. Ibid., 375.
55. Ibid., 376–77.
56. *Chicago Tribune*, 7-2-93.
57. FBI memo, SAC Chicago to ADIC L.A., 1-26-77.
58. Bahrenburg, *Creation*, 14.
59. Ibid., 53.
60. Sharp, *Mr. and Mrs. Hollywood*, 353.
61. Confidential source; also Jim Harwood, "Wasserman, Korshak Figure in NBC H'Wood Crime Report; Dino Cries Foul," *Variety*, 12-17-78; and Moldea, *Dark Victory*, 286.
62. FBI memo, DELETED to SAC L.A., 7-20-76, Korshak file.
63. Kezich and Levantesi, *Dino*, 218; and Bahrenburg, *Creation*, 60.
64. Int. of Fred Sidewater, 5-6-03.
65. Int. of E. Timothy Applegate, 4-12-04.
66. Joyce Haber, *Los Angeles Times*, 11-22-75.
67. *New York Times*, 6-28-76.

Chapter Nineteen

1. Int. of Seymour Hersh, 5-16-03.
2. Int. of Adam Walinsky, 12-3-03.

3. Grutman and Thomas, *Lawyers and Thieves*, 141–54.

4. Int. of MJ Goldblatt, 6-6-04.

5. Int. of confidential source, 12-3-03.

6. Int. of Jan Amory, 3-5-03.

7. Int. of Tom Zander, 12-8-03.

8. Frank Lalli, *New West*, 8-2-76.

9. *Chicago Tribune*, 6-28-76; and *Chicago Sun-Times*, 6-29-76.

10. Int. of Leo Geffner, 3-18-05.

11. FBI airtel, SAC Chicago to SAC L.A., 9-17-76.

12. *New York Times*, 6-30-76.

13. Hentoff, *Village Voice*, 7-19-76.

14. Lalli, *New West*.

15. Ibid.

16. *Congressional Record*, 9-30-76, 17384–85.

17. Moore letter to *New York Times*, 9-13-76. This and other related letters found in various work files (especially Mollenhoff) of the 1986 President's Commission on Organized Crime, located in the National Archives, College Park, MD.

18. Moore, "Was Estes Kefauver 'Blackmailed.' "

19. *New York Times*, 7-1-76.

20. Int. of Tim Applegate, 4-12-04.

21. *Chicago Sun-Times*, 7-9-76.

22. Ibid., 7-4-76.

23. Int. of Marvin Rudnick, 4-2-04.

24. Int. of Tom Mankiewicz, 4-4-03.

25. Int. of Jan Amory, 3-5-03.

26. New Jersey Division of Gaming Enforcement int. of Barron Hilton, 6-22-83.

27. Confidential int.

28. *Chicago Sun-Times*, 7-4-76.

29. Sharp, *Mr. and Mrs. Hollywood*, 354.

30. *New West*, 8-2-76.

31. *Los Angeles Times*, 8-21-76; Carter quoted in Moldea, *Dark Victory*, 278; see also McDougal, *Last Mogul*, 397.

32. FBI airtel, L.A. to SAC New York, 12-14-76.

33. FBI memo, DELETED to SAC L.A., 7-6-77.

34. FBI memo of int., 2-25-76 (#183-118).

35. FBI memo, director to asst. AG, Criminal Division, 12-29-76.

36. Telex, SAC L.A. to director, 10-31-75, *Queen Mary* RICO.

37. Memo, UNDISCLOSED to SAC L.A., 7-13-76, Korshak file.

38. McDougal, *Last Mogul*, 400.

39. *New York Times*, 8-29-76.

40. Ibid., 9-12-76.

41. Demaris, *Boardwalk Jungle*, 278.

42. CCC, Lambie memo to file on Pritzker, 1-6-82.

43. Lernoux, *In Banks We Trust*, 85.

44. Int. of Andy Furfaro, 10-20-24.

45. Quoted in Jim Drinkhall, *Wall Street Journal*, 4-18-80.

46. See especially Lernoux, *In Banks We Trust*, 77–99, and Block, *Masters of Paradise*. For a general overview of international money laundering, see Robinson, *Laundrymen*.

47. "Oversight Hearings into the Operations of the IRS (Operation Tradewinds, Project Haven, and Narcotics Traffickers Tax Program)," *Hearings Before a Subcommittee of the Committee on Government Operations*, House of Representatives, 94th Cong., 1st sess., October 6, November 4 and 11, 1975 (U.S. Government Printing Office, 1976).

48. Confidential int., 5-14-05.
49. See Royce's series on the Pritzkers in the *Kansas City Times*, March 8, 9, and 10, 1982.
50. *Kansas City Times*, 3-10-82.
51. Lewis and Allison, *Cheating of America*, 64.
52. Ibid., 62–64.
53. Summers and Swan, *Arrogance of Power*, 253–59.
54. Ibid.
55. Lewis and Allison, *Cheating of America*, 62.
56. *John and Martha Fogerty v. Kanter et al.*, complaint before the Superior Court of the State of California, County of Santa Barbara, 3-20-78.
57. Graham Nixon, *The Castle Bank of Nassau Story*, http://members.tripod.com/riverising/members-graham/bank.html; and Block, *Masters of Paradise*, 191–93, 314–23.
58. *Billboard*, 5-14-83.
59. *Nassau Guardian*, 12-8-75; and *Los Angeles Times*, 1-28-76.
60. *San Francisco Examiner*, 10-31-76; and *Los Angeles Times*, 6-11-76.
61. The ruling came in the case of Jack Payner, an Ohio businessman who had been charged with failing to report that he had a trust account at Castle. The Justice Department and the IRS used the trial judge's ruling as the basis for ending the investigation in 1977. "IRS v. CIA: Big Tax Investigation Was Quietly Scuttled by Intelligence Agency: Bahamian Bank's Hundreds of U.S. Account Holders Go Unchecked as a Result," *Wall Street Journal*, 4-18-80.
62. Ibid.; see also, U.S. Supreme Court, *United States v. Payner*, 447 U.S. 727 (1980). The 106-page Castle Bank Depositors List made available to author from confidential source.
63. Jonathan Dahl, *Wall Street Journal*, 2-18-87.
64. Block, *Masters of Paradise*, 292.
65. Lernoux, *In Banks We Trust*, 92.
66. "Tax Me If You Can," *Frontline* (PBS, WGBH), 2-19-04.
67. Allison, *Perfectly Legal: Taking Advantage of Holes in the Revenue Net*, http://www.tompaine.com/feature.cfm/ID/4196.

Chapter Twenty

1. Kelley, *His Way*, 437–39; and Sinatra, *Frank Sinatra*, 244–45.
2. Sinatra, *My Father's Daughter*, 158.
3. Kelley, *His Way*, 434.
4. Sinatra, *My Father's Daughter*, 158.
5. Ibid., 199.
6. *Architectural Digest*, December 1998, 184.
7. *Los Angeles Times*, 4-16-80; Kupcinet, *Chicago Sun-Times*, 4-11-80, 7-30-80; and McDougal, *Last Mogul*, 420.
8. *Los Angeles Herald-Examiner*, 7-8-80.
9. Kiernan, *Roman Polanski Story*, 77.
10. Ibid., 97.
11. Brenneman, "Roman, Larry, Sidney, and Me," unpublished.
12. Kiernan, *Roman Polanski Story*, 251.
13. *New York Times*, July 24, 24, and 26, 1977.
14. Dick, *Engulfed*, 146.
15. Ibid., 147.
16. *International Directory of Corporate Histories* (St. James Press, 1998), 1:451–53; see also Bagdikian, *Media Monopoly*, 27–29.
17. Dick, *Engulfed*, 147.
18. *Chicago Tribune*, 6-27-78.

19. Quoted in *Chicago Sun-Times*, 8-28-77.
20. List at http://www.chicagojewishnews.com/lists_chijews.jsp.
21. *Chicago Today*, 5-5-72.
22. *Chicago Sun-Times*, 4-26-73; and *Chicago Today*, 4-25-73.
23. *Chicago Today*, 5-3-74; and *Wall Street Journal*, 5-3-74.
24. *Chicago Sun-Times*, 5-4-74.
25. *Chicago Today*, 5-6-74; *Chicago Sun-Times*, 5-7-74; and *Chicago Tribune*, 5-7-74.
26. *Chicago Today*, 4-22-74.
27. Ibid., 4-23-74.
28. Confidential interview.
29. Paul McGrath, *Chicago Magazine*, November 1973.
30. *Chicago Tribune*, 9-18-79.
31. Ibid., 1-14-83.
32. *Sentinel*, 9-21-89.
33. *Chicago Sun-Times*, 2-5-90.
34. Hefner testimony from his 1983 appeal for a New Jersey casino license, Superior Court of New Jersey, Appellate Division, Case #A-4188-8lTl, "In the Matter of the Application of Playboy-Elsinore Assoc. for a Casino License."
35. Bruck, *When Hollywood Had a King*, 360.
36. UPI wire dispatch, 5-13-78.
37. Moldea, *Dark Victory*, 285.
38. Jack Tobin notes; int. of Dick Brenneman, 12-2-03.
39. *Los Angeles Herald-Examiner*, 9-10-78; also, *Los Angeles Magazine*, January 1979.
40. Witcover, *Marathon*, 333.
41. Int. of Steve Hronek, 1-23-04.
42. Int. of Jim Grodin, 1-24-04.
43. Int. of Brian Ross, 4-19-04.
44. Organized Crime Control Commission, *First Report*, May 1978, obtained from the California State Library in Sacramento (c1690.R4-1978); also, Mike Qualls, "Crime Syndicate: $6.8 Billion Annual Take Told," *Los Angeles Herald-Examiner*, 5-2-78; Bill Farr, "Mafia Making Major California Move," *Los Angeles Times*, 5-3-78; and Robert Lindsey, *New York Times*, 5-3-78.
45. Int. of E. Timothy Applegate, 4-12-04.
46. Mike Qualls, "Alleged Crime Figure Says List 'Pure Politics,' " *Los Angeles Herald-Examiner*, 5-7-78.
47. CCC memo to file from William K. Lambie, re Evelle Younger, 4-16-80; and Moldea, *Dark Victory*, 286.
48. Tobin memo to file (Jack Tobin files), 1-19-69.
49. Mike Qualls, "Younger-FBI Feud Sparks Questions," *Los Angeles Herald-Examiner*, 5-7-78.
50. Int. of Brian Ross, 4-19-04.
51. Int. of Fred Sidewater, 5-6-03.
52. E-mail from Ira Silverman, 4-25-05.
53. Video copies of the program obtained from the Vanderbilt University Television News Archive.
54. FBI teletype, L.A. to director, 8-27-85, Korshak file.
55. "The Brink's Job: U.S. Probing Alleged Mob Link with Movie," *Los Angeles Times*, 12-14-78.
56. Int. of Leo Geffner, 3-18-05.
57. Harry Bernstein, *Los Angeles Times*, 3-23-79.
58. "The Hollywood Park Story," 6-19-05, tape from Vanderbilt University Television News Archives.
59. Quoted in Moldea, *Dark Victory*, 290.
60. *Evening Press* (Binghamton, NY), 7-20-79.
61. *San Francisco Chronicle*, 7-12-79.
62. *Sacramento Union*, 7-15-79.
63. *Chicago Sun-Times*, 7-22-79.
64. *Chicago Tribune*, 3-9-80; also 3-5-80.

65. Hauser testimony before Permanent Subcommittee on Government Affairs, 98th Cong., 1st sess., pt. 3, April 27 and 28, 1983.
66. *Los Angeles Times*, 5-26-79.
67. Kupcinet, *Chicago Sun-Times*, 2-15-80.
68. *Los Angeles Times*, 7-2-81.
69. Jim Drinkhall, *Wall Street Journal*, 8-6-79.
70. Newbart and Pallasch, "The Blues Brothers: 25 Years Later," *Chicago Sun-Times*, 6-24-05.
71. DOJ memo to FBI SAC, L.A., 3-13-80 (183-967-100), copied in Korshak FBI file.

Chapter Twenty-one

1. Robert W. Maitlin, *Newark Star-Ledger*.
2. *October Surprise sources:* Leslie Cockburn, *Out of Control* (New York: Atlantic Monthly Press, 1987); Jean-Charles Deniau and Bani Sadr, *Le Complot des ayatollahs* (Paris: Éditions la Découverte, 1987); Ted Goertzel, "Belief in Conspiracy Theories," *Political Psychology* 15 (1994); Gary Sick, *October Surprise: America's Hostages in Iran and the Election of Ronald Reagan* (New York: Times Books, 1991); Steven Emerson, "No October Surprise," *American Journalism Review*, March 1993; *Joint Report of the Task Force to Investigate Certain Allegations Concerning the Holding of American Hostages by Iran in 1980* (Washington, DC: U.S. Government Printing Office); U.S. Senate, Committee on Foreign Relations, *The "October Surprise" Allegations and the Circumstances Surrounding the Release of the American Hostages Held in Iran* (Washington, DC: U.S. Government Printing Office, 1992).
3. Re convictions: Zeller, *Devil's Pact*, 22.
4. Friedman and Schwarz, *Power and Greed*, 258.
5. FBI summary report, 10-28-83.
6. Williams testimony before the President's Commission on Organized Crime, 1986.
7. Kelley, *His Way*, 458.
8. "Admitted Mafia Killer Asserts in Book That Reagan Aide Is Tied to Syndicate," *New York Times*, 12-25-80.
9. "Kup's Sunday Column," *Chicago Tribune*, 3-8-81.
10. Friedman and Schwarz, *Power and Greed*, 258.
11. Moldea, *Interference*, 419–20; and Moldea, *Dark Victory*, 317–34.
12. Moldea, *Dark Victory*, 324.
13. Evans, *Kid Stays*, 306.
14. Re the charges: *New York Times*, 8-1-80, 9-22-80.
15. Evans, *Kid Stays*, 309.
16. Letter from Gerth and Bergman to DRAM, 1-28-81, author's files.
17. Grutman and Thomas, *Lawyers and Thieves*, 143.
18. Int. of Knut Royce, 4-22-03.
19. *Chicago Tribune*, 2-24-82, 3-8-82.
20. Corbitt, *Double Deal*, 216.
21. *Sources for Playboy-Pritzker:* Playboy-Elsinore Appellate Hearings before Superior Court of New Jersey, A-4188-8lTl, 6-14-83; In re Boardwalk Regency Corp. Application for a Casino License, 90 NJ 361, 369, 1982; Miller, *Bunny*, 333–42; *Wall Street Journal*, various 1982; *Chicago Tribune*, 2-24-82, 12-16-81, 3-8-82, 4-14-82; *Chicago Sun-Times*, 4-8-82; and Johnston, *Temples of Chance*, passim.
22. Miller, *Bunny*, 342.
23. *Chicago Tribune*, 11-24-85.
24. *Ann Arbor News*, 6-8-83.
25. *Chicago Tribune*, 1-12-83.
26. *New York Times*, 1-21-83; *Chicago Sun-Times*, 1-21-83; and *Washington Post*, 1-21-83.
27. Moldea, *Interference*, 367.
28. Int. of Mike Corbitt, 3-19-03.
29. FBI telex, L.A. to director, 1-26-83.

30. Hanley biographical data from the Illinois Police and Sheriff's News Web site, http://www.ispn.org.

31. *New York Times*, 2-20-83.

32. Felch and Tevlick, "Unsung Hero," *American Journalism Review*, 6-29-04.

33. Int. of Frank McCulloch, 1-5-05.

34. Int. of Dick Brenneman, 12-2-03.

35. *Washington Post*, 6-5-87.

36. Int. of Denny Walsh, 1-5-04.

37. *Washington Post*, 7-8-86.

38. Felch and Tevlick, "Unsung Hero."

39. Sharp, *Mr. and Mrs. Hollywood*, 443–47.

40. *Los Angeles Times*, 1-24-84.

41. Int. of Connie Carlson, 10-20-04.

42. Int. of David Robb, 9-14-04.

43. Int. of Dan Moldea, 12-13-04.

44. Int. of E. Timothy Applegate, 4-12-04.

45. Hilton testimony, Division of Gaming Enforcement, 6-22-83.

46. Korshak quoted in draft of unsent Applegate 1997 letter to *Vanity Fair* magazine, supplied to author by Applegate.

47. *Business Week*, January 1988.

48. Deposition of William O. Pessel Jr. before NJ Casino Control Commission, 11-20-84.

49. NJ Division of Gaming Enforcement interview report of Marshall Korshak and David Mendelsohn, 10-18-83.

50. CCC hearings, 2-28-85, 14:2012.

51. Bruck, *When Hollywood Had a King*, 392.

52. Trump, *Trump*, 149–64.

53. See Zion, *Autobiography of Roy Cohn*; and von Hoffman, *Citizen Cohn*.

54. Johnston, *Temples of Chance*, 91.

55. *Los Angeles Times*, 6-27-91.

56. FBI teletype, L.A. to director, 1-11-85, Korshak file.

57. FBI L.A. memo of conversation, 2-14-85 (Korshak file).

58. McDougal, *Last Mogul*, 442.

59. Zeller, *Devil's Pact*, 107.

60. FBI memo summarized in Department of Justice summary of Teamsters RICO investigation, 1-15-81, Korshak FBI file.

61. FBI teletype, L.A. to Boston, 12-9-80, Korshak file.

62. *Vanity Fair*, April 1997.

63. McDougal, *Last Mogul*, 442.

64. Bruck, *When Hollywood Had a King*, 393–94.

65. Brenneman notes.

66. Int. of Dick Brenneman, 12-2-03.

67. *Chicago Sun-Times*, 11-21-85.

68. Williams testimony, 34.

69. Fratianno testimony, 46.

70. Moldea, *Interference*, 348–49.

71. Niklas, *Corner Table*, 28.

72. Gianni Russo, unpublished manuscript, 209–19.

73. Int. of Gianni Russo, 4-28-03.

74. Dannen, *Hitmen*, 272–89.

75. *Sources for the mob and MCA:* Knoedelseder, "Salvatore Pisello: A Shadowy Figure in Records Deals," *Los Angeles Times*, 5-4-86; Michael Orey, "Death of a Mob Probe," *American Lawyer*, July 1988; Dan Moldea, "MCA and the Mob: Did the Justice Department Cut Reagan's Hollywood Pals a Break?" *Regardie's*, June 1988; Knoedelseder, *Stiffed*; Moldea, *Dark Victory*.

76. Quoted in Akst and Emshwiller, "Image Fight: MCA Is Battling Accounts Linking It to Organized Crime," *Wall Street Journal*, 9-12-88.
77. McDougal, *Last Mogul*, 457–58.
78. Transcript of *60 Minutes*, 11-19-89, obtained from CBS.
79. Sharp, *Mr. and Mrs. Hollywood*, 477.
80. Ibid.
81. Int. of Marvin Rudnick, 4-2-04.
82. Sharp, *Mr. and Mrs. Hollywood*, 449.
83. Quoted in McDougal, *Last Mogul*, 446.
84. Int. of Marvin Rudnick, 4-2-04.

Chapter Twenty-two

1. Broccoli, *When the Snow Melts*, 290.
2. Individual Grant Deed from L.A. Recorder's Office, #87-714122, 5-6-87; Cooke: Obit, *Washington Post*, 4-7-97; and Havill, *Last Mogul*, especially 128.
3. *Los Angeles Times*, 1-18-96.
4. *St. Louis Post-Dispatch*, 2-18-89, 8-10-89, 3-26-95.
5. John L. Smith, "The Double Life of Moe Dalitz," *Las Vegas Review-Journal*, http://www.1st100.com/part2/dalitz.html.
6. *Reagan-USSR sources:* Steele, *Limits of Soviet Power*; Smith, *Russians* and *New Russians*; Richard Ned Lebow and Janice Gross Stein, "Reagan and the Russians," *Atlantic Monthly*, February 1994; Kennan, *At a Century's Ending*; Zinn, *People's History*, especially 591–92.
7. Kennan, op-ed, *New York Times*, 10-28-92.
8. "The Quiet Mover and Shaker: The Late Paul Ziffren Was a Hardworking Patriot for Los Angeles," *Los Angeles Times*, 6-4-91.
9. *Los Angeles Times*, 4-4-91.
10. Velie, *Reader's Digest*, July 1960, 114.
11. Int. of Connie Carlson, 10-20-04.
12. Bio of Ken Ziffren compiled from various articles in *Variety* online archives.
13. *Los Angeles Times*, 8-23-92.
14. *Los Angeles Times*, 11-12-92.
15. Sinatra, *My Father's Daughter*, 227.
16. *Variety*, 8-11-93.
17. Int. of David Robb, 9-14-04; and *Hollywood Reporter*, 8-19-94.
18. Bart, *Who Killed Hollywood?*, 117.
19. Int. of Dominick Dunne, 4-19-05.
20. Int. of George Schlatter, 4-20-04.
21. Confidential int., 1-14-05.
22. Int. of Virginia Korshak, 1-20-04.
23. *Chicago Tribune*, 1-20-96.
24. Eugene Kennedy, *New York Times Magazine*, 12-29-96.
25. Int. of Jimmy Murphy, 2-6-04.
26. *New York Daily News*, 1-23-96.
27. *Chicago Jewish News*, 1-26-96.
28. Bruck, *When Hollywood Had a King*, 244.
29. *Los Angeles Times*, 1-22-96.
30. Int. of Gianni Russo, 4-28-03.
31. Bruck, *When Hollywood Had a King*, 356.
32. Int. of George Schlatter, 1-20-04.
33. McDougal, *Last Mogul*, 264.

34. *Guardian* (Manchester, England), 1-23-96.

35. Int. of Mike Wacks, 4-22-03.

36. Int. of Sy Hersh, 5-16-03.

37. McDougal, *Last Mogul*, 327.

38. Jeff Gerth, "Richard Nixon and Organized Crime," in Blumenthal and Yazijian, *Government by Gunplay*, 99.

39. Int. of Edwin Guthman, 1-19-04.

40. Int. of Tom Mankiewicz, 4-4-03.

41. *Beverly Hills Courier*, 1-26-96.

42. Sinatra, *My Father's Daughter*, 283.

43. Lewis and Allison, *Cheating of America*, 62–64.

44. Truell and Gurwin, *False Profits*, 125n.

45. Senate Committee on Foreign Relations, staff int. of Abdar Sakhia, 10-7-91, 102nd Cong., 2nd sess.

46. *New York Times*, 12-11-01.

47. "Shattered Dynasty," *Vanity Fair*, May 2003.

48. *The Pritzkers in the Nineties: Chicago Tribune*, 3-6-04, 4-6-04, 12-29-04; and "Shattered Dynasty," *Vanity Fair*.

49. "Inside the Pritzker Family Feud," *Chicago Tribune*, 6-12-05.

50. *Los Angeles Times*, 6-4-02.

51. *New York Post*, 8-5-04.

52. Sharp, *Mr. and Mrs. Hollywood*, 494.

53. See especially Zwillman's Kefauver testimony.

54. *Los Angeles Times*, 6-4-02.

55. Demaris, *Last Mafioso*, 129–30.

56. See especially Johnston, *California's Gabrielino Indians*; and MacMillan, *Missions*.

Bibliography

Books

Abel, Elie. *The Missile Crisis*. New York: Bantam Books, 1966.

Ahlgren, Gregory, and Stephen Monier. *Crime of the Century: The Lindbergh Kidnapping Hoax*. Boston: Brandon Books, 1993.

Ainsworth, Ed. *Maverick Mayor: A Biography of Sam Yorty of Los Angeles*. Garden City, NY: Doubleday, 1966.

Allen, Steve. *Hi-Ho, Steverino! My Adventures in the Wonderful Wacky World of TV*. Thorndike, ME: Thorndike Press, 1992.

Allen, Steve, with Roslyn Bernstein and Donald H. Dunn. *Ripoff: A Look at Corruption in America*. Secaucus, NJ: Lyle Stuart, 1979.

Andersen, Christopher P. *A Star, Is a Star, Is a Star! The Lives and Loves of Susan Hayward*. Garden City, NY: Doubleday, 1980.

Anderson, Jack, and Fred Blumenthal. *The Kefauver Story*. New York: Dial Press, 1956.

Andrew, John A. *Power to Destroy: The Political Uses of the IRS from Kennedy to Nixon*. Chicago: I. R. Dee, 2002.

Ashkenazi, Abraham. *The Prince: Analytic Notes and Review*. New York: American R.D.M. Corp., 1966.

Bagdikian, Ben H. *The Media Monopoly*. Boston: Beacon Press, 1983.

Bahrenburg, Bruce. *The Creation of Dino De Laurentiis' King Kong*. New York: Pocket Books, 1976.

Baker, Bobby, with Larry L. King. *Wheeling and Dealing: Confessions of a Capitol Hill Operator*. New York: Norton, 1978.

Balio, Tino. *United Artists: The Company Built by the Stars*. Madison: University of Wisconsin Press, 1976.

———. *United Artists: The Company That Changed the Film Industry*. Madison: University of Wisconsin Press, 1987.

Balsamo, William, and George Carpozi Jr. *Crime Incorporated: The Inside Story of the Mafia's First 100 Years*. Far Hills, NJ: New Horizon Press, 1991.

Barlett, Donald L., and James B. Steele. *Howard Hughes: His Life and Madness*. New York: W. W. Norton, 2004. (Prev. published as *Empire*, 1979.)

Barnes, Alan, and Marcus Hearn. *Kiss Kiss Bang! Bang!: The Unofficial James Bond Film Companion*. Woodstock, NY: Overlook Press, 1998.

Bart, Peter. *Who Killed Hollywood? . . . and Put the Tarnish on Tinseltown*. Los Angeles: Renaissance Books, 1999.

Basichis, Gordon. *Beautiful Bad Girl: The Vicki Morgan Story*. Santa Barbara: Santa Barbara Press, 1985.

Beck, Warren A., and David A. Williams. *California: A History of the Golden State*. Garden City, NY: Doubleday, 1972.

Bergreen, Laurence. *Capone: The Man and the Era*. New York: Simon & Schuster, 1994.

Berkow, Ira. *Maxwell Street: Survival in a Bazaar*. Garden City, NY: Doubleday, 1977.

Birmingham, Stephen. *"Our Crowd": The Great Jewish Families of New York*. New York: Harper & Row, 1967.

Biskind, Peter. *Easy Riders, Raging Bulls: How the Sex-Drugs-Rock-'n'-Roll Generation Saved Hollywood*. New York: Simon & Schuster, 1998.

Block, Alan A. *Masters of Paradise: Organized Crime and the Internal Revenue Service in the Bahamas*. New Brunswick, NJ: Transaction Publishers, 1998.

Block, Alan A., and Constance A. Weaver. *All Is Clouded by Desire: Global Banking, Money Laundering, and International Organized Crime*. Westport, CT: Praeger, 2004.

Bluhdorn, Charles G. *The Gulf + Western Story*. New York: Newcomen Society of the United States, 1973.

Blumenthal, Sid, and Harvey Yazijian. *Government by Gunplay: Assassination Conspiracy Theories from Dallas to Today*. New York: New American Library, 1976.

Bollens, John C., and Grant B. Geyer. *Yorty: Politics of a Constant Candidate*. Pacific Palisades, CA: Palisades Publishers, 1973.

Bollens, John C., and G. Robert Williams. *Jerry Brown: In a Plain Brown Wrapper*. Pacific Palisades, CA: Palisades Publishers, 1978.

Bowden, Charles, and Lew Kreinberg. *Street Signs Chicago: Neighborhood and Other Illusions of Big City Life*. Chicago, IL: Chicago Review Press, 1981.

Boyar, Burt, and Jane Boyar. *Why Me?: The Sammy Davis Jr. Story*. New York: Farrar, Straus & Giroux, 1989.

Bradlee, Benjamin C. *A Good Life: Newspapering and Other Adventures*. New York: Simon & Schuster, 1995.

Brashler, William. *The Don: The Life and Death of Sam Giancana*. New York: Harper & Row, 1977.

Brill, Steven. *The Teamsters*. New York: Simon & Schuster, 1978.

Brillstein, Bernie, and David Resin. *Where Did I Go Right?: You're No One in Hollywood Unless Someone Wants You Dead*. Boston: Little, Brown, 1999.

Brittain-Catlin, William. *Offshore: The Dark Side of the Global Economy*. New York: Farrar, Straus & Giroux, 2005.

Broccoli, Albert R., with Donald Zec. *When the Snow Melts: The Autobiography of Cubby Broccoli*. London: Boxtree, 1998.

Brown, Peter Harry, and Patte B. Barham. *Marilyn: The Last Take*. New York: Dutton, 1992.

Brown, Peter Harry, and Pat H. Broeske. *Howard Hughes: The Untold Story*. Cambridge, MA: Da Capo Press, 2004.

Brownstein, Ronald. *The Power and the Glitter: The Hollywood-Washington Connection*. New York: Pantheon Books, 1990.

Bruck, Connie. *When Hollywood Had a King: The Reign of Lew Wasserman, Who Leveraged Talent into Power and Influence*. New York: Random House, 2003.

Bunch, William. *Jukebox America: Down Back Streets and Blue Highways in Search of the Country's Greatest Jukebox*. New York: St. Martin's Press, 1994.

Burton, Hendrick J. *The Jews in America*. New York: Arno Press, 1923.

Byer, Stephen. *Hefner's Gonna Kill Me When He Reads This* . . . Chicago: Allen-Bennett, 1972.

Cahan, Richard. *A Court That Shaped America: Chicago's Federal District Court from Abe Lincoln to Abbie Hoffman*. Evanston, IL: Northwestern University Press, 2002.

Cheshire, Maxine, with John Greenya. *Maxine Cheshire, Reporter*. Boston: Houghton Mifflin, 1978.

Ciccone, F. Richard. *Daley: Power and the Presidential Politics*. Chicago: Contemporary Books, 1996.

Cleland, Robert Glass. *California in Our Time (1900–1940)*. New York: A. A. Knopf, 1947.

Cohen, Adam, and Elizabeth Taylor. *American Pharaoh: Mayor Richard J. Daley: His Battle for Chicago and the Nation*. Boston: Little, Brown, 2000.

Cohen, Mickey, as told by John Peer Nugent. *Mickey Cohen, in My Own Words: The Underworld Autobiography of Michael Mickey Cohen*. Englewood Cliffs, NJ: Prentice Hall, 1975.

Cohn, Victor. *Sister Kenny: The Woman Who Challenged the Doctors*. Minneapolis: University of Minnesota Press, 1975.

Collier, Peter, and David Horowitz. *The Kennedys: An American Drama*. San Francisco: Encounter Books, 2002.

Collins, Gail. *Scorpion Tongues: Gossip, Celebrity, and American Politics*. New York: William Morrow, 1998.

Connors, Thomas. *Meet Me in the Bar: Classic Drinks from America's Historic Hotels*. New York: Stewart, Tabori & Chang, 2003.

Cook, David A. *Lost Illusions: American Cinema in the Shadow of Watergate and Vietnam, 1970–1979*. New York: Charles Scribner's Sons, 2000.

Corbitt, Michael, with Sam Giancana. *Double Deal: The Inside Story of Murder, Unbridled Corruption, and the Cop Who Was a Mobster*. New York: William Morrow, 2003.

Cork, John. *James Bond, the Legacy: Forty Years of 007 Movies*. New York: Harry N. Abrams, 2002.

Cornwell, Rupert. *God's Banker: An Account of the Life and Death of Roberto Calvi*. London: V. Gollancz, 1983.

Cray, Ed. *Chief Justice: A Biography of Earl Warren*. New York: Simon & Schuster, 1997.

Custen, George F. *Twentieth Century's Fox: Darryl F. Zanuck and the Culture of Hollywood*. New York: Basic Books, 1997.

Cutler, Irving. *The Jews of Chicago: From Shtetl to Suburb (Ethnic History of Chicago)*. Urbana: University of Illinois Press, 1996.

D'Abo, Maryam, and John Cork. *Bond Girls Are Forever: The Women of James Bond*. New York: Harry N. Abrams, 2003.

Daniels, Bill, David Leedy, and Steven D. Sills. *Movie Money: Understanding Hollywood's Creative Accounting Practices*. Los Angeles: Silman-James Press, 1998.

Daniels, Roger. *The Decision to Relocate the Japanese Americans*. Philadelphia: Lippincott, 1975.

Dannen, Fredric. *Hitmen: Power Brokers and Fast Money Inside the Music Business*. New York: Vintage Books, 1991.

Davis, John H. *Mafia Kingfish Carlos Marcello and the Assassination of John F. Kennedy*. New York: Signet, 1989.

Davis, Margaret Leslie. *Rivers in the Desert: William Mulholland and the Inventing of Los Angeles*. New York: HarperCollins Publishers, 1993.

Davis, Sammy, Jr. *Hollywood in a Suitcase*. New York: Morrow, 1980.

Davis, Sammy, Jr., Jane Boyar, and Burt Boyar. *Sammy: An Autobiography*. New York: Farrar, Straus & Giroux, 2000.

Demaris, Ovid. *The Boardwalk Jungle*. New York: Bantam Books, 1986.

———. *Captive City: Chicago in Chains*. New York: Lyle Stuart, 1969.

———. *Dirty Business: The Corporate-Political Money-Power Game*. New York: Harper's Magazine Press, 1974.

———. *Judith Exner: My Story*. New York: Grove Press, 1977.

———. *The Last Mafioso: "Jimmy the Weasel" Fratianno*. New York: Bantam Books, 1981.

Denton, Sally, and Roger Morris. *The Money and the Power: The Making of Las Vegas and Its Hold on America, 1947–2000*. New York: Knopf, 2001.

Dick, Bernard F. *Engulfed: The Death of Paramount Pictures and the Birth of Corporate Hollywood*. Lexington: University Press of Kentucky, 2001.

Dietrich, Noah, and Bob Thomas. *Howard, the Amazing Mr. Hughes*. Greenwich, CT: Fawcett Publications, 1972.

Difonzo, Luigi. *St. Peter's Banker*. New York: Watts, 1983.

Donner, Frank. *Protectors of Privilege: Red Squads and Police Repression in Urban America*. Berkeley: University of California Press, 1990.

Dorsett, Lyle W. *The Pendergast Machine*. New York: Oxford University Press, 1968.

Douglas, Helen Gahagan. *A Full Life*. Garden City, NY: Doubleday, 1982.

Douglas, Kirk. *The Ragman's Son*. New York: Simon & Schuster, 1988.

Drosnin, Michael. *Citizen Hughes: In His Own Words, How Howard Hughes Tried to Buy America*. New York: Holt, Rinehart & Winston, 1985.

Dunar, Andrew J. *The Truman Scandals and the Politics of Morality*. Columbia: University of Missouri Press, 1984.

Dunne, Dominick. *The Way We Lived Then: Recollections of a Well-Known Name Dropper*. New York: Crown, 1999.

Dunne, George H. *Hollywood Labor Dispute: A Study in Immorality*. Los Angeles: Conference Publishing Company, 1950.

Dunne, John Gregory. *Delano: The Story of the California Grape Strike*. New York: Farrar, Straus & Giroux, 1967.

Early, Gerald, ed. *The Sammy Davis Jr. Reader.* New York: Farrar, Straus & Giroux, 2001.

Edmonds, Andy. *Bugsy's Baby: The Secret Life of Mob Queen Virginia Hill.* Secaucus, NJ: Carol Publishing Group, 1963.

Edwards, Anne. *Early Reagan: The Rise to Power.* New York: Morrow, 1987.

Ehrenhalt, Alan. *The Lost City: Discovering the Forgotten Virtues of Community in the Chicago of the 1950s.* New York: Basic Books, 1995.

Epstein, Edward Jay. *The Big Picture: The New Logic of Money and Power in Hollywood.* New York: Random House, 2005.

Evans, Robert. *The Kid Stays in the Picture.* New York: Hyperion, 1994.

Exner, Judith, as told to Ovid Demaris. *My Story.* New York: Grove Press, 1977.

Falcone, Giovanni, and Marcelle Padovani. *Men of Honour: The Truth About the Mafia.* New York: Harper-Collins, 1992.

Faulkner, William. *Requiem for a Nun.* New York: Random House, 1951.

Ferrell, Robert H. *Truman and Pendergast.* Columbia: University of Missouri Press, 1999.

Ferriss, Susan, and Ricardo Sandoval. *The Fight in the Fields: Cesar Chavez and the Farmworkers Movement.* New York: Harcourt Brace, 1997.

Fishgall, Gary. *Gonna Do Great Things: The Life of Sammy Davis Jr.* New York: Scribner, 2003.

Fontenay, Charles L. *Estes Kefauver: A Biography.* Knoxville: University of Tennessee Press, 1980.

Fox, Stephen. *Blood and Power: Organized Crime in Twentieth-Century America.* New York: Penguin Books, 1989.

Franco, Joseph (Joe), with Richard Hammer. *Hoffa's Man: The Rise and Fall of Jimmy Hoffa as Witnessed by His Strongest Arm.* New York: Prentice Hall Press, 1987.

Freidel, Frank. *Franklin D. Roosevelt: A Rendezvous with Destiny.* Boston: Little, Brown, 1990.

Fremon, David K. *Chicago Politics Ward by Ward.* Bloomington: Indiana University Press, 1988.

Fried, Albert. *The Rise and Fall of the Jewish Gangster in America.* New York: Holt, Rinehart & Winston, 1980.

Friedman, Allan, and Ted Schwarz. *Power and Greed: Inside the Teamsters Empire of Corruption.* New York: Franklin Watts, 1989.

Friedrich, Otto. *City of Nets: A Portrait of Hollywood in the 1940's.* New York: Harper & Row, 1986.

Frost, David. *"I Gave Them a Sword": Behind the Scenes of the Nixon Interviews.* New York: Morrow, 1978.

Gabler, Neal. *An Empire of Their Own: How the Jews Invented Hollywood.* New York: Anchor Books, 1989.

Gage, Nicholas, ed. *Mafia U.S.A.* Chicago: Playboy Press, 1972.

Garrison, Omar V. *Howard Hughes in Las Vegas.* New York: Lyle Stuart, 1970.

Gehman, Richard. *Sinatra and His Rat Pack.* New York: Belmont Books, 1961.

Giancana, Antoinette, and Thomas C. Renner. *Mafia Princess: Growing Up in Sam Giancana's Family.* New York: Morrow, 1984.

Giancana, Sam, and Chuck Giancana. *Double Cross: The Explosive, Inside Story of the Mobster Who Controlled America.* New York: Warner Books, 1992.

Gomery, Douglas. *Shared Pleasures: A History of Movie Presentation in the United States.* Madison: University of Wisconsin Press, 1992.

Gorbachev, Mikhail. *Memoirs.* New York: Doubleday, 1996.

Gosch, Martin A., and Richard Hammer. *The Last Testament of Lucky Luciano.* Boston: Little, Brown, 1975.

Griswold del Castillo, Richard, and Richard A. Garcia. *Cesar Chavez: A Triumph of Spirit.* Norman: University of Oklahoma Press, 1995.

Grutman, Roy, and Bill Thomas. *Lawyers and Thieves.* New York: Simon & Schuster, 1990.

Guiles, Fred Lawrence. *Legend: The Life and Death of Marilyn Monroe.* Stein & Day, 1984.

———. *Norma Jean: The Life of Marilyn Monroe.* New York: McGraw-Hill, 1969.

Hack, Richard. *Hughes, the Private Diaries, Memos and Letters: The Definitive Biography of the First American Billionaire.* Beverly Hills: New Millennium Press, 2001.

Hamby, Alonzo L. *Man of the People: A Life of Harry S. Truman.* New York: Oxford University Press, 1995.

Hammer, Richard. *The Vatican Connection.* New York: Holt, Rinehart & Winston, 1982.

Hannibal, Edward, and Robert Boris. *Blood Feud.* New York: Ballantine Books, 1979.

Harris, Marlys J. *The Zanucks of Hollywood: The Dark Legacy of an American Dynasty*. New York: Crown Publishers, 1989.

Hartley, Robert E. *Big Jim Thompson of Illinois*. Chicago: Rand McNally, 1979.

Havill, Adrian. *The Last Mogul: The Unauthorized Biography of Jack Kent Cooke*. New York: St. Martin's Press, 1992.

Haygood, Wil. *In Black and White: The Life of Sammy Davis Jr*. New York: A. A. Knopf, 2003.

Hersh, Seymour M. *The Dark Side of Camelot*. Boston: Little, Brown, 1997.

Herzog, Arthur. *Vesco: From Wall Street to Castro's Cuba: The Rise, Fall, and Exile of the King of White Collar Crime*. New York: Doubleday, 1987.

Heymann, C. David. *Poor Little Rich Girl: The Life and Legend of Barbara Hutton*. Secaucus, NJ: Lyle Stuart, 1984.

Hill, Gladwin. *Dancing Bear: An Inside Look at California Politics*. Cleveland: World Pub. Co., 1968.

Hitchens, Christopher. *The Trial of Henry Kissinger*. New York: Verso, 2001.

Hoffa, James R., as told by Oscar Fraley. *Hoffa: The Real Story*. New York: Stein & Day, 1975.

Hoffa, James R., as told by Donald I. Rogers. *The Trials of Jimmy Hoffa, an Autobiography*. Chicago: H. Regnery Co., 1970.

Honegger, Barbara. *October Surprise*. New York: Tudor Pub. Co., 1989.

Hoover, John Edgar. *Masters of Deceit: The Story of Communism in America and How to Fight It*. New York: Henry Holt, 1958.

Hopkins, A. D., and K. J. Evens, eds. *The First 100: Men and Women Who Shaped Las Vegas*. Las Vegas: Huntington Press, 1999.

Horne, Gerald. *Class Struggle in Hollywood, 1930–1950: Moguls, Mobsters, Stars, Reds, & Trade Unionists*. Austin: University of Texas Press, 2001.

Jacobs, George, and William Stadiem. *Mr. S: My Life with Frank Sinatra*. New York: Harper Entertainment, 2003.

Johns, Howard. *Palm Springs Confidential: Playground of the Stars!* Fort Lee, NJ: Barricade Books, 2004.

Johnson, Curt, with R. Craig Sautter. *Wicked City Chicago: From Kenna to Capone*. Highland Park, IL: December Press, 1994.

Johnston, Bernice Eastman. *California's Gabrielino Indians*. Los Angeles: Southwest Museum, 1962.

Johnston, David. *Temples of Chance: How America Inc. Bought Out Murder Inc. to Win Control of the Casino Business*. New York: Doubleday, 1992.

Kelley, Kitty. *His Way: The Unauthorized Biography of Frank Sinatra*. New York: Bantam Books, 1986.

———. *Nancy Reagan: The Unauthorized Biography*. New York: Simon & Schuster, 1991.

Kennan, George F. *At a Century's Ending: Reflections, 1982–1995*. New York: W. W. Norton, 1996.

Kezich, Tullio, and Alessandra Levantesi. *Dino: The Life and Films of Dino DeLaurentiis*. New York: Mirimax Books/Hyperion, 2004.

Kiernan, Thomas. *The Roman Polanski Story*. New York: Delilah/Grove Press, 1980.

Kilian, Michael, and Arnold Sawislak. *Who Runs Washington?* New York: St. Martin's Press, 1982.

Knepp, Donn. *Las Vegas: The Entertainment Capital*. Menlo Park, CA: Lane Pub. Co., 1987.

Knoedelseder, William. *Stiffed: A True Story of MCA, the Music Business, and the Mafia*. New York: HarperCollins, 1993.

Kotkin, Joel. *Tribes: How Race, Religion, and Identity Determine Success in the New Global Economy*. New York: Random House, 1993.

Kotkin, Joel, and Paul Grabowicz. *California Inc*. New York: Rawson, Wade, 1982.

Kupcinet, Irv, with Paul Neimark. *Kup: A Man, an Era, a City*. Chicago: Bonus Books, 1988.

Kushner, Sam. *The Long Road to Delano*. New York: International Publishers, 1975.

Lacey, Robert. *Little Man: Meyer Lansky and the Gangster Life*. Boston: Little, Brown, 1991.

LaGuardia, Robert, and Gene Arceri. *Red: The Tempestuous Life of Susan Hayward*. New York: Macmillan, 1985.

Lait, Jack, and Lee Mortimer. *Chicago Confidential*. New York: Crown, 1950.

Larsen, Lawrence H., and Nancy J. Hulston. *Pendergast!* Columbia: University of Missouri Press, 1997.

Lasky, Victor. *J.F.K.: The Man and the Myth*. New York: Macmillan, 1963.

Lawford, Patricia Seaton, with Ted Swartz. *The Peter Lawford Story: Life with the Kennedys, Monroe, and the Rat Pack*. New York: Carroll & Graf, 1988.

Lawrence, Carol. *Carol Lawrence: The Backstage Story*. New York: McGraw-Hill, 1990.

Lernoux, Penny. *In Banks We Trust: Bankers and Their Close Associates: The CIA, the Mafia, Drug-Traders, Dictators, Politicians and the Vatican*. Garden City, NY: Anchor Press/Doubleday, 1984.

Levy, Jacques E. *Cesar Chavez: Autobiography of La Causa*. New York: Norton, 1975.

Levy, Shawn. *King of Comedy: The Life and Art of Jerry Lewis*. New York: St. Martin's Press, 1996.

Lewis, Charles, Bill Allison, and the Center for Public Integrity. *The Cheating of America: How Tax Avoidance and Evasion by the Super Rich Are Costing the Country Billions—and What You Can Do About It*. New York: Morrow, 2001.

Lewis, Finlay. *Mondale: Portrait of an American Politician*. New York: Harper & Row, 1980.

Linet, Beverly. *Susan Hayward: Portrait of a Survivor*. New York: Atheneum, 1980.

Liston, Robert A. *Sargent Shriver: A Candid Portrait*. New York: Farrar, Straus, 1964.

Littlejohn, David, ed. *The Real Las Vegas: Life Beyond the Strip*. New York: Oxford University Press, 1999.

Longstreet, Stephen. *Chicago: An Intimate Portrait of People, Pleasures, and Power, 1860–1919*. New York: David McKay, 1973.

Loos, Anita. *The Talmadge Girls: A Memoir*. New York: Viking, 1978.

Lundberg, Ferdinand. *The Rich and the Super-Rich: A Study in the Power of Money Today*. New York: Lyle Stuart, 1968.

Lynch, Vincent. *Jukebox: The Golden Age*. New York: Putnam, 1981.

MacMillan, Dianne. *Missions of the Los Angeles Area*. Minneapolis: Lerner Publications, 1996.

MacShane, Frank. *The Life of Raymond Chandler*. New York: E. P. Dutton, 1976.

Madsen, Axel. *Gloria and Joe*. New York: Arbor House/William Morrow, 1988.

Maheu, Robert, and Richard Hack. *Next to Hughes: Behind the Power and Tragic Downfall of Howard Hughes by His Closest Advisor*. New York: HarperCollins, 1992.

Marx, Arthur. *Life with Groucho*. New York: Simon & Schuster, 1954.

Mathison, Richard. *His Weird and Wanton Ways: The Secret Life of Howard Hughes*. New York: Morrow, 1977.

McCarty, John. *Hollywood Gangland: The Movies' Love Affair with the Mob*. New York: St. Martin's Press, 1993.

McClellan, John L. *Crime Without Punishment*. New York: Duell, Sloan & Pearce, 1962.

McCoy, Malachy. *Steve McQueen: The Unauthorized Biography*. Chicago: H. Regnery Co., 1974.

McCullough, David. *Truman*. New York: Simon & Schuster, 1992.

McDougal, Dennis. *The Last Mogul: Lew Wasserman, MCA, and the Hidden History of Hollywood*. New York: Crown, 1998.

———. *Privileged Son: Otis Chandler and the Rise and Fall of the L.A. Times Dynasty*. Cambridge: Perseus, 2001.

McPhaul, Jack. *Johnny Torrio: First of the Gang Lords*. New Rochelle, NY: Arlington House, 1970.

McPhaul, John J. *Chicago: City of Sin*. Beverly Hills: Book Company of America, 1962.

Meites, Hyman L., ed. *History of the Jews of Chicago*. Chicago: Chicago Jewish Historical Society/Wellington Pub., 1990.

Messick, Hank. *The Beauties and the Beasts: The Mob in Show Business*. New York: David McKay, 1973.

———. *Lansky*. New York: Putnam, 1971.

———. *The Mob in Show Business*. New York: Pyramid Books, 1975.

———. *The Politics of Prosecution: Jim Thompson, Marje Everett, Richard Nixon & the Trial of Otto Kerner*. Ottawa, IL: Caroline House Books, 1978.

———. *Secret File*. New York: Putnam, 1969.

———. *Syndicate in the Sun*. New York: Macmillan, 1968.

Messick, Hank, and Joseph L. Nellis. *The Private Lives of Public Enemies*. New York: P. H. Wyden, 1973.

Miller, Marvin. *The Breaking of a President*. Los Angeles: Therapy Productions, 1974.

Miller, Richard Lawrence. *Truman: The Rise to Power*. New York: McGraw-Hill, 1986.

Miller, Russell. *Bunny: The Real Story of Playboy*. New York: Holt, Rinehart & Winston, 1984.

Miller, William "Fishbait," as told by Frances Spatz Leighton. *Fishbait: The Memoirs of the Congressional Door-keeper*. Englewood Cliffs, NJ: Prentice Hall, 1977.

Milligan, Maurice M. *The Inside Story of the Pendergast Machine by the Man Who Smashed It*. New York: Charles Scribner's Sons, 1948.

Mills, James R. *A Disorderly House: The Brown-Unruh Years in Sacramento*. Berkeley, CA: Heyday Books, 1987.

Milton, Joyce, and Ann Louise Bardach. *Vicki*. New York: St. Martin's Press, 1986.

Moldea, Dan E. *Dark Victory: Ronald Reagan, MCA, and the Mob*. New York: Viking, 1986.

———. *The Hoffa Wars: Teamsters, Rebels, Politicians, and the Mob*. New York: Paddington Press, 1978.

———. *Interference: How Organized Crime Influences Professional Football*. New York: Morrow, 1989.

Mollenhoff, Clark. *Game Plan for Disaster: An Ombudsman's Report on the Nixon Years*. New York: Norton, 1976.

———. *Strike Force: Organized Crime and the Government*. Englewood Cliffs, NJ: Prentice Hall, 1972.

———. *Tentacles of Power: The Story of Jimmy Hoffa*. Cleveland: World Publishing Co., 1965.

Monaco, Paul. *The Sixties: 1960–1969*. Berkeley: University of California Press, 2003.

Montgomery, Gayle B., and James W. Johnson. *One Step from the White House: The Rise and Fall of Senator William F. Knowland*. Berkeley: University of California Press, 1998.

Moore, William Howard. *The Kefauver Committee and the Politics of Crime, 1950–1952*. Columbia: University of Missouri Press, 1974.

Munn, Michael. *The Hollywood Connection: The True Story of Organized Crime in Hollywood*. London: Robson Books, 1993.

Murray, George. *The Legacy of Al Capone: Portraits and Annals of Chicago's Public Enemies*. New York: G. P. Putnam's Sons, 1975.

Naylor, R. T. *Hot Money and the Politics of Debt*. Montreal: McGill-Queen's University Press, 2004.

Newmark, Harris. *Sixty Years in Southern California, 1853–1913*. New York: Knickerbocker Press, 1916.

Neff, James. *Mobbed Up: Jackie Presser's High-Wire Life in the Teamsters, the Mafia and the F.B.I*. New York: Atlantic Monthly Press, 1989.

Ng, Wendy. *Japanese American Internment During World War II*. Westport, CT: Greenwood Press, 2002.

Nielsen, Mike, and Gene Mailes. *Hollywood's Other Blacklist: Union Struggles in the Studio System*. London: British Film Institute, 1995.

Niklas, Kurt, as told by Larry Hamm. *The Corner Table: From Cabbages to Caviar, Sixty Years in the Celebrity Restaurant Trade*. Beverly Hills, CA: Tuxedo Press, 2000.

O'Connor, Len. *Clout: Mayor Daley and His City*. Chicago: H. Regnery Co., 1975.

O'Donnell, Pierce, and Dennis McDougal. *Fatal Subtraction: How Hollywood Really Does Business*. New York: Doubleday, 1992.

Pack, Robert. *Jerry Brown: The Philosopher-Prince*. New York: Stein & Day, 1978.

Paper, Lewis J. *Empire: William S. Paley and the Making of CBS*. New York: St. Martin's Press, 1987.

Payne, J. Gregory, and Scott C. Ratzan. *Tom Bradley: The Impossible Dream*. Santa Monica, CA: Roundtable, 1986.

Peretti, Burton W. *The Creation of Jazz: Music, Race, and Culture in Urban America*. Urbana: University of Illinois Press, 1992.

Peters, Charles, and Taylor Branch. *Blowing the Whistle: Dissent in the Public Interest*. New York: Praeger, 1972.

Peterson, Virgil W. *Barbarians in Our Midst: A History of Chicago and Politics*. Boston: Little, Brown, 1952.

Petro, Sylvester. *Power Unlimited: The Corruption of Union Leadership: A Report on the McClellan Committee Hearings*. New York: Ronald Press Co., 1959.

Porrello, Rick. *The Rise and Fall of the Cleveland Mafia: Corn Sugar and Blood*. New York: Barricade Books, 1995.

Powell, S. Steven. *Covert Cadre: Inside the Institute for Policy Studies*. Ottawa, IL: Green Hill Publishers, 1987.

Prince, Stephen. *A New Pot of Gold: Hollywood Under the Electronic Rainbow, 1980–1989*. New York: Charles Scribner's Sons, 2000.

Puttnam, David, with Neil Watson. *Movies and Money*. New York: Knopf, 1998.

Pye, Michael. *Moguls: Inside the Business of Show Business*. New York: Holt, Rinehart & Winston, 1980.

Rakove, Milton L. *We Don't Want Nobody, Nobody Sent: An Oral History of the Daley Years*. Bloomington: Indiana University Press, 1979.

Rappleye, Charles, and Ed Becker. *All American Mafioso: The Johnny Rosselli Story*. New York: Doubleday, 1991.

Raw, Charles, Bruce Page, and Godfrey Hodgson. *Do You Sincerely Want to Be Rich?: The Full Story of Bernard Cornfeld and IOS*. New York: Viking, 1971.

Reagan, Ronald. *An American Life: The Autobiography*. New York: Simon & Schuster, 1990.

Reagan, Ronald, with Richard G. Hubler. *Where's the Rest of Me?* New York: Duell, Sloan and Pearce, 1965.

Reid, Ed. *The Grim Reapers: The Anatomy of Organized Crime in America, City by City*. New York: Bantam Books, 1969.

———. *Mickey Cohen: Mobster*. New York: Pinnacle Books, 1973.

Reid, Ed, and Ovid Demaris. *The Green Felt Jungle*. New York: Trident Press, 1963.

Reynolds, Debbie, with David Patrick Columbia. *Debbie: My Life*. New York: Morrow, 1988.

Robinson, Greg. *By Order of the President: FDR and the Internment of Japanese Americans*. Cambridge, MA: Harvard University Press, 2001.

Robinson, Jeffrey. *The Laundrymen: Inside Money Laundering, the World's Third Largest Business*. New York: Arcade, 1996.

Roemer, William F., Jr. *Accardo: The Genuine Godfather*. New York: Ivy Books, 1995.

———. *The Enforcer-Spilotro: The Chicago Mob's Man over Las Vegas*. New York: Ivy Books, 1994.

———. *Roemer: Man Against the Mob*. New York: Ivy Books, 1989.

———. *War of the Godfathers*. New York: Ivy Books, 1990.

Rogers, Henry C. "A Biography." Unpublished.

Ro'I, Yaacov, ed. *Jews and Jewish Life in Russia and the Soviet Union*. Portland: F. Cass, 1995.

Rothchild, Sylvia. *A Special Legacy: An Oral History of Soviet Jewish Émigrés in the United States*. New York: Simon & Schuster, 1985.

Rothman, Hal. *Devil's Bargains: Tourism in the Twentieth-Century American West*. Lawrence: University Press of Kansas, 1998.

———. *Neon Metropolis: How Las Vegas Started the Twenty-first Century*. New York: Routledge, 2002.

Rothmiller, Mike, and Ivan G. Goldman. *L.A. Secret Police: Inside the LAPD Elite Spy Network*. New York: Pocket Books, 1992.

Russo, Gianni. "Godfathers, Popes and Presidents." Unpublished autobiography.

Russo, Gus. *The Outfit: The Role of Chicago's Underworld in the Shaping of Modern America*. New York: Bloomsbury, 2001.

Salerno, Ralph. *The Confederation: Cosa Nostra and Allied Operations in Organized Crime*. Garden City, NY: Doubleday, 1969.

Samish, Arthur H., and Bob Thomas. *The Secret Boss of California: The Life and High Times of Art Samish*. New York: Crown, 1971.

Scheim, David E. *Contract on America: The Mafia Murders of John and Robert Kennedy*. Silver Spring, MD: Argyle Press, 1983.

Schlesinger, Arthur M., Jr. *Robert Kennedy and His Times*. New York: Ballantine Books, 1978.

———. *A Thousand Days: John F. Kennedy in the White House*. Boston: Houghton Mifflin, 1965.

Schrag, Peter. *Mind Control*. New York: Pantheon Books, 1978.

Schwartz, Barbara, et al., eds. *The Sentinel's History of Chicago Jewry, 1911–1961*. Chicago: Sentinel Publishing Co., 1986.

Sharp, Kathleen. *Mr. and Mrs. Hollywood: Edie and Lew Wasserman and Their Entertainment Empire*. New York: Carroll & Graf, 2003.

Sheridan, Walter. *The Fall and Rise of Jimmy Hoffa*. New York: Saturday Review Press, 1972.

Shore, Dinah. *Someone's in the Kitchen with Dinah*. Garden City, NY: Doubleday, 1971.

Sifakis, Carl. *The Mafia Encyclopedia*. New York: Facts on File, 1999.

Silber, Arthur, Jr. *Sammy Davis Jr.: Me and My Shadow, a Biographical Memoir*. Valley Village, CA: Samart Enterprises, 2002.

Sinatra, Nancy. *Frank Sinatra, My Father*. New York: Pocket Books, 1986.

Sinatra, Tina, with Jeff Coplon. *My Father's Daughter: A Memoir*. New York: Simon & Schuster, 2000.

Sloane, Arthur A. *Hoffa*. Cambridge, MA: MIT Press, 1991.

Smith, Alson J. *Syndicate City: The Chicago Crime Cartel and What to Do About It.* Chicago: H. Regnery Co., 1954.

Smith, Hedrick. *The New Russians.* New York: Random House, 1990.

———. *The Russians.* New York: Times Books, 1983.

Smith, John L. *Of Rats and Men: Oscar Goodman's Life from Mob Mouthpiece to Mayor of Las Vegas.* Las Vegas: Huntington Press, 2003.

Smith, Sally Bedell. *In All His Glory: The Life of William S. Paley, the Legendary Tycoon and His Brilliant Circle.* New York: Simon & Schuster, 1990.

Spada, James. *Peter Lawford: The Man Who Kept the Secrets.* New York: Bantam Books, 1991.

Spoto, Donald. *Marilyn Monroe: The Biography.* New York: HarperCollins, 1993.

Starr, Kevin. *The Dream Endures: California Enters the 1940's.* New York: Oxford University Press, 1997.

Steele, Jonathan. *The Limits of Soviet Power: The Kremlin's Foreign Policy, Brezhnev to Andropov.* New York: Simon & Schuster, 1983.

Stossel, Scott. *Sarge: The Life and Times of Sargent Shriver.* Washington, DC: Smithsonian Books, 2004.

Summers, Anthony. *Goddess: The Secret Lives of Marilyn Monroe.* New York: Macmillan, 1985.

———. *Official and Confidential: The Secret Life of J. Edgar Hoover.* New York: G. P. Putnam's Sons, 1993.

Summers, Anthony, and Robbyn Swan. *The Arrogance of Power: The Secret World of Richard Nixon.* New York: Viking, 2000.

Swados, Harvey. *Standing Up for the People: The Life and Work of Estes Kefauver.* New York: E. P. Dutton, 1972.

Taraborrelli, J. Randy. *Sinatra: Behind the Legend.* Secaucus, NJ: Carol, 1997.

Taylor, Ronald B. *Chavez and the Farm Workers.* Boston: Beacon Press, 1975.

Terrill, Marshall. *Steve McQueen: Portrait of an American Rebel.* New York: D. I. Fine, 1994.

Theoharis, Athan. *From the Secret Files of J. Edgar Hoover.* Chicago: I. R. Dee, 1991.

Thomas, Bob. *King Cohn: The Life and Times of Harry Cohn.* New York: Putnam, 1967.

Thomas, Tony. *Howard Hughes in Hollywood.* Secaucus, NJ: Citadel Press, 1985.

Thrasher, Frederic M. *The Gang: A Study of 1,313 Gangs in Chicago.* Chicago: University of Chicago Press, 1936.

Toffel, Neile McQueen. *My Husband, My Friend.* New York: Atheneum, 1986.

Torgerson, Dial. *Kerkorian: An American Success Story.* New York: Dial Press, 1974.

Tosches, Nick. *Dino: Living High in the Dirty Business of Dreams.* New York: Doubleday, 1992.

———. *Power on Earth.* New York: Arbor House, 1986.

Touhy, Roger, with Ray Brennan. *The Stolen Years.* Cleveland: Pennington Press, 1959.

Truell, Peter, and Larry Gurwin. *False Profits: The Inside Story of BCCI, the World's Most Corrupt Financial Empire.* Washington, DC: Beard Books, 1999.

Truman, Margaret. *Harry S. Truman.* New York: Quill, 1984.

Trump, Donald, with Tony Swartz. *Trump: The Art of the Deal.* New York: Random House, 1987.

Tuohy, John W. *When Capone's Mob Murdered Roger Touhy.* Fort Lee, NJ: Barricade, 2001.

Turner, William W. *Hoover's FBI.* New York: Thunder's Mouth Press, 1993.

———. *Rearview Mirror: Looking Back at the FBI, the CIA and Other Tails.* Granite Bay, CA: Penmarin Books, 2001.

Vaughn, Stephen. *Ronald Reagan in Hollywood: Movies and Politics.* New York: Cambridge University Press, 1994.

Velie, Lester. *Desperate Bargain: Why Jimmy Hoffa Had to Die.* New York: Reader's Digest Press, 1977.

Von Hoffman, Nicholas. *Citizen Cohn.* New York: Doubleday, 1988.

Vorspan, Max, and Lloyd P. Gartner. *History of the Jews of Los Angeles.* San Marino, CA: Huntington Library, 1970.

Weddle, David. *Among the Mansions of Eden: Tales of Love, Lust, and Land in Beverly Hills.* New York: Morrow, 2003.

Weissman, Steve, ed. *Big Brother and the Holding Company: The World Behind Watergate.* Palo Alto, CA: Ramparts Press, 1974.

Wertheimer, Jack. *Unwelcome Strangers: East European Jews in Imperial Germany.* New York: Oxford University Press, 1987.

Wick, Steve. *Bad Company: Drugs, Hollywood and the Cotton Club Murder.* San Diego: Harcourt Brace Jovanovich, 1990.

Wiernik, Peter. *History of the Jews in America.* New York: The Jewish History Publishing Company, 1931.

Wilkerson, W. R. *The Man Who Invented Las Vegas.* Beverly Hills: Ciro's Books, 2000.

Williams, Paul L. *The Vatican Exposed: Money, Murder, and the Mafia.* Amherst, NY: Prometheus Books, 2003.

Wilson, Earl. *Sinatra: An Unauthorized Biography.* New York: Macmillan, 1976.

Winter-Berger, Robert N. *The Washington Pay-Off: An Insider's View of Corruption in Government.* Secaucus, NJ: Lyle Stuart, 1972.

Wirth, Louis. *The Ghetto.* Chicago: University of Chicago Press, 1956.

Witcover, Jules. *Marathon: The Pursuit of the Presidency, 1972–1976.* New York: Viking, 1977.

Wolf, Marvin J., and Katherine Mader. *Fallen Angels: Chronicles of L.A. Crime and Mystery.* New York: Fact on File Publications, 1986.

Woodiwiss, Michael. *Organized Crime and American Power.* Toronto: University of Toronto Press, 2001.

Yablonsky, Lewis. *George Raft.* New York: McGraw-Hill, 1974.

Yallop, David A. *In God's Name: An Investigation into the Murder of Pope John Paul I.* New York: Bantam Books, 1984.

Yule, Andrew. *Fast Fade: David Puttnam, Columbia Pictures and the Battle for Hollywood.* New York: Delacorte Press, 1989.

Zehme, Bill. *The Way You Wear Your Hat: Frank Sinatra and the Lost Art of Livin'.* New York: HarperCollins, 1997.

Zeiger, Henry A. *Frank Costello.* New York: Berkley, 1974.

Zeller, F. C. Duke. *Devil's Pact: Inside the World of the Teamsters Union.* Secaucus, NJ: Carol, 1996.

Zinn, Howard. *A People's History of the United States.* New York: Perennial, 2001.

Zion, Sidney. *The Autobiography of Roy Cohn.* Secaucus, NJ: Lyle Stuart, 1988.

Zolotow, Maurice. *Billy Wilder in Hollywood.* New York: Putnam, 1977.

Zukerman, Michael J. *Vengeance Is Mine: Jimmy "the Weasel" Fratianno Tells How He Brought the Kiss of Death to the Mafia.* New York: Macmillan, 1987.

FBI Files

The following FBI files were obtained for this project under the Freedom of Information Act (FOIA): Anthony Accardo, Jake Arvey, David Bazelon, Charles Bluhdorn, Morris "Moe" Dalitz, John Factor, Al Hart, Murray Humphreys, Marshall Korshak, Sidney Roy Korshak, La Costa Resort, Ronald Reagan, Benjamin Siegel, Jules Stein, and Paul Ziffren.

The FBI's Hoffa Disappearance file was obtained from David Ashenfelter of the *Detroit Free Press*, and the Ronald Reagan-Clark Kerr FBI file was obtained from the *San Francisco Chronicle* Web site.

Miscellaneous Documents

Sidney R. Korshak, birth certificate from Chicago Illinois State File #200223.

Sidney R. Korshak, military records.

Sidney R. Korshak, DePaul University Law School grade record.

Sidney R. Korshak, certificate of death, County of Los Angeles, 39619003663.

John Marshall High School Alumni Association records.

1920 Census, Chicago, Illinois.

1930, Fifteenth Census of the United States.

Annual report, Office of Alien Property, Department of Justice, for fiscal year ended June 30, 1949.

Evelle J. Younger, California attorney general, "Organized Crime Control Commission 1st Report," May 1978.

Castle Bank, IRS master list of depositors.

Select Committee on Assassinations of the U.S. House of Representatives, 95th Congress, 2nd sess., March 1979.

Ralph Everett Stolken, certificate of death from County of Riverside, Riverside, California, 2-6-73.

Dorothy Drake, Last Will and Testament from State of New York, County of Nassau, created 11-7-88, DoD 8-9-90.

Hearings before the Special Committee to Investigate Organized Crime in Interstate Commerce, U.S. Senate, 82nd Congress, 1st sess., pursuant to S. Res. 202 (81st Congress), "A Resolution Authorizing an Investigation of

Organized Crime in Interstate Commerce"; pt. 5: Illinois, September 9; October 5, 6, 7, 17, 18, 19; December 18, 19, 20, 1950; January 5, 19, 1951.

Committee on the Judiciary (House), Subcommittee to Investigate the Department of Justice ("Chelf Committee"), 82nd–83rd Congress; hearings, testimony, and case files. (Also the Frank Chelf Collection at Western Kentucky University.)

Hearings before the Permanent Subcommittee on Investigations of the Committee on Governmental Affairs, U.S. Senate, 98th Congress, 1st sess., with regards to the Hotel Employees & Restaurant Employees International Union; pt. 3: April 27, 28, 1983.

Hearings before the Select Committee on Improper Activities in the Labor or Management Field, 85th Congress, 2nd sess., pursuant to S. Res. 74 and 221 (85th Congress); pt. 33: March 21; July 8, 9, 10, 11, 1958.

Federal Communications Commission report on the telegraph industry, December 1939.

Committee on Expenditures in Executive Departments (House), 80th Congress, 2nd sess., 1948; report and hearings ("Parole Investigation").

Subcommittee of the Committee on Interstate and Foreign Commerce (Senate), 81st Congress, 2nd sess., May 1950; "Transmission of Gambling Information" (race wire) ("McFarland").

Hearings before the Committee on Interstate and Foreign Commerce (House) regarding proposed legislation to prohibit interstate sale of gambling machines (slots, etc.), 81st Congress, 2nd sess., June 1950.

Securities and Exchange Commission hearings in the matter of Parvin Dohrmann Company, Hearing Order 424, 8-21-69.

Securities and Exchange Commission v. Sidney R. Korshak et al., U.S. District Court, Southern District of New York, 69 Civ. 4543, 12-8-70.

The President's Commission on Organized Crime, June 24–26, 1985; "Organized Crime and Gambling."

Appeal to the Superior Court of New Jersey from, regarding Playboy-Elsinore Associates application for a casino license, A-4188-81T1, 7-23-84.

Inquiry into the Illinois Racing Board License No. 402, 6-23-70, 7-24-70.

Universal City Studios, Inc., et al. v. RKO General, Inc., et al., Superior Court of the State of California, No. C 125 242, 6-6-75.

U.S. and Michael J. Sheehy, Special Agent of the Internal Revenue Service, v. Marshall Korshak, U.S. District Court, Northern District of Illinois, Eastern Division, No. 73 C 820, 4-23-73.

U.S. v. Louis Compagna, et al., Federal Court, Southern District, New York.

U.S. v. Schenck & Moscowitz, Federal Court, Southern District, New York. (Supplied by Boris Kostelanetz.)

Sophie White v. Sidney Korshak, Superior Court of Cook County.

Estate of Joseph Glaser, No. 69 P 3458, Docket 160, p. 89, Circuit Court of Cook County, Illinois Probate Division.

Probate of Jules C. Stein, Superior Court of the State of California, County of Los Angeles, Case No. P 664540, 8-1-86, 5-18-88, lawyers' fees, 6-1-88.

Peter Vaira and Douglas P. Roller, "Organized Crime and the Labor Unions," report prepared for the Carter White House, 1978.

State of New Jersey Casino Control Commission, "Plenary Licensing Hearing of Hilton New Jersey Corporation," 1984.

Penthouse International Ltd. v. Dalitz, Los Angeles Superior Court Civil Action No. C-162233.

U.S. v. MCA et al., U.S. District Court, Southern District of California, Central Division, Civil Action No. 62-942-WM.

The papers of Robert Goe and Art White (miscellaneous confidential sources).

Journal Articles

Berry, Kate. "City National Grows into L.A.'s Largest Independent." *Los Angeles Business Journal*, 5/12/03.

Chambliss, William J. "Vice, Corruption, Bureaucracy, and Power." *Wisconsin Law Review* 4 (1971): 1150–73.

Moore, William Howard. "Was Estes Kefauver 'Blackmailed' During the Chicago Crime Hearings?: A Historian's Perspective." *Public Historian* 4 (1982): 5–28.

Peterson, Virgil. "Chicago: Shades of Capone." *Annals of the Academy of Political and Social Science* 347 (May 1963): 30–39.

Rosenthal, Erich. "This Was North Lawndale: The Transplantation of a Jewish Community." *Jewish Social Studies* 22 (1960): 67–82.

Wanklyn, H. G. "Geographical Aspects of Jewish Settlement East of Germany." *Geographical Journal* 95 (1940): 175–88.

Witwer, David. "The Scandal of George Scalise: A Case Study in the Rise of Labor Racketeering in the 1930's." *Journal of Social History* 36 (2003): 917–40.

Index

NOTE: SK refers to Sidney Korshak; RFK refers to Robert R. Kennedy. Bold page numbers refer to pictures.

134, 140; and Truman administration, 90; as U.S. assistant attorney, 133; and Watergate investigation, 409; Ziffren's relationship with, 66, 90, 92, 94, 100, 110–12, 116, 122, 132–34, 140, 240, 244, 377, 404; and Zwillman, 188

BCCI (Bank of Credit and Commerce International), 521–22

Beatty, Warren, 148, 282, 326–27, 330, 383

Beck, Dave, 164, 166, 172, 182

Becker, Edward Nicholas, 130, 142, 207, 214, 225, 312–13, 313n, 322, 336, 419

Bellagio (Las Vegas), 388n, 501n

Benny, Jack, 79, 95, 148, 281, 448n

Bergman, Lowell, 428, 428n, 478–79, 486

Beverly Hills Hotel, 126, 187, 212, 360

Beverly Hilton Hotel (Beverly Hills), 180, 241, 305

Beverly Rodeo Hotel (Beverly Hills), 303–4, 303n, 373

Beverly Wilshire Hotel (Los Angeles), 78, 97, 98, 448

Bioff, Willie, 44, 51–53, 56–63, 74, 117, 143–44, 162, 216, 216n, 435

Bismarck Hotel (Chicago), 32–33, 53, 56–57, 453

The Bistro (Beverly Hills), 281, 283; Chandler (Buff)–SK meeting at, 358; closing of, 514; decor of, 281; and Evans (Bob), 323, 396–97, 477; Everett's choking at, 372; FBI surveillance of SK at, 292; and Hughes-SK relationship, 282; location of, 280; and Moldea investigation, 488; Niklas as manager of, 280; opening of, 280, 281–82; owners/stockholders in, 280–81, 448n; and Polanski arrest, 448; Reagan's "Kitchen Cabinet" at, 305–6, 306n; regular patrons of, 282; Rosselli at, 409–11; and Silverman-Ross series about SK, 460–61; Sinatra-Hart meeting at, 295; SK as original investor in, 280–81; and SK's lady friends, 329, 331; as SK's "office," 1, 255, 282–89, 292, 294, 321, 360, 396–97, 402, 406, 415, 420–21, 423, 425, 448, 456, 467, 488; and Smith-Lansky relationship, 476n; and Wilder, 280

Bistro Gardens, 447–48, 506, 515, 520

Blake, Gene, 259, 261–62, 263

Blakey, G. Robert, 291, 354, 519

Bloomingdale, Alfred, 282, 305, 347, 347n, 361, 436, 478

Bluhdorn, Charles, 319, 423n, 493; death of, 483; and Dutch Sandwich, 402; and Evans, 321–23, 398, 477, 478; as founder of G&W, 318, 319; and The Godfather, 389–90, 393–94, 393–94n; and Hersh investigation, 430, 449–50; and Levin-Transnation, 323; and Paramount Studios, 320–22, 323, 365–68, 398, 404; personality and character of, 318, 319, 321; personal and professional background of, 318–19; and racing, 355, 362; and SEC probe, 449–50; and Sindona, 438; and SK's fees, 406; SK's relationship with, 318, 355; and Sulzberger, 430; and The Valachi Papers, 394. See also Gulf & Western

Bond (James) films, 126, 399–401, 399n, 401, 401n

Brenneman, Richard "Dick," 125, 192–93, 242, 289n, 449, 455, 484, 498 The Brink's Job (film), 424, 424n

Broccoli, Albert Romolo "Cubby," 126, 148, 399–401, 400, 506, 513, 515, 520

Bronfman family, 342, 524

Brown, Edmund "Pat," 243, 282, 284, 285, 298; accomplishments of, 306n; and Bautzer's death, 506; as California attorney general, 136, 146, 237; and Chavez, 300, 304; death of, 520; and Dodger Stadium, 254; and elections, 100, 237–40, 271–72, 306, 347; and Factor, 249; as governor, 239–43; and IOS, 346, 347–48; and Knowland, 237–40; and Lacher, 506; law firm of, 347, 416; mob connections of, 238–39, 241; Mosk appointment of, 243, 243n; and Nixon, 271–72; and Proposition B, 254; and Sinatra, 300; SK's relationship with, 125, 237, 242, 272; and Ziffren, 136, 146, 237, 238–43, 271–72, 510

Brown, Jerry: aspirations of, 415, 465; as "born-again capitalist," 416; and Davis (Gray), 455–56, 455n; early career of, 415; and elections, 414, 415, 455, 512; fundraising for, 454; idealism of, 414–15; and labor unions, 454–55, 454n, 460, 464–65, 469; questionable supporters of, 455; and racetracks, 464–65, 467; SK's relationship with, 125, 415, 454, 466–69, 467, 467n, 472; and Wasserman, 415; and Ziffren's death, 510

Browne, George E., 40, 44, 51–53, 58–60, 63, 74, 117, 162, 174, 228

interview by, **151**; and Shore's death, 513*n*;
and Sinatra, 149, 475; and SK's
philandering, 328, 329; SK's relationship
with, 61–62; and SK's reputation, 122–23;
and SK's role in Supermob, 219; on Stein-
Capone relationship, 43
Kupcinet, Jerry, 62, 62*n*, 295
Kupcinet, Karyn, 294–95, 525

La Costa Country Club (California), 135,
148, 208, 378
La Costa Resort (Carlsbad, California),
224–25, 345, 350, 354, 357, 379, 419, 428,
457, 471*n*, 474, 478–79, 479*n*, 482
Labor Department, U.S., 164, 167, 225–26,
293, 380, 496*n*, 498
labor unions: Allen's documentary about,
285; and congressional investigations,
133–34; expansion of Supermob's
influence in, 162–67; and FBI, 164; and
hotel industry, 69, 97; Jews as leaders of,
23; and *L.A. Times* investigations, 259;
and LAPD, 173; in Las Vegas, 177,
221–25, 299–300, 301*n*, 425, 489, 493;
mob infiltration into, 30–34, 483; and
movie industry, 52–53, 81, 157, 228,
231–37, 436; and Outfit-Gilbert
relationship, 33–34; and politics in
California, 228, 231–37, 239; power of, 22;
and *Queen Mary*, 436–37; and racetracks,
253–54, 360–63; and SK's early legal
career, 31, 32, 34; and sports, 254–55. *See
also specific person or union*
Laemmle, Carl, 76–77, 78
Lamb, Ralph, 226, 256–57, 299, 434, 513
Landmark Hotel (Las Vegas), 225, 311, 375
Lansky, Meyer, 224, 251, 439; banks for, 376;
biopic of, 502; Capone connections with,
25; Cuba/Bahama activities of, 94, 95, 97,
121, 208, 220, 224, 224*n*; and Dalitz, 202,
203, 205, 208, 221*n*, 345; and Genis, 99, 241;
and Greene, 93, 131; and Hart, 142, 342;
Kefauver Committee testimony of, 95, 122*n*;
and Kennedy (Joseph), 221*n*; and Kerkorian,
384; and Kirkeby, 95, 121; Las Vegas
activities of, 126, 195, 200, 205, 208, 219,
310, 338, 339, 344, 345, 347, 384, 471;
lawyers for, 27, 55, 126; and Levin, 340; and
Luciano, 25; and Mexico/Acapulco
ventures, 337, 338, 338*n*, 339, 342, 363–64,
365, 368; and movie industry, 394; and Raft,

150; and Reagan administration, 476*n*;
Schenley connection of, 300; and Siegel, 195,
199, 205, 338; SK's relationship with, 158
Larner, Hy, 139, 418, 482
Las Vegas, Nevada: casino ownership in,
202, 209, 214–15, 223, 265, 315–16; and
Chicago Crime Commission, 206; and
congressional investigations, 212–13; and
FBI, 200, 205, 209, 212, 214, 215, 218, 219,
309, 315–16, 379, 417–18, 433–34; history
of development of, 195–96, 226; IRS
investigation in, 276–77; and Kefauver
Committee, 206, 209; labor activities in,
177, 212, 221–25, 299–300, 301*n*, 353, 386,
425, 489, 492, 493; mob's connection
with, 195–202, 209–20, 222–23, 226, 246,
249, 264–68, 309, 310–12; money
laundering in, 83; organization of casino
dealers in, 301*n*; and Parvin-Dohrmann
deals, 343–48; and SK as double agent,
256–57; skimming in, 177, 201–2, 208,
215, 218–19, 221*n*, 225, 261, 267*n*,
276–77, 296, 309, 311–12, 337, 339, 345,
423, 441, 484; SK's activities in, 69, 148,
194, 202, 207–16, 219–22, 246, 246*n*,
264–68, 279, 299–300, 301*n*, 305, 309–18,
327, 353, 356, 400, 425, 438, 493, 497; and
SK's decline in reputation, 497; Teamsters
Pension Fund funding in, 69, 164, 214,
223–26, 246, 261, 309, 375, 378–79, 438,
455, 479, 492; wiretaps in, 296, 310, 313.
See also specific person, casino, or hotel
Lawford, Peter, 142, 181, 183, 273–74, 330
Lawndale (Chicago), 5–14, 18, 21, 24–26,
24–25*n*, 34–35, 39, 75
Lawndale Enterprises, 41, 240
Laxalt, Paul, 370, 370*n*, 416–18, 473, 475,
476, 484–85, 485*n*, 486
Lazar, Irving "Swifty," 189, 281, 448, 461,
478
Leavitt, Herman "Blackie," 301, 301*n*,
303–4, 407, 455, 469
LeRoy, Mervyn, 79, 253, 279, 336
Levin, Philip J., 323, 340–43, 349, 354–55,
362–65, 368, 369, 371, 376*n*, 384–85
Lewis, Jerry, 117, 118, 149–50, 154, 254
Life magazine, 315, 316, 322, 484, 507
liquor licenses, 250–53
Lombardo, Joey "the Clown," 224, 465–66
Lorimar Telepictures Productions, 224–25,
224*n*, 387*n*, 496

and Goldblatt, 145; and Hoffa/Teamsters, 166–67; and Hyatt hotels, 138–39; LAPD investigation of, 137–38; mob associates of, 67, 69, 131, 137, 188, 204; real estate holdings of, 92–93, 113, 133, 227; SK's relationship with, 67, 188; and Ziffren, 92
Pritzker, Jay A., 92, 109–10, 138, 316, 438, 480, 522
Pritzker family: activities of, 67–68; asset management by, 138; and BCCI, 521; and Castle Bank, 138, 439–43, 480; and Dalitz, 438; dissension within, 522; and FBI, 67, 94, 145; and Hefner, 480–82; heirs of, 527; holdings of, 67–68, 138, 480, 522; and Hyatt hotels, 138–39; and IRS, 499, 521, 522; and Korshak family, 67; and *L.A. Times* investigations, 261–62; Las Vegas activities of, 438, 479; mob connections of, 66–70, 480; and mob infiltration of California, 116, 261; *New York Times* article about, 437–38, 479; philanthropy of, 522–23; political contributions of, 468; and Prudential Insurance, 440, 521; and real estate investments in California, 261; Royce article about, 259, 479–80; SEC probe of, 479; SK's relationship with, 68, 69, 259, 437–38; style of, 138; Supermob role of, 68; and Teamsters, 139, 166–67, 261, 437–38, 479, 480–82
Profaci crime family, 389
Prudential Insurance Company, 440, 521
Pump Room (Chicago), 61, 62, **62**, 167, 179, 183, 280, 282, 288, 294
Purple Gang, 201, 201*n*, 203
Puzo, Mario, 382–83, 388

Qualls, Mike: SK interview with, 458–59
Queen Mary (luxury liner), 436–37

race issues, 38, 433, 451
racetracks, 253–54, 279, 360–65, 371–72. *See also specific track*
Raft, George, 52*n*, 81, 126, 143*n*, 150–52, **151**, 200, 246*n*, 298, 353, 384, 409, 461
Ramada Inn Corporation, 221–22, 343
Rawls, Wendell, 6, 55, 142, 169, 184
Reagan, Nancy Davis, 230–31, 254, **283**, 361–62, **446**, 478, 496, 503, 525
Reagan, Ronald, **47**, **232**, 282, **283**, 287, **307**, 445, **446**, 470, 506; Annenberg as supporter of, 116; and Bergman investigation, 486; and communism, 228–29, 307, 508–9, 508*n*, 509*n*, 525; congressional investigation of, 473–74*n*; "creation" of, 228–32; Davis marriage of, 230–31; death of, 525; and Dodgers, 254; early California years of, 73, 82, 116, 228; early career of, 45, 228; and elections, 306, 348–49, 415, 416, 473–75, 473–74*n*, 475, 485; and FBI, 229, 307–8, 496; and foreign affairs, 473, 473–74*n*, 475, 508–10, 508*n*; and *GE Theater*, 234, 235, 237, 269, 306; as governor, 306–9, 347, 360, 361–62, 403, 404; grand jury testimony of, 487; and Hoffa pardon, 373; and Japanese nationals, 507; joins Republican Party, 271, 305; "Kitchen Cabinet" of, 305–6, 306*n*, 347, 361; and labor activities, 228, 360, 361–62; lady friends of, 48; and Laxalt, 415, 473, 475, 476, 485, 485*n*; and MCA, 116, 157, 228, 231–37, 268–69, 271, 305, 308, 487, 488, 504; Moldea's investigation of, 487–88; and politics in California, 227, 228–37, 254; as president, 308, 471, 475–76, 485*n*, 486, 507, 508–9, 508*n*; and racetrack strike, 360, 361–62; Robb investigation of, 487; and SAG, 116, 157, 229–37, 268–70; "selling" of, 305–9; SK's comments about, 47–48; SK's relationship with, 47–48, 230, 231, 235, 236, 472, 487, 496; and Stein, 45, 47, 228, 237, 308, 478; tax problems of, 232, 269, 308; and taxes for movie industry, 403, 404; and Teamsters, 474, 476, 496; and Trudeau, 468*n*; on TV, 233–34; and University of California, 307–8; war on organized crime of, 476, 499–501; and Wasserman, 47, 48, 228–30, 232–35, 237, 306, 486–88, 503
real estate: in California, 73, 82–86, 89–90, 106, 114, 261, 376, 379, 398; as central to Supermob power, 7; Florida, 249; foreclosures of, 16; of German nationals, 110, 112–13, 132; insider information about, 100, 109–12, 113; investigation of California, 89–90, 242; Japanese, 100–106, 111, 133, 261; and *L.A. Times* investigations, 260–61, 262; and mob infiltration of California, 261; and politics in California, 82, 238–39, 242; and Pritzker holdings, 67–68. *See also* Office of Alien Property; Teamsters Pension Fund; *specific person, corporation, or property*

A Note on the Author

Gus Russo is the author of *The Outfit: The Role of Chicago's Underworld in the Shaping of Modern America* and *Live by the Sword: The Secret War Against Castro and the Death of JFK*. He is an investigative reporter who has worked for various major television networks, including PBS, where he was a lead reporter for the award-winning *Frontline* series.